11 25

13382

INTRODUCTION TO PSYCHOLOGY

LINDA L. DAVIDOFF Essex Community College

INTRODUCTION TO PSYCHOLOGY

McGraw-Hill Book Company ● New York ● St. Louis ● San Francisco ● Auckland ● Düsseldorf
Johannesburg ● Kuala Lumpur ● London ● Mexico ● Montreal ● New Delhi ● Panama ● Paris
São Paulo ● Singapore ● Sydney ● Tokyo ● Toronto

To my favorite friends,
past and present:

my father, Samuel Lee
my mother, Edith Litwack Lee
Carolyn McGill
Susan Morris Hedling
Psyche
Cricket
and especially, Martin

INTRODUCTION TO PSYCHOLOGY

3 4 5 6 7 8 9 0 M U R M 7 9 8 7 6

See Acknowledgments on pages 550–552. Copyrights
included on this page by reference.

This book was set in Baskerville by Black Dot, Inc. The
editors were Jean Smith, Richard R. Wright, and James
R. Belser; the designer was Hermann Strohbach; the
production supervisor was Thomas J. LoPinto; the
photo editor was Inge King. The drawings were
done by J & R Services, Inc.
The printer was The Murray Printing Company; the
binder, Rand McNally & Company.

LIBRARY OF CONGRESS CATALOGING IN
PUBLICATION DATA
Davidoff, Linda L
    Introduction to psychology.
    Bibliography: p.
    Includes index.
    1. Psychology. I. Title.
BF121.D326   150   75-12611
ISBN 0-07-015459-7

CONTENTS

PREFACE

Why another introductory psychology text? Like many teachers, I couldn't find a book that met my needs. Most introductory texts survey many subjects and present comparatively little information about each one. I was looking for a book that presented several important and relevant topics in some depth in each major area of psychology. Further, my ideal book had to be empirical in its approach and organized in such a way that students might understand the process of asking and answering questions about behavior—and it had to at least try to involve students in that process. The book had to be simple, clear, and informal in writing style, without being simple-minded; and it had to include direct quotations and readings to give students the flavor of the original observations, research, or theories. Finally, it had to contain, as an integral part of the text, learning objectives, questions, exercises, and projects to encourage students to learn actively and use psychology. I couldn't find such a text on the market, so I began writing one.

Writing an introductory psychology text is an enormous project. Although the author receives most of the credit, many people contribute significantly to the end product, and I want to thank six people individually.

Psychologist David Andrews reviewed at least one and in most cases two or three drafts of each chapter. His many perceptive comments have greatly improved the logic, coherence, and accuracy of the text.

My colleague Barbara McClinton class-tested several chapters and reviewed one draft. The majority of her excellent suggestions have been incorporated in the final manuscript. She also prepared the first draft of much of the study guide materials which appear throughout the book.

All the McGraw-Hill editors who worked with me were helpful and patient. John Hendry spent a great deal of time teaching me the fundamentals of textbook writing. Jean Smith helped refine the final product; she and Jim Belser supervised all the production details.

My husband, Martin Davidoff, has probably smoothed every smooth sentence at least once and has also caught and helped correct a great many problems in clarity, logic, and organization. Those that remain are not his fault. Besides functioning as my chief critic, he also shared much of the typing, proofreading, literature searching, and innumerable other tasks with me. Most of all, I am grateful to him for remaining encouraging and loving throughout these most hectic two years.

I also want to thank the following psychologists for reviewing particular aspects of the manuscript at various stages and offering constructive suggestions: Barbara Bailey, Hugh Banks, Elaine Bresnahan, Elizabeth Bryan, Clarke Burnham, Gordon Haaland, Mary Ellen Keane, Richard Lerner, Faith Lossiah, Eugene McDowell, Al Orsini, Joanne Pelosi, David Schroeder, Lee Sechrest, Jim Sherry, Anthony Testa, William Wahlin, Ira Weiss, Arno Wittig, Thomas Williams, and Joan Yates.

Finally, I am indebted to the administration at Essex Community College for granting me a year's leave of absence to work on the book and to Pat German and Mary Peck, librarians at Essex, for processing more than five hundred interlibrary loans for me and for being accommodating far beyond the call of duty.

Linda L. Davidoff

TO THE STUDENT

There are a number of study aids within this textbook to help you learn and use psychology. Of these, the most important is the **Study Guide** at the end of each chapter. The guide is designed to help you review what you've learned, deepen your understanding of key points, and test and apply your knowledge. The guide contains six major sections:

1. *Review* (lists of key terms, important research, people to identify, and basic theories). After reading the chapter, test yourself to see if you can define, identify, or describe these items. Look up and study any that give you difficulty. Writing down definitions or descriptions may help you with troublesome material.

2. *Self-Quiz.* When you think you have mastered the material in the chapter, answer the multiple-choice questions on the Self-Quiz. If your answers differ from those in the key, review the appropriate material and/or work the exercises that follow. It's important to note that the Self-Quiz does not cover all the material in the chapter.

3. *Exercises.* If you want extra practice on difficult or confusing material, these exercises should help you. Note that an answer key is provided.

4. *Questions to Consider.* Many of these questions are typical exam questions. Others are intended to stimulate your thinking about the personal or practical implications of the material in the chapter. Another source of practice exam questions is the list of learning objectives at the beginning of each chapter.

5. *Project.* These projects will give you practice using experimental, observational, and survey methods to answer psychological questions.

6. *Suggested Readings.* If you want to learn

more about topics mentioned in a chapter, these readings are a good place to begin. The titles in the list were chosen because they are both informative and enjoyable.

Learning objectives at the beginning of each chapter point out the important topics you'll be encountering. Keep them in mind as you read. (Psychological studies show that people get more from their reading when they know in advance what's important.)

The **Glossary** at the back of the book briefly defines important terms that appear repeatedly. If you need further information, look the word up in the **Index** and refer to the text.

A final suggestion: Before starting the text you might want to jump ahead to pages 235 to 240 for some practical tips on learning and remembering more effectively.

Linda L. Davidoff

1
AN INTRODUCTION TO PSYCHOLOGY

IN THIS CHAPTER
We begin by considering several fundamental questions: What is psychology?
Which historical movements shaped
psychology? What do psychologists believe today? What roles do psychologists play in our society? After reading
this chapter, you should be able to do
the following:

1. Define "psychology"
2. Name, describe, and contrast five
   movements that shaped modern psychology
3. Compare the psychoanalytic, neobehavioristic, cognitive, and humanistic views of psychology
4. Describe the activities that American
   psychologists engage in today
5. Distinguish between psychologists,
   psychiatrists, and psychoanalysts

WHAT IS PSYCHOLOGY?

I get lots of junk mail. Some of it looks like this:

**EXTRAORDINARY NEW DISCOVERIES
IN THE BEHAVIORAL SCIENCES!!!**

**Would you like to understand the secrets of
human nature? Would you like to be happy,
productive, socially successful, wealthy, self-
confident, energetic, self-controlled, and loving?**

OF COURSE YOU WOULD.

**Our revolutionary new book, based on major
breakthroughs in the understanding of human
behavior, can show you how to attain these goals.
It contains:**

> **Five chapters devoted to the three powerful
> forces which determine how and why people
> feel, think, and behave as they do**
> **Six chapters on the six major personality types
> and eight simple rules for building successful
> relationships with people**
> **Four additional chapters on the techniques of
> meaningful and effective human communica-
> tion**

**After reading this book, you need never again
experience anxiety, loneliness, frustration, dissatisfaction, unhappiness, or guilt.**

This chapter opens with these wild claims because many people believe that psychologists make assertions like these. Right now, psychology is still far from being able to make good on these promises, so no ethical psychologist would make them.

A Definition of Psychology

Most students enter a course with some expectations about what it will cover. What do you expect of psychology?

Do you expect to find psychology similar to the "commonsense psychology" that people use every day?

Do you expect psychology to focus primarily on personality, emotion, adjustment, and abnormality?

Do you expect to find in psychology a unified body of knowledge with answers to many practical problems?

Do you expect a scientific approach?

Do you expect to encounter research on the behavior of animals?

We will be focusing on each of these issues shortly, but first, what is psychology? We begin with a definition: _Psychology is the science of behavior._ This definition is accepted by most psychologists, but what does it really mean? Like many definitions, this one isn't fully clear unless you understand the key terms.

The word "behavior" should be interpreted in its broadest sense; that is, as any human or animal process or activity that can be _objectively observed or measured_ (observed or measured in a way that is reasonably free of value judgments, personal preferences, and biases so that impartial observers can agree on the description). Overt behavior, such as thumb sucking, foot jiggling, eating, kissing, and running, can be directly observed. Verbalizations and vocalizations, such as laughing, snoring, and talking, can be heard and accurately recorded. Physiological responses, such as perspiration, respiration, muscle tension, heartbeats, and brain waves, can be measured by electronic equipment. Psychologists are also interested in many important functions such as thoughts, sensations, emotions, needs, motives, personality characteristics, and capabilities that cannot be observed or measured directly. Psychologists call these phenomena _hypothetical constructs_, and they treat them in a special way. These characteristics, conditions, or processes are inferred (guessed at) on the basis of related behavior. Consider intelligence. People talk about intelligence as if it were a tangible entity, but what is intelligence? In actuality, we cannot see it and we do not know what it is. We observe behavior—such as a series of moves that win a chess tournament or a high-scoring performance on an intelligence test—and assume that such behavior reflects the operation of an internal mechanism, "intelligence." At present there is absolutely no way to measure intelligence directly. Let's consider another hypothetical construct: emotion. We cannot observe an emotion. Instead, we observe overt behaviors that seem to be related to the emotion: gestures, facial expressions, postures, and verbal comments; we also observe the general situational context in which the behaviors occur, and then make inferences about the internal emotional state.

In real life, people frequently observe behavior and make inferences about the underlying internal state—usually automatically and without any conscious awareness. For example, if you walk past an acquaintance who does not greet you, you might infer that the acquaintance has the personality characteristic "snobbishness" or the temporary condition "preoccupation" or "fatigue." In studying hypothetical constructs, psychologists do the same thing, but they do it consciously and methodically.

Psychology as a science. When we say that psychology is a *science*, we mean that psychologists gather knowledge about their subject—behavior—using scientific methods such as experimentation and observation, that they also strive to make their studies as objective as possible, and that they accumulate information in an orderly way. Students are rarely prepared to find psychologists so

Figure 1-1. Tears of grief and tears of joy. Cues such as gestures and facial expressions help people infer internal emotional states. (Left: Mark Godfrey, Magnum; right: John Briggs.)

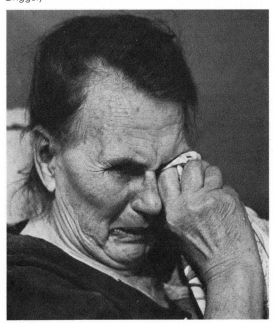 

concerned about being scientific, but there are very good reasons for the scientific approach. Many of them will be clear to you after you've finished Chapter 2. We turn now to some of the other expectations that students frequently bring to their first psychology course.

"Commonsense psychology." We all use "commonsense psychology" as we struggle along from day to day. We try to understand other people. We attempt to predict what this or that person will do next. Most of us have plenty of ideas about how to get control over our own lives and sometimes over the lives of others. In other words, each of us has commonsense psychological "theories" of our own—the best approach for raising children, selling a car, making friends, attracting members of the opposite sex, impressing people, controlling anger. Many commonsense psychology principles are embodied in maxims, old cultural sayings that are handed down from generation to generation. As you read the following list of maxims, mark each one true or false:

Birds of a feather flock together.
He who hesitates is lost.
Out of sight, out of mind.
Look before you leap.
Never too old to learn.
Losers are always in the wrong.

Opposites attract.
Absence makes the heart grow fonder.
The cheerful loser is a winner.
You can't teach an old dog new tricks.

Commonsense psychology, as reflected in these maxims, has at least three significant weaknesses: First, the principles of commonsense psychology are not based on solid evidence. Instead, they are usually accepted because they sound profound, or a positive personal experience has supported the truth of the principle, or some authority—such as Dear Abby, a teacher, a mother, a friend, or a doctor—advocates the principle. Second, the principles of commonsense psychology tend to accumulate haphazardly and uncritically. They have no internal consistency; that is, they often directly contradict one another. (Note that in the maxims above there are five themes with two contradictory statements about each. Were you consistent in your principles?) Third, people do not make systematic attempts to evaluate their commonsense psychology beliefs—to identify the ones that hold true most of the time and discard the others. For all these reasons commonsense psychology does not make sound psychology.

The focus of psychology. Psychology does deal with personality, emotion, adjustment, and abnormality—but not exclusively. Psy-

Figure 1-2. "Commonsense" psychology.

Do birds of a feather flock together?

Or do opposites attract?

chologists also study subjects such as development, learning, measurement techniques, the physiological bases of behavior, sensation, perception, mental processes, intelligence and creativity, motivation, and social influences on behavior. Moreover, although some psychologists focus on questions about particular individuals and their behavior—such as "Can Mary do college-level work?" and "Can Jim and Susan learn to cope with the problems of their marriage?"—many psychologists spend their time trying to answer basic questions of a less immediate, less personal nature, such as the following:

How does confining a child to a crib or playpen during its early years affect its later behavior?

Where and how does the brain store memories?

Do motives influence people's perceptions?

What are the effects of losing sleep?

How is language learned?

What conditions increase the retention of information?

How can intelligence be measured?

What occurs when people feel hungry?

Is aggression influenced by physiology?

How do people cope with anxiety?

What treatment programs help chronic schizophrenics live on their own in the community?

What social conditions lead to prejudice?

How does crowding affect people's behavior?

In later chapters we will be looking at the tentative answers to each of these questions.

Psychology: A unified science? Psychology is neither a clearly unified nor a complete body of knowledge. Psychologists research diverse subjects that are hard to tie together neatly. They also hold diverse philosophical views of what goals psychologists should aim at, what subjects they should study, and what methods they should use. In addition, like many other sciences, psychology is far from being complete. Psychologists do not have final answers to many important questions; in fact, there are many subjects about which psychologists know very little. A great deal of research remains to be done; so you should not expect to find in psychology a single or simple approach to the subject matter or answers to all your questions.

Psychology and animals. Goldfish, cockroaches, worms, crabs, bats, rats, pigeons, armadillos, dogs, cats, monkeys, people, and many other animals serve as subjects in psychological investigations. Students are often surprised and sometimes disheartened to find so much psychological research on animals. Psychologists use animals as research subjects for a number of reasons. Sometimes they happen to be genuinely interested in the behavior of the gerbil or the duck or the kangaroo or the chimpanzee. These are legitimate concerns. As we defined it, psychology is the study of all behavior, not simply human behavior. However, many—perhaps even most—psychologists who study animals are more interested in understanding human behavior. Why would psychologists who are basically interested in human behavior choose to study animal behavior instead?

One reason is ethics. There are many kinds of research that cannot ethically be conducted with people. Consider brain research: To understand how the brain affects behavior, psychologists sometimes remove part of it—in animals, of course. To study the effects of heredity on behavior, psychologists sometimes arrange genetics through animal-breeding programs. Similarly, using animal subjects, psychologists can explore the consequences of potentially destructive experiences such as isolation, crowding, punishment, malnutrition in infancy, or stress during pregnancy.[1]

Moreover, animals have undeniable practical advantages as subjects. They are cooperative, convenient, and easily studied for long periods of time. The big brown bat, for example, weighs 25 grams (nearly 1 ounce), eats very little, has minimal housing requirements, demands no salary, needs no deception, and arrives on time. When the psychologist goes on vacation, the bat can be stored several months in a cigar box in the refrigerator with a little water. When the psychologist returns, the bat is easily thawed in an hour and ready for study (1). Furthermore, specific animals have advantages for particular kinds of research. Pigeons, for example, have

[1]Psychologists also study the effects of the brain, heredity, and stress on human behavior, but they do it less directly. To learn about the brain's relationship to human behavior (a topic we explore in Chapter 4), psychologists sometimes observe people who have sustained limited brain damage. As we will see in Chapter 3, psychologists investigate the effects of heredity on human behavior by comparing the behavioral characteristics of blood relatives of varying degrees of closeness. And they sometimes study the consequences of human stress (discussed in Chapter 11) by observing people who have endured disasters, battered childhoods, prisoner-of-war camps, and so on.

excellent vision—particularly color vision—and thus make good candidates for studies of vision. Fruit flies, on the other hand, are excellent subjects for genetic studies because they reproduce quickly—a new generation appears in less than two weeks. Even the most enthusiastic and dedicated psychologist could not study more than three generations of people in a lifetime (2).

Finally, some psychologists argue that basic processes of behavior are easier to detect in simple animals than in complex people. These researchers assume that many psychological principles apply to both animals and people. To put it another way, they believe that their findings about animal behavior *generalize* to human behavior. There's little doubt that many principles do generalize from animals to people. For instance, animals and people both learn in similar ways, as we will see in Chapter 7. In general, however, few psychologists believe that the principles derived from animal research will explain *all* human behavior.

In this text we will be concerned primarily with people. We will look at studies of animals only when they advance our understanding of human behavior. We turn now to the movements that have given American psychology its present shape.

Figure 1-3. Using animal subjects, psychologists can explore the effects of potentially destructive experiences like crowding. (Left: John Oldenkamp; right: Fujihara, from Monkmeyer.)

FIVE MOVEMENTS THAT SHAPED PSYCHOLOGY

People appeared on earth about 4 million years ago, and they have probably been trying to understand themselves ever since. Aristotle (384–322 B.C.), the Greek philosopher, is sometimes called the Father of Psychology, but speculation about psychological matters did not begin with Aristotle. Hundreds of years before him, the earliest philosophers on record were theorizing about such subjects. We begin our brief view of the shaping of psychology at a much later point in history—in the nineteenth century, when the field called "psychology" emerged. For centuries philosophers had been speculating about the human mind. Physiologists were just beginning to study the brain, the nerves, and the sense organs using scientific methods. Most importantly, Gustav Fechner (1801–1887), an eminent physicist, had shown how mental processes could also be studied by the same scientific methods. Early in the 1850s Fechner had become interested in the relationship between physical stimulation and the resulting sensations people experienced. He was especially fascinated by the sensitivity of the human senses. How bright must a star be to be seen? How loud must a noise be to be heard? How heavy must a touch be to be felt? Fechner devised the necessary techniques to find precise answers to questions like these. When his major work, *Elements of Psychophysics,* was published in 1860, it showed other scientists how experimental and mathematical techniques could be used in the laboratory to study mental processes. Less than two decades later, a German physiologist, Wilhelm Wundt, founded a discipline that he called psychology.

Originally trained as a physician, Wilhelm Wundt (1832–1920) taught physiology for

Figure 1-4. Wilhelm Wundt, 1832–1920. (The Bettmann Archive.)

seventeen years at the University of Heidelberg, Germany. Early in his career Wundt showed an intense interest in behavior—however, at this time the study of behavior had no identity of its own; its subject matter belonged to philosophy. Wundt thought that psychology should become an independent science; so in 1875 he accepted a position as chairman of the Philosophy Department (the department in which psychology was included) at the University in Leipsig, Germany. Wundt is credited with founding the first experimental psychology laboratory in the world four years later in 1879[2]; so in that year psychology became a laboratory science.

Wilhelm Wundt was a solemn, scholarly man. He wrote voluminously—in fact, he published more than 50,000 pages before he died. He believed that psychology should investigate the *elements* of the human mind. In the words of Edward Titchener, Wundt's student:

[2]Is anything ever really the first of its kind? Probably not. Historians can usually find a "forerunner." So it is with psychology laboratories. William James, the American philosopher and psychologist, had a room at Harvard University set aside for psychological experimentation in 1875. A German philosopher named Carl Stumpf is said to have had an "experimental psychology laboratory" even before that—a cigar box full of tuning forks.

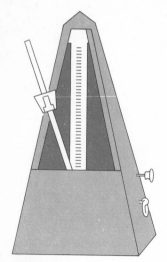

Figure 1-5. Metronome.

The world of psychology contains looks and tones and feels; it is the world of dark and light, of noise and silence, of rough and smooth; its space is sometimes large and sometimes small, as everyone knows who in adult life has gone back to his childhood's home; its time is sometimes short and sometimes long. . . . It contains also the thoughts, emotions, memories, imaginations, volitions that you naturally ascribe to mind . . . mind is simply the *inclusive name of all these phenomena* [3].

How were psychologists supposed to study these mental elements? Wundt and his followers championed a method called *analytic introspection*—a special kind of self-observation. Each self-observer was carefully trained to answer specific, well-defined questions in the laboratory setting. For example, in one study, Wundt and his students listened to the beats of a metronome (a mechanical instrument that makes repeated clicking sounds at an adjustable pace and is used by music students to hold a specific rhythm). As soon as a pattern ended, they immediately reported their sensations and perceptions. Wundt himself recorded that he had the

sensation of an agreeable whole when the clicks ended. He detected a feeling of slight tension as he waited for the clicks to begin. When they increased in rate, he felt mildly excited (4). Proceeding in this general way, Wundt and his followers analyzed many kinds of sensations into their component parts. Remember that they were looking for the basic elements of the mind.

Wilhelm Wundt, Edward Titchener, and Structuralism

In 1892 one of Wundt's most able students, an English psychologist, Edward Titchener (1867–1927), migrated to the United States and took charge of a new experimental psychology laboratory at Cornell University. There he spread Wundt's ideas and became the leader of the movement known as *structuralism*. The structuralists (1) believed that psychologists should study the human mind, primarily sensory experience; (2) emphasized painstaking introspective studies in the laboratory; and (3) aimed at analyzing mental phenomena into elements, discovering the connections between the various elements, and explaining them by locating related structures in the nervous system.

Structuralism had some clear limitations. First, structuralist psychologists advocated one and only one method of study: analyzing people's introspective reports. Since children and animals could not be trained in analytic introspection, they were automatically excluded as subjects. Second, structuralist psychologists considered complex matters such as thinking, language, morality, and abnormal behavior inappropriate subjects for research. Third, they were unwilling to address themselves to practical issues. Very soon other psychology movements arose to remedy these shortcomings.

Figure 1-6. William James, 1842–1910. (Culver Pictures, Inc.)

William James and Functionalism

William James (1842–1910), an eminent American psychologist, taught philosophy and psychology at Harvard University for thirty-five years. He neither led nor followed any psychological movement. His special "system" of psychology came from his own wise and human observations of himself and life. James opposed structuralism because he saw it as essentially inaccurate in its conception of mental processes. The mental processes, James argued, are "personal and unique," "continually changing," "evolving over time," and "selective" in helping the individual adapt to the environment.

In the early 1900s several psychologists at the University of Chicago—including John Dewey (1859–1952), the famous philosopher and educator—were strongly influenced by James's views. Like James, they were interested in the mental processes, particularly in how these processes *functioned* to help people survive in a dangerous world. Moreover, although they disagreed with one another on other issues, they were strongly united in their opposition to structuralism. Identified as *functionalists*, they shared the following beliefs: Psychologists (1) should study the functioning of the mental processes and a large range of other subjects, including the behavior of children and animals, abnormal problems, and individual differences between people; (2) should be free to use both the introspective and objective methods of observation; and (3) should apply psychology to practical pursuits like education, law, and business.

On many basic issues the psychologists in the functional movement went their separate ways. Although diversity and flexibility are attractive characteristics, they make it hard for movements to survive intact. Not surprisingly, functionalism was soon replaced by a new American psychology movement, behaviorism.

John Watson and Behaviorism

John Watson (1878–1958) completed his doctorate in the field of animal psychology at the University of Chicago under a functionalist professor. As a young man, he was very dissatisfied with the prevailing practices of American psychology. He criticized both structuralism and functionalism as follows:

In all other sciences the facts of observation are objective, verifiable and can be reproduced by all trained observers. . . . Psychology, on the other

Figure 1-7. John B. Watson, 1878–1958. (Historical Picture Service, Chicago.)

hand, as a science of "consciousness" has no such community of data. . . . The psychologist's use of "introspection" as its principal method has been another serious bar to progress. . . . All that introspective psychology has been able to contribute is the assertion that mental states are made up of several thousand irreducible units like redness, greenness, coolness, warmth, and the like, and their ghosts called images, and the affective irreducibles, pleasantness and unpleasantness. . . . Whether there are ten irreducible sensations or a hundred thousand (even granting their existence), whether there are two affective tones or fifty, matters not one whit to that organized body of world-wide data we call science [5].

Watson was determined to make psychology a respectable science on par with the other physical sciences. In 1912 he began lecturing and writing to publicize his views. That year the movement known as _behaviorism_ is said to have been born. Watson was a strong backer of the idea that psychologists should be objective; he urged them to study behavior as their subject matter and use the methods of experimentation and observation.

Watson's exciting and forceful prose combined with his unconventional ideas to attract the attention of many psychologists. Consider Watson's famous statement about the environment's important influence on human abilities:

Give me a dozen healthy infants well formed and my own specified world to bring them up in and I'll guarantee to take any one at random and train him to become any type of specialist I might select—doctor, lawyer, artist, merchant-chief, and yes, even beggarman and thief, regardless of his talents, penchants, tendencies, abilities, vocations, and race of his ancestors [6].

Such flamboyance was hard to ignore.

Even Watson's studies were dramatic. Watson taught at Johns Hopkins University in Baltimore, and he occasionally did research at nearby hospitals. In one study he systematically observed and tested newborn infants over the course of their first year of life. Later Watson catalogued their reflexes and emotional responses. On the basis of this study Watson claimed that people begin life with a small repertoire of innate responses. Complex human behaviors, such as personality, thought, emotion, and language, he maintained, were all learned later on by simple conditioning. To prove that fears followed this model, Watson took an eleven-month-old infant named Albert and (with his mother's permission) conditioned him to fear white rats. The psychological community was horrified. Before you judge Watson too harshly, you should know that many later fear-treatment programs have been based, in part, on information acquired in this study. (More details on this experiment are found in Chapter 7.)

Many young American psychologists were attracted to the behaviorist movement. In fact, behaviorism in some form or another dominated American psychology for about thirty years. In general, the early behaviorists believed the following: (1) Psychologists should study behavior. The environment is the most important determinant of simple and complex behavior, abilities, and traits. For that reason, learning is an especially important topic for study. (2) The introspective methods should be abandoned for objective methods such as experimentation, observation, and testing. (3) Psychologists should aim at the description, explanation, prediction, and control of behavior. They should also undertake practical goals, such as advising parents, lawmakers, educators, and business people. (4) Animal behavior should be investigated (along with human behavior) because it is frequently simpler to study and understand than human behavior.

Behaviorism began as an angry movement. As it evolved, its philosophy was clarified, modified, and broadened. The behavioristic approach has had, and continues to have, a profound impact on modern psychology. You may have noticed that our definition and discussion of the nature of psychology were heavily influenced by behavioristic ideas.

Max Wertheimer and Gestalt Psychology

While behaviorism was flourishing in America, gestalt psychology was growing up in Germany. (*Gestalt* is the German word for shape, pattern, or structure.) Like behaviorism, gestalt psychology arose, in part, as a protest against structuralist policies. The gestaltists were particularly unhappy about the structuralists' goal: analyzing the mental processes into simple elements. They argued that psychologists should study *whole phenomena.*

The movement called gestalt psychology is said to have begun in 1912 when Max Wertheimer (1880–1941), a German psychologist at the University of Frankfurt, published a report on some experimental studies of *apparent movement.* If we watch two stationary light bulbs which are appropriately positioned and then turned on and off sequentially (in turn) at the proper rate, we perceive a single moving light (apparent movement). Electric signs containing elements which appear to move demonstrate this phenomenon vividly. In reality, nothing is moving. Rather, thousands of light bulbs are being turned on and off at the proper times. Wertheimer set out to study apparent movement in the laboratory. He put two electric lights on the edge of a table several feet apart. Then he attached a vertical rod to the opposite edge of the same table so that it was equally distant from the two light bulbs. The bulbs cast two separate shadows of the rod on the wall (see Figure 1-9a). When the lights were alternately switched on and off at the proper speed, the two shadows were seen as a single shadow that moved back and forth.

Figure 1-8. Max Wertheimer, 1880–1941. (United Press International Photo.)

After demonstrating this phenomenon, Wertheimer began to investigate the reasons for it. Laboratory study ruled out a number of explanations. Eventually Wertheimer proposed that the phenomenon resulted from the organization of the human brain and eyes which perceive movement under certain conditions of sensory stimulation.

The study of apparent movement demonstrates some of the major characteristics of gestalt psychology:

1. Apparent movement occurs because people impose their interpretations on sensory data. Generally, the gestaltists believed that psychologists should study subjective experience—the meanings people give to the objects and events of their world.

2. Apparent movement was studied by introspective techniques; that is, subjects reported what they saw. The gestalt psychologists believed that introspection was a legitimate method; at the same time they also endorsed the objective methods.

3. Apparent movement cannot be understood by analyzing it into its component events. At any given instant in time one light bulb is on and one is off. In reality, there is no physical motion. The motion exists only in the observer's perception. To understand apparent movement or any

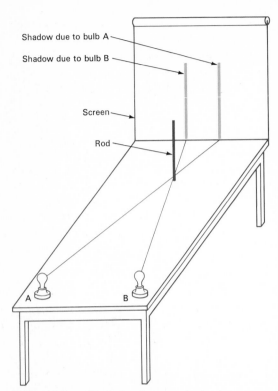

Figure 1-9a. Wertheimer's apparatus to show apparent movement. **b.** The apparent-movement phenomenon produces the effect of the moving news bulletin in Times Square. (Ed Grazola, Magnum.)

other phenomenon, the gestaltists believed that the psychologist must take into account all of the interacting elements in the dynamic environment (*field*)—including the human being who is viewing it. In the case of apparent movement, one must understand the physiological functioning of the observer's eyes and brain as well as the configuration of lights.

For the most part, the gestalt psychologists were interested in questions of whole experience. They insisted that the whole was unique and that it always influenced how people viewed any one part of a situation. In fact, the gestalt slogan became "The whole is greater than the sum of its parts."

The gestalt movement was a strong and

unified one. Its views shaped the direction of psychology in Germany and later influenced psychology in the United States. As we will see, at least two contemporary American movements—humanistic psychology and cognitive psychology—show its marked influence.

Sigmund Freud and Psychoanalytic Theory

The theories of Sigmund Freud (1856–1939), a Viennese physician who specialized in the treatment of neurotic disorders (such as excessive anxiety reactions and physical ailments without a physical basis), are widely accepted by the public—so widely accepted that many people equate psychology with *psychoanalytic theory* (the general name for Freud's theories about personality, abnormality, and treatment). Psychoanalytic theory is, however, only one psychological theory.

The psychoanalytic movement did not resemble the other four movements we have examined in that Freud never attempted to specify goals and methods for psychology. Instead, he proposed a comprehensive personality theory that took shape from his own clinical experience. We will be considering the psychoanalytic movement as a psychology movement because it has been immensely influential inside psychology and because it has attracted a large following among psychologists.

How did psychoanalytic theory originate? In Freud's day medical doctors did not understand and could not successfully treat the neurotic disorders. Freud was interested in both these subjects. As he observed his neurotic patients, he formulated *hypotheses* (tentative explanations) for their behavior. He tried to test these hypotheses as he treated his patients. Drawing on a vast number of clinical observations and on his understanding of himself, Freud gradually formulated a comprehensive and well-integrated theory that explained both the normal and the abnormal personality. We will be looking at Freud's ideas on the development of the normal personality in Chapter 12 and on the abnormal personality in Chapter 14; in Chapter 15, we will examine Freud's recommendations for treating abnormal behavior.

Freud's followers held the following beliefs: (1) Psychologists should study human personality, the laws that govern it, and the experiences that shape it. (2) Unconscious motives, conflicts, fears, and frustrations are considered the important determinants of personality. (3) Early childhood is identified as the critical period during which the personality is formed. (4) Personality can best be studied by observing individual patients in clinical settings as they are treated for their problems.

Special techniques such as dream analysis and interpretation of the patient's free associations were developed to probe beneath superficial behavior to uncover the meaning of that behavior. Using these techniques, psychoanalytic psychologists study their patients' thoughts, dreams, fantasies, preoccupations, mistakes, accidents, emotions, motives, needs, experiences, and memories over a long period of time. Psychoanalytic psychology is still very much alive today both in its original form and in numerous modifications.

FOUR CURRENT VIEWS OF PSYCHOLOGY

Psychology continues to grow and change; it cannot yet be cast into a single mold. Although psychologists do not generally belong to movements today, they still show distinct differences in the ways they approach psychology, and they continue to disagree on some very fundamental philosophical issues.

Figure 1-10. Sigmund Freud, 1856–1939, in his study. (Historical Picture Service, Chicago.)

Even today there is no consensus on goals, on appropriate subject matter, or on the best methods for studying psychological phenomena.

Many psychologists identify to a greater or lesser degree with one of four major points of view—the psychoanalytic, the neobehavioristic, the cognitive, or the humanistic—while many favor an *eclectic* approach—that is, a combination of viewpoints.

The Psychoanalytic Point of View

Many psychologists—especially those who study personality, adjustment, abnormality, and treatment and those who work in clinic settings with psychologically troubled people—take the psychoanalytic point of view. Although there are wide individual variations in their specific beliefs, psychoanalytically oriented psychologists generally hold the views stated in the preceding section.

The following excerpt, which comes from an article by Sigmund Freud, illustrates the general methods that psychoanalytic psychologists frequently use to research a personality process. The reading describes how Dr. Joseph Breuer, Freud's colleague, discovered the significance of certain neurotic symptoms. As you read, try to pinpoint the distinctive features of the psychoanalytic approach.

The investigation of a personality process: The psychoanalytic approach of Sigmund Freud

"I was a student, busy with the passing of my last examinations, when another physician of Vienna, Dr. Joseph Breuer [was beginning to understand and treat an hysterical patient.] . . . Dr. Breuer's patient was a girl of twenty-one, of a high degree of intelligence. She had developed in the course of her two years' illness, a series of physical and mental disturbances which well deserved to be taken seriously. She had a severe paralysis of both right extremities with anesthesia, and at times the same affection of the members of the left side of the body; disturbance of eye movements, and much impairment of vision; difficulty in maintaining the position of the head, an intense . . . nausea when she attempted to take nourishment, and at one time for several weeks a loss of the power to drink, in spite of tormenting thirst. Her power of speech was also diminished, and this progressed so far that she could neither speak nor understand her mother tongue; and, finally, she was subject to states of 'absence,' of confusion, delirium, alteration of her whole personality. . . . The illness first appeared while the patient was caring for her father, whom she tenderly loved, during the severe illness which led to his death, a task which she was compelled to abandon because she herself fell ill. . . .

". . . [Dr. Breuer] noticed that the patient in her states of 'absence,' of psychic alteration, usually mumbled over several words to herself. These seemed to spring from associations with which her thoughts were busy. The doctor, who was able to get these words, put her in a sort of hypnosis and repeated them to her over and over, in order to bring up any associations that they might have. The patient yielded to his suggestion and reproduced for him those psychic creations which controlled her thoughts during her 'absences,' and which betrayed themselves in these single spoken words. . . . Whenever she had related a number of such fancies, she was, as it were, freed and restored to her normal mental life. . . .

"The doctor soon hit upon the fact that through such cleansing of the soul more could be accomplished than a temporary removal of the constantly recurring mental 'clouds.' Symptoms of the disease would [actually] disappear when in hypnosis the patient could be made to remember the situation and the associative connections under which they first appeared, provided free vent was given to the emotions which they aroused. [At this point Freud quotes Breuer directly:] 'There was in the summer a time of intense heat, and the patient had suffered very much from thirst; for, without any apparent reason, she had suddenly become unable to drink. She would take a glass of water in her hand, but as soon as it touched her lips she would push it away as though suffering from hydrophobia. . . . When this had been going on about six weeks, she was talking one day in hypnosis about her English governess, whom she disliked, and finally told, with every sign of disgust, how she had come into the room of the governess, and how that lady's little dog, that she abhorred, had drunk out of a glass. Out of respect for the conventions the patient had remained silent. Now, after she had given energetic expression to her restrained anger, she asked for a drink, drank a large quantity of water without trouble, and woke from hypnosis with the glass at her lips. The symptom thereupon vanished permanently.'

"Permit me to dwell for a moment on this experience. . . . This would be a pregnant discovery if the expectation could be confirmed that still other, perhaps the majority of symptoms, originated in this way and could be removed by the same method. Breuer spared no pains to convince himself of this and investigated the parthogenesis of the other more serious symptoms in a more orderly way. Such was indeed the case; almost all the symptoms originated in exactly this way, as remnants, as precipitates . . . of affectively toned experiences, which for that reason we later called 'psychic traumata.' The nature of the symptoms became clear through their relation to the scene which caused them. They were . . . 'determined' by the scene whose memory traces they embodied, and so could no longer be described as arbitrary or enigmatical functions of the neurosis. . . .

"When a number of years later, I began to use Breuer's researches and treatment on my own patients, my experiences completely coincided with his. . . . If you will permit me to generalize, . . . we may express our results up to this point in the formula: Our hysterical patients suffer from reminiscences. Their symptoms are the remnants and the memory symbols of certain (traumatic) experiences. . . . They cannot escape from the past and neglect present reality in its favor. This fixation of the mental life on the pathogenic traumata is an essential, and practically a most significant characteristic of the neurosis [7]."

The Neobehavioristic Point of View

Today the behavioristic approach is much broader and more flexible than it was in Watson's day. Behaviorists still emphasize the study of behavior, but they have become increasingly interested in complex human processes. Currently, the environment is viewed as only one major determinant of behavior; internal determinants—such as thoughts and perceptions—are also considered important. This new behaviorism is sometimes called *neobehaviorism* to distinguish it from Watson's original approach. We will be using the terms "neobehaviorism" and "behaviorism" interchangeably throughout the text. The major characteristics of the neobehaviorist position are its insistence on (1) asking precise, well-delineated questions; (2) using scientific methods; and (3) doing very careful, accurate research.

Harry Harlow, a psychologist at the University of Wisconsin and a past president of the American Psychological Association, would be labeled neobehavioristic in approach. In this excerpt Harlow describes how he and his colleagues attacked a research problem in "love." As you read, try to specify the characteristics of the neobehaviorist philosophy.

Investigating love in the psychology laboratory: The approach of a neobehaviorist

"Our interest in infant-monkey love grew out of a research program that involved the separation of monkeys from their mothers a few hours after birth. . . . We were particularly careful to provide the infant monkeys with a folded gauze diaper on the floor of their cages, in accordance with Dr. Van Wagenen's observation that they would tend to maintain intimate contact with such soft, pliant surfaces, especially during nursing. We were impressed by the deep personal attachments that the monkeys formed for these diaper pads, and by the distress that they exhibited when the pads were briefly removed once a day for purposes of sanitation. The behavior of the infant monkeys was reminiscent of the human infant's attachment to its blankets, pillows, rag dolls or cuddly teddy bears.

"These observations suggested the series of experiments in which we have sought to compare the importance of nursing and all associated activities with that of simple bodily contact in engendering the infant monkey's attachment to its mother. For this purpose we contrived two surrogate mother monkeys. One is a bare welded-wire cylindrical form surmounted by a wooden head with a crude face. In the other the welded-wire is cushioned by a sheathing of terry cloth. We placed eight newborn monkeys in individual cages, each with equal access to a cloth and a wire mother. . . . Four of the infants received their milk from one mother and four from the other, the milk being furnished in each case by a nursing bottle, with its nipple protruding from the mother's 'breast.'

"The two mothers quickly proved to be physiologically equivalent. The monkeys in the two groups drank the same amount of milk and gained weight at the same rate. But the two mothers proved to be by no means psychologically equivalent. Records made automatically showed that both groups of infants spent far more time climbing and clinging on their cloth-covered mother than they did on their wire mothers. During the infants' first 14 days of life the floors of the cages were warmed by an electric heating pad, but most of the infants left the pad as soon as they could climb on the unheated cloth mother. Moreover, as the monkeys grew older, they tended to spend an increasing amount of time clinging and cuddling on her pliant terry cloth surface. Those that secured their nourishment from the wire mother showed no tendency to spend more time on her than feeding required, contradicting the idea that affection is a response that is learned or derived in association with the reduction of hunger or thirst.

"These results attest the importance—possibly the overwhelming importance—of bodily contact and the immediate comfort it supplies in forming the infant's attachment for its mother . . . [8]."

The Cognitive Point of View

From the 1930s to the 1960s "respectable" American psychologists talked little and cautiously—if at all—about the mind, images, thinking, making choices, solving problems, or other similar *cognitive processes* (mental activities). Watson's behaviorism made these topics taboo. The early behaviorists treated people as if they were "black boxes," which could be understood simply by measuring what went in and what came out—the *stimuli*

Figure 1-11. This infant monkey clings to its terrycloth surrogate mother, though it has nursed on the wire "mother" in the background. (Wisconsin Primate Laboratory.)

in the environment and the *responses* that were made to those stimuli. In the early 1960s cognitive psychologists began to rebel against the old behavioristic model, insisting that psychologists had to come to understand what was going on *inside* the black box—particularly the operation of the mind.

Cognitive psychologists share the following beliefs: (1) Psychologists should study mental processes such as imagery, thought, perception, memory, and language. In studying human problem solving, cognitive psychologists might ask: How do people solve problems? How do changes in the task alter problem-solving behavior? How are problem-solving skills learned? (2) The cognitive processes are assumed to be among the most important determinants of human behavior. (3) Psychologists should try to acquire precise knowledge of these cognitive processes.

In the excerpt that follows, Jerome Bruner, a cognitive psychologist at Harvard University, describes some research on children's cognitive styles. As you read, try to locate the characteristic features of the cognitive approach.

Studying children's cognitive styles in the laboratory: The approach of a cognitive psychologist

"We have been conducting a series of experimental studies on a group of some seventy school children over the last four years. The studies have led us to distinguish [a] . . . dimension of cognitive activity that can be described as ranging from episodic empiricism at one end to cumulative constructionism at the other. . . . One of the experiments employs the game of Twenty Questions. A child—in this case he is between 10 and 12—is told that a car has gone off the road and hit a tree. He is to ask questions that can be answered by 'yes' or 'no' to discover the cause of the accident. After completing the problem, the same task is given him again, though he is told that the accident had a different cause this time. In all, the procedure is repeated four times. Children enjoy playing the game. They also differ quite markedly in the approach or strategy they bring to the task. There are various elements in the strategies employed. In the first place, one may distinguish clearly between two types of questions asked: the one is designed for locating constraints in the problem, constraints that will eventually give shape to an hypothesis; the other is the hypothesis as question. It is the difference between, 'Was there anything wrong with the driver?' and 'Was the driver rushing to the doctor's office for an appointment and the car got out of control?' There are children who precede hypotheses with efforts to locate constraint[s] and there are those who, to use our local slang, are 'pot-shotters,' who string out hypotheses non-cumulatively one after the other. A second element of strategy is its connectivity of information gathering: the extent to which questions asked utilize or ignore or violate information previously obtained. The questions asked by children tend to be organized in cycles, each cycle of questions usually being given over to the pursuit of some particular notion. Both within cycles and between cycles one can discern a marked difference . . . [in] the connectivity of the child's performance. Needless to say, children who employ constraint location as a technique preliminary to the formulation of hypotheses tend to be far more connected in their harvesting of information. Persistence is another feature of strategy, a characteristic compounded of what appear to be two components: a sheer doggedness component, and a persistence that stems from the sequential organization that a child brings to the task. Doggedness is probably just animal spirits or the need for achievement. . . . Organized persistence is a maneuver for protecting our fragile cognitive apparatus from overload. The child who has flooded himself with disorganized information from unconnected hypotheses will become discouraged and confused sooner than the child who has shown a certain cunning in his strategy of getting information—a cunning whose principal component is the recognition that the value of information is not simply in getting it but in being able to carry it. The persistence of the organized child stems from his knowledge of how to organize questions in cycles, how to summarize things to himself and the like.

"Episodic empiricism is illustrated by information gathering that is unbound by prior constraints, that lacks connectivity, and that is deficient in organizational persistence. The opposite extreme is illustrated by an approach that is characterized by constraint sensitivity, by connective maneuvers, and by organized persistence . . . [9]."

The Humanistic Point of View

Humanistically oriented psychologists are united by a common goal: they want to humanize psychology; that is, they want to make psychology the study of "what it means to be alive as a human being [10]." They come from diverse backgrounds: some from clinical settings with psychologically troubled people; some from research settings where they are frequently involved in studying topics such as personality, emotion, development, language, and social behavior. Although humanistically oriented psychologists vary considerably in their individual beliefs, they share the following general attitudes:

1. Although psychologists must gather knowledge, their major goal should be service. Psychologists should help people understand themselves so that they may develop to their fullest potential. They should also aim at expanding and enriching the individual's life.
2. Psychologists should study living *human beings as wholes*, rather than compartmentalizing human functioning into categories such as perception, learning, and personality. Significant human problems—including personal responsibility, life goals, commitment, fulfillment, creativity, spontaneity, and values—should be the subjects of psychological investigations.
3. Psychologists should focus on subjective

Figure 1-12. Abraham Maslow, 1908–1970. (Brandeis University.)

awareness (how people interpret their experiences) since these interpretations are fundamental to all human activity. (This emphasis on the whole person and on subjective human experience reflects the influence of the gestalt movement.)

4. Psychologists should strive to understand the individual, the exceptional, and the unpredictable, as well as the general and the universal. In contrast, psychoanalytic, neobehavioristic, and cognitive psychologists are most interested in discovering general laws of functioning.

5. The specific methods that psychologists adopt are secondary to the problems they choose to study. Consequently, humanistic psychologists use many kinds of research strategies: scientific methods, individual case studies, introspective techniques, and even the analysis of literary works. Because humanistic psychologists believe that intuitive awareness is a valid source of information, they do not hesitate to rely on their own subjective impressions.

In the following excerpt, Abraham Maslow (1908–1970), an important figure in the humanistic movement, describes the beginning of his *self-actualization* (self-fulfillment) research. Note how Maslow's study exemplifies the humanistic approach.

The beginning of self-actualization research: The approach of a humanistically oriented psychologist

"My investigations on self-actualization were not planned to be research and did not start out as research. They started out as the effort of a young intellectual to try to understand two of his teachers whom he loved, adored, and admired, and who were very, very wonderful people. . . . I could not be content simply to adore, but sought to understand why these two people were so different from the run-of-the-mill people in the world. These two people were Ruth Benedict and Max Wertheimer. They were my teachers after I came with a Ph.D. from the West to New York City, and they were most remarkable human beings. My training in psychology equipped me not at all for understanding them. It was as if they were not quite people but something more than people. My own investigations began as a prescientific or nonscientific activity. I made descriptions and notes on Max Wertheimer, and I made notes on Ruth Benedict. When I tried to understand them, think about them, and write about them in my journal and my notes, I realized in one wonderful moment that their two patterns could be generalized. I was talking about a kind of person, not about two noncomparable individuals. There was a wonderful excitement in that. I tried to see whether this pattern could be found elsewhere, and I did find it elsewhere, in one person after another.

"By ordinary standards of laboratory research, that is, of rigorous and controlled research, this simply was not research at all. My generalizations grew out of *my* selection of certain kinds of people. Obviously other judges are needed. So far, one man has selected perhaps two dozen people whom he liked or admired very much and thought were wonderful people and then tried to figure them out and found that he was able to describe a syndrome—the kind of pattern that seemed to fit all of them. . . . The people I selected for my investigation were older people, people who had lived much of their lives out and were visibly successful. . . . When you select out for careful study very fine and healthy people, strong people, creative people, saintly people, sagacious people—in fact, exactly the kind of people I picked out—then you get a different view of mankind. You are asking how tall can people grow, what can a human being become [11]?"

Eventually Maslow made a careful study of forty-nine persons who seemed to exemplify self-actualization. He discovered that they shared many characteristics including an objective perception of reality; the ability to accept themselves, other people, and nature; spontaneity; problem-centeredness rather than self-centeredness; a positive liking for solitude and privacy; independence; resistance to conformity; occasional peak experiences; a deep feeling of sympathy for all mankind; and profound interpersonal relationships with other adults (12).

Synthesis: One Psychology or Many?

Table 1-1 presents the psychoanalytic, neobehavioristic, cognitive, and humanistic views of psychology. Each view contributes important insights. The neobehavioristic approach offers psychology a responsible way of investigating the functioning of people and other animals. The cognitive movement reminds psychologists that the human mind is one of the most fascinating and important of subjects, and the psychoanalytic tradition points to the many mysterious aspects of personality that need thorough exploration. Finally, the humanistic philosophy offers important goals by insisting that psychologists research meaningful questions and use their knowledge for serving people.

AMERICAN PSYCHOLOGISTS TODAY

More than 35,000 Americans currently consider themselves psychologists. As pictured by a recent survey, they are a varied group.

TABLE 1-1. A COMPARISON OF FOUR CURRENT VIEWS OF PSYCHOLOGY

	Psychoanalytic View	Neobehavioristic View	Cognitive View	Humanistic View
Major Goals	Knowledge and service.	Knowledge.	Knowledge.	Service and enrichment primary; knowledge secondary.
Subject Matter	The laws that govern the development of normal and abnormal personality. Motives, conflicts, fears, and frustrations —conscious and unconscious— are also frequently studied.	Any well-defined question about simple or complex animal or human behavior.	The functioning of mental activities (perceptual processes, problem solving, memory, etc.)	Questions about the whole person, subjective human experience, and significant human problems. The extraordinary and individual as well as the usual and universal.
Research Methods	Clinical observations using special psychoanalytic procedures (interpretation of free associations, dream analysis, etc.)	All objective methods (experimentation, observation, testing, etc.)	All objective and introspective methods.	Objective methods, introspective methods, case studies, etc. Intuitive awareness is emphasized.

They range widely in age—from twenty-four to ninety-three. They reside in every American state and possession. Three-fourths of them hold the Doctor of Philosophy degree or a similar professional degree; another 24 percent hold a Master's degree. Only 25 percent of them are women (13). What do they study? What do they do?

What Do Psychologists Study?

Psychology is a vast field, as we have mentioned; and it grows vaster each year. Because no single person can master it all, psychologists tend to specialize in one or more particular subject matter areas. The fields of

specialization within psychology include abnormal behavior, counseling, psychotherapy, child development, adolescence, old age, learning, perception, motivation, emotion, language, thinking, personality, social behavior, the physiological bases of behavior, animal behavior, tests and measurements, psychology applied to industry, psychology applied to education, psychology applied to consumer affairs, psychology applied to the environment. The list goes on and on.

What Do Psychologists Do?

What do psychologists do? A recent survey indicated that about 37 percent of them pri-

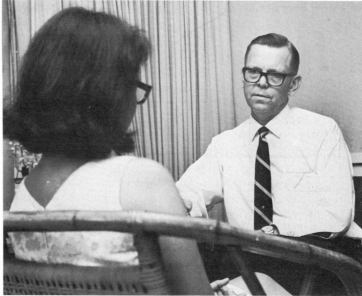

Figure 1-13. The broad range of careers in psychology includes experimental research, such as that done by psychologist Neal Miller shown in his laboratory at Rockefeller University (left), and psychotherapy, shown here at the Counselling Service Center in Singapore. (Left: Dr. Neal E. Miller; right: Fujihira, from Monkmeyer.)

marily teach and/or do research. Nearly 21 percent of them work in clinical settings—doing counseling, psychotherapy, and testing. About 19 percent are mainly administrators; they may direct clinics, research projects, consultant agencies, or training programs. Some 10 percent primarily design, administer, or interpret psychological tests. Only 1 percent principally act as consultants to industry (14).

Psychologists who see themselves primarily as teachers, researchers, or scholars frequently focus their studies on a single subject matter area—such as child development, or language, or personality. On the other hand, many psychologists apply psychological findings from several related subject matter areas to problems in a particular setting such as a school or mental health clinic or in industry. Psychologists are usually known by the setting in which they work or the subject matter which they study. Table 1-2 presents a list of some of the major specialists in psychology.

TABLE 1-2. MAJOR SPECIALISTS IN PSYCHOLOGY

Specialist	Percentage of Total
Clinical psychologist	29
Experimental psychologist	10
Counseling psychologist	10
Educational psychologist	10
School psychologist	9
Industrial and personnel psychologist	7
Social psychologist	3
Developmental psychologist	3
Personality psychologist	2
Psychometric psychologist	2
Engineering psychologist	2
Miscellaneous	13

Source: J. Cates. "Psychology's manpower: Report on the 1968 national register of scientific and technical personnel." *American Psychologist*, 1970, 25, 254–263.

Psychologists, Psychiatrists, and Psychoanalysts

Many people confuse clinical psychologists, psychiatrists, and psychoanalysts. Their roles are quite similar: All three professionals frequently work in clinic settings, diagnosing and treating people with mild and severe psychological problems. The major difference between them is their training. *Clinical psychologists* usually hold a Doctor of Philosophy (Ph.D.) degree in psychology, and they have served an internship in a psychiatric setting. That means that they have studied the areas of normal and abnormal psychology; they have learned to diagnose and treat psychological problems; and they have been trained to do research to further the understanding of these conditions. It is important to note that although many clinical psychologists work in clinical settings, a great many do research and/or teach in colleges and universities.

Psychiatrists, in contrast, hold a Doctor of Medicine (M.D.) degree; in addition, they have served a three- to five-year residency in a psychiatric hospital. Essentially, psychiatrists are physicians (medical doctors) who have been trained to detect and treat various psychological disturbances, using psychological methods as well as drugs, surgery, and other medical procedures.

Finally, we have *psychoanalysts.* About 10 percent of all psychiatrists in the United States call themselves psychoanalysts. In addition to their psychiatric training, they have studied Freud's personality theories intensively and they have learned Freud's special psychoanalytic treatment procedures. They have undergone psychoanalysis themselves. They have also graduated from a recognized psychoanalytic training institute. In theory, anyone could become a psychoanalyst by attending the psychoanalytic training institute and undergoing psychoanalysis; however, in practice, most psychoanalytic training institutes accept only physicians. So psychoanalysis—at least in America—is essentially a subdivision of psychiatry.

STUDY GUIDE 1

Key Terms. psychology, behavior, objective, observation, hypothetical construct, infer (inference), generalize, analytic introspection, apparent movement, field, hypothesis, eclectic, cognitive process, stimulus, response, clinical psychologist, psychiatrist, psychoanalyst.

Important Research. case study of a neurotic young woman (Freud), mother-infant "love" in monkeys (Harlow), cognitive styles (Bruner), self-actualized personalities (Maslow).

People to Identify. Gustav Fechner, Wilhelm Wundt, Edward Titchener, William James, John Watson, Max Wertheimer, Sigmund Freud, Harry Harlow, Jerome Bruner, Abraham Maslow.

Important Theories. structuralism, functionalism, behaviorism (and neobehavioristic approach), gestalt psychology, psychoanalytic theory, cognitive approach, humanistic approach.

Self-Quiz

1. This textbook defines psychology as [**a**] the study of personality; [**b**] the science of behavior; [**c**] the study of how people think, feel, and change; [**d**] the application of research studies to real-life problems.
2. Psychologists study [**a**] people's attitudes and

prejudices; [**b**] personality and abnormal behavior; [**c**] the brain and its functioning; [**d**] all of the above.

3. Wundt and Titchener were important figures in the development of [**a**] functionalism; [**b**] behaviorism; [**c**] gestalt psychology; [**d**] structuralism.

4. The belief that complex human behaviors are learned by simple conditioning is characteristic of [**a**] functionalism; [**b**] behaviorism; [**c**] gestalt psychology; [**d**] structuralism.

5. "Eclectic" means [**a**] based on inferences; [**b**] combining a variety of approaches; [**c**] mildly neurotic; [**d**] an illusion of apparent motion.

6. Clinical observations that emphasize irrational thoughts, dreams, and memories would be characteristic of the _____ approach. [**a**] cognitive; [**b**] neobehavioristic; [**c**] psychoanalytic; [**d**] humanistic.

7. Informal observations on people who are unusually well adjusted would be most likely to come from a psychologist with a _____ approach. [**a**] cognitive; [**b**] neobehavioristic; [**c**] psychoanalytic; [**d**] humanistic.

8. An experimental study of the effect of crowded living conditions on children's aggression would be characteristic of the _____ approach. [**a**] cognitive; [**b**] psychoanalytic; [**c**] neobehavioristic; [**d**] humanistic.

9. The term "cognitive" is roughly equivalent to the term [**a**] "mental"; [**b**] "hypothetical"; [**c**] "observable"; [**d**] "emotional."

10. The most common type of work done by American psychologists is [**a**] psychological testing; [**b**] applying psychology to business; [**c**] teaching and/or research; [**d**] counseling and similar clinical work.

11. Which of the following is true of a psychiatrist but is *not* usually true of a clinical psychologist? [**a**] has an M.D. degree; [**b**] works in a clinical setting (hospital, clinic, or office); [**c**] tries to help people solve personal psychological problems; [**d**] treats a wide range of psychological disorders, mild to severe.

12. What is the main difference between a psychiatrist and a psychoanalyst? [**a**] Only the psychoanalyst is fully qualified to treat mental disorders; [**b**] only the psychoanalyst has an M.D. degree; [**c**] psychiatrists are mostly American but psychoanalysts are usually European; [**d**] only the psychoanalyst has special intensive training in Freud's theories.

13. One of the most basic beliefs of gestalt psychology is that [**a**] the experimental method is the most effective procedure; [**b**] events must be broken down into parts to be studied effectively; [**c**] to be properly understood, events must be studied as whole phenomena; [**d**] psychologists should focus on personality, emotion, motivation, and adjustment.

14. Analytic introspection is [**a**] a method of self-observation used by Wundt and his followers; [**b**] a technique of recalling childhood events; [**c**] the systematic observation and recording of all aspects of an experiment; [**d**] the application of Freud's method of analysis to oneself.

15. Which of the following is *not* a hypothetical construct? [**a**] anger; [**b**] imagination; [**c**] free will; [**d**] language.

Exercises

1. HYPOTHETICAL CONSTRUCTS. A hypothetical construct is a characteristic, condition, or process that cannot be directly observed or measured but is assumed to exist because it has effects that can be directly observed or measured. Hypothetical constructs are called constructs because they are formed or constructed in people's minds. They are called hypothetical because we hypothesize or guess that they exist, although we are not absolutely certain that they do. To make certain you understand what hypothetical constructs are, pick out the hypothetical constructs from this list: [**a**] mental illness; [**b**] an eyeblink; [**c**] personality; [**d**] "the will to live"; [**e**] sex drive; [**f**] the brain; [**g**] the good mood of a friend; [**h**] learning; [**i**] a friend saying, "I feel great today!"; [**j**] heartbeat; [**k**] musical talent; [**l**] intelligence; [**m**] trees and flowers; [**n**] Mother Nature.

2. PSYCHOLOGICAL MOVEMENTS AND POINTS OF VIEW. To help you sort out the ideas of the various movements and points of view in psychology, match the movements or viewpoints with the statements that characterize them.

Movements: structuralism (S), functionalism (F), behaviorism (B), gestalt psychology (G), psychoanalytic theory (P).

_____ **1.** Concentrates on understanding subjective experiences.

_____ **2.** Believes that psychology should study the elements of the mind.

_____ **3.** Focuses on the functioning of normal mental processes.

_____ **4.** Concentrates on studying the human personality, normal and abnormal.

_____ **5.** Urges psychologists to study observable behavior.

_____ **6.** Developed from clinical experiences with neurotic people.

_____ **7.** Sees the environment as the most important influence on development.

_____ **8.** Assumes that much human behavior is caused by unconscious motives, conflicts, and fears.

_____ **9.** Believes that "The whole is greater than the sum of its parts."

_____ **10.** Uses analytic introspection as its major method.

_____ **11.** Urges that psychology be applied to practical problems such as education and business.

Points of View: psychoanalytic (P), neobehavioristic (N), cognitive (C), humanistic (H).

_____ **12.** Studies mental processes either by observation, experimentation, or introspection.

_____ **13.** Concentrates on helping people develop their full potential and become happy, creative individuals.

_____ **14.** Believes that the personality is formed during early childhood.

_____ **15.** Emphasizes subjects such as problem solving, language, and memory.

_____ **16.** Believes that psychologists should study human beings as wholes.

_____ **17.** Uses the methods developed by Freud to study personality.

_____ **18.** Insists on scientific methods to answer precise questions about human and animal behavior.

_____ **19.** Believes that methods are secondary to the problems being investigated.

Questions to Consider

1. Many people—philosophers, poets, novelists, sociologists, politicians, salespeople, and others—are interested in understanding human behavior. What is distinctive about the way psychologists study human behavior?

2. Think of some commonsense psychological assumptions, such as "You can't teach an old dog new tricks" or "Spare the rod, spoil the child." How might a psychologist go about testing such assumptions?

3. Name several hypothetical constructs and tell what behaviors you would observe to learn more about them.

4. Reread the Freud, Harlow, Bruner, and Maslow excerpts carefully and make a list of the clues that reveal each man's philosophical approach to psychology.

5. Suppose that someone tried to convince you that psychologists should not study the behavior of animals, either because experimenting with animals is cruel and unethical, or because no useful information

can be found by studying animals. How would you respond?

6. If you could have joined an early psychology movement, which one might you have joined? Why?

7. Do you find any one current view of psychology more appealing than the others? If you could create an eclectic approach to psychology, what aspects of each viewpoint would you select?

Project 1: Is Psychology Simply Commonsense?

Some people believe that although psychologists do lengthy and involved studies, their findings are predictable from the beginning—are primarily commonsense. The point of this project is to examine this argument and see if there is more to psychology than commonsense.

Method. Answer the questions on the questionnaire that follows. Then administer the questionnaire to several acquaintances. Try to find people who have not taken a psychology course recently and do not read psychology books or magazines regularly. You might make several copies of the questionnaire and let each person write in his or her own answers, or you can read the statements aloud to each person, one at a time, and record their answers.

IS PSYCHOLOGY SIMPLY COMMON- SENSE: A QUESTIONNAIRE

Indicate your opinion by writing True (T) or False (F) beside each statement.

_F_ **1.** Some people never dream at night; others dream very rarely.

_T_ **2.** Anxiety contributes to physical problems like heart attacks and even death.

_T_ **3.** People can learn to control their own brain waves.

_F/_ **4.** Women tend to outperform men on tests of intelligence.

_T_ **5.** Memories can be transmitted from one worm to another by injecting a chemical from one that has learned a particular task into a second that has not.

_____ **6.** A significant correlation between robbery and hard drug use means that hard drugs probably cause many users to become robbers.

_____ **7.** The most effective way to overcome prejudice is to expose people to the members of the group against whom they are prejudiced.

_____ **8.** A newborn infant kept in total darkness for the first two or three years of life would probably never be able to see normally, even with glasses.

_____ **9.** About one out of every twenty Americans now exhibits life-disrupting psychological problems.

_____ **10.** In the majority of cases old-fashioned physical punishment has the fewest disadvantages of any disciplinary technique.

_____ **11.** People who are highly intelligent tend to be highly creative.

_____ **12.** If told by a respectable psychologist to deliver painful electric shocks to another adult as part of a learning experiment, few Americans would obey.

_____ **13.** Most Americans who are currently dissatisfied with their present jobs primarily want better pay and fringe benefits.

_____ **14.** Prison is probably the most effective way for society to rehabilitate criminals.

_____ **15.** When the connections between the right and left sides of the cerebral hemispheres are cut, people behave quite normally except on certain psychological tests.

_____ **16.** Infants whose parents respond frequently to their cries are likely to grow into spoiled tyrants.

Results. Score questions according to the answer key. Give one point for each correct answer, then count the number of correct answers on each questionnaire. This number is the score. Compute the mean score for all subjects (including yourself) by adding all the scores together and dividing by the total number of scores.

Discussion. Consider the following questions:

1. On the average, did people answer more questions correctly than would be expected by chance? (Even if a person knew none of the answers and simply guessed, the individual would be right 50 percent of the time; so you should expect a score of 8 simply by chance.)

2. What conclusions can you reach? (In answering this question take the following issues into account: Are the answers to the questions on the questionnaire readily predictable? Can psychological questions be answered by studying the responses of only two or three people? Does the questionnaire reflect a representative range of psychological topics?)

3. Can you think of other ways to answer the question "Is psychology simply commonsense?"

Suggested Readings

1. Watson, R. I. _The great psychologists: From Aristotle to Freud_ (3d ed.) Philadelphia: J. B. Lippincott Company, 1971. (paperback) Describes the lives and works of historically important psychologists.

2. Keller, Fred S. _The definition of psychology_ (2d ed.) New York: Appleton-Century-Crofts, 1965. An account of the early psychology movements.

3. _A career in psychology._ Washington, D.C.: American Psychological Association, 1975. This pamphlet surveys contemporary psychology, tells what psychologists do, gives the requirements for becoming a psychologist, and presents other career-related information.

4. Kwawiec, T. S. (ed.) "The psychologists," _Psychology Today_, September 1972, 6, 58–64, 66–68, 70, 88. Three prominent contemporary psychologists describe themselves and their careers in psychology.

Answer Keys

SELF-QUIZ
1. b   2. d   3. d   4. b   5. b   6. c   7. d   8. c   9. a
10. c   11. a   12. d   13. c   14. a   15. d.

EXERCISE 1
Hypothetical constructs: a, c, d, e, g, h, k, l. n.

EXERCISE 2
1. G   2. S   3. F   4. P   5. B   6. P   7. B   8. P   9. G
10. S   11. F and B   12. C   13. H   14. P   15. C
16. H   17. P   18. N   19. H.

PROJECT 1
1. F   2. T   3. T   4. F   5. T   6. F   7. F   8. T   9. F
10. F   11. F   12. F   13. F   14. F   15. T   16. F.

PSYCHOLOGY: A SCIENTIFIC ENTERPRISE

IN THIS CHAPTER
We explore psychology as a scientific enterprise—focusing on its scientific goals, principles, and methods. We also look briefly at how psychologists analyze the information they collect. After reading this chapter, you should be able to do the following:

1. Describe four goals of psychology
2. Describe six principles that guide psychological research
3. Describe four descriptive methods
4. Explain the experimental method and identify three classes of events that should be controlled
5. Explain the purpose of statistics and the meaning of seven statistical concepts

INSIDE THE PSYCHOLOGY LABORATORY

If you picked up a psychology journal, you'd probably be impressed by how well disciplined the researching psychologist is. In almost every article you'd find a comprehensive description of relevant past research, logical reasons for the current undertaking, orderly descriptions of the subjects, methods, and major results, and a discussion of those results. You'd probably conclude that the psychologist is a paragon of organization, order, and precision. For the most part you'd be wrong. Journal reports do not deliberately misrepresent the psychologist's work; rather they present a capsule sketch of it—organized tightly under a tidy format. Journal reports rarely—if ever—contain the mundane details of the psychologist's search. In reality, psychologists, like other scientists, usually do a lot of muddling around—getting started,

having to stop, trying, erring, trying again, overlooking the obvious, happening by chance on promising ideas, giving in to concerns of expediency and budget, and so on. In actuality, "people don't usually do research the way people who write books about research say they do research[1]." Indeed, "one of the most striking facts about the history of science is that scientific progress is often made through *capitalizing on misconception, error, ambiguity, and accident*[2]."

The account of a discovery by an eminent pathologist, Lewis Thomas, makes enlightening reading. In 1958, Thomas, then at New York University, made an accidental discovery about how papain, an enzyme, affected cartilage tissue in rabbits' ears. Thomas's account of his progress clearly reveals how scientists — including psychologists — often grapple with problems. (*Note:* Focus on Thomas's procedures; the biological details are not important for our purposes.)

The case of the floppy-eared rabbits

"I was trying to explore the notion that the cardiac and blood vessel lesions in certain hypersensitivity states may be due to release of proteolytic enzymes. It's an attractive idea on which there's little evidence. And it's been picked up at some time or another by almost everyone working on hypersensitivity. For this investigation I used trypsin, because it was the most available enzyme around the laboratory, and I got nothing. We also happened to have papain; I don't know where it had come from; but because it was there, I tried it. . . . What the papain did was . . . produce these bizarre cosmetic changes (The rabbits' ears flopped.) . . . It was one of the most uniform reactions I'd ever seen. It always happened and it looked as if something important must have happened to cause this reaction . . . I chased it like crazy . . . I did the expected things. I had sections cut, and I had them stained by all the techniques available at the time . . . I expected to find a great deal, because I thought we had destroyed something . . . I hadn't thought of cartilage. You're not likely to, because it's not considered interesting . . . I know my own idea had always been that cartilage is a quiet, inactive tissue."

After months of working at the problem—what did papain do to the structure of the tissue in rabbits' ears?—Thomas abandoned his research because he was "terribly busy working on another problem," a problem on which he was "making progress." Besides, Thomas had "already used all the rabbits he could afford."

Several years later while teaching second-year medical students, Thomas stumbled back onto the floppy-eared phenomenon in rabbits. This time he discovered that papain produced changes in the structure of the cartilage tissue itself. Thomas made the discovery this time because he was teaching students and for that reason following correct scientific procedure. Previously, Thomas had neglected to compare normal and papain-injected rabbits' ears (3).

Consider the following questions:

1. Why did Thomas choose papain? trypsin?
2. How did Thomas "chase the cause" of floppy ears?
3. Why didn't Thomas think of cartilage initially?
4. For what reasons did Thomas abandon the research on floppy-eared rabbits?
5. What motivated Thomas to compare normal-eared and floppy-eared rabbit cartilage the second time?

This is probably not the way you ordinarily picture eminent scientists in their laboratories making discoveries. Scientific research is a human enterprise. Like other human undertakings, it sometimes depends on availability and accident; it sometimes is limited by stereotyped notions, preconceptions, conventions, and mundane realities. It is also true that students often have a good effect on scientists—reminding them to follow correct scientific procedure.

As you read, keep in mind that scientists are people, like butchers, bakers, candlestick makers, and others. In fact, they can even be studied.[1]

Figure 2-1. ". . . scientific progress is often made through capitalizing on misconception, error, ambiguity, and accident"—as in the case of the floppy-eared rabbits.

THE NATURE OF SCIENTIFIC PSYCHOLOGY

Although psychologists disagree about what psychology should study, as we saw in Chap-

[1]One study of scientists found that the conventions of the scientific community sometimes stifle innovation and retard the discovery process. The following delinquent practices were cited: The prestige of the scientist affects the fate of the discovery; scientists often have a hard time advancing research in areas outside their own specialization area; older scientists sometimes resist the work of younger ones (4).

ter 1, most psychologists agree that psychology is a science. In this chapter we explore the nature of scientific psychology. We focus first on psychology's scientific goals.

The Scientific Goals of Psychology

Psychologists aim at four basic goals: describing behavior, explaining it, making predictions about it, and, under some circumstances, changing or controlling it.

Description is the most basic goal of any science. The scientist attempts to gather facts about a particular phenomenon in order to put together an accurate picture of it. Psychologists are interested in constructing pictures of behavioral phenomena. When possible, they observe or measure a phenomenon directly. When direct observation is not possible or is extremely difficult, they turn to indirect methods, such as tests, interviews, or questionnaires, to provide information. We will be discussing each of these descriptive methods later in this chapter.

Let's take an example of what we mean by describing behavior. Suppose that two psychologists want to describe the aggression of 30 three-year-olds who attend nursery school A. They might train six observers and place them on the playground during the noon play period each day for a week. Each observer observes five children—counting the num-

ber of times that each child hits, kicks, pushes, bites, slaps, knocks, punches, or otherwise batters another child, adult, or object. At the end of the week, the psychologists can compute an average daily-acts-of-aggression index for each of the thirty children. Now the psychologists have a description of aggressive behavior in nursery school A.

Once psychologists have described a phenomenon, they are usually interested in explaining it. *Explanation* consists of establishing cause-and-effect relationships among the relevant factors. Usually psychologists propose a tentative explanation (an *hypothesis*) and test it by doing controlled experiments. (Controlled experiments are discussed later.) Let's go back to our example. After describing aggressive behavior at nursery school A, the psychologists must construct a reasonable hypothesis to explain its causes. Assume that they interview the children's parents, looking for differences in the routines of children with high and low average daily-acts-of-aggression indexes. Suppose that they learn that children who aggress frequently spend far more hours each day watching violent TV programs than those who aggress relatively infrequently. The psychologists are now in a position to formulate a rational hypothesis: Watching violent TV programs increases aggression in young children. To test their hypothesis, they might run an experiment in nursery school B. After measuring each

Figure 2-2. Psychologists who study behavior such as aggression among young children have four basic goals: description, explanation, prediction, and, under some circumstances, control. (Mimi Forsyth from Monkmeyer.)

child's aggression for a week (so that they can compute an average daily index of aggression for each one), they randomly assign the children to two groups. The children in one group watch violent TV programs ten hours a week for two months; the children in the second group watch neutral TV programs ten hours a week for two months. Each day the psychologists observe the children's aggression during the noon recess period. If the children who watch violent TV programs increase in daily aggression on the average and those who watch neutral TV programs do not, the psychologists would tentatively conclude that their hypothesis is correct: TV violence does play a role in causing aggression in young children.

Once psychologists find some support for a hypothesis, they test the hypothesis further. If it is accurate, it should be able to *predict* behavior in other situations. The psychologists in our example might predict that watching violent TV programs increases aggression in many situations. To check their prediction, they could repeat their experiment at summer camp C and elementary school D.

Finally, psychologists are sometimes interested in influencing or changing a particular behavioral phenomenon. We use the term *control* to refer to this goal. To reduce aggression at nursery school E, the psychologists might ask the parents of highly aggressive toddlers to limit their children's viewing of violent TV programs. If the psychologists observe aggressive behavior at the noon recess both before and after the TV restrictions, they can evaluate their control of the behavior (assuming the parents cooperate, of course).

Principles That Guide Psychological Research

The psychologist's research is guided by a number of scientific principles, the most im-

portant of which are objectivity, precision, empiricism, determinism, parsimony, and tentativeness.

Objectivity. Psychologists strive to be *objective*; that is, they try to keep their personal biases and feelings from affecting their research. Suppose that one of the psychologists in our example happens to be a pacifist. She personally believes that aggression is wrong. This psychologist must make every effort to prevent her biases from influencing her study. She might arrange to have independent observers rate the children on aggression. She might also avoid personally coming in contact with the children—lest she bias their behavior unknowingly.

Precision. Psychologists try to be *precise*. They clearly define what they are studying. (Later we will be talking about their special definitions, *operational definitions*.) Psychologists also describe their subjects, their equipment, their procedures, and their results as accurately as they can. This way other psychologists can *replicate* (repeat) the study—to make sure that the finding is a reliable one. The psychologists who have been studying aggression will write a research report in which they describe the children (their ages, socioeconomic status, intelligence test scores, race, and other important characteristics), the nursery school itself, its teachers, and its geographical location. They will include a copy of the rating scales they used as well as a discussion of how they were designed and evaluated. Finally, they will present their quantitative findings in detail. If other psychologists doubt that the findings are accurate, they can repeat the study following the procedures as closely as possible to see if they obtain the same results.

Empiricism. Psychologists believe that actual sensory experience is the best source of knowledge about behavior. For that reason experiments and observations are the primary tools they use to increase their understanding of behavior. Commonsense and speculation are not considered adequate sources of evidence. Even the most distinguished psychologists must back up their hypotheses with observations and experimental studies. We call this "look and see" attitude *empiricism*. The psychologists at nursery school A did not accept the teacher's word that particular children were aggressive. Nor did they assume that boys are by nature more aggressive than girls—as some child-care experts assert. They made observations.

Determinism. The word *determinism* refers to the philosophical doctrine that all events, including human choices, have a cause. Most psychologists believe that the world is an orderly place where things happen for reasons—some of which they know and some of which they don't. Determinism does not imply that people's decisions and choices are only determined by external circumstances. On the contrary, most psychologists believe that choices, decisions, and other behaviors are caused by a combination of internal factors (such as genetic potentialities, motives, emotions) and external factors (such as pressures from other people, past experiences, and present circumstances). Because of these beliefs, psychologists look for natural explanations for whatever they study; and, accordingly, they display little patience with supernatural explanations such as magic, fate, luck, or God.[2] No matter how mystifying a particular phenomenon appears, psychologists remain confident that there is a natural explanation for it that they will eventually be able to observe or measure. Consequently, most psychologists would not accept the following statements:

> Some people are always depressed. There is *no explaining it*.
> Some people are rich; others are poor. It all depends on *chance*.

Parsimony. Many psychologists strive to be *parsimonious*. In other words, they look for the simplest explanation that fits the observed facts. This means that they do not advance complex, abstract explanations unless simpler ones have proved inadequate. Consider a game that children in many American cities play. They skip over cracks in the sidewalk while chanting simultaneously: "Step on the crack, break my mother's back." Why do children play this game? A parsimonious psychologist might speculate that children simply learn the game from other children. A nonparsimonious psychologist might suggest that children who play this game really hate their mothers and wish them harm. Accordingly, they adopt the opposite stance; that is, they pretend to be concerned about their mothers' safety. In fact, although they appear to be cautiously avoiding sidewalk cracks, they are unconsciously hoping that they will step on them—causing their mothers to be hurt. Let's consider a second example. Recall the psychologists who found that watching a large amount of violent TV increased aggression in children. A parsimonious explanation for this finding would be that children learn violence by watching violent models. A nonparsimonious explanation would be that aggression increases because children feel that their parents are rejecting them by allowing them to watch frightening stories. Subsequently, anger toward their parents causes them to lash out at others around them. In

---

[2]Does this mean that a good psychologist cannot believe in God? Not at all. It simply means that the psychologist does not assert that religious phenomena explain psychological findings. The psychologist might personally believe that the human conscience is a gift from God, but in studying the development of the human conscience, this psychologist would test natural observable causes—such as strict parental disciplinary practices and church attendance. To conduct an objective study, the religious psychologist must treat beliefs as biases and try to keep them from affecting research results.

both our examples, parsimony demands that the psychologist choose the simpler explanation that fits the observed facts.

Tentativeness. Psychologists regard their conclusions as *tentative*; they strive to be open-minded, accepting of criticism, and ready to reevaluate and revise their conclusions if new evidence warrants it. A tentative attitude is realistic for many reasons. Even though psychologists try to perform the most careful observations that they are capable of, they cannot eliminate every potential source of error. Errors can creep in because of complications in the real world, faulty instruments, or improperly designed procedures. Moreover, behavioral phenomena frequently turn out to be more complicated than they initially appear. Through further research,

Figure 2-3. Stress can be operationally defined as exposure to electric shock of a given intensity and duration. In this experiment on stress, one group of rats received electric shocks, which they could turn off by manipulating the wheel. Animals who could control their environment generally developed smaller ulcers than those who had no control. (Dr. Jay M. Weiss, Rockefeller University.)

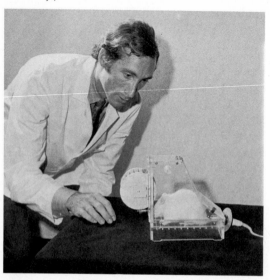

for example, the psychologists studying aggression in children would probably learn that watching TV violence is only one of many factors that increase aggression. (In Chapter 11, we discuss this subject further.) In general, as psychologists extend their research on behavioral phenomena, they usually increase the accuracy of their descriptions and their explanations; and their ability to predict the outcome of specific situations and change or influence behavior also improves. So psychologists need to keep their minds open.

Before the Research Begins

Before psychologists begin their research, they must attend to two very basic issues: They must define their terms, and they must state their questions in such a way that they can be investigated.

Operational definitions. Many everyday words have multiple meanings. Take the statement "We will study severe stress." The "severe stress" could refer to the loss of a parent, extreme cold, separation from a spouse, physical injury, financial problems, conditions of war, or pressure for advancement at work. If psychologists are going to understand one another, they must define their terms precisely. One way to define words precisely is to relate them to the procedures that are used to observe or measure them. This kind of definition is called an *operational definition.*

Job satisfaction can be operationally defined as a score on a particular questionnaire. Stress can be operationally defined as exposure to electric shock of a given intensity and duration. Aggression can be operationally defined as kicks, hits, bites, and knocks. If psychologists defined job satisfaction as a feeling of inner contentment at work, stress as a sense of internal turmoil, and aggression as an impulse to destroy, they would not be using operational definitions. More often than not, psychologists use operational definitions to clarify their terms—so that any interested person knows exactly what they are talking about.

The questions psychologists ask. Psychologists begin their research with questions that arouse their curiosity, questions such as "What does stress do to people?" "What makes people turn to crime?" "How does memory operate?" As these questions stand, they are hard to investigate. Take "What does stress do to people?" What "stress"? What "people"? "Do" in what sense? Before they start their studies, psychologists must limit the scope of their questions so that they can be investigated scientifically. Accordingly, a question such as "What does stress do to people?" might become "How does the threat of extreme pain (a particular stressor) affect people's desires to affiliate with one another (a particular effect)?" "What makes people turn to crime?" might become "Do the majority of juvenile delinquents in Boston come from families with only one parent?"

You may object: "The questions have changed. They're no longer the grand questions they were." That's true. But grand questions cannot be answered as they stand. Grand questions are usually many questions. Take "What does stress do to people?" There are hundreds of stresses; and they affect different organisms at different times in different ways. The many questions cannot be answered at the same time. They must be tackled one by one.

After formulating a researchable question, the psychologist is ready to begin looking for an answer. To *describe* behavior, psychologists turn to one of the descriptive methods. To *explain* behavior, they use the experimental method.

THE DESCRIPTIVE METHODS

One of the psychologist's most basic goals is the accurate description of behavior. Direct observation is the most straightforward way to accomplish this goal.

Direct Observation

Observing psychologists have a conflict. They want to make precise, objective observations. At the same time, they want to observe realistic behavior. It is hard to do both simultaneously. Realistic behavior is more likely to be seen in natural settings. Precision and objectivity are more easily achieved in artificial settings such as laboratories. In the end observing psychologists almost always compromise.

Naturalistic observation. How does a gang leader interact with members of his gang? What are the social practices of the Mundugumors, a native tribe in New Guinea? What characterizes the play of eight-year-old inner-city children? These questions lead to *naturalistic observations*—observations in a natural setting. In making such observations the social scientist is interested, above all, in viewing realistic behavior. Considerations of precision and objectivity are secondary.

The collection of naturalistic observations poses a difficult problem at the onset: how to minimize the observers' presence so that they do not distort the behavior that they are observing. Sometimes the social scientist observes from the sidelines—as inconspicuously as possible. One can watch children while pretending to be absorbed in a book. In some situations concealed movie or videotape cameras or tape recorders can be used to record observations. Another tactic is *participant observation*. The social scientists participate in the activities that they are observing; consequently, they are mistaken by their subjects for members of their own group. In one participant observation, for example, social scientists had themselves admitted to various mental institutions by claiming to hear voices. The staff considered their subsequent writing and record keeping symptomatic of their mental problems (5). More follows on this study in Chapter 14. In another widely known participant observation, social scientists posed as true believers so that they would be accepted by a religious cult that believed that the world would be destroyed by floods and earthquakes on a particular day in December and that only a few faithful members of the group would be rescued by flying saucers. The social scientists planned to remain in the group after the failure of the prophecy to see how the fanatics would alter their beliefs (6).³

Participant observation has an important advantage—close contact with the subjects. However, as observers become more and more involved, they lose their capacity for objectivity. The social scientists who posed as mental patients had to be released from the institutions by their own devices. None of them knew when they would get out. Being awakened on the fifteenth or sixteenth morning by the greeting, "Come on you m----- f-----s, out of bed! [7]" must have heavily taxed their powers of objectivity. Moreover, participant observers may inadvertently influence their subjects' behavior. The "true believing" social scientists found that their presence in the group bolstered the group members' confidence in their fanatic beliefs. So participant observation is not the best way to make naturalistic observations—when there is a choice.

³Although the appointed hour passed without event, the group members did not reject their beliefs. Five hours after the appointed hour the leader of the group announced that the explanation had appeared to him: God had saved the world from destruction because the true believers had spread their faith throughout the world.

After psychologists find a way to observe their subjects without influencing them, they consider whether the observations can be made systematically and recorded precisely and objectively. Sometimes they cannot be. Participant observers, for example, cannot always record as they observe. Frequently they must write down their general impressions at some later time. Many observations on the religious cultists were recorded in this way. Here is a sample.

There is no doubt that the believers really expected a saucer to land in the back yard at four o'clock. By noon, all five of the regular members of the group had removed every scrap of metal from their persons—including zippers, metal clasps, buttons with metal backing, bobby pins, and belt buckles [8].

Sometimes observations in the naturalistic setting can be recorded systematically and precisely. Here is an example: A profoundly retarded adolescent at a state institution had been injuring himself for many years—primarily by slapping his own face. Before beginning a treatment program, psychologists made careful observations. First, they operationally defined the response: They decided to count an act as self-injurious each time the boy's palm came into contact with his face. In the beginning two observers watched the boy. Later their findings were compared to make sure that the response was being consistently counted. Furthermore, the psychologists watched their subject through a one way mirror—to avoid influencing his behavior. Finally, the observations were scheduled for one hour at the same time each day in the same room. This precaution minimized the influences that would have resulted from different rooms, different times of day, and different amounts of time (9).

Clinical observations. Sometimes social scientists observe the people they are treating in clinic settings. Such observations tend to be

Figure 2-4. The room where Freud developed many of his techniques and theories. (Historical Picture Services, Chicago.)

informal and impressionistic. They also run the danger of being biased—since observing clinicians are usually sympathetic to their patients and professionally involved in their progress. To some degree, the roles of committed therapist and objective scientist are incompatible. On the other hand, the intimate relationship of clinician and patient gives the observing social scientist insight into private behavior that is rarely observed under any other circumstances. Later these insights can be systematically investigated.

Clinical observations furnished the basis of Sigmund Freud's theories of personality. Here are Freud's clinical observations on one of his patients.

Frau Cacilie M.: Clinical observations

"When a girl of fifteen, . . . [Frau Cacilie M.] was lying in bed, under the watchful eye of her strict grandmother, the girl suddenly gave a cry; she had felt a penetrating pain in her forehead between her eyes, which lasted for weeks. During the analysis of this pain, which was reproduced after nearly thirty years, she told me that her grandmother had given her a look so 'piercing' that it had gone right into her brain. (She had been afraid that the old woman was viewing her with suspicion.) As she told me this thought she broke into a loud laugh, and the pain once more disappeared. In this instance, I can detect nothing other than the mechanism of symbolization. . . .

"My observation of Frau Cacilie M. gave me an opportunity of making a regular collection of symbolizations of this kind. A whole set of physical sensations which would ordinarily be regarded as organically determined were in her case of psychical origin or at least possessed a psychical meaning. A particular series of experiences of hers were accompanied by a stabbing sensation in the region of the heart (meaning 'it stabbed me to the heart'). The pain that occurs in hysteria of nails being driven into the head was without any doubt to be explained in her case as pain related to thinking. ('Some things come into my head.') Pains of this kind were always cleared up as soon as the problems involved were cleared up. Running parallel to the sensation of the hysterical 'aura' in the throat, when that feeling appeared after an insult, was the thought 'I shall have to swallow this.' She had a whole quantity of sensations and ideas running parallel with each other. Sometimes the sensation would call up the idea to explain it, sometimes the idea would create the sensation by means of symbolization, and not infrequently it has to be left an open question which of the two elements had been the primary one [10]."

Questionnaires, Interviews, and Tests

When psychologists cannot directly observe the behavior they are interested in, they frequently turn to assessment devices: questionnaires, interviews, and tests. These devices allow them to study large numbers of people. Questionnaires (and interviews), in particular, enable the psychologist to investigate what people report concerning their practices, attitudes, feelings, thoughts, beliefs, motives, fears, and other behavior. Psychological tests enable the psychologist to zero in on specific skills. We examine these two devices in more detail.

Questionnaires. The questionnaire is a relatively inexpensive way for psychologists to collect information on what large numbers of people say about some aspect of their behavior. Questionnaires consist of written questions that are easily answered—in two senses. They usually ask for readily available information that requires a minimum of soul searching; and, more often than not, subjects

simply pencil a mark in the appropriate place.

The wording of the questions on a questionnaire is one key to the questionnaire's success. The items below come from a questionnaire on sexual attitudes that appeared in *Psychology Today* in 1969 (11).

"Have any of the following prevented you from freely expressing your sexuality?" (Percentages show proportion responding "yes" to each.)

	Males, %	Females, %
Fear of pregnancy	31	45
Fear of disease	14	7
Social disapproval	20	21
Guilt feelings	23	33
Religious or other moral training	17	22
Other	—	—
None of the above	31	26

"Where did you get most of your information about sex when you were a youngster?"

Parents	8	17
Course in school	3	3
Books	23	23
Friends	64	51
Church	—	1
Other	2	5

Are these good questions? Good questionnaire questions are specific and concrete. When questions on a questionnaire are ambiguous, subjects may interpret them in different ways. When this happens, the responses cannot be correctly assessed. Most psychologists would probably consider the questions above adequately specific and concrete.

Good questions also attempt to eliminate biases, such as a subject's inclination to agree simply to be helpful or to disagree simply to be negative. Each question above presents several response options. Only one is to be endorsed, of course. The subjects cannot mechanically check off "yesses," "nos," "agrees," or "disagrees." So they are likelier to read all the options and pick the one that best reflects them.

Even when the questions on the questionnaire are carefully devised, the results of a questionnaire study are hard to interpret. Written self-reports may or may not be accurate ones. Some people deliberately falsify. Others attempt to present an image they like. Still others may not fully understand how they themselves feel or think or behave.

There is a second important problem. We don't know how well the respondents represent the group we are interested in. For example, the 20,000 respondents to the *Psychology Today* questionnaire may be more open and enlightened than the majority of *Psychology Today* readers, so their answers may not reflect the feelings of the majority. In view of all these problems, psychologists prefer to observe behavior directly when it is possible.

Psychological tests. Psychological tests attempt to measure abilities, personality characteristics, feelings, attitudes, or interests. They vary in form. They may contain written questions or problems to be solved out loud. Some tests are designed to be administered to a large group of people; others are intended for a single individual. The development of a psychological test is an enormously complex undertaking which we will describe in Chapter 9.

Why do psychologists want to measure abilities, personality characteristics, and other similar phenomena? Consider intelligence. For thousands of years people were able to

Figure 2-5. The administration of a psychological test. (Blair Seitz, Editorial Photocolor Archives.)

distinguish the quick-witted from the dull-witted, but they were limited to crude categorization until the creation of the intelligence test provided both an operational definition of, and a way to quantify, intelligence. For the first time psychologists could study "intelligence" systematically. For example, they could test the same children at different ages to see if "intelligence" changed with age. They could also test large groups of men and women to see which was the brighter of the two sexes. We will be looking at intelligence testing and intelligence in Chapter 9. Our point is that tests allow psychologists to describe and study hypothetical constructs that cannot be directly observed.

Tests also improve the psychologist's ability to answer important questions such as "Is Martha personally suited for engineering, or is she better fitted for working with people?" "Will Harry be able to do college-level work?" Being able to answer questions like these makes psychologists effective as diagnosticians and counselors. The following case demonstrates how tests help psychologists diagnose.

The case of Mr. M.

Mr. M., a twenty-five-year-old man, had come from the Deep South to Syracuse, New York, to live with his relatives. He applied almost immediately for a work-training program. During the routine interview which followed, he revealed that he had never learned to read or write; he was so intensely ill at ease that he could hardly talk either—he answered the officials' questions with barely audible "yesses" or "nos." The officials wanted to accept him, but they were in conflict because they didn't know if he was intelligent enough to become a machinist. For this reason, they decided to refer him to a psychologist for an evaluation.

When Mr. M. arrived for his interview with the psychologist, he appeared quite nervous. The psychologist tried to make him feel more comfortable. She asked him about his new home. She volunteered some information about herself. She questioned him about his family, Florida, his schooling, his hobbies, and interests. After an hour's conversation Mr. M. appeared more relaxed and ready for formal testing. He took several tests including the Wechsler Adult Intelligence Scale (a test that assesses general information, social know-how, arithmetical reasoning, abstract thinking, and other intellectual skills). During the testing the psychologist tried to be supportive and friendly. Under these conditions Mr. M. performed as well as the majority of people his own age. His memory and his ability to reason and form concepts were better than average. On the other hand, he did worse than the average person his own age on items that require a conventional educational background (such as "Who wrote the *Iliad*?") and on items that are adversely affected by severe anxiety (such as "Repeat the following digits backward: 9, 7, 3"). So the testing furnished a description of Mr. M.'s current intellectual functioning and a way of interpreting that functioning. Incidentally, Mr. M. was accepted into the program, and he completed it successfully (12).

THE EXPERIMENTAL METHOD

Description is the first step in understanding behavior. Explanation is the second step. The experimental method leads to explanations. Scientists aren't the only ones who use it. Curious children and adults continually experiment. Abigail throws jelly beans in her father's coleslaw and observes his reaction. Harold uses a new study technique for a semester and notes the effect on his grade-point average. Bargain Basement runs an ad on the Late Show for a week and monitors its sales. In each example something is deliberately manipulated (changed or varied), and the effect of the manipulation is assessed. Scientists do exactly the same thing when they perform an experiment. The only difference is that they do it more systematically and they attempt to control the influence of extraneous factors.

The Anatomy of a Psychological Experiment

In March 1964, as Kitty Genovese returned home from work in Queens, New York, at 3 A.M., she was assaulted by a maniac. The young woman screamed in terror. Thirty-eight of her neighbors heard her screams and watched from their windows as she struggled against her assailant. Kitty's cries and pleas for help continued for half an hour before she died. Not a single person called the police during the assault or came to Kitty's assistance. Incidents like this one (and, unfortunately, this case was not an isolated occurrence) are hard to explain. Many social critics assumed that a new kind of person had emerged, a person who "adapted to the pressures caused by the increasing urbanization of life by turning other people into objects, by losing human feeling for them, and by rejecting the moral imperative to help another in distress [13]." Bibb Latané and John Darley,

two psychologists then in New York City, felt that there was a likelier explanation: Knowing that other people are aware of an emergency may simply make each person feel less responsible for taking action—because the responsibility is diffused among them. Think of it this way: If you alone witness an emergency that can be handled by a single individual, you are likely to feel intensely responsible. If you don't take action, you will probably feel quite guilty. If, on the other hand, you are one of many people who witness an emergency, you will probably react differently. Although you may feel somewhat responsible for helping, you can easily say to yourself, "Someone else will probably help." If no one else helps, the guilt is easier to bear—it is shared by many people.

Latané and Darley decided to test the hypothesis that people's perceptions of the number of other bystanders witnessing an emergency affects their willingness to help. The hypothesis relates two concepts or *variables*. In this case the two variables are (1) the subject's perception of the number of bystanders witnessing an emergency and (2) the subject's willingness to help. The hypothesis states that one variable is caused by and therefore depends on the other. In our example, willingness to help is thought to be caused by and consequently to depend on the subject's perception of the number of other witnesses. The dependent variable is known as precisely that—the *dependent variable*. In our example, willingness to help is the dependent variable. In psychological experiments the dependent variable is always some aspect of behavior. The other variable, the one that is thought to influence the dependent variable, is known as the *independent variable*. In our example, the subject's perception of the number of other witnesses is the independent variable. To test the hypothesis, the psychologist manipulates the independent variable and observes and measures its actual effect on the dependent variable.

Figure 2-6. Studies show that bystander apathy and helping behavior are related to the number of witnesses. (Charles Gatewood.)

The hypothesis is formulated. The independent and dependent variables are identified. Now the experimenter begins to think about an *experimental design*—a good way of investigating how the independent variable affects the dependent variable. Latané and Darley decided to set up a situation somewhat like the Kitty Genovese murder. Male and female university students came individually to their laboratory. After arriving each subject was told by an experimental assistant that he or she would be talking to one, two, or five other students in other rooms about personal problems associated with urban college life. The "discussion" took place over an intercom. There was really only one subject, the student who had come to the laboratory. The other "subjects" were taped voices. During the discussion one of the taped "subjects," whom we shall call the "victim," appeared to undergo a serious epilepticlike seizure. The victim called out for help. Some subjects believed that they were the only ones to hear; others felt that one or four other people heard. The experimenters measured how fast the subject reported the emergency. (In other words, the dependent variable, willingness to help, was operationally defined by speed of response to the emergency.)

The Importance of Control in the Psychological Experiment

Recall that the experiment attempts to assess the influence of one and only one kind of variable, the independent variable—in our example, the subject's perception of the number of other witnesses. The most characteristic feature of an experiment is its attempt to *control* all those extraneous factors that might interfere with or obscure the influence of the independent variable. There are many potentially interfering factors that psychologists try to control in designing their experiments.

Controlling the experimental setting. Imagine that the details of the Latané-Darley study varied from day to day. On some days the assistant was a middle-aged man in a suit; on others a flippant, teen-aged boy in jeans. Suppose that the experiment took place at a local fraternity house on some days and at the University Counseling Center on others. Assume also that the experimenter improvised the instructions for each subject. All these variations might have important effects on the subject's measured responses. Since the psychologist is trying to single out the effect of the independent variable, it is best to expose all subjects to the same setting, the same procedures, the same instructions, and the same tasks.

Even though the psychologist keeps the subjects' experience uniform, the specific procedural details may affect every subject's behavior. For example, running the study with a handsome young male experimental assistant may yield different results than running the study with an ugly old male experimental assistant. Because psychologists cannot predict the effects of myriad details, they usually create at least two groups of *subjects* (animals being studied). Sometimes psychologists call their groups *conditions*. One or more groups—the *experimental groups*—are subjected to changes in the independent variable. One or more groups—the *control groups*—are not subjected to such changes. Since the groups are otherwise exposed to the same procedures and setting, differences in their observed behavior have to be due to the independent variable.

Latané and Darley controlled for unwanted influences in the experimental setting by using three groups of subjects—two experimental groups and one control group. All subjects were exposed to the same experimenter, experimental assistant, setting, procedures, and instructions. The control group subjects were led to believe that they would be discussing the problems of urban college life with one other student; the experimental subjects were led to believe that they would be discussing such problems with either two or five other students. In all cases the victim and the other discussants were taped voices; so the discussions were standard, as was the victim's emergency. Only the final debriefing—enlightening the subjects about the true nature of the experiment and dealing with their feelings—followed individualistic lines. Note that the experiences of the subjects in the control and experimental groups varied in only one significant way. Subjects in the control group believed that they were the only witness to the victim's emergency, whereas subjects in the experimental groups believed that varying numbers of people witnessed the emergency along with them.

Controlling the subjects' characteristics. Subjects vary—in heredity, past history, personality, intelligence, sex, age. These subject characteristics might easily obscure the effect of the independent variable. You can grasp the power of subject variables by imagining that one of Latané and Darley's experimental groups contained mostly young men under twenty years of age and that their control group contained mostly married women over forty. Because subject variables are important, the experimenter tries to make certain that the groups of subjects are initially equivalent on all significant personal characteristics (those which might affect the outcome of the study).

There are many ways to do this. One way is to *randomly assign* subjects to groups. In random assignment the assignment of subjects to groups is based on chance, so that each subject in the study has an equal probability of being assigned to any group. When random assignment procedures are used, personal characteristics are approximately equally distributed among groups. This method is most effective when large numbers of subjects are used. One procedure for assigning subjects randomly to groups is well known. The names of all the subjects in the study are placed in a bowl; one by one, they are drawn and designated for a particular group, until each group has the correct number of subjects. Latané and Darley used the random assignment procedure to control subject variables in their study.

There are other ways to control subject variables. *Matching* refers to the procedure of equating the subjects in each group on several significant characteristics. In studying the effects of a diet pill, for example, psychologists might match subjects on pounds overweight, sex, age, and general health. If the investigators place a forty-year-old woman in poor health and approximately 100 pounds overweight in one group, they have to place another forty-year-old woman in poor health and approximately 100 pounds overweight in the second group. Accordingly, each subject in one group is "equated" with another in the other group(s). Matching can only be used when the psychologist has a very large number of potential subjects from which to choose the sample.

The method of *equivalent groups* is a third way to control subject variables. Groups are formed so that the subjects in each group have the same average score on an important characteristic(s). The groups are equivalent in the sense that they begin with the same average score. In studying the effects of a diet pill, for example, the psychologist might divide subjects into groups so that each group averages 100 pounds overweight.

Controlling experimenter effects. In the late 1930s researchers at the Hawthorne Works of the Western Electric Company in Chicago investigated ways to increase their employees' productivity. They studied a group of female workers while systematically

Figure 2-7. The Assembly Test Room of the Hawthorne Works in Chicago, where researchers discovered that attention is an important variable in a psychological experiment. (Harvard University Press.)

varying a number of work practices, such as rest periods, working hours, levels of illumination, and pay incentives. After such manipulations, the women worked more efficiently —even when the working conditions worsened! The researchers finally concluded that attention from the experimenters was the important independent variable—not rate of pay, working hours, or any of the other factors (14). This phenomenon, the influence of attention on performance, is labeled the *Hawthorne effect.*

The careful experimenter strives to pay the same kind and the same amount of attention to all groups in the experiment because variations in attention will probably influence the dependent variable. Recall that in the Latané-Darley study the kind and amount of attention did not vary from group to group.

Sometimes experimenters unknowingly cue their subjects and influence their behavior in the direction of their expectations. This phenomenon, known as *experimenter bias*, is illustrated very clearly by the famous case of clever Hans, a horse who answered addition, subtraction, multiplication, and spelling questions—by stomping the correct number of times with his right forefoot. Early in the nineteenth century an eminent German psychologist, Oskar Pfungst, reported on a series of ingenious experiments that had been designed to discover Hans' secret. Pfungst observed that Hans could solve problems with or without his master's presence, but he made many errors (1) when he could not see his interrogator and (2) when the interrogator did not know how to answer the question himself. As it turned out, Hans responded to subtle unintentional visual cues—among them, almost imperceptible movements of the examiner's head (15).

Similarly, psychologists today sometimes unintentionally influence their subjects' behavior in the direction of their expecta-

tions—by their facial expressions, gestures, and vocal tones. Robert Rosenthal, a social psychologist at Harvard University, has studied these effects systematically. In one study, for example, ten advanced undergraduate and graduate students in psychology were selected as "researchers." Each was assigned twenty students as subjects for a study. The "researcher" showed ten photographs of human faces one at a time and the subject rated the degree of failure or success reflected in the face. All ten "researchers" read identical instructions to their subjects; moreover, they had all been cautioned not to deviate from these written instructions. The purpose of the study, they were informed, was to see if a "well-established finding" could be duplicated. Half the "researchers" believed that the "well-established finding" was that people rated the faces as moderately successful. The other half believed that the "well-established finding" was that people rated the faces as moderately unsuccessful. The researchers, who were the real subjects in Rosenthal's experiment, obtained results in the direction of their expectations. Further investigations have demonstrated that apparently without their knowing it, researchers sometimes cue their subjects by their facial expressions and vocal tones (16). The importance of experimenter effects like these can be minimized if the experiment is run by a neutral person, one who does not know the hypotheses of the experiment or the subject's condition and one who is not personally involved in the outcome of the study.

The subjects' expectations are also important. Physicians have long recognized this fact. That is why they sometimes prescribe sugar pills and water-filled capsules (chemically inert drugs such as these are known as *placebos*) for patients whose complaints cannot be treated more effectively. Many people actually *feel* better after swallowing a placebo—apparently because they *expect* to feel

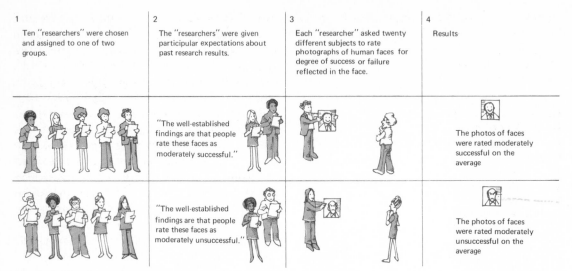

Figure 2-8. The effects of experimenter bias in Rosenthal's experiment.

better. Psychologists use several types of placebos in their experiments to control the expectations of their subjects, their experimenters, or both. In studies of the potency of a particular drug, for example, subjects in the experimental group take the medication of interest and subjects in the control group take a placebo that is identical in appearance. This way both groups begin with similar expectations. Likewise, to control the subjects' expectations in studies of treatment effects, the experimental subjects receive the treatment of interest and the control subjects receive a "placebo" treatment—a different form of treatment. Any procedure used to prevent subjects from knowing what condition they are in is labeled a *single-blind procedure.* When neither experimenter nor subject know the subject's group, we have a *double-blind procedure.* These controls minimize the likelihood that an experiment will turn out in a certain way because the experimenter, the subjects, or both want or expect it to.

The Results of the Experiment

After experimenting, psychologists end up with measurements (sometimes referred to as observations or data) on the dependent variable for all their subjects. Table 2-1 presents a summary of Latané and Darley's data. Statistical analyses showed that subjects who believed that they were either alone or with one other witness came to the victim's aid significantly faster than subjects who believed that there were five other witnesses. Apparently, the independent variable (perceived group size) did affect the dependent variable (speed of helping). (We turn to the topic of statistics and significant differences later in the chapter.)

It is important to note that psychologists usually insist on quantitative measurements for several reasons. First, they lead to clear, exact descriptions. Latané and Darley reported that subjects who perceived themselves alone with the victim responded to his plight

TABLE 2-1. EFFECTS OF GROUP SIZE ON LIKELI-HOOD AND SPEED OF RESPONSE

Group Size (Victim and Subject Are Included)	2	3	6
Number of Subjects	13	26	13
Percentage Responding before End of Fit	85	62	31
Percentage Responding before End of Experiment	100	85	62
Average Elapsed Time before Response, seconds	52	93	166

Adapted from B. Latané and J. M. Darley. *The unresponsive bystander: Why doesn't he help?* New York: Appleton Century Crofts, 1970. P. 97.

after fifty-two seconds on the average—rather than "quite quickly." The reader, of course, would have no way of interpreting the precise meaning of the phrase "quite quickly." Moreover, because numbers have no "good" or "bad" connotations, they are unlikely to project the experimenter's personal biases, whereas adjectives and adverbs may. In addition, numerical data allow the investigator to make subtle discriminations. There were, in fact, only thirty-one seconds difference on the average between the reaction time of those subjects in the two- and three-person groups (victim and subject included). A difference of this magnitude might have been easily overlooked had the "measurements" been impressionistic ones. Finally, as we will see, quantitative measurements allow a refined statistical analysis of the results.

After the data are analyzed, the psychologist interprets them and comes to some general conclusions. Latané and Darley concluded that the unresponsive bystanders in their study were far from apathetic. Many of them appeared to them to be quite anxious about

the victim's welfare. They theorized that all their subjects had been in a state of indecision and conflict. On the one hand, they were genuinely worried about the victim's welfare, they wanted to help, and they felt guilty about not helping. On the other hand, they did not want to overreact, make themselves look foolish, or ruin the study. When subjects believed they were alone with the victim, the first factor far outweighed the second. But the conflict became more sticky when the subjects believed that they had shared the emergency with other witnesses—apparently because the responsibility for helping or not helping could be passed along to other people (17).

Summary

Each of the scientific methods we have examined has advantages and limitations. The descriptive methods provide a clear picture of behavior. They are particularly useful for providing insight into realistic behavior in natural settings. Whenever experimentation is difficult, inconvenient, or impossible, the descriptive methods furnish invaluable information. In addition, they suggest possible explanations which can later be investigated experimentally. In contrast to the descriptive methods, experiments furnish a more precise, focused, and controlled way to investigate cause-and-effect relationships between events. However, since experiments usually occur in laboratory settings, psychologists cannot be certain that human subjects are behaving in a natural way.

Because each procedure has distinct strengths and weaknesses, psychologists usually combine them to study complex psychological events. Take bystander apathy and helping behavior. The investigation of this matter was precipitated initially by naturalistic observations in big cities—report after report that people watched stabbings, beatings, murders, and rapes and did nothing to help the victim. Many puzzled psychologists turned to formal research methods for a better understanding. Some social scientists studied helping behavior experimentally in their laboratories, others set up experiments in natural settings—in alleys (18), in people's homes (19), on superhighways (20), and on beaches (21). Yet other psychologists attacked the problem through psychological testing, trying to find out more about the personality characteristics of people who help and people who don't (22, 23).

The picture we have of bystander apathy and helping behavior is still far from clear. Under certain conditions bystanders do help. Many factors appear to be involved—among them, the bystander's personality and sex, the specific circumstances, the motives aroused, and the presence or absence of other people. This research shows that both descriptive and

Figure 2-9. Ethical questions are continually raised by psychological research on human subjects. In the study pictured, children watched a model behave aggressively toward a Bobo doll. Later they had an opportunity to demonstrate what they had learned. Studies like this one are necessary if psychologists are to understand the conditions that stimulate aggression. (Albert Bandura.)

experimental methods are frequently necessary to achieve an understanding of a complex topic.

ETHICS AND PSYCHOLOGICAL RESEARCH

You may have been surprised to learn that psychologists sometimes observe people without asking their prior permission, deceive them about the real purposes of their studies, and expose them to unpleasant situations like witnessing a simulated epileptic fit. You may have wondered whether psychologists pay any attention at all to ethical considerations.

Psychologists *are* aware of the ethical dilemmas of conducting psychological research, and ethical guidelines have existed for a long time. Recently, the American Psychological Association published a formal canon of ethical principles specifically designed to guide psychologists in research with human participants. This document states that psychologists are responsible for assessing the ethical acceptability of any project that they decide to undertake. If the project is ethically questionable, they are obligated to seek advice. After deciding on a particular course of study, psychologists are expected to do the following:

1. To inform participants in advance about those aspects of the research that might influence their decision to participate and to answer their questions about the nature of the research
2. To inform the participants of the reasons for any necessary deceptions after the experiment is over
3. To respect the participants' freedom to decline to participate in the study or to discontinue participation at any time
4. To clarify the responsibilities of the investigator and participant at the beginning of the study

5. To protect the participants from physical and mental damage, danger, harm, and discomfort (When these risks exist, the investigator must inform the participants and receive their consent before continuing. Research procedures which could cause lasting or severe damage are never to be used.)

6. To clarify the nature of the study and remove misconceptions, once the data are collected

7. To detect and alleviate long-term after-effects, if any exist

8. To keep information collected about research participants confidential (24)

Many questions of ethics are subtle and controversial. Moreover, being human, psychologists occasionally violate their own ethical standards—unintentionally as well as intentionally. So the subject of ethics is continually being debated.[4]

STATISTICS

After observing, experimenting, testing, or interviewing, psychologists emerge with findings that already are, or can usually be arranged, in quantitative form. At this point,

[4]Recently, for example, a British psychologist, A. D. Baddeley, called attention to a study that was performed about ten years ago, as servicemen were flying across the ocean. The subjects in the experimental group were exposed to a simulated emergency. One of the plane's engines was stopped; the men were convinced that the plane would have to make an emergency crash landing in the sea. The servicemen filled out two forms—a kind of will directing the disposition of their personal belongings and a test of their retention of the emergency instructions. Not surprisingly, the subjects who were exposed to stress made more errors than a second group of unstressed controls (25). The results of this study are far less interesting, however, than the ethical issue. Should such a study have been conducted in the first place? Would this study be judged ethical according to the 1973 standards cited above?

the psychologist must sit down with the data—to organize, describe, and interpret the findings. This is what statistics enable the psychologist to do. You should note that the word *statistics* has several meanings: It refers to the various mathematical techniques that provide ways of organizing, describing, and interpreting numerical data; it also refers to the numerical data themselves.

After You've Got Your Data—What Next?

Let's assume that you're a psychologist and that you teach at college Y. You suspect that students who attend class regularly make better grades on their exams than students who attend class irregularly. To test this hypothesis informally, you pick four students at random from your grade book for last semester's Introduction to Psychology course. Your records contain the data shown in Table 2-2. Before you can answer your question, you have to organize the "raw data"—the numbers that you begin with. You need ways to describe these observations more succinctly and more meaningfully.

Let's start with the test data. You have four students and each student has five grades; so you have four groups of five scores. You want to find one number for each student that will give you a picture of his or her performance, a kind of summary number that can represent five scores.

Measures of Central Tendency

A group of scores usually cluster around a central value. Measures of this central value are known as *measures of central tendency*. There are three common ways of measuring central tendency.

1. Most of the time psychologists use the

TABLE 2-2. GRADES AND ATTENDANCE OF FOUR STUDENTS

Student	Grades					Attendance
	Exam 1	Exam 2	Exam 3	Exam 4	Exam 5	(total days)
1	97	83	84	88	92	41
2	79	79	81	78	77	35
3	88	64	69	91	76	36
4	37	67	53	87	82	24

arithmetical average or the *mean*: the sum of all scores divided by the number of scores. To calculate the mean exam grade for student 1, we add the scores for all the tests (97 + 83 + 84 + 88 + 92 = 444); and we divide 444, the sum, by 5, the number of tests. So student 1's mean is 88.8. The mean tells us that student 1's grades center around the value 88.8. To make sure you understand how means are computed, calculate the means for the other students.[5]

2. Sometimes psychologists pick the middle score, the *median*—the number that half the remaining scores fall above and half fall below. To find the median, one ranks the scores in the group from high to low and then counts down to the middle one. If there are two middle scores, as there are when the number of scores is even, one must take the mean of the two middle scores. The median for student 1 is 88. Compute the medians for the other students.[6]

3. Occasionally, psychologists pick the number that appears most frequently in the group of scores. This number is called the *mode*. Modes are used primarily when one or two scores are extremely frequent in a large group of measurements; and when one wishes to talk about the typical score or scores. The mode is inappropriate to use here as the number of scores is small.

[5]The means are 78.8, 77.6, and 65.2 for students 2, 3, and 4, respectively.
[6]The medians are 79, 76, and 67 for students 2, 3, and 4, respectively.

Psychologists compute a measure of central tendency whenever they want to summarize a group of numbers. When the numbers naturally center around a value in the middle, they generally use the mean as the measure of central tendency, because the mean gives each number equal importance. When the numbers naturally pile up at the high or low end of the range of values, psychologists frequently use the median. Let's take an example. Suppose that a good student makes the following grades on her exams: 20, 91, 87, 94, and 92. In this case the student's grades pile up at the high end of the spectrum. If we're looking for a representative score, it makes some sense to select the median rather than the mean. That way the grade of 20, which seems very atypical of this student, will not count so heavily. The median of these scores is 91. The mean is 76.8.

Measuring Variability

Some of the time the mean value reflects the scores quite well. For example, all student 2's exam marks were very close to the mean value 78.8, but the mean for subject 3, 77.6, describes only one of student 3's marks closely. The other grades are either much lower or much higher than this number. If you look at Table 2-2, you can see that the scores of each student *vary* from the mean score to some degree. Frequently, the psychologist is interested in numerically describing *variability*—how much the scores vary from the central value. The psychologist wants to know whether the scores in the group vary a lot or cluster quite closely to the mean, varying only a little. The *standard deviation* is the statistic that psychologists use most frequently to describe variability. The standard deviation indicates the degree that scores vary, on the average, from the mean. A large standard deviation means they vary a lot; a small standard deviation means they vary very little. Variability is frequently an important bit of information to have. When one is evaluating the performance of new airline pilots, for example, *consistently high* performance may be a matter of life and death. Thus, pilots' performance means should be high and their standard deviations should be small.

Consider the variability of the students' exam marks. If you look at Table 2-2, you can see that student 4's marks vary a lot and that student 2's marks vary almost negligibly from the mean value. On the basis of this information, you'd expect to find a large standard deviation for student 4 and a small standard deviation for student 2. If we calculated the standard deviations, you'd see that you are right. Calculating them involves simple (but tedious) arithmetic. As we are more concerned with the concept than with the numerical details, we will not calculate one here.[7]

Describing Relationships:
The Correlation
Coefficient

Our initial question was whether students who attend class regularly make higher exam

grades than students who attend class irregularly. In other words, how are scores on exams related to scores on attendance? Psychologists use a statistic called the *correlation coefficient* to describe relationships between two sets of scores. The correlation coefficient is a number that ranges from −1 to +1. It is usually expressed as a decimal such as +.23 or +.56 or −.79 or −.94.

First, we will discuss the significance of the sign and then of the size of the correlation coefficient. The plus (+) sign indicates that the correlation is positive; that is, when the score on one variable is high, the score on the other variable tends to be high; when the score on one variable is low, the score on the other variable tends to be low. Here are some everyday examples: height is usually positively correlated with weight; that is, men six feet tall tend to weigh more than men five feet tall. Generally speaking, taller people weigh more than shorter people. Similarly, education is positively correlated with income. People with more education tend to make more money than those with less education.

The minus (−) sign indicates that the correlation is a negative one; that is, when the score on one variable is high, the score on the other variable tends to be low. Here are some everyday examples: Number of cavities is negatively correlated with time spent brushing one's teeth each day. When people spend a lot of time in daily dental care, they tend to have fewer cavities. When they spend a relatively small amount of time in this activity, they tend to have a larger number of cavities. Similarly, the number of cigarettes smoked each day is negatively correlated with life expectancy. When the number of cigarettes smoked daily is high, life expectancy is shortened. And vice versa. *Note that negative and positive do not refer to bad and good*; they simply describe the direction of the relationship between the two variables.

The correlation coefficient has another

[7]Should you wish to calculate a standard deviation, the formula is

$$s = \sqrt{\Sigma \frac{X^2}{N} - \overline{X}^2}$$

where s = the standard deviation
    X = each raw score
    $\overline{X}$ = the mean of the raw scores
    N = the number of raw scores

very important characteristic—strength. The strength of the correlation coefficient refers to the likelihood that two scores will be related. A strong correlation means that the relationship between scores holds true for most cases. A moderate correlation means that the relationship between scores holds true for a moderate number of cases. A weak correlation means that the relationship between scores holds true for only a small number of cases. The size of the number indicates the strength of the correlation. A zero correlation means that the two scores vary randomly; that is, there is no relationship between them. A 1.00 correlation is the strongest correlation possible; it signifies that the relationship between the two scores always holds true. Incidentally, psychologists rarely see correlations of ±1.00. In fact, in psychological research correlations of ±.80 to ±1.00 are considered very strong; ±.60 to ±.80 strong; ±.40 to ±.60 moderate; and ±.20 to ±.40 low. Correlation coefficients below ±.20 are probably due to chance.

If we calculated a correlation coefficient between our attendance and average exam scores, we'd come up with a number around +.98. Since the various correlation coefficients are all rather lengthy to compute, we will not compute one here. What does our correlation coefficient mean? It means that there is a very strong positive relationship between attendance and exam scores; so our initial hunch appears to be correct. When attendance is high, students do well on their exams a large percentage of the time; conversely, when they attend class infrequently, they do rather poorly on their exams for the most part.

We must be very careful about how we interpret this relationship. Many people make the mistake of assuming that because two events are related to one another, one necessarily causes the other. High attendance could contribute to high exam scores. Or it could be that something else, such as high motivation to learn, leads to both good study habits (and consequently high exam grades) and regular class attendance.

Correlation and Causation Are Two Different Things

A correlation coefficient shows how two variables are related to one another; it describes how strongly they are related and in what direction. It does not say that one variable causes the other. *Note: Correlations do not show causation.*

Let's take some examples. Although height and weight are positively correlated, height does not cause weight or vice versa. Rather, both are caused by other factors—heredity, nutrition, and disease. Education and income are also positively correlated, but again one does not necessarily cause the other. A lengthy education does not guarantee a high income. Nor does a lot of money automatically result in a large amount of education. In this case each factor contributes to the other. A high income makes it likely that people will be able to pursue their own interests—education may be one of them; and a good education qualifies people for many high income job opportunities. In both cases, many other variables are also involved.

Because significant correlations do not show causation psychologists are very careful to distinguish between correlational and experimental studies. A correlational study is a descriptive study in which the psychologist makes two or more measurements and uses correlational methods to see whether they appear to be related to one another. For example, a psychologist might make observations on personality characteristics and driving records of motorists. Assume that she finds that aggression is positively correlated with number of serious accidents. She cannot conclude that aggression causes accidents.

Figure 2-10. Although height and weight are positively correlated, one does not cause the other.

6 — feet

5 —

4 —

3 —

2 —

1 —

220 lbs.   220 lbs.   220 lbs.   220 lbs.

Only an experimental study can tell whether one factor causes the other.

Samples, Sampling Errors, and Statistical Decisions

Psychologists usually ask such questions as "How does a three-day work week affect *workers'* productivity?" "Do competitive situations make *women* more anxious than they make *men*?" "How does attending kindergarten affect the five-year-old's performance in the first grade?" But the psychologist cannot study all workers, all women, all men, or all five-year-old children. We call the entire group that the psychologist wants to understand the *population*. The portion of the population that is actually studied is known as the *sample*.

Psychologists try to study *representative* samples. That is, they choose a group of individuals who seem to mirror the important characteristics of the population that they are interested in. For example, if they are interested in American voters, they study a cross section of them—choosing a sample that mirrors the whole population on characteristics such as age, sex, race, religion, socioeconomic class, geography, and voting affiliation. In general, social scientists try to select samples that are both large enough and representative enough to tell them about the entire population. When Gallup takes a poll of American voters, for example, he interviews a comparatively small cross section of them, but he chooses his sample carefully, so that he is usually able to predict accurately from his measurements how the population will vote on election day.

Unfortunately, it is very hard to choose a completely representative sample. Sometimes the investigator is limited to one geographical locale—where people happen to be particularly bright or dull or poor or rich or old or young. Sometimes the method used to choose the sample is faulty. In 1936, for example, spokesmen for the magazine *Literary Digest* predicted a clear victory for Alfred Landon, the Republican presidential candidate. The sample on which the predictions were based had been randomly selected from names in the telephone directories and the automobile registration lists, but in those postdepression years such lists did not contain a representative number of Democrats and Republicans. The biasing of the sample in favor of the Republicans showed up dramatically when Franklin Delano Roosevelt won easily in every state.

Even when the sample is quite representative, *sampling errors*, those errors that result from measuring a sample rather than the entire population, still occur. They occur because of chance differences in the selection of individuals from the total population. Because of sampling errors, for example, the voting preferences of a small sample never mirror the exact voting record of the entire population on election day—although they may come close. Similarly, we cannot expect to obtain the same results on four students that we would obtain if we used all seventy-five students. Moreover, had we chosen four different students at random, we'd almost certainly have come up with four different means, four different estimates of variability, and most importantly, a different correlation coefficient between attendance and average exam score. The important point to remember is this: When the sample's size is relatively large in relation to the population and its composition representative, different samples yield similar results. Our estimate of the relationship between exam average and attendance would have been more accurate had we selected a sample of twenty-five students instead of a sample of four.

This brings us to the important subject of *statistical decisions*. When psychologists compare two or more groups of subjects in an experiment, they almost always see differences between the means and standard deviations of their groups. Similarly, when they correlate two measures, they almost always find correlations stronger than .00, but this does not necessarily mean that the differences are substantial ones due to the inde-

pendent variable or that the correlations are meaningful ones due to some relationship between the scores. Differences could be the result of normal sampling errors.

Under what circumstances can psychologists say that a difference or a correlation is truly significant—that it shows the effect of the independent variable or demonstrates that a real relationship exists? Psychologists use *inferential statistics* to make these decisions. Inferential statistics tell the probability of a given result. When the odds are greater than 5 in 100 that a particular result occurred simply because of chance, psychologists usually assume that the result is not to be trusted. This is an arbitrary decision, but it has come to be widely accepted. When the odds are less than 5 in 100 that a particular result occurred simply because of chance, most psychologists assume that the result is a *significant* one— that is, it is assumed to reflect the real effects of the independent variable or to indicate that a real relationship exists. Significant results are considered stable, trustworthy, and highly likely to be replicated if the study is repeated. Latané and Darley used inferential statistics to decide whether the reaction times of their subjects differed significantly from one another. An initial statistical test showed that such large overall differences in variability between groups could be expected by chance less than 1 out of 100 times—clearly, a significant finding. Further statistical tests revealed the probability of specific differences between particular groups: The difference in reaction times between groups with two and three subjects (including victim and subject) had a reasonably high likelihood of being due to chance alone (more than 5 in 100), so the responses of the members in these groups were not judged to be significantly different from one another. The differences between the two- and six-subject groups and the three- and six-subject groups had a low probability of being due to chance (less than 5 in 100), so the reactions of the members of these groups were judged to be significantly different from one another. These statistical results led Latané and Darley to conclude that the independent variable, perceived group size, did influence how quickly an individual came to th

The findings that we will throughout this textbook are *significant*. In other words, the probability is less than 5 in 100 (or 1 in 20) that chance or error could, by themselves, account for them.

STUDY GUIDE 2

Key Terms. description, explanation, hypothesis, prediction, control, objective, precision, replicate, empiricism, determinism, parsimony, tentative, operational definition;

descriptive method, naturalistic observation, participant observation, clinical observation, questionnaire, psychological test;

experimental method, dependent variable, independent variable, experimental design, subjects, conditions, experimental group, control group, random assignment, matching, equivalent groups, Hawthorne effect, experimenter bias, placebo, single blind procedure, double blind procedure, results, data;

statistics, measure of central tendency, mean, median, mode, variability, standard deviation, correlation coefficient, negative correlation, positive correlation, population, sample, representative sample, sampling error, statistical decision, statistical significance, inferential statistics.

Important Research. floppy-eared rabbits (Thomas), bystander apathy (Latané and Darley), Hans the clever horse (Pfungst), experimenter bias (Rosenthal).

Self-Quiz

1. The "floppy-eared" rabbit study demonstrates which of the following? [**a**] Scientific research sometimes depends on materials that just happen to be available at the time; [**b**] mundane realities and stereotyped notions sometimes limit scientific research; [**c**] following correct scientific procedures may lead to discoveries that are missed by haphazard methods; [**d**] all of the above.

2. A hypothesis is best described as [**a**] a scientific method; [**b**] a possible explanation; [**c**] a type of experimenter bias; [**d**] a random guess.

3. Empirically minded psychologists [**a**] base their conclusions on observed facts instead of on guesses or speculations; [**b**] believe in the idea that all events, including human behaviors, are caused; [**c**] pay attention only to the research of other established scientists in their field, regardless of the value of the research; [**d**] are usually flexible and tentative in their conclusions.

4. A parsimonious explanation is always [**a**] tentative; [**b**] the simplest one that fits the observed facts; [**c**] objective and unbiased; [**d**] based on mathematical calculations.

5. The most reasonable operational definition of curiosity given below is [**a**] the number of questions chosen from a comprehensive checklist of questions when the subject is asked to check all items of interest; [**b**] the parents' estimate of how inquisitive the subject was as a young child; [**c**] the subject's reputation for being inquisitive; [**d**] the subject's grade-point average.

6. Which method is most useful for measuring the attitudes of a large group of people? [**a**] naturalistic observation; [**b**] clinical observation; [**c**] an experiment; [**d**] a questionnaire.

7. A psychologist who anonymously joins a submarine crew to study the behavior of men in close quarters is using [**a**] a descriptive method: testing; [**b**] a descriptive method: participant observation; [**c**] a descriptive method: clinical observation; [**d**] the experimental method.

8. A psychologist who inconspicuously observes the play activities of four-year-old children in a nursery school is using [**a**] naturalistic observation; [**b**] participant observation; [**c**] clinical observation; [**d**] the experimental method.

9. A psychologist designs an experiment to find out whether the amount learned in a particular college

course is influenced by the predominance of lecture or discussion. The dependent variable in this study would be [**a**] the students who participated in the study; [**b**] the predominance of lecture or discussion; [**c**] the type of course; [**d**] the amount learned.

10. The major purpose of randomly assigning subjects to groups is [**a**] to make sure that both groups have an equal number of subjects; [**b**] to be fair, to give each subject an equal chance to be in the most desirable group; [**c**] to obtain groups whose members are as different from one another as possible; [**d**] to control for subject variables which might influence the outcome of the experiment.

11. A double-blind procedure [**a**] prevents subjects from knowing which groups they are in; [**b**] prevents the experimenter from knowing which group the subject is in; [**c**] minimizes the effects of expectancies and biases; [**d**] all of the above.

12. Psychologists are sometimes accused of allowing their personal feelings to bias the results of their studies. In actual fact, [**a**] experimenter bias is rarely a problem; [**b**] studies show that experimenters only influence experimental results in studies where subjects must make ratings; [**c**] experimenter bias is a serious problem, but it can be controlled by several strategies; [**d**] the widespread use of the single-blind procedure has made the experimenter-bias problem insignificant.

13. Which is *not* an ethical requirement in psychological research with humans? [**a**] to compensate subjects in some way for their services; [**b**] to explain the nature of the research to the subjects and answer any questions; [**c**] to allow the subjects to drop out of the experiment at any time; [**d**] to detect and alleviate long-term aftereffects.

14. A _____ represents the value around which a group of scores cluster. [**a**] measure of variability; [**b**] measure of central tendency; [**c**] correlation coefficient; [**d**] standard deviation.

15. A statistic which measures how much scores differ from the central value is called the [**a**] correlation coefficient; [**b**] standard deviation; [**c**] mean; [**d**] inferential statistic.

16. Ordinarily, as the weather gets hotter (temperature goes up), people wear less clothing. The sign of the correlation between temperature and number of articles of clothing worn is [**a**] positive; [**b**] negative; [**c**] nonexistent; [**d**] impossible to determine.

17. Suppose an investigator found a correlation of +.63 between the score on a memory test and the number of years of school attendance. One could conclude from this correlation that [**a**] having a good memory causes students to stay in school; [**b**] people with good memories actually spend fewer years in school than those with poor memories; [**c**] people with good memories frequently stay in school longer than people with poor memories, but there is no way to know what causes this relationship; [**d**] people with good memories occasionally stay in school longer than people with poor memories, but there is no way to know what causes this relationship.

18. Suppose that a psychologist at university A conducts a well-controlled experiment and finds out that subjects who take drug X become apathetic and withdrawn, but subjects who take a placebo do not. Also assume that a psychologist at university B replicates the study and obtains the same result. One could conclude that [**a**] drug X appears to cause apathy and withdrawal; [**b**] the placebo was probably ineffective, and different controls should be used in future studies of drug X; [**c**] although subjects who took drug X appear to be apathetic and withdrawn, there is no way to know what causes this; [**d**] more studies are necessary before any tentative conclusions are reached.

19. If we question two hundred women to find out about the attitudes of women in general, the group of two hundred women is called a(n) [**a**] random sample; [**b**] inferential group; [**c**] population; [**d**] sample.

20. A statistically significant result is best described as one that is [**a**] accurate; [**b**] consistent; [**c**] unlikely to have occurred only by chance; [**d**] important.

Exercises

1. OPERATIONAL DEFINITIONS. Operational definitions are precise definitions that relate the concept or object being defined to the procedures that are used to observe or measure it. Any one concept or object may have several possible operational definitions. It is also important to note that operational definitions tend to apply only to certain limited situations. That is, they are rarely general, dictionary-type definitions. This is unfortunate but necessary; it is usually impossible for a definition to be both widely applicable and precise enough for scientific work; so when defining terms for research purposes, psychologists often sacrifice generality for precision.

   To make certain you understand what an operational definition is, operationally define the following terms. You· should be able to think of at least two possible operational definitions for each one (it might help to imagine a very specific situation and ask yourself, "In this situation, how can I tell for certain whether _____ occurs or exists?"): anger, learning, hunger, prejudice, abnormal behavior, creativity, a juvenile delinquent, love.

2. DESCRIPTIVE AND EXPERIMENTAL METHODS. Psychologists choose different research methods to answer different types of questions. When psychologists want to answer the question "What behavior or event occurs under a particular set of circumstances?" they use descriptive methods; when they want to investigate the question "Does X affect, influence, or cause Y?" they do an experiment. Some questions can be studied with either method. For example, in considering whether people in frustrating surroundings are more aggressive than those who are not, you could observe the aggression of people who normally live in frustrating surroundings or administer a questionnaire to such people. You could also answer this question experimentally by selecting a group of people, assigning them at random to two groups, frustrating one group but not the other, and comparing their aggression. When both the descriptive or experimental methods can be used, the experimental method is preferred because it alone gives information about the causes of behavior.

The following exercise is designed to help you make certain you understand how particular methods are chosen to answer particular questions. Use the following abbreviations to indicate the most appropriate method for investigating each question: E—experimental; N—naturalistic observation; C—clinical observation; Q—questionnaire or interview.

_____ **1.** Do men and women differ in their opinions about the importance of federally aided poverty programs?

_____ **2.** Does smoking marijuana cause changes in people's ability to reason?

_____ **3.** Does snacking between meals increase the likelihood of becoming obese?

_____ **4.** What happens at the meetings of a particular juvenile gang?

_____ **5.** How does Gary perceive his childhood?

_____ **6.** How many words does a typical three-year-old use?

_____ **7.** Can students' anxiety about tests be reduced by giving many small quizzes instead of a few large exams?

_____ **8.** Do naturally red-haired people flare up more readily than other people?

_____ **9.** Is a very frightening film more likely than a nonfrightening educational film to convince people to give up cigarette smoking?

_____ **10.** Do teachers' expectations influence their students' learning?

_____ **11.** How does Andrew, a resident at a state mental hospital, typically behave?

_____ **12.** What events make Paul and Jane angry at one another? How do they usually handle their anger?

_____ **13.** Will a particular school program increase children's creativity?

_____ **14.** How do the values of current teen-agers differ from those of their parents?

3. INDEPENDENT AND DEPENDENT VARIABLES. In designing an experiment psychologists are interested in testing their hypothesis—in finding out whether the independent variable(s) cause or influence the dependent variable(s). Although hypotheses can be worded in many different ways, they are usually put in one of the following forms: X (the independent variable) influences Y (the dependent variable). Or a change in X (the independent variable) causes a change in Y (the dependent variable). To practice deciding which variable is which, identify the independent variable(s) (IV) and dependent variable(s) (DV) in each of the following questions.

_____ **1.** Can malnutrition reduce mental ability?

_____ **2.** Do ads featuring beautiful people sell more cosmetics than those featuring "everyday" people?

_____ **3.** Do children learn to read more quickly if their parents read to them frequently?

_____ **4.** Are monkey infants who are isolated from birth from their mothers more socially withdrawn and poorer at problem solving than normally reared monkeys?

_____ **5.** Are objects valued more highly when they are worked for or given free?

_____ **6.** Do social class and sex influence a person's chance of getting a job?

_____ **7.** Are people likely to make more mistakes on a simple task when they are anxious than when they are calm?

4. STATISTICS. For further practice in using statistics, consider the following problem. Assume that you wanted to find out whether a particular study technique influenced children's learning. You assigned eighteen sixth-grade children randomly to two groups. Nine children used the study technique and nine did not. Then you tested each child on a series of learning tasks and computed a "learning score" for each one (10 was the highest possible score.) Your data looked like these:

Study technique group   5, 7, 8, 5, 5, 6, 5, 7, 8.
No study technique group   9, 3, 6, 6, 4, 5, 7, 2, 1.

Calculate (1) the mean, (2) the median, and (3) the mode for each group. A quick way to judge variability is to find the range of scores, the difference between the highest and lowest score. You calculate the range by subtracting the lowest score from the highest score (range = the highest score minus the lowest score). (4) Calculate the range of each group. (5) Although you do not know whether the differences between groups on means, medians, modes, or ranges are statistically significant ones, assume that they are and speculate on how the study technique affected the children's learning.

To find out whether the effect of the study technique was related to any subject characteristics, you would calculate correlation coefficients. *Estimate* the value (.00–.20, .20–.40, .40–.60, .60–.80, .80–1.00) and give the sign of the correlation coefficient that would describe each of the following situations: (6) There was no significant relationship between score on an intelligence test and learning score among children using the study technique: Children with low and high measured intelligence scored equally well. (7) There was a strong relationship between age when the study technique was used and learning score: The younger the child, the higher the learning score. (8) There was a low but significant relationship between learning score before the study technique was used and learning score after the study technique was used: The higher the first score, the higher the second score.

Questions to Consider

1. How could you use naturalistic observation, a questionnaire, and an experiment to study the effects of anxiety on desire for human contact?
2. Collect examples which illustrate how the mass media (newspapers, magazines, scandal sheets, advertisements on television, and so on) abuse statistics. Look for nonrepresentative sampling, conclusions of causation from correlations, assumptions that differences between groups are necessarily significant.
3. Design an experiment to test this hypothesis: Students who have experienced academic success are more likely to perform well in school than students who have experienced failure. What is the independent variable? the dependent variable? How might you operationally define each variable? Be sure to include controls for experimental setting, subjects'

characteristics (including measured intelligence), and possible experimenter effects in your design.
4. Describe some informal experiments which you have conducted (situations where you manipulated some event and observed the effects of the manipulation). What were the independent and dependent variables? Describe the "experimental design." What were the results? Did you make any attempt to control the extraneous factors?
5. Would you consider the Latané and Darley study ethical by the 1973 ethical standards of the American Psychological Association?

Project 2: Making Precise Naturalistic Observations

Many animals, including people, are territorial—that is, they have areas which they consider their own and defend from intruders. People's territories include their homes and such personal possessions as cars and furniture. People also seem to have temporary territories, areas which they "stake out" for a period of time and treat as their own. Some examples of temporary territories include the end of the table at which a person is sitting in a cafeteria, the carrel at which a person is studying in the library, one's sitting space in a chair or on the ground, and any place where one has deposited one's coat and books.

Method. For this project, you will be making two-minute naturalistic observations on five people to answer the question: How do people react to an invasion of a temporary territory? Although you could wait for invasions of people's temporary territories to occur and observe what happens, you can get more information more quickly by structuring the situation—by having a friend or classmate invade the temporary territory.

First, decide what type of temporary territory to invade. If you decide to invade a temporary cafeteria territory, you might ask your accomplice to sit down across from single individuals at cafeteria tables. Your subjects should all be strangers to both you and your accomplice; and the invasion should be carried out in precisely the same way and preferably in the same setting for all five subjects.

Use the checklist below to collect observations. You will be observing bodily movements, signs of discomfort (example: blushing), polite requests to move, challenging comments (example: "Hey, what are you doing here?"), raised voices, irritated or accusing looks, other-directed negative comments (example: "Look at this creep here."), obscenities, and physical violence. Note that you can write in additional behaviors. A convenient way to record your observations is simply to check the appropriate box each time the subject makes that response during the two-minute observation period. By using one column per subject, you can collect all your data on one sheet of paper. After you have collected your data, be sure to inform the subject about the nature of the project.

Results. Count the total number of times each behavior is emitted by all your subjects. Note whether any particular behaviors are more prevalent than others.

Discussion. Be certain to consider the following questions: (1) What do people do when their temporary territories are invaded? (2) Which subject and invader characteristics influenced the findings? Did sex of subject interact with sex of invader? (3) Should other behaviors have been included in the checklist? (4) What problems occurred and how could they have been prevented? (5) Can you now describe how people generally behave when their temporary territories are invaded? (6) Was this study ethical?

Checklist

Behaviors	Subject				
	1 (sex__)	2 (sex__)	3 (sex__)	4 (sex__)	5 (sex__)
Bodily movements					
Signs of discomfort					
Polite requests to leave					
Raised voice					
Dirty looks					
Negative comments					
Obscenities					
Violence					
Other: _____					

Suggested Readings

1. Bachrach, Arthur. *Psychological research: An introduction* (3d ed.) New York: Random House, Inc., 1972 (paperback). Introduction to psychological research by the psychologist who wrote, "People don't usually do research the way people who write books about research say they do research."

2. Doherty, Michael E., & Shemberg, Kenneth M. *Asking questions about behavior: An introduction to what psychologists do.* Glenview, Ill.: Scott, Foresman and Company, 1970. (paperback) This brief book focuses on how to ask researchable questions in psychology; it also looks at some sound research answers to the question, "How do specific stresses affect behavior?"

3. Huff, Darrell. *How to lie with statistics.* New York: W. W. Norton & Company, Inc., 1954 (paperback). Entertaining book about how people abuse statistics.

4. Pomeroy, Wardell Baxter. "Alfred C. Kinsey: Man and method." From "Dr. Kinsey and the Institute for Sex Research." *Psychology Today*, March 1972, 5, 33–40, 72. An associate of Kinsey's describes the interview techniques that Kinsey pioneered.

5. Rosenthal, Robert. "Self-fulfilling prophecy." *Psychology Today,* September 1968, 44–51. Rosenthal describes research which demonstrates that expectations (particularly the experimenter's) affect people's behavior.

6. Warwick, Donald P. "Deceptive research: Social scientists ought to stop lying." *Psychology Today*, February 1975, 8, 38, 40, 105, 106. A social scientist questions the ethics of using deception in research.

7. Bakan, D. "Psychology can now kick the science habit." *Psychology Today*, March 1972, 5, 26, 28, 86–88. A humanistic psychologist argues that psychology must give up its reliance on the scientific methods of the natural sciences.

Answer Keys

SELF-QUIZ
1. d 2. b 3. a 4. b 5. a 6. d 7. b 8. a 9. d
10. d 11. d 12. c 13. a 14. b 15. b 16. b 17. c
18. a 19. d 20. c

EXERCISE 2
1. Q 2. E 3. E 4. N 5. C 6. N 7. E 8. N 9. E
10. E 11. N 12. C 13. E 14. Q

EXERCISE 3
1. IV—malnutrition, DV—mental ability, 2. IV—type of ad, DV—cosmetic buying 3. IV—frequency of parental story-reading, DV—speed of child's learning to read 4. IV—isolation from mothers, DV—monkey's problem solving and sociability 5. IV—the manner in which objects are acquired, DV—value placed on objects 6. IV—social class and sex, DV—being hired 7. IV—degree of anxiety, DV—number of mistakes on simple task

EXERCISE 4

1. Study technique group: 6.2; No study technique group: 4.8.
2. Study technique group: 6; No study technique group: 5.
3. Study technique group: 5; No study technique group: 6.
4. Study technique group: 3; No study technique group: 8.

5. The study technique appears to have increased the average child's learning. It also appears to have minimized differences in learning between children.
6. .00 to $\pm$ .20
7. $-.60$ to $-.80$
8. $+.20$ to $+.40$

THE BEGINNING: HEREDITY, ENVIRONMENT, AND THE EARLY DEVELOPMENT OF THE CHILD

IN THIS CHAPTER
We focus on hereditary and environmental factors that shape the developing infant. After reading this chapter, you should be able to do the following:

1. Describe six factors that continually influence development
2. Describe four methods that scientists use to assess the effects of heredity on behavior
3. Cite evidence that heredity helps shape intelligence and temperament
4. Describe four maternal conditions that affect the developing fetus
5. Define *maturation*
6. Describe how universal sensory and social experiences influence development
7. Cite current research findings on five child-care practices

The *neonate*, as the newborn human baby is called, weighs between 6 and 7 pounds, on the average, and measures between 18 and 21 inches. Early psychologists perceived the infant as homely and incompetent. G. Stanley Hall, one of the first American psychologists to study children systematically, described the human infant as "squinting, cross-eyed, pot-bellied, and bow legged"; and he attributed to it a "monotonous and dismal cry" and "red, shriveled, parboiled skin [1]." William James, another early psychologist, wrote: ". . . assailed by eyes, ears, nose, skin, and entrails at once, [the newborn] feels that all is one great blooming buzzing confusion [2]."

Recent studies of newborn infants have changed psychologists' opinions. The neonate, as it turns out, is not inept at all. It is a responsive organism from the very first; it sees; it hears; it is sensitive to touch; it tastes; and it smells. It also learns—although its learning capacity is rather limited when judged by adult standards.[1] It is equipped with many *reflexive behaviors* (behaviors automatically elicited by stimuli in the environment) that help it to survive. If you put an object in the infant's mouth, it sucks. If you stroke its cheek, it turns its head. It startles to loud, sudden noises. It makes swimming motions when held horizontally and supported by the abdomen. It can also hiccough, vomit, grasp objects in its hands, and cry. During its first eighteen months, the baby will be "transformed from a crying, squirming, reflexive creature into a coherent, coordinated, and planful child [5]." The child, of course, will continue to develop throughout its lifetime.

We begin our study of psychology by examining the developmental process. We are in the domain of *developmental psychology*, the branch of psychology that investigates the evolution of physical structure, behavior, and psychological functioning in people and other animals from any point after conception to any point before death. In later chapters we will deal with the early development of perception, thought, language, personality, and complex modes of social behavior. We turn now to the developmental process itself.

Heredity and Environment: The On-going Interactions

Heredity and environment continuously influence the development of people and other

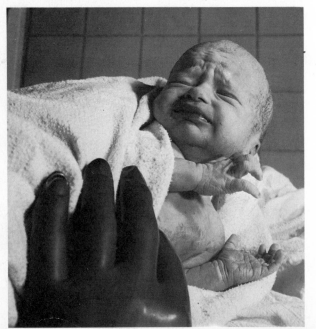

Figure 3-1. The neonate is not inept, as early psychologists believed: it sees, it hears, it is sensitive to touch; it tastes, it smells, and it learns. (Wayne Miller, Magnum.)

[1]There is no question that experience influences the newborn's behavior; in this broad sense, infants learn. They are capable of making new associations between events. For example, if a sugar solution is paired fifty times with an air puff, which makes an infant blink, a normal infant will blink at least some of the time when the sugar solution is presented alone (3). Neonates also alter their responses when doing so leads directly to pleasurable consequences. For example, an infant of several days can modify its sucking pattern to increase its milk supply (4).

animals. At conception heredity "programs" human potentialities into the embryo. At the same time the environment (experience) is also influencing the developing person. The genes themselves operate within the environment of a cell. The embryo grows into a fetus within the intrauterine environment. Conditions in either environment may alter human structures and/or behaviors. Both heredity and environment continue to influence human development as infants grow to adulthood and old age. Donald Hebb, a psychologist at McGill University, has organized the hereditary and environmental factors underlying development into six categories:

1. Heredity—the animal's physical inheritance.
2. The chemical prenatal environment—the environment that surrounds the developing fetus—in people, the intrauterine environment.
3. The chemical postnatal environment—chemical influences like nutrition, water, oxygen, and drugs, to which the animal is exposed after birth.
4. Constant sensory experiences—those experiences which occur both before and after birth that are normally inevitable for all members of a particular species. (After birth, for example, people ordinarily experience alternation of light and dark, changing visual patterns, sounds of human voices, and physical contact with other human beings.)
5. Variable sensory experiences—those experiences which vary from animal to animal depending on their peculiar circumstances.
6. Traumatic physical events—events that destroy an organism's cells. If fortunate, an animal may never be exposed to these experiences (6).

In this chapter we focus on some of these major influences. We begin with heredity.

HEREDITY AND DEVELOPMENT

How does heredity influence the development of intelligence and temperament? This question belongs within the domain of *behavior genetics*, (the psychological discipline that attempts to understand how heredity influences behavior) Note that this subject is only one aspect of how heredity affects development. Before we proceed, you need to review some basic facts about genetics. (For more detailed information, you may want to consult a biology textbook.)

1. Technically, each life begins at conception when the father's *germ cell*, the *sperm*, unites with the mother's *germ cell*, the egg or *ovum*, producing a single cell, known as the *zygote*.
2. The nucleus of the zygote contains forty-six minute particles, called *chromosomes* (from the Greek words meaning "colored bodies"). The twenty-three chromosomes supplied by the germ cell of each parent furnish the genetic link between parent and child. Although chromosomes exist in most other bodily cells, only those in the germ cells are involved in transmitting physical characteristics.
3. Each chromosome in the zygote's nucleus carries thousands of even smaller particles called *genes*. We will consider the gene the basic unit of heredity. Composed of a complex chemical substance, *deoxyribonucleic acid* (*DNA*, for short), genes direct the production of *enzymes*, complex organic substances that control all chemical reactions within the body including the formation of proteins. The proteins are the basic components of blood, muscle, tissues, organs, and all other bodily structures. Through their control of the enzymes and protein production, genes direct the development of internal and external bodily

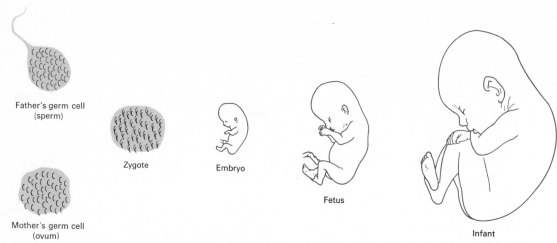

Figure 3-2. Technically, a person's life begins at conception when the father's germ cell, the sperm, unites with the mother's germ cell, the egg or ovum. The fertilized ovum divides again and again, forming a mass of cells which gradually develops into the structures of the human infant. For the first six to eight weeks following conception the cell mass is known as an embryo; after three months it is called a fetus.

structures—duplicating those structures inherited from the parents.

4. People and other animals inherit broad species characteristics. The human embryo develops a set of human structures that make human responses and capacities possible. Because we inherit opposing thumbs, for example, we learn to manipulate tools quite easily; similarly, the inheritance of large cerebral cortexes allows us to process vast amounts of information.

5. At the same time, people and other animals also inherit a set of unique characteristics. An individual may inherit a tendency to grow tall or short, to have straight hair or curly hair, to be immune or susceptible to poison ivy, and so on.

6. Each parent contributes half of his or her chromosomes to each child—with each child receiving a different combination. For this reason each family member is genetically unique. There is one exception to this rule: Identical twins, triplets, and so on—individuals who come from the split-

ting of a single zygote—are genetically identical. It is important to note that most twins are fraternal twins; that is, they come from the unions of different eggs and sperms; consequently, they do not resemble each other any more than most brothers and sisters do. It should now be apparent that people exhibit varying degrees of genetic similarity. The members of a particular family exhibit a high degree of genetic similarity, but only identical twins are genetically identical. Unrelated individuals, on the other hand, exhibit a low degree of genetic similarity.

7. The geneticist's understanding of the functioning of heredity varies from species to species. Fruit-fly heredity is so precisely understood that scientists can assign most fruit-fly traits to specific genes and identify the location of those genes on particular chromosomes. In fact, they can breed almost any specifiable kind of fruit fly. Human heredity, in contrast, is much less well understood. Why? With fruit flies

scientists are dealing primarily with *discrete* characteristics; that is, the animal has or does not have a particular trait. Blue eyes are a discrete characteristic; so is curly hair. In contrast, many human characteristics, especially psychological and behavioral ones, are *continuous*; that is, they exist in degrees. Every human being has some degree of motor coordination, no matter how ungainly he or she is. Similarly, every human being has some degree of intelligence. Continuous characteristics like these are thought to be influenced by numerous genes, each making a small contribution. The genetics of continuous characteristics is very difficult to investigate. There is a second complication. Many human characteristics depend on factors other than heredity. Consider athletic prowess. Heredity may contribute a potentiality for long limbs, large muscles, and acute vision, but if a person does not practice, he or she will not develop athletic skills.

We turn now to psychologists' efforts to understand how heredity helps shape intelligence and temperament.

Early Attempts to Study the Effects of Genetics on Behavior

In 1865 an eminent English physician, mathematician, geographer, inventor, and scientist named Francis Galton made one of the first systematic investigations of the influence of genetics on behavior. Galton had an equally illustrious cousin named Charles Darwin. According to a popular story, Galton was struck by family resemblances: Greatness obviously ran in his own family. Did it have a genetic basis? To research this question, Galton collected data on the family members of prominent men in science, law, the military,

politics, and the ministry. He found that the families of these outstanding men often contained a greater number of distinguished members than chance alone could account for. He also discovered that close blood relatives were more likely to be outstanding than distant ones. Galton felt that the data were best explained by assuming that genetics was responsible for productivity. He minimized the fact that prominent people probably furnished their children with great social and educational advantages.

A second early researcher, American psychologist H. H. Goddard, embarked on a similar enterprise in the early 1900s. Goddard, however, was interested in the genetic basis of stupidity, debauchery, and vice. He confined his studies to the offspring of a Revolutionary war soldier known as Martin Kallikak. Kallikak had sired two lines of descendents—one by a feeble-minded woman who worked in a tavern and a second by a woman from a respected family. The descendents of the first match reputedly

Figure 3-3. Sir Francis Galton, 1822–1911. (The Bettmann Archive).

"excelled only in dereliction [negligence, delinquency] and stupidity." The descendents of the second match were solid citizens of reputation and accomplishment. Goddard used the testimony of local townsfolk to evaluate each Kallikak. Here is an example:

The field worker accosts an old farmer—"Do you remember an old man, Martin Kallikak (Jr.) who lived on the mountain-edge, yonder?" "Do I? Well I guess! Nobody'd forget him. Simple, not quite right here (tapping his head) but inoffensive and kind. All the family was that. Old Moll, simple as she was, would do anything for a neighbor. She finally died—burned to death in a chimney corner. She had come in drunk and sat down there. Whether she fell over in a fit or her clothes caught fire, nobody knows. She was burned to a crisp when they found her. That was the worst of them, they would drink. Poverty was their best friend in this respect, or they would have been drunk all the time" . . . [7].

Goddard's observations do not provide strong evidence for the role of heredity on behavior. Why not? In the first place, we don't know whether the townspeople's reports are reliable or valid. Moreover, as in Galton's study, the effects of heredity have not really been isolated from the effects of environment. Impoverished conditions, lack of opportunity, and "derelict" family models can probably lead to dereliction and apparent stupidity, regardless of heredity. Nevertheless, these early family studies performed one important function: they aroused curiosity and stimulated better research.

The Method of Twin Study

Galton introduced the method of twin study some twenty years after his study of family eminence. It was a great improvement over the family study method. The logic of the twin study method is this: Identical twins have identical sets of genes; fraternal twins are no more genetically similar than other brothers and sisters. Both identical and fraternal twins usually grow up in a nearly identical environment. They inhabited the uterus together, and since they are the same age at the same time, they are likely to be treated similarly by family members, friends, and relatives. Thus, observed differences between identical twins can be due only to different experiences, whereas observed differences between fraternal twins can be due to different genetics, different experiences, or both; so we have a natural experiment. If identical twins resemble each another more closely on a particular characteristic (on the average), psychologists conclude that heredity is a major determinent of that characteristic. On the other hand, if fraternal twins are as similar to each another as identical twins (on the average), then heredity is not considered an important determinant of that characteristic (see Figure 3-4).

Although these assumptions are widely accepted, some psychologists argue that because identical twins share similar characteristics, they are more likely to be treated alike than fraternal twins. In other words, identical twins have both a more similar heredity and, under most circumstances, a more similar environment. To meet this criticism investigators sometimes compare identical twins who have been reared in different homes to fraternal twins reared in the same home.

The twin study method has been repeatedly used to study the inheritance of intelligence. Intelligence is commonly defined as a potential for learning, reasoning, understanding, and solving problems. The difficulties begin when psychologists try to assess that potential. Right now they have to measure intelligence indirectly because it cannot be measured directly. Usually, they devise problem-solving tasks and score a person's performance on those tasks. Performance on particular tasks, however, is influenced by many factors, including motivation and past

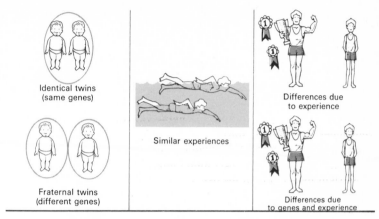

Figure 3-4. The rationale behind twin studies.

If identical twins resemble one another more closely on characteristic X than fraternal twins, the characteristic can be assumed to have a genetic basis.

If fraternal twins resemble one another as closely on the characteristic as identical twins, then the characteristic cannot be assumed to have a genetic basis.

learning; so keep in mind that when psychologists ask, "What is the genetic basis of intelligence?" they are really asking, "Does performance in a specific problem-solving situation seem to be determined, at least in part, by heredity?" (We look at intelligence and intelligence testing in more detail in Chapter 9.)

Numerous studies find that white middle-class families tend to resemble one another rather closely on intelligence test perform-ance. Moreover, the greater the genetic similarity between two people, the more similar their intelligence test scores are likely to be. Figure 3-5 summarizes the results of fifty-two studies of family similarity on intelligence test performance. The numbers at the top of the figure are correlation coefficients (see Chapter 2). They show the degree to which pairs of individuals obtain similar scores. A correlation of 1.00, you'll recall,

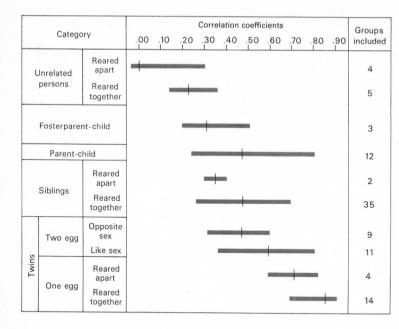

Category		Correlation coefficients	Groups included
		.00 .10 .20 .30 .40 .50 .60 .70 .80 .90	
Unrelated persons	Reared apart		4
	Reared together		5
Fosterparent-child			3
Parent-child			12
Siblings	Reared apart		2
	Reared together		35
Twins / Two egg	Opposite sex		9
	Like sex		11
Twins / One egg	Reared apart		4
	Reared together		14

Figure 3-5. Correlation coefficients for intelligence test scores from fifty-two studies. The horizontal lines show ranges, and the vertical lines represent medians. (From Erlenmeyer-Kimling and Jarvick, 1963.)

shows total agreement; a correlation coefficient of .00 indicates no relationship between scores. Looking at Figure 3-5, you can see that when the intelligence test scores of two unrelated persons reared apart are compared, the correlations range from approximately .00 to .30, indicating that the two sets of scores have a low (possibly inconsequential) positive relationship. When identical twins reared apart are compared, correlations range from approximately .60 to .80, demonstrating that the intelligence test performances of identical twins are strongly positively related. As you look over Figure 3-5, you can see that as people become more genetically similar, there is a corresponding increase in the correlation, indicating an increase in the similarity of their intelligence test scores.

Can you see any evidence that environment also influences intelligence? Note that for all genetic relationships, intelligence test scores are more alike when people are reared together. We will have more to say about the

environment's effects on intelligence later in this chapter. On the basis of data like these, many psychologists believe that genes influence human intelligence.

Studying Genetic Abnormalities and Behavior

Psychologists use another tactic to study the effects of heredity on behavior. They make systematic observations on people with known genetic abnormalities to see whether consistent mental abilities or deficiencies are displayed. A number of strong correlations between specific genetic abnormalities and particular patterns of performance on mental tests are known to exist. Some examples: One psychologist has found that the missing X chromosome in Turner's syndrome tends to be associated with above-average verbal abilities and below-average abilities to visualize three-dimensional objects in space (8). Observations of 167 families showed that a single recessive gene on the X chromosome appears to influence people's spatial abilities (9). Down's syndrome (also known as Mongolism) is caused by an extra chromosome, and it leads to many problems, among them a large overall deficiency in general mental ability. A study of the growth and development of children with Down's syndrome showed that regardless of training, such individuals consistently attained IQs in the moderately retarded range (10). We could add many examples to this list. The point is that specific genetic factors are almost certainly linked to specific mental functions in people.

The Method of Selective Breeding: Maze-bright and Maze-dull Rats

Another way to study the effects of genetics on behavior is selective breeding. Psychologists cannot selectively breed people, so they work with animals—frequently with rats. In selective breeding the investigator breeds two pairs of animals—one pair is particularly outstanding and the other pair is particularly poor on a certain behavioral characteristic—like speed in learning their way through a maze. High-scoring offspring of the high scorers are repeatedly bred with each other; similarly, low-scoring offspring of the low scorers are also repeatedly bred with each other. The breeding program continues for several generations. If a particular behavior is genetically determined, psychologists should find that after breeding for a number of generations, the high scorers consistently breed offspring with high scores on the behavior and the low scorers consistently breed offspring with low scores on the behavior. In 1940 R. C. Tryon, a psychologist at the University of California, performed a classic selective-breeding study to see if maze learning, presumably an intellectual ability in rats, had a genetic basis. Tryon bred maze-bright rats, rats who made comparatively few errors in learning to run a maze, and maze-dull rats, rats who made a great many errors on the same maze. His selective-breeding program continued for eighteen generations. Careful measurements at the end of the program showed no overlap between groups. The dullest maze-bright rat did better in maze running than the brightest maze-dull animal (11). Apparently, maze learning in rats has a genetic basis.

The Study of Infant Differences

Psychologists use yet another strategy to understand the influence of heredity on behavior. They measure particular psychological characteristics in newborn infants before they are influenced by their postnatal environments, and they continue to assess these same characteristics as their subjects develop throughout childhood. If a specific characteristic persists in a large number of subjects, psychologists infer that the characteristic was—at least partly—determined by heredity. Observations from this perspective may support or cast doubt on findings from other sources, but this procedure cannot be considered conclusive. Note that neonatal behavior could be the result of experiences in the intrauterine environment or during delivery. Moreover, the persistence of characteristics observed in infancy can be explained in several ways, as we will see.

For centuries, mothers have been insisting that their newborn babies differ. Psychologists, in contrast, long viewed neonates as essentially identical. In recent years it has become clear that mothers were right all along. Neonates show stable, measurable individual differences. For example, some are easygoing: They sleep, lie quietly in their cribs, or babble softly to themselves most of the time. Others appear to be perpetually upset: They thrash about vigorously, sleep fitfully, and yell loudly for long periods of time (12). Infants' sensory thresholds also differ: Some babies respond to minimal sensory stimulation; others require intense sensory stimulation before they react (13). Female infants, for example, flex their toes at lower intensities of electrical current than male babies do, indicating that they are probably more sensitive to pain (14). Similarly, neonates vary in their reactions to stress and discomfort. Their responses may be mild or intense. They also differ qualitatively. When hungry, for example, infants may show an increase in heart rate, or a rapid change in skin temperature, or they may vomit, or break out in rashes, or flush (because of increased blood pressure) (15).

About fifteen years ago three physicians, Alexander Thomas, Stella Chess, and Herbert Birch, decided to study the early behavioral reactions of approximately 140 infants to see if they persisted over time and to determine how they interacted with specific environmental factors. Through interviews with parents they obtained detailed descriptions of each infant's behavior beginning when each subject was two or three months old. They rated each baby on nine aspects of temperament: extent of motor activity (activity level), degree of regularity of functioning (rhythmicity), response to new situations (approach or withdrawal), response to altered situations (adaptability), intensity of reaction, level of stimulation necessary to evoke a response (responsiveness), general quality of mood, distractability, and span of attention and persistence at an activity. Thomas, Chess, and Birch continued to assess these characteristics at frequent intervals throughout childhood. They found that temperament traits persisted over a ten-year period for many—but not all—of the children.

The investigators also distinguished three temperament patterns, which they labeled "easy," "difficult," and "slow to warm up." "Easy" infants gave their parents few problems. They had sunny dispositions. Their

Figure 3-6. Temperamental differences that appear early in infancy frequently persist through childhood. Here a highly active, "difficult" child "gets into everything," while an "easy" child causes parents few problems. (Erika.)

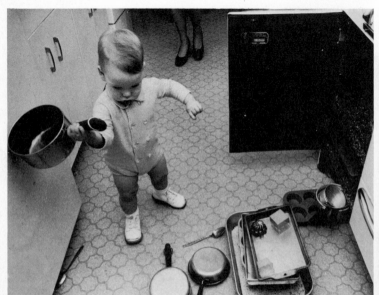

eating and sleeping patterns were regular. They were quick to adapt to new routines, new foods, and new people. Moreover, they continued to be characterized in this way as they grew throughout childhood. Of the sample 40 percent was classified "easy." "Difficult" infants, in contrast, were hard on their parents. They were disagreeable, fussy, and hard to manage. They slept and ate irregularly. They rejected new foods, and they withdrew from new situations. Frustration sent them into tantrums. They cried a lot. Above all, they were loud and intense. "Difficult" infants continued to be "difficult" as they grew older. Of the sample 10 percent was labeled "difficult." A third group of infants was characterized as "slow to warm up." These children were somewhat negative in mood; they adapted slowly to new situations; and they withdrew when exposed to new stimuli. Throughout their childhood they continued to display these same characteristics. Of the sample 15 percent was classified in the "slow to warm up" category. It is important to note that more than one-third of the infants were not sufficiently consistent to be included in one of these groups.

Thomas, Chess, and Birch made an important discovery as they studied their infants in childhood. Out of forty-two children who required professional attention for behavioral problems, 70 percent had been initially classified "difficult," whereas only 18 percent had been categorized "easy." In short, the child's temperament, as assessed in infancy, related very strongly to the child's later adjustment (16).[2] This study supports the no-

tion that temperament characteristics are at least partly determined by heredity and can be reliably detected early in infancy.

Note that the findings that temperament characteristics are frequently consistent can also be explained by interacting environmental factors. The neonate's behavior influences its parent's initial attitudes and reactions. Subsequently, parental behavior further strengthens the child's behavior. A "difficult" infant, for example, may evoke feelings of frustration, anxiety, or anger in its parents. Consequently, the parents may treat their "difficult" baby harshly or inconsistently. The child finds such parental behavior distressing, and it becomes unhappier and harder to get along with—perpetuating the cycle.

Twin studies also support the hypothesis that certain temperament characteristics have a genetic basis. Genes seem to have something to say about whether people are actively friendly and outgoing (extroverted) or shy, reserved, and withdrawn (introverted) (18, 19). Similarly, temperament characteristics which affect mental health appear to be influenced by heredity. One twin study has shown, for example, that neuroses characterized by anxiety, depression, obsession, and withdrawal have a substantial genetic component (20). There is also strong evidence that heredity contributes to severe psychotic disorders, particularly schizophrenia (21).

In sum, studies of twins, persons with genetic abnormalities, neonates, and selectively bred rats indicate that heredity plays some role in the development of intellectual abilities and temperament characteristics.

[2]Thomas, Chess, and Birch argue that children require differential treatment and that the sooner such treatment begins the better—for everyone's adjustment. "Difficult" and "slow to warm up" infants need consistent, patient, nonpunitive parents who understand their baby's tendency to reject the new. Such children do best when they are encouraged to try new experiences and when they are given plenty of time to get used to unfamiliar situations. Older children continue to require differential treatment. A child who becomes intensely absorbed in his own activities should not be expected to come immediately when called. An active child should not be forced to sit quietly on a long automobile trip. Thomas, Chess, and Birch believe that many psychological problems can be prevented if parents adjust their child-rearing practices to their child's temperament (17).

THE INTRAUTERINE ENVIRONMENT AND EARLY DEVELOPMENT

The mother "houses" her child within her uterus for its first forty weeks (approximately). The uterus, the infant's earliest environment, is an important one that can actualize or thwart the child's genetic potential. The mother's health, diet, drug use, and emotional state create a chemical environment which contributes to the shaping of the unborn child.

Disease, especially when it is accompanied by fever, disrupts the stability of the intrauterine environment and can injure the fetus. For example, when mumps, influenza, or rubella (German measles) are contracted during the first three months of pregnancy, they frequently have serious effects on the developing child. After conception the organ systems of the embryo develop in a fixed order. As each system develops, it is maximally vulnerable to disruption. We call these periods of rapid growth during which the organism is unusually vulnerable to the effects of the environment *sensitive (critical) periods.* If the environment is favorable (and if there are no genetic defects), then the system develops properly. If the environment is unfavorable, the developing system may be adversely affected. Surveys show that if the mother develops rubella during the early weeks of her pregnancy, her child has a 60 percent likelihood of being born abnormal in some way. Because the fetus's heart, nervous system, and sense organs are developing rapidly at this time, congenital heart disease, eye defects, deafness, and mental retardation often result (22). Unborn infants can also catch illnesses such as smallpox, chicken pox, and mumps from their mothers.

The mother's nutrition also influences her developing child. When mothers are seriously malnourished, they cannot maintain an adequate food supply for their fetuses. Much research supports this notion. In one study, for example, investigators observed 210 pregnant women who were attending a clinic at the University of Toronto. All the women had been on inadequate diets for the first four to five months of their pregnancy. At this point in their pregnancies 90 of the women received supplements to make their diets adequate, and the other 120 women continued to eat as previously. The investigators compared both the pregnancies and the infants of the two groups. Mothers on good diets were in better health throughout their pregnancy than mothers on inadequate diets. They experienced fewer complications such as anemia, toxemia (a condition of unknown origin characterized by swelling limbs and associated with kidney and circulatory problems), threatened and actual miscarriages, premature births, and still births. Their labor was five hours shorter on the average. Moreover, their infants had better health records immediately after birth and for the entire first six months of their lives (23). Although research on animals links low-protein diets with anatomical defects of the central nervous system (24), scientists do not know whether people are affected in a similar way. Infants who are likely to have experienced gross protein deficiency in utero usually come from poor homes. Poverty brings with it added exposure to illness and stress. Consequently, the separate effects of diet, illness, and stress cannot usually be isolated from one another in people.

Drugs in the mother's blood stream are usually passed along to the child. Although the consequences of certain drugs are well documented, the effects of countless others—such as nose drops, aspirin, insecticides, room fresheners, and the like—are not well understood. A tragedy of massive proportions occurred recently with the tranquilizer thalidomide. Mothers who took thalidomide

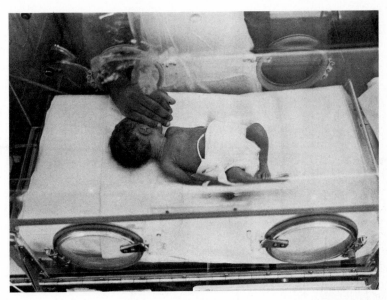

Figure 3-7. This child of a heroin-addicted mother began going through acute withdrawal immediately after birth. (Charles Gatewood.)

early in their pregnancies delivered stillborn or grossly deformed infants. When pregnant women use quinine, it sometimes produces congenital deafness in their babies. The neonates of narcotics addicts are frequently born addicted themselves—displaying acute withdrawal symptoms, irritability, trembling, and vomiting. Psychologists have systematically studied the effects of sedating drugs, those given prior to and during delivery to reduce the mother's distress. When mothers take a depressant such as pentobarbital within ninety minutes of delivery, their newborn infants display a shorter span of attention (they look at pictures more briefly) than babies of mothers who have not taken such drugs within ninety minutes of delivery (25). Whether these drugs have permanent effects is not known. However, some researchers believe that heavy doses of sedatives can produce asphyxiation and brain damage (26).

The consequences of cigarette smoking are becoming clearer. One group of researchers studied 2,736 pregnant women before they gave birth and found that the rate of premature deliveries related to the duration of the mother's smoking history: 11.2 percent for nonsmokers, 13.6 percent for those who had begun smoking during pregnancy, and 18.6 percent for chronic smokers. The incidence of premature deliveries also increased as the *amount* of cigarettes smoked increased. In addition, the infants of smokers weighed less than those of nonsmokers regardless of duration of the pregnancy, the child's sex, or the mother's age, work history, education, or score on a psychosomatic complaint scale (27). Studies such as this one lead psychologists to believe that smoking affects fetal development and onset of labor. Note that we are dealing with a correlational study; so we cannot be certain of these conclusions.

Mothers undergoing severe stress also appear to create problems for their unborn children. Pregnant women, like other people, respond to emotions such as rage or anxiety, with an autonomic reaction that includes the massive outpouring of adrenal hormones (see Chapter 11). These hormones enter the fetus's blood stream. Some researchers believe that excessive adrenal hormones may damage the fetus permanently. When psychologists subject pregnant rats to severe stress,[3] the rats give birth to fearful timid offspring who perform poorly at learning mazes and exploring open fields (28). When human mothers undergo emotional crises (such as the death or injury of a loved one), the movements of their fetuses increase several hundred percent. When mothers remain upset for several weeks, their fetuses continue moving around at the exaggerated tempo (29). Correlational studies also indicate that emotional distress in mothers during pregnancy is associated with irritability, intestinal problems, and excessive crying in babies during early infancy (30). Although we do not know that these effects persist, it looks as if the infants of mothers suffering prolonged or severe emotional upsets get off to a bad start.[4]

From this brief review it should be clear that the sojourn in the intrauterine environment is an important one which helps shape the physical and behavioral characteristics with which the neonate is born.

MATURATION

The behavior of infants all over the world develops in much the same order. The neonate smiles almost randomly at first. At approximately six weeks of age, infants begin to smile regularly whenever they see human faces. Babies of about six months acquire strong attachments to family members and fears of strangers. Early motor behavior also develops in a fixed sequence. Normal babies—regardless of their circumstances—roll over before they sit with support. A little later, they sit by themselves. Later yet, they stand while holding on. Very few children sit up before they roll over or stand before they sit. Language, perceptual abilities, and intellectual and learning skills also appear on a universal timetable.

It is important to note that although many early behavior patterns follow a regular sequence, individual children reach various milestones at different ages. Figure 3-8 shows the extent to which children vary in motor development. Notice that some babies are close to three months ahead of others in achieving particular skills.

These universal behavioral sequences depend to a large extent on heredity. At the time of conception genetics sets certain potentialities for the organism's structural and functional development, which are only partially complete at the time of birth. The infant's body and nervous system will continue to grow throughout its lifetime. Psychologists frequently use the term *maturation* to refer to (the emergence of behavior patterns that depend on the development of body and nervous system structures) In recent years it has become clear that environmental factors also play a large role in maturation. Before birth the intrauterine environment influences the developing fetus. After birth the infant's genetic endowment interacts with its chemical environment (nutrition, drugs, oxygen, and so on) to make it physically ready to learn new responses at particular *sensitive periods* early in its development. If the external environment provides constant sensory experiences (normally inevitable opportunities to learn and a minimum amount of

---

[3]In this study the severe stress was created by sounding a buzzer and then presenting a strong shock to a group of female rats. After the animals had learned to associate the two events, they were taught to avoid the shock by making a particular response as soon as the buzzer sounded. Then they were mated. After becoming pregnant, the rats were exposed periodically to the buzzer—without being allowed to make the avoidance response. According to the investigator, they appeared to be intensely anxious.

[4]Note once more that we cannot conclude that a mother's emotional stress *causes* emotional signs in her infant. Emotionality in mothers is merely *correlated* with emotionality in infants. Their common genetic inheritance could cause both the mother's and child's emotional behavior.

stimulation and practice), then motor, language, sensory, social, and intellectual skills develop in an orderly way. Thus, at least four types of developmental factors—heredity, chemical prenatal, chemical postnatal, and constant sensory experiences—actually influence the process psychologists call maturation. We focus now on some of the normally inevitable sensory and social experiences that interact with heredity and the early chemical environments to influence maturation.

Universal Sensory Experiences and Early Development

Even before birth infants experience sensory stimulation from contact with parts of their own bodies and the uterine wall and from vibrations in the fluid that surrounds them. After birth, sensory stimulation increases tremendously. The infant hears countless sounds—everything from its own breathing to the roar of the crowd at the football game on the family TV. It kicks its limbs and clenches its fists; it handles soft blankets, crumbly cookies, and plastic toys. Its parents provide more stimulation—by rocking, patting, caressing, smiling, and talking to it.

Studies in the laboratory show that animals need all kinds of sensory stimulation when they are young if they are to be able to perceive adequately later on. If they are deprived of specific sensory experiences during infancy, their later perceptual skills are frequently defective. (We explore this topic further in Chapter 5.) In one study, for example, a group of psychologists reared a chimpanzee with cardboard cuffs over its forearms and lower legs until it was 2½ years old. The cuffs permitted the animal to move its arms and legs, but they prevented the ordinary tactile experiences of touching its own body and feeling objects in the environment. This tactile deprivation seems to have

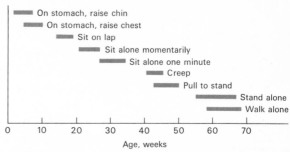

Figure 3-8. Ages at which human infants develop important motor skills. (From Shirley, 1931.)

had many effects on the chimpanzee's later behavior. It sat in unusual postures; it seemed somewhat insensitive to pain; and it had trouble learning in situations where it had to use tactile cues (31). Apparently, although normal genes and favorable intrauterine experiences ensure the proper development of sensory structures (eyes, ears, skin receptors, and the like), sensory experiences are essential if an animal is to be able to use these capabilities.

How could psychologists investigate whether sensory stimulation is essential for human

Figure 3-9. Here a chimpanzee sits and gestures normally, behavior contrasting sharply with the actions of chimpanzees raised wearing cardboard cuffs that prevented normal tactile experiences. (Yerkes Regional Primate Research Center of Emory University.)

infants? Unfortunately, some institutional settings, such as certain orphanages, provide infants with dull, barren environments and little stimulation; so the question is not impossible to explore. Of course, even in the bleakest of institution settings, infants receive some sensory stimulation. Accordingly, we can only examine the effects of relative, and not absolute, sensory deprivation on people. Also note that deprivation in a barren orphanage is multiple; that is, children are deprived of sensory stimulation, of motor stimulation, of a mother, and of social relationships.

In 1962 Sally Provence and Rose Lipton, pediatricians who were then at Yale University, published a study that compared seventy-five family-reared infants with seventy-five reared in an orphanage. The orphanage was clean, well lit, heated, and adequately ventilated, but eight to ten infants shared only one attendant for eight hours each day. During the remaining sixteen hours, no one was present except at feeding time, when an attendant propped up bottles, heated formulas, and changed diapers. For stimulation each infant had a simple rattle or some beads—occasionally a stuffed toy. That was all. No one talked to these infants, rocked them, smiled at them, tended to their needs, responded to their crying, or reacted to them as individuals in any way.

The differences between the infants reared in the orphanage and those reared normally at home became apparent when the babies were about four months old. The institutionalized infants rarely babbled, cried, or cooed. When picked up, they felt stiff and wooden—like "sawdust dolls," as one observer put it. By the time they were eight months old, they had little interest in toys or in their surroundings. They spent much of the time rocking themselves—perhaps in an attempt to provide their own sensory stimulation.

Their faces appeared bland, disinterested, expressionless, and solemn. Their movements were inhibited. They lacked vigor. When they were frustrated, they cried passively or turned away; they rarely attempted to surmount problems by themselves. They did not speak till very late. By the age of ten months, the orphanage-reared children were very noticeably retarded in many areas. One gets a good overall impression of these children from observers' comments on Teddy, a ten-month-old child. One observer stated: "The light in Teddy has gone out." Another observer added, "If you crank his motor you can get him to go a little; he can't start on his own (32)." The findings of Provence and Lipton are similar to the findings of many other investigators. Children reared in unstimulating environments during the first year of life often appear to become retarded with respect to motor skills, language development, intellectual development, expression of emotions, and capacity for strong, lasting emotional attachments.

But what causes these effects? Is it sensory deprivation? motor deprivation? social deprivation? the absence of a mother? or some combination of factors? Presently, psychologists believe that sensory stimulation is directly related to intellectual development. The evidence is impressive, but not universally accepted. A Harvard University developmental psychologist, Jerome Kagan, and an associate, Robert Klein, studied children as they grew up in Guatamalan villages. They found that Guatamalan babies of $5\frac{1}{2}$ to $11\frac{1}{2}$ months resembled those seen in bleak institutional settings in the United States: They were frequently listless, apathetic, and retarded on tests of intellectual skills. Contact with their mothers was frequent, so they were not deprived of social experience nor of a mother. On the other hand, they lived in dark huts for the first year of life. They could

Figure 3-10. Children raised in orphanages frequently appear to be apathetic and listless, as if "the light has gone out."

not visually explore their environment nor practice reaching, creeping, crawling, or manipulating objects. Their parents did not actively interact with them much, and they did not have attractive toys to stimulate them. Kagan and Klein believe that lack of sensory variety and restricted opportunities to act and explore during the first year were the critical factors which produced the early retardation (33). In other studies infants reared from birth without their mothers in communal settings such as Israeli kibbutzim and Russian nurseries were compared with children reared in middle-class homes. The communal babies grew up under highly enriched sensory conditions, and they attained at least the same, and sometimes a higher, developmental level—intellectually, as well as physically, socially, and emotionally—as children reared in middle-class homes (34,35). So several observations support the hypothesis that sensory stimulation during an early sensitive period affects the development of intelligence.

Are the effects of early sensory deprivation reversible? Several observations indicate that they are. Once the Guatamalan children walk, for example, they leave their huts and find stimulation in the outside world. By age ten, they are "gay, alert, and intellectually competent children whose performance on memory, perception, and reasoning tests . . . [are] comparable to those of children in the United States [36]." The effects of early deprivation tend to persist only when later experiences are also restrictive and unstimulating, as the experimental study which follows demonstrates vividly.

Sensory stimulation and intelligence:
A radical experiment

In the 1930s Harold Skeels, a psychologist for a number of State Mental Health Institutions in Iowa, noticed the story of two young orphan girls. As infants in an Iowa orphanage, the girls had been judged hopelessly retarded and transferred to a home for the mentally retarded. After six months in the new setting, each girl had made remarkable and totally unexpected progress. When Skeels investigated further, he found that the children had been "adopted" by adoring mentally retarded "mothers" and "aunts" who played with them, fussed over them, and took them on trips; so the children had received far more affection, attention, and sensory stimulation in the "home" than they had received previously in the crowded orphanage. Had it actually altered their intellectual functioning?

Skeels attempted a radical experiment to answer this question. He had thirteen more "hopelessly retarded" children (the experimental group) transferred from the orphanage to the home for the mentally retarded. At the time of their transfer, the children had an average age of one year and seven months and an average intelligence quotient of 64.3 (which puts them squarely in the retarded category). Twelve children who remained at the orphanage served as a control group. These children had an average age of one year and five months and an average intelligence quotient of 86.7 (which puts them in the "dull normal" category). After two years both groups were retested. The experimental group had gained 28.5 intelligence quotient points on the average. They were now functioning in the average range of intelligence. The control group had lost 26.2 intelligence quotient points on the average. They were now functioning in the retarded range.

Thirty years later Skeels followed up on his original subjects. He found that the thirteen experimental children had fared well. They had attained a median education of twelfth grade. None were wards of state institutions; all were either employed or housewives. Eleven were married. The twelve control children had been less successful. Four were still wards of state institutions; one had died in that status. They had attained a median education of third grade. Six held jobs; only one was married (37).

This study suggests that when children are deprived of sensory stimulation at an early age, they retain the capacity for normal intellectual development if their later environment is stimulating. On the other hand, when early deprivation is followed by a bleak and unstimulating later environment, children are not likely to recover. A recent investigation by Wayne Dennis indicates that there may be a sensitive period for sensory stimulation effects. When children from a Beirut orphanage were adopted into foster homes before the age of two, they recovered almost entirely, it appeared, from their earlier retardation. When children were adopted at ages later than two, some degree of intellectual retardation persisted (38).

How does sensory stimulation work? What does sensory stimulation do? Some remarkable studies with rodents indicate that sensory stimulation actually alters the brain. Mark Rosenzweig, a psychologist at the University of California, and his associates work with several strains of rats, lab mice, and gerbils. At some specific age, usually after weaning, three male animals (rats, for example) are taken from each of about a dozen litters and randomly assigned to one of the following conditions:

1. *An enriched environment.* In this condition several rats live together in a large cage that contains a number of objects to play with. Each day they receive a new set of play things.
2. *An impoverished environment.* In this condition each rat lives alone in a small cage.
3. *A standard laboratory environment.* In this condition several rats live together in an adequately sized cage.

At the end of some time period (a few days to a few months), the rats are killed; their brains are removed, dissected, and analyzed biochemically.

Rosenzweig and his associates find that enrichment actually affects the structure of the brain. The brains of rats who have been reared in a varied sensory environment actually weigh more and contain more brain enzymes associated with memory and learning. These studies have been repeated nu-

merous times, and the effect is undoubtedly a real one. Moreover, sensory enrichment is beneficial both for rats who have not yet been weaned and for adult rats (39). Perhaps human brains also grow bigger and manufacture more enzymes associated with learning and memory when they are exercised by a stimulating and complex environment.

Universal Social Experiences and Early Development

Social animals, including people, nurture and protect their young. Under ordinary circumstances, the young form strong bonds of attachment to their parents during early sensitive periods near birth. The bond ensures that the young animal remains near its parents where it can be nurtured and protected. Many of the initial studies of these early attachments—how they're formed and what consequences they have for the animal's future behavior—began on birds.

Imprinting in birds and other animals. Birds such as geese, chickens, turkeys, and ducks, who walk as soon as they hatch, follow almost any moving thing to which they are exposed within the first hours after birth. This tendency to follow peaks at differing times (at about seventeen hours after birth in chickens) and then becomes less and less likely (at three or four days the chicken becomes fearful and does not follow unfamiliar moving objects). This early following behavior has drastic consequences for the animal's later social and sexual behavior. The nature of the followed object seems to determine the animal's later choice of friends and mates. For example, when turkeys are reared by people from birth, they will often choose to court a person rather than a turkey later on. Konrad Lorenz, an Austrian ethologist, named the early following behavior, which reflects the learning of an initial social attachment, *imprinting*. To demonstrate the process, Lorenz took the eggs of a greylag goose and divided them into two groups. He allowed the mother to hatch one group, while he himself hatched the second group in an incubator. The greylag goslings in the incubator group became imprinted on Lorenz. They followed him initially; they came to regard him as their rightful parent; when frightened they sought him out. The goslings in the control group saw their mother upon hatching, followed her, and formed an attachment to her (40). Here is Lorenz's teacher's vivid description of what happens to goslings hatched in an incubator:

Without any display of fear, [the goslings] stare calmly at human beings and do not resist handling. If one spends just a little time with them,

Figure 3-11. Ethologist Konrad Lorenz is followed here by greylag goslings that had imprinted on him. (Thomas McAvoy, TIME-LIFE Picture Agency.)

it is not so easy to get rid of them afterwards. They pipe piteously if left behind and soon follow reliably. It has happened to me that such a gosling, a few hours after removal from the incubator, was content as long as it could settle under the chair on which I sat. If such a gosling is carried to a goose family accompanied by goslings of the same age, the result is usually the following: . . . One can . . . rapidly deposit the orphan gosling among . . . [the other geese] and retreat hastily. Aroused as they are, the parents naturally regard the tiny newcomer as their own offspring at first and will attempt to defend it as soon as they see and hear it in the human hand. But the worst is to come: *The young gosling shows no inclination to regard the two adults as conspecifics:* The gosling runs off, piping, and attaches itself to the first human being that happens to come past; it regards the human as its parent [41].

Laboratory studies of imprinting indicate that it is a complicated kind of learning that occurs not only in birds, but also in certain insects, fish, and mammals. It tends to take place during a *sensitive period* after birth, which varies with the species—for mallard ducks between thirteen and sixteen hours, for lambs between one and seven days, for puppies between three and twelve weeks. Psychologists have been particularly interested in what brings the sensitive period to an end. One possibility is that the fear of strangers that develops in infants of many species near the close of this period interferes with the inclination to follow and helps terminate the imprinting process. It is important to note that in some animals later experiences with members of a species can reverse the effects of imprinting. For example, birds imprinted on people may form social and sexual bonds to other birds after having appropriate experiences with birds later in their lives.

Attachment in monkeys. In the late 1950s Harry Harlow, a psychologist at the University of Wisconsin, became interested in the basis for the human infant's attachment to its mother. Harlow and his associates decided to study attachment formation using rhesus monkeys as subjects. They took monkey infants from their mothers at birth and put each one in a cage with two new "mothers"— cylindrical wire forms, one of which was covered with soft, absorbent terry cloth; the other was simply left bare. Both mothers had long tapered bodies to which the infants could cling. One had a "breast" and gave milk. (The nipple of a bottle of milk protruded from its chest.) The other had no breast and gave no milk. Four baby monkeys nursed on the terry cloth "mother"; another four nursed on the wire "mother." Regardless of which mother provided nourishment, the monkey babies spent most of their time cuddling and climbing on the cloth mother; and the infants always clung to the cloth mother in threatening situations. Clearly, contact with a soft and comfortable agent ("contact comfort") was more important than nursing in the infant's formation of an attachment to its mother (42). (See Chapter 1 for Harlow's description of this study.)

Harlow's monkey infants had been deprived of a real mother during the sensitive period for the formation of social attachments (somewhere between three and six months of age in rhesus monkeys). Note that their experience parallels that of the institutionalized children of whom we spoke earlier. Both groups have experienced a minimum of sensory stimulation and almost no social stimulation. Although the infant monkeys seemed healthy and normal enough to Harlow at the time of this study, they were "without question socially and sexually aberrant" as adolescents and adults. They frequently exhibited compulsive habits like skin pinching, moving in circles, clasping their own arms, and rocking back and forth. Sexually, they were failures. They did not orient themselves correctly for mating. Not surprisingly, they were unable to mate successfully. They were social recluses as well. In adulthood they showed no interest in other monkeys. They did not even interact with one another when caged together. Attempts at forced matings led to vicious fights (43). Recently, Robert Heath, a medical researcher at Tulane University, has found abnormal electrical activity in the brains of isolated monkeys. So there is actually indirect evidence that social and sensory isolation damages the brain (44).

Are the effects of early social isolation reversible? A recent study shows that in some instances they are. Rhesus monkeys were isolated from other animals for the first six months of life. At this time they showed the typical peculiar social habits noted above. All the monkeys were then given "intensive therapy." Infant female monkeys were placed in each isolate's cage. Very gradually the infants

Figure 3-12. Adolescent and adult monkeys show abnormal behavior patterns when reared in isolation during the first six months of their lives. Here an adult isolate bites itself as the photographer approaches. (Robert O. Dodsworth; Wisconsin Primate Laboratory.)

approached and began clinging and directing play responses at the isolate. Eventually the isolates began to reciprocate. After twenty-six weeks of "therapy," the isolates were displaying normal social behavior (45).

Attachment in people. What about human infants and their social attachments? Several studies show that it is easy to establish positive relationships with human infants between the ages of six weeks and six months. During this sensitive period babies smile at people and even at masks of human faces. By approximately six months of age (sometimes considerably later) many babies stop smiling at people they do not know; the majority display marked fears of strangers. The changes taking place during this five-month stretch are not well understood, but many psychologists believe that it is an imprintinglike period during which human infants form attachments to the people who surround them. Afterwards, the fear of the new and unfamiliar may inhibit the formation of strong social bonds (46).

What attaches the human infant to the person who cares for it? One study suggests that two factors are important for strong human attachments: (1) the degree to which the caretaker responds to the infant's crying and (2) the total amount of stimulation which the caretaker provides. The kind of stimulation can be varied—physical contact, conversation, visual stimulation, or the presentation of interesting objects (47). A more recent study suggests that frequent and sustained physical contact is very important for the growth of a healthy attachment (48).

There are, of course, no rigorous experimental studies of human social attachments in infancy. Instead, psychologists rely on observations of mothers and infants in home settings and during separations and on observations of apparent social neglect in institutions. One investigator, for example, compared children reared in an understaffed orphanage for the first three years of life and subsequently adopted into foster homes with children who'd been reared from birth in foster homes. The findings in this study included the following: The children reared from birth in the orphanage were characterized in case notes as emotionally cold, isolated, and incapable of forming lasting personal relationships. They were more intensely active; they stole, fought, and destroyed things more frequently than children reared from birth in foster homes. The investigator concluded that the absence of social relationships during the sensitive period may have affected the children's ability to form genuine attachments to other people (49). This conclusion is an uncertain one for several reasons. The children reared from birth in the orphanage were probably exposed to many kinds of deprivation, so we cannot isolate the effects of social deprivation alone. Moreover, even if social deprivation was responsible for the observed results, we cannot be sure that the damage was irreversible. Had the three-year-old orphans received intensive warm contact from their foster parents, they might have recovered their capacity for meaningful attachments.

In this section we have focused on the importance of the sensory and social experiences which parents ordinarily provide for their infants. We have seen that when children and other animals are deprived of these experiences during early sensitive periods, intellectual and social skills may fail to develop normally. We turn now to child-rearing practices, one of many variable sensory experiences, which also influence children's development.

REARING CHILDREN

A child's development is profoundly influenced by its individual experiences in a particular culture as a member of a particular family. All societies have unwritten but widely held expectations for their children. Our culture emphasizes self-reliance and independence. We teach children to walk, to control elimination, to feed, and to dress themselves when they are very young. Our culture also values intellectual achievement and self-assertiveness. Consequently, we demand that young children learn to read, to write, to calculate, and to form concepts; we are continually urging them to "do their best," so that they can be "first." British children, in contrast, are taught, above all, to control their antisocial instincts and impulses. Many agricultural societies emphasize responsibility, obedience, and cooperation, whereas hunting cultures tend to train their children's motor skills at an early age. Generally, then, early child-rearing practices reflect the nature of the society.

Parents are the agents of *socialization*; that is, parents usually guide their children toward behaviors, values, goals, and motives that the culture considers appropriate and discourage those behaviors, values, goals and motives of which the culture does not approve. Self-styled "authorities" in many societies advise parents on the "proper ways" to rear their children. Psychologists have been studying child-rearing practices for a relatively short time—since the 1940s. It is difficult to obtain systematic and objective data on child-rearing practices; so our findings are highly tentative. With this warning we turn to some current research findings on several child-care subjects.

Feeding the Baby

For years people have been debating the relative merits of breast and bottle feeding. The research indicates that it doesn't make any real difference which way the baby is fed—as long as the mother is comfortable with the method she is using (50,51). When mothers show signs of tension in the feeding situation, their babies also show signs of tension. When mothers are relaxed, their babies tend to be calm too. The relationship is the same—regardless of method (52). One notable authority sums it up like this: "The truth is that the emotional health of both mother and baby is best served by whatever generates the most pleasure between the two, the greatest closeness and affection, one for the other [53]."

Toilet Training

Toilet training is usually the parent's first attempt to curb the child's natural inclinations. The child is expected to learn to control an involuntary reflex. Initially, it automatically releases its sphincter muscles as soon as it feels tension from a full bladder or bowel. The child must learn to control this natural response, go into the bathroom, and use the toilet properly. That is asking a lot of a young child. It must be ready neuromuscularly; it must also be able both to understand and communicate its own needs. Ordinarily, this is not possible until the child is eighteen months old.

The research indicates that toilet training proceeds most smoothly when parents encourage gradual control and minimize conflict. Waiting until the proper age, giving instructions, watching for signs and immediately taking the child to the toilet, allowing the child to learn by observing others, and bestowing warmth and approval for success—all seem to make toilet training easier (54). Rigid toilet training, where frequent punishment, coldness, and rejection are associated with the toileting routine, appears to lead to hostility, chronic bed-wetting, and other behavioral problems (55,56).

When Infants Cry

Crying is one of the infant's major ways of communicating with its parents. However, unlike smiling, cooing, and other communicatory gestures, most parents find crying unpleasant. Child-care experts—current and past—have encouraged parents to be wary of responding to their infant's cries. The rationale is that if parents continually respond immediately whenever the baby cries, the infant learns that crying pays off and it becomes a spoiled, fussy tyrant whose continual demands enslave the parents. Does responding to an infant's cries really have these effects? How could psychologists find out?

Until recently most studies of this subject focused on parental responses to excessive crying in older children. Psychologists did not have data on the consequences of parental responses to normal infant crying. In 1972 Silvia Bell and Mary Salter Ainsworth, developmental psychologists at Johns Hopkins University in Baltimore, published an impor-

tant study on twenty-six infants and their mothers. Bell and Ainsworth trained observers to make home visits and observe both infant behavior—including frequency of crying—and mother-infant interactions—including how quickly and in what manner the mother responded to crying. Each infant-mother pair was subsequently observed for several hours at frequent intervals throughout the infant's first year. Bell and Ainsworth's findings indicate that when mothers ignore their young infant's crying, their babies cry more frequently and persistently later in their first year. On the other hand, when mothers respond quickly to their infant's crying—especially by picking the infant up and initiating close physical contact—the child cries less frequently later in its first year. Bell and Ainsworth view crying in infancy as a communication signal. By responding to the child's cries, the parent is answering; the child learns that it is competent and that it can affect the behavior of others. Accordingly, its methods of communication develop further, and it begins to use more mature forms of communication (57). It is important to note that the responsive mothers in the Bell and Ainsworth study attended to their babies when they were *not crying*, as well as when they were. If infants are attended to *only* when they cry, they may very well turn into "big cry babies" later.

Talking to Children

Parents sometimes adopt the philosophy, "Children are to be seen and not heard." Psychologists generally disagree. Children must be seen, talked to, and heard, or they do not communicate very well later on. Many studies show that talking to children is important for their language development. For example, one investigator found that when working-class mothers read to their children ten minutes a day, their children gained more

Figure 3-13. When parents respond quickly to their infant's crying, their babies cry less frequently later in their first year. (Wayne Miller, Magnum.)

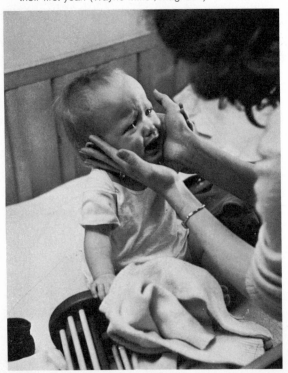

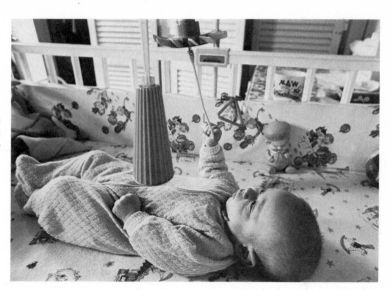

Figure 3-14. Infants nurtured in stimulating environments attain competence at an early age. (Shelly Rusten.)

competence in all areas of speech than working-class children who were not read to (58). The family's *style* of talking also influences the child's later thinking, problem-solving, and learning skills. Some families tend to use *restricted codes* of communication: Their sentences are short, simple, unfinished, implicitly understood, and limited both in concepts and in information. Other families use *elaborated codes*: Their sentences are individualized for a specific situation and person, precise, and particular; they allow a more complex range of thought; and they discriminate between intellectual and emotional content. For example, imagine a child playing noisily when the doorbell rings. The mother with a restricted style says, "Be quiet!" The mother with an elaborated style says, "Please be quiet for a minute. I want to talk to Mrs. Jones, and I won't be able to hear what she's saying unless you stop that racket." In the first instance, the child is asked only to comply; in the second instance the child is given the opportunity to follow several ideas and exercise its mind. There is evidence that these communicative styles shape the child's later cognitive abilities (59).

Rearing Competent Children

Competent children anticipate consequences, plan and carry out complex projects, understand complex sentences, and are generally capable of dealing with problems. Children usually attain competence at an early age—between ten and eighteen months in the United States, according to one researcher. Professor Burton White, Director of the Harvard University Preschool Project, has studied the mothers of competent children looking for those characteristics which produce competence. This is White's conclusion:

Our most effective mothers do not devote the bulk of their day to rearing their young children. . . . What they seem to do, often without knowing exactly why, is to perform excellently the functions of designer and consultant. By that I mean they design a physical world, mainly in the home, that is beautifully suited to nurturing the burgeoning curiosity of the one to three year old. It is full of small manipulable, visually-detailed objects. . . . It contains things to climb. . . . It includes a rich variety of interesting things to look at. . . .

. . . This mother sets up guidelines for her child's behavior which seem to play a very important role in his development. . . . The child is encouraged in the vast majority of his explorations. When the child confronts an interesting or difficult situation, he often turns to his mother for help. Though usually working at some chore, she is generally nearby. He then goes to her and usually, but *not always*, is *responded* to by his mother with help or shared enthusiasm plus, occasionally an interesting, naturally-related idea. These ten- to thirty-second interchanges are usually oriented around the *child's* interest of the moment. . . . It is in experiences of this kind that I believe an infant's intrinsic curiosity is effectively expanded by these skillful mothers. . . . [These mothers] get an enormous amount of teaching in "on the fly," and usually at the child's instigation [60].

Summary: Heredity, Environment, and Early Development

1. Experience and heredity continually interact to influence development. We conceptualized the factors in the developmental process, following Hebb's lead, as genetics, the chemical prenatal environment, the chemical postnatal environment, constant sensory experiences, variable sensory experiences, and traumatic influences.
2. Heredity affects behavior and psychological functioning through its impact on bodily structures—like the nervous system, the muscles, the sensory receptors, and the endocrine glands.
3. A species inheritance gives an animal broad behavioral propensities; an individual inheritance structures unique potentialities.
4. Family, twin, genetic abnormality, and

selective-breeding studies indicate that certain problem-solving skills may be influenced by genetics.
5. Certain temperament characteristics present in the neonate seem to endure. This finding, supported by the results of twins studies, suggests that such characteristics are influenced by heredity, though it is also possible that parental attitudes and reactions strengthen them.
6. An animal is maximally sensitive to the effects of the environment during early sensitive periods when it is growing rapidly.
7. The child's earliest environment is the uterus. Harmful experiences there, such as maternal disease, malnutrition, smoking, drug taking, and stress, seem to prevent the human infant from achieving its full genetic potential.
8. Normal human babies all over the world develop motor, perceptual, social, intellectual, and language skills in approximately the same sequence. Apparently, heredity and environment make the organism physically ready to learn particular behaviors during specific sensitive periods. Then, if the sensory environment provides minimal opportunities and stimulation, these skills develop in an orderly way. Gross sensory deprivation frequently leads to perceptual and intellectual deficits. Early social neglect, which usually accompanies early sensory deprivation, seems to produce social deficiencies later on. These deficiencies can sometimes be reversed.
9. Variable sensory experiences also affect the child's development. Many child-care practices appear to have specific behavioral consequences.

STUDY GUIDE 3

Key Terms. neonate, reflexive behavior, heredity, chemical prenatal environment, chemical postnatal environment, constant sensory experiences, variable sensory experiences, traumatic physical events, behavior genetics, sperm, ovum, zygote, chromosome, gene, DNA, enzyme, discrete characteristic, continuous characteristic, twin study method, identical twins, fraternal twins, selective breeding, sensitive period (critical period), maturation, sensory stimulation, sensory deprivation, imprinting, attachment, socialization, restricted codes, elaborated codes.

Important Research. inheritance of intelligence in the Kallikak family (Goddard), breeding for intelligence: maze-bright, maze-dull rats (Tryon), temperament differences in infants (Thomas, Chess, and Birch), comparison of family-reared and orphanage-reared infants (Provence and Lipton), sensory-deprived infants in Guatamala (Kagan and Klein), stimulation of "hopelessly retarded" infants (Skeels), sensory stimulation and brain structure (Rosenzweig), imprinting (Lorenz), "motherless" monkeys (Harlow), attending to baby's crying (Bell and Ainsworth), mothers of competent children (White).

Self-Quiz

1. Hearing human voices is an example of which of Hebb's developmental categories? [**a**] chemical postnatal; [**b**] chemical prenatal; [**c**] constant sensory; [**d**] variable sensory.

2. The difference between discrete and continuous characteristics is that [**a**] discrete characteristics rarely occur; continuous ones are relatively common; [**b**] discrete characteristics are influenced by the environment; continuous ones are not; [**c**] discrete characteristics act only at certain times; continuous ones influence the organism throughout its lifetime; [**d**] discrete characteristics are either present or absent; continuous ones exist in degrees or varying amounts.

3. Thomas, Chess, and Birch found that early temperament characteristics [**a**] depended almost entirely on the parents' behavior; [**b**] persisted from infancy to ten years or longer in many cases; [**c**] generally disappeared by the time the children were ready to start school; [**d**] depended almost entirely on heredity.

4. Improving the diet of mothers who were malnour-

ished during the first half of pregnancy [**a**] produced healthier mothers and healthier babies; [**b**] made the mothers healthier but did not help the babies, who were still less healthy than normal; [**c**] produced healthier babies, but left the mothers with the same number of health problems; [**d**] decreased only the number of premature births.

5. Tryon increased the maze-learning ability of rats by [**a**] selectively breeding "maze-bright" rats; [**b**] creating a special enriched environment for rats; [**c**] giving rats practice in many different mazes; [**d**] selectively breeding "maze-dull" rats.

6. The process called "maturation" [**a**] usually refers to the changes that occur during puberty; [**b**] is best understood as the emergence of behavior patterns which depend almost entirely on heredity; [**c**] is best understood as the emergence of behavior patterns which depend primarily on heredity, chemical prenatal, chemical postnatal, and constant sensory factors; [**d**] depends for the most part on physical traumas which occur during sensitive periods.

7. Mothers' smoking during pregnancy is correlated with [**a**] increases in infectious diseases in infancy; [**b**] increases in number of premature deliveries and in low-birth-weight babies; [**c**] decreases in mother's milk production and in infant's digestive problems; [**d**] all of the above.

8. Children reared from infancy in an unstimulating environment such as an understaffed orphanage [**a**] appear to be normal except in forming social attachments; [**b**] appear to be normal, but do not perform well in school; [**c**] show signs of retardation—socially, intellectually, emotionally, and on motor skills—before the age of one year; [**d**] show signs of retardation in language and social development by the age of two years, but not before.

9. Studies indicate that the undesirable effects of an unstimulating environment [**a**] can be overcome if the environment is made more stimulating before the age of two; [**b**] can be overcome if the environment is made more stimulating at any age up to puberty; [**c**] cannot be overcome after six months in such an environment; [**d**] depend entirely on the individual child: some children are seriously affected; others are not.

10. The process by which some birds and other animals form social attachments by following anything that moves is called [**a**] maturation; [**b**]

bonding during the sensitive period; [**c**] imprinting; [**d**] social stimulation.

11. Monkeys reared away from their mothers and other monkeys did *not* show which of the following? [**a**] poor physical health; [**b**] abnormal social behavior; [**c**] abnormal sexual behavior; [**d**] compulsive habits such as rocking.

12. Harlow found that the most important influence on infant monkeys' formation of a social attachment was [**a**] food and nursing; [**b**] bodily movement; [**c**] the mother's behavior when the infant was in danger; [**d**] contact with a soft and comfortable agent (contact comfort).

13. The Bell and Ainsworth study suggests that frequently picking up a crying baby [**a**] is likely to make the baby cry more often later on; [**b**] is likely to make the baby cry less often later on; [**c**] has no effect on the amount of crying, but makes the baby smile more often; [**d**] has no effect on the amount of crying, but increases the loudness of crying.

14. Children develop better language and thinking skills when parents [**a**] use elaborated codes of communication; [**b**] read to their children daily; [**c**] design a home environment which contains a wide variety of interesting things; [**d**] all of the above.

15. Burton White found that mothers best helped their preschool children develop intellectual skills (competence) by [**a**] devoting most of the day to stimulating the child; [**b**] deliberately planning short lessons and spending several hours each day teaching the child; [**c**] designing a home with lots of interesting things to see and do and spending many short, informal moments "consulting" with the child about interesting or difficult situations—usually at the child's instigation; [**d**] providing a safe, secure environment and surrounding the child with playmates.

Exercises

1. HEBB'S CATEGORIES OF FACTORS INFLUENCING DEVELOPMENT. Hebb revised the traditional two-factor (heredity, environment) view of development to take into account six types of events that contribute to development. To make certain that you understand the classification system, label the following events according to the category to which they belong. Use the following abbreviations: (H—heredity, C pre—chemical prenatal, C post—chemical postnatal, CS—constant sensory, VS—variable sensory, T—

traumatic). All of these items apply to a child unless stated otherwise.

_____ **1.** Seeing other people
_____ **2.** Having blue eyes
_____ **3.** Feeling water on the skin
_____ **4.** Speaking English
_____ **5.** Breaking an arm
_____ **6.** Breathing polluted air
_____ **7.** Playing poker
_____ **8.** Taking aspirin
_____ **9.** Tranquilizers in the mother's blood stream before the infant's birth
_____ **10.** Eating protein
_____ **11.** Hearing human voices
_____ **12.** Being male or female (genetic sex)
_____ **13.** Level of the hormone adrenalin in the mother's blood stream before birth
_____ **14.** Attending a particular high school

2. TWIN STUDY. Reread the description of the rationale behind twin studies. Then analyze the results of the following imaginary studies to determine whether heredity appears to influence the behavior being studied. If heredity appears to be exerting some influence, designate the item H.

_____ **1.** In a study of attitudes toward premarital sex, the following correlations are obtained: identical twins +.63; fraternal twins +.67; nontwin siblings (brothers and sisters) +.64; and nonrelated people −.14.
_____ **2.** In a study of manual skills, the following correlations are obtained: identical twins +.86; fraternal twins +.46; nontwin siblings +.41; and nonrelated people +.08.
_____ **3.** In a study of extroversion-introversion, the following correlations are obtained: identical twins +.46; fraternal twins +.34; nontwin siblings +.30; nonrelated people +.10.

Questions to Consider

1. Assume that you are designing an orphanage for children. What specific early experiences would be essential? How would you provide them?

2. Suppose you wanted to study the effects of parents' disciplinary practices on children's conscience development. How would you do it? What are some of the difficulties you would encounter in using parental interviews or surveys, direct observations, experiments? Could these methods be combined to yield more satisfactory results?

3. Ask one of your parents to rate your behavior in infancy on the nine aspects of temperament listed on page 70. Has your temperament remained the same? Do you think that you fit into one of the three personality categories: "difficult," "slow to warm up," or "easy"? Speculate on the reasons for consistencies or inconsistencies in your development.

4. Everyone recognizes that parents influence the behavior of their babies. How do babies influence the behavior of their parents?

5. Says Burton White, "The vast majority of educated women in this country don't know what the hell they are doing when they have a child. We just don't prepare our women or our men for parenting." Do you agree? What should be done? Consider: Should parents be licensed for parenting? On what basis should licenses be granted?

6. Carefully observe some parent-child interactions. How do parents guide their children toward culturally appropriate behaviors, goals, values, and motives and discourage socially inappropriate ones?

Project 3: Child-rearing Opinions: Mothers vs. Nonmothers

Most people, regardless of age, sex, or parental status (parent or nonparent), have opinions about the proper ways to rear children. In this project you will be conducting a survey to see whether parents and nonparents show consistent differences in their child-rearing opinions.

Method. The following questionnaire contains statements about children and child-care practices. Find six cooperative married female subjects approximately the same age who have never taken a psychology course nor read widely in child psychology; three should be mothers; three should not be mothers. Read the questions on the questionnaire to each woman individually and record her opinions by writing A (agree) or D (disagree) in the appropriate spaces.

Results. For each item record the majority opinion for mothers and nonmothers and write that opinion on the line marked M below the appropriate box. The answer key represents current widely accepted opinions among psychologists based on research and clinical observations. Count the number of items on which the majority of nonmothers and psychologists agree. Count the number of items on which the majority of mothers and psychologists agree.

Discussion. Consider the following questions. (1)

Were there any items on which both mothers and nonmothers agreed? Speculate on the reasons for these similarities. (2) Did mothers and nonmothers disagree on particular questions? Examine these items carefully. Speculate on the reasons for the differences. (3) Does being a mother appear to increase one's expertise about children and child care? (4) What sorts of factors besides parental status influence the responses of your subjects? How could these extraneous factors have been controlled? (5) Do you think fathers and nonfathers would respond differently? Explain.

CHILD REARING AND CHILDREN: A SURVEY

Does the subject *tend to* agree (A) or disagree (D) with the following statements?

Mothers   Nonmothers

1. Babies are very similar at birth. They don't develop different characteristics for several months.

2. Babies should be breast-fed, not bottle-fed.

3. Babies should be attended to when they cry.

4. Problems in early childhood such as frequent bed wetting, thumb sucking, fears of imaginary animals or the dark, and occasional nightmares suggest that the child probably has the beginnings of some serious psychological problems.

5. Women almost always do a better job as mothers when they stay home with their children than when they work outside the home.

1 2 3 1 2 3

M_____ M_____

6. Providing young infants (younger than eight months) with interesting bright objects is basically a waste of time and money.

1 2 3 1 2 3

M_____ M_____

7. All married women should have children.

1 2 3 1 2 3

M_____ M_____

8. Unborn babies are affected by their mother's emotional state.

1 2 3 1 2 3

M_____ M_____

9. It is best for everyone if a child is toilet-trained by eighteen months.

1 2 3 1 2 3

M_____ M_____

10. When they cannot be watched *carefully*, children under 2 should be confined to small areas of the home or to cribs or playpens.

1 2 3 1 2 3

M_____ M_____

11. No matter how well meaning parents are, they are too close to their children to be able to help them with their psychological problems.

1 2 3 1 2 3

M_____ M_____

12. Although talking to infants may be fun for the parents, it really doesn't help children until they have learned to talk themselves.

Suggested Readings

1. Scott, John Paul. *Early experience and the organization of behavior.* Belmont, Calif.: Brooks/Cole Publishing Company, 1968 (paperback). A psychologist presents research on the effects of early experience on developing animals (including people).

2. Lipsitt, Lewis P. "Babies: they're a lot smarter than they look." *Psychology Today*, December 1971, 5, 70–72, 88–89. Discussion of how infants learn.

3. Thomas, Alexander, Stella Chess, & Herbert Birch. "The origin of personality." *Scientific American*, 223 (2), August 1970, 102–109. Description of the research on temperament differences in infants.

4. Rabkin, Leslie Y. & Karen Rabkin. "Children of the kibbutz." *Psychology Today*, September 1969, 3, 40–46. Discussion of the Israeli kibbutz and the research which shows that children can thrive in an enriched communal environment.

5. Harlow, Harry F., Margaret K. Harlow, & Steven J. Suomi. "From thought to therapy: Lessons from a primate laboratory." *American Scientist*, September–October, 59, 1971. A description of an ingenious series of research studies on monkeys, how they form attachments, and how isolation affects their "mental health."

6. Hawkins, Robert. "It's time we taught the young how to be good parents (and don't you wish we'd started a long time ago?)" *Psychology Today*, November 1972, 6, 28, 29, 36, 38–40. A psychologist argues for compulsory parent training programs.

Answer Keys

SELF-QUIZ
1. c 2. d 3. b 4. a 5. a 6. c 7. b 8. c 9. a
10. c 11. a 12. d 13. b 14. d 15. c

EXERCISE 1
1 CS 2. H 3. CS 4. VS 5. T 6. C Post 7. VS
8. C Post 9. C Pre 10. C Post 11. CS 12. H
13. C Pre 14. VS

EXERCISE 2
2. H 3. H

PROJECT 3
1. D 2. D 3. A 4. D 5. D 6. D 7. D 8. A 9. D
10. D 11. D 12. D

THE PHYSIOLOGICAL BASES OF BEHAVIOR

IN THIS CHAPTER
We focus on how physiology affects behavior. Our physiology determines whether we move on two legs or four, whether vision, or smell, or some other sense guides our perceptions, whether we make bodily motions, grunt, or talk to communicate with others, and how much information we can absorb and process. We will concentrate on two topics from physiological psychology: (1) the brain and its role in memory and (2) the endocrine system and its role in shaping stereotypic masculine and feminine behavior. After reading this chapter, you should be able to do the following:

1. Specify the subject matter of physiological psychology
2. Explain how neurons transmit information
3. Describe four methods which psychologists use to study the relationship between the brain and behavior
4. Describe three memory systems
5. Describe where and how the brain may store long- and short-term memories
6. Explain how the androgens organize the brain and subsequent sex-typed behavior
7. Cite evidence that social and psychological factors influence sex-typed behavior

The man with a shattered world

Sublieutenant Zasetsky, aged twenty-three, suffered a head injury [from a gunshot wound] 2 March 1943 that penetrated the left parieto-occipital area of the cranium. The injury was followed by a prolonged coma and, despite prompt treatment in a field hospital, was further complicated by inflammation . . .

This brain injury produced many abrupt and dramatic changes in Zasetsky's behavior. One symptom of this injury was fragmented vision. Zasetsky described the problem like this:

Ever since I was wounded I haven't been able to see a single object as a whole—not one thing. Even now I have to fill in a lot about objects, phenomena, or any living thing from imagination. That is, I have to picture them in my mind and try to remember them as full and complete—after I have a chance to look them over, touch them, or get some image of them.

Parts of Zasetsky's body appeared distorted to him. He wrote:

Sometimes when I'm sitting down I suddenly feel as though my head is the size of a table—every bit as big—while my hands, feet, and torso become very small. When I close my eyes, I'm not even sure where my right leg is; for some reason I used to think (even sensed) it was somewhere above my shoulder, even above my head . . . .

In addition, Zasetsky's perception of space was disturbed. In his own words:

Ever since I was wounded I've had trouble sometimes sitting down in a chair or on a couch. I first look to see where the chair is, but when I try to sit down I suddenly make a grab for the chair since I'm afraid I'll land on the floor. Sometimes that happens because the chair turns out to be further to one side than I thought.

Many of Zasetsky's other mental abilities were also impaired. He lost his ability to read and write. He had trouble following the meaning of a conversation or understanding a simple story. Although he had been an excellent student, he could not cope with the complex ideas of grammar, arithmetic, geometry, and physics. Zasetsky wanted desperately to relearn. He had to begin again from scratch, but because his brain was not intact, he had to find ways to compensate for abilities he no longer had. Zasetsky describes a frustrating geometry lesson like this:

M. B., a young man who recently got his degree in philosophy, tried to teach me geometry. At first he used a text from the middle school to explain some concepts in geometry like "point," "line," "plane," and "surface." Then he began to discuss theorems. Now the strange thing was that I remembered I once knew these theorems, even though I couldn't understand any of them. . . . While he talked I just kept saying "yes, yes" as though I understood everything, though I couldn't follow any of his explanations. I couldn't catch the words he was using or understand them. I had to rely mostly on pictures—drawings and sketches of figures. Without them, none of the verbal explanations "got through" to me. I always had to compare the writing above the sketches—"This is a line, a point, a plane"—with the actual drawing. But I still can't explain or define any of these concepts no matter how many times I go over the explanations . . . [1].

Wounds heal, but damaged brain cells do not grow back again. Although Zasetsky kept working for more than twenty-five years, he never recovered his lost abilities.

These excerpts come from a Russian psychologist's biography of a gunshot victim who was treated and observed for approximately twenty-five years. The brain is the single most important physical regulator of behavior. It controls basic life processes such as breathing and digestion. It provides for continuing needs such as those for food and sleep. It is centrally involved in the operation of the senses. It enables people to process information: to understand, to remember, to speak, to write, and to reason. Injury to the brain can remove any or all these abilities, as Zasetsky's unhappy case shows.

We are entering the area of *physiological psychology*. Physiological psychologists study the physical foundations of sensation, perception, learning, memory, motives, and emotions. They also research genetics and physical conditions, such as epilepsy and ulcers, which are intertwined with behavior. In this chapter we will be exploring the physiological basis of human memory and *sex-role behavior* (characteristically masculine and feminine behavior). Before we begin, we look briefly at the nervous system, of which the brain is a vital part.

THE NERVOUS SYSTEM: AN OVERVIEW

The nervous system organizes the functioning of all living organisms. In this chapter we will be considering two major subsystems

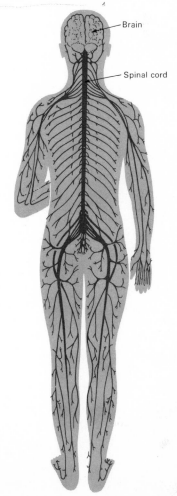

Figure 4-1. The nervous system. The nervous system is comprised of billions of neurons (nerve cells). Neurons within the brain and spinal cord form the central nervous system; neurons outside the brain and spinal cord form the peripheral nervous system. Many neurons begin in one system and end in the other.

Brain

Spinal cord

of the nervous system: (1) the central information-processing component, the *central nervous system (CNS)*, and (2) the network of communication lines that bring information into and out of the CNS, the *somatic nervous system* of the *peripheral nervous system (PNS)*.

The Peripheral Nervous System

The peripheral nervous system is composed of (1) the *autonomic nervous system*, whose functions we consider in Chapter 11 where we deal with emotion, and (2) the *somatic nervous system*, which we consider here. The somatic nervous system contains two types of pathways: *sensory pathways*, which carry information from sensory cells in the skin to the CNS, and *motor pathways*, which carry

Figure 4-2. Some basic features of a neuron.

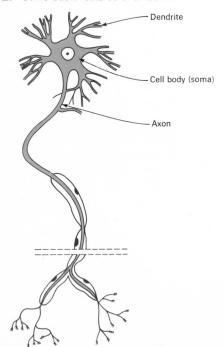

- Dendrite

- Cell body (soma)

- Axon

"orders" from the CNS to the muscles and glands that carry the "orders" out.

How Are Messages Transmitted?

How does the peripheral nervous system transmit messages? To understand the process, we must look at the basic unit of the nervous system, the *neuron,* or nerve cell. Although neurons vary considerably in structure, a typical neuron looks something like the diagram shown in Figure 4-2.

The neuron consists of a main cell body, called the *soma*, and branching fibers that distinguish it from all other cells. The neuron is completely covered by a *cell membrane*, which regulates everything that passes in and out of the neuron. The branching fibers consist of many *dendrites*, which reach out to pick up information from other neurons, and an *axon* (sometimes as long as 3 feet), which transmits information to other neurons, to muscles, and to glands.

Some 10 billion to 15 billion neurons make up the human nervous system. Cell bodies that perform similar functions are frequently located near one another. Those which regulate appetite, for example, cluster together to form a "brain center." The neuron fibers also bunch together forming pathways that lead from the sense organs to the CNS, throughout the CNS, and from the CNS to the muscles and glands.

How are messages initiated? That is, how is information introduced into a sensory pathway? Suppose someone squeezes your hand. If the squeeze is sufficiently intense, sensory cells will translate the event into nerve impulses, the language that the brain understands. To initiate a nerve impulse, the stimulus must exceed a particular intensity (the *threshold*). If the stimulus is too weak (below the threshold), the cell does not *fire* (produce a nerve impulse). It is important to note that the cell either fires or does not fire; the intensity of the nerve impulse has nothing to do with the intensity of the stimulus.

Let's assume that the squeeze is vigorous enough to stimulate the neuron to fire. What next? The neurons code the characteristics of the hand squeeze into their own electrochemical language. A strong stimulus might cause a cell to fire many bursts of electrochemical energy per second; a weak stimulus might cause it to produce only a few bursts per second. Moreover, when the stimulus is strong, a large number of sensory neurons respond by firing; conversely, when it is weak only a small number produce electrochemical bursts. Furthermore, the neurons themselves are specialized so that only particular ones respond to particular types of stimulation.

How do neurons transmit their electrochemical messages? Although neurons are, in fact, highly interconnected, let's construct a simplified model that will help us visualize their action. Imagine that three neurons—

N1, N2, N3—are chained together as shown in Figure 4-3. An axon fiber of N1 is located very close to a dendrite of N2. Similarly, an axon fiber of N2 is located near a dendrite of N3. The small gap that separates the axon fiber of one neuron from the dendrite of another is called a *synapse*. How does a nerve impulse travel through a neuron and across a synapse? When a neuron is not transmitting nerve impulses, its cell membrane maintains a delicate balance—keeping certain electrically charged particles inside the cell, others outside, and allowing yet others to flow freely in both directions. If an external stimulus, such as a nerve impulse from a hand squeeze, arrives, say via N1, the membrane loses its control, and electrically charged particles are redistributed throughout the neuron. When we talk about firing, we are really talking about this redistribution of charged particles. The charge redistribution causes certain chemicals, called *transmitter substances*, to be

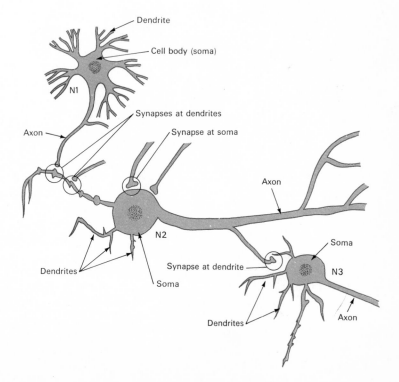

Figure 4-3. Three interconnected neurons. (From Kimble, 1965.)

Dendrite

Cell body (soma)

N1

Axon

Synapses at dendrites

Synapse at soma

Axon

N2

Soma

Synapse at dendrite

N3

Dendrites

Soma

Dendrites

Axon

secreted into all the synapses of N2. The transmitter substances alter the membrane at the other end of the synapse—like the one at N3—raising or lowering N3's firing threshold.

In actuality, neurons are not connected to one another in the simple sequential arrangement of our model. Instead, the axon and dendrites of a single neuron synapse with the dendrites and axons of thousands of neighboring neurons. Moreover, whether or not a neuron fires is based upon what happens at all its synapses, not simply one, as we implied; that is, a nerve cell fires when the quantity of

Figure 4-4. Three layers of the brain in evolutionary perspective. (From Hilgard, Atkinson, and Atkinson, 1975.)

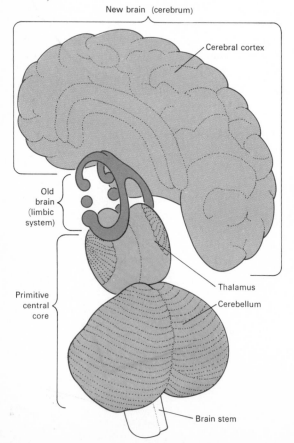

New brain (cerebrum)

Cerebral cortex

Old brain (limbic system)

Primitive central core

Thalamus

Cerebellum

Brain stem

transmitter chemicals in its synapses that lower the firing threshold (*excitatory transmitters*) is significantly greater than the quantity of transmitter substances that raise its threshold (*inhibitory transmitters*).

Eventually, information about the strong hand squeeze, coded in nerve impulses, reaches the brain. The brain interprets and processes the information and decides what should be done. Then it fires its "orders"—again in the form of nerve impulses—back through the spinal cord and down through the motor pathways to the muscles and glands.

Impulses in the central nervous system are behind all our thoughts, our feelings, our needs, and our actions. The neurons in our bodies continually fire as long as we live. They respond to inputs from both our external environment and our internal physiological environment; and they are active, even when we lose normal consciousness as in sleep (see Chapter 6).

The Central Nervous System

The central nervous system consists of the spinal cord and brain. The *spinal cord* serves two major functions. It coordinates certain *reflexes* (automatic responses, such as withdrawing one's hand when it touches a hot stove and gagging when something is caught in the throat) and it carries messages to and from the brain. The *brain,* "a grotesque enlargement at the top end of the spinal cord [2]," is the master decision-making organ of the body. Although it looks like a single organ, it is really a collection of structures that perform diverse administrative functions.

Figure 4-4 shows the human brain in evolutionary perspective. The human brain can be conceptualized as composed of three layers: (1) a primitive central core, (2) the old brain (or the limbic system), which evolved upon this core, and (3) an outer layer, the new brain (or the cerebrum), which evolved upon the old brain layer. Brain centers in the *central core* control routine, continually operating activities such as digestion, circulation, respiration, and certain reflex movements that are basic to the functioning of primitive and sophisticated animals alike. The *limbic system* structures are involved in seeking satisfaction for the body's recurring needs for food, water, sleep, sex, and protection. The *cerebrum*, the most recently evolved division of the brain, is more highly developed in mammals than in other creatures and is most highly developed in humans. This brain region integrates incoming information with previously acquired information, and it is involved in complex processes such as talking, thinking, remembering, and learning.

Like the peripheral nervous system, the central nervous system is made up of neurons. Their cell bodies are generally smaller, their axons shorter, and their dendrites more numerous than those in the PNS; so the CNS contains many more densely packed, highly interconnected neurons than the other parts of the nervous system.

The following brain structures are particularly interesting to psychologists because they play an important role in human behavior.

The cerebral cortex. Whenever you look at a picture of the human brain, you see mostly cerebral cortex, as in Figure 4-5. "Cerebrum" is the Latin word for brain; "cortex" for rind or bark. Accordingly, the *cortex,* as the *cerebral cortex* is usually abbreviated, is the covering of the cerebrum. The cortex consists of layers of neurons arranged in "wrinkles, folds, and convolutions . . . [which] give the impression that nature has gone to considerable extremes to pack into the limited space available as much yardage of this sheet material as possible [3]." If the cortex were stretched out flat, its surface would cover nearly 6 square feet. All incoming information about the sensory world—sights, sounds, tastes, and feelings—goes to specific *sensory regions (projection areas)* of the cortex. *Motor regions* within the cortex control the skeletal muscles that initiate behavior (see Figure 4-6). The majority of the human cortex (some 90 percent of it) is taken up by *association areas*, regions that integrate incoming

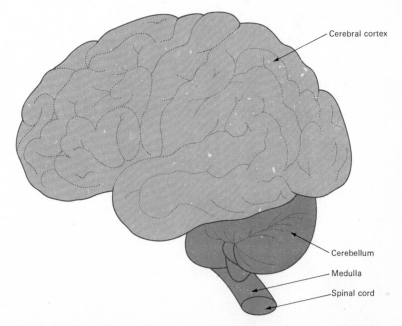

Figure 4-5. The human brain: side view showing the extent of the cerebral cortex.

Cerebral cortex

Cerebellum

Medulla

Spinal cord

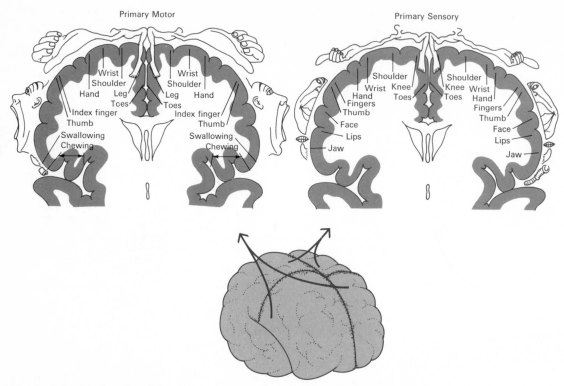

Figure 4-6. The location of the primary motor and sensory areas of the cortex. Two parallel cross sections through the cerebrum are shown: a motor cross section and a sensory cross section. In the distorted figures, known as homunculi, the size of each body part represents the amount of cortex devoted to controlling the functions associated with that part. As you can see, mouths and hands receive high priority from the cortex. (Adapted from Penfield and Rasmussen, 1950.)

information and coordinate the decision-making process. Humans have more association area in their cortex than any other animal.

Each human cortex has a similar arrangement of crevices and ridges. Looking down on the cortex, as in Figure 4-7, we see a deep crevice that divides it into two nearly symmetrical halves—the *cerebral hemispheres*. Physically, these two hemispheres are almost mirror images of one another. Each functions as a separate brain with its own sensory and motor areas. The right hemisphere controls the left half of the body; the left hemisphere controls the right half of the body. Each

hemisphere is further divided by crevices and ridges into four lobes: the *frontal lobe*, the *parietal lobe*, the *temporal lobe*, and the *occipital lobe* (see Figure 4-7). We will look at the functioning of several of these lobes later.

The reticular formation. The *reticular formation* is a massive network of neurons in the primitive central core of the brain. It begins at the top of the spinal cord and continues up through the brain stem to the lower part of the cerebrum, as we see in Figure 4-8. The word "reticular" comes from the Latin word meaning "netlike." One of the main functions of the reticular formation appears to be an

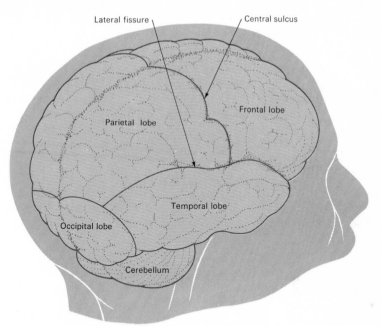

Figure 4-7. Looking down on the human cortex.

alerting one. When scientists electrically stimulate a cat's reticular formation, the cat suddenly appears attentive. When the reticular formation is removed, a cat lapses into a coma, a permanent state of inattention, from which it is not likely to recover. The reticular formation alerts the cortex to important sensory information. Studies show that receptor cells send messages to the cortex by two major routes. Sometimes messages are sent directly to the appropriate sensory projection area; at other times they are sent by way of the reticular formation. The cortex usually ignores sensory information that comes to it directly, while it pays close attention to sensory messages that come by way of the reticular formation. Apparently, the reticular formation warns the cortex when information is important and requires attention.

The limbic system. The *limbic system* includes those brain structures shown in Figure 4-9. "Limbic" comes from the Latin word meaning "border," and the limbic system occupies the inner border of both cerebral hemispheres. The structures of the limbic

Figure 4-8. The reticular formation. In this cross section of the brain, the reticular formation is indicated in gray. Note that the nerve fiber which joins the sense organ to the sensory area of the brain extends up through the reticular formation. When a stimulus travels along this pathway, the reticular formation can alert the entire brain, as indicated by the arrows.

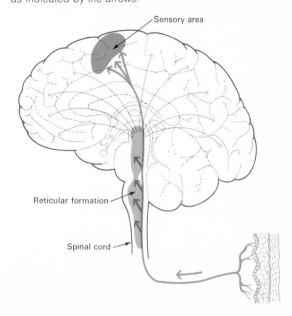

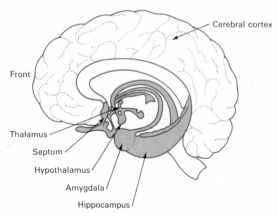

Figure 4-9. The limbic system (in blue).

system function together, along with the cortex, to influence motives and emotions, especially primitive ones. Because the cortex, the center of voluntary control, can inhibit the electrical activity in the limbic system, our emotions are never simply blindly determined by these lower brain centers. In other words, people do have control over their emotions. One limbic system structure, the *amygdala*, influences aggression, as we will see in Chapter 11. The *hypothalamus*, another limbic structure no bigger than a peanut in humans, exerts control over the posterior pituitary gland. Together the hypothalamus and pituitary gland interact to regulate endocrine gland functioning. As we will see later in this chapter, they also control our sexual physiology and influence our sexual behavior. Additionally, the hypothalamus influences eating, drinking, sleeping, and aggressive behavior.

How Do Psychologists Study the Relationship between the Brain and Behavior?

Scientists have been investigating the relationship between the brain and behavior since the early 1800s. At that time a young European physician named Franz Joseph Gall spread the belief that specific abilities and traits were *localized* (located) in particular regions of the brain. Gall reasoned that the brain was like a muscle. As particular parts were exercised, they developed, grew larger, and eventually pushed outward toward the scalp. To understand where particular functions were localized in the brain, Gall believed that it was necessary to find people with highly developed characteristics and explore their scalps for corresponding bumps. And that's what Gall did. For example, he found that several thieves had bumps just over their ears. Because the thieves were continually trying to acquire other people's goods, Gall reasoned that acquisitiveness must lie just over the ears. Using similar logic, Gall concluded that sexuality was located in the back of the head and destructiveness behind the ears. Gall called his brain study method *phrenology* (a word he coined from Greek words that mean the study of the mind). Phrenology became quite popular in the United States, and one hundred years passed before scientists showed that Gall had been wrong.

Today the four methods discussed below are used to explore the relationship between the brain and behavior.

1. Brain researchers *observe the behavior of brain-diseased or brain-injured people.* Diseases such as tumors and injuries such as gunshot wounds sometimes damage limited areas of brain tissue. From studying the symptoms that result, scientists can infer the role that the damaged brain structure played. For example, physicians have observed that when shells or bomb fragments injure the anterior (front) portion of the *occipital* area of the brain (a region known as the "secondary visual cortex"), people continue to see the parts of objects as clearly as previously, but they can no longer synthesize the parts into

complete wholes. Their world appears incoherent and fragmented. If presented with a picture of eyeglasses, for instance, people with this injury will see a curved attachment, a circle, a cross bar, a circle, and a second curved attachment. When asked to name what they have seen, they may guess "bicycle." Because they no longer perceive whole objects, they have trouble recognizing the meaning of visual stimuli (4). This was one of Zasetsky's problems.

2. Using surgical techniques, brain researchers *remove or destroy particular parts of an animal's brain,* observe what the animal does or does not do once the structure is gone, and infer what that structure ordinarily does. In the late 1930s, for example, Heinrich Klüver and Paul Bucy removed the *temporal lobes* including parts of the *amygdala* of wild rhesus monkeys, who were characterized by their short tempers and their readiness to aggress at the slightest provocation. After the monkeys recuperated from the operation, Klüver and Bucy noted that their personalities were drastically changed. They were so gentle and peace loving that they did not aggress even when directly attacked. They also exhibited signs of hypersexuality. The males mounted everything in sight, and the females were receptive to sex with such unlikely suitors as water faucets. The hunger drives of these monkeys were also disordered. Instead of disregarding inedible objects, as normal monkeys do, they attempted to chew up metal bolts when they were mixed with their peanuts. Apparently, the temporal lobes and amygdala are involved in directing motivated behavior such as eating, sex, and aggression (5).

3. Brain researchers *stimulate particular regions in the brain* using chemicals or electrical current. The resulting behavior gives information about the functioning of those regions. When patients undergo certain types of brain surgery under local anesthesia, for example, surgeons sometimes stimulate particular areas of their exposed brains with a mild electric current—with the patients' permission. Contrary to what you might expect, patients do not experience any discomfort whatsoever even though they are wide-awake during the surgery. (There are no pain receptors in the central nervous system.) Instead they respond to the mild current with varied sensations and perceptions. Using these procedures, Wilder Penfield, a Canadian neurosurgeon, has discovered that stimulation in the *temporal lobe* of the association cortex produces reports of past experiences in a small but significant number of patients. Patients report both sound sequences, like music or conversation, and visual events. Curiously, they describe the experience not as remembering, but as "seeing again" or "hearing again" or "living through a past moment [6]." Here is the way one of Penfield's patients responded to stimulation of the temporal lobe:

There was a piano there and someone was playing. I could hear the song, you know. It is a song I have sung before but I cannot find out quite what the title of the song is. That was what I was trying to do when you finished stimulating [7]!

The stimulation technique has enabled neurosurgeons to draw maps of the human cortex giving information on how various regions function.

4. Brain researchers *use electrical recording techniques.* As we have mentioned, mild electrical activity occurs continuously throughout the brain as the nervous system performs its many functions. Scientists can hone in on this electrical activity by attaching *electrodes* (usually needles or flat

metal bits that conduct electricity) to the brain or scalp. Connected to a measuring device, the electrode enables scientists to record the brain's electrical activity. To measure the activity of a single neuron as it responds to a particular event, investigators implant *microelectrodes* (tiny electrodes one-thousandth of a millimeter in size) directly into a specific neuron. They put larger electrodes inside the brain or some-where on its surface to measure the summed electrical responses of many neurons. Finally, psychologists often use a machine called an *electroencephalograph* (EEG) to record electrical activity throughout even larger regions of the brain. To make these large-scale recordings, electrodes are simply glued to the subject's scalp.

THE BRAIN AND MEMORY

The case of H. M.: A man who could not remember.

At age seven a young boy, H. M., sustained a head injury; later he began to experience minor seizures. The seizures became increasingly frequent and severe until, at the age of twenty-seven, H. M. could no longer hold a job. As a last resort radical bilateral medial temporal lobe surgery on the hippocampus (part of the limbic system, see Figure 4-9) was performed to bring H. M. relief.

A memory impairment was immediately apparent following surgery. H. M. did not recognize members of the hospital staff, except for the hospital surgeon, whom he'd known for several years. Furthermore, he did not recall and could not relearn his way to the bathroom. Nor could he remember daily happenings around the hospital.

H. M.'s ability to recall daily occurrences did not improve. When he and his family moved to a new house, he did not learn the new address and could not find his way home alone. Day after day he worked the same jigsaw puzzles and read the same magazines. Each time the contents were new and unfamiliar.

Some aspects of H. M.'s memory were still intact. H. M. remembered his early past vividly; he could also remember small bits of information for short periods of time. The surgery had not affected other abilities: H. M.'s capacity to respond emotionally appeared to be unchanged; he behaved perfectly appropriately in social situations; and his speech was as intelligible as previously. Curiously, H. M. actually scored slightly higher on tests of intelligence following surgery.

The following incident pinpoints the selective nature of H. M.'s memory deficit. On one occasion, H. M. was asked to remember the digits 5, 8, 4; and he was allowed to sit quietly without interruption. By making elaborate associations, H. M. managed to remember the digits for fifteen minutes—but he remembered no longer. Minutes later he could not recall the digits or the train of associations that had helped him recall them; he couldn't even remember that he'd been assigned the digit-recall task at all (8).

H. M.'s case, which we will be discussing later, reminds us that memory is linked to the brain. For centuries, scientists have believed that long-lasting physical changes called *memory traces*, or *engrams*, occur in our brains each time we perceive, experience, or learn. Although no one has ever seen an engram, brain researchers continue to believe that literally billions of them are stored throughout each human brain. In this section we explore the following questions: Is there more than one memory-making process? Where does the brain store mental representations of experience? How does it store them?

Is There More Than One Memory-making Process?

Try the following exercises:

1. Shut your eyes, then open them as briefly as possible, then shut them again. Notice that the image, which you picked up while your eyes were open, remained with you for a short period of time after you closed your eyes the second time.
2. Recall the directions given in exercise 1.
3. Describe what you did on your last birthday.

These exercises are designed to make you use several different kinds of memory. As you may have surmised after reading the case of H. M., the process we ordinarily call memory is not a single unitary one. Rather, there are at least three distinct types of memory systems. Each system has different characteristics and is probably based on a different physiological mechanism. One memory system that few people are aware of is the *sensory representation system*. People make brief sensory representations of all sensory stimuli, fleeting memories that are erased after a fraction of a second. You may have already demonstrated for yourself what psychologists mean by a sensory representation by performing the first exercise. After you closed your eyes you continued to see an image—for an instant. The ability to make sensory representations of the world comes from the nature of the perceptual system.

Another memory system helps us retain information for short periods of time— seconds and even minutes—before losing it. Exercise 2 was designed to make you use this memory system, which psychologists call the *short-term memory system*. When holding a conversation, we remember the most recent sentences that were spoken. After looking up a new phone number, we usually remember the numbers long enough to dial. The memories in this system are *not* sensory representations. We do not simply retain sights or sounds. Instead we remember our interpretation of the sensory data: numbers or meaningful words, for example. Our short-term memory is capable of retaining about seven items of information at a time. However, by *rehearsing* (repeating the information) we can keep information in our short-term memory indefinitely. H. M.'s short-term memory system was still intact as evidenced by the fact that he could retain information for fifteen minutes using rehearsal.

Certain short-term memories are filed in a *long-term memory system.* Many short-term memories—such as our own phone numbers—are probably rehearsed so often that they are converted into long-term memories. At the same time, new bits of information are continually being added to the long-term memory storage without deliberate effort. You can probably recall what you did last Sunday, even though you made no conscious effort to remember at the time. Dramatic or vivid events also leave impressions which remain in our memories. Currently, psychologists do not know precisely how information is transferred from the short-term memory system to the long-term memory system, but they do know that the brain needs to operate without being disturbed for a period of time if short-term memories are to be remembered later. Certain experiences such as head injuries, epileptic attacks, electroconvulsive shock (passing a nonlethal amount of electric current through an organism's brain), certain drugs, and certain illnesses massively disrupt neural activity in the brain. These experiences usually produce a memory loss for events that immediately precede them, but not for more distant memories, a phenomenon known as *retrograde amnesia.* Many psychologists believe that the memory loss results in these cases because the brain does not have the time it requires to transform, or *consolidate,* its short-term memories into long-term ones.

The human brain may be something like an enormous videotape recorder that is continually recording and then storing experiences in hundreds of file cabinets in a warehouse. Each file cabinet is crammed with bits of information that have been accumulating over a lifetime. A number of observations support this metaphor. Most of us have encountered some stimulus that triggers a "long-forgotten" memory. A particular odor might remind you of a building you once visited ten years ago or more. Penfield's brain-stimulation work (described earlier) also suggests this hypothesis. So do abundant clinical anecdotes: People who have suffered strokes, for example, sometimes revert to "forgotten behavior" such as speaking a language they haven't spoken for fifty years. Similarly, people under hypnosis sometimes remember minute details of early childhood incidents.

If so many experiences are stored in our brains, what is forgetting? Many psychologists believe that there may be more than one forgetting process. With sensory and short-term memory, the memory seems to die out (*decay*), leaving no permanent impression. On the other hand, memories in long-term storage appear to remain but become difficult to *retrieve* (recover), possibly because recent memories and past memories interfere with each other. A memory of a new gym locker combination may keep a person from retrieving a memory of an old combination. Similarly, if you studied French in high school and later attempted Russian in college, you might have noticed that French words (old memories) often come to mind instead of the Russian equivalents (recent memories) that you were searching for. In terms of our metaphor, although information in long-term memory may remain in storage somewhere in the warehouse, it may be misfiled, filed in some difficult-to-reach location, or lost. We will be discussing some of the practical aspects of retrieving information in Chapter 8.

The case of H. M. demonstrated that these memory processes depend on mechanisms within the brain. Having lost his *hippocampus* on both sides, H. M. appeared to lose his ability to convert short-term, language-related memories into long-term memories. H. M.'s case raises a question: Where are memory systems located within the brain? Psychologists have been searching for the answer to this question for at least fifty years. Most of their efforts have focused on the long-term memory system.

Where Are Long-term Memories Stored?

Many sensory and motor skills are regulated primarily by specific cortical regions. Vision, for example, is localized primarily in the occipital lobes (see Figure 4-7). What about our long-term memories?

What Karl Lashley learned from his rats. Karl S. Lashley (1890–1958), a student of John Watson's and an important psychologist in his own right, spent much of his life searching for the neural basis of memory. Lashley used white rats as his experimental subjects. First, he taught them to find their way through complex mazes, then he surgically removed parts of their cerebral cortexes. After the rats recuperated from the surgery, Lashley retested them to see if they remembered the mazes. He found that the more cortex he removed, the longer it took the rat to relearn the maze, a measure of memory. The remarkable thing was that the rats' memories did not seem to depend on any specific area of the cortex. Rats simply appeared to need a certain *amount* of cortex. Lashley's research indicates that memories are redundant; that is, that they are duplicated over and over again and stored throughout the entire cortex and not in specific locations (9).

Many of Lashley's studies dealt with rats and primarily with memory for visual experiences. What about higher animals such as people and other types of long-term memory?

What our human cerebral hemispheres know and remember. Important biological structures often come in pairs: We have two eyes, two arms, two kidneys, and two cerebral

hemispheres. It would actually be more correct to say that the cerebrum has two halves. As we mentioned before, these two halves are nearly structural mirror images of one another with parallel centers for vision, hearing, and other sensory and motor skills. As we stated, each hemisphere tends to be associated predominantly with one side of the body. The right half of the cerebrum controls the left side of the body and receives its sensory information from it; the left half serves the same functions for the right side of the body. Recent research shows that the two hemispheres store different information about the same experience in different ways.

Under ordinary circumstances the *corpus callosum*, a massive network of nerve fibers, (see Figure 4-10) joins the two hemispheres, giving each access to the information and memories of the other. Part of remembering may consist of putting together different aspects of a memory from different parts of the brain. Our knowledge about this subject comes largely from the work of Roger Sperry, a physiological psychologist at the California Institute of Technology, and his associates, who began studying the corpus callosum in the early 1950s. Sperry and his colleagues worked initially with cats, rats, and monkeys. Later they observed people with "split brains." When seizures threaten the lives of epileptics or force them to live like vegetables and when drugs and normal surgical procedures do not help, neurosurgeons sometimes sever the connection between the two hemispheres as a last resort. For reasons that are not fully understood, this operation usually stops the seizure activity almost entirely. However, the epileptic patient emerges from surgery with a split brain. Roger Sperry and his associates have observed split-brain people extensively to learn more about how the two human hemispheres function.

Because the visual system is frequently used to test the functioning of the two hemi-

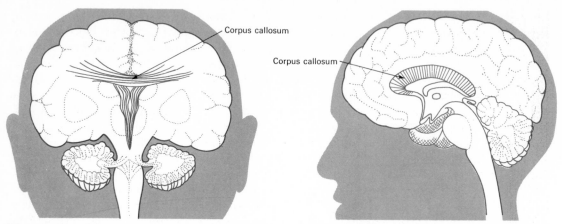

Figure 4-10. The corpus callosum joins the two brain hemispheres giving each access to the information and memories of the other.

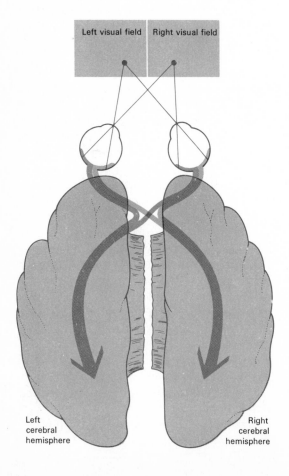

spheres, it is necessary to understand a little about its anatomy. As people look straight ahead, the lens of each eye projects objects in the right visual field onto the left side of each retina. Similarly, each lens projects objects in the left visual field onto the right side of each retina. The *retina*, the light-sensitive membrane at the back of the eyeball, contains neurons that convey nerve impulses describing visual objects to the brain. Information in the right visual field is channeled to the left cerebral hemisphere and information in the left visual field is channeled to the right cerebral hemisphere. In right-handed people, the left hemisphere is the dominant one (see Figure 4-11).

People with split brains function quite normally on the surface. In fact, people who are born without a corpus callosum may never detect the abnormality. However, refined laboratory tests that restrict information to one hemisphere of the brain demonstrate pecu-

Figure 4-11. Information in the right visual field is channeled to the left cerebral hemisphere, and information in the left visual field is channeled to the right cerebral hemisphere.

liarities in their behavior. When split-brain patients observe objects in their dominant (usually right) visual field, they rarely have trouble naming them. Similarly, if a pencil is placed in their dominant (usually right) hand, they can identify it by name instantly. This information is channeled to the dominant (usually left) side of the brain, where language is localized. But if a picture is projected onto the split-brain patient's nondominant visual field, the patient reports seeing only a flash of light and denies having seen any details. Similarly, if a pencil is placed in the nondominant hand and the patient is asked to name it, the individual may reply that the hand feels numb. Something is obviously wrong. At first it appeared that the nondominant hemisphere did not recognize objects. As it turns out, the problem is not one of recognition. If an object is put in the split-brain patient's nondominant hand and he or she is asked to find it in a bag of other objects, the individual has no problem doing so. Similarly, although split-brain patients cannot describe pictures flashed to their nondominant visual field, they can gesture to show their function. For instance, if we show such individuals a scissors, they can make a cutting motion. They can also draw what they have seen. They simply cannot describe it with words (10). (See Figure 4-12.)

What does this mean? Evidently higher animals such as people have two parallel specialized information-processing systems. The dominant cerebral hemisphere is responsible for language. It is analytic and logical. The nondominant hemisphere cannot name or write, though it does recognize some written words and it can obey spoken commands. It also recognizes and remembers objects long enough to find them when they are mixed in with other objects. Research shows that the nondominant hemisphere is also centrally concerned with emotional experiences and is adept at both conceptual-

izing spatial relationships and remembering tactile sensations (11). Ordinarily, the corpus callosum allows both hemispheres to pool their skills and share their information and memories.

It is interesting to note that the two halves of the cerebrum function in split-brain people as two independent brains whose goals are sometimes contradictory. Physiological psychologist Michael Gazzaniga described

Figure 4-12. A picture of a spoon is presented in the left visual field. The input goes to the right hemisphere (usually nondominant). Though the spoon can be retrieved from behind a screen with the left hand, the split-brain patient cannot say what has been picked up. If the spoon had been presented to the right hand or right visual field, the input would go to the left hemisphere (usually dominant) and the split-brain patient would make the verbal response, "spoon." (Adapted from Gazzaniga, 1970.)

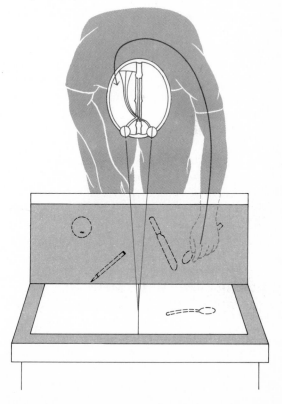

one case who "would sometimes find himself pulling his pants down with one hand and pulling them up with the other. Once, he grabbed his wife with his left hand and shook her violently, while with the right trying to come to his wife's aid in bringing the left belligerent hand under control. Once, while I was playing horseshoes with the patient in his back yard [Gazzaniga reports], he happened to pick up an axe leaning against the house with his left hand. Because it was entirely likely that the more aggressive right hemisphere might be in control, I discreetly left the scene—not wanting to be the victim for the test case of which half-brain does society punish or execute [12]."

Psychologist Robert Ornstein has suggested that everyone is pulled in two directions by the two modes of consciousness that result from these two cerebral hemispheres. When we are under the control of the dominant hemisphere, we behave as rational, analytic beings: We are interested in language; we are logical; and our ideas follow one another sequentially. When the nondominant hemisphere takes charge, we tend to function in an intuitive and subjective way. We become involved in fantasy, art, emotionality, and mystic experiences; and our ideas come spontaneously. To feel complete, Ornstein believes, people must allow both aspects of their consciousness to express themselves (13).

Lashley's and Sperry's research suggests that the brain makes memories throughout both cerebral hemispheres, giving people and other animals a high degree of flexibility should their brains be injured.

How Does the Brain Store Memories?

How does the brain store memories? That is, what structural or chemical or electrical changes occur in our brains to record our experiences. We don't know the answers to this question, but we have some promising theories.

The immediate memory systems. Many psychologists believe that the immediate memory systems—sensory representation and short-term memory—both depend on activity within the neurons. The process of short-term memory might operate something like this. Imagine that your teacher is assigning a homework problem: number 4 on page 83. You have to retain this information long enough to turn to page 83 in your book and locate and mark problem number 4. What happens in your nervous system? As the teacher mentions the number, it is coded by the sensory neurons and transmitted to neurons in the brain where short-term memory is probably localized. One widely held theory postulates that brain neurons are arranged in loops, as pictured in Figure 4-13. The theory also states that particular neuron loops respond only to specific stimuli—for example, there may be a loop that responds to the number "83" and another loop that responds to the number "4." When a loop is activated, the neurons fire in turn, continuing full circle, again and again for a brief period of time after the stimulus ends—accounting for short-term memory. Forgetting occurs when the reverberation decays after a varying number of cycles. Why do the cells stop reverberating? To understand one likely explanation for the decay process, consider the plight of one neuron within the loop—neuron A—as it responds to number 83. Whether or not neuron A fires depends not only on the activity of the neuron preceding it in the loop but also on the electrical activity of all the other neurons with which it is interconnected. If such reverberating loop arrangements exist in our brains, each neuron probably belongs to thousands of different loops; each loop probably contains large numbers of neurons; and the neurons in each

Figure 4-13. The reverberating loop theory of short-term memory.

loop are probably interconnected in complex ways. Therefore, electrical activity in these other neurons could cause neuron A to fire out of turn, or not to fire when its turn comes, thereby ending the reverberating electrochemical activity.

Making long-term memories. How is a short-term memory consolidated into a long-term memory? One possibility is that the brain changes structurally, as it records a new memory. For example, it might make new synapses. Another possibility is that it stores its long-term memories chemically, perhaps in the synaptic junctions. One widely held hypothesis states that *ribonucleic acid (RNA)* is the molecule responsible for recording long-term memories. Genetic information about each individual organism is stored in large molecules of *deoxyribonucleic acid (DNA)*. A second molecule, RNA, transfers information from DNA to the cells of the body. Many scientists reason that if RNA can transfer information from DNA, it might also be

capable of storing long-term memories. RNA seems to be a likely candidate for this role for other reasons. It is involved in synthesizing the *proteins,* substances that regulate the operation of the neuron, control its reaction rates, and synthesize and break down its transmitters. Moreover, the structure of RNA varies; and as it varies, it produces different proteins. Accordingly, learning may alter the structure of RNA molecules, producing changes in the proteins of the neurons, which lead to modifications of neuron communication patterns—a likely basis for long-term memory storage.

There is quite a bit of evidence to support this hypothesis. Some of it comes from Swedish biologist Holger Hydén, who has used rats as his subjects in several ingenious investigations. As humans are right- or left-handed, so rats are right- or left-pawed. Hydén trained rats to use their nonpreferred paws to retrieve food from a narrow tube. Each rat received two 25-minute training sessions per day until it had learned the task well. Then it

was killed, and its brain was chemically analyzed. Hydén found that the RNA in each cell
was greater in weight and different in structure on the learning side of the brain when
compared with either the untrained side of
the same brain or the brain of an untrained
rat, one who had only one or two days of
training.

In a second study, Hydén trained rats to
walk a tightrope at a 45-degree angle. When
he later analyzed their brains, he found that
the RNA content of the *vestibular nuclei*, brain
cells engaged in the perception of gravity and
in maintaining equilibrium, had increased
and changed in structure. The brains of rats
who were simply rotated back and forth and
up and down in a special apparatus also
increased their RNA concentration, but the
structure of their RNA did not change (14).
Both studies indicate that RNA appears to be
involved in coding and storing experience.

If memory is rooted in brain RNA, then
scientists may be able to transfer memory
by transferring RNA from one animal to
another. For more than ten years, James
McConnell, a psychologist at the University
of Michigan, studied this issue. He used a
curious type of freshwater worm known as a
planarian. Planaria (plural of planarian) have
several remarkable abilities. The first one of
note is that if they are cut into as many as six
pieces, each bit will grow into a complete
animal (an "identical twin" of the original) in
approximately two weeks. In some early studies McConnell taught planaria to tense up
when exposed to light by a training procedure known as respondent conditioning (we
will be examining respondent conditioning in
Chapter 7). Ordinarily, planaria do not tense
up when they are exposed to light, but they
do tense up when given a mild electric shock.
So McConnell and his associates presented a
light, and shortly afterward, a mild electric
shock. After many pairings (150 to 200),
planaria began anticipating the shock by tens-

ing up as soon as the light was presented.
Technically, we say that they were conditioned.

As this point, McConnell and his colleagues
cut their learned planaria in half. After each
half had regenerated a new tail or a new
head, it was tested to see if it remembered the
response. Sure enough, the tail-regenerated
planaria performed just as well as the head-
regenerated planaria. Both needed significantly fewer trials to relearn the tensing response than animals who had never learned it
in the first place. Apparently, chemical
changes had occurred during learning
and had spread throughout the entire
organism (15). Some later evidence suggested that these changes had involved
RNA. In further studies McConnell and his
colleagues found that memory could also be
transferred from one animal to another. In
one experiment, previously conditioned
planaria were ground up and fed to naive
worms who had never before been trained
(the experimental group). At the same time,
naive planaria were ground up and fed to a
second group of naive planaria (the control
group). As expected, the experimental
worms learned more rapidly than the control subjects (16).

These results astounded brain investigators
and stimulated a flood of research on memory transfer. McConnell's studies were harshly
criticized at first. However, over the years,
many scientists using more refined experimental procedures have obtained similar results with planaria and other animals, such as
rats and mice. The role of RNA in such
memory transfers remains a controversial
subject.

Currently, we can give no final answer to
the question of how the brain stores long-
term memories. Permanent memories may be
encoded by RNA in proteins or represented
by structural changes. Only further research
can provide an answer.

Summary: The Brain and Memory

1. There are at least three distinct memory systems: a sensory representation system, a short-term memory system, and a long-term memory system.
2. The entire cerebrum appears to be involved in both learning and memory.
3. The two human cerebral hemispheres process and store different information; under ordinary circumstances the corpus callosum, which connects the two hemispheres, permits them to share their learning and their memories.
4. It is not yet clear precisely how the brain stores memories. Reverberating loops of neurons in the brain may account for short-term memories and sensory representations.
5. A brain appears to need to function without disturbance for a period of time to consolidate short-term memories into long-term memories.
6. Long-term memories may be stored by structural changes in the brain or in RNA.

THE ENDOCRINE SYSTEM AND SEX-TYPED BEHAVIOR

The nervous system is an animal's primary internal coordinating system; it enables animals to register, analyze, and respond appropriately to stimuli in the external world. The *endocrine system* is a second internal coordinating system. Composed of ductless glands that secrete chemical substances, called *hormones,* directly into the blood stream, the endocrine system regulates the animal's internal environment (see Figure 4-14).[1] The hormones

[1] Recent studies suggest that the pineal gland secretes serotonin and melatonin; the functions of these hormones in people remain uncertain.

travel throughout the body controlling various processes including metabolism, growth, and sexual development and influencing emotionality and vitality. The nervous system and the endocrine system continually interact. Sometimes the nervous system stimulates the release of hormones; sometimes the release of hormones stimulates the nervous system. Internal bodily conditions can also trigger the release of hormones.

Males in many species, including our own, tend to be more aggressive, more active, and more independent than females. Is there some physiological basis for these differences? Research on both animal and human infants suggests that some sex-typed behavior is evident at the beginning of life and probably reflects inborn biological inclinations. Male rhesus monkey infants, for example, do much more biting, hitting, pushing, shoving, yanking, and grabbing than female rhesus infants do, whereas female rhesus infants tend to be shy, passive, and withdrawn (17). Similarly, male human babies tend to be physically active whereas female human babies tend to be physically passive in early infancy (18). In this section we examine how sex hormones influence the brain and sex-typed behavior. We will also focus briefly on the role that the environment plays in shaping sex-typed behavior.

Sex Hormones and Sex-typed Physical Characteristics

Sex hormones, chemical substances that affect sexual development and sexual behavior, are produced by the *gonads,* or sex glands—*ovaries* in the female and *testes* in the male. In addition, the *adrenals,* endocrine glands that are on top of the kidneys, also secrete *sex hormones* beginning at puberty (at approximately ten to fourteen years of age in humans). The gonads and adrenals function

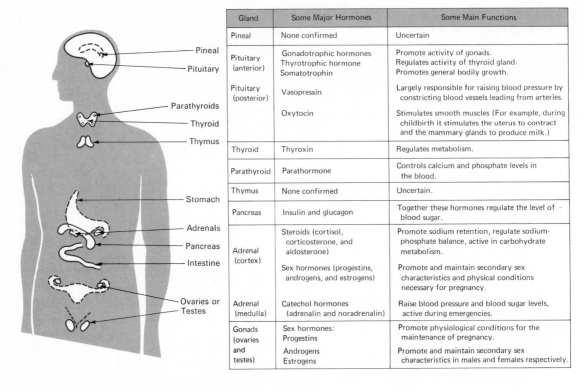

Gland	Some Major Hormones	Some Main Functions
Pineal	None confirmed	Uncertain
Pituitary (anterior)	Gonadotrophic hormones Thyrotrophic hormone Somatotrophin	Promote activity of gonads. Regulates activity of thyroid gland. Promotes general bodily growth.
Pituitary (posterior)	Vasopressin	Largely responsible for raising blood pressure by constricting blood vessels leading from arteries.
	Oxytocin	Stimulates smooth muscles (For example, during childbirth it stimulates the uterus to contract and the mammary glands to produce milk.)
Thyroid	Thyroxin	Regulates metabolism.
Parathyroid	Parathormone	Controls calcium and phosphate levels in the blood.
Thymus	None confirmed	Uncertain.
Pancreas	Insulin and glucagon	Together these hormones regulate the level of blood sugar.
Adrenal (cortex)	Steroids (cortisol, corticosterone, and aldosterone)	Promote sodium retention, regulate sodium-phosphate balance, active in carbohydrate metabolism.
	Sex hormones (progestins, androgens, and estrogens)	Promote and maintain secondary sex characteristics and physical conditions necessary for pregnancy.
Adrenal (medulla)	Catechol hormones (adrenalin and noradrenalin)	Raise blood pressure and blood sugar levels, active during emergencies.
Gonads (ovaries and testes)	Sex hormones: Progestins	Promote physiological conditions for the maintenance of pregnancy.
	Androgens Estrogens	Promote and maintain secondary sex characteristics in males and females respectively.

Figure 4-14. The location of the endocrine glands and the main effects of some of the major hormones that they secrete. Note that some glands occur in pairs, such as the testes and ovaries. Note also that hormones from the same gland sometimes serve very different functions.

together to regulate the growth of sexually mature and sexually responsive men and women.

Regardless of your sex, your gonads and adrenals both produce *estrogens* and *progestins*, the feminine sex hormones, and *androgens* (including testosterone), the masculine sex hormones. The estrogens and androgens are almost totally responsible for what are called primary and secondary sex characteristics. *Primary sex characteristics* are the actual sex organs—in females, the ovaries, the vagina, and the uterus; in males, the testes and the penis—structures that are usually present at birth. *Secondary sex characteristics* are those which develop at puberty, including the growth of breasts and the broadening of

hips in young women and the growth of facial and body hair and the deepening of the voice in young men. If the male fetus's testes manufacture either too much estrogen or too little androgen, the male infant may actually be born with female genitals. If a young boy's adrenals or testes secrete an excessive proportion of the estrogens during puberty, the boy may exhibit feminine secondary sex characteristics such as a hairless face and overdeveloped breasts. On the other hand, if the boy's testes or adrenals manufacture either too much androgen or too little estrogen, he may develop body hair, a beard, a deep voice, and other secondary sex characteristics at a very early age. Similarly, too much androgen or too little estrogen will masculinize the female fetus. If this condition exists during or after puberty, the girl may develop facial hair and a deep voice. Too much estrogen or too little androgen before puberty will cause a young woman to develop feminine secondary sex characteristics at an early age.

Early Sex Differences: Genes and Gonads

The differentiation of male and female—physically and behaviorally—is a complex process. In the beginning, at the moment of conception, the *genetic sex* of the embryo is determined by one pair of chromosomes—the sex chromosomes. Mothers give their embryos an X chromosome. If the father contributes a second X chromosome, the embryo develops as a genetic female. If the father contributes a Y chromosome, the embryo develops as a genetic male. Genetic sex is only the first step in a long chain of processes. Initially, the embryo is capable of developing either ovaries or testes. The Y chromosome causes the development of testes. The X

chromosome causes the development of ovaries.

After the gonads have formed, they begin producing sex hormones, and the sex hormones now occupy the prominent role in sexual differentiation. The androgens, particularly *testosterone* which is primarily secreted by the testes, are probably the most influential sex hormones. If the androgens are present, they structure the development of masculine reproductive organs; feminine reproductive organs are suppressed. In the absence of the androgens, the embryo develops feminine reproductive organs; masculine reproductive organs are inhibited. Thus, females are made automatically, unless the androgens are present. Evidently, "nature's primary impulse is to make a female—morphologically [structurally] speaking at least [19]." (See Figure 4-15.)

The Androgens, Rat Brains, and Rat Behavior

More than thirty-five years ago, Carroll Pfeiffer, an endocrinologist then at the Yale

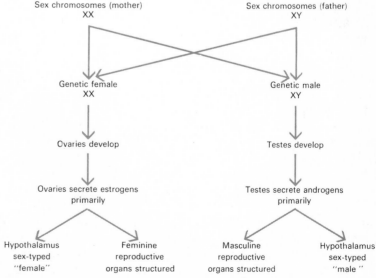

Figure 4-15. Early sexual differentiation.

University School of Medicine, began systematically studying the early effects of the gonads to see how they affected rats' later sexual identities. Pfeiffer removed the testes of newly born male rats and replaced them with transplanted ovaries. Similarly, he removed the ovaries of neonatal (newborn) female rats and replaced them with transplanted testes. Finally, he also grafted the opposite set of gonads onto some sexually intact newborn rats, so that each animal had two complete sets of gonads (see Figure 4-16). Pfeiffer was particularly interested in observing how these changes would affect the adult rats' hormonal functioning. Ordinarily, adult mammals show very consistent patterns. The female's hormonal pattern is cyclical, repeating itself every five or six days in rats; every twenty-eight days in human females. The male does not exhibit cyclical hormonal patterns.

When Pfeiffer examined his rats at maturi-ty, he found that the androgens had exerted the deciding influence. Genetic males (XY) without testes showed a cyclic hormonal pattern at maturity. Genetic males with both testes and ovaries, and genetic females (XX) with testes (with or without ovaries) did not show the cyclic hormonal pattern at maturity. In other words, when androgen was present during early infancy it caused the noncyclic masculine pattern; otherwise the organism functioned as a female.

Pfeiffer believed that androgen had sex-typed the pituitary gland. As it turned out, he was mistaken. Subsequent research has demonstrated that the early presence or absence of androgen alters neural circuits in the hypothalamus, sex-typing them "male" or leaving them "female." The hypothalamus then assumes permanent control over the pituitary with regard to sex (20). There is a sensitive period for these effects (see Chapter 3). In

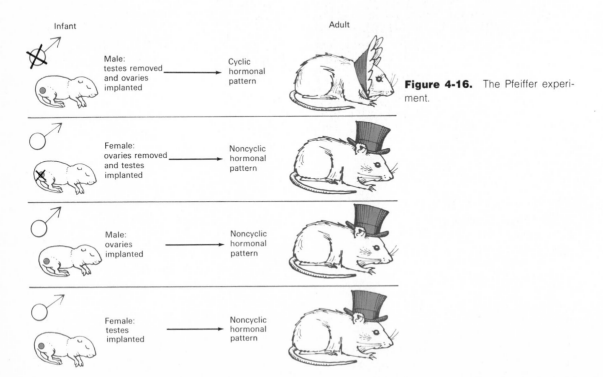

Infant   Adult

Male: testes removed and ovaries implanted → Cyclic hormonal pattern

Figure 4-16. The Pfeiffer experiment.

Female: ovaries removed and testes implanted → Noncyclic hormonal pattern

Male: ovaries implanted → Noncyclic hormonal pattern

Female: testes implanted → Noncyclic hormonal pattern

onkeys, hamsters, and humans it begins
.iortly before birth; in rats, slightly after
birth. Before and after this period, androgen
does not alter the nervous system and the
animal's subsequent hormonal patterns.

Research studies using animals suggest that
sex-typed behavior patterns may also be programmed in during the early sensitive period. The androgens and estrogens which are
produced as the animal matures appear to
excite or inhibit the expression of these previously established patterns. Let's look again at
the rat. Male and female rats show consistent
behavioral differences. For instance, both
sexes have their own specific complementary
behavioral role in copulation. During mating,
normal males mount, thrust, and ejaculate,
whereas normal females show various forms
of receptive posturing. In addition, males
and females differ in the ways they exercise,
react in large open enclosures, and respond
to threat and to newborn rat pups. If we
tamper with the androgens during the early
sensitive period, we can reverse the natural
order of things—we can create female rats
with the capacity to behave like male rats and
male rats with the capacity to behave like
female rats. Then, if we inject them at puberty with the sex hormones of the opposite sex,
they exhibit the behavioral patterns typical of
that sex. Similar results have been obtained
with guinea pigs, rabbits, dogs and monkeys.
What about people?

The Androgens, Human Brains, and Human Behavior: The Case of the Hermaphrodite

The first pediatric endocrine clinic in the
world was established at Johns Hopkins Hospital in Baltimore, Maryland, in the early
1950s. The clinic sometimes serves children
with birth defects of the sex organs or ambiguous sexual anatomy (*hermaphroditism*). John

Money, a medical psychologist engaged
psychohormonal research at the clinic, a
his associates have been studying childr
with sex anatomy problems for more th
twenty years. Money and one colleague, Ar
Ehrhardt, studied twenty-five young g
who had been exposed to excessive androg
levels during the early sensitive period sh
ly before birth—in some cases because c
genetic defect and in others because of dr
used to treat pregnancy complications. T
twenty-five fetally androgenized girls, as
will call them, received corrective surger
birth to feminize their anatomy and cortis
therapy to assure appropriate feminine
ondary sexual development. Each infant
considered "female" by her family and re
accordingly.

Money and Ehrhardt matched t
twenty-five subjects with a control grou
twenty-five normal girls on age, intellige
socioeconomic background, and race. T
they interviewed and tested all the girls
ages ranging from four to sixteen—to
which sex role they preferred. Their mot
were also questioned. Money and Ehrh
found that the behavior of the fetally an
genized subjects differed from that of
normal controls. They regarded themse
and were more frequently regarded by
families and peers, as tomboys; they shov
greater preference for energetic play
team games, functional, utilitarian clot
and traditionally masculine toys; and
were less excited about babies and child
and more enthusiastic about a care
adulthood. Money and Ehrhardt concl
that the pervasive tomboyishness of th
tally androgenized group was most sat
torily explained by the early influenc
androgen in masculinizing their brains
It is possible, however, that the fetally a
genized girls were not treated entirel
normal girls by their families.

What about feminized males—male

prived of androgen at the sensitive period, born feminized; surgically and hormonally corrected as male, and labeled and reared male? Such feminized males do not exist. The early fetal lack of androgen cannot be fully corrected at birth because the necessary surgery and hormone therapy have yet to be perfected. There is some research, however, on genetic males (XY) who have been feminized by a clinical condition known as the androgen-insensitivity syndrome. In this condition androgen is present during the sensitive period, but a genetic defect prevents the fetus from utilizing it. The masculine internal reproductive structures begin to develop but do not become complete. Consequently, the male is born with feminized genitals; he is likely to be identified, labeled, and reared female. Once the truth is discovered, as it usually is, these males are given feminine hormones and corrective surgery to further feminize their bodies—since experts believe that they have a better chance to adjust in the feminine role. Since these genetic males have not been exposed to androgen during the early critical period, their central nervous systems have not been organized along masculine lines; and accordingly they should not display masculine behavior patterns. Do they?

Money and Ehrhardt studied ten genetic males with this syndrome. Each was being reared as female. The information which Money and Ehrhardt collected showed that nine of these "boys" conformed to the female stereotype: for the most part, they enjoyed homecrafts, were interested in clothing and adornment, played with feminine toys as children, wished to be wives, had dreams of rearing families, and exhibited strong interests in infants and their care. These androgen-insensitive "males" were clearly more "feminine" in their behavior than the fetally androgenized females (22). These studies point to the importance of androgen

at the early critical period in ⌐ human brain and influencin₍ human behavior.

Learning, Culture, and Sex-typed Behavior

Human males and females are probably b₍ with different behavioral tendencies, they ar also shaped by distinctive psychological and social forces. American men are *expected to be* independent, active, aggressive, competitive, nonconforming, and impersonal; while the trend may be changing, American women are generally *expected to be* dependent, passive, conforming, and emotional (23). Accordingly, men and women are exposed to differing standards for appearance, behavior, sexuality, and academic and vocational achievement. Recent evidence indicates that American mothers begin the shaping process shortly after birth. In one study, Michael Lewis, a psychologist at the Fels Research Institute in Yellow Springs, Ohio, and his associates observed mother-infant interactions when infants were three, six, and thirteen months of age. During the last observation period, the mothers sat in a chair for fifteen minutes watching their children play. Observers behind a one-way mirror recorded how frequently mother and child vocalized, looked at one another, and established physical contact or proximity. After fifteen minutes a barrier was placed between mother and child so that the child's reaction to the separation could be observed. Data obtained from the entire study showed that as early as twelve weeks the mothers were talking to and looking at their infant girls more than their infant boys. However, during the first six months, the infant boys were kept in greater physical contact; after that the situation was reversed. So the boys had their physical contact early; they were on their own early while the girls were still being sheltered and coddled. Not sur-

prisingly, at the age of thirteen months, boys and girls were already behaving quite differently. The boys played vigorously with toys and nontoys such as door knobs and light switches, they talked little to their mothers, and they tackled the barrier by themselves. The girls, in contrast, stayed close to their mothers, they talked to them frequently, and their play was more passive. Typically, they handled the barrier problem by sobbing in the middle of the room (24). Note that these findings can be attributed to early sex typing by the androgens, as well as to learning or a combination of the two.

Parents are not the only teachers of appropriate sex-typed behavior. Influencial members of the society—teachers, politicians, clergy, physicians, and mental health experts—reiterate the society's sex-role policy. So do the mass media—books, magazines, advertisements, TV programs (see Figure 4-17).

In America men hold the leadership and prestigious roles, women the menial ones. One index that reflects this convention is the

Figure 4-17. Stereotyping of women in 1,200 TV commercials. (*The New York Times*, 1972.)

In 37.5% women were men's domestic adjuncts

In 22.7%—demeaned housekeepers

In 33.9%—dependent on men

In 24.3%—submissive

In 16.7%—sex objects

In 42.6%—household functionaries

In 17.1%—unintelligent

pattern of advanced degrees. In America women hold only one of ten Ph.D.s and only one of sixteen M.D.s (25). America is, by no means, atypical. Men hold the important jobs and enjoy more privileges and status than women in most societies. One investigator who studied ninety-six nonliterate cultures found that women dominated only four or five, shared equal status in several more, but in the vast majority of cases the cultures were dominated by men. Similarly, in most cultures women play the nurturant and obedient role; men the self-reliant and achieving one (26).

These findings lead some people to conclude that the status quo is ordained by biology and is the natural order of things. Many social scientists, arguing against this position, assert that sex roles developed as a response to specific conditions of life. Our own sex-role standards probably originated at a time when strength was necessary for survival. Men have a greater muscle-to-fat ratio than women, even at birth. They also tend to be taller, heavier, and consequently, physically stronger. In a world where staying alive depended on physical strength, men were better suited than women for particular tasks such as hunting food, protecting families, clearing land, and herding. Women assumed the roles that required less strength—cooking and cleaning, notable among them—and they bore and took care of children. This specialization of labor was once necessary. As conditions changed, other role arrangements became possible (and many would argue, desirable).

Margaret Mead, an eminent cultural anthropologist, was one of the first to show that typical male and female sex roles can vary markedly from culture to culture. In the early 1930s she visited New Guinea where she studied three primitive tribes which displayed three distinct sex-role patterns:

We found the Arapesh—both men and women—displaying a personality that, out of our historically limited pre-occupations, we would call maternal in its parental aspects, and feminine in its sexual aspects. We found men, as well as women, trained to be cooperative, unaggressive, responsive to the needs and demands of others. We found no idea that sex was a powerful driving force either for men or for women. In marked contrast to these attitudes, we found among the Mundugumor, that both men and women developed as ruthless, aggressive, positively-sexed individuals, with the maternal cherishing aspects of personality at a minimum. Both men and women approximated to a personality type that we in our culture would find only in an undisciplined and very violent male. Neither the Arapesh nor the Mundugumor profit by a contrast between the sexes: The Arapesh ideal is the mild, responsive man, married to the mild, responsive woman; the Mundugumor ideal is the violent aggressive man married to the violent, aggressive woman. In the third tribe, the Tchambuli, we found a genuine reversal of the sex-attitudes of our own culture, with the woman, the dominant, impersonal, managing partner, the man the less responsible and the emotionally dependent person. These three situations suggest, then, a very definite conclusion. If those temperamental attitudes which we have traditionally regarded as feminine—such as passivity, responsiveness, and a willingness to cherish children—can so easily be set up as the masculine pattern in one tribe, and in another to be outlawed for the majority of men [and women], we no longer have any basis for regarding such aspects of behavior as sex-linked.

We are forced to conclude that human nature is almost unbelievably malleable, responding accurately and contrastingly to contrasting cultural conditions [27].

Mead's work suggests that regardless of innate physiological differences, the roles of men and women are extremely flexible and are not limited to particular patterns.

Summary: The Endocrine System and Sex-typed Behavior

1. Genes endow male and female embryos with different sex chromosomes that structure the development of the appropriate set of gonads. The hormones secreted by the gonads direct further sexual differentiation.
2. In the male the testes produce large quantities of the androgens, causing the masculine reproductive organs to develop. At a sensitive period near birth the androgens also organize the male fetus's hypothalamus and possibly other central nervous system structures.
3. When no hormones or femin mones are present during the period, feminine reproductive organs are structured. The effects of the estrogens on the brain are uncertain.
4. A brain which has been organized by the androgens mediates masculine sex-typed behavior patterns in animals (including people). When a brain has not been organized by the androgens, animals are likely to display feminine sex-typed behavior patterns.
5. Social and psychological factors also play an extremely important role in shaping masculine and feminine human behavior.

STUDY GUIDE 4

Key Terms. physiological psychology, central nervous system (CNS), peripheral nervous system (PNS), autonomic nervous system, somatic nervous system, sensory pathway, motor pathway, neuron, soma, dendrites, axon, threshold, fire, synapse, transmitter substances, spinal cord, brain, central core, limbic system, cerebrum, cerebral cortex, sensory regions, motor regions, association areas, cerebral hemispheres, frontal lobes, parietal lobes, temporal lobes, occipital lobes, reticular formation, amygdala, hypothalamus, localized, phrenology, lesion, electrode, microelectrode, electroencephalograph (EEG);

hippocampus, memory trace (engram), sensory representation system, short-term memory system, long-term memory system, retrograde amnesia, consolidate, retrieve, corpus callosum, split brain, reverberating loop, decay, ribonucleic acid (RNA), deoxyribonucleic acid (DNA), proteins, vestibular nuclei;

endocrine system, hormone, sex hormones, gonads, ovaries, testes, adrenals, estrogens, progestins, androgens, testosterone, primary sex characteristics, secondary sex characteristics, puberty, genetic sex, chromosomes, sexual identity, sex-typed behavior, hermaphrodite, fetally androgenized girls, androgen-insensitivity syndrome.

Important Research. removal of the temporal lobes in monkeys (Klüver and Bucy), electrical stimulation of the brain (Penfield), effects of brain surgery on rats' memories (Lashley), split-brain research (Sperry), RNA and memory storage (Hydén), transfer of learning in planaria (McConnell), transplanted gonads and sexual identity (Pfeiffer), early sex hormones and sex-typed behavior (Money and Ehrhardt), differences in parental treatment of boys and girls (Lewis), sex roles in other cultures (Mead).

Self-Quiz

1. One major function of the peripheral nervous system is to [a] mediate complex processes such as thinking and remembering; [b] coordinate basic reflexes; [c] relay information to and from the central nervous system; [d] seek satisfactions for the

body's recurring needs for food, water, sleep, sex, and protection.

2. Compared with a weak stimulus, a strong one may cause a neuron to [**a**] secrete a larger quantity of transmitter substances; [**b**] fire more intense nerve impulses; [**c**] fire more frequently; [**d**] fire longer-lasting nerve impulses.

3. Neurons in the body fire [**a**] continually, as long as we are alive; [**b**] only when we are awake; [**c**] when we are awake or when we are dreaming; [**d**] when an outside event stimulates them.

4. Brain centers in the central core control [**a**] information about bodily needs for food, water, sleep, and sex; [**b**] routine activities such as blood circulation, digestion, and breathing; [**c**] simple associative processes involving previously learned information; [**d**] complex associative processes such as thinking and learning new information.

5. The cerebral cortex has all of the following *except* [**a**] association areas; [**b**] reflexive behavior areas; [**c**] sensory regions; [**d**] motor regions.

6. The limbic system, along with the cerebral cortex, controls [**a**] motives and emotions; [**b**] alertness and attention; [**c**] memory; [**d**] sensory functions.

7. Which technique has been widely used to draw "maps" showing how the parts of the human brain function? [**a**] Experimental brain lesions; [**b**] studies of accidental brain injury; [**c**] electrical recording using the EEG; [**d**] electrical stimulation.

8. The memory problem of H. M., who underwent brain surgery to control his seizures, was largely due to a loss of [**a**] long-term memory; [**b**] intelligence; [**c**] the ability to make sensory representations; [**d**] consolidation abilities.

9. When Lashley taught rats complex mazes, then removed parts of their cerebral cortexes, he found that [**a**] amount of memory loss depended on what part of the cortex had been removed; [**b**] amount of memory loss depended on how much of the cortex had been removed; [**c**] the rats were unable to relearn any mazes; [**d**] the rats could relearn simple mazes but not complex ones.

10. If a common object is observed in the left visual field of a right-handed person after a split-brain operation, the person can [**a**] easily name the object; [**b**] easily choose a matching object by touch, but cannot name it; [**c**] rarely identify it in any way; [**d**] easily describe, but not name, the object.

11. The nondominant cerebral hemisphere plays a major role in [**a**] emotional experiences; [**b**] controlling the right side of the body; [**c**] language; [**d**] arithmetic and logic.

12. The results of McConnell's planaria experiments suggest that [**a**] memories can be transmitted chemically from one animal to another; [**b**] memories are contained in RNA; [**c**] memories are made through structural changes in the synapses between neurons; [**d**] planaria are incapable of remembering complex information.

13. Hormones are [**a**] chemicals that endocrine glands secrete directly into the blood stream; [**b**] chemicals that control bodily processes such as metabolism and growth; [**c**] chemicals that can stimulate the nervous system; [**d**] all of the above.

14. If a girl is exposed to too much androgen shortly before birth, she [**a**] is likely to develop masculine characteristics and behavior; [**b**] is likely to develop feminine characteristics and behavior prematurely; [**c**] will probably become a lesbian or be asexual; [**d**] will probably not be affected physically or behaviorally.

15. Genetic males who become feminized physically because of the androgen-insensitivity syndrome and are then reared as girls usually [**a**] remain masculine in personality characteristics and habits; [**b**] discover that they are genetically male and assume the masculine role; [**c**] develop feminine habits and interests; [**d**] fail to adjust to either a masculine or a feminine role.

Exercise

CENTRAL NERVOUS SYSTEM FUNCTIONS. In the following list, match each function with the central nervous system structure that controls it (remember that many structures may have more than one function). Use these abbreviations: spinal cord—SC; central core—Core; limbic system—LS; cerebrum—C; cerebral cortex—CC; reticular formation—RF; occipital lobes—OL; temporal lobes—TL; hippocampus—H; corpus callosum—Call.

_____ 1. Wrinkled outer layer of the cerebrum that contains sensory, motor, and association areas.

_____ 2. Carries messages to and from the brain.

_____ 3. Appears to help convert short-term memories into long-term memories.

_____ 4. Plays a role in the control of vision.

_____ 5. Helps keep animals alert and attentive.

_____ 6. Most recent brain division to evolve; integrates complex cognitive processes.

_____ 7. Coordinates many reflexes.

_____ 8. Pathways connecting right and left cerebral hemispheres permitting them to share learning and memories.

_____ 9. Receives incoming information about sights, sounds, and feelings.

____ **10.** Controls routine processes such as digestion and breathing.

____ **11.** When electrically stimulated, memories of past experiences sometimes occur.

____ **12.** Influences motives and emotions (along with the cerebral cortex).

Questions to Consider

1. Explain why psychologists study physiology.

2. Do you think that all human behavior will someday be explained in terms of underlying physiological processes?

3. Have any personal experiences convinced you that memories remain within the brain but become difficult to retrieve?

4. Enumerate the advantages (benefits) and disadvantages (costs) of current American sex roles. How could you design new sex roles for men and women which are consistent with physiology but do not force people into narrow stereotypes?

Project 4: Right and Left Gazing and Right and Left Thinking

Studies show that the right and left cerebral hemispheres are responsible for different functions. The dominant hemisphere (the left in right-handed people) may be described as primarily responsible for analytic, rational thinking and language, whereas the nondominant hemisphere may be described as primarily responsible for conceptualizing spatial relationships and comprehending emotional experiences. Psychologist Robert Ornstein suggests that eye movements provide a clue to this specialization of the hemispheres. Ornstein and his associates have observed that right-handed people tend to gaze in one direction (usually toward their right) when thinking about logical or verbal problems, and toward their left when thinking about spatial problems. (For more details about Ornstein's work, see Robert Ornstein. "Right and left thinking." *Psychology Today*, May 1973, 6, 87–92.) The purpose of this project is to test Ornstein's directed-gazing hypothesis.

Method. Choose six cooperative subjects. Do not use people who are in your psychology class or who are likely to know about Ornstein's research. Explain to the subjects that they will be participating in a small research study, but do not tell them the purpose of the research until after you have made your observations. You will be testing each subject one at a time.

Set up a space for making observations. It must be quiet and free from all distractions. Have your subject face you directly. (It is absolutely imperative that you not sit off to one side.) Sitting on opposite sides of a table works well.

Tell your subject that you will be asking six questions one at a time and that you will be writing down the answers. Do not carry on any further conversation with the subject during the questioning period. Ask each subject the following questions:

1. (Analytic-verbal) Define the word "conscience."

2. (Analytic-verbal) Spell the word "parallel."

3. (Analytic-verbal) How much is 8 times 13?

4. (Spatial) Which way does George Washington face on a quarter?

5. (Spatial) Describe the way the furniture is arranged in your bedroom.

6. (Spatial) Give instructions to go from your home to _____. (Insert "work," "school," or another familiar place) using the same mode of transportation as usual.

Vary the order of the questions. Use the order shown in data sheet 1 for three subjects and the order shown in data sheet 2 for three subjects.

Make up data sheets for your subjects like the ones shown. Observe and record the predominant direction in which each subject gazes as he/she thinks about each question. You are interested in the subject's right or left, *not* your right or left. Be sure to find out whether each subject is right or left handed.

Results. In what direction did each subject gaze predominantly for the analytic-verbal questions? for the spatial questions? Did your results agree with Ornstein's? That is, did the majority of right-handed subjects gaze right in thinking about analytic-verbal questions and left in thinking about spatial questions? Did the majority of left-handed subjects gaze left in thinking about analytic-verbal questions and right in thinking about spatial questions?

Discussion. Consider the following questions.

1. Did you obtain support for Ornstein's findings?

2. How can positive findings be interpreted? Do they prove that the two cerebral hemispheres are specialized in function? What do they suggest?

3. If your results did not support Ornstein's findings, speculate on possible reasons.

4. Could your own expectations have influenced your subjects' behavior?

5. What problems occurred? How could this study be better designed?

6. What was the point of varying the order of the questions?

DATA SHEETS (one needed for each subject)

Sheet 1

Question Number	Direction of Gaze	Subject is _____ handed
1 (AV)	_____	
4 (S)	_____	
5 (S)	_____	
2 (AV)	_____	
6 (S)	_____	
3 (AV)	_____	

Sheet 2

Question Number	Direction of Gaze	Subject is _____ handed
6 (S)	_____	
3 (AV)	_____	
2 (AV)	_____	
5 (S)	_____	
1 (AV)	_____	
4 (S)	_____	

Suggested Readings

1. Wooldridge, Dean. *The machinery of the brain.* McGraw-Hill Book Company, 1963 (paperback). Wooldridge describes the brain and research on its functioning.
2. Isaacson, Robert L. "When brains are damaged." *Psychology Today*, January 1970, 3, 38–42. Discussion of animal studies which demonstrate the different effects of brain damage on infants and adults.
3. Gazzaniga, Michael. "The split brain in man." *Scientific American*, August 1967, 217, 2, 24–29. Survey of research investigations on patients with split brains.
4. Howe, M. J. A. *An introduction to human memory.* New York: Harper & Row, Publishers, Incorporated, 1970 (paperback). A brief introduction which covers recent memory research.
5. Norman, Donald A. *Memory and attention.* New York: John Wiley & Sons, Inc., 1969. Very readable discussion of memory and attention. Emphasizes broad issues of human information processing.
6. Bermant, Gordon, & Julian M. Davidson. *Biological bases of sexual behavior.* New York: Harper & Row, Publishers, Incorporated, 1974 (paperback). A comprehensive introduction to the subject. Takes an evolutionary perspective and emphasizes neurological, hormonal, and environmental determinants of sexual behavior.
7. Money, John, & Anke Ehrhardt. *Man and woman, boy and girl.* Baltimore: The Johns Hopkins Press, 1972 (paperback). A discussion of sexual differentiation drawing on research in genetics, embryology, and endocrinology, as well as psychology and anthropology. Difficult in spots.
8. Rosenberg, B. G., & Brian Sutton-Smith. *Sex and identity.* New York: Holt, Rinehart and Winston, Inc., 1972 (paperback). Explores the development of sex roles from many perspectives.

Answer Keys

SELF-QUIZ
1. c 2. c 3. a 4. b 5. b 6. a 7. d 8. d 9. b
10. b 11. a 12. a 13. d 14. a 15. c

EXERCISE
1. CC 2. SC 3. H 4. OL 5. RF 6. C 7. SC
8. Call 9. CC, RF 10. Core 11. TL 12. LS

PERCEIVING

IN THIS CHAPTER

We focus on perceiving, the process by which people take in information about the world surrounding them. After briefly describing the physiological processes underlying perception, we turn to vision to illustrate two characteristics of perceptual processes: (1) their high level of organization and (2) their dependency on both innate and environmental factors. We also explore the question: Does extrasensory perception exist? After reading this chapter, you should be able to do the following:

1. Explain the role of the sensory systems, the brain, and attention in perception
2. List three principles that people use to organize their perception of form and ten cues that they use to organize their perception of depth and distance
3. Cite evidence that seeing is influenced by genetics, experience, active learning, light, deprivation of patterned sensory stimulation, experience within a culture, and psychological states
4. List arguments for and against the existence of extrasensory perception

One bright May morning in the spring of 1953, Aldous Huxley, the writer, swallowed four-tenths of a gram of mescaline. Huxley was playing guinea pig. An investigator remained with him and recorded their conversations. Later Huxley described his perceptual experiences under mescaline.[1]

"What about spatial relationships?" the investigator inquired. . . .

It was difficult to answer. True, the perspective looked rather odd, and the walls of the room no longer seemed to meet in right angles. But these were not the really important facts. The really important facts were that spatial relationships had ceased to matter very much and that my mind was perceiving the world in terms of other than spatial categories. At ordinary times the eye concerns itself with such problems as *Where?— How far?—How situated in relation to what?* In the mescaline experience the implied questions to which the eye responds are of another order. Place and distance cease to be of much interest. The mind does its perceiving in terms of intensity of existence, profundity of significance, relationships with a pattern. I saw the books, but was not at all concerned with their positions in space. What I noticed, what impressed itself upon my mind was the fact that all of them glowed with living light and that in some the glory was more manifest than in others. In this context, position and the three dimensions were beside the point. Not, of course, that the category of space had been abolished. . . . Space was still there but it had lost its predominance [1].

We define *perception* as the process of extracting information from the environment. We make perceptions automatically and unconsciously. Our senses take in raw data— data on sights, sounds, smells, and textures in the world around us. Both the senses and the brain organize and interpret the data. What we perceive depends on both processes. Perhaps William James put it more clearly: "Part

[1]The book that resulted (*The doors of perception.* New York: Harper & Row, 1954) makes very interesting reading.

of what we perceive," he wrote, "comes through our senses from the object before us, another part . . . always comes out of our own head [2]." Huxley's perceptions under mescaline show these processes at work. Huxley's senses are probably bringing in the raw data as they ordinarily do; the organizational processes which order and interpret these data appear to be affected by mescaline.

People usually assume that their perceptions of the world are accurate: that they reflect precisely what is out there. It can easily be demonstrated that perception involves interpretation and that interpretation produces distortions.

Is the middle character in Figure 5-1a the letter B or the number 13? Is the middle character in Figure 5-1b an A or an H? In both these cases the context clearly influences what we see when we look at the same sensory stimulus.

Which horizontal line in Figure 5-2 looks longer? Most people find that the upper line looks longer, but both lines are precisely the same length (see page 133 for an explanation).

We turn now to the physiological basis of perception.

THE PHYSIOLOGICAL BASIS OF PERCEPTION

How does perception operate? The perceptual process depends on both the sensory systems and the brain. The sensory systems

Figure 5-1. Context influences our perception of sensory stimuli.

receive information from the environment, convert the information into nerve impulses, process some of the information, and send most of it via nerve fibers to the central nervous system. The central nervous system plays the major role in information processing.

The Sensory Systems

Our bodies are equipped with a number of specialized information-gathering systems. These systems, which we call *senses*, enable us to perceive the surrounding environment. The early Greek philosopher Aristotle believed that there were five senses—vision, hearing, taste, smell, and touch. It took more than two thousand years to discover that there were more. Contemporary scientists have catalogued more than ten distinct senses. Touch turned out to be composed of four different skin senses, which detect pressure, warmth, cold, and pain. Two additional senses were not included at all in the traditional five: the kinesthetic sense and the vestibular sense. The *kinesthetic sense* depends on receptors in the muscles, tendons, and joints that inform people about the positioning of the body and its parts as they move. If you close your eyes and bend your fingers, for example, this sensory system makes you aware of the movement. The *vestibular sense* depends on receptors in the boney parts of the skull in both inner ears. It informs people about the movement and positioning of the head and body when they move on their own and when they are propelled through space by cars, planes, boats, and so on.

How do the senses operate? Each sense has a detection element called a *receptor*, a single cell or group of cells that respond to specific kinds of energy. Cells in the eyes respond to certain light photons, a form of electromagnetic energy called visible light. Cells in the ears respond to vibrations in the air, a form

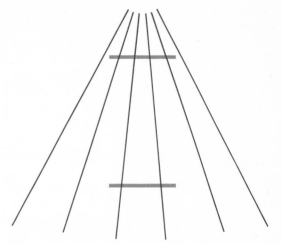

Figure 5-2. A visual illusion based on cues from linear perspective.

of mechanical energy called sound. Each receptor is responsive to a narrow range of stimuli. Receptors in our eyes, for example, respond to visible light, which is a tiny fraction of the electromagnetic energy spectrum. The electromagnetic spectrum also includes radio waves, gamma rays, infrared rays, and ultraviolet rays, but we cannot see these other rays.[2] Similarly, receptor cells in the ears respond to vibrations of matter in the approximate range of 20 to 20,000 cycles per second. Mechanical vibrations extending into the millions of cycles per second frequently occur, but we cannot hear them.

Each time a receptor is stimulated by energy in the environment, it behaves like a *transducer*, a device that converts energy from one form to another. If the incoming energy is sufficiently intense, it triggers nerve impulses that carry coded information about various features of the stimulus along nerve fibers to the brain (see Chapter 4).

Other cells within the sensory system serve an information processing function. We consider vision to illustrate, after we look briefly

[2] We actually have another sense, the warmth sense in the skin, that responds to infrared radiation.

at the anatomy of the eye. A few of the basic parts of the eye—those with which we will be concerned—are shown in Figure 5-3. The human eye can be pictured as a dark chamber with an opening in front, the *pupil*, which admits light. The *iris*, the colored disk surrounding the pupil, controls the amount of light entering the chamber by changing the size of the pupil. When lighting conditions are dim, the iris causes the pupil to become larger, allowing more light to enter the eye. Under conditions of intense illumination, the iris causes the pupil to contract to reduce the amount of light. The visible part of the eye is covered by a transparent covering, the *cornea*. The cornea protects the eye and focuses images of objects in the visual field onto the rear inner surface of the eye, the *retina*. The *lens*, located behind the pupil, also helps focus incoming visual images onto the retina. Incidentally, the images that fall on the retina are inverted and reversed from left to right. The retina itself is composed of multiple layers of light-sensitive receptor cells called *rods* and *cones*. These cells convert the incoming light rays into nerve impulses that are subsequent-

Figure 5-3. Some basic parts of the human eye.

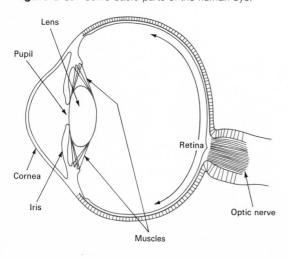

ly channeled to various centers in the brain by the fibers that make up the *optic nerve.*

How does the eye process information? In 1959, Jerome Lettvin, Humberto Maturana, Warren McCulloch, and W. H. Pitts, scientists at the Massachusetts Institute of Technology, published a classic study on the frog's visual system. The study demonstrated that the frog's brain receives material that has been highly processed and organized into specific patterns within the frog's retina. Lettvin and his associates immobilized frogs, one at a time, and placed and moved small objects around in their visual field. Electrodes implanted within the frog's optic nerve measured "what the frog's eye told the frog's brain." The investigators discovered that no matter how complex or subtle the stimulus, receptor cells in the frog's eyes detected only four distinct pieces of information, which were channeled via four distinct groups of fibers to the *tectum* (the frog's chief visual brain center): (1) Sustained contrast detectors honed in on the general outlines of objects in the frog's environment. (2) Moving edge detectors gathered information about suddenly moving objects. (3) Net dimming detectors registered sudden decreases in light (like those that might occur when an enemy attacked). (4) Net convexity detectors responded only when small, round, dark objects darted near the frog's eye. (This last system enables frogs to capture flying bugs.) In short, the frog's eye analyzes and extracts important survival-related information from its visual field and sends the information to its brain. The eyes of higher animals, such as people, work on the same principle: They help reduce the amount of useless information that reaches the brain, thereby increasing the chance that people will attend to important stimuli. However, in higher animals less information is processed in the eyes and more is processed in the brain.

The Brain

Most sensory information processing takes place in the cortex in higher animals. Through studies of cats David Hubel and Torsten Weisel, physiologists at the Harvard Medical School, have learned something about how the cortex processes visual information. Hubel and Weisel placed anesthetized cats in front of a wide screen on which they projected patterns of light. Microelectrodes in the visual portion of the cat's cortex recorded the responses of individual cortical cells to the various light patterns. Hubel and Weisel discovered that the visual cortex seemed to be organized like a beehive. Tiny columns, composed of thousands of cells, extend from its surface to its center. Information from a small region in the visual field projects onto a small area on the retina that is, in turn, represented by a specific *cortical column.* Each cortical column contains specialized cells that respond to different features in the visual field. Cells near the surface respond to information about particular shapes, edges, lines, or slits at particular angles. Cells farther back respond to more complex information such as moving edges, corners, or parallel lines. Cells even deeper integrate the various inputs. Changes in the visual field produce changes in the pattern of firing in cells of the corresponding cortical column. The brain deciphers the coded nerve impulses from the cortical columns, combines and integrates them, compares them with past impressions, makes decisions, and initiates appropriate actions.

Attention and Perception

During every waking moment enormous numbers of sensory stimuli compete for our attention. We do not attend equally to all of them. Like a movie camera, we selectively focus first on one event and then on another; the stimuli that are not in the center of our attention form a background. At a party, for example, we listen to one conversation while the others blur together, forming a background noise of which we are only dimly aware. Should someone call our name, however, our attention easily shifts at once to the new stimulus. Similarly, as you read, you are probably at least vaguely aware of your surroundings; perhaps of the position in which you are sitting, the temperature of the air, the color of the walls, noises, other people, and so on. We define *attention* as a selective openness to a small portion of impinging sensory phenomena. We continually select a small trickle of incoming sensory impressions to attend to. But what directs our attention? Needs, interests, and values, determine, in part, what will attract and hold our attention. The teacher absorbed in a lecture may hardly notice the bell signaling the end of class. The student who is looking forward to lunch and the companionship of friends is keenly aware of the same stimulus. The physiology of the brain and sensory systems also determines how attention is focused. All animals attend to the objects and events in the environment and particularly to those that are novel, unexpected, intense, or changing. This perceptual style has important survival value: It allows animals to locate and manipulate objects in space, to move without collisions, and to respond to unexpected dangers. If animals attended to everything at once, important survival cues would probably be lost amidst the clutter.

Summary: The Physiological Basis of Perception

1. People have at least ten senses, which help them gather information about the sensory world.

complicated systems. They
and process information.
sensory information to the
system for further infor-
...tion processing.

3. Living things attend selectively to only a small portion of the sensory stimuli which impinge upon them. The focus of their attention is influenced by their internal needs, interests, values, and goals and by the physiology of their eyes and brains, which have evolved to detect environmental stimuli that are novel, unexpected, intense, or changing.

THE PERCEPTUAL SYSTEMS: EMPHASIS ON VISION

The ten senses can be grouped into five major perceptual systems, following the lead of James J. Gibson, a sensory psychologist at Cornell University: a basic orienting system, an auditory system, a haptic (skin) system, a

taste-smell system, and a visual system (3). (See Table 5-1). Although all these systems are important, vision gives people most of their information about the environment. In fact, when sensory information is contradictory, people usually believe their eyes. Also, because it is very accessible for study, more research exists on the visual system, and, consequently, it is better understood, than any other perceptual system. For these reasons we focus now on vision to illustrate two characteristics of perceptual processes: (1) their high level of organization and (2) their dependency on both innate and environmental factors.

THE ORGANIZATION OF VISUAL PERCEPTION

The things of the world register on the retina of the eye as patterns of colored shapes; yet we see clear, distinct objects which are meaningfully related to one another. Why? The

TABLE 5-1. THE FIVE MAJOR PERCEPTUAL SYSTEMS

System	Types of Information Obtained or Responded to	Sense(s) Involved
Basic Orientation	Direction of gravity, acceleration	Vestibular (primarily)
Auditory	Nature and location of sound	Hearing
Haptic	Mechanical encounters, object shapes, material states (solidity or viscosity), temperature	Pain, pressure, heat, warmth, kinesthetic
Taste-Smell	Odors, nutritive values	Taste, smell
Visual	Location, shape, identity, and movement of objects and animals	Sight

Adapted from: J. J. Gibson. *The senses considered as perceptual systems.* Boston: Houghton Mifflin, 1966.

Figure 5-4. The shape of the clock is perceived as circular even when it is viewed from different angles.

data that our senses bring in are continually being internally organized, usually so rapidly and automatically that we are completely unaware of the organizing process itself. While high on mescaline, Aldous Huxley became intensely conscious of organizing principles. Questions such as Where? How far? and How situated in relation to what?—questions that ordinarily structure everyone's perception of space—stopped organizing Huxley's perceptions. In this section we turn to some of the principles that ordinarily structure visual perception in people and, apparently, in many other animals. As we shall see later on, these principles seem to depend both on inborn physiological mechanisms within the sensory and nervous systems and on experience.

The Perception of Objects

The following principles organize our perception of objects:

Constancy. We regard the size, shape, and color of an object as being constant. In other words, even though we view an object from a different angle, or at a different distance, or under different conditions of illumination, it does not appear to change shape, size, or color. Some examples: A person viewed from close or far is judged the same height. A circular clock face viewed from the side still appears circular, even though it projects an elliptical image on the retina. Similarly, white sheets in a dimly lit room continue to look white even though they reflect less light than in bright sunlight (see Figure 5-4).

Figure-ground relationships. We tend to see objects (or *figures*) standing out from a background (or *ground*) whenever we look around. Figures seem to own the contour that is common to figure and ground and to be in front of the ground. A figure may stand out because it seems nearer, more objectlike, more vivid, more definitely shaped, or more solidly colored than the ground (4). Even when the field lacks clear boundaries and visual stimuli run into one another, we manage to extract figures from the background. No clear boundaries form on the retina, as you look at Figure 5-5. Yet once you have distinguished the gray tree frog, it will immediately stand out from the background every time you look at this picture. As long as our senses and brains are operating normally, one figure always stands out from a ground. The figure in Figure 5-6 fluctuates. Sometimes we see two faces on a vague white background. At other times we see a vase on a featureless blue background. The reversals occur spontaneously and are hard to control. Still, although we alternate between the two figures, only one figure dominates at any one time.

Grouping. We tend to unify separate elements into patterns. The following rules are among those that govern our groupings:

1. *Similarity*: Visual elements with the same color, shape, or texture are seen as belonging together. In viewing Figure 5-7a most people report seeing alternating rows of light and dark squares rather than forty-

Figure 5-6. Reversals in perception of figure and ground sometimes occur spontaneously.

19
12
18
12
30

Figure 5-5. Even when the visual field lacks clear boundaries and visual stimuli run into one another, we manage to extract figures—in this case, the tree frog—from the background. (New York Zoological Society.)

nine squares. Similarly, we see alternating lines of triangles and squares in Figure 5-7*b*.

2. *Symmetry or Good Figure*: Visual elements that form regular, simple, symmetrical shapes are seen as belonging together. When they view Figure 5-8, most people report seeing two overlapping squares, rather than two irregularly shaped figures and a triangle.

3. *Proximity*: Visual elements near one another are seen as belonging together (see Figure 5-9). Proximity leads us to organize pattern (*a*) into columns, pattern (*b*) into

rows, and pattern (*c*) into diagonals that run from top right to bottom left or from top left to bottom right.

4. *Continuity*: Visual elements that form smooth regular patterns are seen as belonging together. We see the dots in Figure 5-10 form smooth curves. When the curves cross, the eye does not become confused; rather it continues in the same direction.

5. *Closure*: Incomplete objects are usually seen as complete (a tendency known as *closure*). The disconnected lines in Figure 5-11 are usually perceived as complete objects. Even when images of objects cross the blind spot (a point on the retina where

Figure 5-7. Visual elements with the same color or shape appear to belong together.

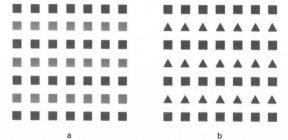

a   b

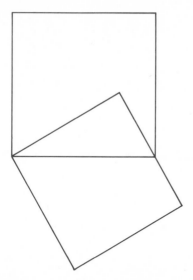

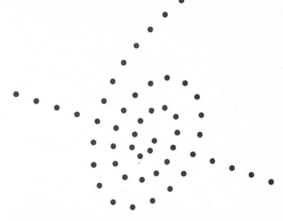

Figure 5-10. Smooth, regular patterns are perceived as continuous.

Figure 5-8. Simple symmetrical forms appear to belong together.

there are no visual receptor cells), objects look complete and uninterrupted.

The Perception of Depth and Distance

The surface of the retina is like a movie screen. It registers images in two dimensions:

Figure 5-9. Proximity influences the perception of figures. (From Dember, 1960.)

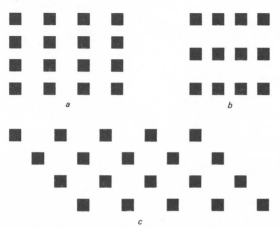

left-right and up-down. Yet people and other animals perceive a three-dimensional world. How are our perceptions organized to do this? We use a number of *cues* (sources of information), including the following:

Physiological cues. Because the eyes are located in different positions, each retina registers a slighly different visual image. This phenomenon is known as *binocular disparity.* Evidently, the brain is able to use the information contained in the two different two-dimensional images to reconstruct a three-dimensional world.

Figure 5-11. Even when lines are broken, objects are perceived as complete.

Another depth cue, of less practical importance, is *convergence*. As our eyes fixate on a nearby object, they turn in toward one another; the kinesthetic feedback from the eye muscles gives people some idea of how distant an object is. Both convergence and binocular disparity are *binocular depth cues* (cues that depend on the operation of both eyes).

Even if we didn't have two eyes, we would still perceive depth by *monocular depth cues* (cues that require the operation of only one eye). As we look at an object, the lens system of the eye focuses the incoming light rays onto the retina by a process called *accommodation*. Muscles in the eye either relax, allowing the lens to become thicker to focus nearby objects, or contract, causing the lens to become flatter to focus distant objects. The brain receives different kinesthetic sensations from the eye muscles. Because there are only minimal changes in the amount of accommodation beyond the distance of a few feet, this cue is not effective for estimating large distances.

Cues from movement. Whenever we move, our field of vision changes and objects that are close to us seem to move with greater speed than distant objects. We call this important monocular depth cue *motion parallax*. Motion parallax is very vivid when we are driving down a highway. Fence posts by the road seem to fly by at high speed, while trees in the distance glide by slowly. The relative motion of objects gives us stable cues to their distance.

Pictorial cues. A number of additional monocular depth cues depend on the rules of perspective that have enabled artists to portray three-dimensional scenes on flat canvases for centuries. These rules are based on the principles that guide the perception of objects. They include the following six pictorial cues.

1. *Perceived size*: Whenever we see a familiar object, we can roughly gauge its distance by noting the size of our retinal image. When the image is relatively large, we assume that the object is near; when the image is relatively small, we assume that the object is distant (see Figure 5-12). We judge the shoes to be near, the man more

Figure 5-12. Because of their relative sizes, we perceive the shoes as being close, the man more distant, and the woman farthest from us. (Annan Photo Features.)

Figure 5-13. These railroad tracks converging in the distance illustrate the depth cue, linear perspective. (John Briggs.)

distant, and the woman farthest from us.

2. *Linear perspective*: Consider the railroad tracks in Figure 5-13. We know that the distance between the tracks is constant and that the tracks are therefore parallel. However, the tracks appear to converge. Why? Examine the railroad ties between the tracks. The nearby ties cast a relatively large retinal image. Distant ties, although physically the same size, cast a smaller retinal image, as we just discussed. Therefore, the distant parts of the tracks appear closer to each other. The apparent change in the size of objects at different distances from the eye produces the depth cue known as *linear perspective*.

Recall the second illusion (Figure 5-2), which we presented at the beginning of the chapter. In viewing this figure, we tend to assume that the converging vertical lines represent parallel lines (like those which define a highway or railroad) receding into the distance. Because of this interpretation, the upper horizontal line appears to be farther than the lower line. Since the horizontal lines project equal-

sized images on the retina, the laws of perspective cause us to perceive the upper (more distant) line as longer.

3. *Light and shadow*: When light from a specific source, like the sun, strikes a three-dimensional object, it illuminates the side(s) of the object facing the light source and leaves the other side(s) in shadow. The pattern of light and shadow gives the observer the impression of three dimensionality (see Figure 5-14).

4. *Aerial perspective*: Haze usually present in the atmosphere makes distant objects ap-

Figure 5-14. Light and shadow create the impression of three dimensionality. (R. Trachtman.)

Figure 5-15. Because of aerial perspective, the "hazy" buildings seem most distant.
(Bahnson, from Monkmeyer.)

pear bluish, blurred, and indistinct. For this reason we perceive distinct objects as being close, and hazy objects as being distant (see Figure 5-15).

5. *Texture gradients*: Objects in the visual field show gradual changes in texture as they become more distant; they appear coarse nearby and finer as the observer looks farther into the distance (see Figure 5-16). The stones near the observer stand out separately; those farther away tend to blend together.

6. *Interposition*: Objects sometimes obstruct the view of other objects. We perceive the complete object as being closer than the obstructed object (see Figure 5-17).

Summary: The Organization of Visual Perception

1. We are continually organizing the information we take in from the visual world that surrounds us.

2. Our perception of objects is structured by principles such as constancy, figure-ground and grouping.

3. To perceive a three-dimensional world people rely on physiological cues such as binocular disparity, convergence, and accommodation; cues from movement such as motion parallax; and pictorial cues such as perceived size, linear perspective, light

Figure 5-16. Stones in the foreground are distinct, those in the distance blurred. Texture gradients like this one provide important depth cues. (Annan Photo Features.)

Figure 5-17. Obstructed objects appear to be farther away than nonobstructed objects. (Harris Corporation, Cleveland, Ohio, and Litho-Krome Company, Columbus, Georgia.)

and shadow, aerial perspective, texture gradients, and interposition.

THE DETERMINANTS OF VISUAL PERCEPTION

In this section we examine the determinants of visual perception. We look first at the visual world of the young infant to learn whether visual organizing tendencies appear to be at least partly inborn.

The Visual World of the Infant

It is known that young infants respond to light, color, and movement, but do they organize their sensations into recognizable forms, patterns, and objects in a three-dimensional world? Or are they simply bombarded by moving patches of color and light; that is, is their visual world a "blooming, buzzing confusion," as William James put it? In the early

1950s Robert Fantz, a psychologist then at the University of Chicago, became interested in investigating whether infants perceive form. In his early studies Fantz used chickens as subjects. He arranged for chicks to hatch in darkness. Immediately afterward he and his associates presented them with various geometrically shaped objects encased in clear plastic containers that eliminated cues of touch, smell, and taste. Each time the chicks pecked at one of the objects, an electrical circuit recorded the peck. More than one thousand chicks were observed, and approximately one hundred objects were used. The data showed that newly hatched chicks had strong pecking preferences: They clearly favored spheres to pyramids, flat circles to flat triangles, spheres to flat circles, and objects of one-eighth inch to any other size (see Figure 5-18). Evidently, chickens are born perceiving shape, size, and three dimensionality and preferring objects that resemble seeds and grains. These perceptions and preferences help them survive.

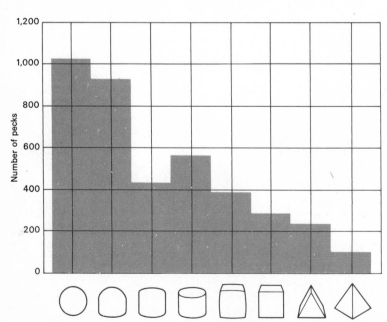

Figure 5-18. When 112 newborn chicks were allowed to peck at simple geometrical objects, they showed a clear preference for spheres during the first forty minutes of visual experience. (After Fantz, 1961.)

Figure 5-19. An improved version of Fantz' "looking chamber." The infant is placed in a semiupright adjustable seat facing the stimuli. An observation hole and mirror allow two experimenters to see the infant's eyes and observe the reflections of the stimuli on the pupils. (Robert L. Fantz.)

Fantz and his associates turned next to human infants. They used an apparatus called a "looking chamber" similar to the one pictured in Figure 5-19. Each infant was placed on its back in a comfortable crib inside the chamber. Test objects were attached to the ceiling of the chamber (which was uniform in color and illumination). The investigator watched the infant's eyes through a peephole in the ceiling. When tiny mirror images of the form appeared over the infant's pupil, the researcher knew that the infant was looking directly at the object. Fantz reasoned that if the infant spent a lot of time gazing at a particular object, then the infant must be able to recognize it.

In an initial experiment Fantz and his coworkers tested thirty infants at one to fifteen weeks of age. They presented four pairs of patterns in a random order while measuring the total time that the baby looked at each one. The pattern pairs included a bull's-eye and stripes, a checkerboard and solid-colored square, a solid-colored cross and a solid-colored circle, and two solid-colored triangles. The results (see Figure 5-20) showed that infants spent more time gazing at complex pairs. Moreover, the relative appeal of each pattern seemed to depend on its complexity. Other investigators have found similar results

at even earlier ages (5). Apparently, the perception of patterns appears at a very early point in development.

Do young infants also perceive depth? To research this question Eleanor Gibson and Richard Walk, psychologists at Cornell University, constructed a simulated cliff which they named a "visual cliff" (see Figure 5-21). A board spans the center of a heavy glass tabletop. On one side of the board, checkerboard-patterned material extends flush with the under surface of the glass, and the side appears solid. On the other side of the board, the same patterned material lies against the floor, causing this side to appear to drop off like a cliff. The sheet of glass eliminates tactile information, air currents, and echoes that might otherwise warn the infant of the drop; so the apparent drop is signaled only by visual cues—hence the name "*visual cliff*."

Rats, birds, turtles, chickens, cats, sheep, goats, dogs, chimpanzees, and human infants have all been tested on this apparatus, using the same general procedure: The animal is placed on the center board between the deep and shallow sides of the cliff and observed. If it avoids the deep side consistently, presumably it perceives depth. Land animals consistently avoid the deep side at a very early age,

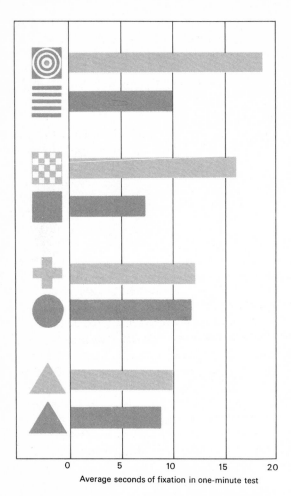

Average seconds of fixation in one-minute test

Figure 5-20. When infants are shown two patterns, they spend more time looking at the complex pattern than at the simple one. When patterns are of similar complexity, infants prefer curved to straight designs. The results shown were obtained from ten weekly tests on twenty-two infants. (After Fantz, 1961.)

even when they have had no opportunity to *learn* about either depth or distance. Rat infants, reared in darkness, for example, avoid the cliff immediately, even when it is their first visual experience. Several hours after birth, when chickens and goats first move about well enough to be tested, they too avoid the cliff. Nonland animals, such as sea turtles, do not avoid the deep side. Gibson

and Walk have discovered that day-old chicks and dark-reared rats use motion-parallax cues to discriminate depth. In the case of the visual cliff, motion parallax makes the pattern on the shallow side move more rapidly across the animal's visual field than the pattern on the deep side whenever the animal moves. It is not surprising that depth perception appears at the time that a land animal begins moving around. After all, the land animal's world contains many dangerous edges—holes, ravines, and cliffs—which the animal must avoid if it is to survive (6).

We humans are also land animals. What about our infants? Thirty-six human infants were tested on the visual cliff when they were

Figure 5-21. Human infants who are just beginning to crawl are quite consistent in avoiding the "deep" side of the "visual cliff." (Lawrence Rothblat.)

just beginning to crawl, at ages between six and fourteen months. The infant's mother stood twice at either end of the cliff beckoning her child to her. Twenty-seven infants moved off the center board. Of those twenty-seven, twenty-four willingly crawled to their mothers on the shallow side and refused to crawl to her on the deep side. Only three infants came when their mothers called them onto "the cliff." Apparently, human infants also perceive depth as soon as they can move about by themselves (7).

Do human infants perceive depth at younger ages? Size constancy is closely related to depth perception. Consider two cubes that project different-sized images on the retina. If we have reason to believe that the two cubes are the same size, then we must conclude that the cube projecting the smaller image is more distant. However, if we have reason to believe that the two cubes are the same distance, then we must conclude that the cube projecting the smaller image is, in fact, smaller.

T. G. R. Bower, a psychologist currently at Edinburgh University, and his colleagues studied size constancy and depth perception in six- to eight-week-old human infants. The infants were observed individually as they lay on a table. A white cube (approximately 12 inches on a side) was placed approximately 1 yard from the infant's eyes. Every time the infant turned its head left, the experimenter popped up, peek-a-booed (a reward), and disappeared quickly (see Figure 5-22). After a number of trials the infant learned to turn its head to the left each time the 12-inch white cube appeared at a distance of 1 yard.

To test the infant's perceptions, Bower introduced three new stimuli (1) an identical cube at a greater distance (about 3 yards), (2) a larger white cube (approximately 36 inches on a side) placed at the same distance (about 1 yard), and (3) a larger white cube (approximately 36 inches on a side) placed at a greater distance (about 3 yards). Note that the 36-inch cube at 3 yards projected the same size retinal image as the original 12-inch cube at 1 yard. Bower reasoned that if any of these stimuli looked similar to the original cube, then they too should elicit a head-turning response.

What were the results? The infants turned their heads left most frequently to the original cube at the original distance; they responded second-most frequently to the identical cube placed 3 yards away. Evidently they recognized the cube even at the further distance and found it most similar to the original stimulus. The infants responded next-most frequently to the 36-inch cube at one yard, and least frequently to the 36-inch cube at 3 yards. Evidently, the infants perceived the last stimulus as very different from the original one, even though it projected an identical image on the retina. Bower concluded that young infants have size constancy: They respond to real size and distance as early as six weeks of age (8).

In sum, the infant studies we have discussed show that some of the principles that organize people's perceptions appear very early and are probably influenced, at least in part, by genetic factors.

The Environment and Perception

Do environmental factors also affect the organization of perception? Psychologists study this issue in a number of ways: (1) by measuring the perceptual skills of infants and adults (frequently animals) after depriving them of potentially important experiences, (2) by observing how people adapt to severe perceptual distortions, (3) by examining the perceptions of members of different cultures, and (4) by exploring how motives, values, and emotions influence perceptual judgments. We turn to each of these topics.

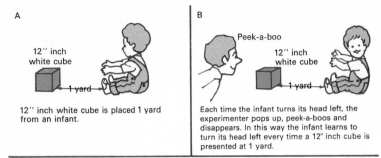

A

12" inch
white cube

← 1 yard →

12" inch white cube is placed 1 yard
from an infant.

B

Peek-a-boo
12" inch
white cube

← 1 yard →

Each time the infant turns its head left, the
experimenter pops up, peek-a-boos and
disappears. In this way the infant learns to
turn its head left every time a 12" inch cube is
presented at 1 yard.

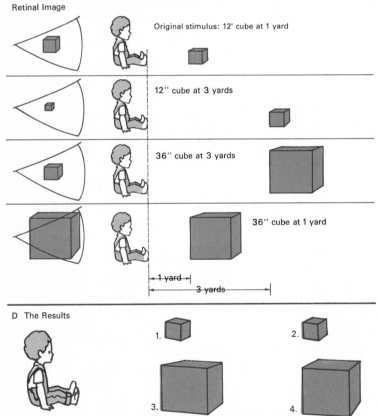

C   The questions
     a. Will the infant respond to any cube at one yard ?
     b. Will the infant respond to the 12-inch cube at any distance ?
     c. Will the infant respond to any cube at any distance as long as it
        projects an identical retinal image ?

Retinal Image

Original stimulus: 12" cube at 1 yard

12" cube at 3 yards

36" cube at 3 yards

36" cube at 1 yard

← 1 yard →
← 3 yards →

D The Results

1.   2.   3.   4.

Figure 5-22. Bower's study of size constancy.

Depriving animal infants of visual experiences. Does light affect the organization of perception? In 1942 Austin Riesen, a psychologist then at the Yerkes Laboratories of Primate Biology in Florida, began to investigate this question. Riesen studied chimpanzee infants because he could not study human ones. Chimpanzees make excellent subjects because, like humans, they are intelligent, adaptable, and strongly dependent on vision for sensory information. Riesen and his colleagues took two newborn chimpanzees and raised them in darkness for sixteen months. When they emerged from the darkness

. . . both chimpanzees showed extreme visual incompetence. Their reflex responses indicated that their eyes were sensitive to light. . . . But both chimpanzees failed to show any visual responses to complex patterns of light until after they had spent many hours in illuminated surroundings. They did not respond to play objects or their feeding bottles unless these touched some part of the body. They did not blink at a threatening motion toward the face. When an object was advanced slowly toward the face, there was no reaction until the object actually touched the face, and then the animal gave a startled jump [9].

What was responsible for these effects? Did darkness prevent the animal from learning important skills? Or did it cause important structures to atrophy because they had not been used? Later studies support the second explanation: Prolonged darkness results in the loss of many retinal ganglion cells (neurons whose axons connect the retina to the rest of the nervous system) (10).[3]

A number of studies show that exposure to particular visual patterns such as horizontal and vertical lines is also essential for later perception. In 1969 British psychologists Colin Blakemore and Grahame Cooper raised two newborn kittens under some unusual conditions. One kitten saw only vertical white lines for six months, whereas the other kitten saw only horizontal white lines for the

same period of time. When the vision of the horizontal-deprived cat was tested by having it cross an obstacle course of vertical slats, the cat easily avoided the obstacles. When it was placed in an environment of horizontal obstacles, the cat bumped into almost every slat "in sight"—as if it did not see them. The vertical-deprived cat performed in the opposite way—easily avoiding horizontal slats and bumping into vertical slats. Blakemore and Cooper discovered that neurons in the vertical-deprived cat did not respond to vertical edges and neurons in the horizontal-deprived cat did not respond to horizontal edges, as they would in cats reared under normal circumstances. Evidently, experience in a particular environment can alter the developing central nervous system (12). Recent studies show that the first two to three months of the cat's life are a sensitive period (see Chapter 3) for visual development. During this period exposure to verticals and horizontals must occur—as little as thirty-six hours of exposure is sufficient—if the animal's perception is to develop normally.

Several studies show that moving around actively is also necessary for the development of visual skills. In one study Richard Held and Alan Hein, psychologists working at the Massachusetts Institute of Technology, raised pairs of kittens in darkness until one member of the pair, designated the active kitten, had sufficient strength and coordination to pull the other kitten, designated the passive kitten, in a gondola apparatus (see Figure 5-23). The gondola exposed both the active and passive kitten to the same visual patterns. Both kittens moved, but only the active kitten, the one pulling the gondola, was able to coordinate vision and movement. After thirty hours of experience (three hours each day) in the gondola apparatus, the kittens' perceptual skills were tested. The active kitten showed normal perceptual skills: It chose the shallow side of the visual cliff; it blinked at approaching objects; and it extended its forepaws

---

[3]Prolonged darkness or exposure only to diffuse light (light but not patterns) may also damage other aspects of the visual system. One study found that when the eyes of newborn kittens were kept closed for two months or covered with a translucent shield that admitted only diffuse light, retinal cells which are specialized to excite visual cortical cells in response to lines and edges in the visual field permanently lost this capability (11).

Figure 5-23. The active and passive kittens received the same visual stimulation, but only the active kittens developed normal sensory motor skills during the course of the experiment. (Ted Polumbaum.)

when moved gently downward toward the table's edge. The passive kitten had not developed these normal responses (13). This and other studies show that the development of visual-organizing skills depends on feedback from motor responses. In other words, seeing seems to require a period of active learning.

The adult and temporary sensory deprivation. We have seen that visual perception can be disturbed in infancy by depriving the infant of important experiences. Can it also be disrupted at later stages of development? To answer this question Austin Riesen took a seven-month-old chimpanzee named Faik who had been raised under normal conditions and had excellent visual skills and put him in a dark room where he lived an active and otherwise normal life until the age of twenty-four months. At twenty-four months, Faik returned to his daylight living quarters for testing. Riesen soon discovered that Faik "had lost all ability to utilize vision in his interplay with the environment. He no longer recognized the feeding bottle, and failed to look at objects or persons, either stationary or

moving. . . . Even in direct sunlight Faik failed to grimace or close his eyelids; [Faik's] . . . recovery of vision [was] slow and is still only partial [14]." This study shows that extreme deprivation can disrupt perception even at an advanced point in development. In this case physical damage to Faik's sensory system was probably responsible for the observed results.

Can limited sensory deprivation disturb the perception of human adults? Jails and prisoner-of-war camps sometimes subject people to extremely restricted sensory environments. So do certain routine military, civil, and industrial jobs where workers do little more than watch pointers, press buttons, and turn dials for eight hours at a time. Does prolonged exposure to such monotonous, relatively unpatterned sensory environments, affect the organization of perception? In 1951 psychologist Donald Hebb began systematically investigating this question. In one study Hebb and his associates paid subjects $20 a day to lie on a foam rubber pillow on a comfortable bed in a lighted cubicle. To screen out patterned visual stimulation, the subjects wore plastic visors. Cotton gloves and cardboard cuffs restricted their sense of touch. The only sound they heard was the humming of an exhaust fan. Brief excursions to the toilet and time out for meals were their only relief from the dull routine. Would you like to earn $20 a day by lying in bed under these conditions? You may be surprised to learn that most subjects found it exceedingly difficult and unpleasant. In fact, many of them refused to continue with the experiment after two or three days.

Hebb and his associates found that the monotonous sensory environment dramatically affected behavior, physiology, and perception. After several days of sensory isolation approximately two-thirds of the subjects reported seeing simple images such as flashes of light, dots, and geometrical patterns, while one-third of the subjects reported seeing images and scenes, like "a procession of squirrels with sacks over their shoulders marching purposefully across a snowfield and out of the field of vision [15]." Perhaps this was the body's way of providing more stimulation for itself.

Even after emerging from sensory isolation many subjects reported perceptual distortions: The entire room seemed to be in motion, vertical and horizontal edges curved, colors glowed, and objects changed shape and size (16). Since this study there have been more than one hundred investigations of sensory deprivation. Many investigators find that when people are exposed to a monotonous, relatively unpatterned sensory environment, their perceptions (visual, auditory, tactile, and so on) are temporarily impaired (17). Evidently, continual patterned stimulation is important for the normal operation of our perceptual systems.

Adapting to a distorted perceptual world.
Since the nineteenth century psychologists have been studying how people adapt to perceptual distortions to investigate the influ-

ence of learning on perception. In the 1890s George Stratton, a psychologist at the University of California, made the first systematic observations on perceptual adaptation. Stratton served as his own subject. In one study he wore special spectacles containing an intricate system of lenses and mirrors that turned the world upside down and backward (reversed from left to right). Stratton wore the spectacles about eleven hours a day every day for eight days, removing them only before going to sleep. Stratton's diaries tell us a great deal about his experiences. On the first day the things of the world looked upside down, unstable, and in motion; and, as we'd expect, Stratton had a hard time moving around. He wrote:

Almost all movements performed under the direct guidance of sight were laborious and embarrassed. Inappropriate movements were constantly made. . . . At table the simplest acts of serving myself had to be cautiously worked out. The wrong hand was constantly used to seize anything that lay to one side. . . . The unusual strain of attention in these areas, and the difficulty of finally getting a movement to its goal, made all but the simplest movements extremely fatiguing [18].

Gradually, Stratton began to adjust, finding it progressively easier to get around in his new world. By the fifth day he noted:

At breakfast, with the lenses on, the inappropriate hand was rarely used to pick up something to one side . . . I usually took the right direction without reflecting and without the need any longer of constantly watching my feet [19].

After eight days Stratton had adjusted so well to his topsy-turvy world that he had problems readjusting to the normal uninverted world again.

Since Stratton's early adventures with inverting lenses, psychologists have found that people can adjust, in time, to many kinds of visual distortions. We can adapt to a visual field that is both upside down and backward and to one that is tilted or shifted left, right, up, or down. We can also adapt to a world where straight lines are curved and right angles obtuse or acute and to split worlds that are blue on one side and yellow on the other or compressed on one side and expanded on the other.

What do we mean "adapt"? Although adaptation varies from person to person, there is a general pattern. When subjects first put on distorting lenses, they feel disoriented. They may reach down instead of up or right instead of left. They continually trip over objects in their path. Locating a book on a table and climbing up stairs are gargantuan undertakings. Gradually, people become accustomed to the new look of things, and they learn to use information automatically; they might see a chair displaced on the right, for example, and make the correct bodily adjustment to avoid bumping into it—without conscious effort. Some subjects slip back into a fairly normal routine. Then, when they first remove the lenses after a long period of time, they feel dizzy and disoriented. The old uninverted world looks strange; objects appear tilted or highly illuminated or moving. And they must adjust once again.

Does the distorted world actually look normal to people? The answer is not completely clear. There's no doubt that people grow accustomed to their new perceptions and that things stop looking peculiar. But getting used to something peculiar is one thing; seeing the peculiar as normal is quite another. The distorted world usually has a mixed-up nature: it is perceived partly in the old and partly in the new way. With lenses that reverse up and down, for example, people might see snow falling up on trees. Similarly, when people attend closely to their perceptions, they frequently become aware of these peculiarities.

How do people adapt to a distorted world?

We do not understand the adaptation process very well, but it appears that internal changes occur. Some studies indicate that the subjects' position sense of their own bodies changes (20). Stratton makes this notion clear in writing that "the limbs began actually to feel in the place where the new visual perception reported them to be . . . I could at length feel my feet strike against the seen floor, although the floor was seen on the opposite side of the field of vision from that to which at the beginning of the experiment I had referred these tactual sensations [21]." That is, vision may be educating the sense of touch and the real adaptation may be taking place in the tactile system. Other studies indicate that people actually *see differently* when they remove the lenses (22).

Culture and perception. Experiences in a particular environment also influence the way people organize their perceptions. Consider the BaMbuti pygmies who live in dense tropical forests in the Congo where distant views are rare. The longest distance most pygmies ever see is from the tops of trees—a hundred feet to the ground. One sophisticated young pygmy, Kenge, traveled with a visiting anthropologist, Colin Turnbull, to an open plain where Kenge saw miles into the distance for the first time in his life. Here is Turnbull's account of this event:

Kenge looked over the plains and down to where a herd of about a hundred buffalo were grazing some miles away. He asked me what kind of insects they were, and I told him they were buffalo, twice as big as the forest buffalo known to him. He laughed loudly and told me not to tell such stupid stories, and asked me again what kind of insects they were. He then talked to himself, for want of more intelligent company, and tried to liken the buffalo to the various beetles and ants with which he was familiar.

He was still doing this when we got into the car and drove to where the animals were grazing. He watched them getting larger and larger, and though he was as courageous as any Pygmy, he moved over and sat close to me and muttered that it was witchcraft. . . . Finally, when he realized that they were real buffalo he was no longer afraid, but what puzzled him still was why they had been so small, and whether they really had been small and had so suddenly grown larger, or whether it had been some kind of trickery [23].

Why didn't Kenge show size constancy? Do pygmies lack this organizing principle? Or has limited experience affected Kenge's perceptual judgments? Let's phrase this question in a more general way: Does experience in a specific environment usually mold an individual's perceptual judgments? To investigate this issue, psychologists Marshall Segall, Donald Campbell, and Melville Herskovitz presented visual illusions (see Figure 5-24) to people living in American and European cities and people living in so-called primitive African and Philippino tribes. Each subject was asked to judge which dark line was longer. As it turned out, Americans and Euro-

peans were frequently susceptible to obtuse- and acute-angled illusions (illusions a and b), whereas native Africans and Philippinos were not. Native Africans and Philippinos, on the other hand, were frequently deceived by horizontal-vertical illusions (illusions c and d), whereas Americans and Europeans were only moderately susceptible to them.

One neat (but tentative) explanation for these findings is that experiences in a particular environment influence visual judgments. Americans and Europeans live in an environment filled with rectangular structures; unconsciously they tend to view acute- and obtuse-angled figures, such as illusions a and b, as if they represent three-dimensional rectangular forms.

Let's look closely at illusion a. The arrow-like figures, shown in Figure 5-24, can be seen as "skeletons" of corners of a building. Figure 1 appears to be a nearby corner; figure 2 appears to be a distant corner. In reality, the two lines project images of equal size on the retina. The laws of perspective tell us that under these conditions, the distant

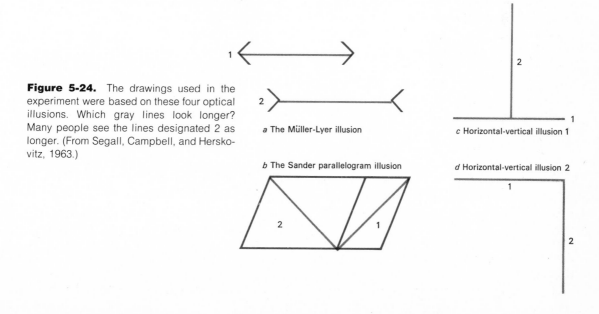

Figure 5-24. The drawings used in the experiment were based on these four optical illusions. Which gray lines look longer? Many people see the lines designated 2 as longer. (From Segall, Campbell, and Herskovitz, 1963.)

a The Müller-Lyer illusion

b The Sander parallelogram illusion

c Horizontal-vertical illusion 1

d Horizontal-vertical illusion 2

Figure 5-25. The arrowlike figures of the Müller-Lyer illusion can be seen in the distant and nearby corners of a building. (John Briggs.)

one must be longer. Consequently we see line 2 as longer than line 1. (See Figure 5-25.)

On the other hand, many Africans and Philippinos live on open, flat plains and are used to seeing intersecting roads or paths. Paths that extend from the observer into the distance are foreshortened (that is, they are longer than they look). In viewing illusions *c* and *d*, many native Africans and Philippinos may view the vertical lines as foreshortened pathways extending far into the distance (24).

Let's reconsider Kenge's experience with the buffalo. We have seen that people base their perceptual judgments on past experi-

ence in a particular environment, so it should not be surprising that Kenge could not relate the image on his retina to apparent distance to achieve size constancy in a situation where the distance surpassed his usual experience. Incidentally, these observations demonstrate quite clearly that size constancy is influenced by environmental factors.

Psychological states and perception. Psychological states also influence perception. More than twenty years ago a study of student perceptions of an important college football game demonstrated this effect very vividly. Psychologists Albert Hastorf and Hadley Cantril had samples of undergraduates from both participating schools—Dartmouth College and Princeton University—watch the same motion picture of the important game. As the students watched, they rated each team's rule violations, judging each one as "mild" or "outrageous." Princeton students saw the Dartmouth players make twice as many violations as their own players and rated most of them "outrageous." Dartmouth students, on the other hand, saw Dartmouth players make the same number of violations as the Princeton players and rated half of them "mild."[4] Apparently, motives, emotions, values, and goals had caused students to perceive the same events differently, emphasizing those incidents that had personal significance for them (25). It probably comes as no surprise that people perceive complex, emotionally charged interpersonal events subjectively. We'd assume that arguments, accidents, and love affairs are similarly perceived, but what about the simple incidents and simple objects of everyday life? A number of studies show that psychological states influence even these perceptions—usually unconsciously—and that this phenomenon can be observed in young children (26).

Summary: The Determinants of Visual Perception

1. Young infants detect form and depth at a very early age. Evidently visual perception, like other perceptual systems, is partly organized by innate factors.
2. Experience also plays a role in organizing perception. In the case of vision, light is

essential for the maintenance of retinal ganglion cells.
3. Experiences such as the seeing of horizontal and vertical lines and the active coordination of vision and movement also influence the development of visual skills.
4. Prolonged deprivation of patterned stimulation disturbs human perception.
5. Humans and other primates (apes, monkeys, and lemurs) are capable of adapting to distorted perceptual inputs.
6. Daily experiences in a particular environment organize perceptual habits and influence new perceptual judgments.
7. Subjective psychological states relating to motives, emotions, values, and expectations influence people's perceptions of both complex and simple events.

EXTRASENSORY PERCEPTION

Up until now we have been concerned with perceptual processes that depend on known sensory systems. We turn now to the question: Do other kinds of perception exist? We will look at evidence based on anecdotes (personal accounts) and on well-controlled laboratory studies.

In 1961 *This Week* magazine reported the following story: A twenty-one-year-old girl was returning home along a country road when a man leaped out from behind a stone storehouse and assaulted her with a hammer. According to the article, the police immediately contacted a psychic named W. H. C. Tenhaeff to ask if he could help identify the criminal. Accompanied by Gerard Croiset, another psychic, Tenhaeff went to the police station. There Croiset picked up the hammer which the police had found at the scene of the crime, squeezed its handle, and concentrated very hard.

[4]Dartmouth was, in fact, penalized 70 yards and Princeton was penalized 25 yards; both sides were penalized on additional plays.

"The criminal," he announced, "was tall and dark and about thirty years old, . . . [with] a somewhat deformed left ear." Croiset added that the hammer belonged to another man living nearby in a small white cottage.

Several months later [according to the article] the police picked up a tall, dark, 29 year old man on another morals charge. His badly scarred and swollen left ear led to questioning about the first attack. Finally, he admitted assaulting the girl with the hammer. He said he had borrowed it from a friend, who, the police discovered, lived in a white cottage . . . [27]

Is this a bonafide incident of extrasensory perception? C. E. M. Hansel, a psychologist at the University of Wales, contacted the burgomaster of the village to verify the facts. As it turned out, the magazine story and the real story disagreed. Several important differences were the following: The psychics were not immediately contacted by the police; they were approached some six weeks after the incident by a group of concerned townspeople. At that time the crime had already been highly publicized and there was already a local suspect (who eventually confessed to the crime). Croiset made many predictions. Several turned out to be correct and several turned out to be incorrect. The suspect, for example, was young, but he had two perfectly normal ears; and no one ever found out where the hammer came from (28). Even when they come from seemingly reliable sources, personal accounts are not necessarily trustworthy.

You probably noted that some of Croiset's statements were accurate. But can you logically assume that ESP is the proper explanation? Not unless you have ruled out four likelier alternatives: *chance, rational inference, acute sensory perception*, and *fraud*. First, it is entirely possible that Croiset made a lucky guess. A guess of "dark" and "young" will be right some percentage of the time. After all, criminals have to be light or dark and young or old. (It's like guessing the toss of a coin. If you say "heads," you will be right 50 percent of the time. Predictions, truly based on ESP, should have a higher probability of being correct than random guesses.) Unfortunately, we don't know anything about Croiset's "ESP batting average." Rational inference could also account for Croiset's successful statements. It does not require any extraordinary ability to know that old men and women rarely commit violent crimes. Acute sensory perception could explain Croiset's success in other situations; that is, like many so-called fortune-tellers and mind readers, Croiset may excel at interpreting ordinary sensory cues such as signs of tension, joy, fear, and anger. Recall Hans, the horse we described in Chapter 2, who made correct responses by noting almost imperceptible movements of the interrogator's head. Some people and some horses are quite sensitive to sensory cues. Fraud is another possibility that must be considered. Croiset might actually have heard about the suspect from conversations with townspeople.[5] Before we can conclude that extrasensory perception is responsible for a particular judgment, we have to eliminate these likelier possibilities. The only way we can do this is by making controlled observations.

Legitimate scientists are currently investigating extrasensory perceptual phenomena

---

[5]In some well-known ESP studies subjects have used magicianlike tricks to deceive the investigator. In other studies the investigators themselves have been dishonest. In June 1974, for example, a highly respected research director at the Institute for Parapsychology at Duke University admitted to tampering with his automated equipment to make it appear that rats could influence an electromechanical device by *psychokinesis* (the power to move material objects using mental powers).

Figure 5-26. ESP cards.

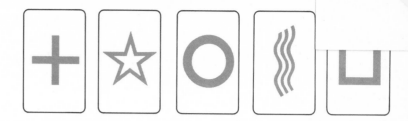

in laboratories and universities throughout the United States, England, and the Soviet Union. Joseph Banks Rhine, formerly a botanist, became interested in ESP research in the early 1920s. One of the most productive of American ESP researchers, Rhine founded the Parapsychology Laboratory at Duke University in 1940, and he has conducted most of his research there. Many of Rhine's studies use a deck of twenty-five ESP cards (see Figure 5-26). Each card contains one of five symbols: a circle, a rectangle, wavy lines, a star, or a plus sign. There are five cards of each kind. Rhine's studies proceed along the following lines: The cards are shuffled. In experiments that deal with knowing the thoughts of another (*telepathy*), the investigator chooses a card and looks at it, then the subject "guesses" the symbol. In *clairvoyance* experiments, those that deal with seeing something that cannot be seen, the investigator chooses a card and without looking at it, places it face downward, then the subject "guesses" the symbol. In experiments that deal with knowing the future (*precognition*), the subject "predicts" the symbol that will appear, then the investigator chooses the card. Strict precautions are usually taken to avoid cheating. These studies show that some subjects can guess symbols on cards with a consistency that cannot be attributed to chance.

Careful studies using other kinds of stimuli in a wide variety of settings also find evidence that certain people have perceptual abilities that cannot currently be explained. Recently, for example, two physicists at the Stanford Research Institute in California conducted several unusually well-controlled investigations. In one series of experiments, the Israeli psychic Uri Geller "received" and reproduced target pictures drawn by scientists at remote locations.

At the beginning of each experiment Geller was placed in a room that was visually, acoustically, and electrically shielded from the target material and personnel involved in the experiment. To eliminate the possibility of preexperimental cuing, each target picture was chosen and drawn after Geller had been isolated. Moreover, Geller did not know the identity of the persons selecting the target nor the method of target selection, which varied throughout these sessions. To guard against biased scoring the target pictures and Geller's drawings were submitted to two independent scientists at the Stanford Research Institute for matching. The results were impressive: The judges matched all ten of Geller's drawings with the appropriate target drawings. As you can see from Figure 5-27, five of them were astoundingly accurate. The odds against chance accounting for Geller's performance are more than 1,000,000 to 1 (29). Studies such as this are beginning to convince many scientists that unidentified perceptual modalities exist and may some day be explained.

Do these studies prove that extrasensory perception exists? Many psychologists believe

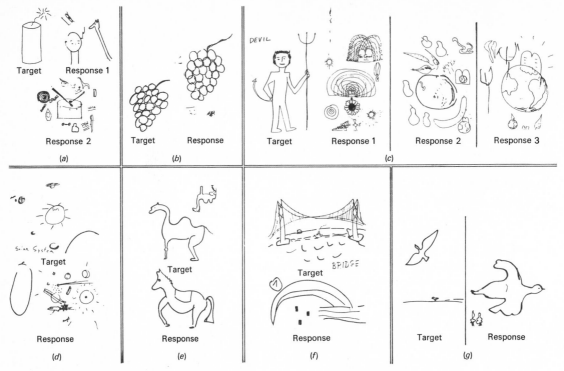

Figure 5-27. Target pictures and responses drawn by Uri Geller during the Stanford Research Institute Study. (Targ and Puthoff, 1974.)

that they do; many others remain skeptical;[6] so our question remains a question. Only careful systematic observations under controlled conditions will tell us more.

[6]Skeptical psychologists cite the following problems: (1) Experimental findings are inconsistent; that is, subjects tend to obtain high ESP scores on some occasions (and not on others), with some procedures (and not with others), and with some investigators (and not with others.) (2) ESP experiments are too rarely designed to completely rule out alternative explanations. (3) The reporting of ESP experiments is frequently haphazard—omitting important features of the experimental setting or presenting discrepant versions of the methods used (30).

STUDY GUIDE 5

Key Terms. perception, senses, kinesthetic sense, vestibular sense, receptor, transducer, pupil, iris, cornea, retina, lens, rods, cones, optic nerve, cortical columns, attention, constancy, figure-ground, grouping, similarity, symmetry (good figure), proximity, continuity, closure, binocular disparity, convergence, binocular depth cues, monocular depth cues, accommodation, motion parallax, perceived size, linear perspective, aerial perspective, texture gradients, interposition, looking chamber, visual cliff, sensory isolation, sensory deprivation, inverting lenses, adaptation, rational inference, acute sensory perception, fraud, telepathy, clairvoyance, precognition.

Important Research. information processing in the frog's eye (Lettvin, Maturana, McCulloch, and Pitts), organization of the visual cortex (Hubel and Weisel), form perception in chicks and human infants (Fantz), the visual cliff (Gibson and Walk), size constancy in infants (Bower), chimps reared in darkness (Riesen), cats reared with either vertical or horizontal lines (Blakemore and Cooper), cats reared without coordinated vision and movement (Held and Hein), loss of visual ability after extended darkness (Riesen), sensory isolation (Hebb), adapting to an upside-down world (Stratton), observations of the BaMbuti pygmies (Turnbull), culture and responses to visual illusions (Segall, Campbell and Herskovitz), influence of motives and emotions on perception (Hastorf and Cantril), investigating an ESP report (Hansel), laboratory research on ESP (Rhine), ESP abilities of Uri Geller (Stanford Research Institute).

Self-Quiz

1. What is the main difference between sensations and perceptions? [**a**] Perceptions are more accurate than sensations; [**b**] people make more perceptions than sensations; [**c**] perceptions involve interpretations; sensations do not; [**d**] perceptions are part of the sensation process.
2. At least _____ distinct senses are currently recognized. [**a**] 12 [**b**] 5 [**c**] 7 [**d**] 10.
3. A transducer [**a**] speeds up nerve impulses; [**b**] converts energy from one form to another; [**c**] carries information from the eye to the brain; [**d**] integrates sensory information within the brain.
4. Hubel and Weisel found that cats [**a**] have columns of specialized cortical cells which respond to specific visual stimuli; [**b**] process most visual information in their retinal cells; [**c**] process most visual information in the fibers which channel information from the eye to the cortex; [**d**] have columns of specialized cortical cells which respond to four different types of survival-related information.
5. You perceive a mailbox as having the same shape regardless of whether you see it from the front or from the side. This is an example of [**a**] constancy; [**b**] grouping; [**c**] continuity; [**d**] similarity.
6. As you look into the distance, the edges of the road appear to be closer together. This is an example of [**a**] convergence; [**b**] linear perspective;

[**c**] a binocular depth cue; [**d**] motion parallax.
7. An object is perceived as closer if it partially blocks the view of another object. This distance cue is called [**a**] aerial perspective; [**b**] light and shadow; [**c**] binocular disparity; [**d**] interposition.
8. Fantz demonstrated that infants perceive form when he showed that they [**a**] consistently reached out for some forms and not others; [**b**] cried when a preferred form was taken away; [**c**] spent more time looking at complex than simple forms; [**d**] also perceive depth.
9. When tested on the visual cliff, [**a**] normally reared land animals usually avoid the deep side from birth; [**b**] normally reared land animals usually avoid the deep side as soon as they can move around on their own; [**c**] some animals avoid the deep side as soon as they can move around, but others do not avoid it until later; [**d**] sea-turtles, rats, and goats avoid the deep side from birth, but humans, cats, dogs, and chimps must learn to avoid the deep side.
10. Bower trained infants to turn their heads left every time an approximately 12-inch cube was presented at a distance of about 1 yard. When Bower later tested the infants using a variety of other stimuli, he found that they [**a**] did not respond at all to any of the new stimuli; [**b**] responded most often when an approximately 36-inch cube was placed about 9 feet away (same size retinal image as the original stimulus); [**c**] responded most often when a 12-inch cube was placed 9 feet away; [**d**] responded most often when a 36-inch cube was placed 3 feet away.
11. Blakemore and Cooper found that kittens reared for six months in an environment of vertical white lines [**a**] showed normal vision; [**b**] had deteriorated retinas; [**c**] behaved as if they could not see horizontal lines; [**d**] could see lines of any slant, but had a strong preference for vertical patterns.
12. When paid to lie on a comfortable bed and do nothing under conditions of sensory deprivation, most subjects [**a**] found the situation very unpleasant, and many of them later experienced perceptual distortions; [**b**] became a little restless after two or three days, but were not seriously distressed; [**c**] found the situation boring and refused to continue after a single day; [**d**] were seriously affected—80 percent reported long-lasting perceptual problems.
13. Cross-cultural studies of people's responses to visual illusions suggest that [**a**] people perceive these illusions similarly all over the world; [**b**] learning in a particular environment influences perception; [**c**] children perceive similarly, but adults do not; [**d**] perceptual differences appear to

be due to hereditary differences between "primitive" and "sophisticated" peoples.

14. According to research studies, motives and emotions [**a**] affect perception, even in children; [**b**] affect the perceptions of adults, but not those of children; [**c**] affect perception only in interpersonal situations; [**d**] rarely affect perception.

15. Which of the following is *not* true about ESP research? [**a**] Reporting of results is sometimes haphazard; [**b**] some people who claim to have ESP powers are frauds who cheat or use tricks; [**c**] some ESP experiments are not designed to rule out other possible explanations such as chance or intelligent guessing; [**d**] as a group American psychologists do not believe in ESP, so ESP research is rarely done in this country.

Exercises

1. ORGANIZATION OF VISUAL PERCEPTION. Review the principles that organize an animal's visual perception of objects. Then match each principle with the corresponding definition or example, using the following abbreviations: constancy—CON; figure-ground—FG; grouping—G; symmetry—SY; proximity—P; similarity—SI; continuity—CONT; closure—CL.

_____ **1.** Tendency to organize separate elements into patterns according to various "rules."

_____ **2.** Elements forming smooth, flowing patterns seem to go together.

_____ **3.** Perceiving a bowl as round regardless of the angle at which it is viewed.

_____ **4.** Elements near each other seen as belonging together.

_____ **5.** Elements with the same shape or texture seem to belong together.

_____ **6.** Clear boundaries not needed to see objects standing out from backgrounds.

_____ **7.** Incomplete objects seen as complete.

_____ **8.** Tendency to see simple, regular forms amidst more irregularly shaped figures.

2. PERCEPTION OF DEPTH AND DISTANCE. Match each distance cue with the corresponding definition or example: binocular disparity—BD; convergence—C; binocular depth cue—BDC; monocular depth cue—MDC; accommodation—A; motion parallax—MP; perceived size—PS; linear perspective—LP; light and shadow—LS; aerial perspective—AP; texture gradient—TG; interposition—I.

_____ **1.** Blurred, hazy objects seem more distant.

_____ **2.** As we move, close objects seem to move by more quickly than distant ones.

_____ **3.** An object that partially blocks the sight of something else appears closer than the object being blocked.

_____ **4.** The distance of a familiar object is judged by noting the size of the retinal image which it casts; the object is assumed to be near when the image is relatively large.

_____ **5.** Depends on information from the eye muscles about the turning in of the eyes.

_____ **6.** Any visual depth cue that can be used when one eye is covered.

_____ **7.** Any visual depth cue that requires both eyes.

_____ **8.** Distant lines appear to converge.

_____ **9.** The surface of an object looks coarser when it is nearby than when it is distant.

_____ **10.** Depends on the slightly different images cast on each retina.

_____ **11.** With the sun behind you, the brighter side of an object seems nearer.

_____ **12.** The thickness of the lens changes as the eye focuses on near and distant objects.

Questions to Consider

1. What is the difference between sensation and perception?

2. Comment on the statement: People and other animals see with their brains not with their eyes.

3. Seat yourself near a window and choose two objects in view—one near and one far. Identify some of the cues which inform you about distance.

4. If Kenge lived in an open plain for a period of time, what do you think would happen to his ability to judge the size of distant objects?

5. People born with congenital cataracts sometimes regain their vision through surgery. Do you think that people who regained their vision at age five would perceive in the same manner as people born with normal vision?

6. How would you go about studying how two family members perceived the events of an argument in which they were involved?

7. Think about the factors that direct and attract attention. Consider needs, interests, values, and novel, unexpected, changing, or intense stimuli. How could college teachers catch and keep students' attention in class?

Project 5: Expectations and Perceptions

People frequently show preferences for foods and drinks which are labeled with a particular brand name. Although some of these preferences are undoubtedly based on taste differences between products, many are probably the result of expectations. That is, many people probably prefer their favorite brand because they expect to like it better. Expectations may be the primary factor that makes a $12 bottle of wine taste better than one that costs $1.25. The purpose of this project is to test the hypothesis indirectly: Expectations influence people's taste perceptions.

Method. You will need three cooperative subjects to participate in this project. Tell each subject that you are studying taste preferences. Do not tell them the real purpose of the study until you have collected your observations. You will need information about each subject's food brand preferences in advance. Ask each subject to tell you their favorite brand (in terms of taste) of cola, beer, coffee, milk, frozen orange juice, or soup. Choose one of these items and buy five different brands of it. (You may want to share supplies with your classmates!)

You will be testing your subjects one at a time. You will be presenting brands of one product to each subject in a way that disguises the identity of the product. The product should be served at the same temperature and in the same kind of container. Wrap the original containers in heavy paper or keep them hidden. Have a glass of water for the subject to drink in between tastings—to remove the old taste. Also make arrangements to present each brand in the order given on the data sheet and to record each subject's judgments on a similar data sheet.

Once you are ready to begin making your observations, bring the subject into your "laboratory," seat him/her at a table, and blindfold him/her so that differences in appearance will not bias the judgments. Present the substances to the subject in the predetermined order one at a time. Allow the subject to taste each substance twice. Then have the subject rate the taste of the substance on a 1 to 5 scale: 1—poor, 2—fair, 3—average, 4—good, 5—excellent. After each substance has been rated, ask the subject if this is the one that was previously described as his/her favorite.

Results. For each subject compute the mean rating for each brand. Did subjects rate their favorite brands highest? Are subject's ratings for the same brand consistent on both trials? Could people accurately guess their favorite brands?

Discussion. Consider the following questions:

1. What extraneous factors did the procedures control?
2. Note that you used a single-blind method (see pages

44–46). How might a double-blind method have improved the accuracy of the findings?
3. What problems arose and how could they have been eliminated?
4. Were certain brands judged consistently good or poor? What is the most parsimonious (simplest) explanation for this finding?
5. Were certain brands judged inconsistently? Speculate on the reasons.
6. Do your observations show that people can consistently identify their favorite brands by taste? Or do your observations suggest that under ordinary circumstances people's favorite brands are probably based on expectations and other psychological factors and not on taste?
7. Think of other ways that psychologists could study the effects of expectations on perceptions using a different sensory modality.

DATA SHEET (one needed for each subject)

Brand	Rating (1–5)	Is This the Favored Brand?
A ( )		
C ( )		
E (favorite:)		
D ( )		
B ( )		
E (favorite:)		
C ( )		
A ( )		
D ( )		
B ( )		

Suggested Readings

1. Gregory, Richard L. *Eye and brain.* New York: McGraw-Hill Book Company, 1970 (paperback). Discusses matters like visual illusions, the evolution of the eye, color vision, and the role of learning in seeing.
2. Droscher, Vitus B. *The magic of the senses.* New York: Harper & Row, Publishers, Incorporated, 1971 (paperback). On the perceptual systems of animals, including the auditory system of bats and the navigational systems of birds and bees.
3. Teuber, Marianne. "Sources of ambiguity in the prints of Maurits C. Escher." *Scientific American*, July 1974, 231,1, 90–104. Teuber discusses the prints of a late Dutch artist which deliberately use psychological research on the perception of objects and space. Amply illustrated.

4. Bower, T. G. R. "The object in the world of the infant." *Scientific American*, October 1971, 225, 12, 30–38. Bower describes his own ingenious research investigations on infants' perceptions of stationary and moving objects.

5. Gibson, Eleanor, & Richard Walk. "The visual cliff." *Scientific American*, April 1960, 202, 64–71. Gibson and Walk report on their now classic work with infants and other animals on the visual cliff.

6. Koestler, Arthur. *The roots of coincidence*. New York: Random House, Inc., 1973. Reviews research in parapsychology and describes some of the strange findings of modern physics which may help explain phenomena such as telepathy, clairvoyance, and psychokinesis.

Answer Keys

SELF-QUIZ
1. c 2. d 3. b 4. a 5. a 6. b 7. d 8. c 9. b
10. c 11. c 12. a 13. b 14. a 15. d

EXERCISE 1
1. G 2. CONT 3. CON 4. P 5. SI 6. FG 7. CL
8. SY

EXERCISE 2
1. MDC, AP 2. MDC, MP 3. MDC, I 4. MDC, PS
5. BDC, C 6. MDC 7. BDC 8. MDC, LP 9. MDC, TG 10. BDC, BD 11. MDC, LS 12. MDC, A

6

STATES
OF
CONSCIOUSNESS

IN THIS CHAPTER
We focus on several states of consciousness. We turn first to sleep and dreaming—two closely related, universally experienced states that are automatically triggered from within. Then we examine meditation and marijuana intoxication—states that are usually reached by specific procedures. After reading this chapter, you should be able to do the following:

1. Describe five stages of sleep and explain how they unfold throughout the sleep period
2. Cite evidence that people need REM and non-REM sleep
3. Summarize what psychologists know about the frequency of dreams, dream content, and the reasons people dream
4. Describe how consciousness and physiology change during meditation and identify three factors that contribute to the effects of meditation
5. Describe how consciousness changes during marijuana intoxication and cite the probable causes

In the summer of 1960 Carlos Castanada, who was then studying anthropology at the University of California, traveled to Mexico to gather information about medicinal plants. On his way he met don Juan Matus, an old Indian with a reputation for being an expert on such matters. During the following year their friendship grew slowly. Eventually, don Juan told Castanada that he was a sorcerer and that he'd decided to make Castanada his apprentice. In a series of books Castanada has described how the sorcerer taught him to view the world with freshness and wonder. In one consciousness-altering lesson Castanada learned how to *not do.* (We use the word "consciousness" to refer to a person's total subjective awareness of world and self.)

When don Juan first mentioned *not doing,* Castanada was puzzled, as you or I might have been. Don Juan explained what *not doing* meant by giving an example. When looking at a tree, people tend to focus on the foliage; they do not look at the spaces between the leaves nor at the shadows which the leaves cast. The sorcerer instructed his pupil to concentrate on the shadows of the leaves, beginning with a single branch and working his way over the entire tree.

You might try this exercise for yourself. It works especially well with trees or plants, but any object will do. Concentrate first on the shadows of one small part, then continue over the entire object. After several moments of intense concentration, you should find that you see the object as a pattern of shadows. The effect is striking. Apparently, the world as we know it depends on our perceptual habits. When these habits change, the appearance of the world also changes.

Don Juan explained to Castanada that sorcerers apply *not doing* to everything in the world. In don Juan's view, *not doing* leads to power, the power that comes from knowing that all doing (perceiving) is arbitrary and unreal and that the only real thing is the being inside each person that is going to die (1).[1]

Our ordinary way of perceiving helps us survive. As we saw in Chapter 5, our sensory systems and brain tend to pick from countless stimuli that surround us those which are novel, unexpected, intense, or changing, and those which are related to our needs. Our ordinary consciousness is not only *selective,* it is also *organized* to attain a relatively stable view of the world so that we can perceive immediately what is important and act quickly. But ordinary consciousness is not the only mode of consciousness. As William James recognized more than seventy years ago:

Our normal waking consciousness, rational consciousness as we call it, is but one special type of consciousness, whilst all about it, parted from it by the filmiest of screens, there lie potential forms of consciousness entirely different. We may go through life without suspecting their existence; but apply the requisite stimulus, and at a touch they are there in all their completeness . . . [2].

For thousands of years people have been experimenting with consciousness altering. By smoking or ingesting drugs or by engaging in activities such as chanting, whirling, fasting, or breathing quickly, many people have been able to produce radical changes in their body chemistry and catapult themselves into startling new realities. Don Juan used a different strategy. He taught his pupil Castanada how to control his consciousness through perceptual exercises; that is, through changing the ways he ordinarily viewed the world.

Although we sometimes alter our consciousness deliberately, our consciousness

---

[1]Some people believe that don Juan is a figment of Castanada's imagination. Castanada insists that he is real. The truth about don Juan's status really doesn't matter. Whether he exists or not, the ideas he voices deserve our consideration.

also changes without our direct intervention. Every day it alters dramatically as we sleep. It also varies subtly throughout each day. Sometimes our consciousness is intuitive; we seem to be attuned to mystery, beauty, music, art, emotion, the body, and our orientation in space. At other times our consciousness is rational and analytic. We focus on intellectual matters, on logic, on clear expression, on facts, and on reality. These differing modes of awareness may reflect the temporary dominance of one cerebral hemisphere (see Chapter 4). Our consciousness also changes with variations in fatigue and attention. When you feel drowsy and dull, for example, you might catch yourself staring into space and find that you have not been registering the sights and sounds around you or thinking about anything in particular. When you feel alert, in contrast, the things of the world appear especially vivid and clear. Similarly, moods—such as depression and joy—also color our awareness of reality.

States of consciousness are difficult to investigate; researchers must depend—to a large degree—on subjects' self-reports concerning their thoughts, reveries, sensations, and perceptions. The self-report method has a number of limitations, which we discussed in Chapter 2. Describing an unusual state of awareness poses several additional problems. Because our language developed to report what we perceive with our ordinary waking consciousness, it may be inadequate for describing our perceptions in other states. Moreover, subjects often cannot remain in states like sleep and simultaneously communicate about their experiences. In addition to self-report data, psychologists usually make behavioral and physiological measurements because they are less affected by bias. To study the hypnotic state, for example, psychologists might measure heartbeats, brain wave activity, or pain threshold to shock both before and after the induction of the state.

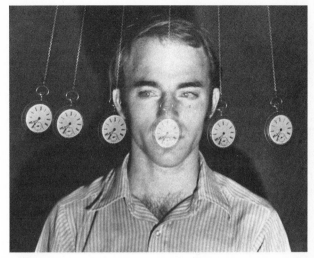

Figure 6-1. Hypnosis is one state of consciousness that psychologists study. (Mimi Forsyth, from Monkmeyer.)

The relationship between physiological changes and states of consciousness is not always clear. In some cases—as in the use of heroin—physiological changes probably account to a large degree for the state. In other cases, the physiological changes may result from the unusual state of awareness. The state of meditation, for example, lowers oxygen consumption.

We will begin our discussion of states of consciousness by considering the state of sleep.

THE STATE OF SLEEP

A period of sleep and a period of waking organize the days of our lives. The sleep-waking cycle interweaves with many other bodily cycles known as *biological rhythms*. These rhythms vary from fractions of a second to a year and perhaps longer. On the average our heart beats slightly quicker than once every second; respiration requires several seconds to complete its cycle; body temperature cycles on a daily schedule; and the menstrual cycle of the human female reappears on a monthly timetable. Generally we are unaware of the vast majority of these rhythms, but we are sometimes sensitive to their effects. Consider body temperature which drops to a low point between 1 and 7 A.M. There is some evidence that this roughly twenty-four-hour cycle determines how people feel when they wake up. If your body temperature begins to rise before you do and reaches a "normal" level by the time you're out of bed, you probably awaken feeling alert and ready to work. If your body temperature is still rising after you are awake and moving about, the chances are that you feel groggy and only half alive for your first hour or so.

There is good reason to believe that biological rhythms affect both the subtle and not-so-subtle variations in our waking consciousness. Consider the following case of manic-depressive psychosis:

Dr. F. A. Jenner in Sheffield, England, has been watching a former boxer from Yorkshire who became manic-depressive after a bad accident in the 1950s. For twenty-four hours he is overactive, talkative, sometimes testy, with grandiose ideas about science and the world; typically, at some time in his sleep he changes. He awakens feeling lethargic and bleak, rises reluctantly, later than usual, and falls asleep earlier that night. For eleven years this man has lived in a clinic, eating a controlled diet and being measured and tested every day for physiological changes that might match behavior. . . . When he stayed in bed on a liquid diet, he showed a forty-eight-hour alternation of weight, urine volume, and volume of red blood cells. It appears that the amount of fluid within and around cells was shifting with his moods. Fluid retention within and around nerve and other cells has been thought to be controlled by a balance of charged elements. The sodium and potassium content of this man's saliva and urine did coincide with his alternating moods . . . [3].

When normal people record their feelings at various times of the day for several months in a diary, they sometimes observe regular periods of lucidity, productivity, drowsiness, inefficiency, and irritability. Such knowledge can be quite useful: "In Japan, the Ohmi Railway Company has stored in a computer the biorhythms of each of its 500 bus drivers. At the beginning of each shift, drivers scheduled to have 'bad' days are given a card reminding them to be extra careful. In their first biorhythmic year, 1969, Ohmi's drivers achieved a 50 percent drop in accidents, a downward trend that has continued . . . [4]."

Where do biological rhythms come from? Originally, scientists suspected that the great rhythms of the universe (like the daily cycle of the sun or the monthly cycle of the moon) ruled our individual rhythms, but subsequent research on people, rats, and other animals has not supported this hypothesis. For example, when people are isolated in caves and deprived of external time cues—clocks, routines, light, or dark—and they are free to schedule meals, activity, and rest as they like, they maintain rather consistent individualistic sleep-waking cycles of slightly more than twenty-four hours. Usually, they vary from twenty-four to twenty-six hours (5). In some cases they adopt a roughly forty-eight, seventy-two, or even ninety-six-hour sleep-waking cycle (6). (Note that these numbers are all multiples of twenty-four.) It is doubtful that a habit is simply persisting, since the studies have lasted up to five and a half months. Rather, it appears that biological rhythms are woven into our physiology and that we simply use external cues to "reset" them each day.

We turn now to what psychologists know about the state of sleep. We will explore the following questions: How do psychologists study sleep? What happens when we sleep? Do we need to sleep and why? What happens when we dream? Who dreams? What do dreams signify? Finally, why do people dream?

Figure 6-2. Wearing sunglasses to protect their eyes, subjects in a study of the effects of prolonged darkness on bodily functions emerge from a cave in central France. (Wide World Photos.)

How Do Psychologists Study Sleep?

Men and women have been speculating about sleep for thousands of years and investigating it scientifically for approximately thirty-five years. The scientific study of sleep was made possible by the invention of the *electroencephalograph* (EEG), an instrument that measures the electrical activity occurring within the neural circuits of the brain (see Chapter 4). The EEG works like this: small conductive electrodes, usually bits of metal, are pasted to specific positions on a person's head. Differences in electrical potential between the electrodes due to electrical activity inside the skull are amplified and recorded on a roll of continuous graph paper. In short, the EEG makes it possible to "see" the electrical activity of the brain. A sample EEG recording, an *electroencephalogram*, appears in Figure 6-3.

In 1937 scientists discovered that there were systematic changes in the brain's electrical activity both before and during the course of sleep. Since that time they have been using the EEG to study sleep as an on-going moment-to-moment activity. Sometimes they monitor the sleep of animals. Sometimes they pay human volunteers to sleep in a *sleep*

laboratory for a number of nights. The first sleep laboratories were opened in the 1950s. Today they exist by the dozens in hospitals

Figure 6-3. EEG patterns during wakefulness and sleep. (Adapted from Jasper, 1941.)

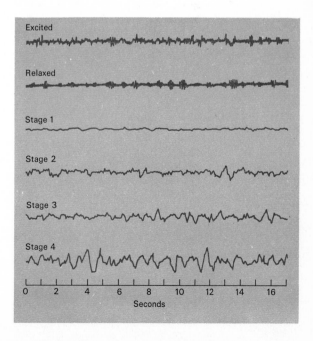

and universities. Typically, each laboratory contains private sleeping compartments for the sleepers and extensive electronic equipment for monitoring the sleepers' physiological responses. Most of our knowledge of human sleep comes from studying thousands of sleep-laboratory volunteers.

What Happens When People Sleep?

A picture of sleep has been pieced together slowly by numerous sleep researchers. It is clear now that sleep is not a unitary activity but a sequence of repeated stages—each representing particular kinds of brain and body activity. A presleep stage—stage 0, as it is sometimes called—occurs as we begin to fall asleep. At this time we are less responsive than usual to sensory stimulation; our muscles loosen up; and our brains frequently show a high level of *alpha activity* (brain activity in the 8 to 12 hertz [cycles per second] band). See line 2 in Figure 6-3. Alpha activity is associated with pleasantly relaxed feelings.

Figure 6-4. Physiological responses of this subject are monitored electronically in William Dement's sleep laboratory. (Dennis Galloway, *Hospital Practice.*)

In stage 0 we are on the threshold of sleep. If aroused, we report thoughts, images, and dream fragments. On the average, it will take us half an hour to attain the state scientists call sleep.

Two separate and distinct types of sleep— *non-REM sleep* and *REM sleep*—occur each night. The term *REM* sleep stands for rapid eye movements, one of the distinguishing features of REM sleep. First we discuss non-REM sleep.

Non-REM sleep. There are four stages of non-REM sleep:

STAGE 1 DROWSINESS—This brief period, lasting only a few minutes, occurs once as sleep begins and may be considered a continuation of stage 0 sleep. People are still falling asleep. They are easy to awaken, and, if awakened, probably are unaware that they have been sleeping. During this phase sensations of floating, images, vague thoughts, and dreamlike fragments continue to be common. (We turn to these experiences later on.) The sleeper's body is more relaxed than previously. Low-amplitude, fast, irregular waves now predominate on the EEG (see Figure 6-3).

STAGE 2 LIGHT SLEEP—Sleep is deeper. The sleeper is more relaxed and harder to awaken than in stage 1. During the initial periods of light sleep, the eyes roll slowly or remain still. There may be hallucinations such as flashes of light, crashes, shots, or sensations such as falling. The nocturnal jerk (a sudden, uncoordinated jerk of the body) sometimes occurs at the beginning of light sleep. Bursts of fast (12 to 14 hertz) waves, called *spindles*, begin to appear on the EEG (see Figure 6-3).

STAGE 3 DEEP SLEEP—People sink still deeper into sleep. They have become quite unresponsive to sounds and are difficult to awaken. Spindles and low-amplitude, fast waves are interspersed with high-amplitude, slow waves (2 hertz or less) on the EEG (see Figure 6-3).

STAGE 4 DEEPEST SLEEP—Totally relaxed now, people rarely move. They are oblivious to the outside world and very hard to awaken. A number of sleep irregularities—sleep walking, night-mares, and bed wetting—occur during this deep-sleep phase. High-amplitude, slow waves predominate on the EEG (see Figure 6-3).

REM sleep. During REM sleep the eyes dart about beneath the closed lids. REM sleep is also characterized by many seemingly contra-dictory characteristics. For instance, during this stage scientists see small, fast, irregular brain waves that suggest high cortical activity and wakefulness, yet the sleeper is as unre-sponsive to most outside stimulation as dur-ing stage 4 non-REM sleep. REM sleep is also characterized by intense autonomic nervous system activity. The body acts as if it is handling an emergency. Breathing is rapid and sporadic, the heartbeat is quick and irregular, the blood pressure is elevated, and the body secretes large quantities of the adre-nal hormones. Generally, there are penile erections in men. Although some muscles jerk and twitch, many are totally relaxed—so relaxed that the sleeper may feel temporarily paralyzed if awakened from this stage. REM sleep is remarkable for yet another reason; it frequently signals the occurrence of dream-ing (a topic we turn to shortly). REM sleep has only one stage; for reasons that will soon become clear, we call it stage 1 REM.

How do these sleep stages fit together? Brain-wave studies show that, in general, sleepers wind their way back and forth se-quentially through these levels of sleep: 1, 2, 3, 4, 3, 2, 1. During the first cycle the sleeper passes through stage 1 non-REM sleep on the way to deeper sleep levels. All subsequent periods of light sleep are periods of stage 1 REM. Each time the whole cycle is repeat-ed—approximately four to six times a night—stage 4 sleep is shorter and stage 1 REM sleep is longer. Sometimes stage 4 sleep drops out altogether. In general, our deep sleep is concentrated into the first few hours of the night, whereas REM sleep predomi-nates in the early morning hours. In young adults stage 1 non-REM sleep makes up some 5 percent of our total night's sleep; REM sleep occupies slightly less than 25 percent; stage 2 roughly 50 percent; and stages 3 and 4 the remaining 20 percent. Research also shows that each individual has a characteristic sleep pattern that deviates in minor ways from the general pattern and changes slightly from night to night.

Do People Need Sleep?

How do you feel after staying awake all night? Generally, people feel "sleepy." That term usually translates into "uncomfortable," "irritable," and "less efficient." But is sleep really necessary for well-being? One way to find out how much people need sleep is to observe their behavior and monitor their physiological responses before and after sleep deprivation. Surprisingly, the results of deprivation studies vary. When people are totally deprived of sleep for three or more nights, a substantial minority—some 25 to 40 percent—report hallucinations and delu-sions (7). The experience of Peter Tripp, a New York City disc jockey, furnishes a vivid illustration of this tendency. In 1959 Tripp decided to subject himself to two hundred hours without sleep to raise money for polio research. He set up his broadcasting head-quarters in Times Square in a glass Army recruiting booth. A team of psychologists,

Figure 6-5. Disc jockey Peter Tripp nears his 200th hour without sleep. (Wide World Photos.)

psychiatrists, and physicians attended him—administering tests at regular intervals. After a little more than forty-eight hours without sleep, Tripp saw cobwebs in his shoes, and specks on a table looked like bugs. After one hundred hours without sleep, Tripp's mental agility declined to the point where he could hardly recite the alphabet. At the same time he began to see grotesque visions: A nurse dripped saliva. A doctor appeared to be dressed in a "suit of furry worms." Finally, after two hundred hours without sleep, Tripp began to believe that the attending physicians were conspiring to drive him insane and to send him to jail (8).

In contrast to Tripp, the majority of people respond to sleep loss with comparatively mild symptoms. The case of a seventeen-year-old high school student named Randy Gardner, who subjected himself to 264 hours without sleep for a science fair project on sleep deprivation, illustrates this reaction. Attended by friends, physicians, and sleep researchers, and comparatively free of stresses or pres-

sures, Randy's reactions were rather tame. He felt nauseated on day 3; his memory lapsed and his ability to concentrate diminished on day 4. On day 7 his speech was slurred. At one point Randy began to see himself as a brilliant black football star (9). (He wasn't.) Note that Randy's symptoms are similar to, though milder than, Tripp's.

After reviewing more than one hundred studies on sleep deprivation, Wilse Webb, a sleep researcher and psychologist, has concluded that scientists have not yet found physiological systems which are highly sensitive to sleep loss. On the other hand, behavioral deficits almost always appear when people stay awake for several days: They work more slowly and take longer to react. They also find it more difficult to do complex or prolonged tasks (10). People appear to be more likely to develop serious, psychoticlike symptoms in response to sleep deprivation under the following conditions: (1) When the circumstances that replace sleep are stressful; when much energy must be expended; when illness is present; when alcohol or drugs are involved. (2) When the subject and/or the experimenter *expects* dire effects. (3) When the environment is gloomy and/or depressing. (4) When the subject initially has serious underlying psychological problems (11).

Does sleep loss have serious long-term effects? We don't yet know the answer to this question. On the surface, the long-term consequences appear to be rather mild. Instead of sleeping day after day to make up for nights of lost sleep, subjects generally sleep some 12 to 15 hours and wake up refreshed. After only one night of sleep, sleep-deprived subjects perform at 90 percent of their former level on cognitive tasks. On the other hand, feelings of fatigue persist for two to three days; mild physiological irregularities may continue for several weeks: subjects may find they spend more or less time in particular sleep stages (12).

Initially, sleep researchers believed that sleep deprivation studies would tell them why sleep is needed. So far, they haven't, and the question of why we need sleep remains unanswered. There are, of course, many hypotheses. Some researchers believe that during sleep the body replenishes important chemical substances, substances necessary for basic life processes such as tissue repair, growth, and the synthesis of proteins. Others think that sleep provides a rest for the neural systems involved in higher mental processes such as memory and learning. Yet others feel that the sleep cycle may have evolved as a way of immobilizing the body at a time when food gathering and protection against predators were likely to be difficult. The state of our current knowledge on the question—why do animals need sleep?—has been eloquently summed up by one sleep researcher:

We knew a great deal more about why we sleep before the present plethora of sleep research, than we know now. Shakespeare . . . could blithely give his functional analog "Sleep that knits up the ravell'd sleave of care" without fear of contradiction. Nowadays we ask: exactly what is being raveled; is care necessary for the raveling; what is being knit up; and how does the knitting process work? To all of which, the answer is: we don't know [13].

What Does REM Sleep Have to Do with Dreams?

In the early 1950s University of Chicago sleep researchers Eugene Aserinsky and Nathaniel Kleitman discovered a relationship between REM sleep and dreams in the course of investigating an entirely different issue. Aserinsky and Kleitman were monitoring the eye movements of adult volunteers to see if they were a reliable indicator of depth of sleep when they discovered that rapid eye movements followed a definite pattern. The activity began some sixty minutes after sleep onset, continued about ten minutes, and recurred at ninety-minute intervals throughout the remainder of the night, lasting for approximately twenty-five minutes each time. Most intriguingly, these movements coincided with a particular type of alert and excited brain activity. Aserinsky and Kleitman suspected that these movements might be the sleepers' reactions to the imagery of their dreams. To find out if dreaming actually occurred at this time, they awakened their volunteers during the various phases of sleep and asked them to describe what they had been experiencing. Subjects reported dreams 74 percent of the time after awakening from REM sleep and only 7 percent of the time after awakening from non-REM sleep (14).

It is important to note that dreamlike activity also occurs throughout the stages of non-REM sleep. Dreamlike fragments are particularly prominent during sleep onset—stage

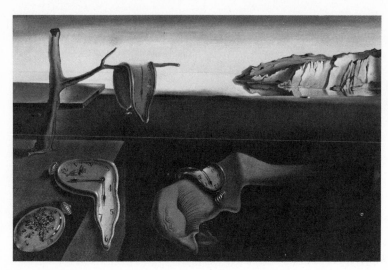

Figure 6-6. Bizarre, dreamlike imagery emerges in surrealistic paintings such as Salvador Dali's *The Persistence of Memory.* (1931. Oil on canvas, 9½ × 13″. Collection, The Museum of Modern Art, New York, Given anonymously.)

0—and during stage 1 non-REM sleep. When people are awakened during these stages, they report three kinds of subjective experiences which appear to occur sequentially. The *intact ego state* is experienced first. During this state our thoughts are logical and realistic; we can discriminate what is in our mind from what is external to us. For example, one subject reported, "I was thinking about the lab secretary typing out my transcripts." The second state is known as the *destructuralized ego state*. During this state we lose contact with reality and our mental content is bizarre. One subject reported: "I was observing the inside of a pleural cavity. There were small people in it, like in a room. The people were hairy, like monkeys. The walls of the pleural cavity are made of ice and slippery. In the midpart there is an ivory bench with people sitting on it. Some people are throwing balls of cheese against the inner side of the chest wall." Finally, people pass through a *restructuralized ego state*. Once again our mental content is plausible, but during the reported experience we appear to lose contact with external reality. For example, one subject reported, "I was driving a car, telling other people they shouldn't go over a certain speed limit [15]."[2]

Who Dreams?

Many people claim that they never dream. Do they dream without realizing it? Or are dreamers a special group of people? Psychologists have investigated this issue by observing large numbers of so-called nondreamers in sleep laboratories. There they monitor their subjects' sleep, wake them up when EEG and eye-movement records signal REM, and ask them what they were just experiencing. Sleep researchers find that even people

[2]The Eastern religious tradition believes that people can control and use the images of the sleep-onset period and stage 1 non-REM to foster personal growth. Unfortunately, these dreamlike fragments last only a few moments and are quickly forgotten. If you'd like to remember them, you might try the following procedure: As you settle down for a nap or for the night, lie on your back so that you can rest your elbows on the bed. Elevate one of your forearms to a vertical position. Then allow yourself to drift off. As your body prepares to enter stage 2 light sleep, your arm will fall because muscle tone disappears at this time. That will wake you up so that you can write down your thoughts and images.

who swear they never dream report dreams under these conditions. In fact, to date, although thousands of subjects have been studied, researchers have yet to find a single person who never reports a dream. It is not only virtually certain that every person dreams, it is probable that we all dream approximately four to six times every night.[3]

What's in a Dream?

For a long time dream interpretation belonged exclusively to the poets and the prophets. Scientists have been on the dream scene now for more than twenty years. They use two methods to collect dreams. Sometimes they simply ask their subjects to record their own dreams in a makeshift diary upon awakening. Using such a procedure, they can gather a vast number of dream reports relatively quickly and inexpensively. Unfortunately, when people write their own reports, they are likely to do so long after the dream—when distortion and forgetting become serious obstacles to accuracy.

Dream researchers also collect dreams in the laboratory—by monitoring their subjects' EEG and eye movements and waking them for a dream report after REM periods. (We refer to this method as the *EEG-REM method*.) Although this procedure is likelier to yield accurate dream reports, it has several drawbacks: It is time consuming and expensive, and dreams collected under these cir-

cumstances frequently contain less vivid imagery than home dreams, as well as many references to the experimental setting and the electronic paraphernalia.

Currently, sleep researchers know a lot about the content of people's dreams. In 1951 Calvin Hall, a psychologist and director of the Dream Research Institute of Miami, Florida, conducted one of the first systematic, large-scale studies of dream content by having essentially normal people record their dreams upon awakening. After collecting and analyzing some 10,000 dreams, Hall discovered that, for the most part, normal people dreamed of engaging in familiar activities in familiar places with familiar people. One interesting finding was that dreams tended to be emotionally negative on balance; that is, hostile acts outnumbered friendly ones 2 to 1. Moreover, anger, apprehension, and fearfulness characterized 64 percent of the dreams, but happy dreams occurred only 18 percent of the time (18).

Many studies show that dreams also reflect the dreamer's cultural experiences. For example, the dreams of American men and women show the clear-cut sex-role differences that our culture sanctions. Men dream about automobiles, tools, weapons, and money more often than women do. Women, on the other hand, tend to dream primarily about people, household objects, clothing, and flowers. Similarly, whereas men tend to be physically aggressive, active, and interested in sex in their dreams, women are likely to express their aggression subtly and emphasize verbal interactions and emotions in their dreams (19). Furthermore, dreams collected in other cultures reflect the conventions of the culture. Just as the Cuna Indians tend to be less aggressive than other Nicaraguans, so their dreams contain less aggressive imagery (20).

As we'd expect, people also dream about those issues or events that are important to

---

[3]People are probably not the only organisms that dream. Most animals show REM cycles, although a few—including fish, reptiles, and amphibians—do not. In addition, there is convincing evidence that at least some animals see images during their REM sleep. For example, researchers have recorded electrical activity in the visual center of the cat's brain during REM sleep (16). Even more to the point, when monkeys are reared in a totally dark environment and learn to press a lever every time a visual image is presented, they sometimes lever-press spontaneously during REM periods—presumably responding to the visual images of their dreams (17).

them. Pregnant women tend to dream increasingly about their pregnancy (21). Several California psychologists, Louis Breger, Ian Hunter, and Ron Lane, have shown that current stresses also appear in dreams. They investigated two conditions of intense personal involvement and high arousal— surgery and sensitivity-group participation. Both before and after the arousing event, subjects' dreams were collected in the laboratory using the EEG-REM method. The psychologists found that these intense experiences left their mark on dream content (22).

Environmental events that occur as we dream also influence what we dream about. In one study, for example, dreamers were exposed near the beginning of the REM cycle to a 1,000-cycle-per-second tone, a flashing 100-watt light bulb, and a spray of cold water. The investigators tried not to awaken their subjects until the end of the REM cycle (they didn't always succeed). In any case, the stimuli were incorporated identifiably into approximately 25 percent of the subjects' dreams (23). Other sleep researchers have sent subjects to sleep in their laboratories hungry, thirsty, or filled with spicy foods to determine how these bodily states affect dreams. Typically, references to hunger or thirst appear in a small but significant portion of the dreams (24).

Not all determinants of dream content are as easy to predict as those we have mentioned so far. For example, it now appears quite likely that physiological factors, such as body temperature, also play a role in determining what people dream about. In 1965 Paul Verdone of the National Institute of Health reported that early dreams were vague and bland and tended to focus on recent events. As the night continues and the sleeper's body temperature drops, dreams become vivid and intense and tend to center on events in the distant past. As temperature rises again toward morning, dream content emphasizes the recent past once again (25).

Sleep researchers continue to learn more and more about the mysterious state we call dreaming, but our understanding is still far from complete. Despite the contrary assertions of many self-styled authorities, the truth is that no one knows exactly how dreams are pieced together and precisely what they reflect. Psychologists should be able to learn more about this topic, once they can answer a more fundamental question: Why do people dream?

Why Do People Dream?

What function does dreaming fill? Psychologists have approached this basic issue in several ways. Long before they knew that REM periods existed, they looked for clues to the purpose of dreaming within the dream. Sigmund Freud was one of the first scientists interested in understanding why dreams occur and what they signify. Scanning the dream's fragmented and bizarre mingling of past and present motives, memories, thoughts, and emotions, Freud proposed that dreams were produced by people's unconscious impulses to gratify drives or fulfill wishes that could not be gratified or fulfilled in reality. According to Freud, the dream narrative, the *manifest content* of the dream, disguised and dramatized hidden desires and motives which formed the real meaning, the *latent content* of the dream. The "evidence" for Freud's explanation came from his psychotherapy sessions: As patients recounted their dreams and free-associated to the various dream elements, they frequently discovered unconscious thoughts and needs. Does such material really constitute evidence? Probably not. As Freud's critics assert, dreams are vague, easily distorted, or embellished, and readily interpreted in many ways. Consequently, people can find in dreams what they expect to find or what they want to find. Furthermore, it can be argued that the scientist cannot discover the purpose of dreaming simply by analyzing the dream itself because what we dream about is not necessarily related to why we dream. Memories, motives, thoughts, and emotions may be the subject matter of our dreams for a very simple reason: These phenomena may be the only stuff the brain has to work with while we sleep.

In looking elsewhere for an explanation of dreaming, modern sleep researchers have concentrated primarily on the well-established facts about REM sleep. One intriguing finding is that birds, mammals, primates, and people all experience significantly higher percentages of REM sleep in their fetal and infant stages than in youth and adulthood. This observation suggests that REM sleep may function in the maturation of the central nervous system. Note that this hypothesis implies that REM sleep (and dreaming) may serve a less important function in adulthood.

Other researchers believe that REM sleep may play a role in restoring brain processes after intense energy expenditure in psychological—as opposed to physical—pursuits. The fact that intense stimulation of the reticular formation in the laboratory (an event that occurs naturally when people use their brains to cope with stress, to learn, to think, to concentrate, and so on) leads to increased time in REM sleep supports this possibility. On the other hand, if REM sleep functions in psychological adaptation, children and adults should increase their REM sleep at times of intense learning, but this does not usually happen.

William Dement, a prominent sleep researcher now at Stanford University, and his associates have explored the function of REM sleep more directly. Dement's group reasoned that if REM sleep is essential for some

purpose, then depriving people of REM (and only REM) sleep, should result in clear-cut deficiencies that pinpoint its function. In an initial study published in 1960, Dement woke people up every time they began a REM stage. After prolonged REM deprivation, the subjects became irritable and anxious; they complained of increasing hunger and of difficulty concentrating. Moreover, when they were allowed to sleep without interruption, they increased the length and frequency of REM sleep beyond that observed before deprivation. These effects were not observed

Figure 6–7. Researchers in the sleep laboratory of William Dement at Stanford University. (Dennis Galloway, *Hospital Practice.*)

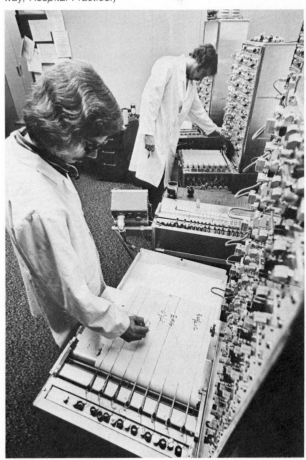

when people's sleep was interrupted the same number of times during non-REM stages (26).

Subsequent replications of this study were disappointing. It now appears that healthy, normal human subjects frequently show no waking consequences when deprived of REM sleep (although their post deprivation sleep frequently shows a marked lengthening and increased frequency of REM sleep) (27). In contrast to people, the selective deprivation of REM sleep in animals produces clear changes in motive-related behavior, particularly sexuality. REM-deprived male cats, for instance, persist in mounting inappropriate sex objects—such as other male cats who are both awake and fully anesthetized. Such studies pointed initially to an exciting hypothesis. There is evidence that energy for basic biological drives continually accumulates in the brain. It appeared that REM sleep might be serving a drive-regulating function, something like a *safety valve*—allowing excess energy to be discharged in the form of dreams without behavioral consequences (28).

Some recent drug research casts grave doubts on the safety valve theory of REM sleep. Late in the 1960s, it came to light that certain drugs used to treat anxiety neurotics and depressives have the side effect of suppressing REM sleep. When people remained on these drugs a year and longer (living without REM sleep for the entire time), there were no noticeable effects on their waking behavior (29,30). However, the various component parts of REM sleep—particular brain waves, rapid eye movements, central nervous system arousal, muscle relaxation, etc.—separated from one another and appeared in other phases of sleep or waking. These findings have led researchers to conclude—at least tentatively—that REM sleep is a conglomeration of separate processes, each serving particular functions (31). In this context dreaming may simply be the by-product of all these many simultaneous physiological activities.

In conclusion, the question of the function of REM sleep, which is indirectly the question of why we dream, has not been resolved. It continues to be one of the most exciting challenges for future sleep research.

Summary: The State of Sleep

1. The approximately twenty-four-hour sleep-waking cycle interweaves with many other biological rhythms.
2. Sleep researchers study sleep as a moment-to-moment process by continuously monitoring the electrical activity of the brain and the physical responses of the body as animals and human volunteers sleep in laboratories.
3. Sleep researchers usually differentiate between two important kinds of sleep: non-REM sleep and REM sleep.
4. Apparently, people need to sleep—although sleep scientists don't know why. Sleep deprivation produces a wide range of effects. So far no physiological system has been found to be especially sensitive to sleep loss. On the other hand, behavioral deficits appear consistently when sleep is lost.
5. The activity we call dreaming occurs primarily during REM sleep, although dreamlike fragments also appear during non-REM sleep.
6. Everyone dreams, but not everyone recalls their dreams. Dreams appear to reflect the dreamer's everyday reality in a particular role in a particular culture. Concurrent events, stresses, and memories all influence dream content. So apparently do physiological factors.
7. Sleep scientists continue to research the question: What functions does REM sleep fulfill?

We turn now to two states of consciousness which people deliberately induce.

THE STATE OF MEDITATION

The drum begins to beat, the caller begins to call a high-pitched flamenco-type air, and slowly the concentric circles begin to revolve in opposite directions. Then the sheik calls out, "Ya Haadi!" (O Guide!) and the participants start to repeat this word. They concentrate on it, saying it at first slowly, then faster and faster. Their movements match the repetitions.

I noticed that the eyes of some of the dervishes took on a far-away look, and they started to move jerkily as if they were puppets. The circles moved faster and faster until I (moving in the outer circle) saw only a whirl of robes and lost count of time. Now and then, with a grunt or a sharp cry, one of the dervishes would drop out of the circle and would be led away by an assistant to lie on the ground in what seemed to be an hypnotic state. I began to be affected and found that, although I was not dizzy, my mind was functioning in a very strange and unfamiliar way. The sensation is difficult to describe and is probably a complex one. One feeling was that of a lightening; as if I had no anxieties, no problems. Another was that I was a part of this moving circle and that my individuality was gone; I was delightfully merged in something larger . . . [32].

Turkish dervishes whirl in circles, Buddhists concentrate on their breathing, and yogis comtemplate specific objects—all to enter an unusual state of consciousness called *meditation.* What is meditation? What critical experiences lead to this state? These are the questions we turn to now.

What Is Meditation?

We define *meditation* as a state of consciousness brought on by diverse techniques that aim at separating the self from daily life, turning off normal analytic consciousness, and attaining an "overall perspective of 'Unity' and 'Humanity as one organism' [33]." The meditator usually follows special procedures or exercises to reach the state. The various meditation exercises can be classified into two categories. In *concentrative meditation* people attempt to restrict their awareness to a single unchanging source of stimulation for a specified time period. Meditators may gaze continually at an object, concentrate on a bodily process such as their breathing, listen to themselves chant aloud, or silently repeat a word or phrase. The dervish's dance is also a form of concentrative meditation. This intense concentration is supposed to lead to a clear positive feeling that is sometimes called, in Indian terminology, "the void" or "emptiness." In this state all active perceptions and thoughts of an analytic nature stop. This sensation lasts no more than several minutes, but it seems timeless to the participant, who feels refreshed afterward and more able to sense life directly.

The second type of meditation is referred to as *"opening up."* Its goal is to make people more aware of their external environment, more closely related to their daily activities,

Figure 6-8. A Tokyo housewife breaks her daily routine with a period of meditation. (Rene Burri, Magnum.)

and more alert. For instance, in "right-mindedness," a Buddhist practice in this category, people are asked to

[B]e aware and mindful of whatever you do, physically or verbally, during the daily routine of work in your life, private, public, or professional. Whether you walk, stand, sit, lie down, or sleep, whether you stretch or bend your limbs, whether you look around, whether you put on your clothes, whether you talk, or keep silent, whether you eat or drink—even whether you answer the call of nature—in these and other activities you should be fully aware and mindful of the act performed at the moment . . . [34].

The Nature of Meditation

Psychologists and others are currently studying the nature of meditation in their laboratories—frequently by inviting people with or without previous experience to meditate under observation. In one such study subjects responded to a campus newspaper ad offering them forty-five minutes of instruction in Zen meditation every weekday for two weeks. The volunteers practiced concentrating on their breathing, particularly on the movements of their stomachs as they breathed in a natural and relaxed way. After each session, they were interviewed about their subjective experiences. Later, on the basis of their interview responses, each subject was classified as a high, moderate, or low responder. The high responders had experienced feelings of nonstriving, calm, and great detachment both in feelings and thoughts—at least once. The moderate responders had been aware of an intensification of bodily sensations—especially those associated with breathing. The low responders, in contrast, had experienced only occasional relaxation, along with fogginess and dizziness (35). Table 6-1 shows the responses reported by the various meditators.

What about the physiological effects of meditation? Two experimenters, Robert Wallace and Herbert Benson, tackled this issue by inviting thirty-six experienced meditators to their laboratories at the University of California in Irvine and at Harvard Medical School in Cambridge. Each subject spent part of a session in transcendental meditation[4] and part in a normal quiet, nonmeditative state. In this way subjects served as their own controls. Continuous measures of blood pressure, heart rate, rectal temperature, skin resistance, and brain waves were taken. In addition, samples of blood were collected and analyzed for oxygen consumption and carbon dioxide elimination. During meditation the human body appeared to be characterized by a pattern of highly relaxed, wakeful activity. Specifically, the metabolic rate was unusually low and, consequently, oxygen consumption, carbon dioxide elimination, and the rate and volume of respiration were all reduced. The heart also slowed significantly, while blood lactate production showed a marked decrease. (The presence of excessive blood lactate is associated with feelings of intense anxiety [37].)

As we noted in Chapter 4, the brain is electrically active as long as we are alive. Does the nature of this electrical activity change as people enter meditation? In the study just cited and in numerous others, investigators have found that the alpha brain rhythm predominates during meditation. High alpha

[4]Transcendental meditation (TM) is a widely practiced yoga technique developed by the Maharishi Mahesh Yogi and taught by instructors whom he personally trains. Because of this arrangement, the TM technique is quite uniform. Generally, people practice a simple exercise for fifteen to twenty minutes each day: They sit in a comfortable position with their eyes closed until they perceive a "suitable" noise or thought that they then allow their minds to "experience." Through TM people expect their thoughts to rise to "a finer and more creative level in an easy and natural manner [36]." For more on TM, see Maharishi Mahesh Yogi. *Transcendental meditation: Serenity without drugs.* Signet, 1968 (in paperback).

TABLE 6-1. FREQUENCY OF PARTICULAR RESPONSE PATTERNS TO ZEN MEDITATION

Classification of Responders	Number of Subjects	Patterns				
		Dizziness, Fogginess	Relaxation, Calmness	Pleasant Bodily Sensations	Vivid Breathing Sensations	Concentration, Detachment
High	6	0	2	3	4	6
Moderate	10	2	3	8	5	0
Low	12	6	8	0	0	0
Total	28	8	13	11	9	6

Source: After E. W. Maupin. Individual differences in response to a Zen meditation exercise. *Journal of Consulting Psychology*, 1965, 29, 139–145.

activity is associated with feelings of being pleasantly blank, floating, peacefulness, rest, and comfort. Additionally, memories, illusions, and dreamlike fragments are also frequently reported during alpha. As you'll recall, high alpha activity is also observed during the sleep-onset stage. The alpha state is considered so pleasant in and of itself that many nonmeditators learn to initiate its onset, using biofeedback (see Chapter 7).

How Concentrative Meditative Exercises Affect Consciousness

Three factors—sensory input, relaxation, and expectations—appear to contribute to the effects of meditative exercises.

Sensory input. Ordinarily, the muscles in the eyes produce small, continual, involuntary movements known as *optical nystagmus*; so, under normal circumstances, images on the retina are kept in continual motion. Some scientists believe that optical nystagmus prevents receptor elements from becoming fatigued by spreading the excitation over a wide area. Many concentrative meditative exercises ask that participants restrict their vision to a specific unchanging object. This

means that during meditation images are sometimes maintained stably on the retina for comparatively long periods of time. What are

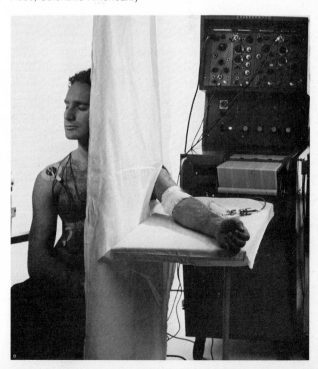

Figure 6-9. While this subject meditates, continuous measurements are made of physiological processes such as heart rate and blood pressure. At ten-minute intervals, a catheter in his left arm draws samples of arterial blood, which are analyzed for oxygen and carbon dioxide content, acidity, and lactate production. (Ben Rose, *Scientific American.*)

the consequences of stabilizing the retinal image? To investigate this question in the laboratory, psychologists have built an optical device that casts the same image on the retina at all times. After prolonged exposure to a stable visual image, subjects report that the image disappears momentarily from time to time. Simultaneously, alpha brain wave activity is observed in these subjects (38). Precisely the same phenomenon seems to be occurring during concentrative meditation.[5]

Relaxation. The techniques of meditation emphasize relaxation. Relaxation may affect consciousness in several ways. Generally, people feel calmer and more serene when they relax on a daily basis. In addition, the contrast between their low-arousal consciousness during meditation and their ordinary waking perceptions may intensify the later ones, making them appear sharper and clearer than previously. It is also possible that the engrossing meditative state gives people a "vacation" from their ordinary consciousness. Then when they "return home," their old perceptions appear fresh and different.

Expectations. Expectations also contribute to the positive emotional experience that ordinarily accompanies meditation. Meditators are striving for unusual changes in consciousness that they regard as highly desirable. Expectations have powerful effects on people's emotions, as we will see in Chapter 11. In this case, expectations probably influence people to interpret their physiological and subjective state as "joyful." The same sensations might be interpreted as neutral in a

laboratory setting or as frightening if they appeared spontaneously.

We turn now to the state of consciousness which accompanies marijuana intoxication.

THE STATE OF MARIJUANA INTOXICATION

[The] subject goes to washbasin and runs water . . . You think that's something, wait til you hear the cold. (runs water again) . . . you know, the . . . trouble is that . . . the present is more interesting now than events in the past. I mean the idea of sitting here and talking about something that's already happened instead of . . . happening now—instead of just being now—the present—is kind of ridiculous. . . . It's interesting to wonder what you could tell from the room. . . . The tape recorder has been going rather steadily. The room . . . the room is just so goddam confused and noisy—noisy in a visual sense. This whole thing—it's hard to get a sense of it at all. It's just kind of like an absolute random collection of things . . . [40].

These ramblings come from a subject in a laboratory experiment who is high on marijuana. *Marijuana* (grass, pot), the name for various preparations of the Indian hemp plant *Cannabis sativa*, is generally smoked and more rarely eaten for its mind-altering effects. The use of marijuana in the United States was relatively restricted until the early 1960s, when large numbers of college students discovered its existence and began experimenting with it. Currently, experts estimate that some 27 million Americans have tried marijuana at least once and that approximately half that number continue to use it regularly (41).

People have been taking substances to alter their consciousness for thousands of years. In fact, written accounts of opium use date back four thousand years before Christ. In this section we focus on the state of consciousness

[5]We see the same effect in sensory deprivation studies (see Chapter 5). When subjects wear halves of table tennis balls over their eyes, as they frequently do in such studies, the balls create a uniform patternless visual field. After prolonged exposure to this field, subjects frequently report temporary loss of vision while exhibiting an increase in alpha brain wave activity (39).

that people experience when under the influence of one such mind-altering substance—marijuana. Many of the same sensations characterize intoxication with other substances.[6] We turn to two questions: How does consciousness change during a marijuana high? How does marijuana affect consciousness?

How Consciousness Changes during a Marijuana High

To learn more about the subjective sensations experienced during a marijuana high, Charles Tart, a University of California psychologist, prepared a questionnaire that contained 206 descriptions of possible marijuana effects and distributed it through informal channels. Each statement was followed by adverbs such as "usually," "very often," "sometimes," "rarely," and "never." Experienced users (primarily college students who had used marijuana a dozen times or more) were asked to indicate, by checking the appropriate adverb, how frequently a particular effect generally occurred in the past six months. Subjects also checked how stoned they were when the effect first occurred: just stoned, fairly stoned, strongly stoned, very strongly stoned, or maximum stoned. Of the 206 questionnaires, 153 were returned. In general the data demonstrated that marijuana users agree on the subjective effects of marijuana intoxication:

Sense perception is often improved, both in intensity and in scope. Imagery is usually stronger but well controlled, although people care less

[6]A clever investigator gave experienced marijuana users an intravenous infusion of either alcohol or neutral saline (the solutions were introduced directly into their veins) while they smoked either a placebo or a marijuana cigarette. As it turned out, the subjects could not tell the difference between a marijuana high and an alcohol high (42).

about controlling their actions. Great changes in perception of space and time are common, as are changes in psychological processes such as understanding, memory, emotion, and sense of identity [43].

Does consciousness under a marijuana high change with degree of intoxication? The responses of experienced marijuana users are summarized in Figure 6-11. Many users report becoming restless when barely intoxicated on marijuana, although this restlessness usually disappears within minutes. As people smoke more marijuana, feelings of calm and openness frequently appear. At this intermediate level of intoxication, people also begin to feel that their sensory systems are keener, that their sensitivities to other people are more acute, and that peak performance on any project is likely. Spontaneous insights,

Figure 6-10. An estimated 27 million Americans have smoked marijuana at least once for its consciousness-altering effects. (Paul Conklin, from Monkmeyer.)

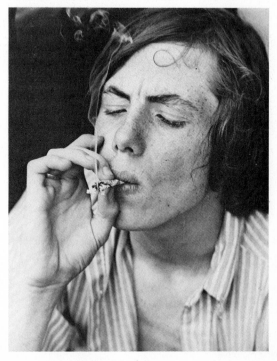

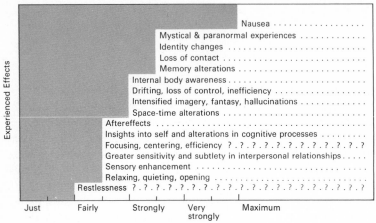

Figure 6-11. Some commonly reported effects of marijuana and the minimal level of intoxication necessary for their occurrence. The minimal level is that at which 50 percent of experienced users report the initial occurrence of the effect. All effects, except those followed by question marks, tend to continue at higher levels of intoxication. (From Tart, 1971.)

unusual associations, and novel thoughts commonly arise at this time; people view problems from new perspectives. These changes, in combination, seem to convince marijuana users that they are functioning more creatively than ordinarily.

If people continue to smoke, they reach a state of strong intoxication. Time seems to slow down; fantasy and imagery are intensified. At still higher levels of intoxication, they may hallucinate (see images, hear voices, and so on), although they are usually aware that the hallucinations are unreal. As thinking drifts off and the user loses the ability to focus on a specific topic, the old feelings of efficiency may give way to feelings of inefficiency. In addition, users sometimes experience an intense awareness of their internal bodily processes (like the beating of their hearts or their breathing).

As users move toward very high levels of marijuana intoxication, their memory spans shrink. Sometimes they lose contact with their environment and become preoccupied with internal imagery and mental processes. During this period of strong to very strong intoxication, users' feelings of personal identity may fade, intensifying their awareness that

they are part of Humanity or the World and not simply particular human beings with particular histories. Mystical experiences also take place at this level of intoxication. If people continue to smoke, nausea and vomiting are likely to result (44).

We've looked at the experiences that a majority of marijuana users report. Are these reports valid? Do marijuana users really feel what they say they feel? This question is hard to answer. A few studies that have measured the performance of people high on marijuana on certain tasks support the validity of these self-reports. For example, subjects high on marijuana consistently overestimate time intervals in the laboratory (45). Incidentally, rats high on marijuana also perform more slowly than usual. After smoking marijuana, people also perform more poorly on tasks that involve remembering for a short period of time, thinking in sequence, or keeping long-term goals in mind (46).

How Marijuana Affects Consciousness

In 1969 Andrew Weil, Norman Zinberg, and Judith Nelsen, psychologists at the Boston

University School of Medicine, published research that sheds some light on how marijuana affects consciousness. They observed seventeen male college students in their twenties in a neutral experimental setting. Nine of their subjects had never smoked marijuana before; eight were experienced users of the drug. The inexperienced subjects were taught the proper smoking technique; then in three subsequent sessions, they smoked either two high-dosage marijuana cigarettes, two low-dosage marijuana cigarettes, or two placebo marijuana cigarettes (made from the male cannabis plant). A double blind procedure was used so that neither the subjects nor the experimenter knew at the time which cigarette the inexperienced subjects were smoking. The experienced subjects were all tested once on the high-dosage cigarettes. Since conditions were not the same for the two groups of subjects, the differences between them must be regarded as tentative and suggestive. All the experienced users became intoxicated on the high-dosage cigarettes both in their own judgment and in the judgment of the experimenters. In marked contrast, only one inexperienced subject had an intense experience on the high-dosage marijuana cigarettes. (Interestingly, this subject had been extremely eager to become high.) The other naïve subjects reported minimal subjective effects, no euphoria, and no marked distortions, except for the slowing of time. Their reports after high dosages of marijuana make this point clear:

SUBJECT 1: "It was stronger than the previous time (low dose) but I really didn't think it could be marijuana. Things seemed to go slower."

SUBJECT 6: "I'd felt a combination of being almost drunk and tired, with occasional fits of silliness—not my normal reaction to smoking tobacco."

SUBJECT 8: "I felt faint briefly, but the dizziness went away, and I felt normal or slightly tired. I can't believe I had a high dose of marijuana [47]."

Moreover, a recent study shows that experienced marijuana users sometimes become high after smoking placebos and that they have trouble distinguishing the effects of placebos from those of relatively potent marijuana cigarettes (48).

How can these results be interpreted? Many psychologists believe that they support a multifactor explanation of marijuana's effects on consciousness. Under ordinary circumstances the drug interacts with the nervous system to create a potential for particular experiences. (The effects of marijuana on the nervous system are not well understood.) Then social-psychological factors (such as setting, mood, past experience, and personality of the user) shape the nature of the experience.

Although the drug itself obviously had some effect on the novice marijuana users in the Weil-Zinberg-Nelsen study, the neutral setting, inhibitions, anxieties, and/or lack of skills in noticing and enhancing subtle bodily effects probably account, at least in part, for the subjects' rather bland perceptions. Similarly, social-psychological factors must be playing some role in the chronic marijuana users' highs on placebo cigarettes. Expectations may be altering perceptions. Respondent conditioning could also be involved. The sight and smell of marijuana have been repeatedly associated with inhaling potent marijuana and experiencing a special state of consciousness. Eventually, the sight and smell of marijuana alone may become sufficient to elicit the altered state. Table 6-2 shows the drug and nondrug factors that appear to influence whether people have good or bad drug trips.

TABLE 6-2. VARIABLES WHICH MAXIMIZE THE PROBABILITY OF GOOD OR BAD DRUG TRIPS

	Variables	Good Trip Likely	Bad Trip Likely
Drug	Quality	Pure, known	Unknown drug or unknown degree of (harmful) adulterants
	Quantity	Known accurately, adjusted to individual's desire	Unknown, beyond individual's control
Long-term Factors	Culture	Acceptance, belief in benefits	Rejection, belief in detrimental effect
	Personality	Stable, open, secure	Unstable, rigid, neurotic, or psychotic
	Physiology	Healthy	Specific adverse vulnerability to drug
	Learned drug skills	Wide experience gained under supportive conditions	Little or no experience or preparation, unpleasant past experience
Immediate-user Factors	Mood	Happy, calm, relaxed, or euphoric	Depressed, overexcited, repressing significant emotions
	Expectations	Pleasure, insight, known eventualities	Danger, harm, manipulation, unknown eventualities
	Desires	General pleasure, specific user-accepted goals	Aimlessness, (repressed) desires to harm or degrade self for secondary gains
Experiment or Situation	Physical setting	Pleasant and esthetically interesting by user's standards	Cold, impersonal, "medical," "psychiatric," "hospital," "scientific"
	Social events	Friendly, nonmanipulative interactions overall	Depersonalization or manipulation of the user, hostility overall
	Formal instructions	Clear, understandable, creating trust and purpose	Ambiguous, dishonest, creating mistrust
	Implicit demands	Congruent with explicit communications, supportive	Contradict explicit communications and/or reinforce other negative variables

Source: C. Tart. *On being stoned: A psychological study of marijuana intoxication.* Palo Alto, Calif.: Science and Behavior Books, 1971, P. 246.

WHY PEOPLE CHOOSE TO ALTER THEIR CONSCIOUSNESS

The states of consciousness achieved by meditation techniques and marijuana intoxication are similar in several respects. In both states people alter the normal reducing function of their senses and increase the amount of information to which they are open. Further, through both meditation and marijuana intoxication people perceive themselves as united with others. Similarly, both experiences introduce people to a slower-paced, more

relaxed reality. Why should people seek to alter their consciousness in these ways? Psychologist Robert Ornstein believes that there are three major reasons:

1. Ordinary rational consciousness fails to make people aware of the sensory, aesthetic, and emotional aspects of life that they want to understand more fully.
2. Ordinary consciousness is analytic; that is, it separates the self from the world. A shift toward viewing oneself as interconnected with life and with other people may be comforting at this time in history when survival seems to depend on our solving

worldwide problems such as nuclear war, overpopulation, famine, and pollution.

3. These states provide people with fleeting moments of peace and quiet—experiences that are far too rare for too many (48).

Summary: The States of Meditation and Marijuana Intoxication

1. People in our culture use meditation and marijuana as tools to deliberately alter their ordinary waking consciousness.

2. In meditation diverse techniques help people obtain a perspective of unity, capture a sense of clarity, and make themselves more sensitive to their daily experiences. During concentrative meditation the meditator's body shows a complex pattern of physiological responses that indicate deep relaxation. Stable sensory input, relaxation, and positive expectations appear to contribute to the effects of meditation.

3. A large number of people use chemical substances to alter their consciousness. Marijuana, one of the more popular substances in our own culture, appears to produce changes in sensory perceptions of time and space, in imagery, and in mental processes. Marijuana's effects on consciousness probably depend on complex interactions between physical factors such as the drug and the user's nervous system and social-psychological factors such as setting, learning, and expectations.

STUDY GUIDE 6

Key Terms. state of consciousness, biological rhythm, electroencephalograph (EEG), electroencephalogram, alpha activity, spindles, non-REM sleep, REM sleep, intact ego state, destructuralized ego state, restructuralized ego state, EEG-REM method, manifest content, latent content, meditation, concentrative meditation, "opening up," optical nystagmus, *Cannabis sativa.*

Important Research. sleep deprivation (Webb), REM sleep and dreams (Aserinsky and Kleitman), content of dreams (Hall), REM-sleep deprivation (Dement), physiological effects of meditation (Wallace and Benson), marijuana experiences (Tart), novice and experienced marijuana users (Weil, Zinberg, and Nelsen).

Self-Quiz

1. States of consciousness are difficult for scientists to investigate because [**a**] the consciousness of most people rarely varies; [**b**] they have no physical correlates; [**c**] research must depend largely on self-reports about events that are difficult to describe in words; [**d**] few people are willing to be subjects in experiments which attempt to alter their consciousness.

2. An electroencephalograph measures [**a**] the electrical activity of the brain; [**b**] the electrical activity of the heart; [**c**] any biological rhythm; [**d**] several physical events, such as brain activity, heart rate, and blood pressure.

3. REM sleep is *not* characterized by [**a**] increased blood pressure and heart rate; [**b**] dreaming; [**c**] being easily awakened; [**d**] small, fast, irregular brain waves.

4. Alpha activity is associated with [**a**] deep sleep; [**b**] periods of dreaming; [**c**] being wide awake and alert; [**d**] pleasantly relaxed feelings.

5. Virtually all people dream [**a**] several times every night; [**b**] once a night; [**c**] at least once every two or three nights, although they may not remember dreaming; [**d**] occasionally, but the amount of dreaming varies widely—some people dream sev-

eral times a night, others only once or twice a week.

6. Which is *not* a factor contributing to serious, psychoticlike symptoms following sleep deprivation? [**a**] alcohol and drugs; [**b**] age; [**c**] expectations of ill effects; [**d**] previous psychological problems.

7. To make up for several nights of sleep loss, subjects generally [**a**] sleep twelve or fifteen hours a night for as many nights as sleep was lost; [**b**] make up the total number of hours lost, either all at once or spread out over several nights; [**c**] sleep twelve to fifteen hours in a single twenty-four-hour period and recover completely; [**d**] sleep twelve to fifteen hours in a single twenty-four-hour period and recover 90 percent of their former mental abilities.

8. After the initial non-REM stage 1 sleep period, what is the typical order of sleep stages? [**a**] 2, 3, 4, 3, 2, 1 (REM)—occurs once before people awaken; [**b**] 2, 3, 4, 3, 2, 1 (REM)—entire sequence is repeated several times throughout the night; [**c**] 2, 3, 4, 1 (REM), 2, 3, 4, 1 (REM)—entire sequence is repeated several times throughout the night; [**d**] 4, 3, 2, 1 (REM)—entire sequence is repeated several times throughout the night.

9. Dream content is known to be influenced by all the following *except* [**a**] important issues or events in the dreamer's daily life; [**b**] external events like flashing lights; [**c**] biological states like hunger or body temperature; [**d**] the dreamer's intelligence.

10. The manifest content of a dream refers to the [**a**] characters in the dream; [**b**] emotional content of the dream; [**c**] "story," or what happens in the dream; [**d**] hidden desires and meanings underlying the "story" of the dream.

11. Which is *not* a widely held theory of why people dream? [**a**] to help develop the central nervous system; [**b**] to gratify wishes that cannot be fulfilled in "real life"; [**c**] to restore brain processes after heavy psychological use; [**d**] to make sleeping a rewarding experience, so people will sleep often and not exhaust their bodies.

12. In comparing meditation with an ordinary quiet state, Wallace and Benson found that meditation was associated with all of the following *except* [**a**] slower heart rate; [**b**] lower metabolic rate; [**c**] lower level of a blood chemical associated with anxiety; [**d**] lower level of alpha brain waves.

13. Which is *not* a factor described in the text as contributing to successful meditation? [**a**] use of certain drugs; [**b**] relaxation; [**c**] reducing small involuntary eye movements; [**d**] positive expectations.

14. A marijuana high [**a**] cannot be distinguished from an alcohol high by experienced users when the appropriate controls are used; [**b**] intensifies sensory experiences and alters the sense of time; [**c**] may be difficult for inexperienced users to achieve; [**d**] all of the above.

15. Which is *not* a condition that increases the chance of a good marijuana experience? [**a**] positive expectations; [**b**] past conditioning of the taste and smell of marijuana with pleasure; [**c**] a culture which perceives marijuana as harmful; [**d**] a stable, healthy personality.

Exercise

STAGES OF SLEEP. To test your knowledge, match the stages of sleep with their characteristics. Use the following abbreviations: stage 0—presleep (0); stage 1—drowsiness (1D); stage 1—REM (1R); stage 2—light sleep (2); stage 3—deep sleep (3); stage 4—deepest sleep (4).

_____ 1. Brain waves characteristic of wakefulness and high cortical activity.

_____ 2. Relaxation and high level of alpha activity on EEG.

_____ 3. Spindles begin to appear on EEG.

_____ 4. Rapid movements of the eyes.

_____ 5. Occur only at the beginning of the night's sleep.

_____ 6. May begin with a sensation of falling.

_____ 7. Sleeper most difficult to awaken.

_____ 8. Fast heart rate and breathing; high blood pressure.

_____ 9. Occurs just before stage 4 in nightly cycle.

_____ 10. Occurs just after stage 4 in nightly cycle.

_____ 11. Vague thoughts, floating sensations, and dreamlike fragments frequently reported when awakened.

_____ 12. Dreaming usually reported when awakened.

_____ 13. About half total sleep time of young adults.

_____ 14. Sleep irregularities such as sleep walking, nightmares, bed wetting occur.

Questions to Consider

1. Does your consciousness vary cyclicly? Try keeping a diary for a week, rating each hour as alert, sluggish, or neutral. Taking your temperature each hour to see whether it is related to mood might also prove interesting. Do you have regular cycles of alertness and sluggishness?

2. If you wanted to catch and remember one dream each

night, how could you do it? How could you catch all the dreams of a single night?

3. Watch a sleeping dog or cat and try to observe REM. You might also waken the animal during REM and non-REM periods to see if the animal behaves differently upon awakening at these two times.

4. Would meditation be a good alternative for drug users?

5. Marijuana alters an animal's awareness of time. How could you test this hypothesis?

6. Some people seem to prefer their ordinary rational consciousness, whereas others prefer more unusual states. How do you think these two different groups of people vary in personality, attitudes, and background?

Project 6: The Dreams of REM and Non-REM Periods

Many researchers find that subjects report vivid dreams a large percentage of the time when awakened from REM sleep and only a small percentage of the time when awakened from non-REM sleep. The purpose of this project is to verify these findings and to collect dream reports for further analysis.

Method. Find two subjects who have little trouble falling asleep and enlist their cooperation ahead of time by explaining the purposes and procedures of this project. You will be observing your subjects individually.

Make up a data sheet for each subject like the one shown.

Let the subject go to sleep in a quiet room. Leave a dim light on so that you can see what is going on. If your subject has trouble falling asleep with another person in the room, leave the room for about fifteen minutes. Record the time when the subject first appears to be asleep. (Breathing tends to be slow and rhythmic at this time.) Now watch the subject's eyes. When they begin to dart about (the activity is clearly visible even though the lids are tightly closed), record the time, then wait five or ten minutes to awaken the subject. Record the time. Then ask the subject the following questions:

Were you dreaming? (If yes, proceed with the other questions.)
Were you dreaming in color?
What were you dreaming about? (characters, events, and places?)
What seemed to be motivating the characters?
What was the overall emotional tone of the dream? (happy, fearful, angry, etc.?)
Was the dream ordinary or bizarre?
How long did the dream seem to last?

Record the answers to these questions on your data sheet. Let the subject return to sleep. Wait about a half hour. Awaken the subject again when there are no rapid eye movements and question him/her again. Repeat the same procedure during one more REM and one more non-REM period.

Results and discussion. Consider the following questions:

1. Did dreams occur more often during REM periods than during non-REM periods? If not, can you explain your negative results by procedural problems? Was there any difficulty in deciding what to call a dream? Explain.

2. Did REM periods occur at the predicted times throughout the night?

3. Did your subjects dream in color?

4. Can you relate the content of the subjects' dreams to events, people, or places in their lives? Did the motives of the dream characters correspond to motives which the subjects appear to have? Talking to the subject about these dreams (the next day!) may give you some clues.

5. Were most of the dreams you collected negative or positive in emotional tone?

6. Were most of the dreams you collected ordinary or bizarre?

7. Did the subjects' ideas of how long the dreams had lasted correspond to time in the REM stage before the awakening?

8. Did any of the dreams seem typical of intact, destructuralized, or restructuralized ego states?

9. Suppose you were a full-time dream researcher. How might you modify this procedure to make dream collection more efficient and more reliable?

DATA SHEET FOR DREAM COLLECTION (one needed for each subject)

	Was the Subject Dreaming?
Time when subject fell asleep _____	
Time of first REM period _____	
Time of first REM awakening _____	yes ___ no ___
Time of first non-REM awakening _____	yes ___ no ___
Time of second REM period _____	

Time of second REM awakening

_____ yes _____ no_____

Time of second non-REM awakening _____ yes _____ no_____

Make four blocks like the following:

Dream number _____

Color? _____

Content (characters, events, places)? _____

_____

_____

Motives of characters? _____

Overall emotional tone? _____

Ordinary or bizarre? _____

Estimated length of dream? _____

Suggested Readings

1. Keen, Sam. "Sorcerer's apprentice." *Psychology To-day*, December 1972, 5, 90–92, 95, 96, 98, 100, 102. Interview with Carlos Castanada concerning how he learned to reach higher states of consciousness.
2. Ornstein, Robert. *The psychology of consciousness*. San Francisco: W. H. Freeman and Company, 1972 (paperback). Through accounts of research, Eastern literature, and personal experience, Ornstein examines what is known about consciousness with an emphasis on meditation and other unusual states.
3. Luce, Gay Gaer. *Biological rhythms in human and animal physiology*. New York: Dover, 1971. (paperback) A science writer discusses research on biological rhythms focusing on their effects on learning, job performance, mood, vulnerabilities to stress and disease, and medical treatment.
4. Dement, William C. *Some must watch while some must sleep*. San Francisco: W. H. Freeman and Company, 1974 (paperback). A sleep researcher describes current sleep and dreaming research, much of it his own.
5. Snyder, Solomon. "Work with marihuana: Effects." *Psychology Today*, May 1971, 4, 37–40, 64–65. Summary of research on marihuana's effects.
6. Campbell, Colin, Gary Schwartz, & Leon Otis. "The facts on transcendental meditation." *Psychology Today*, April 1974, 7, 37–51. A description of current research on transcendental meditation, focusing primarily on what makes it work and who benefits from it.

Answer Keys

SELF-QUIZ
1. c   2. a   3. c   4. d   5. a   6. b   7. d   8. b   9. d
10. c   11. d   12. d   13. a   14. d   15. c

EXERCISE
1. IR   2. 0   3. 2   4. IR   5. 0, ID   6. 2   7. 4, IR
8. IR   9. 3   10. 3   11. 0, ID   12. IR   13. 2   14. 4

BASIC LEARNING PROCESSES

IN THIS CHAPTER
We explore several basic learning processes that produce relatively permanent changes in the ways people and other animals behave. These fundamental learning processes often occur without people deliberately attempting to change and without their even being aware that any changes are occurring. We examine three processes: respondent conditioning, operant conditioning, and observation learning. The activities that people ordinarily call learning—such as learning to read or memorizing poetry—illustrate complex cognitive types of learning. We focus on this type of learning in Chapter 8. After reading this chapter, you should be able to do the following:

1. Describe how respondent behavior is acquired, reinforced, extinguished, recovered spontaneously, generalized, and discriminated
2. Explain how fears can be learned and unlearned by respondent conditioning principles
3. Describe how operants are reinforced, shaped, extinguished, and recovered spontaneously
4. Cite five principles that lead to the effective and humane use of punishment and five disadvantages of using punishment
5. Describe how people learn by observation and whom they model

Every year coyotes eat countless numbers of sheep, causing large financial losses for sheep ranchers in the Western United States. Consequently, sheep ranchers are among the most avid of the coyote's enemies, and they slaughter large numbers of coyotes each year. But killing coyotes causes new problems because coyotes serve several valuable functions: They consume gophers, squirrels, rabbits, mice, and other rodents that might otherwise eat the grass and other grains that feed the sheep. Moreover, if rodent and rabbit populations grow unchecked, they overrun the countryside.

In 1972 two psychologists, Carl Gustavson and John Garcia, joined forces to see if they could engineer a more satisfactory solution to the coyote problem. They devised a program to teach coyotes an aversion (a distaste) for lambs, using a fundamental learning process known as respondent (classical) conditioning. As we will see, when one event repeatedly precedes a second event which automatically evokes a particular response, the first event often begins to evoke a similar response. Gustavson and Garcia observed that wild coyotes ate hamburger meat with gusto. Several days later they laced some hamburger meat with lithium chloride, a drug that in-

Figure 7-1. Coyotes fed lamb meat tainted with nausea-producing lithium chloride were taught an aversion to lamb.

duces nausea and vomiting. After devouring this meal, the coyotes became quite ill; later, when presented with perfectly good hamburger meat, they sniffed, retched, rolled on the meat, urinated on it, or buried it. Apparently, they had learned to associate hamburger meat with an upset stomach.

Could the coyotes be taught an aversion to lamb? Three coyotes participated in a second study. After observing that these coyotes did, in fact, attack and devour live lambs, the psychologists gave them minced lamb meat tainted with lithium chloride wrapped in fresh lamb hide. A second such meal followed for two of the animals. After these experiences with tainted lamb meat, the coyotes were given an opportunity to attack a live lamb. Instead of attacking, the animals began retching (1). Eventually a learning-based program, like this one, may help solve the sheep rancher's coyote problem.

A preschool child named Mark was clumsy and inept at physical activities. For that reason, apparently, he spent most of his outdoor time wandering aimlessly from activity to activity. Whenever he tried to play with other children, his poor physical skills disrupted their games. Mark's teachers were concerned. If Mark couldn't participate in recreation, he might never develop important social skills.

Mark's teachers observed Mark's behavior carefully for nine days. During this observation period Mark played alone in the sandbox or pursued other similar activities about 75 percent of the time; approximately 25 percent of the time he simply stood around or watched other children; he played actively less than 1 percent of the time. After these observations were collected, the teachers decided to use a different basic learning process known as *operant conditioning* to try to increase the time Mark spent in physical play. Every time Mark came near the monkey bars, the teacher on duty rewarded him by talking to him, smiling at him, or bringing him more equipment. As we will see, when rewards immediately follow a behavior, they tend to increase the frequency of the behavior. As expected, Mark began spending much of his time near the monkey bars. Eventually, he began climbing on them. At this point the teacher on duty gave Mark her personal attention only for climbing. After nine days of this treatment Mark was spending approximately 67 percent of his outside time climbing and he was climbing skillfully; so the teachers began using their attention to reward other forms of vigorous play. This simple program had lasting effects: Mark was still playing actively approximately 50 percent of the time when he returned to school the following fall (2).

A psychologist named Robert O'Connor worked with twelve severely socially withdrawn preschool children. He was interested in finding out if the children could learn appropriate social behavior by observing another withdrawn nursery school child engage in social activities. Learning through observation is a third basic learning process.

O'Connor divided the twelve children into two groups. One group watched a film on dolphins. The other watched a film that depicted a shy child in eleven situations. Initially, the shy child in the movie observed another child (or other children) engaged in some activity; eventually the shy child joined in and received encouragement from the other children or the narrator. The play became more vigorous and the number of children increased from scene to scene. For example, the child in the first scene shared a book with another, whereas the child in the last scene joined a group of children tossing a toy. After the children had watched the film, O'Connor observed their play. The children who had viewed the dolphin movie remained withdrawn; the children who had viewed the shy child in social activities increased both the number and quality of their interactions with other children (3).

In these cases psychologists and teachers have used three basic learning processes to change behavior. We discuss these learning processes in detail in this chapter, but first, what do psychologists mean by the word "learning"?

Figure 7-2. Shy children can learn social skills through observation learning. (Leonard Freed, Magnum.)

What Do Psychologists Mean by "Learning"?

Psychologists define *learning* as a process that occurs inside the organism and leads to relatively permanent changes in behavior that can be attributed to experience. The learning process is not well understood. It seems likely that during learning chemical and electrical changes occur within an animal's nervous system—stamping in associations, skills, ideas, and information.

It is important to note that behavior changes cannot always be attributed to experience. Other factors—such as fatigue, drugs, changes in motivation, and maturation—also alter behavior. The effects of fatigue, drugs, and motives tend to be brief—in contrast to those of learning. After a good night's rest the effects of a sleepless night usually vanish. The influence of a drug wears off after some well-defined period of time, and the person behaves as before. The effects of motivation are also temporary ones. The small child who is hungry for supper may whine and howl until dinner is served. But after the need is filled, the child typically stops whining.

Changes in behavior also result from the growth of the body and nervous system. Such maturational changes (see Chapter 3) tend to appear at certain times in development and do not depend on any *specific* experiences. For example, the newborn human infant can without any prior training grasp anything that touches its fingers. This response must be largely attributed to physical development. As long as the environment is within normal limits, the response appears. Many other responses such as smiling, walking, and talking result from a combination of maturation and learning.

The Importance of Learning

Learning is an important influence on all living creatures. As we saw in Chapter 3, experience begins to shape the developing organism at conception. As time goes on, experience plays a powerful and increasingly important role in molding behavior. The more complex the animal, the more impressively learning contributes to its shaping, but even primitive animals learn. For instance, when hatched, fish are already largely adapted to their world. Heredity has programmed them with instinctive behaviors that serve them well under many circumstances, but not under all circumstances. Hatchery-reared fish, for example, learn to associate shadows with food because the arrival of the attendant, who casts a shadow at the edge of their pool, precedes all their meals. Naturally, every time they see a shadow, they swim to the surface of the pool. When these fish are released in streams, they continue to behave in this way, so they do not last long. To help these creatures, psychologists have devised survival-training programs. A mild electric current is passed through the surface of the hatchery pool each time the shadow appears, so the fish receive a shock if they approach close to the surface of the water. After a number of pairings of shadow and shock, hatchery fish learn to avoid shadows. Consequently, these educated fish fare much better in the wild with raccoons, bears, and fishermen (4). Thus, even rather simple animals can, and sometimes must, learn.

Learning in its broadest sense—the effect of experience on behavior—is such an important topic in psychology that a great many psychologists are involved, in one way or another, in studying it. Some representative learning interests of various areas of psychology are shown in Table 7-1.

Performance: The Measure of Learning

In general, psychologists measure learning by observing changes in behavior. These changes in behavior are called *performance*. It is

TABLE 7-1. WHO STUDIES LEARNING?

Area of Psychology	Some Typical Concerns
Experimental	1 How does the scheduling of rewards influence an animal's learning? 2 Does punishment interfere with further learning?
Cognitive	1 How do people learn to solve problems? 2 How do children learn their language?
Physiological	1 What goes on in the nervous system as people learn? 2 Do physical defects keep mentally retarded children from learning at a normal rate?
Developmental	1 Can newborn infants learn? 2 How do children learn sex roles?
Educational	1 Do students learn best when grouped by ability? 2 What factors cause students to fail to learn?
Social	1 How do people learn prejudices? 2 Is aggression learned or innate?
Clinical	1 How do people learn bad habits like fears, addictions, or criminal activities? 2 How can poorly adjusted people learn more adaptive ways of coping with their problems?
Industrial	1 How can foremen learn effective management techniques? 2 What programs can most effectively equip the hard-core unemployed with useful vocational skills?

Adapted from Table 4-1 in L. E. Bourne & B. R. Ekstrand. *Psychology: Its principles and meanings.* Hinsdale, Ill., Dryden, 1973. P. 88.

important to keep in mind that performance and learning are two separate phenomena. Learning is a process that occurs inside an organism, whereas performance is a visible demonstration that learning has occurred. Psychologists use performance as a measure of learning out of necessity. Since they cannot observe or measure learning directly, they need an indirect measure. Performance is the most practical indirect measure available.

Unfortunately, performance is not a completely satisfactory measure of learning. Much learning takes place without any observable behavior; that is, much human learning is *latent*; it becomes evident only when some occasion arises for using it. As you read, for example, you pick up all kinds of information that may, at some future date, affect your behavior. As you see and hear, you also continually learn. An announcer on the radio may report that it will rain later in the afternoon. At that moment you may say

or do nothing that demonstrates your learning, but at 4 o'clock in the afternoon, you may don your raincoat and get your umbrella before setting out for the library. When psychologists devise a situation that forces an animal to perform, the performance may or may not reflect what the animal has learned. It's all too easy to think of situations where performances do not reflect learning very well. For example, many people freeze on tests and perform poorly even though they may be able to reproduce large amounts of information a short time before and after they are asked to perform.

We turn now to three basic learning processes. We begin with respondent conditioning.

RESPONDENT CONDITIONING

All animals are "prewired" with automatic responses or reflexes called *respondents*. Respondents are triggered by events that immediately precede them. Salivating, startling, blinking, gagging, feeling nauseated, feeling afraid, slowing or speeding the heart, and lowering or raising the blood pressure can be respondents. When something gets caught in your throat, you gag; the sudden loud report of a rifle produces a startle response. Note that we do not seem to have a choice about whether or not to make respondents. They tend to occur automatically in response to particular kinds of stimulation.

The Conditioning of Respondents

A respondent can be transferred to a situation in which it does not ordinarily occur by a method called *respondent conditioning* (*classical conditioning*). Startling, a response frequently made to thunder, is easily transferred to the sight that usually precedes thunder, lightning. Feeling nauseated, another respondent, is easily transferred from a bout of food poisoning to the food that preceded that experience. How do these transfers take place?

Four elements are involved in respondent conditioning: (1) The first element, the *unconditioned stimulus* (*US*), automatically produces a particular respondent. Let's take a common example. The unconditioned stimulus—food in the mouth—automatically elicits the respondent—salivation—in people and in other animals. (2) The *unconditioned response* (*UR*) is the respondent that is automatically elicited by the unconditioned stimulus—in this case, salivation. (3) A *neutral stimulus*— any event, object, or experience that does not elicit the unconditioned response to begin with—is paired with the unconditioned stimulus. Assume that the sound of a bell—a neutral stimulus—precedes eating lunch at noon every day. (4) Finally, after the neutral stimulus has been closely followed by the unconditioned stimulus (sometimes once,

usually many times), it comes to evoke a response that is similar to, but milder than, the unconditioned response. This response is called the *conditioned response* (*CR*). In this case, the mere sound of the noon bell would elicit *mild* salivation, the conditioned response. At this point psychologists call the neutral stimulus the *conditioned stimulus* because it has been "conditioned" to elicit a new response (see Figure 7-3).

Let's take a second example that can occur in real life. Having one's teeth pulled or filled (an unconditioned stimulus) produces pain (an unconditioned response). The dentist begins as a neutral stimulus. After the dentist is paired several times with these painful procedures, the mere sight of the dentist may evoke a conditioned fear response (see Figure 7-4).

The History of Respondent Conditioning: Pavlov and His Dogs

Ivan Petrovich Pavlov (1849–1936), a Russian physiologist, is credited with the discovery of respondent conditioning.[1] (Accordingly, respondent conditioning is sometimes called *Pavlovian conditioning*.) Pavlov and his associates were studying digestive secretions, among them, salivation. Because Pavlov was a meticulous scientist, he noted that his dogs were salivating to stimuli other than food— such as the feeder's footsteps and the sight of the feeder. These inexplicable salivations, nuisances at first, increasingly occupied Pavlov's attention. Eventually, Pavlov and his associates set up a simplified version of the

---

[1]An American graduate student named E. B. Twitmeyer working on his dissertation at the University of Pennsylvania published the first written report on respondent conditioning in 1904. No one paid any attention to Twitmeyer, and he did not follow up systematically with additional research.

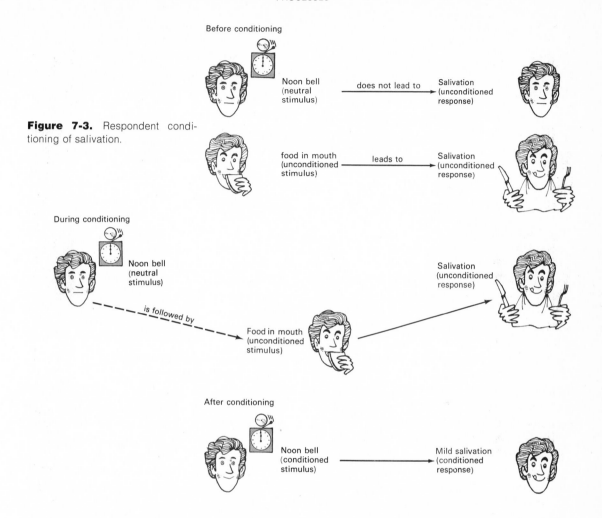

Figure 7-3. Respondent conditioning of salivation.

situation that had produced the peculiar salivations, taking care to remove as many contaminating factors as they could. They used the apparatus pictured in Figure 7-5.

Prior to their study Pavlov and his associates performed a minor operation on each dog. They diverted the dog's saliva through its cheek into a tube so that it could be easily measured. Once the dog recovered from surgery, they put it on a stand and restrained it in a harness. Then they permitted the animal to become accustomed to the experimental situation. After the dog had relaxed a bit, they measured its salivary reactions to both food in the mouth (the unconditioned stimulus) and a tone (the neutral stimulus). The animal salivated considerably when the food was placed in its mouth, and it salivated negligibly when the tone was presented. Once these measurements were made, the conditioning trials began. Pavlov sounded the tone and presented the food soon afterward—all by remote control. Fifty such pairings occurred over the course of several weeks. As a

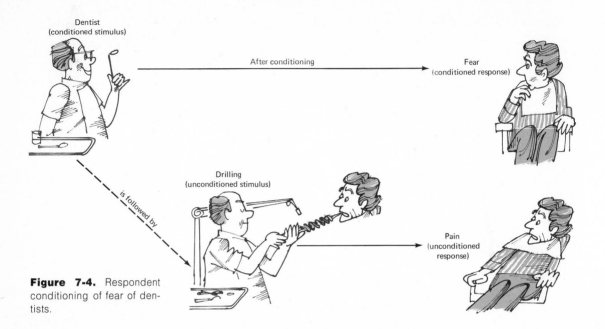

Dentist
(conditioned stimulus)

After conditioning

Fear
(conditioned response)

is followed by

Drilling
(unconditioned stimulus)

Pain
(unconditioned
response)

Figure 7-4. Respondent conditioning of fear of dentists.

result, the dog increased both the amount and the speed of its salivating following the tone. Apparently, the nuisance salivations had arisen from the accidental pairings of food and the stimuli immediately preceeding the food.

The Characteristics of Respondent Conditioning

Russian and American psychologists have studied respondent conditioning intensively in their laboratories. Generally, they select a

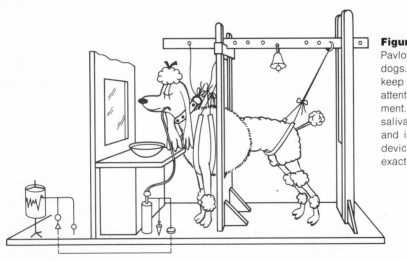

Figure 7-5. Apparatus used by Pavlov to condition salivation in dogs. The restraining harness helps keep the dog in place and directs its attention to the events of the experiment. A tube runs from the dog's salivary glands through its cheek and into a glass container where a device (in the lower left) records the exact amount of salivation.

simple unconditioned stimulus, such as a puff of air or meat powder. The simple unconditioned stimulus evokes a simple unconditioned response, such as an eyeblink or salivation. Psychologists also choose simple neutral stimuli, such as tones, lights, or buzzers. The selection of simple stimuli and responses keeps the procedures straightforward and ensures that accurate measurements can be made.

Imagine that you are a psychologist and that you want to condition the eyeblink reflex in a human subject. Suppose that you select a fixed tone as the neutral stimulus. You'd begin with some measurements. You must see if the puff of air, the unconditioned stimulus, automatically elicits an eyeblink, the unconditioned response. You must also make certain that the neutral stimulus, the tone, does not elicit the unconditioned response. Once you have checked these measurements, you are ready to begin.

Acquisition. The conditioned response is *acquired* after the neutral stimulus is paired with the unconditioned stimulus—usually repeatedly. Acquisition is most efficient when the neutral stimulus precedes the unconditioned stimulus by about a half second. Thus, you would present the tone and follow it with the presentation of the puff of air about a half-second later, continuing to follow one stimulus with the other until your subject acquired the eyeblink response following the tone. A *reinforcement* is an event that increases the probability that a particular response will occur. In respondent conditioning the pairing of the neutral stimulus with the unconditioned stimulus is considered reinforcement for the conditioned response.

Extinction and spontaneous recovery. Once the subject has acquired an eyeblink response to the tone, you could expect it to continue as long as the conditioned stimulus is followed

Figure 7-6. The basic principles of respondent conditioning have been used successfully in toilet-training devices like the one pictured above. Here a loud tone is emitted from the case attached to the waist of the child's clothing whenever any moisture touches a grid sewn into the child's training pants. The tone alerts the child. Eventually, the youngster begins to pay attention to bladder and bowel tension, the bodily states that consistently precede the tone.

by the unconditioned stimulus. If the conditioned stimulus is presented alone many times in succession, then the conditioned response is no longer reinforced and will probably decline in frequency until it occurs no more frequently than it did prior to conditioning. Psychologists call this phenomenon *extinction*. It is important to note that even though a conditioned response may disappear, it is not erased entirely. Pavlov discovered that when he brought his experimental subjects back into the laboratory after extinction had occurred and presented them with the conditioned stimulus, they frequently made the conditioned response. The reappearance of a previously extinguished conditioned response following a rest period is known as *spontaneous recovery*. If you repeatedly presented the tone alone without the puff of air in your eyeblink conditioning study, your subject's eyeblink response to the tone would soon drop out. If your subject returned to the laboratory several days later, presenting the tone alone might once again elicit an eyeblink response.

Stimulus generalization. The spreading of a conditioned response to events that are similar to the conditioned stimulus and to aspects of the situation where the response was initially conditioned is known as *stimulus generalization*. In our example, you might find that after conditioning, the subject blinks at louder and softer sounds than the one used during the conditioning procedure. Similarly, the subject might also blink every time he or she sees a psychology laboratory.

Stimulus discrimination. Although animals generalize, they also learn to discriminate; that is, they learn to respond to one stimulus and to inhibit that response to a second similar stimulus. You could teach your subject to discriminate between high- and low-pitched tones by pairing the puff of air with high-pitched tones and withholding the puff of air with low-pitched tones. In real life we continually learn discriminations. For example, if we touch a hot stove, we are burned, whereas we do not receive burns from cold stoves; so we learn to fear only hot stoves.

We have described some of the fundamental characteristics of respondent conditioning. We turn next to the role of respondent conditioning in learning fears.

THE RESPONDENT CONDITIONING OF FEARS

Newborn human infants fear loud noises, sensations of falling, and pain. At approximately six months of age a fear of strange people and places usually develops. These first fears—of noise, pain, falling, and strangeness—seem to be inborn responses to potential dangers that help infants survive. The cries of the frightened infant are likely to bring a parent or another concerned person to remove the baby from potential danger. Older children exhibit a larger range of fears: among them are imaginary creatures, the dark, robbers, death, certain animals, being alone, heavy traffic, water, fire, and jail (5). Most of these fears are acquired by learning—many by respondent conditioning.

How do people learn fears by respondent conditioning? If a neutral event is paired repeatedly (sometimes once is enough) with one of the four stimuli that automatically elicit fear, the neutral event itself may begin to elicit fear. Let's take an example. A child comes close to drowning in a swimming pool. In this case the swimming pool is paired with the near drowning, a stimulus that evokes pain. After that, the mere sight of the swimming pool may evoke fear, the conditioned response. Because of stimulus generalization all bodies of water may come to elicit a fear response.

People do not need to have an actual frightening experience with a neutral stimulus to learn to fear it. If the sight of water or the word "water" is frequently paired with frightening stories, descriptions, or warnings, a person may also develop a conditioned fear response. Sometimes respondent conditioning is even more indirect. For example, a boy might sense that his parents are uneasy whenever they are around water, and this uneasiness may upset the child. If the boy is frequently upset around water, he himself may eventually come to fear water. Many human fears appear to be established by direct or indirect forms of respondent conditioning (see Figure 7-7).

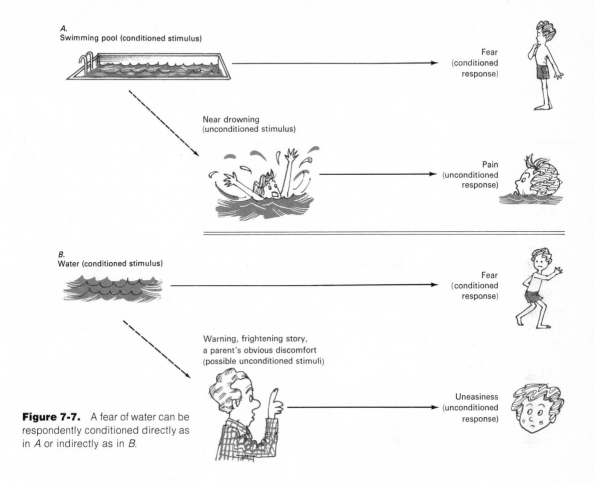

A.
Swimming pool (conditioned stimulus)

Fear
(conditioned
response)

Near drowning
(unconditioned stimulus)

Pain
(unconditioned
response)

B.
Water (conditioned stimulus)

Fear
(conditioned
response)

Warning, frightening story,
a parent's obvious discomfort
(possible unconditioned stimuli)

Uneasiness
(unconditioned
response)

Figure 7-7.   A fear of water can be respondently conditioned directly as in *A* or indirectly as in *B*.

Little Albert: Learning Fear in the Laboratory

Psychologists can establish fears in a controlled laboratory setting using respondent conditioning procedures. In 1920 John Watson, the founder of behaviorism (see Chapter 1), and Rosalie Rayner, one of his graduate students (and later his wife), conducted what is believed to be the first conditioning experiment on human fear. Watson and Rayner studied an eleven-month-old child named Albert, the son of a nurse employed by a nearby hospital for invalid children. Albert was "an infant with a phlegmatic disposition

[not easily excited], afraid of nothing 'under the sun' except a loud sound made by striking a steel bar [6]." Before the experiment began, testing revealed that Albert was not afraid of rats, rabbits, dogs, monkeys, burning newspapers, or toys.

One day as Albert was playing on a mattress in their psychology laboratory, Watson and Rayner took a white rat from a basket and presented it to Albert. Albert reached for the rat. As he reached, one of the experimenters struck a steel bar with a hammer just behind Albert's head, making a loud sound. Albert, we are told, "jumped violently and fell forward, burying his face in the mattress."

TABLE 7-2. CONDITIONING FEAR IN ALBERT

Trial	Presentation	Response
1	Rat alone	Albert reached for the rat but did not touch it.
2	Rat + Noise	Albert startled and fell over.
3	Rat + Noise	Albert startled and fell over.
4	Rat + Noise	Albert startled and fell over.
5	Rat alone	Albert withdrew and whimpered.
6	Rat + Noise	Albert withdrew and whimpered.
7	Rat + Noise	Albert withdrew, whimpered, and cried.
8	Rat alone	Albert cried and crawled away very rapidly.

Adapted from J. B. Watson & R. Rayner. Conditioned emotional reaction. *Journal of Experimental Psychology.* 1920, 3, 1–4.

After Albert recovered, he reached again for the rat. Again one of the experimenters struck the bar. This time Albert "jumped violently, fell forward, and began to whimper." The experimenters gave him no further trials that week.

One week later, however, Albert returned to the psychology laboratory and the conditioning continued. Table 7-2 shows the events that occurred at this time.

As you can see, it took Albert a total of seven conditioning trials on two separate days to learn to fear white rats. Further testing revealed that the fear was fully intact a month later. Moreover, the simple conditioned fear had spread to other objects by stimulus generalization. Albert had also come to fear a white rabbit, a sealskin fur, cotton wool, a dog, and a Santa Claus mask (7). This experiment had challenged a major psychological principle—that fears necessarily developed because of traumatic interpersonal circumstances and were always symbolic of complicated conflicts. Watson and Rayner had demonstrated quite clearly that fears were sometimes a matter of simple learning.

When the general public heard about this experiment, they were outraged. To make matters worse, Albert's mother removed Albert from the hospital before Watson and Rayner could make amends. They had planned to remove Albert's fear—by conditioning.

Peter and the Rabbit: Unlearning Fear in the Laboratory

In the course of studying children's fears, one of Watson's associates, a psychologist named Mary Cover Jones, discovered Peter. Peter looked like "Albert grown a bit older." He was thirty-four months old. He was healthy and normal in every way—except for exaggerated fears of rabbits, rats, fur coats, feathers, and cotton wool. In short, he was a perfect subject for another study—a study of fear deconditioning. Jones arranged for Peter to come into a playroom each day for a daily play period with three children who did not fear rabbits. Peter was also given favorite foods to eat. During at least part of the play period a rabbit was kept in the room. In the course of his treatment Peter passed through the following stages:

A. Rabbit anywhere in the room in a cage causes fear reaction
B. Rabbit 12 feet away in a cage tolerated
C. Rabbit 4 feet away in a cage tolerated
D. Rabbit 3 feet away in a cage tolerated
E. Rabbit close in cage tolerated
F. Rabbit free in room tolerated
G. Rabbit touched when experimenter holds it
H. Rabbit touched when free in room
I. Rabbit defied by spitting at it, throwing things at it, imitating it
J. Rabbit allowed on tray of high chair
K. Squats in defenseless position beside rabbit
L. Helps experimenter to carry rabbit to its cage
M. Holds rabbit on lap
N. Stays alone in room with rabbit
O. Allows rabbit in play pen with him
P. Fondles rabbit affectionately
Q. Let's rabbit nibble his fingers [8].

We can explain Peter's new learning by either of two respondent-conditioning principles: *extinction* or *counterconditioning*. Jones had presented the conditioned stimulus (rabbit) without the unconditioned stimulus (an unpleasant experience) repeatedly until the conditioned response (the fear) ceased (*extinction*). At the same time Jones had paired the conditioned stimulus (rabbit) with new unconditioned stimuli (playing with children and eating). Since the new unconditioned stimuli evoked a new unconditioned response (happy, comfortable, relaxed feelings), rabbits came to be associated with a new conditioned response (a pleasant emotional response). We call this phenomenon *counterconditioning* (see Figure 7-8). In Chapter 15 we discuss systematic desensitization, a technique based on counterconditioning principles that helps people overcome anxiety-related problems.

Summary: Respondent Conditioning

1. All animals exhibit automatic responses or respondents that can be transferred to situations in which they did not occur originally, by a learning process called respondent conditioning.

2. Four elements are involved in respondent conditioning. A neutral stimulus, later known as a conditioned stimulus, is paired, usually repeatedly, with an unconditioned stimulus that automatically elicits a respondent, an unconditioned response. Eventually, the conditioned stimulus comes to elicit a conditioned response—one similar to, but milder than, the unconditioned response.

3. The conditioned response exhibits a number of characteristics. It is acquired by pairing the neutral stimulus with an unconditioned stimulus. If the unconditioned stimulus does not follow the conditioned stimulus regularly, the conditioned response usually extinguishes, although it will sometimes recover spontaneously. The conditioned response frequently spreads by generalization to stimuli that are similar to the conditioned stimulus.

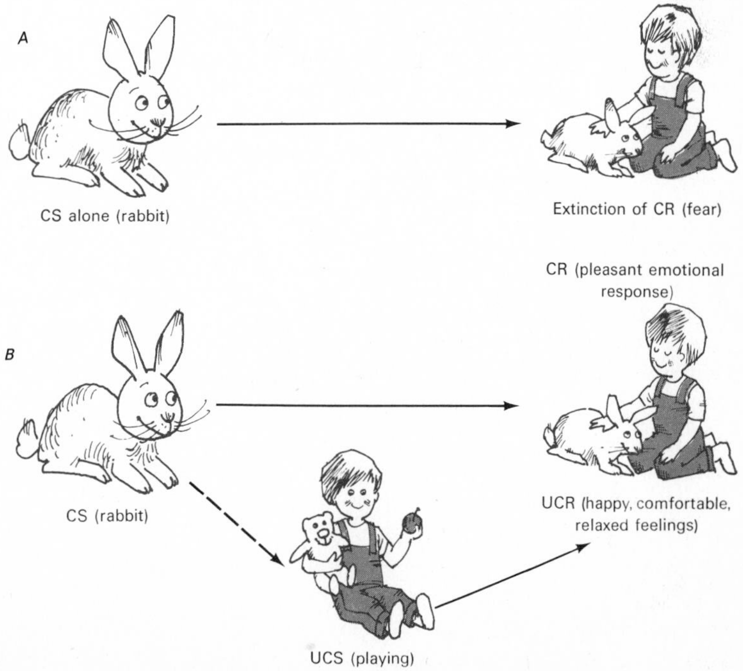

Figure 7-8. The conditioning process used by Jones can be explained by extinction as in *A* or by counterconditioning as in *B*.

A

CS alone (rabbit)

Extinction of CR (fear)

CR (pleasant emotional response)

B

CS (rabbit)

UCS (playing)

UCR (happy, comfortable, relaxed feelings)

Animals also learn to discriminate: to respond to one stimulus and not to respond to other similar stimuli with a particular response.
4. People can learn and unlearn simple fears by respondent conditioning principles.

OPERANT CONDITIONING

We turn now to a second basic learning process, operant conditioning, or the conditioning of operants. Unlike respondents, *operants* are active responses, such as walking, dancing, talking, kissing, writing poetry, drinking beer, gossiping, and playing Parcheesi. Although we perform operants under certain appropriate circumstances, we usually feel that we have control over them. No antecedent event automatically causes us to dance or drink beer or gossip. Nevertheless, although operants appear to be spontaneous, many of them are, in fact, controlled—at least to some degree—by the consequences that have followed them in the past. If an operant has been generally followed by events the organism considers pleasant, then it is likely to be repeated under similar conditions; if an operant has been generally followed by events the organism considers unpleasant, then it is not likely to be repeated under similar circumstances. When the frequency of an operant is modified by its consequences, we say that it is *conditioned*. Throughout our daily lives operants are continually being conditioned—frequently we are unaware of the process. As you talk to a friend, the friend fidgets and looks around the room, and you change the subject. Your parents comment on how nice your jacket looks, and you find yourself wearing that jacket increasingly frequently. A teacher writes "good work" at the top of a paper, and you continue working hard in that class. In each of these cases the probability that a particular operant will occur has been modified by the consequences that follow it.

Thorndike and His Cats: The Importance of Consequences

At about the same time that Ivan Pavlov was working with salivating dogs, an American psychologist, Edward Lee Thorndike (1874–1949), was working with hungry cats. Thorndike was interested in finding out how cats and other animals learn to solve problems. He placed hungry cats in puzzle boxes (cages from which a cat could escape by a simple act, such as manipulating a cord, pressing a lever, or stepping on a platform). Fish were placed within view just outside the cat's cage. Thorndike closely observed the behavior of many cats in numerous boxes. Later he summarized his observations:

When put into the box the cat would show evident signs of discomfort and an impulse to escape from confinement. It tries to squeeze through any opening; it claws and bites at the bars or wire; it thrusts its paws out through any opening and claws at everything it reaches; it continues its efforts when it strikes anything

Figure 7-9. One of Thorndike's puzzle boxes. When the cat pulls the loop, the door is released and the animal can reach the food.

loose and shaky; it may claw at things within the box. It does not pay very much attention to the food outside, but seems simply to strive instinctively to escape from confinement. . . . For eight or ten minutes it will claw and bite and squeeze incessantly. . . . The cat that is clawing all over the box in her impulsive struggle will probably claw the string or loop or button so as to open the door. And gradually all the other non-successful impulses will be stamped out and the particular impulse leading to the successful act will be stamped in by the resulting pleasure, until, after many trials, the cat will, when put in the box, immediately claw the loop or button in a definite way [9].

Thorndike believed that cats and other animals learned to escape from puzzle boxes by *trial and error learning*. Initially the animal tried out various instinctive responses. Successful responses became more frequent. Thorndike believed that they were "stamped in" by the pleasure of success. Unsuccessful responses became less likely. According to Thorndike, they were "stamped out" when they did not produce a desirable result. Thorndike believed that this general process characterized the way all animals, including people, solved problems. Thorndike was one of the first psychologists to emphasize the importance of consequences in learning.

B. F. Skinner and Operant Technology

Burrhus Frederick Skinner (b.1904), an American psychologist at Harvard University, has been an important figure in the study of operant behavior. Like John Watson, Skinner insists that observable behavior is the only appropriate concern of the psychologist; he has been looking for the lawful processes in operant behavior since the late 1920s. Skinner believes that it is easier to find these laws by studying the behavior of simple animals in simple situations; so his studies frequently

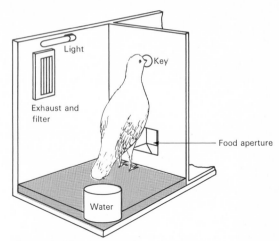

Figure 7-10. A pigeon in a Skinner box.

involve precise investigations of the bar pressing of rats or the key pecking of pigeons in an operant conditioning apparatus, usually called a *Skinner box* (see Figure 7-10).

The Skinner box—one of Skinner's inventions that is now stock apparatus in all experimental psychology laboratories—is a small cage equipped with a bar or key, a light, a food tray, and a food-releasing mechanism. The box provides a distraction-free environment for teaching small animals. Typically, a rat or pigeon is placed in the box and trained to press a bar or peck a key. Each time the animal performs the desired response, a pellet of food is released into its food tray. The experimenter can influence the rat's rate of bar pressing or the pigeon's rate of key pecking by manipulating the conditions under which the food pellet is released.

Exhaustive studies using this simple model have enabled Skinner and other psychologists to discover many of the factors that influence operant learning. Applying this knowledge, Skinner and his followers have taught animals some extraordinary "tricks." For example, they have trained pigeons to walk in figure eights, to hop on one foot, to play table tennis, to guide bombs, and to inspect drug capsules, but Skinner should not be pictured as a frivolous trickster. His contributions to the understanding of operant learning are vast. Moreover, his work has led to the development of a sophisticated body of operant conditioning techniques that help parents, teachers, and psychologists perform their roles more effectively.

PRINCIPLES AND APPLICATIONS OF OPERANT CONDITIONING

As we look at the principles of operant conditioning, we will also point out how parents, teachers, and psychologists apply them to solving problems with children. The application of operant learning and other experimental laboratory procedures to the changing of human behavior is known as *behavior modification*. Behavior modification is used today in many diverse settings—in nursery schools, day-care centers, classrooms, homes, mental health clinics, mental institutions, prisons, nursing homes, stores, and factories (see Chapter 15). The term "behavior modification" is probably an unfortunate one, because it conjures up images of brain washing and thought control. In actuality, behavior modification is more accurately depicted as a body of teaching techniques. In the past, teachers, parents, and psychologists—people who "teach" others—have been rather inefficient. The sophisticated understanding of learning makes more effective teaching possible. In other words, these techniques give the experts a new kind of expertise.

We turn now to operant conditioning principles and their applications.

Reinforcement

Reinforcement or *reinforcer* refers to an event that increases the probability that a particular response will increase in frequency.[2] In operant conditioning responses are reinforced both by the presentation or removal of particular consequences. If Cathy talks more frequently than usual about skiing after Jim's close attention to her skiing stories, then we would call Jim's attention a reinforcer. If Sally cleans her room more frequently than usual to end her mother's nagging, then removing the nagging is also a reinforcer. When the *presentation* of an event *increases* the likelihood of a particular behavior, we call the event a *positive reinforcer*. When the *removal* of an event *increases* the likelihood of a particular behavior, we call the event a *negative reinforcer*. Note that "positive" and "negative" refer to the presentation or removal of an event; they do not connote good or bad. Nor do they refer to increasing or decreasing the probability of the behavior that they follow. All reinforcers by definition *increase* behavior.

There are no absolute positive or negative reinforcers. What is reinforcing in any particular case depends on the individual animal and the situation. If a dog sits on command quite regularly when the act is followed only by a pat on the head and a "good girl," we'd call the affection and praise reinforcers. Similarly, if a student reads his assignments every night to improve his grades, we'd call grades reinforcers. A woman who works on weekdays in the cafeteria is probably reinforced by money. The child who combs his hair before coming to the dinner table may be reinforced by the absence of scolding comments.

The kinds of reinforcers. *Primary* or *unlearned reinforcers* are stimuli that are innately powerful in increasing the probability of behavior. These reinforcers are usually effective because they satisfy basic physiological

[2]Note that reinforcement has precisely the same meaning in both respondent and operant conditioning. Only the manner in which the responses are reinforced in the two kinds of learning differs.

needs. Food, water, sex, and the avoidance of pain can function as primary reinforcers. *Conditioned reinforcers*, on the other hand, acquire the power to reinforce behavior through respondent conditioning—they have been paired with primary reinforcers many times. The dollar bill is an example. The dollar bill has been repeatedly associated with the acquisition of food, shelter, and material objects. That's probably why the dollar bill is such a good reinforcer for so many people. Gold stars, report card grades, and bus tokens also function as conditioned reinforcers.

We will consider social reinforcers a third category of reinforcer. A pat on the back, a smile, attention, approval, prestige, praise, and affection can function as *social reinforcers*, reinforcers that depend on other people. Some psychologists believe that social reinforcers are conditioned reinforcers; others consider them primary reinforcers. Regardless of their classification, they are frequently very influential in modifying human operant behavior.

The scheduling of reinforcement. What is the most effective way to administer reinforcement? B. F. Skinner and other psychologists have investigated the scheduling of reinforcement and they have found that it has an important influence on how fast animals learn, how frequently they respond and pause, and how long they continue to respond once reinforcement stops.

In general, psychologists find that reinforcers seem to be most effective when they occur immediately after the behavior that they are intended to increase.[3] Psychologists have also learned that *continuous reinforcement*—reinforcement that occurs after every correct response—seems to be the quickest way to teach a new response. It is easy to

reinforce a rat in a Skinner box continuously by immediately following every bar press with a food pellet. It is harder to reinforce an adult or child continuously. When reinforcement does not follow every correct response, psychologists call it *partial reinforcement*. Although continuous reinforcement is the quickest method for teaching an initial response, partial reinforcement makes responses persist longer when reinforcement becomes unpredictable or stops altogether. In life many reinforcers come to people on fairly regular partial reinforcement schedules. People are sometimes reinforced after making *a particular number* of correct responses. Psychologists call this kind of schedule a *ratio schedule*. Ratio schedules are designated *fixed* when the reinforcement occurs after a definite number of correct responses. Some factories pay their workers on a piece-rate basis, so much money for so many goods. Farmworkers are frequently paid on a fixed-ratio schedule, say $2 for a bushel of apples. The fixed-ratio schedule produces a relatively high rate of responding. However, psychologists have noted that laboratory animals usually pause after each reinforcement, and during the pause they do not respond at all. Informal observations suggest that people on fixed-ratio schedules also take breaks following reinforcement (see Figure 7-11*a*).

The gambler playing a slot machine never knows when the next response will produce a payoff. This type of ratio schedule is called a *variable-ratio schedule*, because the reinforcement is delivered following a varying number of correct responses. The number of correct responses required for reinforcement varies randomly about some average value. Many reinforcements in real life—such as achievement, recognition, and profit—come to us on this kind of schedule. The variable-ratio schedule produces an even higher response rate than the fixed-ratio schedule. Moreover, animals tend to respond more constantly on this schedule. Apparently, the uncertainty

---

[3]Verbal animals such as human children also learn efficiently from delayed reinforcers, as long as they are reminded periodically that the reinforcer will be forthcoming (10).

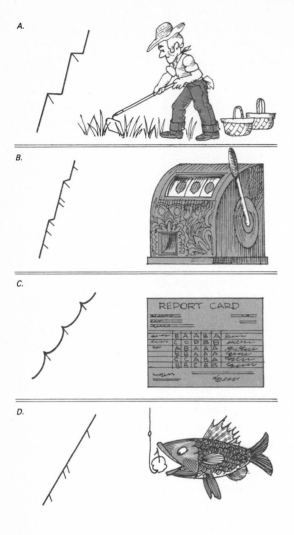

Figure 7-11 *a* The fixed-ratio schedule results in a generally high rate of responding; however, there is usually a pause after each reinforcement, during which the animal does not respond at all. *b* The variable-ratio schedule produces a high response rate with very little pausing. The overall response rate produced by a variable-ratio schedule is higher than that produced by a fixed-ratio schedule. *c* The fixed-interval schedule generates a distinctive pattern of responding known as a "scallop." The response rate is lowest immediately after reinforcement. It gradually increases in rate, reaching its high just before the next reinforcement becomes available. *d* A variable-interval schedule results in a moderate rate of responding with minimal pausing between responses.

keeps them working steadily (see Figure 7-11*b*).

The *interval schedules of reinforcement* depend on the passage of time. That is, reinforcement is provided after two conditions are satisfied: First, a particular interval of time must elapse since the previous reinforcement. Second, a correct response must occur after the time interval. When the time interval between reinforcements is constant, psychologists label the schedule a *fixed-*

interval schedule. When parents use dinner desserts to reinforce their children's eating of vegetables, they are using a fixed-interval schedule. The child is rewarded for eating vegetables (the correct response) every twenty-four hours (the fixed interval). Authors are sometimes reinforced for writing books on fixed-interval schedules. The publisher agrees to make a payment every three months (the fixed interval) so long as the writer is working diligently (the correct response). The fixed-interval schedule generally produces a variable rate of responding. After reinforcement the rate is low. It increases steadily during the interval until it reaches a high immediately before the next scheduled reinforcement (see Figure 7-11*c*).

In many situations the time interval between reinforcements varies randomly about some average value. Psychologists call this reinforcement schedule a *variable-interval schedule.* Compliments are frequently given on a variable-interval schedule. After a good performance on a paper or quiz (the correct response) every two weeks or so (the variable interval), a teacher may comment on how sharp your answers are. Fish also seem to bite on this kind of schedule, reinforcing the fisherman at varying intervals for his patience. The variable-interval schedule produces a constant, but only moderately high, rate of responding (see Figure 7-11*d*).

Shaping

Through the proper use of a positive reinforcement strategy called *shaping* (or the *method of successive approximations*), people and other animals can be taught new responses. In the beginning the trainer positively reinforces a behavior that only faintly resembles the desired responses. As this behavior increases in frequency, the training agent becomes more selective and only reinforces behavior that resembles the goal more closely. When this behavior becomes frequent, the trainer becomes more selective once again. The process continues until the goal behavior itself is conditioned. Parents sometimes use shaping intuitively to teach their children new responses. Consider walking. Once a baby stands, its parents no longer fuss over it for simply standing. It is expected to progress—perhaps to take steps while holding on. After attaining this goal, the baby learns to take more steps with less support. Eventually, it learns to take steps on its own. After each accomplishment, the parents revise their expectations upward and the child must accomplish more before the parents become excited and enthusiastic. The following case shows how psychologists used shaping to treat a serious speech problem in a child.

Shaping speech: A case study of Charles

A troubled four-year-old child, whom we will call Charles, was referred to a psychiatric hospital for diagnosis and treatment. Charles could speak only a few words; he was extremely active, negative, and destructive; and he was intensely frightened of people. Charles had heard very little spoken English because his parents rarely communicated with one another and when they did, they spoke a mixture of German, Hebrew, and English. Moreover, Charles had frequently been beaten and locked in his room—hearing no voices whatsoever for long periods of time.

The psychologists at the psychiatric hospital made friends with Charles and then they began shaping his language skills. In the beginning one psychologist took Charles into a playroom where they played together with toys, books, and other objects. Every time Charles said any word at all, the psychologist acted very interested and repeated what Charles had said. After a while Charles was using his few words more frequently. The psychologist went on to the next step: he held up an object and named it. Charles had to say, "Gimme _____." Each time he said it, the psychologist reinforced him by praise, candy, and the object itself. Reinforcement was no longer given for a simpler response. After some time at this game, Charles became quite proficient at asking for common objects. Then the psychologist changed the game again. Now Charles had to imitate specific words in order to receive reinforcement. The psychologist showed Charles an object or a picture and named it. When Charles repeated the word, he received candy, praise, and several minutes of free play. As soon as he understood the names of many common objects, the psychologist began on colors. And so on. The psychologists spent more than 100 hourly sessions teaching Charles to talk over a twenty-month period. At the time that Charles was discharged to a new foster home, he spoke entirely in sentences. He had also learned to trust people (11).

Extinction

When the reinforcement for a particular response is withdrawn, the response gradually

Figure 7-12. Shaping is used to teach speech to autistic children. Here immediate positive reinforcement, in this case food, is given to the child whenever he correctly imitates a particular sound. (Allan Grant.)

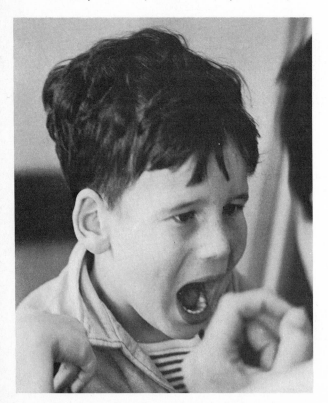

declines in frequency until it occurs no more frequently than it did prior to conditioning. This process is labeled *extinction.* In operant conditioning, as in respondent conditioning, extinction occurs when the reinforcer that is maintaining a behavior is removed. In real life people learn many operants that later extinguish because they are not reinforced. For example, many young children are taught to be polite. Their parents praise them whenever they say "please" or "thank you." If the child's good manners go completely unnoticed later on, they are likely to disappear altogether. On the other hand, parents, husbands, wives, sisters, and brothers frequently attend to one another's annoying habits. Parents pay attention to their children when they have temper tantrums. A married person attends wholeheartedly to a spouse who is complaining about the house or the meals. A teen-ager lectures a younger sibling who causes embarrassment in front of friends. Inadvertently, the attention may serve as a reinforcer and strengthen the behavior that it was intended to discourage. In these cases, inattention—removing the reinforcer that maintains the behavior—will usually extinguish the undesired behavior. Responses that have been extinguished sometimes reappear again after some time. This reappearance, known as *spontaneous recovery,* also occurs in respondent conditioning. Here is an example of extinction and spontaneous recovery in operant conditioning.

Extinguishing tantrum behavior:
A case study of Robert

A child, whom we will call Robert, was seriously ill for the first eighteen months of his life. While he was sick, he received a large amount of attention and care. Not surprisingly, he became accustomed to this state of affairs. By the time he reached twenty-one months Robert was healthy, but he had become a household tyrant guarding numerous privileges and comforts. His behavior was especially distressing to his family at bedtime, when he demanded undivided attention and cried and fussed if his adult companion (parent or aunt) left the room before he had fallen asleep. Because Robert fought sleep as long as he could, his family usually spent one-half to two hours each bedtime waiting for him to let himself fall asleep.

A psychologist helped the family work out a plan to modify Robert's behavior. The parents and the aunt were instructed to put Robert to bed pleasantly in a "leisurely and relaxed fashion." After the pleasantries, the adult left the bedroom and closed the door. Robert, outraged at this violation of protocol, would cry, scream, and fuss. The adults were to exercise extreme self-control and ignore him entirely.

As it turned out, Robert's family had strong nerves, and was able to stick with the plan. It took over a week for Robert to stop crying at bedtime, but by the tenth night, Robert no longer "whimpered, fussed, or cried, when the adult left the room"; in fact, he smiled.

Unfortunately, about one week after Robert's crying had been extinguished, it recovered—apparently spontaneously. In any case, Robert screamed and fussed after his aunt tucked him in. In a weak moment, the aunt gave in: She returned to Robert's side and stayed there until he fell asleep. After this incident, it took nine additional sessions of ignoring tantrum behavior to extinguish the response a second time. Figure 7-13 shows how the treatment program progressed. Two years after treatment, a follow-up study indicated that Robert's behavior had changed in a lasting way. He had had no further temper tantrums at bedtime (12).

Punishment

Ordinarily, people define certain unpleasant procedures—such as spanking, isolation, or the removal of privileges—as punishments. In contrast to common practice, psychologists say that *punishment* occurs when, and only when, a specific response is followed by an event that reduces its frequency. Either the presentation of an unpleasant event or the removal of a pleasant event may function as punishers so long as they reduce the frequency of the response they follow. For example, when some parents spank their children

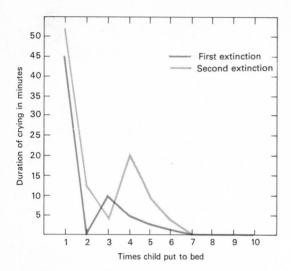

First extinction

Second extinction

Figure 7-13. Amount of crying during two sets of extinction trials. (From Williams, 1959.)

people's negative reactions, can be designated *social punishers*. Psychologists do not know if social punishers are innately aversive or if they acquire their aversiveness by being associated with primary punishers. It is important to note that punishers, like reinforcers, vary according to the individual. What decreases the frequency of one animal's behavior does not necessarily decrease the frequency of another's.

Punishment has been studied both in the laboratory and in real-life settings. Several general principles can be abstracted from the research findings.

1. The more consistently punishment is administered for the same behavior, the more effectively the behavior is suppressed (13). In other words, punishing a response only some of the time is not a good way to eliminate it. In fact, partial punishment tends to make punished responses persist, since the response is reinforced by its natural consequences some percentage of the time.
2. Punishment should be administered immediately after the response-to-be-eliminated occurs. The further removed the punishment is in time and space from the response-to-be-eliminated, the less effective it appears to be, other factors being equal (14).
3. The briefer the period of punishment, the more effective it is. Prolonged punishment causes adaptation. This is particularly true with mild physical punishment (15). Making children stand in the corner for hours is probably a poor practice for this reason.
4. Mild punishment works well both on rats and on children when the subject is provided with an alternative way of behaving that is positively reinforced. Simply punishing "bad" behavior is never enough. If the animal does not know another appropriate response, it may simply return to the

(present a spanking) after mischievous behavior, their children do not repeat the mischief again—at least not in the presence of their parents. Similarly, when "talking back" is followed by the withholding of dessert, some children stop "talking back." This latter kind of punishment sounds superficially like extinction. Actually, the two procedures are quite different. Extinction demands the removal of the specific reinforcing stimulus that is maintaining the response. In punishment any related or unrelated positive event can be removed. We will be using the terms "punishment" and "punisher" interchangeably.

Like reinforcers, punishers can be divided into several classes. Some punishers are *primary* or unlearned. Loud noises and pain-inducing stimuli are innately aversive. Some punishers are *conditioned*; in other words, they have been paired with unlearned punishers until they have become unpleasant in and of themselves. Words such as "no" and "don't" are in this category; so are report card grades such as "F." Punishers such as ridicule, disapproval, or criticism, which depend on punished behavior. A child who fights to attract its parents' attention might be isolated in its bedroom for several minutes after each outburst and reminded that the parents will pay attention to it when it behaves more appropriately.

5. Mild punishment can also be used to transmit information. For example, a mild punishment, such as saying "no," can be used to signal a child that its noisy behavior is unacceptable and cue it to select a more appropriate behavior—quiet play.

Although punishment is undoubtedly an effective way of weakening or eliminating undesirable behavior (16), its disadvantages frequently outweigh its advantages. Here are some of the problems associated with punishment:

1. Events that are likely to decrease the frequency of a behavior may be perceived as anxiety-arousing; so punishing procedures frequently elicit anxiety. Anxiety, as we will see in Chapter 11, can interfere with an animal's ability to perform or learn.

2. Punishment always involves an undesirable consequence to the recipient. To escape or avoid punishment, animals frequently learn to make socially maladaptive responses. Consider a common example. A teacher confronts a student with the fact that he cheated on a test. The student may be very tempted to escape humiliation and possible failure (punishing events) by ly-

ing. To avoid an angry lecture designed to decrease coming in late at night, a young girl may learn to physically avoid her parents.

3. If the punishing procedure involves pain, then it may elicit aggression. As we see in Chapter 11, many animals respond to pain with aggression, apparently automatically. If a child is aggressive to begin with, a painful punisher may increase the likelihood of aggression.

4. Physical punishment provides an aggressive model. By observing adults aggress, children learn that aggression is an acceptable way of handling anger.

5. Severe physical punishment can get out of hand and damage the recipient; severe social punishment (ridicule and humiliation) can permanently injure the recipient's self-esteem.

Because of these undesirable side effects, most psychologists are reluctant to advocate the use of punishment. However, when used in conjunction with positive reinforcement for desirable behavior, mild punishment can be recommended—especially after all other methods have failed. The strategy of mild punishment for "bad" behavior combined with positive reinforcement for "good" behavior is particularly efficient in decreasing problem behaviors that are either very frequent or intensely destructive. The following case shows how punishment can be used effectively.

Punishing a "brat" named Mitch: A case study

Mitch was an exceedingly difficult three-year-old "brat." He often pulled his clothing from his closet and his dresser. He had numerous temper tantrums. He wrote on the walls. He rode his tricycle around the living room. He put small objects in the drain pipes. He took food from the refrigerator and spread it on the floor. He threw rocks and bricks. He broke dishes. He climbed on the furniture. He also knocked over store displays. To make matters worse, Mitch's parents had no control over their son. He did not respond appropriately to "no." He simply ordered his parents to "shut up."

But Mitch was not all bad. He played with his toys ten minutes a day, and he picked them up afterward. He helped his mother set the table. He washed his hands when they were dirty. He said "please" and "thank you." He was also toilet trained. Moreover, he went to bed at 8 o'clock each night and slept soundly all night long. When Mitch was good, his parents were so relieved that they went into another room to savor the moment of peace.

Mitch's parents had tried everything to cope with their son's "bad" behavior. Usually, they were quite indulgent. Their major tactic was to appease Mitch at any cost. To control the property destruction, they had either removed or tied down anything that Mitch could break. The house contained nothing but furniture. The doors were tied shut with rope. Mitch's parents watched their son's destructive behavior with bated breath. On rare occasions when they lost their self-control, they spanked Mitch hard, but spankings didn't accomplish anything constructive either. After a spanking Mitch laughed and engaged in a behavior that surpassed his previous one in "badness."

Mitch's parents finally contacted a psychologist named Martha Bernal then at the UCLA Neuropsychiatric Institute. Bernal and her associates trained Mitch's parents to use the following behavior-modification techniques:

1. Destructiveness and physical aggression were to be immediately followed by punishment. A technique known as "time out" was specifically recommended. "Time out" is an abbreviation for the phrase "time out from positive reinforcement." The method involved removing Mitch from a reinforcing set of circumstances every time he misbehaved in specified ways. At these times he was taken immediately to a "time-out room"—a room devoid of any interesting objects or people—for a short period, usually five to ten minutes. After Mitch had served his time, he was released, and the punishment was over.
2. Temper tantrums were to be totally ignored. Mitch's parents were to act blind, deaf, and dumb.
3. All good behavior was to be immediately positively reinforced by affection, praise, approval, and attention.

Treatment lasted about four months. Mitch improved, and the improvement lasted. One year later, Mitch was still cooperating most of the time. His temper tantrums were down near zero. His destructiveness had decreased from a high of twenty-three incidents in one day to an average of two per day (17).

OPERANT CONDITIONING AND INTERNAL BODILY RESPONSES: BIOFEEDBACK

Traditionally, internal bodily responses such as heartbeat, blood circulation, and stomach contractions have been considered involuntary reactions controlled by the events that precede them (respondents). In 1967 Neil Miller, a psychologist at Rockefeller University in New York City, and his coworkers astounded the psychological community by demonstrating that animals as lowly as the rat could learn to regulate these processes directly when they were rewarded for doing so.[4] Rats were paralyzed by drugs so that they were unable to move their muscles or even breathe without the help of a respirator. Then, every time a rat made a specified internal bodily response—for example, slowed its heart rate—Miller and his associates delivered a powerful reinforcer, a jolt of electricity to the pleasure center in the rat's brain (see Chapter 11 for more information on this subject). To obtain this reinforcer, paralyzed rats learned to control their heart rate, stomach contractions, quantity of blood in the stomach walls, blood pressure, rate of urine formation in the kidneys, and several other internal responses (18). This work stimulated an enormous amount of research designed to learn whether or not people could also learn to control their internal bodily responses. A substantial body of evidence now indicates that people can learn to regulate internal bodily processes. Operant conditioning techniques are used to train internal responses by a procedure known as *biofeedback*.

What does the term "biofeedback" mean?

[4]Note that this demonstration blurs the distinction that we have made between operants and respondents; however, these distinctions are still very useful for understanding and studying the basic learning processes.

Figure 7-14. Placing a child in a time-out room can be an effective punishment. (Mimi Forsyth, from Monkmeyer.)

The eminent mathematician Norbert Weiner defined feedback as "a method of controlling a system by reinserting into it the results of its past performance [19]." *Bio*feedback teaches a person to control a particular *bodily part* by providing systematic information or feedback as to what that part is doing. (Many psychologists think of the feedback as a conditioned reinforcer.)

How does biofeedback work? In one study several psychologists at Harvard University trained normal college students to raise or lower their systolic blood pressure in a single experimental session. The subjects did not know which bodily function was to be changed or in what direction the change was to occur. Experimental subjects received informational feedback for either increases

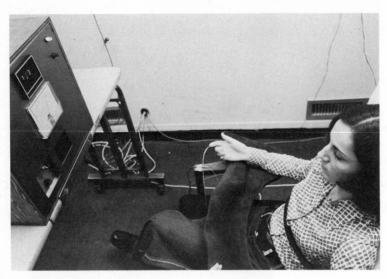

Figure 7-15. Biofeedback training can teach people to control bodily functions such as blood pressure and heart rate. In this setup at Rockefeller University, feedback is provided by a flashing light and fluctuating needle indicator. (John Briggs.)

or decreases in blood pressure, whereas control subjects received informational feedback randomly. Every time blood pressure changed in the desired direction, a tone sounded and a light flashed. All subjects received the same instructions: Make the light flash as much as you can. For every twenty flashes, the subjects were given an added incentive—an opportunity to view a pleasant photograph. The results turned out as the psychologists had predicted. Subjects who received feedback for decreasing their blood pressure, decreased it significantly; subjects who received feedback for increasing their blood pressure, increased it significantly; and subjects who received feedback randomly kept their blood pressure at a level midway between the two experimental groups. Curiously, the experimental subjects managed to control their blood pressure without realizing that they had done so and without knowing the direction in which their blood pressure had changed (20).

The possibilities for using biofeedback training are numerous. Psychologists and physicians employ these techniques to help people master many psychophysiological problems, including insomnia, anxiety, ten-

sion headaches, migraines, chronic pain, epilepsy, paralyzed muscles, backache, asthma, diabetes, alcoholism, elevated blood pressure, and heart irregularities. They can also teach people to control their state of mind. Someday they may also be able to increase creativity and learning ability. Although biofeedback research is still in an early experimental stage and many problems and gaps in knowledge remain to be worked out, its future looks very promising.

Summary: Operant Conditioning

1. When the probability that an operant will be repeated in a particular situation is modified (increased or decreased) by the events that follow it, we call the process operant conditioning.
2. Positive and negative reinforcement *both increase* the probability that an operant will be repeated in the future.
3. Shaping, a positive reinforcement strategy, establishes new operants.
4. When the reinforcer that maintains a particular operant is removed, the frequency of the behavior declines, a process known

as extinction. Sometimes operant behavior that has been extinguished recovers spontaneously.

5. Punishment, which *decreases* the probability that an operant will be repeated in the future, has many disadvantages. However, when mild punishment is used appropriately, in conjunction with positive reinforcement, the frequency of an undesirable behavior can be reduced.

6. Recently, psychologists and physicians have been using biofeedback procedures to help people gain control over certain psychophysiological responses.

OBSERVATION LEARNING

When a relatively enduring change in behavior results in large part from observing the behavior of another, psychologists label the basic learning process *observation learning* (or *imitation*, or *modeling*, or *social learning*). Primitive animals such as rats and chickens learn by observation; so do complex primates such as humans. Nobody knows why humans and other animals imitate, but imitative responses can be observed very early—as early as several weeks in human infants—and it is probable that imitation is an inborn tendency in most animals. Without any doubt, humans learn many important lessons by observing one another. Infants learn vocabulary and patterns of speech; children learn writing and reading, physical routines, social etiquette, and sex-typed behavior. Adults learn roles as parents, workers, and marital partners. How do people learn by observation?

How People Learn by Observation

Albert Bandura, a psychology professor at Stanford University, and his associates have done a great deal of research on observation learning. Bandura believes that the following processes are involved:

Acquisition. The observer is exposed to a model who is behaving in a particular way. The observer attends to the behavior and recognizes its distinctive features.

Retention. The behavior is actively stored in memory.

Performance. The behavior is accepted as appropriate and the observer reproduces it, guided by memory.

Consequences. Once the behavior is performed, it is conditioned by operant principles; that is, it meets with consequences which increase or decrease its frequency (21).

Note that observation learning is a more complex basic learning process than operant or respondent conditioning.

Who Models Whom?

In 1962 the Washington *Post* reported the case of an eleven-year old boy who joined a pack of dogs, ran on all fours, and barked with his canine companions each night (22). When someone models the family dog, it makes the newspaper. In general, people tend to be more selective in choosing their models. Through experimental studies psychologists have identified several factors that make a particular model likely to be copied. It turns out that people are more likely to imitate high-status than low-status models. Competent successful executives, for instance, are more likely to be modeled than Bowery bums. People who have power over important resources are also frequently imitated. Parents control the important sources of pleasure in their children's lives—candy, money, bedtime, and TV. This may be one reason why children so often imitate their parents. People are also more likely to copy

TABLE 7-3. A COMPARISON OF THREE BASIC LEARNING PROCESSES

	Respondent Conditioning	Operant Conditioning	Observation Learning
What Occurs during the Learning Process?	A particular respondent comes to be evoked by a formerly unrelated stimulus through the following process. Before: Neutral stimulus does not lead to unconditioned response. During: Neutral stimulus is paired with unconditioned stimulus. (Unconditioned stimulus leads automatically to unconditioned response.) Afterward: Neutral stimulus (now called a conditioned stimulus) leads to conditioned response.	The frequency of a particular behavior is altered by the following process: A response occurs; the consequences which follow the response increase or decrease the probability that the same response will be repeated in similar situations in the future.	A response is observed (acquired) and retained. Eventually it is performed. The principles of operant conditioning then influence its frequency of occurrence.
Is the Learner Reinforced?	Yes. The pairing of the conditioned stimulus and unconditioned stimulus reinforce the conditioned response.	Sometimes. (Whenever the consequences which follow the response *increase* its probability.)	The learner is not reinforced for acquiring the response although the model may be reinforced. Later, when the response is performed, the learner may be reinforced directly.
Does the Learner Make a Response Voluntarily?	No.	Yes.	Yes, but not necessarily immediately.
Do Higher Mental Processes Appear to Be Involved in the Learning Process?	No.	Not necessarily.	Yes. Judgments are made about whom to model and when to perform an observed response.
Who Learns by This Method?	All known animals, including humans.	Most animals, including humans.	Many animals, particularly primates and especially people.

the responses of models with whom they identify—people of the same sex and similar age, socioeconomic background, education, and values. Observers' emotional states also affect their susceptibility to the model's influence. Moderate emotional arousal heightens the learner's susceptibility to most kinds of learning. That is, when people are excited, fearful, or angry—in moderation—they are more likely to learn by any learning process. On the other hand, extreme emotional arousal usually interferes with learning (see Chapter 11). It should be noted that, in general, people tend to be rather conservative in imitating others. That is, they tend to imitate only those behaviors which fit in with their life styles (23). Table 7-3 presents a comparison of respondent conditioning, operant conditioning, and observation learning.

STUDY GUIDE 7

Key Terms. learning, performance, latent learning, respondent, respondent conditioning (classical conditioning, Pavlovian conditioning), unconditioned stimulus, unconditioned response, neutral stimulus, conditioned response, conditioned stimulus, acquisition, reinforcement, extinction, spontaneous recovery, stimulus generalization, stimulus discrimination, counterconditioning;

operant, operant conditioning, trial-and-error learning, Skinner box, behavior modification, reinforcement, positive reinforcer, negative reinforcer, primary reinforcer, conditioned reinforcer, social reinforcer, schedule of reinforcement, immediate reinforcement, continuous reinforcement, partial reinforcement, fixed-ratio schedule, variable-ratio schedule, fixed-interval schedule, variable-interval schedule, shaping (method of successive approximations), extinction, spontaneous recovery, punishment, primary punisher, conditioned punisher, social punisher, biofeedback;

observation learning (imitation, modeling, social learning), acquisition, retention, performance, consequences.

Important Research. respondent conditioning of salivation (Pavlov), respondent conditioning of fear (Watson and Rayner), counterconditioning and/or extinction of fear (Jones), trial-and-error learning in puzzle boxes (Thorndike), learned control of internal processes (Miller), biofeedback in the laboratory (Harvard research group).

Self-Quiz

1. Psychologists define learning as [**a**] any process which increases the intelligence and creativity of an individual; [**b**] relatively permanent changes in behavior that occur as a result of teaching; [**c**] the modification of behavior by conditioning; [**d**] an internal process producing relatively permanent changes in behavior which can be attributed to experience.

2. Psychologists generally infer learning from changes in [**a**] self reports; [**b**] latent learning; [**c**] performance; [**d**] motivation.

3. A respondent is a [**a**] voluntary response; [**b**] verbal response; [**c**] conditioned response; [**d**] reflex elicited by an event that precedes it.

4. A person who once experienced no fear of airplanes became quite fearful of them after being in an airplane during an attempted hijacking. The conditioned response in this example is [**a**] refusing to go on an airplane; [**b**] fear (of airplanes); [**c**] airplanes; [**d**] fear (aroused by the hijacking).

5. The conditioned stimulus in question 4 is [**a**] fear of airplanes; [**b**] the hijacking; [**c**] airplane associated with hijacking; [**d**] the hijackers themselves.

6. If the conditioned stimulus is presented many times alone, [**a**] the frequency of the conditioned response returns to its preconditioning level; [**b**] extinction occurs; [**c**] the conditioned stimulus becomes a neutral stimulus again; [**d**] all of the above.

7. Which of the following would definitely *not* be learned by respondent conditioning? [**a**] liking the color yellow; [**b**] learning to play the violin; [**c**] fearing bees and wasps; [**d**] overcoming anxiety about taking tests.

8. Thorndike believed cats learned to escape from a puzzle box by [**a**] observation; [**b**] trial and error; [**c**] respondent conditioning; [**d**] the method of successive approximations.

9. Every time a teenage girl uses foul language, her father leaves the room. The girl uses more and more foul language. Psychologists would consider

the girl's foul language [**a**] a respondent; [**b**] a maladaptive habit; [**c**] a positive reinforcer; [**d**] an operant that has been increased in frequency by the father's leaving-the-room behavior.

10. In question 9, the father's leaving-the-room behavior is a _____ for his daughter's foul language. [**a**] punisher; [**b**] positive reinforcer; [**c**] negative reinforcer; [**d**] partial reinforcer.

11. To teach a boy to dress himself, his mother gives him gold stars on a chart for every article of clothing he puts on by himself. The mother is delivering [**a**] conditioned reinforcers on a continuous reinforcement schedule; [**b**] primary reinforcers on a variable-ratio schedule; [**c**] conditioned reinforcers on a partial-reinforcement schedule; [**d**] social reinforcers on a continuous-reinforcement schedule.

12. To improve her husband's cooking, a woman decides to reinforce (with attention and praise) the first good meal he cooks each week. She is delivering [**a**] social reinforcement on a fixed-interval schedule; [**b**] social reinforcement on a variable-interval schedule; [**c**] social reinforcement on a fixed-ratio schedule; [**d**] conditioned reinforcement on a fixed-interval schedule.

13. A mother decides to stop her young daughter's naptime crying by ignoring it. After a few days the girl stops crying at naptime. Then one afternoon, for no apparent reason, she cries again at naptime. This is probably an example of [**a**] shaping; [**b**] extinction after continuous reinforcement; [**c**] extinction and stimulus generalization; [**d**] extinction and spontaneous recovery.

14. Which is *not* a good rule to follow when using punishment to control behavior? [**a**] use it consistently for the same behavior; [**b**] make it last a fairly long time so that the individual will remember it; [**c**] use it immediately; do not make the individual wait for it; [**d**] reinforce an acceptable alternative behavior.

15. Biofeedback techniques can teach people voluntary control of [**a**] bodily processes such as heart rate and blood pressure; [**b**] memory; [**c**] most diseases; [**d**] motor skills.

Exercises

1. DISTINGUISHING BETWEEN THE BASIC TYPES OF LEARNING. Students sometimes have difficulty seeing the differences between the basic types of learning—particularly between respondent and operant conditioning. If you have this problem, study Table 7-3. Note that respondent conditioning involves the modification of more or less involuntary, reflexlike responses, whereas operant conditioning involves the modification of deliberate, voluntary responses, except during biofeedback training. Also consider the timing of the reinforcement in both types of conditioning. In respondent conditioning, reinforcement precedes the response to be strengthened; in operant conditioning it follows the response to be strengthened.

It is important to note that the three basic types of learning frequently combine with one another. The combination of respondent and operant conditioning is so common that it is sometimes given its own name: two-factor learning. Consider how a small boy might acquire a fear of bees and a behavioral response to bees. The sight of a bee does not bother the boy initially, but after he has been stung, the sight of the bee is paired with the pain of the sting and the boy becomes frightened of bees. Whenever the boy sees a bee, he runs away, a voluntary response which is reinforced by the fact that it reduces the fear of being stung. Both respondent and operant conditioning have contributed to the boy's total response to bees.

Identify the type(s) of learning in each of the following examples. Use these abbreviations: RC—respondent conditioning; OC—operant conditioning; Obs—observation learning.

_____ **1.** A mother scolds her little girl, saying, "That's enough! In fact, it's too much!" When her baby brother makes her angry, the little girl tells him, "That's enough! In fact, it's too much!"

_____ **2.** A dog runs into the kitchen salivating every time it hears the sound of the can opener.

_____ **3.** A little boy flinches and feels anxious every time he sees the strap that he is beaten with.

_____ **4.** Music evokes a peaceful, joyful feeling in a certain woman. The church to which the woman belongs has a very fine choir and organist. Every time the woman enters the church, she feels a peaceful, joyful feeling.

_____ **5.** On registration day a confused college student sees a large crowd walking toward a building. She walks toward the building too.

_____ **6.** A nine-month-old baby says "ma ma." The parents get very excited. The baby says "ma ma" increasingly frequently.

_____ **7.** When a particular teacher writes on the board, the chalk squeals. Every time her students see a stick of chalk, they shudder.

_____ **8.** A boy studies his spelling list for half an hour. On the spelling test he gets 100 percent and a gold star. Now he studies half an hour before every spelling test.

_____ **9.** A girl watches a cowboy on TV earn $100 by winning a fist fight. The next day the girl hits a neighbor boy because she wants his quarter. The neighbor boy lets the girl have the quarter.

_____ **10.** A man gets very angry whenever someone yells at him. His mother-in-law yells at him frequently. The man now experiences negative feelings whenever he sees his mother-in-law.

_____ **11.** A woman became very sick after eating a spoiled frozen spaghetti dinner. Now she feels slightly nauseated whenever she sees spaghetti in the grocery store. She has been avoiding the grocery aisle that contains spaghetti.

_____ **12.** In driving, people step on their brakes every time they see a red light.

2. ELEMENTS OF RESPONDENT CONDITIONING. If you have trouble identifying the four basic elements of respondent conditioning, practice by identifying the elements of respondent conditioning in examples 2, 3, 4, 7, 10, and 11 of Exercise 1.

3. PRINCIPLES OF RESPONDENT CONDITIONING. To practice distinguishing the various processes of respondent conditioning, match the following terms with the appropriate events: unconditioned stimulus (US), unconditioned response (UR), neutral stimulus (NS), conditioned stimulus (CS), conditioned response (CR), acquisition (A), reinforcement (R), extinction (E), spontaneous recovery (SR), stimulus generalization (SG), stimulus discrimination (SD).

Whenever Sally's teacher opens the window, the cold air makes Sally shiver and break out in goose bumps. After two weeks Sally shivers slightly whenever the teacher simply walks toward the window.

_____ **1.** Teacher walking toward the window on the first day Sally is in class.

_____ **2.** Teacher walking toward the window after two weeks of conditioning.

_____ **3.** Sally shivers slightly whenever her teacher walks toward the window.

_____ **4.** Sally shivers and gets goose bumps when the window is opened.

_____ **5.** Cold air from the open window.

_____ **6.** Sally doesn't shiver when another student walks near the window.

_____ **7.** Sally shivers when a substitute teacher walks near the window.

_____ **8.** The two-week period during which Sally is conditioned.

For several weeks Sally's teacher stands near the window often but does not open it. After a while Sally stops shivering when the teacher stands near the window. On the first day after Christmas vacation, Sally once again shivers when the teacher stands by the window, even though the teacher has not opened it.

_____ **9.** The reduction in frequency of the "shiver" response.

_____ **10.** Sally shivers on the first day after vacation.

4. PRINCIPLES OF OPERANT CONDITIONING. To review the various processes of operant conditioning, match the following terms with the appropriate events: operants (O), behavior modification (BM), extinction (E), positive reinforcement (PR), shaping (S), spontaneous recovery (SR), punisher (P).

Terry's parents want to teach Terry good table manners. In the past Terry's good table manners have been ignored and his bad ones attended to. A psychologist recommends that Terry's parents praise Terry's good table manners and ignore his bad table manners and that they set higher and higher standards for their praise as Terry masters elementary skills.

_____ **1.** Ignoring bad table manners makes them decrease in frequency.

_____ **2.** Praising good table manners makes them increase in frequency.

_____ **3.** Setting higher and higher standards for positive reinforcement to condition more complicated skills.

_____ **4.** Although food throwing generally disappeared, it reappeared unexpectedly one morning.

_____ **5.** Good manners, bad manners.

5. TYPES OF REINFORCEMENT. To practice distinguishing between different types of reinforcers and reinforcement schedules, match the following terms with the appropriate examples: positive reinforcement (PR), negative reinforcement (NR), primary reinforcer (PR R), social reinforcer (SR), conditioned reinforcer (COND R), continuous reinforcement (CONT R), partial reinforcement (PART R), fixed-ratio schedule (FRS), variable-ratio schedule (VRS), fixed-interval schedule (FIS), variable-interval schedule (VIS), punisher (P).

_____ **1.** Presenting candies for the first correct imitation after a one-minute interval has elapsed since the last reinforcement increases the frequency of correct imitations.

_____ **2.** Using the word "good" after the fourth, ninth, fifteenth, eighteenth, etc., sit-on-command increases a dog's frequency of sitting on command.

_____ **3.** Following a child's fifth, tenth, fifteenth, twentieth, etc. right answers by a penny increases the frequency of the child's correct answers.

_____ **4.** Giving a two-year-old a lollipop after each successful visit to the bathroom increases the child's frequency of correctly using the toilet.

_____ **5.** Presenting a food pellet following a bar press after a varying number of minutes have elapsed since the last reinforcement increases the frequency of the rat's bar pressing behavior.

_____ **6.** To avoid her mother's occasional nagging, Tillie brushes her teeth every morning.

_____ **7.** Frequent yelling at a particular little boy for fighting increases the youngster's fighting behavior.

_____ **8.** Occasional attention increases a teenager's joking around.

_____ **9.** A young girl has been coming home before midnight more frequently since her parents have been taking away her driving privileges every time she is late.

_____ **10.** To avoid the loud buzzing sound which is triggered by failing to fasten seatbelts in particular cars, many people form the habit of wearing their seatbelts.

Questions to Consider

1. People frequently say that learning has occurred. What have they probably observed and what inferences are they making?

2. What similarities do the three types of basic learning share? How do they differ from one another?

3. How could you use respondent-conditioning procedures to remove a young child's fear of swimming pools? Assume that the child almost drowned once in a swimming pool.

4. Reread the description of educating fish in a hatchery. There are elements of both respondent and operant conditioning in this situation. Can you identify them? How could you teach fish to avoid fish hooks?

5. Design a shaping strategy to teach a ten-year-old child who hates doing homework and loves playing outside to do an hour of homework a day.

6. Many people have automatic positive or negative emotional responses to particular people, to particular groups of people, and to particular signs (like the peace sign or a raised clenched fist). How might respondent conditioning account for these emotional responses?

7. If you were a teacher, how might you schedule reinforcement to keep your students working at a high steady rate?

8. Speculate about the possible effects on children of watching violent TV models. How could you study whether or not watching violent TV models actually causes children to behave more aggressively?

9. Do you consider the use of conditioning techniques to change the behavior of other people ethical? Under what conditions would there be ethical problems?

Project 7: The Operant Conditioning of Smiling

People are continually modifying one another's behavior usually without being aware that they are doing so. The purpose of this project is to use operant conditioning principles deliberately to change the frequency of a social behavior, smiling.

Method. Find three cooperative subjects who have never taken a psychology course and rarely read about psychology. Tell the subjects that the project will take about half an hour and involve reading and reciting sentences. Also tell them that you cannot reveal the purpose of the study until after you have collected your observations.

You will be observing each subject individually, recording how frequently the subject smiles under the following three conditions: (1) when you neither encourage nor discourage it (baseline), (2) when you smile after the subject smiles, a potential reinforcer (reinforcement), and (3) when you withhold the potential reinforcer (extinction). Your behavior during the first and last periods will be the same. Each period will last ten minutes.

Make a data sheet for each subject like the one shown. Each number stands for a sentence. It may be necessary to add sentence numbers. You should conduct your observations in a quiet room that is free from distractions. Sitting across a table from your subject is probably ideal. You will need your psychology textbook.

Have the subject begin on page 365 and continue through the text until thirty minutes have elapsed. The subject should read a sentence aloud, then look up, and recite the sentence as accurately as possible. You will be recording how frequently the subject smiles during each recitation. You might simply make a slash for each smile next to the appropriate sentence number. It is important that you maintain a neutral expression at all times except during the reinforcement period when you will follow each of the subject's smiles by smiling yourself. Maintaining a neutral expression is difficult to do so you should practice beforehand.

After you have collected your observations, explain the project to the subject.

Results and discussion. For each subject count and compare the number of smiles during the baseline, reinforcement, and extinction periods. Then consider the following questions:

1. Did the frequency of each subject's smiling increase (past that observed during the baseline period) during the reinforcement period and decrease (approaching that observed during the baseline period) during the extinction period?
2. How can your results be explained?
3. Might factors besides conditioning have influenced the number of times your subject smiled? Explain. (Consider length of sentences, content of sentences, subject fatigue, experimenter bias, etc.) How could these factors be controlled in a more careful study?
4. Were your subjects aware that they were being conditioned? If yes, what effect did it appear to have?
5. How would operant conditioning in real life differ from this laboratory version?
6. Did any problems occur? How might they have been avoided?
7. Did you think that this project had ethical problems? Explain.

DATA SHEET

Baseline
(ten minutes)

1	5	9	13	17	21
2	6	10	14	18	22
3	7	11	15	19	23
4	8	12	16	20	24

Reinforcement
(ten minutes)

1	5	9	13	17	21
2	6	10	14	18	22
3	7	11	15	19	23
4	8	12	16	20	24

Extinction
(ten minutes)

1	5	9	13	17	21
2	6	10	14	18	22
3	7	11	15	19	23
4	8	12	16	20	24

Suggested Readings

1. Gustavson, Carl, & John Garcia. "Aversive conditioning: Pulling a gag on the wily coyote." *Psychology Today*, August 1974, 8, 68–72. Two psychologists report on research in which respondent conditioning is used to control the eating and killing habits of wild animals—particularly coyotes.
2. Whaley, Donald, & Richard Malott. *Elementary principles of behavior.* New York: Appleton-Century-Crofts, 1971 (paperback). An unusually readable introduction to operant and respondent conditioning principles filled with clinical case studies which illustrate how the principles operate.
3. Gray, Farnum, Paul Graubard, & Harry Rosenberg. "Little brother is changing you." *Psychology Today*, March 1974, 7, 42–46. Students are taught to use behavior modification procedures to modify the behavior of their teachers and friends.
4. Skinner, B. F. *Walden II.* New York: The Macmillan Company, 1948 (paperback). A novel about a utopian community where life is guided by operant conditioning principles.
5. Becker, Wesley C., *Parents are teachers.* Champaign, Ill.: Research Press, 1971 (paperback). Designed to help parents master the principles of operant conditioning and become more effective teachers of their children.
6. Jonas, Gerald. *Visceral learning: Toward a science of self control.* New York: The Viking Press, Inc., 1973 (paperback). Introduction to the operant conditioning of the autonomic nervous system, focusing on the research of Neal Miller.
7. Liebert, Robert, John Neale, & Emily Davidson. *The early window.* New York: Pergamon Press, 1973 (paperback). Three psychologists discuss research on how TV models influence children's behavior.

Answer Keys

SELF-QUIZ

1. d   2. c   3. d   4. b   5. c   6. d   7. b   8. b   9. d
10. c   11. a   12. a   13. d   14. b   15. a

EXERCISE 1
1. Obs   2. RC, OC   3. RC   4. RC   5. Obs   6. Obs, OC   7. RC   8. OC   9. Obs, OC   10. RC   11. RC, OC   12. OC

EXERCISE 2
2. US—food in mouth, UR—salivation, CS—sound of can opener, CR—salivation
3. US—beating, UR—pain, flinching, CS—sight of strap, CR—anxiety, flinching
4. US—music, UR—peaceful, joyful feelings, CS—church, CR—peaceful, joyful feelings
7. US—squealing chalk, UR—shudder, CS—sight of chalk, CR—shudder

10. US—yelling, UR—anger, CS—mother-in-law, CR—negative feelings
11. US—spoiled spaghetti dinner, UR—nausea, vomiting, CS—sight of spaghetti, CR—slight nausea

EXERCISE 3
1. NS   2. CS   3. CR   4. UR   5. US   6. SD   7. SG
8. A   9. E   10. SR

EXERCISE 4
1. E   2. PR   3. S   4. SR   5. O

EXERCISE 5
1. PR, PR R, PART R, FIS   2. PR, SR, PART R, VRS
3. PR, COND R, PART R, FRS   4. PR, PR R, CONT R, FRS
5. PR, PR R, PART R, VIS   6. NR, SR, PART R
7. PR, SR, PART R   8. PR, SR, PART R
9. NR, COND R, CONT R   10. NR, PR R, CONT R, FRS

COGNITIVE PROCESSES

IN THIS CHAPTER

We examine several cognitive processes. We look first at thinking and problem solving, then at language, and finally at the learning of verbal material. After reading this chapter, you should be able to do the following:

1. Outline Piaget's theory of mental development
2. Describe three features that are common to most models of the problem-solving process
3. Explain how the stimulus situation, past learning, images, words, strategies, and level of arousal influence the problem-solving process
4. Trace the development of language in early childhood
5. Contrast the language usage of chimpanzees and children
6. Describe the factors that increase people's efficiency at putting information into and retrieving information from memory

Last night my brain was crammed with lofty thoughts. . . . My mind was never so fertile. Ten thousand words on any theme . . . would have been easy for me. That was last night. This morning I have only one word in my brain and I cannot get rid of it. The word is 'Teralbay.' 'Teralbay' is not a word which one uses much in ordinary life. Rearrange the letters, however, and it becomes a common word. A friend—no, I can call him a friend no longer—a person gave me this collection of letters as I was going to bed and challenged me to make a proper word of it . . . 'Teralbay'—what does it make? . . . When I die, 'Teralbay' will be written on my heart. While I live, it shall be my telegraphic address. I shall patent a breakfast food called 'Teralbay'. I shall say 'Teralbay' when I miss a 2-foot putt. . . . I have no doubt that after hours of immense labor, you will triumphantly suggest 'rateable.' I suggested that myself, but it is wrong. There is no such word in the dictionary . . . So I hand the word over to you. Please do not send the solution to me, for by the time you read this, I shall either have found it out or else I shall be in a nursing home. . . . Just a moment. I think I have it now. T-R-A- No . . . [1]. (from A. A. Milne, 'A lost masterpiece,' 1920.)

The solution to the anagram is presented in footnote 1.

Psychologists use the term *cognitive processes* to refer to complex mental activities such as using language, thinking, reasoning, solving problems, conceptualizing, remembering, imagining, and learning verbal material. Human beings spend more time in cognitive activities and tend to be far better at them than any other animal. Like Milne's nameless protagonist, many people walk around absorbed in lofty and not-so-lofty thoughts much of the time. The cognitive processes usually play a *mediating role* between environmental stimuli and responses that people make to these stimuli. In other words, they usually influence how people behave. We do not simply respond automatically like robots

¹The letters in "Teralbay" can be rearranged to make the word "betrayal."

to events around us. Presumably, cognitive processes were at least in part responsible for the observable groaning, moaning, and guessing of Milne's protagonist. The cognitive processes share another characteristic: They are inevitably private events that cannot be directly observed. We did not observe the thoughts of Milne's problem solver; we cannot even observe our own thoughts. We learn about the cognitive processes by their products—by what people say and do and write. As a matter of fact, we learn about our own thoughts in the same way. Also note that cognitive processes are frequently interwoven. To solve the anagram, Milne's character probably rearranged the letters mentally. He might also have worked through a hypothesis or two, such as recalling words that end in -*ly*. Images, memories, reasoning, and language were undoubtedly involved in the problem-solving process. Finally, the cognitive processes are activities that are initiated and controlled by the learner—in contrast to respondent and operant conditioning and observation learning, which are largely controlled by others in the environment. In Milne's story, the hero's hours of immense labor are his own doing—even though he blames his friend. We turn now to thinking.

THINKING

What is thinking? Psychologists use the word "thinking" in the same way that most other people do: as a general label for mental activities such as reasoning, solving problems, remembering, and conceptualizing. Most thinking is hard to categorize. Our thoughts ramble along. During our waking hours, ideas mingle with memories, images, fantasies, and associations. Dreaming might be a continuation of this type of daytime thinking. William James labeled this relatively *undirected* type of mental activity *stream of consciousness*.

In novels we sometimes enter a character's stream of consciousness, as in the following excerpt from *Ullyses* by James Joyce.

I love flowers Id love to have the whole place swimming in roses God of heaven theres nothing like nature the wild mountains then the sea and the waves rushing then the beautiful country with fields of oats and wheat and all kinds of things and all the fine cattle going about that would do your heart good to see rivers and lakes and flowers all sorts of shapes and smells and colors spring up even out of the ditches prim-roses and violets nature it is as for them saying theres no God I wouldnt give a snap of my two fingers for all their learning why dont they go and create something . . . [2].

When psychoanalytic therapists ask their pa-tients to free-associate (see Chapter 15), they are asking the patient to do some undirected thinking. Occasionally, undirected thinking appears to lead to creative achievement (see Chapter 9). For the most part psychologists have studied *directed thinking*, thinking that is aimed at a particular goal, such as reasoning, problem solving, or concept learning. Direct-ed and undirected thinking involve some of the same mental processes—memory, imagi-nation, and association. In contrast with un-

directed thinking, directed thinking is usually highly controlled, tied to a specific situation or problem, and evaluated by external stan-dards.

The human infant is a creature of reflexes; its thinking appears to be quite limited. The human adult is a subtle and sophisticated thinker. How does the capacity for thought develop?

The Development of Thinking

Jean Piaget, an eminent Swiss psychologist, has spent approximately fifty years studying the mental development of children. Piaget became interested in this subject when he noticed that children made consistent mis-takes on intelligence tests. He questioned children about their reasonsing and discov-ered that they actually thought *differently*, not simply *less*, than adults did. On the basis of numerous observations of what children say and do in problem-solving settings, Piaget has formulated a comprehensive theory about how thinking develops. Basically, Piaget be-lieves that the human infant is born with both the need and the ability to adapt to the

Figure 8-1. Psychologist Jean Piaget observing Swiss children at play. (Yves Debrainie, from Black Star.)

environment. As children interact with the environment, they learn to cope with its demands; their mental capacities develop automatically. Piaget calls this mental-growth process *adaptation*. Adaptation, as Piaget defines it, is composed of two subprocesses: assimilation and accommodation. Most of the time children *assimilate* (take in) information that is well within their mental grasp and categorize it in terms of what they already know. For example, Piaget writes:

At twenty-one months Jacqueline saw a shell and said "cup." After saying this, she picked it up and pretended to drink. . . . The next day, seeing the same shell, she said "glass," then "cup," then "hat," and finally "boat in the water." Three days later she took an empty box and moved it to and fro saying "motycar" [3].

Occasionally, children encounter problems that are somewhat beyond their reach. Under these circumstances they must *accommodate*, create new strategies or modify or combine old strategies to handle the new problem. The process of accommodation stretches the child's mind and makes it grow. Here is Piaget's description of an instance of accommodation:

At 16 months, 5 days, Laurent [Piaget's son] is seated before a table and I place a bread crust in front of him, out of reach. Also, to the right of the child I place a stick about 25 cm long. At first Laurent tries to grasp the bread without paying any attention to the instrument, and then he gives up. I then put the stick between him and the bread; it does not touch the objective but nevertheless carries with it an undeniable visual suggestion. Laurent again looks at the bread, without moving, looks very briefly at the stick, then suddenly grasps it and directs it towards the bread. But he grasped it toward the middle and not at one of its ends so that it is too short to obtain the objective. Laurent then puts it down and resumes stretching out his hand towards the bread. Then, without spending much time on this movement, he takes up the stick again, this time at one of its ends (chance or intention?), and draws the bread to him. . . . Two successive attempts yield the same result.

An hour later I place a toy in front of Laurent (out of his reach) and a new stick next to him. He does not even try to catch the objective with his hand; he immediately grasps the stick and draws the toy to him [4].

Piaget believes that thinking develops in the same unvarying sequence of stages in all children, although the age at which a particular child passes through a particular stage varies. During each stage the child shows characteristic mental assumptions and capabilities that can be broadly identified as follows:

STAGE 1: SENSORIMOTOR STAGE (birth to approximately two years). During these first twenty-four months infants develop some important cognitive capabilities; they learn to act to solve a variety of problems. They discover that specific actions have specific consequences. Kicking, for example, gets rid of heavy blankets. Bouncing makes objects suspended above the crib dance about. In the beginning "out of sight" is equivalent to "nonexistent": When the rattle falls on the floor, it is gone. During the sensorimotor period the infant learns that objects continue to exist, even when they aren't immediately present. The infant develops another ability—the ability to find new uses for old objects. The game of drop-the-bear-to-watch-mother-pick-it-up-again can be exasperating evidence of this particular capability. Imitation is another achievement of the sensorimotor period. At this time the child learns to imitate complex new responses quite precisely—even when the model is absent.

STAGE 2: PREOPERATIONAL STAGE (approximately two to seven years). During the preoperational stage children become capable of thinking about their environment; that is, they develop the ability to manipulate symbols (like words) that represent the environment. Before this time they have been restricted to direct interactions with the environment itself. The major achievements of this stage include the development of language, the ability to understand simple concepts (for example, Fido, Blacky, and Spot are all dogs), and the ability to see one object as representing another (a stick as a sword or a doll as a baby). Children at this stage are *egocentric* (self-centered); they see the world strictly from their own perspective; they cannot understand differing points of view.

STAGE 3: STAGE OF CONCRETE OPERATIONS (approximately seven to eleven years). During this stage the child learns to use logic (as opposed to simple sensory information) to understand the nature of things. For example, when milk is poured from a tall, thin glass to a short, wide glass, the preoperational child feels that the amount of milk has actually decreased. The child who has entered the stage of concrete operations learns that sensory properties like size or shape can change without affecting more basic properties like quantity. The child's ability to categorize and classify objects also expands at this time. Although children in this stage are logical in dealing with concrete objects, they are not yet capable of dealing logically with abstract ideas. For example, they cannot solve problems by thinking of possible solutions and mentally eliminating those that are obviously incorrect.

STAGE 4: STAGE OF FORMAL OPERATIONS (approximately eleven to fifteen years). During these years children develop the ability to reason, to see implications, to understand abstract logic, and to

Figure 8-2. A child in the preoperational stage believes that when liquid is poured from a tall, thin glass to a short, wide one, the quantity decreases. (S. Wells.)

test hypotheses in their minds. The child emerges from this stage with a set of adult thinking abilities.

Is Piaget's analysis accurate? Some psychologists believe that it is; others are skeptical. Piaget is sometimes criticized for using small numbers of subjects for certain observations and for confusing children's ability to use language with their ability to use logic. Moreover, many psychologists believe that Piaget has drastically underestimated the importance of a specific environment and specific training in shaping the child's thinking skills.

Piaget's work centers on the development of directed-thinking skills in children. We turn now to the nature of one directed-thinking skill—problem solving—focusing this time on adults.

PROBLEM SOLVING

Try to solve the problems in Figure 8-3 before reading on. As you attempt each problem, speak aloud or write what you are thinking. Then try to identify the various processes that go into problem solving.

A

"Given, a human being with an inoperable stomach tumor. We know that if we apply certain rays, with sufficient intensity, the tumor can be destroyed. The problem is: How can these rays, at the required high intensity, be applied to the tumor without at the same time destroying the healthy tissue which surrounds the tumor?" (After Duncker, 1945.)

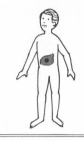

Figure 8-3. How would you solve these three problems? (Solutions are on p. 244.)

B

You are seated in front of a table on which you see kitchen matches, a candle, and a small matchbox filled with thumbtacks. Using these materials, try to affix the candle to the wall and light it. (After Glucksburg and Weisburg, 1966.)

C

You are given the following arrangement of sixteen matches. Move only three matches to create a sixteen-match arrangement of four equal-size squares.*

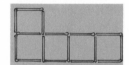

Problem solving is a directed-thinking skill which uses information and experience to generate new responses. Since psychologists cannot observe directly what is going on in problem solving, they frequently ask people to think aloud as they solve problems such as these in the laboratory. Later they analyze the verbal accounts. Although different models of the problem-solving process emerge from such analyses, they tend to share the following features: The problem solver interprets the problem; she or he formulates and embarks upon a plan to solve the problem; eventually she or he evaluates the solution.

The first step in the problem-solving process is interpreting (*representing*) the problem. An initial representation of a problem is likely to include an attempt to understand the problem's goals, conditions, and data. How did you represent the inoperable stomach tumor problem? You might represent this problem as one of eliminating the tumor without destroying healthy tissue. Conceptualizing a problem correctly makes it likelier that the learner will achieve a correct solution. An incorrect representation will make the problem harder to solve. The problem presented in Figure 8-4 makes this point very clearly.

Try to form a representation of the problem in Figure 8-4 before reading on. If you represent the problem in Figure 8-4 in terms of the *distance* the bird must fly, the problem becomes extremely difficult to solve. If you represent the problem in terms of the *amount of time* the bird must fly, then the problem becomes relatively easy.[2]

What do people *do* to solve problems? Sometimes they use *images*; that is, they visualize the problem's solution. To solve the match problem, for example, many people

[2]The trains must travel one hour before they meet, so the bird will fly 100 miles at its current rate of 100 miles per hour.

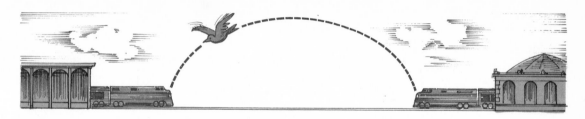

Figure 8-4. Two trains, fifty miles apart, start toward each other at the same time. As they start, a bird springs into the air from the engine of the first train and flies ahead to the engine of the second train. When it reaches the second train, it turns around and flies back to the first train. The bird continues flying back and forth until the trains meet. If each train travels at the rate of twenty-five miles per hour and the bird flies at the rate of one hundred miles per hour, how many miles will the bird fly before the trains meet?

"test" different configurations by visually rearranging the matches in their minds. Sometimes *language* mediates the problem-solving process. Consider the candle problem. When words are used to label the objects appearing in the problem, more people consider potential uses for the box and solve the problem than when the labels are not supplied at all (5). The inoperable stomach tumor problem is likely to be approached by a plan, a *strategy*. When student subjects talked aloud as they attempted to solve this problem in the laboratory, the investigator, Karl Duncker, found that the students used similar problem-solving strategies. After carefully defining the problem, they formulated a number of possible approaches, called *general solutions*, each of which could be expressed in the form: "If such and such could only be achieved, the problem could be solved." One student produced three general solutions: "avoid contact between rays and healthy tissue," "desensitize the healthy tissue," and "lower the intensity of the rays on their way through the healthy tissue." Next the students refined their general solutions into more detailed plans, called *functional solutions*. One student's functional solutions included "displace tumor toward surface," "inject desensitizing chemical," and "give weak intensity in periphery and concen-

trate in place of tumor." The students then searched for very specific concrete ways to apply the functional solution(s), called *specific solutions*. One student produced the specific solutions: "Use pressure to displace tumor toward the surface" and "use lens to concentrate the rays at the tumor." If students failed to achieve a correct solution, they usually backtracked (6).

Finally, the problem solver reaches a solution. If the goal is very clear, then there is little question as to when the problem is solved. Solutions to many problems are not clear-cut; people vary on what constitutes an acceptable solution to a particular problem. To prove this point the famous gestalt psychologist Wolfgang Köhler presented people with the problem in Figure 8-5. Try to solve the problem before reading on.

Did you consider the problem solved as soon as you filled in the blanks? Many people do not (7). They want to know *why* subtract-

Figure 8-5. What are the missing numbers? (After Köhler, 1969.)

1	4	9	16	25	36	49	64
0	1	4	9	16	25	36	49

1	3	5	7	9

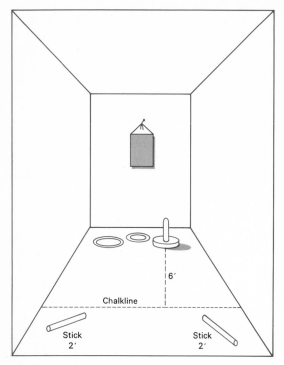

Figure 8-6. The ring problem: Can you put the two rings on the peg while remaining behind the chalkline? You can move around the room and use anything you see—except when picking up the rings and putting them on the peg. (After Scheerer, 1968.)

ing each successive square produces a set of odd numbers. They look for a general rule.

We turn now to some of the factors that influence the problem-solving process.

The Structure of the Problem

All problems have a structure; that is, they contain *elements*—objects, events, or other stimuli—that are organized in time and space. The structure of a problem can facilitate or retard the problem-solving process.

Before reading further, try to solve the ring problem (see Figure 8-6), then check the footnote to make sure your solution is cor-

rect.[3] In the ring problem all the problem elements—two sticks, a chalk line 6 feet in front of a peg and two rings, and a piece of cardboard hanging from a string on the wall—are present together at the same time in the visual field, and there are no irrelevant elements to distract you. When a problem is cluttered with irrelevant elements, problem solving is retarded.

Suppose that the ring problem had been presented as shown in Figure 8-7. It would take time and effort to explore possible uses for each additional object, so the problem-solving process would be more difficult, and it would take more time. Sometimes irrelevant elements are so distracting that they prevent people from solving a problem altogether.

The spatial arrangement of the problem elements also influences the problem-solving process. Problem solving is more difficult when the elements of the problem are not present together in the same visual field—when they are separated from one another in either space or time, or both. In real life, time and space usually separate the elements of most problems.

Some problems require that people use an element of a problem in a novel way. When the elements are present in groupings that emphasize their conventional functions, problem solving is frequently retarded (see Figure 8-8).

When the string hangs on the nail by itself very few subjects fail to solve the ring problem. When the string is used to suspend a sheet of cardboard, an old calendar, or a cloudy mirror, a larger percentage of subjects fail to solve the problem. When the string is used to suspend more functional objects such as a sign, a clear mirror, or a current calen-

---

[3]The problem is most easily solved by tying the two sticks together with the string from the cardboard and using the new longer stick to lift each ring onto the peg.

dar, more than half the subjects fail to solve the problem (8). In these instances the function of the string is firmly fixed by its context; that is, subjects are reminded of their past experiences with strings as supports; consequently, they are unlikely to think of using the string in a novel way. Psychologists label this phenomenon *functional fixity*, which is defined as a tendency to see a particular object as fixed in function (largely because of past experience) and to fail to perceive new and flexible uses for it.

How else does past learning effect problem solving?

Past Learning and Problem Solving

Past learning sometimes supplies necessary bits of information for solving a particular problem. It would be easy to compute the distance your car could travel on one tank of gasoline, for example, if you'd learned some simple algebra and knew the car's gas tank capacity and the number of miles the car averages per gallon. When past learning facilitates learning or problem solving, psychologists label the effect *positive transfer*.

Sometimes past learning in several situations increases general problem-solving abilities. In these cases of positive transfer, psychologists say that subjects have acquired a *learning set* or that they have *learned to learn*. Psychologist Harry Harlow demonstrated this phenomenon quite clearly in monkeys more than twenty years ago. He presented his subjects with discrimination problems. In each problem the monkey had to select one of two small stimulus objects. The stimulus objects—aspirin tins, small jars, bottle caps, soap dishes—varied from problem to problem. One choice yielded food; the other did not. The animals had two trials to work each problem. Since there were only two possible

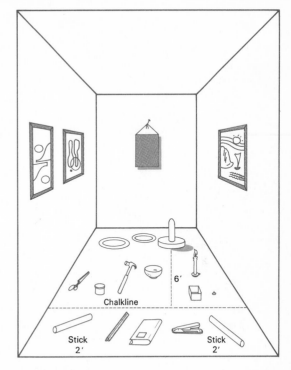

Figure 8-7. When a problem is cluttered with irrelevant elements, problem solving is usually retarded. (After Scheerer, 1968.)

correct answers, it was easy to see if the animals were acquiring general rules, such as "If correct on trial 1, choose the same object again on trial 2; if incorrect on trial 1, choose

Figure 8-8. It is relatively easy to solve the ring problem when the string hangs simply from a nail. It is relatively difficult to solve the problem when the string is used to support one of the other items. (After Scheerer, 1968.)

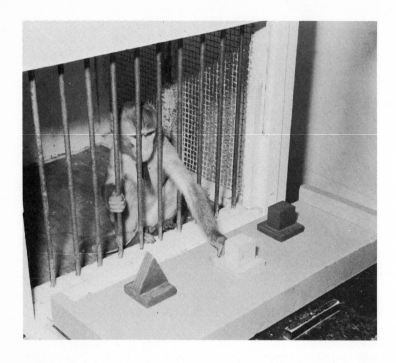

Figure 8-9. After working many discrimination problems, monkeys learn general problem-solving skills. (Wisconsin Primate Laboratory.)

the other object on trial 2." Harlow presented each animal with more than three hundred discrimination problems in all. The data showed that the subjects became increasingly skilled at making new discriminations as they worked more tasks. Evidently, the monkeys were learning general problem-solving skills: to follow rules and to pay attention (9).

Like monkeys, people also learn to learn. After taking several tests, for example, students usually acquire some general test-taking skills, like the ability to guess ahead of time what questions are likely to appear on a test and the ability to read and interpret test questions. Similarly, with experience, civil engineers become adept at solving sewerage and highway problems and auto mechanics at diagnosing and curing car ailments.

Just as learning sets can facilitate problem solving, they can also impede it by making the learner likely to respond in rigid, stereotyped, or mechanical ways in particular situations. When past learning retards new learn-ing or problem solving, psychologists label the effect *negative transfer*. To demonstrate negative transfer, try to solve the problems in Figure 8-10 before reading on.

Past learning is likely to interfere with your ability to solve both of these puzzles. Consider the riddle first. Because of past experience many people assume that the surgeon must be a man. Frequently that assumption is so firmly established that the possibility that the surgeon might be a woman (the mother) is never entertained. Now consider the dot problem. The conventions in most dot games forbid people to extend lines past the edges formed by the dots. Because of past experience many people never consider the actual solution.[4]

In a classic study A. S. Luchins, a psychologist then at New York University, used the problems shown in Figure 8-11 to demonstrate how a set formed by past learning can

[4]See p. 244 for the solution to the dot problem.

A.

A doctor and his son were involved in an automobile accident. The doctor was killed while the son was badly injured. The boy was brought to the hospital for surgery. The surgeon there exclaimed "I can't operate on him, he's my son." How is this possible?

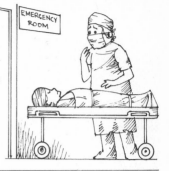

Figure 8-10. Two problems illustrating the effects of negative transfer.

B.

Connect the nine dots by drawing four straight lines without lifting your pencil from the paper.

hinder efficient problem solving. Please solve these problems *in order* before reading on.

Subjects in the experimental group solved all eight problems in succession. In the course of solving problems 2 through 6, many of them formulated an efficient strategy: Take B, subtract A, then subtract 2 C. Once people began using this formula, a majority of them continued to use it mechanically, even on problems 7 and 8 where the most efficient solutions are simple subtraction and simple addition. (Did you solve problems 7 and 8 directly?) Subjects in a control group solved problem 1, then problems 7 and 8. In contrast to the experimental subjects, they solved problems 7 and 8 directly and efficiently 100 percent of the time (10).

Arousal and Problem Solving

In 1945 a psychologist named H. G. Birch studied the relationship between hunger and problem solving in young chimpanzees. Birch deprived his subjects of food for periods of

two, six, twelve, twenty-four, thirty-six, or forty-eight hours; then he observed their performance on problem-solving tasks that required the animals to rake in food with a stick. Birch found that when chimpanzees had been deprived of food for short periods

Figure 8-11. In each problem obtain the specified amount of water by using the two or three empty jars whose volumes are given. (After Luchins, 1942.)

Problem	Jar A	Jar B	Jar C	Volume desired
1	29	3	3	20
2	21	127	3	100
3	14	163	25	99
4	18	43	10	5
5	9	42	6	21
6	20	59	4	31
7	23	49	3	20
8	15	39	3	18

of time, they were easily distracted and they often engaged in behavior that was irrelevant to solving the problem. They simply were not sufficiently interested in the problem to remain with it. In contrast, chimpanzees who had been deprived of food for long periods of time concentrated so intently on the goal that they frequently failed to see important parts of the stimulus situation. These highly aroused chimpanzees also screeched and staged temper tantrums more frequently than the other chimpanzees, displaying an inability to endure frustration and failure. The chimpanzees who were only moderately hungry made flexible, goal-directed responses (11). This study suggests that *arousal* (degree of alertness and excitement) has an important effect on problem-solving capabilities.

What about people? Numerous studies indicate that people behave like chimpanzees in a large number of learning and problem-solving situations. In general, human learning and problem solving both improve as arousal increases up to some optimal point. After that point, increased arousal results in decreased efficiency. When people are highly aroused because of failure, frustration, stress, strong needs, or emotions, for example, their ability to solve problems is usually disrupted. More on the subject of anxiety level and learning later in this chapter and in Chapter 11.

Summary: Thinking and Problem Solving

1. Thinking skills appear to develop in a relatively well-defined sequence of stages as children interact with their environment.
2. Problem solving is a directed thinking skill that uses information and experience to generate new responses.
3. To study problem solving, psychologists have people think aloud as they solve problems in a laboratory setting.

4. Psychologists have identified three processes that usually occur as people try to solve problems: (1) Learners represent (interpret) the problem. (2) They use images, language, and strategies in their attempt to solve the problem. (3) They evaluate their solution to make certain that it is satisfactory.
5. The structure of the problem can retard or facilitate problem solving. Problems are generally more difficult to solve when they contain elements that are (1) irrelevant, (2) isolated in time and/or space, or (3) grouped according to their conventional functions when they must be used in novel ways.
6. Past learning can facilitate problem solving by providing needed information or general problem-solving skills. Past learning can also result in learning sets which make people more rigid and consequently less efficient at solving problems.
7. In general, moderate arousal produces optimum efficiency in problem solving. Very high and very low arousal usually reduce efficiency.

We will be focusing now on language, a cognitive process which is closely related to thinking. Normal children and adults code and store many events in their brains, using language descriptions. Language also helps people think about many of their experiences. Although thinking is greatly facilitated by language, it does not depend on language. Animals think; so do the deaf who are severely retarded in learning to use language. Understanding of language, in turn, depends on thought. It requires the understanding of grammatical rules, such as knowing when to add "s" to make a noun plural, the ability to form abstract concepts such as "intention" and "freedom," and the capacity to grasp relationships such as "similar to" and "smaller than."

LANGUAGE

Most animals, including people, communicate with one another in several ways. The simplest kind of communication is *reflexive*. Reflexive communication consists of stereotyped behavior patterns, such as reflexes, expressive gestures, and signs of emotion, which often convey important information even though they were not intended specifically for that purpose. Wasp larvae in one species, for example, extend their heads from their cells whenever they are hungry; this gesture stimulates the worker wasps to supply them with food. Female dogs in estrus secrete a chemical substance that informs male dogs that they are ready and may be willing to mate; the substance also tells the male where the female is located. Posturing by the female dog (like the positioning of her tail) tells the male whether or not she is willing to mate. Posturing—like certain other gestures, facial expressions, movements, and sounds—is an example of *purposive* communication, communication that sets out to affect the receiver of the information. Horses lower their ears and bare their teeth to frighten their enemies. Baboons present their hindquarters to signify friendliness.

Language is the most sophisticated kind of purposive communication. A *language* systematically relates symbols (sounds, letters, or signs) to meaning and provides rules for combining and recombining the symbols to convey various kinds of information. We say that language is sophisticated because it is incredibly open and flexible. The English language, for example, contains nearly a million words that can be combined and recombined to make approximately 100,000,000,000,000,000,000,000 different twenty-word sentences (12). All known human societies, even isolated and primitive ones, have developed complete languages. It is also impressive that people acquire their native language almost effortlessly: As young children, they learn sounds, words, and *grammar* (how to combine the sounds and words meaningfully to make phrases and sentences) without any systematic teaching or planning long before they go to school. Psychologists are primarily interested in two aspects of language: how it is acquired and how it is used. The study of these subjects is known as *psycholinguistics*. In this section we look at the acquisition of language in children and in chimpanzees so as to better understand what makes human language a distinctive cognitive process.

THE ACQUISITION OF LANGUAGE

All over the world children develop the basics of a grammatical language in two short years—between the ages of $1^1/_2$ and $3^1/_2$. How do they do it?

From Sounds to Words

Newborn infants tend to be rather noisy. Basic reflexive communication patterns appear immediately. The infant cries when it is uncomfortable and coos when it is pleased. Moreover, as it exercises its muscles, it also moves its jaws, tongue, vocal cords, and lips, producing other random noises. Up until the age of six months, all human infants—regardless of nationality, race, environment, or learning ability—vocalize approximately the same amount and produce approximately the same sounds, from French trills to German gutterals. Ordinarily, young infants also show acute auditory discrimination. There is some evidence that normal human infants of only twelve hours move in rhythm with the language spoken around them (13). By a month of age the normal baby can differentiate between voiced consonants like B and

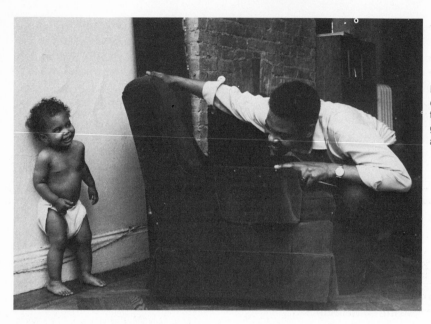

Figure 8-12. *Many parents unknowingly reinforce their young children's language by joy, enthusiasm, and affection. (Erika.)*

unvoiced consonants like P (14). Clearly the necessary capabilities for developing a language are present at a very early age.

From six to twelve months children do a lot of *babbling* (playing with sounds). They imitate and practice the sounds that they hear. By their first birthday they are usually making a distinctive set of sounds that mimic the stress and pitch patterns of those around them. Near the end of their first year children begin to understand the meanings of words. When a child has reached this stage, she will most likely look at her mother if someone says "Mom" and not at her father or at her stuffed squirrel. At about this same time children also begin using single words meaningfully—frequently to convey whole ideas. The utterance "Papa," for example, may be interpreted as meaning "Here is Papa," or "Come here, Papa," or "Where is Papa?" In the next six months the child's vocabulary will grow rapidly. Several kinds of learning shape this early vocabulary that typically consists of the names of objects and

people. In the beginning *observation learning* is very important. Children imitate the words that others say. Meanings become attached to these words as they are *associated* repeatedly with particular objects or events. Let's take some examples. A mother says the word "bear" every time she holds up a teddy bear. A father says the word "no" and pairs it with a slap on the hand every time the child throws its rattle on the floor. In this last instance *respondent conditioning* is occurring. The word "no" is being paired with a slap, an event that automatically elicits the respondent pain; so that the word "no" eventually acquires the capacity to elicit discomfort. Gradually, the sounds of many words will be linked in the child's mind with particular objects, events, and emotional experiences.

Operant conditioning also plays a role in the early acquisition of language. Many parents unknowingly *positively reinforce* their young children's new utterances with attention—bursts of joy, enthusiasm, and affection. In addition, many parents actively *shape* their children's vocabularies, again probably unknowingly. When the child produces a random noise that sounds like a word ("meh," for example), the parent smiles and repeats a closer approximation to the word ("Ma" and later "Mama"). The child will probably imitate the new closer approximation—partly because of the innate propensity to imitate and partly because of the parent's reinforcing response.

Initially, young children use words as if they refer to a large range of objects. The word "papa," for example, may be used for every man—uncle, milkman, and neighbor. One two-year-old child grew up with a Saint Bernard named Sam and called all dogs "Sam." Gradually, parents teach their children *discriminations* by giving them the appropriate labels for the people, objects, and events around them: "This is papa; that is uncle; that is the milkman."

From Words to Sentences: The Development of Grammar

As the child gets around on its own, it begins to interact more with the world. There are noisy things to shake and bang, cuddly things to hold, tasty things to eat. People and objects appear, disappear, and change. The child begins to combine words to keep pace with its growing needs to understand and communicate new ideas. At 1½ to 2 years of age children all over the world begin creating two-word utterances in an abbreviated or *telegraphic* language that they have never heard before. For example, an English-speaking child may say—"All-gone shoe" and "Bye-bye dirty." In fact, even when the child tries to mimic an adult, it produces the same telegraphic utterances (15):

ADULT'S SENTENCE	CHILD'S IMITATION
Where does that go?	Where go?
What's dolly's name?	Dolly name?

These two-word utterances sound deceptively simple, like mere random word combinations. On the contrary, they are meaningful and grammatical sentences which preserve word order, but leave out articles, prepositions, auxiliary words, prefixes, suffixes, and other parts of speech. The simple sentence, for example, has three elements: an *agent or subject*, like "Mary," an *action or verb*, like "feeds," and an *object* which receives the action, like "lamb." At first children combine two elements at a time: for example, action and object ("Feed lamb"), agent and action ("Mary feed"), and agent and object ("Mary lamb") (16). Children use two-word sentences for a large number of purposes:

1. To *identify* and *name* objects, the child might say "Here truck" or "It ball."
2. To express the *concept of quantity*, the child might say "More milk" or "Another bang" or "All-gone cookie."
3. To express *possession*, the child might say "Daddy coat."
4. To express *negation*, the child might say "Not shoe."
5. To express *location* (to say that something is on or in something else), the child might say "Baby highchair."
6. To *join* two things, the child might say "Daddy mommy."
7. To *modify* a noun, the child might say "Red truck."

Already the child appears to have acquired some rudimentary rules of grammar.

In the next few years children's speech will become less and less telegraphic as children begin to fill in the gaps of their sentences with prepositions, articles, and auxiliary words. Although few children (and few adults) can state the rules of grammar, children acquire basic grammatical rules in a fairly stable order. As you might expect, they learn easily understood rules first, such as how to form the past tense of a verb (Mary *looks* now, but if she did it yesterday, she look*ed*) and how to form the plural of a noun (there is one duck; if more appear, there will be several duck*s*). Later, children acquire more difficult rules, such as how to form irregular past tenses (such as "sing, sang, sung") and irregular plurals (such as "oxen" and "geese"). Children will also add many new words to their vocabularies.

How do psychologists know that children learn grammatical rules and not simply individual cases? They can demonstrate in the laboratory that children know and use grammatical rules to produce grammatically correct sentences that they could never have heard before. In 1958, for example, Jean Berko, a linguist at Radcliffe College, studied ninety-four children four to seven years of age. Berko showed each child a picture and asked the child to complete sentences such as the following:

PLURAL 1: "This is a wug. Now there is another one. There are two of them. There are two _____". (See Figure 8-13.)

TENSE 11: "This is a man who knows how to mot. He is motting. He did the same thing yesterday. What did he do yesterday? Yesterday he _____."

POSSESSIVE 21: "This is a niz who owns a hat. Whose hat is it? It is the _____ hat."

In general, Berko's study showed that children apply grammatical rules to new material—even when that material is total nonsense (16)! Later studies have confirmed these findings (17).

Figure 8-13. Figures used in the Berko study. (After Berko, 1958.)

This is a wug.

Now there is another one.
There are two of them.
There are two_____.

How can the acquisition of grammar be explained? Psychologists have been feuding over this question for a long time. B. F. Skinner, the well-known behaviorist, emphasizes the role of learning. Noam Chomsky, a prominent linguist at the Massachusetts Institute of Technology, emphasizes the role of genetics. Chomsky believes that although learning may account for the acquisition of vocabulary, pronunciation, and other superficial aspects of language, children acquire grammar because they are "preset" to learn it. Psychologist Donald Hebb and his associates have taken a "middle of the road" position. They believe that genes give the human infant the capacity to babble, to develop complex auditory discriminations, to deal with symbols, to generalize and to abstract, and they give it a need to communicate. The environment, on the other hand, provides the infant with necessary experiences—the sounds of other human voices, the sound of its own voice, and the sensations felt in its own throat as it vocalizes.

Consider how a child might learn a grammatical rule—say, how to make a singular noun plural. Every time Ella sees one finger, she learns to say "finger"; every time she sees two or more fingers, she learns to add the terminal z sound to produce the word "fingers." Similarly, whenever she sees one cookie, she learns to say "cookie"; whenever she sees two or more, she learns to add a terminal z sound to produce the word "cookies." At some stage in development Ella begins to *generalize* (to abstract general principles from specific cases). She comes to understand that just as two fingers are also two things, two or more of any object are also two or more things. She also comes to associate the terminal z sound with the general concept of two or more similar things. At this point Ella automatically adds the terminal z sound to the singular noun whenever she encounters two or more similar objects. Currently, many psychologists agree with Hebb that language development reflects both heredity and learning and that the acquisition of grammar, in particular, seems to result from the child's active efforts to extract a system of rules.

As we mentioned before, all known human societies have developed a complete language system. Is the human capacity for language unique? Or can other animals also learn a language?

Teaching Chimpanzees a Language

Psychologists have been trying to teach language to chimpanzees for a long time. In the 1940s, for example, two psychologists, Keith and Cathy Hayes, gave a chimpanzee named Vicki six years of intensive speech training with disappointing results: Vicki mastered only four recognizable words. These early efforts failed largely because chimpanzees have different vocal apparatus and different vocal behavior than people and not because chimpanzees are necessarily incapable of using a language. In the wild, chimpanzees communicate extensively but mostly by gestures. In 1966 Allan and Beatrice Gardner, psychologists at the University of Nevada, took this fact into account and became the first successful teachers of a language-using chimpanzee. The Gardners taught a chimpanzee named Washoe to use the *American Sign Language* (*ASL*), the gestural language that many deaf Americans use. During that same year David Premack, a psychologist at the University of California in Santa Barbara, and Ann Premack, a free-lance writer, began using operant conditioning techniques to train a chimpanzee named Sarah to "talk" by manipulating magnetized plastic chips of varying sizes, shapes, and colors. Sarah learned to combine more than 130 symbols to make meaningful sentences. More recently a

team of researchers at the Yerkes Primate Research Center in Atlanta led by a psychology professor, Duane Rumbaugh, have been training a chimp named Lana to read and write on a special typewriter with fifty keys. Each key on Lana's typewriter contains a different white geometrical pattern and colored background and represents a single word in "Yerkish." Using operant conditioning techniques, Lana has been trained to answer questions and to make requests like "Please machine give piece of banana." A projector is attached to Lana's keyboard so that she can see the symbols as she punches them. A computer also attached to the keyboard, rewards Lana when she combines words meaningfully, and records and analyzes all her word sequences. Recently, Lana has begun asking spontaneous questions such as "What is this?" or "What name of this?" There is no longer any question that chimpanzees can learn a variety of "languages." Let's return to the story of Washoe.

Project Washoe

In June 1966 Beatrice and Allan Gardner began training Washoe, a wild-born, approximately year-old chimpanzee, to use American Sign Language. The Gardners treated Washoe like a human child. She lived in a trailer that was furnished like a home. Two human companions kept her company during her waking hours, signing to her and to one another in ASL as they all interacted in play, at meals, and during "child-care" routines. After several months of exposure to the ASL gestures, Washoe apparently *learned* some signs simply by *observation.* Here is an example. After each meal Washoe had to brush her teeth. If she tried to leave her seat, her companions signed, "First toothbrushing, then you can go." Washoe had never made the toothbrush sign herself. Months after the project began, Washoe was visiting at the

Figure 8-14. Washoe asks for a soda, using ASL (R. A. Gardner and B. T. Gardner.)

Gardners' home. She found her way to the bathroom and climbed on top of the counter. There she saw a mug filled with toothbrushes and she spontaneously signed "toothbrush."

Washoe learned most of her signs by a process called *molding*: Washoe's hands and arms were placed in the proper signing position in the presence of the object or action that the sign represented. To teach Washoe the sign for "tickle," for example, the Gardners held Washoe's hands and put them through the appropriate movements while tickling her. Washoe also learned a number of signs by *operant conditioning*. For instance, every time Washoe wanted to open a door, she held up both hands and banged on the door. The sign for "open" happens to be two open hands palm down side by side, moved apart gradually and rotated to palms up. Washoe's banging was actually a beginning. The Gardners waited for Washoe to place her hands on the door and then lift them. Sometimes they prompted her. Then they rewarded the correct approximation by opening the door. Eventually, the Gardners shaped a response that resembled the open sign (18).

Washoe's language is quite impressive. By

1973 she had acquired a vocabulary of approximately 160 words (19). Her use of words is even more intriguing than the sheer size of her vocabulary. Washoe uses signs spontaneously to name objects, to make requests, and to conduct simple conversations like the following one:

ROGER: What you want?
WASHOE: Tickle.
ROGER: Who tickle?
WASHOE: Dr. Gardner.
ROGER: Dr. Gardner not here.
WASHOE: Roger tickle.

Washoe's mistakes show something about her concepts. She signs "flower," for example, in the presence of a tobacco pouch and in kitchens with cooking food (20). She also uses her words in new and appropriate contexts. When her friend and teacher, psychologist Roger Fouts, refused to take Washoe with him on one occasion, Washoe signed "dirty Roger." Prior to this incident, she had used the dirty sign primarily for soiled items or feces (21).

Washoe began combining signs approximately ten months after her training began, signing utterances such as "open hurry," "more food gimme," and "hug come hurry." The following incident, recorded by a writer who visited Washoe at her new home, the Institute for Primate Studies at the University of Oklahoma, conveys some of the flavor of her language: Washoe was standing in the midst of a pond on a small island surrounded by other chimpanzees. She begged psychologist Roger Fouts to come and get her by signing: "Roger ride come gimme sweet eat please hurry hurry you come please gimme sweet you hurry you come ride Roger come give Washoe fruit drink hurry hurry fruit drink sweet please please . . . [A plane flew overhead just then and Washoe signed:] "You me ride in plane [22]."

Researchers at the Oklahoma Primate Institute are currently training more chimpanzees to use ASL. They are studying many fascinating questions such as the following: How do chimpanzees conceptualize? Will chimpanzees spontaneously use ASL to communicate with one another? Will chimpanzee mothers reared with ASL teach ASL to their offspring?

The Language of Chimpanzees and Children: A Comparison

We have seen that chimpanzees can learn a language. Is a young chimpanzee's use of language similar to a child's? (Keep in mind that chimps and children learn language under different sets of circumstances; so our comparison is a rough one.) Chimpanzees and children show many similarities in their use of language:

1. They both practice "words" when they're alone as they are learning to "speak."
2. They both acquire large vocabularies. (Children acquire larger ones—the average five-year-old uses more than five thousand words.)
3. They both transfer old words to new situations. (Recall Washoe's use of the sign "dirty.")
4. They both use words in appropriate combinations which they have never seen before. (A University of Oklahoma chimpanzee named Lucy labeled watermelon the "water fruit" and radishes the "cry hurt food.")
5. They both learn rules of word order. (Lucy knows the difference between "Roger tickle Lucy" and "Lucy tickle Roger.")
6. They both talk about things that are not physically present, and they both grasp relationships such as "same as," "different," and "if—then."

Chimpanzees and children also show some striking differences in their use of language:

1. Chimpanzees do not naturally learn a language that we know of when reared with people or with other chimpanzees. Teaching a chimpanzee language is an arduous undertaking which requires enormous planning and work.
2. Chimpanzees do not explore and use language with the same obvious pleasure and enthusiasm of the young child. As a matter of fact, chimpanzees are frequently "not in the mood" to use language.
3. Chimpanzees tend to use language spontaneously for one major purpose: to ask people to act, usually to fulfill needs like those for food, social contact, or sensory stimulation, though Lana's interest in names suggest that chimpanzees may have other uses for language. Children use language for many more purposes.
4. Laboratory studies indicate that adult chimpanzees think in an egocentric and intuitive way at about the same level as the preoperational child. This suggests a rather severe limit on the chimpanzee's potential for language use.

Thus, although people are not the only animals that can learn to use a language, they are still by far the most sophisticated users of language.

Summary: The Acquisition of Language

1. All known human societies have developed a language.
2. Children acquire language in an orderly way. Newborn infants vocalize to exercise their muscles and to express comfort and discomfort. In the last half of the first year babies babble a great deal. During this period they acquire increasing control over the sounds they make. By their first

birthday, they are usually beginning to understand and use words meaningfully.

3. Children of eighteen to twenty-four months combine words in grammatical two-word utterances that serve many purposes. During the next two years, they expand their sentences as they continue to acquire basic rules of grammar.

4. Both genetics and learning influence the acquisition of grammar.

5. While chimpanzees can learn to use a language, their use of language appears to be severely limited by their conceptual abilities. People are unquestionably the most sophisticated users of language.

We turn now to verbal learning.

OPTIMIZING VERBAL LEARNING

Once children have learned a language, much of their later learning depends on that language. Reading, writing, and other "school" subjects such as history, science, and literature obviously depend on it. So does the learning that comes from reading the newspaper, watching television, or listening to the radio. As we mentioned before, people tend to code many of their experiences into language. The term *verbal learning* refers to all language-related learning, learning that involves the use of words. The nature of verbal learning—what goes on in the head as people learn—is not well understood. Consider reading, the enormously complex achievement that is basic to many kinds of verbal learning. To read people must first recognize marks on a piece of paper as distinctive symbols (letters); group the marks into units (words); code the units into meanings (phrases and clauses); link the meanings together; remember the meanings; and inter-

pret the current meanings by integrating them with past meanings. Reading clearly involves many complex cognitive skills.

When psychologists use the term *verbal learning*, they are really talking about all the processes involved in putting information, coded in language, into memory and taking that information out of memory again. We therefore will focus first on the memory process itself.

The Memory Process

Currently, psychologists view memory as composed of three processes: encoding, storage, and retrieval. *Encoding* refers to the initial transformation of the stimulus-that-is-to-be-remembered into images or words, so that it can be stored. The black letters in a textbook and the sounds that the teacher makes are transformed by your eyes, ears, and brain into images and words, as you perceive. The images or words are stored or recorded in the brain. As we noted in Chapter 4, the brain has at least three distinct ways of storing information. The *sensory memory* operates for the shortest period of time recording information as it is received by the senses. It holds a sensory picture up to about one-half second. We maintain information in *short-term memory* for several seconds to several minutes. By repeating or attending to that information, we can keep it in the short-term system even longer. *Long-term memory* is a third way of storing information. Many dramatic or vivid events leave impressions that remain in our memories. In other cases we repeat bits of information like the number of days of the year, our own address, or our social security number so frequently that they become permanent. In a well-known study, psychologists Roger Brown and David McNeill demonstrated that people seem to be in close touch with the long-term memory system. Brown and McNeill asked college students to identify words from definitions like the following: (1) the name of the waxy substance derived from sperm whales and (2) the name of the small boats used in harbors and rivers in China and Japan.[5] Some subjects recalled the correct word immediately; others could not identify the word at all; a third group of subjects believed that they knew the right word but simply couldn't recall it (the *tip-of-the-tongue* phenomenon, or *TOT*). Brown and McNeill discovered that subjects in the TOT state were frequently able to recall the correct number of syllables of the word, some of its letters (usually its first or last ones), its sound, its most accented syllable, and its perceptual properties (such as how "tall" its letters were) (23). This and other studies show that people seem to know what information is and isn't stored in long-term memory.

People also seem to know how difficult it will be to retrieve a particular bit of information. *Retrieval* refers to the sometimes difficult task of locating stored information. Most of the time the process functions reasonably efficiently and we are hardly aware of its existence. At other times we know that we know something, but we cannot retrieve it without actively working at it. The working frequently involves recalling strings of related information and gradually reconstructing the data that we are searching for. You can demonstrate the reconstructive nature of retrieval for yourself by trying to recall out loud what you did four weeks ago Sunday evening.

We turn now to two important practical questions: How can people put verbal information into long-term memory more efficiently? How can they retrieve verbal in-

formation from long-term memory more effectively?

Putting Information into Memory: Efficient Learning

Research shows that the following factors influence verbal learning.

Attention. Some students "study" while simultaneously listening to the radio and fantasizing about the approaching weekend. Can people learn without paying attention? To study this issue in the laboratory several psychologists presented subjects with two different tasks. Through earphones to one ear people heard words which they had to repeat aloud immediately. Simultaneously, through earphones to the other ear they heard common English words. Afterward, they were tested to see if they remembered the common English words. As it turned out, the subjects had no memory of them whatsoever. A later study showed that the common English words had been retained in short-term memory for about thirty seconds, before disappearing—apparently without a trace (24).

Other studies demonstrate that although people can learn to some extent when they are not focusing their attention wholly on particular verbal material, they learn more quickly and thoroughly when they concentrate. Attention seems to be important for transferring information from short- to long-term memory.

Organization. When people dump facts into their long-term memory in mere random fashion, they have a hard time learning and an extremely hard time retrieving the material when they later need it. A study by Stanford University psychologist Gordon Bower demonstrates this quite clearly. Bower pre-

[5]Ambergris; sampan.

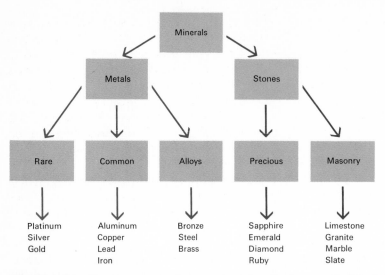

Randomized list of source words:

Ruby	Gold
Bronze	Platinum
Lead	Aluminum
Sapphire	Iron
Limestone	Diamond
Slate	Steel
Silver	Granite
Emerald	Copper
Marble	Brass

Figure 8-15. Words are easier to memorize when they're organized in the form of a hierarchial tree than when they're listed in random order. (After Bower, 1970.)

sented words to one group of subjects in random order and to another in the form of a hierarchial tree (see Figure 8-15). Both groups of subjects spent the same amount of time studying and memorizing the words. The subjects who had studied the hierarchial tree outperformed the others (25). The implications are clear. It is easier to recall information if it has been organized in some logical way. Instead of learning isolated details about the memory process, for example, the student might make a chart which shows what each subprocess does and how it relates to the other subprocesses.

Mnemonic strategies are devices that organize material by associating it with rhymes, images, meaningful stories, or past information, making it easier to remember. "Thirty days has September . . ." helps many people remember the number of days in each month. The musical notes in the spaces of the treble clef are more easily recalled if they are linked with the word "FACE." Incidentally, you might want to use a mnemonic strategy to remember the word "mnemonic," if you've

never encountered the word before. The word "mnemonic" rhymes with the word "demonic" and is a "demon" to pronounce.

Numerous studies show that mnemonic strategies can help people retain information in the laboratory. In one study, psychologists Gordon Bower and Michael Clark gave subjects lists of ten totally unrelated nouns to learn in order. Whereas the control subjects received no particular instructions on how to proceed, the experimental subjects were told to make up stories that incorporated the nouns in order. One of the stories of one experimental subject read: "One night at DINNER I had the NERVE to bring my TEACHER. There had been a FLOOD that day, and the rain BARREL was sure to RATTLE. There was, however, a VESSEL in the HARBOR carrying the ARTIST to my CASTLE." On a test of retention the experimental subjects recalled almost seven times more words than the control subjects did (26).

Mnemonic devices are probably most useful for memorizing lists of items that are not meaningfully related to one another, such as parts of anatomy, lists of words and long numbers.

Active participation. After reading an assignment over once, many students expect the information to be automatically absorbed, but that expectation is unrealistic. Studies in the laboratory show that active participation is frequently necessary for the mastery of complex verbal material. Teaching machines and *programmed learning materials* capitalize on this well-known finding (see Figure 8-16). Typically, these devices present learners with a small amount of material at a time. Questions follow, forcing people to test their understanding actively before proceeding to new material. The correct answers are provided, giving learners immediate feedback about their performance so that they know precisely what requires further practice or clarification.

One strategy for *actively* studying textbooks, which many students find helpful, is known as the *SQ3R program.* The phrase SQ3R summarizes the five steps of the study technique: survey, question, read, recite, review.

STEP 1: SURVEY—The student first obtains an overview of the chapter by looking at the behavioral objectives, the chapter outline, the headings, and the summaries within the chapter. Studies in the psychology laboratory show that when people have information in advance on what they're expected to learn (termed an *advance organizer* by psychologist David Ausubel), they are better at comprehending complex verbal material. If you know how a chapter is organized, you have an idea of what to expect, and you are likelier to read with a sense of direction.

STEP 2: QUESTION—People seem to remember material better when they are asking and answering questions. It stimulates them to think about what they are reading and it directs them to important information. One way to formulate questions is to take the headings of each section and turn them into questions. For example, at the beginning of this chapter you saw the heading "thinking," which might have been converted into the question "How do psychologists use the

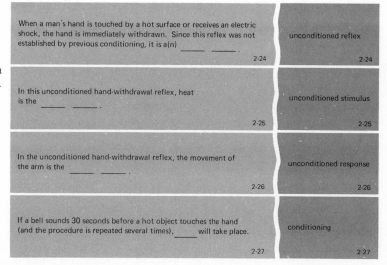

Figure 8-16. An excerpt from a programmed psychology text. (Holland and Skinner, 1961.)

word 'thinking'?" The second heading reads: "The Development of Thinking." It could have been turned into the question "How does thinking develop?" Similarly, you might question yourself on the meaning of key terms as you read along.

STEP 3: READ ACTIVELY—Many students simply run their eyes over the page. It is important to read actively, trying to answer the questions you have formulated as you go along.

STEP 4: RECITE—After reading each section, it is helpful to try to repeat aloud or write down (with the book closed) the important information that you have learned. Reciting gives people a good idea of what they don't remember and/or don't understand. Students who cannot recite the important points under a given heading should reread the section until they can. A classic study shows that people retain more information when they spend equal amounts of time reading and reciting, as opposed to simply reading and rereading (27). The recitation procedure is also important because it gives the student practice in retrieving information—a behavior that is likely to be required in class discussions and on exams.

STEP 5: REVIEW—After reading and reciting the important points under each heading, the student should review the chapter as a whole. There are many ways to review. You might read over notes that you have made during reading. You might turn the headings into questions once again and recite the answers, or you might reread to make sure that you haven't left anything out or to refresh your memory.

The SQ3R method was worked out and thoroughly tested at Ohio State University. Studies indicate that when the method is used conscientiously, it improves the performance of both good and poor students.

• **Massed versus spaced practice.** Is it better to cram your studying into one long session the night before an exam? Or is it better to spread your studying out? Psychologists have studied this issue indirectly by investigating two kinds of practice: massed and spaced. *Massed practice* refers to crowding the learning into one practice period without a rest; *spaced practice* refers to distributing the learning over short practice periods with rest periods in between. So far the laboratory results do not support the uniform superiority of either method. Massed practice seems to be best for learning verbal material that is coherent, organized, or highly meaningful—for reading stories, for memorizing speeches, and for solving problems, for example. Massed practice immediately before an exam actually has several advantages for test takers. Forgetting follows a definite pattern: It tends to occur most rapidly soon after learning takes place. After learning a list of one hundred vocabulary words, for example, you'd probably remember only forty-five words an hour later, about thirty words a day later, and twenty-five words a week later. People who cram at the last moment capitalize on this characteristic of memory. They also capitalize on motivation—so long as their motivation has not reached panic proportions.

On the other hand, spaced practice is better for acquiring motor skills and learning verbal materials which are loosely connected (example: the separate chapters of a textbook) (28). Moreover, when studying is distributed over several days, the learner has better control over other key practices—attention (there are distinct limits to how long people can profitably concentrate on a single activity), organization, active participation, and repeated practice or overlearning (a subject we will take up in a moment). When studying for exams a combination of these two procedures is probably most effective.

Overlearning. Do the grinds who overstudy for each test benefit? Or are they wasting their time? To put the question more generally: Does practice beyond the point of mastery, or *overlearning*, increase the learner's retention of the material? In another classic study subjects memorized several lists of single syllable nouns. Then they were divided into three groups. One group (the 100 percent overlearning group) continued to practice the list for the same amount of time it had taken them to learn it initially. A second group (the 50 percent overlearning group) continued to practice for half that amount of time. A third group (the no overlearning group) did not practice any additional time at all. The results of the study are summarized in Figure 8-17. (29) Note that overlearning led to superior retention. Note also that moderate overlearning as demonstrated by the 50 percent overlearning group increased retention quite substantially; and continuing to practice to 100 percent overlearning improved retention only a small additional amount. These results suggest that there is a point of diminishing returns—that students might benefit from practicing a moderate amount of time beyond the point of bare mastery. Discussions, debates, and projects involving newly learned material are interesting ways to overlearn.

Using reinforcement. Parents sometimes use praise or prizes or money to reward their children's efforts to learn. When parents reward their children immediately after each small accomplishment, they are using positive reinforcement (see Chapter 7) to increase the likelihood that the child will study. Two gen-

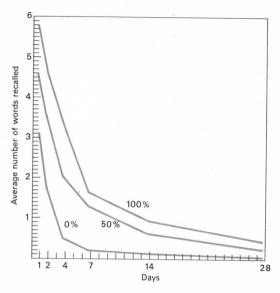

Figure 8-17. The effects of overlearning. (After Krueger, 1929.)

eral kinds of positive reinforcement increase the probability of studying and learning: *intrinsic positive reinforcement* and *extrinsic positive reinforcement*. Positive reinforcement is said to be *intrinsic* to a task when it is the natural and inevitable result of simply engaging in the task. Some people learn because they enjoy acquiring information and take pride in being knowledgeable. Positive reinforcement is said to be *extrinsic* when it is not the natural and inevitable outcome of simply engaging in a task but comes from outside the task. Some people learn because they like getting good grades, or because they want a degree, a gold star, or someone else's approval.

Students who do not find intrinsic reinforcement in learning can systematically use extrinsic reinforcement to increase the likelihood that they will study and learn. A student might plan a reasonable daily schedule, then reinforce himself or herself immediately following the completion of a small amount of work by doing something enjoyable—such as taking a five-minute coffee break, talking on the phone to a friend, or listening to a record. The big problem in self-reinforcement is keeping the reward *contingent* (dependent) on executing the assignment. It is very easy to cheat.

Taking Information Out of Memory: Effective Retrieval

After learning, people frequently face some kind of "test." The day comes when they must retrieve the information that has been learned from memory and use it. Research shows that retrieving is easier under the following conditions:

When people have practiced retrieving. In studying for tests, for example, students should practice retrieving information in the form that will be needed for the test. If one is going to take an essay exam, it makes sense to try writing short paragraphs. If there will be a vocabulary drill in French class, it makes sense to quiz oneself on vocabulary words.

When the information has been organized during learning. We have already mentioned the importance of organizing material during learning. When the learner organizes the material, the retrieval of one piece of information tends to lead to the retrieval of related pieces of information.

When retrieval cues are readily available. Retrieval is usually cued by key words, ideas, or images. Sometimes the event is difficult to identify; at other times, it is obvious. Compare the questions "Discuss the factors that influence problem solving" and "Discuss the role of the following factors on problem solving: the stimulus situation, past learning, and level of arousal." It is easy to see that the second question provides cues that should stimulate the recall of information—especially if the material has been organized under these headings. Students can provide their own retrieval cues by organizing test material under key words and memorizing the key words.

When anxiety is low. High anxiety usually interferes with complex tasks such as verbal learning, and it frequently makes retrieval extremely difficult. Many students experience test anxiety; they become so anxious in the testing situation that their "minds go blank," and they cannot retrieve the information that they need. We will be looking at anxiety in Chapter 11; in Chapter 14, we will describe a behavior modification technique, called systematic desensitization, that helps people cope with anxiety.

Summary: Optimizing Verbal Learning

1. Psychologists view memory as composed of three processes: encoding, storage, and retrieval.
2. Verbal material is put into memory and retained most efficiently when it is attended to, organized, actively practiced, and overlearned. When studying for exams some combination of massed and spaced practice is probably most effective.
3. The systematic use of extrinsic positive reinforcement can increase the frequency of study behavior when intrinsic positive reinforcement for this behavior rarely occurs.
4. Retrieval is most effective when people have practiced retrieving, when the information has been organized during learning, when retrieval cues are present, and when anxiety is relatively low.

STUDY GUIDE 8

Key Terms. cognitive processes, mediating, undirected thinking, stream of consciousness, directed thinking, adaptation, assimilation, accommodation, sensorimotor stage, preoperational stage, egocentric, stage of concrete operations, stage of formal operations, image, strategy, general solution, functional solution, specific solution, elements, functional fixity, learning set (learning to learn), positive transfer, negative transfer, arousal, reflexive communication, purposive communication, language, grammar, psycholinguistics, babbling, observation learning, respondent conditioning, operant conditioning, positive reinforcer, shaping, discrimination, telegraphic speech, American Sign Language (ASL), molding, verbal learning, encoding, storage, sensory memory, short-term memory, long-term memory, tip-of-the-tongue phenomenon (TOT), retrieval, attention, organization, mnemonic strategy, programmed-learning materials, SQ3R program, advance organizer, massed practice, spaced practice, overlearning, intrinsic reinforcer, extrinsic reinforcer, contingent, retrieval cue.

Important Research. problem-solving strategies (Duncker), learning to learn (Harlow), arousal and problem solving (Birch), children's understanding of grammar (Berko), teaching sign language to a chimp (Gardner and Gardner), teaching a plastic-symbol language to a chimp (Premack and Premack), teaching keyboard language to a chimp (Rumbaugh), tip-of-the-tongue phenomenon (Brown and McNeill), learning without attention, organization of memory (Bower), mnemonic devices (Bower and Clark), the effects of overlearning.

Basic Theories. Piaget's theory of mental development; the views of Skinner, Chomsky, and Hebb on the origin of grammar.

Self-Quiz

1. Which is *not* usually considered a cognitive process? [**a**] conditioning; [**b**] using language; [**c**] reasoning; [**d**] imagining.
2. The development of language and the ability to use symbols occur during the_____ stage. [**a**] concrete operations; [**b**] formal operations; [**c**] sensorimotor; [**d**] preoperational.
3. Which of the following statements is *not* included in Piaget's theory of mental development? [**a**]

Older children solve problems more quickly than younger children do; [**b**] preschool children have difficulty imagining how people take points of view different from their own; [**c**] children cannot use systematic methods to solve problems until approximately ten to eleven years of age; [**d**] children think differently than adults.
4. Duncker found that solutions to complex problems typically occur in which order? [**a**] functional, specific, general; [**b**] general, functional, specific; [**c**] functional, general, specific; [**d**] specific, functional, general.
5. Harlow found that monkeys who had had experience solving particular types of problems solved further problems of the same type very efficiently. He called this phenomenon [**a**] functional fixity; [**b**] an elemental strategy; [**c**] encoding; [**d**] a learning set.
6. Some people believe that learning how to play the piano interferes with learning how to type later. This is an example of [**a**] functional fixity; [**b**] positive transfer; [**c**] negative transfer; [**d**] the effects of massed practice.
7. Birch found that chimpanzees were most efficient at solving problems under conditions of _____ arousal. [**a**] no; [**b**] very little; [**c**] moderate; [**d**] maximal.
8. Using gestures and postures to communicate meaning is an example of_____ communication. [**a**] reflexive; [**b**] purposive; [**c**] formal; [**d**] telegraphic.
9. Which is *not* a language-related skill of children less than six months old? [**a**] combining sounds in sentencelike intonation patterns; [**b**] vocalizing the sounds found in all languages; [**c**] moving in rhythm with the language spoken around them; [**d**] discriminating the sound of B from the sound of P.
10. According to Chomsky's theory of language development, [**a**] most language is learned by operant conditioning; [**b**] humans are genetically "preset" to learn grammar; [**c**] most language is learned by respondent conditioning; [**d**] societies have different languages because of differences in heredity.
11. When Berko asked children to complete sentences using nonsense words, she found that they [**a**] used nonsense words in grammatical ways; [**b**] used nonsense words in nongrammatical ways; [**c**] had no idea what nonsense words meant or how to use them; [**d**] used nonsense words grammatically

only at young ages; children five or older were bewildered by the task.

12. In contrast to chimpanzees, children [**a**] spontaneously use language for many purposes; [**b**] practice "words" when they are alone; [**c**] transfer old words to new situations and combine old words to convey new meanings; [**d**] form concepts and "talk" about objects that are not present.

13. Locating information stored in memory is called [**a**] encoding; [**b**] retrieval; [**c**] probing; [**d**] advance organizing.

14. The five steps of the SQ3R method (in order) are [**a**] survey, question, read, review, reread; [**b**] skim, question, read, reorganize, review; [**c**] survey, question, read, retrieve, reread; [**d**] survey, question, read, recite, review.

15. Massed practice is better than spaced practice for [**a**] learning highly organized verbal material; [**b**] acquiring motor skills; [**c**] long-term retention—in general; [**d**] maintaining attention and alertness.

Exercise

PIAGET'S THEORY. To test your knowledge of Piaget's theory, match the terms with the definitions and examples that follow: adaptation (AD), assimilation (AS), accommodation (AC), egocentric (E), sensorimotor stage (SM), preoperational stage (PO), stage of concrete operations (CO), stage of formal operations (FO).

_____ **1.** Developing new ideas or changing old ones to fit new information.

_____ **2.** Although young children know their own right and left hands, they confuse the right and left hands of a person facing them.

_____ **3.** Seeing a seashell for the first time and processing it in terms of a cup.

_____ **4.** Children see a lion for the first time and change an idea of "cat" to include big cats.

_____ **5.** A child with a room full of toys has a hard time understanding that his mother sees a new toy as an unjustifiable expense.

_____ **6.** The mental growth process itself.

_____ **7.** Children see a Siamese cat for the first time and add it to a mental category "cat."

_____ **8.** Numbers 4 and 7 combined.

At what stages are the following cognitions likely to first appear?

_____ **9.** Comprehending that a toy exists even though it cannot be seen.

_____ **10.** Understanding that the amount of juice stays the same when it is poured from a tall glass to a short one.

_____ **11.** Learning that kicking removes blankets.

_____ **12.** Understanding simple concepts such as "the category man includes father, brother, and uncle."

_____ **13.** Learning to imitate the words others say.

_____ **14.** Understanding and using abstract logic.

_____ **15.** Being logical when dealing with physical objects but not with abstract ideas.

_____ **16.** Developing language.

_____ **17.** Speculating about the possible solutions to a problem.

Questions to Consider

1. Define positive and negative transfer; give two personal examples of each.

2. Can you think of any times when a learning set has helped or hindered your problem-solving efforts?

3. Consider the relationship between arousal and problem solving. How could this information help students perform better on tests?

4. From a distance, watch a group of people as they communicate with one another. Observe the varied forms of purposive communication (besides language) that are used.

5. Design a program to teach language to a severely retarded child who has never learned to speak. Be sure to consider the research on teaching language to chimpanzees.

6. Describe the various principles derived from verbal-learning research which can be applied to improving study skills. Devise a coordinated study plan, based on these principles, which would be both efficient and motivating for you.

Project 8: Observing
Children's Thinking

After systematically observing the problem-solving behavior of children at different ages over many years, Piaget and his associates have concluded that children think differently than adults. The purpose of this project is to examine the cognitive processes that characterize children at particular ages and corresponding stages of mental development.

Method. Choose four subjects—two subjects in each of two age ranges, five to six and eight to nine. Be sure to explain the project to the children's parents and obtain their permission. Make certain that each child can count to ten, and ask each child individually if he/she would be willing to play several games with you. Find a quiet setting that is free from distractions for making the observations.

You will be testing each child individually on two tasks. For children aged five and six, use the conservation-of-number and volume tasks; for children aged eight and nine, use the conservation-of-volume and the logical problem-solving tasks (these tasks, including props and procedures, are described below). The tasks can be tricky, so gather the props and practice the procedures beforehand. The child should be able to solve the first but not the second problem. It is very important, however, *not to tell* the child whether he/she is right or wrong. Simply record the child's responses and behave as though they are perfectly normal answers (they probably will be!).

Results and discussion. As you look over your observations, consider the following questions:

1. Did your findings support those of Piaget and his associates? That is, (1) were the two children in each age range similar in their cognitive tactics and (2) were they able to solve the problem suitable for their age range and not the one suitable for older children?
2. How can your findings be explained? How would Piaget explain them? If your observations did not support Piaget's, speculate on the reasons.
3. Can you think of explanations besides Piaget's why children fail to solve problems as adults do? Consider whether children might misunderstand the problems. Might they lack interest in solving the problems "correctly"?
4. Did your subjects' backgrounds vary? Might specific environments influence children's problem-solving tactics? Explain.
5. When children are tested on problems appropriate for younger children, a common response is, "Why do you ask me such simple questions?" According to Piaget, why should a task designed for a five-year-old seem so simple and obvious to an eight-year-old?

TASKS FOR OBSERVING CHILDREN'S THINKING

Conservation-of-number Task

Preoperational children learn—usually at about the age of five or six—that the number of objects stays the same even when the objects themselves are rearranged.

Younger children think that changing the arrangement changes the number.

Props: Fourteen to sixteen identical small objects such as pennies, buttons, beads, or poker chips.

Procedure: Arrange the objects side by side in two rows that are equal in number of objects *and* in length. Ask the child, "Do both rows have the same number of_____, or does one row have more?" (If the child says that one row has more, have him/her rearrange the objects until both rows look the same. Proceed only when both you and the child agree that the two rows have the same number of objects.)

Now, as the subject watches, spread out the objects in one row so that one row is longer than the other (keep the number of objects in each row the same.) Repeat the question, "Do both rows have the same number of_____, or does one row have more?" After the child answers, ask "Why?" Record the child's responses.

Conservation-of-volume Task

Children in the stage of concrete operations learn that the amount of a fluid remains the same even if it is placed in a differently shaped container. Children younger than eight rarely take two dimensions, such as height and width, into account at once; they usually judge the amount of a fluid by one dimension, frequently height.

Props: Three water glasses: two should be identical; the third should have distinctly different dimensions.

Procedure: Arrange the glasses side by side. Fill both identical glasses to an equal height with a liquid, preferably juice or colored water. Ask the child, "Do both glasses have the same amount of_____, or does one glass have more?" If the child thinks that one glass has more, make adjustments until you both agree that they are equal.

Now pour the liquid from one of the identical glasses into the different-sized glass as the subject watches. Then ask, "Do both glasses have the same amount of_____, or does one have more?" After the child answers, ask "Why?" Record the child's responses.

Logical Problem-solving Task

Being able to test hypotheses logically is characteristic of people who have reached the stage of formal operations, a stage which starts at perhaps ten or eleven and continues through adulthood. You will be asking your subjects to figure out the factors that influence the speed of a swinging pendulum. Be sure to try the task out on yourself before testing anyone else.

Props: You will need two strings, about 24 inches long, and five or six identical objects to use as weights, such as sewing machine bobbins, nuts (the kind that go with bolts), or keys. Use objects that can be easily tied to the end of a string. You will also need a place to tie your pendulum so that it can swing freely. Taping the strings to the bottom of a tabletop will work.

Procedure: Tie one weight to the end of each string. Then demonstrate to the subject how both pendulums may be swung at once. Set both pendulums in motion at the same time. Let the subject practice until he/she can release both pendulums at once. Then ask the subject, "What determines how fast the pendulum swings? See if you can figure out all the things that influence its speed." If you receive a blank stare or quick incorrect answer, suggest that the subject play around with the pendulums and the weights to see if he/she can discover the answer to the question.

Observe how the subject goes about solving the problem. Record these observations. The final answer is not especially important. According to Piaget's theory, people in the stage of formal operations can logically try out hypotheses to solve the problem. In approaching the pendulum problem, they should systematically test the effects of changing the amount of weight, length of string, etc. Younger children attempt to solve the problem by guessing and usually give incorrect answers without systematically testing out hypotheses.

Suggested Readings

1. Posner, M. *Cognition: An introduction.* Glenview, III.: Scott, Foresman and Company, 1973 (paperback). A brief introduction to research on memory, thinking, problem solving, and other cognitive processes.

2. Evans, R. *Jean Piaget: The man and his ideas.* New York: E. P. Dutton & Co., Inc., 1973. A collection of materials on Piaget, including an interview with Piaget, a summary of Piaget's ideas, and a short autobiography.

3. Adams, J. L. *Conceptual blockbusting: A guide to better ideas.* San Francisco: W. H. Freeman and Company, 1974 (paperback) Delightful, involving book on creative problem solving.

4. Morgan, C., & J. Deese. *How to study* (2d ed.) McGraw-Hill Book Company, 1969. A practical guide to sound study techniques that takes the psychology of verbal learning into account.

For more information about specific "talking" chimpanzees, see:

5. Gardner, A., & B. Gardner. "Teaching sign language to a chimpanzee." *Science*, August 15, 1969, 162, 664–672.

6. Premack, A. J., & D. Premack. "Teaching language to an ape." *Scientific American*, October 1972, 227, 92–99.

7. Rumbaugh, D., T. Gill, & E. C. von Glassersfeld. "Reading and sentence completion by a chimpanzee." *Science*, November 16, 1973, 182, 731–733.

Answer Keys

SELF-QUIZ
1. a 2. d 3. a 4. b 5. d 6. c 7. c 8. b 9. a
10. b 11. a 12. a 13. b 14. d 15. a

EXERCISE
1. AC 2. E 3. AS 4. AC 5. E 6. AD 7. AS
8. AD 9. SM 10. CO 11. SM 12. PO 13. SM
14. FO 15. CO 16. PO 17. FO

Solution to stomach tumor problem (Figure 8-3A)
One solution to the inoperable stomach tumor problem is to focus several low-intensity x-ray sources located at different positions onto the tumor. This will produce a high intensity of radiation at the tumor and a low intensity at other points on the body. A second solution is to aim a single x-ray source at the tumor while rotating the body so that the total exposure at the tumor will be high and the total exposure at other points on the body will be low.

Solution to candle problem (Figure 8-3B)
The correct solution involves tacking the box to the wall so that it can serve as a platform for the candle.

Solution to match problem (Figure 8-3C)

Solution to dot problem (Figure 8-10B)

INTELLIGENCE AND CREATIVITY

IN THIS CHAPTER
We examine how intelligence is defined and measured and how measured intelligence varies with age, personality, and sex role in our culture. We also look at differences in measured intelligence between social classes and racial groups and what those differences mean. Finally, we focus on how creativity is defined and measured and on training programs which attempt to teach creativity. After reading this chapter, you should be able to do the following:

1. Explain how definitions of intelligence differ
2. Describe the requirements of a good intelligence test
3. Explain why psychologists disagree about the validity of current intelligence tests
4. Describe how measured intelligence varies with age, personality, and sex role in our culture
5. Describe and cite supporting evidence for believing that environmental causes produce differences in measured intelligence between poor people and others
6. Explain why it is currently impossible to attribute differences between racial group performances on intelligence tests to genetics
7. Describe how psychologists define, measure, and train creativity

Margaret and Rebecca

At age six Margaret spent her second year in kindergarten trying once again to master the reading readiness materials. She had trouble manipulating a pencil, folding paper, coloring within lines in a coloring book, and distinguishing one symbol from another. Although Margaret usually appeared to be listening attentively, she rarely understood the teacher's instructions. After a second year in kindergarten Margaret was placed in a special public school class, and there she remained. In her first six years she learned a number of simple skills, such as naming colors, counting, adding, subtracting, and reading elementary materials. In high school Margaret concentrated on homemaking, particularly on sewing, cooking, and ironing. She learned to perform these tasks quite adequately as long as an adult supervised her work and helped her out if a problem arose. When Margaret graduated from high school, she did not look for a job; she preferred to remain at home with her mother doing housework and making dolls and Christmas decorations to sell at a nearby church.

Rebecca was an alert baby. By the time she was three years old, she was reading by herself. She learned easily and quickly throughout her school career. In the third grade, for example, Rebecca tested some six grades ahead of herself in arithmetic. By the time she entered the seventh grade, she was reading college-level material. Rebecca taught herself Chinese during one summer. At the age of fifteen she wrote a book of poems which was later published. Rebecca was also distinguished as an adult. After completing a doctorate in biology, she was hired by a highly respected State University to teach and do research. There she made a number of apparently noteworthy contributions in her own specialized area.

Who is more intelligent—Rebecca or Margaret? Most people would probably agree that Rebecca appears to be intelligent and Margaret appears to be intellectually limited. Consider a more difficult case, Rickey Ponce de Leon.

Boy with I.Q. of 55 is genius at piano

"Los Angeles (UPI)—When Rickey Ponce de Leon sat down to play, the audience hushed, then listened in awe to the impressive organ rendition he pounded out with fingers of a musical virtuoso.

"The teen-ager is mentally retarded with an IQ of 55. Yet the Filipino youth was the featured soloist at the 25th-anniversary banquet of the Exceptional Children's Foundation here.

"Considered a musical genius, de Leon can play about 1,000 songs from memory, is adept with seven instruments and composes excellent music—yet displays a retardate's poor muscle coordination when he is away from his music.

"Robert Shushan, local director of the foundation, introduced the youth as a 'gifted, retarded individual' who is an 'exceptional example' showing that mental retardates can perform well under the right conditions.

"'[W]hen he seats himself at the console of an electronic organ a miracle happens,' said Mr. Shushan, 'poor coordination disappears, replaced by excellent independence in the use of all four limbs, playing keyboard and pedal board [1].'"[1]

Is Rickey Ponce de Leon intelligent? What is intelligence? Try to define it for yourself before reading on. Some psychologists define intelligence as an ability to learn or profit from formal instruction; others define it as an ability to adapt effectively to the environment. Some psychologists see intelligence as a cluster of relatively distinct abilities, such as memory, reasoning, and verbal fluency; others emphasize certain general abilities such as those required for using language, forming abstract concepts, and reasoning. Some psychologists believe that the limits of intelligence are fixed by heredity; others believe that experience plays an important role in its development. In sum, psychologists do not agree on the nature of intelligence: on how to define it; on whether it consists of one general ability or many separate abilities; or on how much it depends on heredity and environment. We will define the construct *intelligence* as an overall ability to "act purposefully, to think rationally, and to deal effectively with the environment [2]." We will assume that

this ability consists of many relatively distinct capacities. We will also assume that intelligence is determined by both hereditary and environmental factors (see Chapter 3 for evidence that both heredity and environment influence intelligence).

Although psychologists do not agree on the nature of intelligence, tests to measure the characteristics included in some of the major definitions have been developed. Scores on these "intelligence tests" are widely used to define intelligence operationally. We begin by looking closely at how psychologists measure intelligence.

THE MEASUREMENT OF INTELLIGENCE

The problem—how to measure intelligence—has baffled some very intelligent people. Consider the efforts of the illustrious American psychologist James McKeen Cattell (1860–1944). In 1890 Cattell published a "mental test" that sampled abilities like the greatest possible squeeze of the hand, the quickest possible movement of the right hand and

[1]Rickey would probably be classified as an idiot savant, a person who tests mentally retarded but possesses several above-average abilities. The condition is relatively rare and not well understood.

arm, and the point at which pressure causes pain. This test did not work out.

The First Intelligence Test

Alfred Binet (1857–1911), the leading French psychologist of his day, began his work on mental tests at about the same time as Cattell. In the beginning, Binet and his associates measured children's sensory and motor skills. Soon they discarded these tasks and collected and developed new ones that were designed to measure vividness of imagery, length and quality of attention, memory, quality of aesthetic and moral judgments, and the abilities to find logical errors and comprehend sentences. Binet believed that these separate but related capabilities were the basis of intelligence.

Binet's test-making project was given a big push by some practical pressures. In 1904 Binet was appointed to a governmental commission to investigate the problems of retarded children in the public school system in Paris. Binet concluded that if retarded children could only be identified and placed in special schools, they could be taught more effectively. Accordingly, he began working on a test that could distinguish those children who could not benefit from ordinary schooling from those children who could. How did Binet proceed? He evaluated the many test items that he had previously collected by presenting each one to a small number of children. Only those items which distinguished between older and younger children of apparently similar intelligence or between apparently brighter and duller children of the same age were kept. Using this general strategy, Binet amassed a number of test items with discriminatory power. He then arranged the items in order of difficulty by age level—there were problems that the average five-year-old had been able to solve; problems that the average six-year-old had

been able to solve; and so on. Binet used some of the following items: At age three: point to the nose, the eyes, and the mouth, repeat two digits; give family name; and enumerate objects in a picture. At age seven: point to the right hand, describe a picture, identify the missing part, execute three commands, count coins, and name four primary colors. At age fifteen: repeat seven digits, find three rhymes for a particular word in one minute, and interpret various facts and pictures (see Figure 9-1).

Binet's test was administered to each child individually. The examiner simply asked the subject questions and recorded the answers. Later the child's performance was compared with the performance of other children of the same age. Binet designed his test so that an average child at a particular age could solve approximately 50 percent of the problems designed for children in that age group and all the problems designed for younger children. Retarded children generally solved fewer problems, brighter children more problems, than average children their own age. On the basis of their test performance, children were assigned a *mental age* score. A ten-year-old who performed like the average ten-year-old received a mental age score of ten. A ten-year-old who performed like the average six-year-old received a mental age score of six. Binet used the difference between the mental age and the chronological age as the measure of intelligence. Children were considered retarded if their mental ages were two years below their chronological ages. It is important to note that Binet's intelligence test (and many later tests, as well) operationally defined intelligence as one's performance on a specific test in comparison to the performance of others in the same age group.

The IQ and Intelligence

Lewis Terman (1877–1956), an American psychologist at Stanford University, pro-

Figure 9-1. Test items used on the first intelligence test (Binet-Simon Scale, 1905).
A and *B*: "Which is prettiest?" (age five level). *C*: "Identify the missing part." (age seven level).

duced a widely accepted revision of Binet's test in 1916. At that time he adopted the concept of *intelligence quotient* (IQ), which had been introduced by the German psychologist William Stern, as an index of intelligence. The IQ is simply a concise way of expressing relative performance on an intelligence test. An IQ on the Stanford-Binet, as Terman's revision was called, is computed in this way: The test taker receives a precise number of months' credit for each correct answer. The points are added together; the sum is labeled *mental age* (MA). (The point values awarded for each task were chosen so that average people's mental age scores will equal their chronological ages.) The person's mental age is then divided by the person's *chronological age* (CA), and the result is multiplied by 100 to yield an IQ; that is, IQ = (MA/CA) × 100. As an example, consider the intelligence-test performance of a ten-and-one-half-year-old girl who achieves a mental age score of 10 years 8 months. To compute her IQ we divide her mental age score, 10 years 8 months, by her chronological age, 10 years 6 months, and multiply the result by 100. So this ten-and-one-half-year-old girl has an approximately average IQ of 102.

Many people tend to use the term IQ as if it were identical to the term intelligence. In actuality IQ and intelligence are quite different concepts. Intelligence, as we have defined it, is an overall capacity for particular mental activities that cannot be measured directly. The IQ, on the other hand, is a number that indicates how a person performed on a particular test as compared to others in the same age bracket. Don't fall into the trap of equating the IQ with intelligence.

Designing an Intelligence Test

The Stanford-Binet is only one of a great many intelligence tests in wide use today. Some of these tests are administered individually, such as Binet's original scale. Others have been developed for use in groups. Most tests are intended for specific categories of people such as infants, preschoolers, older children, adolescents, adults, the blind, the hard of hearing, etc. Some mental tests require verbal answers; others require nonverbal responses, such as matching identical pictures or stringing beads in a particular order.

Designing a good intelligence test is an extremely complicated undertaking. The test items must be selected carefully so that they satisfy a number of criteria:

1. The items must call for skills that are within the repertoire of the average individual for whom the test is intended. Consider an intelligence test for the American adult. The average American adult writes, speaks, and understands standard English; so items that require these skills would be judged fair. On the other hand, calculus does not fall within the repertoire

of the average American adult; so its use would be judged unfair.

2. The items must be relatively interesting so that everyone will be motivated to work at solving them. Consider the item "count backwards by 1,000 beginning with 1,000,000." Success on such an item might more accurately measure the ability to withstand boredom than intelligence; so it is not a good item.

3. Ideally, the entire set of test items should not favor or discriminate against any subgroup of people for whom the test is intended. Questions calling for a knowledge of farm implements favor rural people and discriminate against city dwellers. Questions which require the visualization of spatial relationships (see Figure 9-2 for an example) discriminate against females and favor males. Because it is difficult to find items that are totally nondiscriminatory, test designers frequently try to balance the bias by providing favored items for each group.

4. In the case of children's intelligence tests, items chosen should discriminate between children of different ages so that the percentage of children giving the correct response increases with age. Consider the task "Define the word 'revenge.'" If we find that 20 percent of the ten-year-old group is successful on the task, we'd require a larger percentage of the eleven-year-old group to respond correctly and an even larger percentage of the twelve-year-old group to give the correct answer before using the item.

5. Finally, each item on an intelligence test must relate to total performance on the entire test; that is, success or failure on a particular item should be correlated with success or failure on the remaining items. If each item measures intelligence, then people who succeed in performing a particular item should do better on

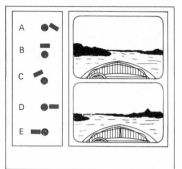 

Figure 9-2. Items from the Guilford-Zimmerman Spatial Orientation Test. The subject marks the answer which shows how the position of the boat's prow in the bottom picture has changed in relation to its original aiming point in the top picture. The boat's prow is represented by the bar; the original aiming point by the dot. The answers are D and B.

the test, in general, than people who fail that item.

Once the test questions are chosen, the test designer turns to other considerations. The test should be objective, reliable, and valid.

Objectivity. Test designers try to design objective tests. A test is considered *objective* when the examiner's biases do not influence the test taker's score on each item. Objectivity is enhanced by providing the examiner with the correct solutions to each problem and/or comprehensive, detailed scoring criteria.

Reliability. The test designer tries to produce a test which has high reliability. The term *reliability* is roughly synonymous with the term *consistency*. When tests are reliable, repeated measurements of the same phenomenon with the test yield similar results. One kind of reliability in which psychologists are interested is known as *test-retest reliability*. To determine test-retest reliability, the test designer administers the same test twice to the same group of people. The second testing usually occurs several weeks to several months after the first. The two different scores will be similar if the test's test-retest reliability is high. If a person achieved an IQ of 150 one week on a particular intelligence test and an IQ of 70 several weeks later on the

same test, the test would be considered unreliable; no one would have any confidence in its ability to measure intelligence. When people take the Stanford-Binet twice, with several weeks intervening between testings, the two scores are usually strongly positively correlated, approximately .80 to .98—demonstrating that the Stanford-Binet is a reliable test (3).

Validity. The test designer is also interested in producing a *valid* test, one that measures what it is intended to measure. A test can be reliable without being valid. A student, for example, might score in the seventies on each of his weekly psychology quizzes, showing that the quiz is a reliable indicator of something for that student, but does the quiz necessarily measure knowledge of the psychology chapter? It could be measuring the teacher's consistent opinion of the student's work. The designer of an intelligence test looks for evidence that the test really measures intelligence.

To assess a test's validity psychologists investigate the question: Does performance on the test correlate highly with other criteria of intelligence. Although there are no clear-cut criteria of intelligence on which all psychologists agree, many psychologists reason that grades in school, scores on achievement tests and on other intelligence tests, vocational success, and success in college reflect intelligent functioning. They assume that if an intelligence test really measures intelligence, then people who score highly on it should do well in these other situations which also appear to depend on intelligence. Similarly, people who do poorly on the intelligence test should also do poorly in these other situations. We will discuss the validity of currently used intelligence tests later on in this chapter.

The test designer must now specify how the test is to be administered and how the results should be interpreted.

Standard administration. Suppose that a particular intelligence test for children is administered differently to each child who takes it. Imagine that an examiner gives some subjects three items to practice on and others none. Suppose he explains the instructions at great length to some testees and only reads them over once to others. These differing practices are likely to cause differences in performance. The test can be pictured as a kind of experiment. Just as an experimenter wants to measure the influence of one variable—the independent variable—the test examiner wants to measure the influence of one phenomenon—in the case of an intelligence test, the subject's intelligence.

For this reason, the test designer provides standard procedures to which all test examiners adhere. This way performance on the test can be assumed to reflect the subject's characteristics and not the examiner's procedures.

4 **Norms.** Eventually, the test designer tries out the test items on a large sample of people whose characteristics (age, sex, social class, race, and so on) are similar to those of the population for whom the test is intended. This practice permits test designers to further evaluate the suitability of each test item. It also provides them with *norms*, information on the test performance of a large group of people. Without norms, psychologists have no way of interpreting an individual's test score. Consider the norms in Figure 9-3. The figure shows how a group of 3,184 native-born white American children performed on the Stanford-Binet in 1937. This information gives test examiners a common frame of reference for evaluating the intelligence test performance of other subjects. Suppose a child in Ohio achieves a Stanford-Binet IQ of 125. Psychologists in Mississippi and Maine will not only agree that the score is unusually high, they will also agree that roughly 7 percent of the group, on which the

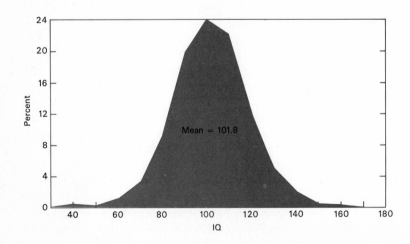

Figure 9-3. Distribution of Stanford-Binet Intelligence Test scores for 3,184 children. (After Terman and Merrill, 1960.)

norms were gathered, performed this well or better.

Taking an Adult Intelligence Test Today

The Wechsler Adult Intelligence Scale (WAIS) is widely used today to evaluate the intelligence of adults. Psychologist David Wechsler introduced the prototype in 1939. The test, which was subsequently revised in 1955, consists of eleven subtests. Six *verbal subtests* contain tasks which assess abilities that depend on language. Five *performance subtests* contain tasks which assess abilities that depend on nonverbal thinking and practical problem-solving skills. The items on each subtest are arranged in order of difficulty from easy to hard. Table 9-1 describes each subtest and the ability that appears to be measured.

A trained examiner administers the WAIS to a single individual, delivering standard instructions, asking standard questions, and recording the test taker's responses as precisely as possible. Afterward, the examiner evaluates those responses by comparing them with a set of criteria which accompanies the test and assigns the subject a score on each of the eleven subtests. The score indicates how the person's performance on each subtest compares with that of others in the same age bracket. This information allows the examiner to construct a profile of a particular individual's intellectual strengths and weaknesses (see Table 9-2). Finally, the total score is converted into an IQ. The IQ on the WAIS also represents the subject's relative performance; that is, the performance of each test taker is compared with the performance of a representative sample of people in the same age bracket—those on whom the norms were originally gathered. The subject who performs as well as 50 percent of the people the same age receives an average IQ—100. An individual who performs better than 98 percent of the people the same age receives an IQ of 130 or higher. An individual who performs more poorly than 98 percent of the people the same age receives an IQ of 69 or lower. Table 9-3 shows how various IQ scores are classified on the WAIS and what percentage of people tend to fall within each category.

The Validity of Current Intelligence Tests: A Controversy

Are currently used intelligence tests valid? Do they measure intelligence? As we noted before, psychologists assess validity by seeing whether performance on an intelligence test correlates positively with other criteria of intelligence. The problem is finding good criteria of intelligence. Currently, psychologists tend to correlate intelligence test scores with measures of educational and social success, but these measures reflect motivation, opportunity, learned skills, and other variables besides intelligence. Let's temporarily put this issue aside and look at the results of validity studies.

Many investigators find significant positive correlations between performance on intelligence tests and other criteria of social and educational attainment. Intelligence tests frequently agree with the judgments of educators as to whether an individual is mentally retarded. They are also positively correlated (approximately .50 on the average, which is considered good for a validity correlation coefficient) with measures of academic achievement; that is, people who score high on intelligence tests frequently receive high grades in elementary school, high school, and college. Low scorers, on the other hand, frequently receive low grades in these academic situations (4). Intelligence test performance also shows a low positive correlation

TABLE 9-1. THE SUBTESTS OF THE WAIS

Verbal Subtest	Nature of the Tasks	Ability(ies) Measured (roughly)
Information	Questions that call for general information; e.g., "How many wings does a bird have?" "Who wrote *Paradise Lost*?"	General knowledge
Comprehension	Questions that call for knowledge of practical matters; e.g., "What should you do if you see someone forget his book when he leaves his seat in a restaurant?" "What is the advantage of keeping money in a bank?"	Practical information and social judgments
Arithmetic	Questions that require the manipulation of numbers; addition, subtraction, and simple algebra; e.g., "Three men divided eighteen golf balls equally among themselves. How many golf balls did each man receive?"	Concentration and arithmetic reasoning
Similarities	Questions that require that two items be compared for their essential similarity; e.g., "In what way are a lion and a tiger alike?" "In what way are an hour and a week alike?"	Logical and/or abstract ability
Digit Span	Questions that ask the testee to repeat from memory two to nine digits—forwards or backwards.	Attention and rote memory
Vocabulary	Questions that ask the testee to define words such as "umbrella" and "conscience."	Learning ability, verbal information, and general range of ideas
Performance Subtest	Nature of the Tasks	Ability(ies) Measured (roughly)
Digit Symbol	The testee must learn a symbol for each of nine digits. Then he or she is presented with a series of digits and asked to write the corresponding symbol beneath each one.	Speed of learning and writing symbols
Picture Completion	Incomplete pictures are presented. The testee must specify the essential part that is missing.	Visual alertness and visual memory
Block Design	Designs are presented. The testee must use small wooden blocks to duplicate them.	Ability to analyze the whole into its component parts and to form an abstract design
Picture Arrangement	Three to six small pictures are presented in a random order. The testee must rearrange them to make a sensible story.	Ability to comprehend and size up a social situation
Object Assembly	Puzzlelike parts of an object are presented. The testee must put them together quickly to make a whole object.	Ability to put together concrete forms.

with occupational proficiency across many types of jobs. In other words, people who score high on intelligence tests frequently do well on their jobs—at least in their employer's estimation. Conversely, people who score low on intelligence tests frequently do poorly on

TABLE 9-2. PROFILE OF PHILLIP'S WAIS SUBTEST SCORES

Subtests	Scaled Scores	Ability(ies) Measured (roughly)
Verbal Scale	Very Low Average Very High	
Information	0 1 2 3 4 5 6 7 8 9 10 11 12 13 14 15 ⑯ 17 18 19	General knowledge
Comprehension	0 1 2 3 4 5 6 7 8 9 10 11 12 13 ⑭ 15 16 17 18 19	Practical information and social judgments
Arithmetic	0 1 2 3 4 5 6 ⑦ 8 9 10 11 12 13 14 15 16 17 18 19	Concentration and arithmetic reasoning
Similarities	0 1 2 3 4 5 6 7 8 9 10 11 12 ⑬ 14 15 16 17 18 19	Logical and/or abstract ability
Digit Span	0 1 2 3 4 5 6 7 8 ⑨ 10 11 12 13 14 15 16 17 18 19	Attention and rote memory
Vocabulary	0 1 2 3 4 5 6 7 8 9 10 11 12 13 14 15 16 ⑰ 18 19	Learning ability, verbal information, and general range of ideas
Performance Scale		
Digit Symbol	0 1 2 3 4 5 6 7 8 ⑨ 10 11 12 13 14 15 16 17 18 19	Speed of learning and writing symbols
Picture Completion	0 1 2 3 4 5 6 7 8 9 10 11 12 ⑬ 14 15 16 17 18 19	Visual alertness and visual memory
Block Design	0 1 2 3 4 5 6 7 8 9 10 11 12 13 14 ⑮ 16 17 18 19	Ability to analyze the whole into its component parts and to form an abstract design
Picture Arrangement	0 1 2 3 4 5 6 7 8 9 10 ⑪ 12 13 14 15 16 17 18 19	Ability to comprehend and size up a social situation
Object Assembly	0 1 2 3 4 5 6 7 8 9 10 11 12 ⑬ 14 15 16 17 18 19	Ability to put together concrete forms

Age 22   Verbal IQ 116   Performance IQ 114   Full Scale IQ 116

their jobs (5). Furthermore, studies indicate that people who graduate from high school receive a mean IQ of approximately 110; those who graduate from college attain a mean IQ of 120, while those who go on to graduate school and earn a degree achieve a mean IQ of 130 (6). (You should note that these average values apply to groups and that individuals within these groups overlap considerably.) Finally, intelligence test performance also correlates positively with overall socioeconomic achievement: People with high incomes and high-status jobs (such as physicians, lawyers, and scientists) generally score high on intelligence tests, whereas people with low incomes and low status jobs (such

as porters, domestics, and laborers) frequently score low (7). These findings are supported by thousands of studies; so scores on intel-

TABLE 9-3. INTELLIGENCE CLASSIFICATIONS

IQ	Classification	Per cent Included
130 and above	Very superior	2.2
120–129	Superior	6.7
110–119	Bright normal	16.1
90–109	Average	50.0
80–89	Dull normal	16.1
70–79	Borderline	6.7
69 and below	Mental defective	2.2

Source: D. Wechsler. WAIS manual. New York: The Psychological Corporation, 1955. P. 20.

ligence tests enable psychologists to make predictions about people's performance in various academic, social, and vocational situations. From this point of view intelligence tests can be considered valid.

Although no one questions that performance on an intelligence test is a good predictor of performance in numerous situations, many psychologists question the basis for that prediction. In other words, do intelligence test scores correlate significantly with other criteria because they both measure intelligence or is there another explanation? Psychologists are divided on this issue.

Consider the position of one prominent intelligence test critic, Harvard University psychologist David McClelland. McClelland argues that the intelligence test measures the credentials and skills that upper and middle-class socioeconomic status gives certain members of society. He writes:

Belonging to the power elite not only helps a young man go to college and get jobs through contacts his family has, it also gives him easy access as a child to the credentials that permit him to get into certain occupations. Nowadays, those credentials include the words and word-game skills used in Scholastic Aptitude Tests [8].

McClelland and others believe that performance on intelligence tests does not predict real competence to cope effectively with the world, so much as it predicts success as defined by middle-class American standards.

Let's return to our initial question. Are current intelligence tests valid? The question is not easy to answer. Although the currently used tests of intelligence do predict certain kinds of competence, it is not entirely clear that they measure intelligence as we defined it (as an overall ability to act purposefully, to think rationally, and to deal effectively with the environment). For this reason we will distinguish throughout the chapter between the concept of intelligence and the concept of measured intelligence (performance on an intelligence test).

Before we leave the subject of intelligence testing, we turn to one more question: Are there other ways to measure intelligence?

The Alternatives

Psychologists are currently trying to develop other ways of measuring intelligence. Some intelligence test designers follow traditional procedures but aim at creating *culture-fair* tests, tests that attempt to minimize the discrimination against particular ethnic and social groups. Culture-fair tests try to provide tasks that do not depend on language or school achievement (see Figure 9-4). They do not pressure the subject by demanding high speed; they often give the test taker practice on each task to minimize the advantages or disadvantages of previous experience or inexperience. Typically, culture-fair tests are also administered in a familiar environment by an examiner of the same ethnic background using the language the subject knows.

Psychologists at the University of Montreal Institute of Psychology are exploring another alternative: They are developing revolutionary intelligence tests for children based on the findings of Jean Piaget. As we saw in Chapter 8, Piaget has shown that children's thinking becomes increasingly more sophisticated with age. The test makers at the Institute of Psychology oppose traditional intelligence tests which simply compare one child with others at the same age on what they believe to be arbitrary skills and bits of knowledge. They believe that it is more meaningful to pinpoint the child's current level of intellectual development—the level at which the subject is currently thinking.

How do these Piagetian test makers measure the level of thought? They evaluate the

Figure 9-4. Sample questions used on a culture-fair intelligence test. (After Cattell, 1968.)

1. Which one of these is different from the remaining four?

2. Which of the five figures on the right would properly continue the three on the left? That is, fill in the blank.

3. Which of the figures on the right should go into the square on the left to make it look right?

4. In the figure on the left, the dot is outside the square and inside the circle. In which of the figures on the right could you put a dot outside the square and inside the circle?

Answers: 1–3, 2–5, 3–2, 4–3.

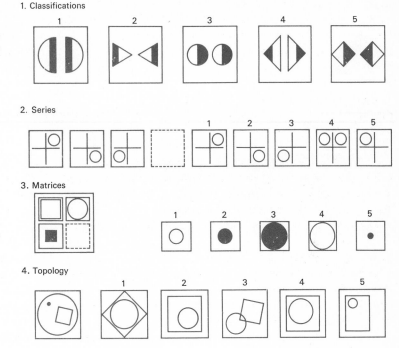

1. Classifications
2. Series
3. Matrices
4. Topology

quality of the child's thinking in experimental situations such as the following:

5 The child sits at a table with a small tank of water on it. The examiner picks up . . . a nail, lets the child feel it if he wants to, and says, "If we put this nail in the water, will it go to the bottom, or will it remain on the water?". . . . Then the child puts the nail in the water to see what it will do. It sinks, of course, to the bottom. The examiner says, "Why does it go to the bottom, do you think? [9]"

The test makers in Montreal believe that performance on tasks such as this one can lead to a better understanding of both the individual child and the general processes underlying intellectual functioning.

There are some other interesting alternatives. John Ertl, director of the University of Ottawa's Center for Cybernetic Studies, has developed an electronic device that is supposed to measure intelligence directly. Ertl

6 believes that the more quickly the brain processes information, the more intelligent the person is. The test is simple. The test taker sits in a chair wearing a helmet lined with electrodes which run to a computer and EEG equipment (see Figure 9-5). Lights are flashed on a screen. The gadgetry measures the time it takes these flashes of light to produce changes in the subject's brain waves. After one minute and 100 flashes of light, Ertl comes up with a person's average score. The shorter the average score, the more efficient the brain, and supposedly the more intelligent the person. Ertl himself has found highly significant negative correlations between his electronic measure and IQ on the WAIS ($-.88$ and $-.76$) (10). Recent studies, however, have failed to replicate these results; so whether or not Ertl's device really measures something like intelligence remains to be demonstrated.

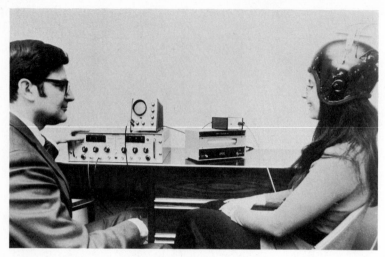

Figure 9-5. John Ertl using an electronic device, the Neural Efficiency Analyzer, which he developed to measure intelligence. (*APA Monitor.*)

In any case, psychologists are aware of the problems of measuring intelligence in the traditional ways, and many of them are looking for better tests.

Summary: The Measurement of Intelligence

1. The first widely used intelligence test, designed by Alfred Binet at the turn of the twentieth century, measured performance on a wide variety of intellectual tasks. Binet assumed that the intellectually dull child would pass fewer items and the intellectually bright child more items than the average child of the same age. The same rationale underlies most intelligence tests in current use today.
2. The IQ is a numerical index that describes performance on an intelligence test in relation to others the same age.
3. An intelligence test must satisfy a number of requirements. Its items must be selected according to definite criteria: They are supposed to be interesting, nondiscriminatory, within the repertoire of the average test taker, and related to total perfor-

mance on the test. In the case of children the problems should discriminate between subjects of different ages. In addition, test designers strive for objectivity, reliability, and validity. They also provide standard administration procedures, and they gather norms on a representative sample of intended test takers.
4. Although traditional tests of intelligence are valid predictors of performance in many academic, social, and vocational situations, it is not certain that they are valid measures of an overall capacity to act purposefully, think rationally, and deal effectively with the environment.
5. Psychologists are currently exploring new ways to measure intelligence.

VARIATIONS IN MEASURED INTELLIGENCE

Psychologists know quite a bit about how people perform on traditional intelligence tests under a large number of circumstances. In this section we look more closely at some of their findings. We turn first to how measured intelligence varies with age.

Measured Intelligence and Age

How does measured intelligence vary with age? Performance on intelligence tests generally improves as children grow older until it reaches a peak somewhere between the ages of eighteen and twenty-five. However, because the IQ itself evaluates performance in relation to age, it usually remains rather stable from test to test, once a child has passed the age of approximately five. Accordingly, children who attain superior IQs at age six usually attain superior IQs at age sixteen. Similarly, six-year-olds who perform at average and below-average levels also tend to maintain their relative positions. This does not mean that measured intelligence never changes at all.

How can psychologists study the effects of age on measured intelligence? Two general strategies are used. Sometimes psychologists do *cross-sectional* studies: They might pick out representative samples of ten-year-olds, twenty-year-olds, thirty-year-olds, forty-year-olds, and so on, and compare their performance on intelligence tests. There is a problem in evaluating the results of cross-sectional studies. The various groups have been born at different times and they have been exposed to consistently different general life experiences, such as depressions, wars, and television; so age is not the only factor that systematically influences their test performance. *Longitudinal studies,* those which study the same individual at two or more points in time, avoid this problem; so although longitudinal studies are relatively expensive and time-consuming, they are currently the preferred way to estimate the effects of age on measured intelligence.

Does measured intelligence fluctuate during childhood? Although there are no predictable age-related patterns of growth or decline in measured intelligence in childhood, IQ changes do occur even during the school years (between the ages of nine and eighteen) when IQs are relatively stable. Psychologist Marjorie Honzik reported that the IQs of 85 percent of the children in one longitudinal study, the Berkeley Guidance Study, varied ten or more points on the eight intelligence tests that were administered during these years. The IQs of nearly 10 percent of the children varied as many as thirty points or more. Correlations between intelligence test performance in the late teens and at twenty to thirty years of age were about .70 (11). Whereas some IQs improve, others decline and others show both tendencies.

Does measured intelligence decline as people age? To answer this question Honzik compared intelligence test scores for subjects in the Berkeley Guidance Study at ages eighteen and forty and for subjects in a second longitudinal study, the Oakland Growth Study, at ages seventeen and forty-eight. She found that mental abilities maintained themselves and that some even increased. Both men and women gained IQ points on tests which measured vocabulary, information, and comprehension. Interestingly, Honzik noted that older women seemed to need a lot of reassurance and encouragement to bolster their confidence so that they would complete the intelligence test. Honzik suggests that as women age, cultural and sex-role expectations may interfere with their test-taking ability and generally depress their test performance (12).

What happens to measured intelligence in old age? In 1956 K. Warner Schaie, a University of Southern California psychologist, began investigating this issue carefully. Schaie administered intelligence tests to five hundred subjects ranging in age from twenty-one to seventy. Seven years later Schaie and Paul Baltes, a psychologist at Pennsylvania State University, readministered the same tests. In analyzing the results they looked closely at four different kinds of intellectual ability:

CRYSTALLIZED INTELLIGENCE—skills acquired through education and through culture; for example, numerical skills, information, and social know-how.

COGNITIVE FLEXIBILITY—the ability to shift from one way of thinking to another; for example, providing an antonym or synonym for a word, depending on whether the word appears in capital or lowercase letters.

VISUAL-MOTOR FLEXIBILITY—the ability to shift from a familiar to an unfamiliar pattern on visual-motor tasks; for example, copying words while interchanging capitals and lowercase letters.

VISUALIZATION—the ability to organize and process visual material; for example, finding a simple figure in a complex figure.

Schaie and Baltes found that as people grew older, they declined primarily on one intellectual ability—visual-motor flexibility. Cognitive flexibility did not show age-related changes, whereas visualization and crystallized intelligence frequently improved with age, even in people over seventy (13).

Later investgators find similar results: Declines in old age seem to occur primarily on visual-motor tasks which require speed. Performance on intelligence tests does not necessarily decline even at age eighty. The results depend on the test and the individual. Although the measured verbal abilities of some eighty-year-olds decrease, those of others actually increase (14).

Regardless of age, measured intelligence does appear to decrease five or six years before people die. Several groups of psychologists have found that when older people are tested at frequent intervals, they decline abruptly on certain intellectual skills about five years before they die—despite the fact that they appear to be in good health at the time of testing (15). We may speculate that certain brain functions may actually be altered as death approaches, disrupting particular intellectual abilities.

Measured Intelligence, Personality, and Sex Role

In 1958 Lester Sontag, Charles Baker, and Virginia Nelson, psychologists at the Fels Research Institute of Human Development at Antioch College in Yellow Springs, Ohio,

Figure 9-6. The cognitive skills required for activities such as playing chess do not necessarily decline in old age. (Irene Bayer, from Monkmeyer.)

studied the cases of two hundred children who had been tested each year for more than twenty years on the Stanford-Binet Intelligence Scale. Over the course of those years, the IQs of many of these children had changed. The psychologists looked for personality characteristics that might account for gains and losses in IQ. They found that emotional dependence on parents and femininity were both associated with IQ losses. Curiosity, emotional independence, verbal aggressiveness, persistence in efforts to master difficult and challenging problems, and competitiveness in ordinary interactions were all associated with increases in IQ (16). The psychologists suggested that these later characteristics are associated with the masculine role in our society, a role that probably facilitates learning and contributes to intellectual mastery. Findings that American men are more likely than American women to show increases in IQ support this hypothesis (17, 18).

Are these IQ increases primarily the result of inborn differences between the sexes? Or are they shaped for the most part by our culture? Many psychologists believe that differential shaping is responsible. The reasoning is straightforward: Women in our culture are encouraged to be helpless, dependent, and unthinking—qualities which could not help them perform intelligently in achievement situations. Men, on the other hand, are generally encouraged to be self-reliant, independent, and logical—qualities which are likely to enhance learning and intellectual mastery in most situations.

These findings raise a second question. Do American males generally outperform American females on intelligence tests? The answer to this question is no. There are no significant overall IQ differences between the sexes in our culture, partly because the items on most intelligence tests were initially selected so that the test would be equally difficult for both sexes. However, men and women do display their own consistent intellectual strengths. In general, women do better on test items that require verbal ability, vocabulary, and rote learning, whereas men excel on items that require the visualization of spatial relationships and arithmetic reasoning (19). These patterns may reflect underlying genetic capabilities, environmentally shaped achievements, or some combination of the two.

Poverty and Measured Intelligence

Lower-class children and adults average twenty to thirty IQ points below middle- and upper-class children and adults on intelligence tests (20). Psychologists do not agree on how to explain these findings. Some believe that the discrepancies in performance are, at least partially, genetically determined and that socioeconomic status is a direct result of inborn intelligence. In Chapter 3 we presented evidence that measured intelligence is partly determined by heredity, but our evidence applied only to the white middle class. Studies of the intelligence test performance of the poor show that the environment influences their scores to a much greater extent than it influences those of the white middle class (21).

How could the environment create differences in measured intelligence between the poor and others? One possibility is that the early experiences of many poor children stunt their intellectual growth. Unquestionably, numerous intelligence-arresting physical conditions—malnutrition, lead poisoning, and disease, for example—are more prevalent among low-income families than among those who are better off financially. The effects of the social-psychological climate of poverty are open to debate. Some psychologists believe that the homes of the poor are likelier than middle-class homes to be confused and chaotic—crowded, noisy, disorganized, and tense. They go on to speculate that under these conditions poor children will be less likely than middle-class children to learn that their behavior produces predictable consequences. Therefore, the argument goes, they are less apt to attempt to cope with problems; accordingly, they are less likely to develop their intelligence. Other psychologists assume that the poor child is frequently understimulated (roughly comparable to a child in an orphanage) (see Chapter 3). They assume that many poor parents are likely to be malnourished, unhealthy, tired, uncomfortable, unfulfilled in their physiological and social needs, and worried much of the time. As a result, they probably spend less time than middle-class parents helping their children to develop their abilities. Moreover, if their own education and language are limited and if their own abilities were never cultivated, such parents may not know how to help their children develop their minds.

A particularly well-planned study of a comprehensive early education program provides support for an environmental explanation of intelligence test differences between poor and middle-income people. After surveying a Milwaukee slum area, social scientists Rick Heber and Howard Garber found that mothers with IQs below 80—who made up 45.5 percent of their sample—reared 78.2 percent of the children with IQs below 80. Heber and Garber hypothesized that the low-IQ mothers were providing their normally intelligent offspring with an impoverished environment that pulled their IQ down. Note that heredity could also have explained the children's low measured intelligence.

Heber and Garber began an ambitious six-year project aimed at trying to prevent retardation. They identified forty mothers with IQs below 70 and randomly assigned each one to an experimental or control group. As soon as one of the mothers returned home from the hospital with a newborn infant, treatment began. The mothers

in the experimental group were visited by a staff member from the Infant Education Center. Once rapport was established, the staff member introduced the mother to a special enrichment program where she received occupation, homemaking, and babycare training. At the same time the infant was picked up each morning and transported to the Infant Education Center for the entire day. There the infant took part in an intensive program which stimulated sensory, cognitive, and language skills. Infants of the mothers in the control group grew up under ordinary circumstances except for occasional testing. The results were impressive: At age 5½ the experimental children achieved an average IQ score of 124, while the control children attained an average IQ score of 94 (see Figure 9-7). On the basis of previous data the IQ scores of the children in the control group are expected to decline progressively.

Heber writes:

We have seen a capacity for learning on the part of young children surpassing anything, which previously, I would have believed possible. The trend of our present data does engender the hope that it may prove to be possible to prevent the kind of retardation which occurs in children reared by parents who are both poor and of limited ability (22).

Many shorter, less intensive preschool education programs find similar results: Poor children make impressive gains on intelligence tests when enrolled in programs that emphasize language and cognitive skills. Unfortunately, these gains are rarely maintained unless the parents are actively involved and the child's environment also changes or unless the special program continues. In any case such programs support the hypothesis that the early environment does have an important influence on measured intelligence.

You may have noticed that there is a prob-

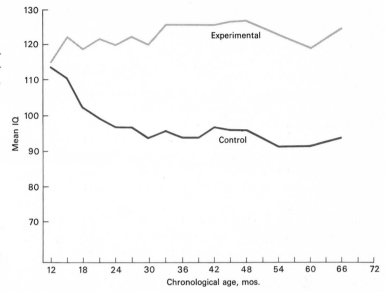

Figure 9–7. Mean IQ performance of the experimental and control subjects. (After Heber et al., 1972.)

lem in interpreting the data from studies of unprepared. They have never before been early education programs. We could assume that the children's basic intellectual capacity is changing and that the gains on the intelligence test reflect these underlying changes, or we could assume that the children are simply learning particular skills which the intelligence test measures, while their cognitive capacity is remaining the same.

A large number of psychologists believe in this latter possibility. They argue that poor children are cognitively competent and that they simply do not acquire the particular intellectual skills which are measured by traditional intelligence tests. They reason that middle- and upper-class children begin school with a head start—they are psychologically prepared for it. Frequently, they have learned to listen, to sit quietly for long periods of time, and to obey authority figures. They have often been "primed to learn." Enthusiastic parents have taught them verbal skills—to say the alphabet, to count, or to write their names, for example.

Many lower-class children begin school with a handicap—they are psychologically

unprepared. They have never before been required to sit and pay attention for long periods of time, to behave politely, or to obey authority figures. Moreover, when children are hungry and tired, they may not be good at these activities. Poor children are less likely to have learned academic skills from their parents. The survival and other life skills that they have learned—such as how to secure enough food to eat, how to protect oneself, and how to care for an infant—may not be valued in the school setting.

The rest of the story is quite predictable. The middle-class children like the teacher and the teacher likes them; so, on the whole, they have relatively positive experiences at school. Their teachers and their parents hold high expectations for their school success; so they are encouraged to achieve academically and intellectually. Many lower-class children, in contrast, dislike the alien routines of the classroom, which seem to have little relevance to their lives. The middle-class teacher is likely to perceive the children unfavorably. Consequently, the children find their experiences in school negative and frustrating.

Many poor children are neither expected nor encouraged to achieve academically or intellectually (as defined by society).

Robert Rosenthal, a psychologist at Harvard University, and his associates have shown that expectations can affect intelligence. In the mid-1960s Rosenthal and Lenore Jacobson selected an elementary school from a lower-class neighborhood in south San Francisco; at the beginning of the year they gave the children in each classroom a nonverbal intelligence test. The teacher was told that the psychologists were measuring "intellectual blooming." After the test, Rosenthal and Jacobson *randomly* chose 20 percent of the children in each classroom and labeled them "intellectual bloomers." The psychologists gave the names of the "bloomers" to their teachers, informing them at the same time of the remarkable gains that could be expected. The differences between "bloomers" and "nonbloomers," of course, was solely in the teacher's mind. Eight months later Rosenthal and Jacobson returned to the school and retested the children. The "bloomers," whether low or high in ability, had all "bloomed" at least moderately, gaining four IQ points more, on the average, than the control subjects, the "nonbloomers [23]."

The interpretation of this study has been controversial; more than two hundred replications have been attempted. A sizable proportion of them show a small but significant effect. Some of these recent studies suggest that teachers translate their expectations into behavior—without necessarily being aware of it. When teachers expect children to "bloom," they tend to create warmer social-emotional climates for them. They give them more feedback. They teach them more material. They question them more; they give them more opportunities to respond (24). When children are expected to perform in an average way, they are more apt to be ignored. In fact, there is evidence that should such children achieve (contrary to the teacher's expectations), they are likely to be labeled "troublemakers (25)." It is probably not too farfetched to speculate that children who are negatively viewed by their teachers perceive themselves as intellectually inadequate and their academic work as both unpleasant and frustrating. One study indicates that children who are poor and black may be negatively perceived by their teachers more frequently than other children—even when the teachers themselves are black (26). Given negative teacher expectations, the odds that children from low-income families will achieve intellectually—at least by society's standards—are rather slim.

Soon after children enter kindergarten, their socioeconomic status may seal their fate. The snowball effect begins. Upper- and middle-class children progress farther, and lower-class children slip farther behind in school-related skills that the society defines as intelligence. It is quite possible that the intelligence test performance of lower- and middle-class children and adults simply reflects this reality.

The traditional intelligence test and the testing situation are other factors that may contribute to the discrepancy in IQ scores between the poor and others. In the case of children, the middle-class child is likely to feel comfortable with the middle-class examiner, interested in the schoollike tasks of the intelligence test, and motivated to do well; but poor children are likely to feel ill at ease with the examiner, uninterested in the test items, and unmotivated to perform to the best of their ability. Even more importantly, perhaps, children from an inner city ghetto or a rural slum may not understand the vocabulary, the instructions, and the middle-class situations which they are expected to evaluate. The following question appears on a widely used children's intelligence test: "What would you do if you were sent to the store by your mother to buy something and you found the store didn't have it?" "Go to another store" (the correct answer) may be the best answer for the middle-class child, but is it necessarily the most intelligent response for the child reared on an Indian reservation or in the inner city? The child on an Indian reservation may not have another store to go to. For the ghetto child going to a store on the next block may be dangerous and therefore unadvisable. In short, many psychologists believe that traditional intelligence tests simply do not tap the insights, skills, and competencies of lower-income people.

Race and Measured Intelligence

A 1966 review of some 380 studies concluded that whites score higher than blacks on intelligence tests by some ten to twenty IQ points on the average (27). Although there is some evidence that the IQ discrepancies may be lower, few psychologists question that differences exist. The real issue is: What is responsible for them?

Arthur Jensen, a respected educational psychologist at the University of California at Berkeley, believes that the differences are largely inherited. In a now famous article in *The Harvard Educational Review,* "How much can we boost IQ and scholastic achievement?" (1969), Jensen argued:

1. Studies of blood relatives, especially those of identical twins reared apart (same heredity, different environment), lead to statistical estimates that approximately 75 to 80 percent of the variations which individuals exhibit on intelligence tests can be explained by genetic factors. These estimates have led Jensen to conclude that heredity is roughly twice as important as

environment in determining measured intelligence.

2. Blacks not only make lower scores on traditional intelligence tests, they also score their points differently from whites. They excel at tasks that require rote learning and memory, whereas whites excel at tasks that require abstract thinking and reasoning. Jensen believes that these findings support the hypothesis that blacks and whites as groups have inherited a different kind of intellectual ability as well as a different capacity for intellectual achievement.

3. If intelligence was simply suppressed in blacks because of environmental conditions, compensatory educational programs for poor blacks should have brought their intelligence-test scores up to those of whites. According to Jensen, black genes *may* make this goal unrealistic (28).

The majority of psychologists disagree with Jensen's interpretation of the intelligence test data for a variety of reasons. Many of them challenge Jensen's assumption that current intelligence tests measure intellectual capacity for all groups. They argue that the traditional tests simply provide a measure of performance on specific mental tasks and that they are clearly unfair to both poor and ethnic minority groups. Blacks fall in at least one and often in both of these categories; so the test is not a fair measure of their real intellectual capacity.

White people can better understand what taking an intelligence test in an unfamiliar culture means by sampling an item or two from the Dove Counterbalance General Intelligence Test which appears in Figure 9-8. This test was designed by black sociologist Adrian Dove to demonstrate to the white community that it is absurd to evaluate a black ghetto child by white middle-class standards.

1. A "handkerchief head" is: (a) a cool cat, (b) a porter, (c) an Uncle Tom, (d) a hoddi, (e) a preacher.

2. Which word is most out of place here? (a) splib, (b) blood, (c) gray, (d) spook, (e) black.

3. A "gas head" is a person who has a: (a) fast-moving car, (b) stable of "lace," (c) "process," (d) habit of stealing cars, (e) long jail record for arson.

4. "Down-home" (the South) today, for the average "soul brother" who is picking cotton from sunup until sundown, what is the average earning (take home) for one full day? (a) $.75, (b) $1.65, (c) $3.50, (d) $5, (e) $12.

5. "Bo Diddley" is a: (a) game for children, (b) down-home cheap wine, (c) down-home singer, (d) new dance, (e) Moejoe call.

6. If a pimp is up tight with a woman who gets state aid, what does he mean when he talks about "Mother's Day?" (a) second Sunday in May, (b) third Sunday in June, (c) first of every month, (d) none of these, (e) first and fifteenth of every month.

7. "Hully Gully" came from: (a) East Oakland, (b) Fillmore, (c) Watts, (d) Harlem, (e) Motor City.

8. If a man is called a "blood," then he is a (a) fighter, (b) Mexican-American, (c) Negro, (d) hungry hemophile, (e) Redman or Indian.

9. Cheap chitlings (not the kind you purchase at a frozen-food counter) will taste rubbery unless they are cooked long enough. How soon can you quit cooking them to eat and enjoy them? (a) 45 minutes, (b) two hours, (c) 24 hours, (d) one week (on a low flame), (e) one hour.

10. What are the "Dixie Humming-birds?" (a) part of the KKK, (b) a swamp disease, (c) a modern gospel group, (d) a Mississippi Negro paramilitary group, (e) Deacons.

11. If you throw the dice and seven is showing on the top, what is facing down? (a) seven, (b) snake eyes, (c) boxcars, (d) little Joes, (e) 11.

12. "Jet" is: (a) an East Oakland motorcycle club, (b) one of the gangs in "West Side Story," (c) a news and gossip magazine, (d) a way of life for the very rich.

13. T-Bone Walker got famous for playing what? (a) trombone, (b) piano, (c) "T-flute," (d) guitar, (e) "Hambone."*

*Those who are not "culturally deprived" will recognize the correct answers are 1. (c), 2. (c), 3. (c), 4. (d), 5. (c), 6. (e), 7. (c), 8. (c), 9. (c), 10. (c), 11. (a), 12. (c), 13. (d).

Figure 9-8. The Dove Counter-balance General Intelligence Test. (Copyright © Newsweek, Inc., 1968.)

Some psychologists believe that the whole issue of black versus white intelligence is impossible to investigate. They assert that one cannot study the intelligence of different racial groups accurately because pure races are virtually nonexistent. Some people classified white have black ancestry; similarly, many blacks have white ancestry.

In addition, Jensen's misinterpretation of a statistical concept keeps many psychologists skeptical about his conclusions. Recall that Jensen asserted that 75 to 80 percent of the variability seen on intelligence tests could be accounted for by genetic factors. This estimate, known as a *heritability index*, was taken from studies of predominantly white middle-class American twins. It is a well-accepted statistical fact that heritability is not an intrinsic property of a trait but of the population in which it occurs (29). In other words, the heritability index is computed for particular groups and cannot be automatically applied to other groups. Although the intelligence test scores of white middle-class Americans may be heavily influenced by genetic differences, the intelligence test scores of other groups cannot be assumed to follow the same pattern. When a heritability index was recently computed on 1,521 pairs of twins from disadvantaged groups in the Philadelphia school system, the results showed that heredity accounted for practically none of the measured differences between lower-class children. Apparently, as we stated before, intelligence test performance among poor people (and a high percentage of blacks are poor) is much more decisively influenced by their environment than that of middle-class whites (30).

This study and others support the hypothesis that although the innate intellectual capacity of blacks and whites may be essentially the same, blacks do not perform as well as whites on intelligence tests on the average because of disadvantaged environmental conditions. Poverty is one important factor. So are the long-range cumulative effects of unequal opportunity, inferior education, and social, legal, and political discrimination.

Finally, Jensen's claim that compensatory educational programs should be expected to bring the average black IQ up to that of the average white IQ probably rests on unsound reasoning. The basically unhealthy conditions which often surround black children can not possibly be righted by a single summer or winter program.

We have mentioned only a few of the major criticisms of Jensen's position. Can we come to any conclusions as to whether or not blacks and whites differ in innate intellectual capacity? It should be clear by now that at least two problems make the question currently impossible to answer: (1) Traditional intelligence tests have clear cultural biases which favor white middle- and upper-income people. (2) The environmental conditions which stimulate intellectual ability (as defined by society) are unquestionably unequal for the two racial groups.

The race and intelligence controversy has raised an important side issue. Jensen's work was not motivated by either racist or political motives. He was exploring a question which interested him. Still, many of Jensen's conclu-

sions have been distorted, misstated, and dramatized by the popular press to support racist claims. Should scientists study issues such as this one—issues which have so much potential for abuse? What do you think?

Summary: Variations in Measured Intelligence

1. Once a child passes the age of five, the IQ usually remains stable; however, IQs can and do change—sometimes to a marked degree. Measured intelligence does not appear to decline in middle age, and many intellectual abilities appear to be maintained in old age until shortly before death. In very old age the stability of measured intelligence varies with the individual and the test.

2. Personality characteristics such as verbal aggression, competitiveness, persistence, and independence are associated with increases in IQ. American males are more likely than American females to show such personality-related IQ increases.

3. Although American males and females attain the same average IQ on intelligence tests, they display different intellectual strengths.

4. Poor children and adults score twenty to thirty IQ points, on the average, below middle- and upper-income children and adults. This finding may be explained in several ways: Poor people may have less inherent intellectual ability. On the other hand, the diverse conditions associated with poverty may depress intellectual functioning, or they may simply interfere with the development of those traditional skills that intelligence tests measure—without necessarily damaging basic cognitive capacities.

5. A fair comparison of the innate intellectual abilities of blacks and whites appears to be presently impossible because of inher-

ent biases in current intelligence tests and unequal environmental opportunities for the development of the abilities that are measured by intelligence tests.

We turn now to a second cognitive ability, creativity.

CREATIVITY

Mozart described the process of creating music in the following way:

When I am, as it were, completely myself, entirely alone, and of good cheer—say, traveling in a carriage, or walking after a good meal, or during the night when I cannot sleep; it is on such occasions that my ideas flow best and most abundantly. *Whence* and *how* they come, I know not; nor can I force them. Those pleasures that please me I retain in memory, and am accustomed, as I have been told, to hum them to myself. If I continue in this way, it soon occurs to me how I may turn this or that morsel to account, so as to make a good dish of it, that is to say, agreeably to the rules of counterpoint, to the peculiarities of the various instruments, etc. [31].

Creativity is a mysterious capability. Mozart did not understand it; psychologists are just beginning to. For a long time creativity was assumed to be a special type of intelligence. Currently, creativity and intelligence are viewed as two quite distinct mental abilities. Intelligence, as assessed by traditional intelligence tests, can be characterized as *convergent thinking,* the ability to follow accepted patterns of thought and arrive at single correct solutions to particular problems. Creativity can be characterized as *divergent thinking,* innovative and original thinking that deviates from customary patterns and results in more than one correct solution to particular problems. The two abilities are only moderately related. The measured intelligence of creative writers, artists, mathematicians, and sci-

entists, for example, is almost always above average. Yet, within any single group, measured intelligence does not predict how creative a particular individual will be. A scientist with an IQ of 130, for example, may be considered highly creative by her colleagues, while another with an IQ of 180 may not be considered creative at all. We will assume that creativity is a distinct capacity which people possess in varying degrees, enabling them to produce original ideas that are both adaptive (serve a useful function) and fully developed. Can creativity be measured?

The Measurement of Creativity

Many psychologists have devised creativity tests which measure various divergent thinking skills. Psychologists Michael Wallach and Nathan Kogan measured creativity in fifth graders by having them work gamelike tasks and scoring them on the number of unique responses that they produced.

The procedures involved such matters as requesting the child to suggest possible uses for each of several objects, or to describe possible ways in which each of several pairs of objects are similar to each other. For example, in one procedure the child was to suggest all the different ways in which we could use such objects as a newspaper, a cork, a shoe, a chair. "Rip it up if angry" was a unique response for "newspaper," while "make paper hats" was not unique. In another, he was to indicate similarities between, for example, a potato and a carrot, a cat and a mouse, milk and meat. "They are government inspected" was a unique response for "milk and meat," while "they come from animals" was not unique. In yet another, he was to indicate all the things that each of a number of abstract drawings might be. For a triangle with three circles around it, "three mice eating a piece of cheese" was a unique response, while "three people sitting around a table" was not unique. For two half-circles over a line, "two haystacks on a flying carpet" was a unique response, while "two igloos" was not unique [32]. [See Figure 9-9.]

Figure 9-9. Children's responses to abstract drawings. (From Wallach and Kogan, 1967.)

Unique: "Foot and toes"
Common: "Table with things on top"

Unique: "Three mice eating a piece of cheese"
Common: "Three people sitting around a table"

Unique: "Lollipop bursting into pieces"
Common: "Flower"

Unique: "Two haystacks on a flying carpet"
Common: "Two igloos"

Adult creativity tests usually assess similar divergent thinking skills. Figure 9-10 presents items which have been used to assess creativity in adults.

How would you characterize these tests? An educational psychologist Philip Vernon has observed that creativity tests frequently consist of "rather trivial verbal jugglery and involve nothing like the prolonged agony of the creative writer or composer, nor the scientist's intense drive and concentrated application of technical expertise [33]." Are these creativity tests valid? Do people recognized as especially creative perform more ably on them than people who appear to be less creative? Psychologists at the Institute of Personality Assessment and Research of the University of California at Berkeley have attempted to answer questions such as this one in the course of studying especially creative people. Typically, they have asked writers, business people, artists, mathematicians, scientists, architects, and others to pick their most creative peers. The highly creative nominees then come to the Institute from all over the United States. There they are observed, tested, questioned, and rated on various characteristics and compared with less creative people in the same educational category. Numerous studies find that the creativity test performances of highly creative and less creative people cannot be distinguished (34)— although the groups do show distinct differences in personality and interests. Descriptive statements that have been found to differentiate between highly creative and less creative individuals include the following.

Appears to have a high degree of intellectual capacity
Genuinely values intellectual and cognitive matters
Values own independence and autonomy
Is verbally fluent; can express ideas well
Enjoys esthetic impressions; is esthetically reactive
Is productive; gets things done
Is concerned with philosophical problems; for example, religion, values, the meaning of life, and so forth
Has high aspiration level of self
Has a wide range of interests
Thinks and associates to ideas in unusual ways; has unconventional thought processes
Is an interesting, arresting person
Appears straightforward, forthright, candid in dealings with others
Behaves in an ethically consistent manner; is consistent with own personal standards [35]

Apparently, divergent thinking is only one aspect of creativity. Personality, motivation,

(B) 9. Problems with Educational System

"List below problems you see with our educational system. Do not discuss or solve these problems. Just *list* as many problems as you can think of."

(G) 1. Seeing Different Meanings

"In this test each given word has a number of different possible meanings. Your task is to think of as many different meanings of each given word as you can."
SAMPLE WORD: Scale

(G) 3. Possible Jobs

"As the Inter-Planet Express prepared to land on Mars, the tourists were discussing a new custom developed by the Martians. Since the first settlers had arrived from earth, the Martians had taken to wearing emblems to show what each person's job is.

"As the tourists looked through the videoscope, they saw one Martian wearing the emblem shown below. (Line drawing of a shining light bulb within a circle.)

 'Electrical engineer,' said one of the tourists. 'Light bulb manufacturer,' said another. 'Maybe a bright student,' a third tourist suggested.

"In this test you will see more of the emblems that the Martians wore. Imagine that you are one of the tourists. Think of as many possible jobs as you can which might be indicated by the emblems. If you are not sure whether one of your ideas is reasonable, write it down anyway and try to think of another idea."

(G) 6. Apparatus Test

"In this test you will be given names of objects that are familiar to everyone. Your task is to suggest two improvements for each of the objects. Do not suggest an improvement that has already been made. You do not need to worry about your ideas being possible, so long as they are sensible.

"It is not necessary to explain your reason for a suggested improvement. Your suggestions should be specific. A suggested improvement like 'The object should be made more efficient,' is too general to be acceptable.

A.

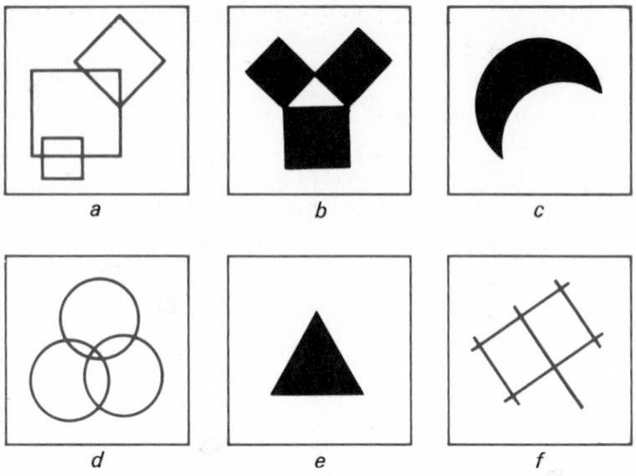

B.

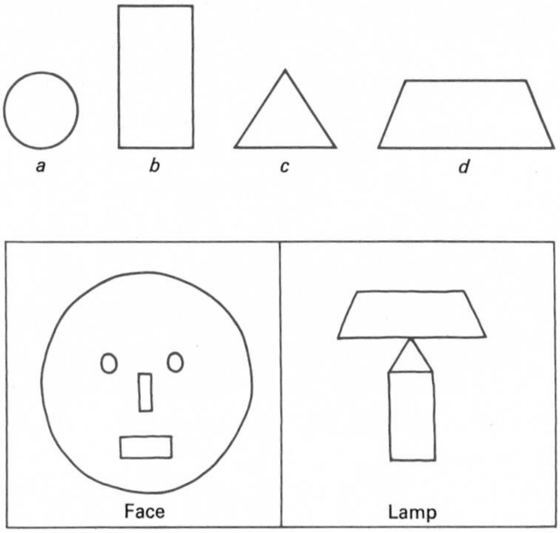

C.

Figure 9-10. Examples of items which appear on creativity tests for adults. (*A*) Verbal items (from Parnes and Noller, 1973). (*B*) Identifying similarities. Figures such as these are presented and people are asked to find as many similarities as they can. Two possible answers are BCE (black) and ABD (three parts) (from Guilford, 1967). (*C*) Constructing objects. People are asked to combine forms like these to make specific objects. Two responses are shown. (Courtesy of the Sheridan Psychological Services, Inc.)

and other intellectual factors also influence actual creative achievement.

Teaching Creativity

Many psychologists believe that the habits which make creative achievement likely are partially learned and can be enhanced by formal training. Consequently, programs have been developed to teach creativity to people of all ages. In the majority of these programs people learn various divergent thinking skills, such as the four techniques illustrated below. This material comes from a creativity guidebook which was designed for eighth graders by psychologists Gary Davis and Susan Houtman. (You'll understand the methods better if you try to work the exercises yourself.)

1. Part-changing Method—Students are invited to identify the main parts or attributes of some phenomenon and to think of different ways to change each one. For example:

   Three parts (or qualities) of common classroom chalk are color, shape, and size. . . . Invent some new kind of chalk by listing 15 different *colors* (and don't forget striped chalk, like the striped tooth paste), ten different *shapes*, and five *sizes*. Try to think of *different* ideas and don't worry about whether or not they are any good [36].

2. Checkerboard Method—Students are asked to make a checkerboard and to enter words and phrases on the vertical and horizontal axes. After the checkerboard is complete, the student examines each combination. For example:

   Your gym teacher has decided to give you a final exam in which you have to make up a new sport or game. Use a *checkerboard* to help you do this by putting materials or equipment along the top and things the players do (running, batting, kicking, etc.) down one side [37].

3. Checklist Method—The student is invited to apply a checklist of seven items to the design of a new product. Here is the checklist:

   Change color
   Change size
   Change shape
   Use new or different material
   Add or subtract something
   Rearrange things
   Identify a new design

4. Find-something-similar Method—The student is invited to solve a problem by thinking of other things in the world that accomplish the same goal. For example,

   Imagine your school has a parking problem

(which it probably does). Let's find ideas for solving this problem by thinking of how bees, squirrels, ants, shoe stores, clothing stores, and so on "store things [38]."

One particularly ambitious program designed to stimulate the creativity of adults was developed by Sidney Parnes and Ruth Noller, psychologists at the State University College at Buffalo. Parnes and Noller selected 150 experimental and control subjects at random from 350 students who had applied for the Creative Studies program. In their freshman and sophomore years the experimental subjects took four courses in Creative Studies; the control subjects did not take the courses. The experimental subjects were involved in discussions, films, lectures, projects, and exercises which emphasized creative problem solving, using their imagination, and becoming more aware of themselves and their potential for creative achievement. Before and after the training program both groups were measured and compared on various tests of mental ability and creativity. The experimental group significantly outperformed the control group on nine of the thirteen final measures (39).

Creativity programs apparently can teach people to produce unusual responses and to solve problems more flexibly. These skills increase creativity as measured by creativity and achievement tests of various kinds, but do they enhance actual creative achievement? That is, do they lead to the production of serious pictures, poems, scientific achievements, and the like? The answer to this important question is not known.

Summary: Creativity

1. Psychologists consider creativity an ability distinct from intelligence.
2. Creativity is often measured by assessing people's performance on tests of divergent thinking. Current research indicates that

creativity involves abilities other than divergent thinking—personality, motivation, and other intellectual skills are believed to be important.

3. Psychologists try to train creativity by providing experiences that emphasize the practice of divergent-thinking skills. Although such programs increase measured creativity, it is not certain that they increase actual creative achievement.

STUDY GUIDE 9

Key Terms. intelligence, mental age, chronological age, intelligence quotient (IQ), Stanford-Binet test, objectivity, reliability, test-retest reliability, validity, standard administration, norms, Wechsler Adult Intelligence Scale (WAIS), verbal subtests, performance subtests, measured intelligence, culture-fair test, cross-sectional study, longitudinal study, crystallized intelligence, cognitive flexibility, visual-motor flexibility, visualization, Dove Counterbalance General Intelligence Test, heritability index, convergent thinking, divergent thinking, creativity.

Important Research. development of the first useful intelligence test (Binet), stability of IQ scores (Honzik), measured intelligence in old age (Schaie and Baltes), measured intelligence and approaching death, personality and measured intelligence (Sontag, Baker, and Nelson), early education and measured intelligence (Heber and Garber), teachers' expectancies and measured intelligence (Rosenthal), race and measured intelligence (Jensen), measurement of creativity (Wallach and Kogan), studies of creative people (University of California research group), teaching children to be creative (Davis and Houtman), teaching adults to be creative (Parnes and Noller).

Self-Quiz

1. Which definition of intelligence do the majority of psychologists accept? "Intelligence is _____." [a] the ability to act purposefully, think rationally, and deal effectively with the environment; [b] a cluster of abilities including memory, reasoning, and verbal fluency; [c] a score on an IQ test; [d] none of the above: psychologists do not agree on any one definition of intelligence.

2. Binet developed an intelligence test to [a] identify the severely retarded; [b] identify children who could and could not benefit from public school education; [c] identify brain-damaged children; [d] find out if younger and older children were equally intelligent.

3. If you compare scores on an intelligence test with other measures of intelligent functioning, such as grades in school, you are measuring [a] objectivity; [b] reliability; [c] validity; [d] norms.

4. IQ is not significantly correlated with [a] job status; [b] sex; [c] job performance; [d] grade-point average in high school.

5. Which is not described in the text as a possible way of measuring intelligence? [a] Measuring how quickly the brain responds to flashes of light; [b] administering a traditional intelligence test; [c] comparing a child's language with standards derived from Chomsky's theory; [d] comparing a child's thinking with standards derived from Piaget's theory.

6. A study comparing the mental abilities of six-, ten-, sixteen-, and thirty-two-year-old subjects at one point in time would be considered a(n) _____ study. [a] cross-sectional; [b] age-sampled; [c] longitudinal; [d] age-normative.

7. In a study of the stability of children's IQ scores, Honzik found that [a] scores were quite stable for six years; [b] scores were quite stable for twelve years; [c] scores of 85 percent of the children changed more than ten points during the school years; [d] scores of 85 percent of the children changed more than five points during the school years, but less than 20 percent changed more than ten points.

8. Schaie and Baltes found that as people grow older, the only mental ability that declines noticeably is [a] number skills; [b] ability to shift from one way of thinking to another; [c] ability to organize visual material; [d] ability to shift from a familiar to a new pattern on visual-motor tasks.

9. Which is not true of the Milwaukee early education project of Heber and Garber? [a] Mothers of all subjects had IQs of 70 or less; [b] mothers, as well as children, received an enrichment program; [c] at five years of age, children in the experimental group averaged thirty points higher than those in the control group on intelligence tests; [d] at eight years of age, the IQs of the control-group subjects were almost equal to those of the experimental-group subjects.

10. Rosenthal found that children's IQ scores can be raised simply by [**a**] giving the children frequent intelligence tests; [**b**] improving the children's self concepts; [**c**] telling their teachers that they will "bloom"; [**d**] giving parents interesting books to read to their children.

11. The type of thinking measured by most intelligence tests is called [**a**] convergent; [**b**] crystallized; [**c**] divergent; [**d**] flexible.

12. The heritability index estimates [**a**] the extent to which variability on a measured characteristic in a particular population can be explained by heredity; [**b**] the extent to which a particular characteristic is determined by heredity; [**c**] the probability that two groups have similar genetic capabilities; [**d**] the probability that two groups have dissimilar genetic capabilities.

13. Which is ordinarily *not* a characteristic of a creative person? [**a**] Has a wide range of interests; [**b**] is quiet and reserved; [**c**] values independence; [**d**] expresses ideas well.

14. Attempts to teach creativity [**a**] have improved subjects' performance on a variety of creativity measures; [**b**] have produced individuals who go on to make important creative contributions to the arts and sciences; [**c**] have generally been unsuccessful; [**d**] have been successful with children but not with adults.

15. If you give the same people the same test twice, you are most probably measuring the_____ of the test. [**a**] reliability; [**b**] validity; [**c**] objectivity; [**d**] standardized administration.

Exercises

1. COMPUTING AN INTELLIGENCE QUOTIENT. To practice computing intelligence quotients, calculate the IQ in each example:

   1. Joe is fourteen years old; he performs like a child of 10.0 on an intelligence test.
   2. Twelve-year-old Bonnie has a mental age of 12.0.
   3. Six-year-old Sam has a mental age of 8.0.
   4. Nancy is eight years old, and she performs slightly better on an intelligence test than children her own age and attains a mental age of 8.5 years.

2. THE CHARACTERISTICS OF A GOOD TEST. To test your knowledge of the characteristics of a good test, match the following terms with the characteristics below: objectivity (O), reliability (R), validity (V), standard administration (SA), norms (N).

____ **1.** Consistency.
____ **2.** Insures that all individuals are given a particular test in roughly the same way.
____ **3.** Information about the performance of many people on a particular test.

____ **4.** Tells whether the test measures what it is supposed to measure.
____ **5.** Occurs when the test scores are not influenced by the tester's biases.
____ **6.** Helps the psychologist to interpret an individual's score on a particular test.
____ **7.** Increases when the tester is provided with criteria for judging the correct answers.
____ **8.** Can be measured by giving the same test twice.
____ **9.** In the case of creativity tests, can be measured by comparing scores on the creativity test with actual creative achievement.

Questions to Consider

1. After considering the various definitions of intelligence on page 247, define intelligence and defend your definition. Explain the advantages and disadvantages of other definitions of intelligence. If you were designing an intelligence test, what would you include on your test? How does your definition of intelligence influence the design of your test?

2. Describe traditional and recent intelligence tests. List the advantages and disadvantages of each. Which intelligence test(s) do you prefer? Why?

3. Define reliability and validity. Describe how psychologists might measure the reliability and validity of the Dove Counterbalance General Intelligence Test, using the group for which it was designed—black inner-city American children?

4. Do you consider traditional intelligence tests valid? What other criteria can be used to validate an intelligence test besides those on pages 251–256?

5. Rosenthal demonstrated that teacher's expectations can influence children's scores on intelligence tests. How do you think parents' expectations affect measured intelligence? How could this issue be studied?

6. If you were in charge of a well-funded experimental education project, what kind of program would you design to increase permanently the measured intelligence of poor children?

7. Poverty is associated with low measured intelligence. The correlation can be interpreted as furnishing support for two hypotheses: (1) a poor environment contributes to low measured intelligence and (2) low measured intelligence contributes to poverty. Correlations do not demonstrate cause-and-effect relationships. How could psychologists study these hypotheses using experimental methods?

8. Design a test of creativity. How could you check its reliability and validity?

Project 9: Evaluating an Intelligence Test

Many tests have been devised to measure intelligence. Some are more useful than others. Whether a test is useful or not depends on its objectivity, reliability, validity, ease of administration, scoring, etc. The purpose of this project is to evaluate the usefulness of a simple intelligence test, the draw-a-person (DAP) test.

Method. Find three cooperative children at varied ages between three and fourteen years of age. Ask each child if he/she would be willing to make some drawings. Explain the project in detail to the child's parents and obtain their permission. Each child should be tested individually in a quiet place free from distractions. Give the subject a piece of plain paper and a pencil and ask him/her to "draw the best person you can." If the subject draws only a head, request that the entire person be drawn. Two or three days later, ask each subject to draw another person, again "the best person you can" under the same conditions.

Results. Although it requires training and practice to score a draw-a-person test accurately, the drawings can be roughly evaluated by considering the following questions:

1. Are head, neck, eyes, eyebrows, nose, mouth, hair, ears, arms, hands, fingers, correct number of fingers, legs, feet, trunk, and clothing present? Count one point for each of the above items present. Give one extra point if both hands have five fingers. (Possible total sixteen points.)
2. Are these body parts placed correctly? Count one point for each correctly placed body part. (Possible total fifteen points.)
3. Are these body parts drawn in proportion? Count one point for each body part that is drawn in proportion. (Possible total fifteen points.)

   Each drawing may receive up to forty-six points.

   To judge reliability, compare the two pictures of each subject using the criteria above. Are the scores similar?

   To judge validity, compare the highest scoring pictures of all three subjects. Are there substantial differences in the quality of the three drawings? Do these differences correspond to the ages of the subjects? Do these differences correspond to your idea of the subject's comparative mental ability?

Discussion. Consider the following questions:

1. How useful is the draw-a-person test? Is it easy to administer and interpret? Is the interpretation likely to be free of bias? Is the test reliable? valid?
2. What additional checks of reliability might you make?
3. How could you formally test the validity of the draw-a-person test?
4. What factors besides intelligence might influence a subject's score on the draw-a-person test?
5. Why might the draw-a-person test be less valid with adult than children subjects?

REFERENCE: Harris, D. B. *Children's drawings as measures of intellectual maturity.* New York: Harcourt, Brace & World, Inc., 1963.

Suggested Readings

1. Matarazzo, J. *Wechsler's measurement and appraisal of adult intelligence* (5th ed.) Baltimore: The Williams & Wilkins Company, 1972. Discusses problems in defining intelligence and designing intelligence tests; also describes the literature on how measured intelligence varies with age, sex, personality, social class, race, etc. Excellent source, but likely to be difficult for most beginning students.
2. Jensen, A., B. Rice, & T. Dobzhansky. "Race, intelligence, and genetics." *Psychology Today*, December 1973, 7, 80–101. In this collection of articles a psychologist and a geneticist discuss evidence for and against genetic differences in intelligence between races, and a journalist explores a side issue—the consequences of investigating topics like this one.
3. Baltes, P. B., & K. W. Schaie. "Aging and IQ: The myth of the twilight years." *Psychology Today*, March 1974, 7, 35–40. A survey of the research on what happens to intelligence in old age.
4. Voyat, G. "IQ: God given or man-made?" *Saturday Review*, May 1969, 17, 52, 73–75, 86–87. A very clear comparison of the ideas of Jensen and Piaget on intellectual development. The relative value of traditional intelligence tests and the new Piagetian intelligence tests is considered.
5. Rosenthal, R. "The Pygmalion effect lives." *Psychology Today*, September 1973, 7, 56–63. A summary of recent research on teachers' expectations and the effects of these expectations on students.
6. Vernon, P. (ed.) *Creativity: Selected readings.* Middlesex, England: Penguin, 1970 (paperback). A diverse assortment of studies by leaders in this area: on creative children and adults, attempts to measure creativity, and programs to train creativity. Also includes introspective material by a number of creative artists.

Answer Keys

SELF-QUIZ
1. d 2. b 3. c 4. b 5. c 6. a 7. c 8. d 9. d 10. c 11. a 12. a 13. b 14. a 15. a

EXERCISE 1
1. 71 2. 100 3. 133 4. 106

EXERCISE 2
1. R 2. SA 3. N 4. V 5. O 6. N 7. O (also R and V) 8. R 9. V

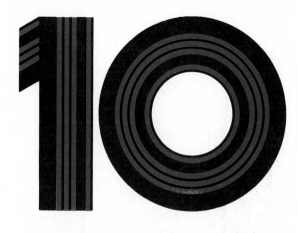

10
MOTIVATION

IN THIS CHAPTER
We begin by looking at the nature of motives and at some of the problems that arise when psychologists study motives. Then we focus on three motives: hunger, sex, and the achievement motive. After reading this chapter. you should be able to do the following:

1. Describe the relationship between needs, motives, and behavior
2. Describe four important types of motives
3. Explain why human motives are difficult to study
4. Explain how physiology, learning, and culture influence when people eat and stop eating and what foods they prefer
5. Describe how heredity, early eating practices, external food-related cues, and underexercising contribute to obesity
6. Describe how physiology, experience, and learning influence the human sex drive and human sexual practices
7. Explain how psychologists measure the achievement motive
8. Discuss the origin of the achievement motive and its influence on the behavior of men and women

In the early twentieth century, motives became an important subject in psychology, largely because of the efforts of William McDougall (1871–1938), an eminent British psychologist. McDougall believed that motives, or "instincts" as he called them, were irrational, compelling, inherited forces which shaped virtually everything people did, felt, perceived, and thought. Many early psychologists accepted McDougall's general view of instincts and set to work trying to identify the specific instincts which might account for all behavior. In 1908 McDougall himself published a list of twelve basic human instincts which included flight, repulsion, curiosity, pugnacity, self-abasement, self-assertion, child rearing, reproduction, hunger, gregariousness, acquisitiveness, and constructiveness (1). Many psychologists were dissatisfied with McDougall's brief list and proceeded to add other instincts—so many, in fact, that by 1924 a sociologist surveying the psychological literature found literally thousands of behaviors that had been classified as "instincts." The lists included "instincts" to be moral, to estimate the age of each passerby as one walks down a street, and to avoid eating apples in one's own orchard (2). Clearly, the concept of instincts was out of hand. One critic noted sardonically:

Man is impelled to action, it is said, by his instincts. If he goes with his fellows, it is the "herd instinct" which actuates him; if he walks alone, it is the "anti-social instinct"; if he fights, it is the instinct of pugnacity; if he defers to another, it is the instinct of self-abasement; if he twiddles his thumbs, it is the thumb-twiddling instinct; if he does not twiddle his thumbs, it is the thumb-not-twiddling instinct. Thus everything is explained with the facility of magic—word magic [3].

By the late 1920s most psychologists agreed that it was absurd to label every behavior an instinct. Such labeling did not contribute to

any real understanding of why organisms behaved as they did. After all, labeling is not explaining. The value of categorizing and classifying was also questioned. Instead, two other tasks appeared more important: (1) explaining the nature of a motive and (2) conducting scientifically sound investigations of specific motives. For more than thirty years psychologists have been concentrating their energy in these directions.

A Note on Terminology

Needs, motives, drives, and *instincts* are all hypothetical constructs whose existence is inferred from behavior. Psychologists use each of these terms in a specific way. We use the term *need* to refer to a bodily or felt social-psychological deficiency. We use the term *motive* to refer to an internal arousing state which results from a need and usually activates behavior aimed at fulfilling that need. We use the term *drive* to label certain motives such as hunger which appear to arise from fundamental physiological needs.

The term *instinct*, defined as an inborn drive which arouses complex behavior, has a controversial status. Some psychologists would like to see the term banned from our language because it implies that behavior patterns are innate, as they very rarely are, and because the term is frequently offered as an explanation when it is merely a label. On the other hand, many psychologists argue that the term instinct should be used—as long as it is used cautiously—to refer to certain behavior patterns in animals which appear to be (1) largely unlearned (those which appear without special experiences in the normal course of development), (2) typical of a single species, and (3) elicited by the presence of a particular stimulus pattern. For example, the adult male three-spined stickleback, a European fish, instinctively attacks other male sticklebacks during the mating period. The stickleback's aggression is generally labeled instinctive because experiments show that it does not depend on any particular prior experiences, it occurs regularly in all tested male sticklebacks of a particular age, and it is elicited by a highly specific stimulus configuration—any object at all with a red underside and a head-down position (see Figure 10-1).

How Do Motives Operate?

Psychologists assume that motives activate or arouse behavior. How do they operate? Let's look first at the *basic* or *primary drives*, motives which activate behavior aimed at fulfilling fundamental biological needs such as those for food, temperature regulation, water, and so on. In *The Wisdom of the Body* (published in 1932) physiologist Walter Cannon described the remarkable manner in which an animal's various bodily systems automatically maintain proper *equilibrium* (balanced) conditions. In people, for example, internal temperature is kept within certain critical limits centered about 98.6 degrees Fahrenheit and the concentration of elements such as salt, sugar, and calcium in the blood is automatically maintained at relatively constant levels. The body's self-regulating tendency is known as *homeostasis* (from the Greek words meaning "home state"). Whenever the automatic mechanisms in the body are unable to maintain a balanced state, a need is triggered in ways not fully understood. The need apparently activates a motive which causes the animal to take action to correct the imbalance.

We will assume for now that all motives operate in a similar way (see Figure 10-2). When a person's state departs from some internal reference level—which may be genetically programmed, learned, or a combination of the two—a need is stimulated. The

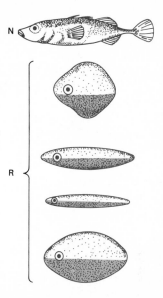

Figure 10-1. Five stickleback models: N is a carefully made true-to-life stickleback model without a red belly. The crude models, labeled R, have red bellies. In laboratory tests model N is less frequently attacked than the other models. (After Tinbergen, 1951.)

need activates a motive, and the motive triggers behavior which is usually directed at satisfying the need. If the behavior succeeds in satisfying the need, an equilibrium state returns. For example, when blood sugar concentration drops below a certain reference level, the body requires energy, the hunger motive is activated, and food-searching and food-consuming behavior become likely. After eating, blood sugar concentration rises and the body returns to its equilibrium with respect to energy.

This model is oversimplified, of course, but it serves a useful function. It enables psychologists to break down their grand question—How does a motive operate?—into some more manageable questions such as: How does a need activate a motive? How do motives produce behavior? And what roles do learning and physiology play in these various

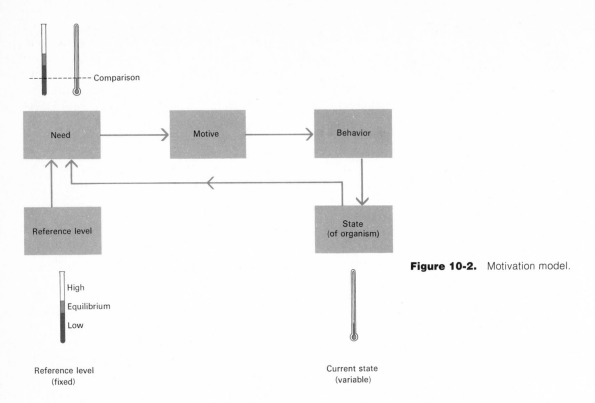

Figure 10-2. Motivation model.

processes? We turn now to several important types of motives.

Some Important Types of Motives

Psychologists are currently studying the following types of motives.

Basic drives. As we mentioned before, basic drives activate behavior aimed at satisfying the body's needs for oxygen, water, food, sex, urination, defecation, and pain avoidance. Later in this chapter, we will be looking closely at hunger and sex. Now we look briefly at pain avoidance. We define *pain* as a

specific sensation—such as stinging, burning, aching—which is distinctly unpleasant and is frequently associated with tissue damage. In actuality this sensation serves a very useful function. It signals danger and arouses a basic drive to remove its source.[1] Laboratory animals will learn many arbitrary responses, such as bar pressing or key pecking, to avoid

[1]Medical records indicate that a few individuals are born without pain sensitivity. This deficiency can lead to the neglect of serious injuries or diseases which may result in permanent bodily damage or even death. For instance, one seven-year-old girl without pain sensitivity had a special problem with burns. On several occasions the smell of burning flesh alerted her parents to the fact that she was leaning casually on a hot stove. Only direct parental intervention saved the child (4).

or escape pain resulting from electric shock. The motive to avoid pain is so strong that it sometimes leads people to confess to crimes that they did not commit, to betray friends and family, or to violate their most cherished ideals.

Sensory stimulation, manipulation, and exploration. An enormous amount of research shows that people and other animals require stimulation. When people are deprived of sensory stimulation, for example, for a prolonged period of time in prisoner-of-war camps, tedious jobs, or sensory-deprivation studies (see Chapter 5), they actively create their own—by daydreaming, singing, rehearsing past memories, talking to themselves, engaging in trivial routines, or even hallucinating. Recent research suggests that a person's stimulation-seeking behavior is relatively consistent; for example, a person who prefers spicy or unusual food is likely to favor complex designs to simple ones and to volunteer for unusual experiments. Some psychologists believe that each individual is genetically programmed for a particular optimum level of stimulation. Whenever the actual amount exceeds or falls below this level, people experience a need which activates a drive leading them to increase inadequate stimulation or to reduce overly intense stimulation (5).

The motive to explore and manipulate the environment, which is frequently called *curiosity*, is probably related to the need for sensory stimulation. A great deal of experimental evidence shows that monkeys have a basic curiosity motive. They will work a puzzle for no other reward than that which is intrinsic in doing it. They will learn a complex response for the opportunity to view their surroundings, in the same way that they will learn to obtain food when they are hungry or to avoid electric shock (6). Similarly,

curiosity appears to be an important motive for human behavior. Human infants normally scan their surroundings; it is obvious to observers that new sights and sounds excite them. Typically, young children are eager to mouth, touch, bite, and take apart the objects around them. Such varied adult pursuits as reading novels, climbing mountains, and conducting scientific research are probably also motivated—to some extent—by the need to explore and manipulate.

Social motives. People are social animals; that is, throughout their lives, they require contact with other people. Much of their behavior appears to be directed toward satisfying numerous social motives—to feel loved, accepted, approved, and esteemed, for example. From the very first, the human infant depends on others for survival—for warmth, food, water, and safety. If it were possible to design a computer to take care of these needs, infants would probably survive, but they would not develop normally without the sensory and social stimulation which adults usually provide, as we saw in Chapter 3. Parental warmth and acceptance also appear to be critical for successful adjustment in childhood and in later life. In fact, when children feel loved, conditions such as severe poverty, physical handicaps, and harsh discipline—which might otherwise impair development—appear to cause relatively little damage (7). Most psychologists believe that people continue to require human relationships all their lives. Some support for this notion comes from observations on a group of volunteers—scientists, military officers, and enlisted personnel—who gathered scientific data in the Antarctic for approximately a year. Occasionally, when individuals were particularly troublesome, the group ignored them completely. Isolates developed the "long eye" syndrome: They could not sleep;

they were prone to outbursts of crying; they neglected their personal hygiene and daily routines; and they appeared aimless and apathetic. As soon as the individual was accepted once again by the group, these symptoms of severe depression disappeared (8).

Growth motives. The motives we have discussed so far cannot explain why people strive for excellence or why they create symphonies or sophisticated theories about the origin of the universe. To explain this kind of behavior many psychologists assume that people have a need to develop and acquire competence and to actualize all their various potentials. This need presumably arouses a *growth* (or actualization) motive. Some psychologists believe that growth needs are programmed into our genes. Support for this idea comes from the observation that children all over the world struggle to coordinate their bodily movements, to talk, and to reason at approximately the same age—regardless of their specific circumstances. The late humanistic psychologist Abraham Maslow believed—and many other psychologists continue to believe—that growth motives lie at the core of human development. Maslow's evidence consisted primarily of observations which indicated to him that healthy children

"enjoy[ed] growing and moving forward, gaining new skills, capacities, and powers [9]." Other psychologists believe that behavior aimed at growth may be dictated—at least in part—by learning. American school children, for instance, are likely to strive for excellence in sports or academics because our society values these activities.

Maslow worked out a highly regarded motivational theory which integrates the growth needs (which he calls self-actualization needs) with other important needs. According to Maslow, people are born with five need systems, as shown in Figure 10-3.

The various physiological needs are placed at the bottom of the hierarchy. They are the most primitive needs, in Maslow's estimation, because they aim at remedying gross deficiencies necessary for bare survival. The need for safety is somewhat less primitive. Needs for love and belonging follow. Near the top of Maslow's hierarchy is the need to be esteemed—by oneself and others. The need for self-actualization comes last; it is the least primitive need and Maslow considered it the most important. Maslow believed that the lower needs tended to be more compelling and more insistent than the higher ones. He also thought that people worked their way up through the various motive systems. Tired and hungry people, for example, are caught up in their own physiological needs. Consequently, they cannot experience need states higher on the hierarchy. Once the physiological needs are satisfied, needs to feel protected, free of danger, and secure become apparent. When these needs are achieved, people seek to love and be loved. After these needs are fulfilled, they strive for status; they want to feel valued in their community, at work, and at home; and they want to respect themselves. Finally, people search for self-actualization: They struggle to realize their potential capabilities and to fulfill their ideals. Maslow believed that actualization needs

Figure 10-3. Maslow's hierarchy of needs.

which enhanced—and did not merely preserve life—predominated in healthy personalities, whereas deficiency needs (the other four need systems) predominated in unhealthy personalities. The evidence for Maslow's theory is controversial; no one has yet found a satisfactory way to investigate the concept of a needs hierarchy scientifically.

We have enumerated some important types of motives which psychologists are currently investigating. We focus now on some of the problems psychologists encounter when they study motives.

Special Problems in Studying Motives

Motives are difficult to study because they cannot be directly observed and their characteristics must be inferred from behavior. To study the motives of laboratory animals, such as rats, psychologists frequently deprive their subjects of something they need and assume that the animal's subsequent behavior will provide information about the motive that has been aroused to fulfill the need. For example, psychologists might isolate mature male from mature female rats for several weeks to activate a motive for sex. To assess the strength of the motive, the researchers might measure (1) how quickly their deprived subjects perform a specific response such as bar pressing, which they have learned will gain them access to a receptive female or (2) how much pain their subjects will endure— perhaps by crossing an electrified grid—to reach a receptive female.

Human motives are much harder to investigate through behavioral observations for a number of reasons:

1. A particular behavior can be aroused by several different motives or a combination of motives. Consider the act of reading this textbook. Your reading may be motivated by social motives such as a motive to comply with orders, to attain recognition, or to avoid failure and subsequent humiliation. On the other hand, you might be reading to satisfy growth motives—to increase your own understanding— or you might be reading for stimulation.

2. Diverse behaviors may satisfy the same need. You might fulfill a need to achieve excellence by becoming a track star, robbing a bank, solving a difficult mechanical problem, or capturing a rare butterfly.

3. Finally, motives do not always produce behaviors which lead to the satisfaction of a given need. Consider the plight of a small town adolescent girl with a need to love and be loved. She may not believe that there are suitable candidates around and spend most of her time daydreaming. Or, although she might be fascinated by the town's most eligible bachelor, she may not express her motive in behavior because she is anxious, or because she feels that she has no chance of success, or because she believes that she lacks the appropriate skills, or because she has other conflicting motives. In sum, particular human behaviors do not necessarily reflect the existence of the particular motives present.

An alternative to observation is the self-report method, but it also poses problems. The most serious one is that people are often *unaware* of their own motives. Sigmund Freud believed that people blocked their threatening motives, especially those concerned with sex or aggression, from conscious awareness. Many psychologists agree that people are frequently unaware of their motives—for a great variety of reasons. Obviously, people cannot accurately report what they are ignorant about.

To see how psychologists overcome these problems we turn to research on three motives—hunger, sex, and the achievement motive.

HUNGER

Eating is an important activity in all societies, particularly so in our own. Although many Americans overeat, statistics also indicate that a large number of them deliberately undereat. A 1964 survey showed that 25 percent of all Americans were watching their diets (10). Why is eating so important? Why do people eat? The answers to these questions lie, of course, in understanding the drive we call hunger. In this section we examine the biological and social-psychological factors which shape and control the hunger drive in people. We focus on the following questions: What physiological mechanisms regulate the hunger drive? How do learning and culture influence the hunger drive? How do specific hungers (appetites or drives for particular foods) arise? Finally, What causes obesity?

Physiological Mechanisms That Regulate the Hunger Drive

All animals need food to meet their daily requirements for energy, growth, and tissue repair. Although very few animals consciously regulate their food intake, most of them manage to consume the precise amount of food needed to accomplish these tasks—and no more. This is a rather miraculous feat when you consider what it involves. To maintain a constant body weight the number of calories a person takes in each day must balance the number of calories used. Every time we consume 3,500 calories more than we use, we gain a pound. Every time we forgo 3,500 calories that we need, we lose a pound. If people err by only 100 calories each day (by

eating an extra ounce of cheese or half a chocolate bar or by omitting a twenty-minute walk), they gain 10 pounds each year—50 pounds in five years. How do people and other animals know when to eat and when to stop eating?

The stomach, the mouth, and the throat. Many people link the hunger drive with the growling and groaning of their stomachs (stomach pangs) which frequently precede meals. So did early psychologists who were following the lead of physiologist Walter Cannon, who had demonstrated that the subjective sensations of hunger correlated with the presence of stomach contractions. In an ingenious study, Cannon had persuaded his research assistant, A. L. Washburn, to swallow a thin rubber balloon. Once the ballon reached Washburn's stomach, it was inflated so that it touched his stomach walls. Then, whenever Washburn's stomach contracted, the balloon was pinched, the air inside was compressed, and the air pressure at the end of the tube was recorded. While this was going on, Washburn was pressing a telegraph key, also attached to a recorder, every time he felt a hunger pang (see Figure 10-4). Analysis of the recordings showed that the reported hunger pangs and stomach contractions coincided quite consistently. Similar findings on additional human subjects led Cannon to the conclusion that stomach contractions were the prime mechanism signaling the brain of the body's need for food (11).

Soon after Cannon published his theory, contradictory evidence began to accumulate. When scientists took hungry rats and severed the sensory nerves joining their stomachs to their brains, they expected the surgery to radically interfere with the rats' ability to experience hunger, but it didn't. The rats continued to search for food, as though they were still hungry (12). Even when their stomachs were removed, rats became hungry—in

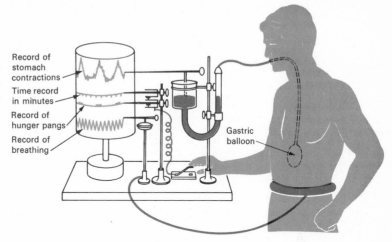

Figure 10-4. The apparatus used by Cannon to record stomach contractions and hunger pangs simultaneously. (After Cannon, 1934.)

Record of stomach contractions

Time record in minutes

Record of hunger pangs

Record of breathing

Gastric balloon

fact, more often than previously because they had less space to store their food (13). Later it was discovered that stomach contractions could occur persistently without hunger sensations (14). Observations such as these made it very clear that hunger signals did not originate primarily in the stomach.

It now appears that stomach contractions are learned by respondent conditioning (see Chapter 7). After a meal our stomachs must churn the food to digest it. When we eat regular meals each day, our brains seem to anticipate approximately an hour beforehand that our stomachs must get ready to work on the food. Accordingly, our brains send neural signals to alert the stomach muscles. These muscles then contract, producing the gnawing sensations which other parts of the brain interpret as signs of hunger.

The stomach does play a modest role in the short-term control of the hunger drive. After a normal amount of food is ingested, the stomach becomes distended. The distension of the stomach is one state our brains monitor to judge when we are full and should stop eating. The brain, working in conjunction with the mouth and throat, also monitors our intake. After a reasonable quantity of gulps or swallows—before any of the nutritive ma-

terials have been absorbed into the blood stream—the brain signals us to stop eating.

The composition of the blood. If the stomach does not signal the brain of hunger, what does? There is a good possibility that the composition of the blood serves this function. After a meal, powerful chemical substances in our saliva and stomachs, called *enzymes*, break the food down into protein, sugar, and fat molecules which the body can utilize. Within a few hours after a meal the molecules pass through the lining of the small intestine and are absorbed into the blood stream and circulated to the body's cells. One kind of sugar molecule, called *glucose*, is essential for supplying cells with energy. Scientists have found that the concentration of glucose in the blood stream is relatively high after a meal when people feel full and relatively low when people have not recently eaten and feel hungry. Laboratory studies also show that when rats who have just eaten a large meal receive an injection of insulin (a hormone ordinarily secreted by the pancreas which lowers the concentration of glucose in the blood stream), they begin to eat again—no matter how recently and how much they just ate. Other studies also suggest that glucose level is one of

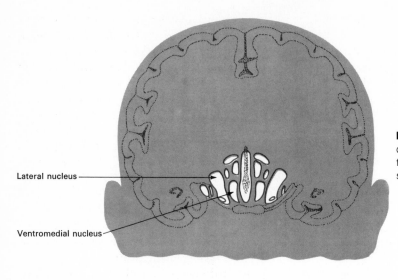

Lateral nucleus ——————

Ventromedial nucleus ——

Figure 10-5. The hypothalamus, consisting of groups of nerve cells in the central portion of the brain, is shown in white.

the important signals which tell the brain when it is time to eat and stop eating.

Figure 10-6. Removal of the ventromedial nucleus of the hypothalamus causes animals to overeat till they reach a size some three to four times their normal weight. (Dr. Neal E. Miller.)

The hypothalamus. The bundle of nerve cells called the *hypothalamus* lies in the central portion of the brain (see Figure 10-5). The hypothalamus contains cells which are sensitive to the concentration of glucose in the blood. When the glucose level drops very low, certain cells in the *lateral nucleus* of the hypothalamus, sometimes referred to as the "*feeding center*," become active and animals typically feel hungry. When scientists electrically stimulate these cells, they elicit feeding behavior—even in animals that have just eaten an enormous quantity of food. Moreover, the removal of the feeding center causes appetite loss; in fact, under these conditions animals may die of starvation even when food is readily available, unless they are fed forcibly. On the other hand, when the blood sugar level is high, cells in the *ventromedial nucleus* of the hypothalamus, sometimes referred to as the "*satiety center*," begin to fire rapidly and animals feel full. When scientists electrically stimulate these cells, animals stop feeding—even when they are literally starving. As we'd expect, the removal of this structure causes extreme overeating, until animals, like the rat pictured in Figure 10-6, reach a gigantic size some three to four times their normal weight. Recent studies suggest that these hypothalamic centers do not simply induce eating or its cessation; rather, they interact with each other and with other brain mechanisms to regulate the organism's weight level. An animal with a ventromedial lesion maintains its weight at a higher than normal level, whereas an animal with a lesion in the lateral nucleus maintains its weight at a lower than normal level (15).

The cerebral cortex. Although the exact nature of the link between the hypothalamus and higher brain centers is unclear, it is certain that higher brain centers are active in regulating the hunger drive. In 1971, Philip Teitelbaum, a physiological psychologist at the University of Illinois, published a study which showed that if rats with lesions in the feeding center were kept alive by forced feeding, they eventually began eating again of their own accord. When such animals were later deprived of a functioning cerebral cortex, they returned to their noneating pattern (16). The *cerebral cortex* probably interprets hypothalamic activity and initiates feeding behavior.

Do central brain mechanisms also direct the human hunger drive? In the late 1960s psychologist Eliot Stellar and two associates at the University of Pennsylvania devised a technique to explore this issue without opening up the brain. They had college student subjects come to their laboratory each morning for a liquid breakfast. Subjects in the first condition (oral intake) sucked Metrecal through a long straw from a container which was kept out of sight. Those in the second condition (pumped oral intake) pressed a button to pump Metrecal through the straw directly into their mouths, and subjects in the third condition (stomach intake) pressed a button to deliver Metrecal directly into their stomachs via a nasal tube. Note that people in

the oral-intake condition had cues about total intake from sucking and swallowing, those in the pumped oral-intake condition did not have the sucking cues, and those in the stomach-intake condition had neither sucking nor swallowing cues. The results showed that the subjects in the pumped oral- and stomach-intake conditions controlled their total intake of Metrecal approximately as accurately as those in the oral-intake condition. Interestingly, people in the stomach-intake condition could not specify what cues they had used. This study supports the notion that a central brain mechanism monitors many different physical systems to regulate the human hunger drive (17).

The physiology of the hunger-drive–regulating system is complex and by no means totally understood. In addition to these physiological mechanisms, a large number of other physical factors—such as disease and level of activity—also influence when we eat and when we stop eating. To complicate the picture further, learning and other social-psychological variables play an important role in regulating the human hunger drive.

Learning, Culture, and the Hunger Drive

Children learn a great many lessons about when to eat and when to stop eating from their families and cultures. The majority of these lessons are subtle. Parental practices establish how much food constitutes a serving and how many servings to allow per meal. Parents may also teach the child what state of stomach distension to label "full." For some "full" is signified by a heavy, painful, filled-with-lead sensation; for others, a much milder feeling suffices. Parents also set standards for how frequently and on what occasions eating is appropriate. Many children, for example, are taught to snack after school, before bed, and while watching television. Children may also be encouraged to eat under more unusual circumstances. Consider the following case. A mother might encourage her adolescent daughter to "eat a little something and you'll feel better" every time the girl appears to be unhappy or bored. Eating is pleasurable, and it typically takes the girl's thoughts off her unpleasant emotional state. It also pleases her mother. Eating under such circumstances is therefore reinforced by these pleasant consequences, so it is likely to occur frequently in similar situations. The adult who feels an "irresistible impulse" to eat during every emotional crisis is probably the product of this kind of conditioning. Learned associations also play a role in determining when people eat. If particular places or activities are associated repeatedly with eating certain foods, the places and activities themselves sometimes elicit feelings of hunger for the food. Movies and popcorn, football games and hot dogs, and TV and potato chips are common examples of this type of learning.

Current social conventions also influence when people eat. Still stuffed with breakfast, you might take coffee and a donut to be sociable at a coffee break. Or you might eat dessert at a dinner because it is offered and because refusing might be construed as "rude" or "unfriendly," even though you are not hungry.

Human hunger, then, is frequently controlled by *external food-related cues* like these. (We call these cues "external" because they are not directly related to internal physiological hunger cues such as hunger pangs, dizziness, or fatigue.) External food-related cues include the appearance of attractive food, the sight of others eating, the taste or aroma of a favorite dish, and particular places, times, or emotions. All these events can trigger eating even when people are satiated.

The Origin of Specific Hungers

Rats, cats, cows, pigs, chickens, and many other animals choose a well-balanced diet if they are allowed to pick their meals from a wide range of foods. Many animals also show specific hungers which lead them to actively seek out substances in which their diets are deficient. If psychologists put rats on a fat-free diet, for example, and then give them a choice between eating fat, sugar, or wheat, the animals show a marked preference for fat. Rats will also make up for deficiencies in sugar, protein, thiamine, riboflavin, salt, phosphorus, and calcium by showing specific hungers for foods high in these substances.

How do animals know what foods to choose? We do not understand the entire explanation for specific hungers, but taste appears to be an important variable. Some recent research indicates that certain taste preferences may be inborn (18). Moreover, when the taste nerves of rats with dietary deficiencies are severed, the animals stop correcting for the deficiencies. If the deficiencies are sufficiently severe, they may die, even though the foods that will correct the deficiency are available (19).

What about people? People appear to exhibit similar self-regulating tendencies—at least under certain conditions. One physician found that when infants chose their diets from a wide assortment of natural foods (harmful foods were not presented), they grew and thrived. In some cases, they even compensated for physiological deficiencies (20). People with Addison's disease, a condition which progressively destroys the adrenal cortex and prevents the retention of salt, frequently experience cravings for foods high in salt, such as ham and sauerkraut. In one case a thirty-four-year-old man with the disease put a $1/8$ inch layer of salt on his steak and mixed a half-glass full of salt with his tomato juice. Similarly, children with parathyroid deficiencies sometimes eat chalk, plaster, and other substances high in calcium; people with pernicious anemia may crave and consume enough liver to keep themselves reasonably healthy (21). We could cite many more examples. Note how well these specific hungers fit our model of motivation: A dietary deficiency causes the body to depart from an internal reference level producing a need for a particular substance. Presumably, the need arouses a drive and the drive activates behavior which returns the body to its equilibrium state.

Do specific hungers usually keep our diet balanced? How can we account for the drug addict or the alcoholic who forgoes food altogether or the adolescent who subsists on soft drinks, candy bars, ice cream, and the like? Obviously many food preferences are either learned or altered by experience. Psychologists at the Miami University in Ohio demonstrated this fact quite clearly. They gave female rats garlic-laced water while they were pregnant and nursing their young. Later, infants of these rats were compared with normally reared rats to see if they preferred plain or garlic-tasting water. Only rats whose mothers had quenched their thirst on garlic-laced water selected it (22). This study and others show that food-taste habits can be acquired at early ages and that animals can learn to prefer foods of dubious nutritional value.

The eating habits of various cultures provide additional informal evidence that tastes are heavily influenced by learning. One nutrition expert, Dorothy Lee, writes:

We do not recognize dragon-flies as human food; the Ifugao do. They eat three species of dragon-fly, as well as locusts which are boiled, then dried, then powdered and stored for food. They eat crickets and flying ants which they fry

in lard. They eat red ants and water bugs and a variety of beetles. I doubt that I would recognize these insects as food, however hungry I might be. On the other hand, I regard milk as food, a fluid which some cultural groups regard with disgust and as akin to a mucous discharge [23].

Inborn taste preferences probably helped primitive people select a balanced nutritious diet and avoid poisonous substances long before food experts arrived on the scene. Although biologically based taste preferences may continue to guide people's diets—at least over the long run—there is little question that learning in a culture and a family frequently override these preferences.

The Causes of Obesity

Approximately 35 to 40 percent of all middle-aged Americans are considered obese (24). The term *obese* is applied to people who have accumulated an excessive amount of adipose tissue (fat). The amount of adipose tissue is difficult to measure; so physicians usually label people who are 20 percent or more over their ideal weight "obese." What does obesity have to do with motivation? Obesity results when the controls on eating fail to operate correctly and people overeat—take in more calories than their bodies need to maintain an ideal weight. Although the word "obesity" is generally written as a singular noun, it might be more accurate to write it as a plural one, "obesities." In the mouse alone more than a dozen different genetically determined obesities have been identified. Mice also become excessively overweight when scientists put them on high-fat diets, or keep them immobile, or inject them with various chemicals, or alter their central nervous systems by surgery. The story is similar in human beings. Research indicates that obesity runs in families in patterns which suggest that heredity is involved. Early eating practices also appear to influence whether we will be fat or lean; so do our adult eating and activity patterns. In short, obesity is a complex condition with many causes.

Early eating practices. Studies by Jules Hirsch, a researcher at the Rockefeller Institute in New York, suggest that eating practices in infancy, childhood, and adolescence may shape the adult's figure. In an early study Hirsch separated the twenty-six offspring of two rat mothers into two groups, an affluent group of four and a deprived group of twenty-two. The rat pups then suckled in the large or small group throughout their infancy. At the time of weaning, the affluent subjects were all consistently fatter than the deprived subjects. What happened from this point was less predictable. The deprived and affluent rats were now offered the same quantity of food each day under standard laboratory conditions. Surprisingly, the deprived rats stayed slim; the affluent rats remained fat. Hirsch later found that the affluent rats had accumulated greater numbers of fat cells and that each cell was larger due to greater deposits of fat (25).

Studies on people confirm these results (26). The number of fat cells which adults carry around with them is established at an early age. Once the fat cells are manufactured, they cannot be removed. Some scientists believe that people who have been obese in childhood and who have consequently accumulated a large number of fat cells are likely to have an especially difficult time losing weight. People who have been obese as children have probably also developed eating habits that are likely to keep them fat.

External food-related cues and overeating. Many psychologists believe that overeating, alone or in combination with other factors, is the major cause of the current American obesity epidemic. This leads to the question—What causes overeating? Studies by Stanley Schachter, a psychologist at Columbia University, and his colleagues have provided some answers to this question. In a typical early study, obese and lean subjects came individually to the laboratory on an empty stomach. (They had been asked to omit either lunch or dinner.) After their arrival, half the subjects in each group were given sandwiches to eat so that they would be full; the remaining subjects were not fed and continued to be hungry. All the subjects were told that the psychologists were studying taste. Their task was to rate crackers in terms of how salty, cheesy, garlicky, etc. they tasted. They were told to help themselves to as many crackers as they needed to form an accurate impression. The rating procedure was a ruse. The investigators were really interested in how many crackers their lean and obese subjects would eat when their stomachs were empty or full. As you might suspect, the lean subjects ate more crackers when their stomachs were empty than when they were full. In contrast, the obese subjects consumed the same number of crackers under both conditions, suggesting that they were not "in touch" with their internal physiological state (27) (see Figure 10-7).

Much evidence substantiates the notion that overweight people are frequently insensitive to the state of their bodies in hunger-related situations. For example, there is a high positive correlation between the presence of stomach contractions and subjective reports of hunger in people of normal weight, but obese people report hunger only slightly more frequently when their stomachs are contracting (28). Moreover, although the internal turmoil produced by a fear-arousing experience generally interrupts the eating of slim people, it does not appear to affect the eating of stouter ones (29).

Schachter's studies also support the hypothesis that obese people appear to be ex-

Figure 10-7. The experimental design and results of Schachter's study.

1. Each subject came to the laboratory hungry.

2. Half of the lean and half of the obese subjects were given roast-beef sandwiches; the remaining subjects did not receive anything to eat.

3. The subjects were told that the study concerned taste. They were asked to rate five types of crackers and told that they could eat as many as they needed to make an accurate judgment.

4. The results: average number of crackers eaten by subjects in each group.

tremely sensitive to external food-related cues such as the sight of an attractively prepared food, the taste of food, the presence of others eating, or the places or times of usual meals (30); so overweight people may have a harder time resisting such temptations, no matter how recently they just ate.

Although oversensitivity to external food-related cues and undersensitivity to internal food-related cues could be the direct result of a physiological abnormality—say, in the hypothalamus or in some other part of the hunger-regulating machinery—in most cases these sensitivities are probably the result of experience. In contemporary America external food-related cues are everywhere tempting everyone. Few Americans ever find themselves far from a vending machine, a canteen, a short-order food joint, or a restaurant. Food is not only highly visible and readily available in our environment, it has also assumed an important role in human relationships—as a major recreation, as a way of celebration, and as a gesture of hospitality, friendship, and love. In view of these circumstances, it is hardly surprising that many people overeat and become fat.

Underexercising. At the same time that it is easy for Americans to overeat, it is also easy for them to be underactive. Although contemporary life can be hectic and tiring, it is often not physically exerting. We drive to work, to the grocery, and to the corner mailbox. We set dials, push buttons, and turn knobs as machinery provides most of the labor in homes, on farms, in cities, and in factories. In our modern technological society energy expenditure has become less and less necessary for survival. Jean Mayer, an eminent Harvard nutritionist, believes that underactivity may be a major cause of the current obesity epidemic in our country. Although everyone knows that exercise burns calories, Mayer's studies suggest that exercise serves an even more important function. In one study a group of rats was forced to exercise on a treadmill from one to ten hours each day for several weeks, while their food intake and body weight were measured. Later these experimental animals were compared with control subjects who had been left in their cages undisturbed for the same period of time. The rats who had been left in their cages ate more food than they needed and gained weight. The rats who had exercised for more than six hours each day ate less food than they needed and lost weight, whereas the rats who had exercised from one to six hours each day increased their food intake just enough to compensate for their increased energy expenditure. These results support the idea that an extreme lack of activity leads to overeating and overweight. They also show that bodily mechanisms may maintain weight quite accurately and precisely over a wide range of energy expenditure, but fail at the two extremes (31).

Summary: Hunger

1. Many physiological mechanisms play a role in regulating the hunger drive. The higher brain centers appear to monitor food intake and the distension of the stomach. In addition, structures in the hypothalamus (which appear to function to maintain weight at a particular level) detect the glucose concentration in the blood and send messages to the cerebral cortex to initiate or terminate feeding accordingly.
2. Hunger is also regulated by learning and experience in a particular culture. In our own culture many external food-related cues influence when we eat and when we stop eating.
3. Specific biologically based hungers moti-

vate many animals to eat a balanced nutritious diet and avoid poisonous substances. Taste preferences are also governed by learning. In people, unfortunately, learning and experience appear to be able to override the internal self-regulating mechanisms which call for a balanced diet.
4. Genetics, early feeding practices, external food-related cues, and underexercising all contribute to overeating and consequently to obesity.

THE SEX DRIVE

Although no one can live indefinitely without food, we could probably all survive an entire lifetime without sex. Of course, the human race would not survive. Psychologists usually classify the motive for sex as a basic physiological drive, because it is rooted in both the brains and endocrine systems of all higher animals and directed toward physiological goals—orgasm and reproduction. Although we consider sex a basic drive, learning and experience also play an important role in shaping sex-related behavior, especially in people. We will consider the following questions: What is the physiological basis for sexual motivation? How do experience and learning influence human sexual drives and practices?

The Physiological Basis of Sexual Motivation

The sex drive of lower animals appears to be primarily controlled by physiology. How do we know? When psychologists electrically stimulate a particular area of the male rat's posterior hypothalamus, they elicit a copulation response—if a receptive female is present. If the psychologists continue stimulating this area, the male rat copulates over and over again (32). Similar procedures evoke sexual behavior in complex animals such as monkeys. There is also considerable evidence that high concentrations of sex hormones in the blood stream elicit simple, stereotyped sexual behavior in lower animals. The female rat, for example, is receptive to the sexual advances of the male only at the time of her estrus cycle when her estrogen level is high and her eggs are ready to be fertilized, typically once every four or five days. At this time her aroused state leads to tension and restless activity; if she is placed near a male rat, she is likely to seek copulation actively by presenting herself in the proper receptive posture. Similarly, if psychologists inject a physiologically immature female rat with ovarian hormones, she will display mature sexual behavior. Aged female rats whose production of sexual hormones has ceased will once again make sexual responses if treated with ovarian hormones (33).

The sexual behavior of the male rat also appears to be controlled by his hormones, but to a lesser degree. In contrast to the female, he engages in sexual behavior as a juvenile, long before he is capable of the entire sexual act. When scientists castrate him (remove his testes and consequently shut off his major supply of sex hormones, the androgens) after puberty, his sexual activity is reduced but not completely abolished. When rats are castrated before puberty, their sexual behavior does not persist (34).

Is the human sex drive similarly controlled by physiological mechanisms? The answer seems to be to some extent, but by no means entirely. To investigate this issue psychologists have gathered information on patients who have undergone sex-related surgery, often for malfunctioning or diseased glands. In 1959, for example, Johan Bremer, the medical director of a hospital in Oslo, Norway, assessed the effects of castration on 157 Norwegian men. Of his subjects 74 reported

feeling "asexual" (no desire for intercourse) shortly after the surgery. Another 29 reported the same effect at some time during their first postoperative year. The remaining 54 claimed to be sexually active (both desirous and capable of intercourse) in the years following surgery. It is important to note that although castration reduced sexual activity in every case without exception, it did not necessarily terminate it (35). As a matter of fact, castrated men have been known to remain sexually active for twenty years and more. Moreover, many elderly men are still sexually competent even though their bodies have stopped producing large quantities of the androgens. Other studies show that men with undersized testes who are receiving testosterone replacement therapy (testosterone is the chief androgen hormone) frequently report increased sexual desire and activity (36).

The case of the human female is similar. Her sexual arousal also appears to be related to her hormonal level, but again not completely. Curiously, it is the androgens, the male sex hormones, that appear to influence her sex drive (37). When women undergo testosterone therapy after hysterectomies or during menopause, they frequently report increases in their sexual desire and activity (38). Of course, the sex drive of a woman is not completely under the control of her physiology. Women are not simply sexually receptive on particular days of peak hormonal activity; and both before puberty and after menopause—times when the ovaries are relatively inactive—women are often sexually responsive.

The human sexual response. Since the human sex drive is at least partly controlled by hormonal mechanisms, we would expect the human sexual response to be somewhat uniform. In the 1950s gynecologist William

Masters and psychologist Virginia Johnson began studying human sexual behavior in their laboratory. Initially, they paid prostitutes to undergo various sexual experiences (chiefly masturbation) while their physiological responses were recorded. Later they studied people as they engaged in heterosexual intercourse and other sexual practices—making simultaneous physiological measurements on each individual before, during, and after orgasm.

Although people vary widely in the specific ways that they satisfy their sexual drive, Masters and Johnson found that when sexually aroused, the human body exhibits a consistent pattern of physiological responses. The pattern can be divided into four stages: excitement, plateau, orgasm, and resolution. This simple classification is useful in conceptualizing a highly complicated process.

During the *excitement* phase, the sex drive builds rapidly or slowly depending on how aroused the person feels. At the same time there is increased muscular tension and vasocongestion (filling of the tissues with fluid) in response to sexual stimulation. Physiological changes (such as erection in the male and vaginal expansion and lubrication in the female) ready the body for the sex act.

The *plateau* phase follows. The muscles of the body continue to tighten and the blood frequently gathers at the body's surface. Men exhibit a single pattern: The excitement builds up to a high point, levels off, and is maintained for varying lengths of time. Women show several possible patterns. They may build up to a plateau as the man does, build up directly to orgasm, or remain in the plateau stage until resolution without orgasm.

The *orgasm* lasts several seconds, and it appears to play the same physical role for both men and women. It brings relief to blood swollen areas and tightened muscles which otherwise cause discomfort. Men's or-

gasms are physiologically similar. Masters and Johnson believe that women also experience one type of orgasmic reaction which varies widely in duration and intensity.[2]

The last stage of the sexual response is the *resolution*. During this phase, the body returns to its normal state as blood congestion is relieved and tightened muscles relax (41).

The Environmental Basis of Human Sexual Behavior

Although the human sex drive is inborn, the behavior patterns which satisfy it are not. Human sexual behavior is actively shaped by particular experiences within a particular culture. In our own society, as in most others, a tangle of laws, rules, conventions, and convictions regulate sexual conduct. Typically, societies teach their members which sexual prac-

[2]Masters and Johnson's comments on women's orgasms surprised many people. The traditional point of view among professionals and the general public alike had been that women didn't require orgasms. "After all, many women didn't experience them and still enjoyed sex," it was argued. Masters and Johnson countered that the double standard had interfered with the ability of many women to experience full physical sexuality and that women required orgasms physically in the same way that men did and were fully capable of them.

Women's orgasms are becoming less and less mysterious. Data from a study of 1,000 married women suggest that a woman's ability to experience orgasm depends on some simple straightforward parameters such as marital happiness, length of foreplay, and intromission. When intromission lasts sixteen minutes or more, only 5.1 percent of the women in this study failed to report experiencing orgasm; under these conditions over 80 percent of the women reported experiencing orgasm at least half of the time (39). Apparently, women are also particularly susceptible to psychological distractions during the sex act and must concentrate their undivided attention on their sexual experience to become aroused. In support of this observation one investigator found that women who reported being able to focus on their own physical sensations and on erotic fantasies during the sex act also reported orgasms a higher percentage of the time than other women (40).

tices are acceptable; that is, when, where, how, under what circumstances, and with whom people can express their sexuality. Anthropologists have noted wide disparities in the sex practices that various societies condone or condemn. People in the Melanesian Islands, for example, actively encourage homosexual activity in their adolescent boys (42). Among the Trobrianders, Sironon, Duson, and Plains Cree, lovers spend hours grooming and delousing one another as stimulation for sexual intercourse (43). Within a single society the various subgroups also adhere to distinctly different sexual customs. For instance, in the 1940s Alfred Kinsey, the famous investigator of American sexual practices, and his colleagues found that poorly educated, low-income groups tended to view any sexual activity besides coitus as perverse and distasteful; whereas well-educated, high-income groups experimented widely with sexual practices (44).

Our own society teaches contradictory attitudes toward sex. Whereas experts tell us that sex is both normal and healthy, and the mass media play up the glamour of sexuality, the Victorian heritage remains strong. Many parents actively discourage their children from expressing their sexuality. The child's many other training agents—relatives, teachers, religious leaders—frequently share the parents' attitude that sex is somehow "wrong," "dirty," or "unsavory." It is highly probable that the inhibition of sexuality in early childhood has a negative effect on adult sexual adjustment. In reviewing several cross-cultural studies one investigator found that societies which were relatively tolerant of children's sexuality had fewer adult complaints of impotence and frigidity (45). Further support for this hypothesis comes from informal clinical observations which indicate that when parents fail to accept their children's sexuality, problems—sexual inhibitions, chronic anxiety over sex, and sexual deviance—commonly

arise at some later date. Experimental data on dogs suggest a direct cause-and-effect relationship between early punishment for sexuality and later sexual inhibitions. In one study young male puppies were severely punished every time they mounted or nosed the genitals of other puppies (normal puppy behavior). As adults, these punished dogs refrained from making sexual advances to females in heat (46).

Cultures probably influence the sexual adjustment of their members by shaping their expectations, thoughts, and feelings about sex. Two popular American stereotypes are only beginning to change. American men are frequently expected to be virile Don Juans, continually interested in sex and ready to perform at any time. American women are often expected to inhibit their sexuality to conform to cultural standards for ladylike behavior. These expectations make sex frightening for large numbers of people. Men are sometimes afraid of not being able to perform as expected; women of humiliation, rejection, or loss of love. Fear, as we will see in Chapter 11, stimulates the secretion of particular hormones which ready the body to face an emergency. This bodily reaction tends to interfere with sexual arousal.

The many differences in sexual behavior that are seen within a particular culture are undoubtedly learned. In some cases the learning is direct: People are instructed by parents, friends, books, or teachers on appropriate sexual behavior. Certain kinds of sexual behavior are also reinforced or punished by the reactions of other people. Respondent conditioning appears to be particularly important in determining the people, places, and circumstances that elicit sexual arousal. When a stimulus, such as a particular perfume, which does not initially arouse sexual feelings, is paired with a satisfying sexual experience, the stimulus itself may become sexually-arousing. Similarly, if a pleasant sexual encounter occurred in a glue factory, the sights and smells of the glue factory might later evoke sexual arousal. *Fetishes* (special objects which some people consider essential for full sexual satisfaction) appear to originate when a particular object is accidentally paired with a pleasurable sexual experience. In one case a young woman complained to her counselor that she needed to wear high-heeled shoes to engage in satisfying sexual intercourse. It gradually emerged that as a youngster the young woman had frequently dressed in her mother's high-heeled shoes. Whenever she had squatted, her genitals had rubbed against the shoes and the shoes had consequently become associated with sexual pleasure.

Homosexuality and lesbianism may repre-

Figure 10-8. Lesbians Barbara Love (left) and Sidney Abbott, coauthors of *Sappho Was a Right-On Woman,* a book that examines the social, political, and psychological climate of their lives. (Chie Nishio, Nancy Palmer Photo Agency.)

sent yet another instance of respondent conditioning. In 1974 it was estimated that approximately 4 million men and between 1 million and 2 million women in the United States regarded themselves as homosexuals or lesbians (47). Hormonal, genetic, and other biological variables can account for only a tiny fraction of these cases (48). Respondent conditioning is a plausible explanation if we assume that all human beings are normally capable of choosing persons of either sex as sex partners. Many psychologists reason that most Americans become heterosexual because our society generates strong pressures which move men and women toward one another. However, when satisfying sexual experiences with members of the opposite sex fail to occur or satisfying sexual experiences with members of the same sex occur repeatedly, individuals of the same sex may come to be associated with sexual fulfillment. At the same time cognitive factors probably enter in. Once a person begins to view himself or herself as "homosexual" or "lesbian," the label colors the self-image and affects sexual fantasies. It probably also influences the person's choice of friends and, consequently, the nature of future relationships. The preference for a partner of the same sex may be stamped in even more strongly if experiences with the opposite sex are unpleasant or fear-arousing and keep the person from associating with that sex. Thus the basic learning dynamics of homosexuality and lesbianism may include both positive respondent conditioning to members of the same sex and negative respondent conditioning to members of the opposite sex.

Summary: The Sex Drive

1. Sex is a biological drive which is necessary for species survival.
2. The sexual behavior of most lower animals appears to be largely controlled by their

physiology. Physiology also plays some role in regulating human sexual conduct but the effects of learning and experience are also important.

3. People learn sexual attitudes and practices through social norms, direct instruction, reinforcement, punishment, and respondent conditioning.

THE ACHIEVEMENT MOTIVE

The hunger and sex drives are clearly necessary for survival—for the individual person or the entire human race. In addition, both are rooted in physiology. The achievement motive, or the *need to achieve* as researchers generally call it, may be defined as a motive to pursue excellence, to accomplish lofty goals, or to be successful in difficult tasks. The achievement motive is not obviously necessary for survival today, and it has no obvious physiological basis. Psychologists categorize this motive in various ways. When the satisfaction of a particular individual's potentialities is considered the goal, then the achievement motive is considered a *growth motive.* When competition between people is stressed, then the achievement motive is classified as a *social motive.*

How does the achievement motive fit our motivation model? Presumably, certain people experience a need to achieve—probably because of experiences in a particular culture and a particular family, as we shall see. That felt need arouses a motive, and the motive activates behavior aimed at satisfying the need. The attainment of excellence probably reduces the need—at least to some extent. Although the need may be reduced by various successes, it is unlikely that any one attainment ever satisfies the need completely.

In this section we look first at how psychologists measure the achievement motive, then we explore the research on how it arises and how it influences the behavior of men and women.

Measuring the Achievement Motive

Can you think of any ways to measure the achievement motive? Many students initially suggest, "Measure how much people actually achieve," but, as we have mentioned before, motives are not automatically translated into relevant behavior. You may know people who appear to have a strong motive to achieve but who lack the ability, perseverance, opportunities, or freedom from anxiety to pursue their achievement needs.

In the 1930s a Harvard psychologist named Henry Murray came up with an ingenious method for measuring social motives. Murray believed that people's motives might be accurately reflected in what they ordinarily thought about—when they were not under pressure to think about anything in particular. The problem was to pinpoint these everyday thoughts. Psychologists could ask people, of course, but as we have mentioned repeatedly, self-reports are not always valid. Murray decided to ask people to tell stories about certain pictures, like the one shown in Figure 10-9. Most of the pictures depicted a single person or group of people in an ambiguous situation. The subject answered such questions as What is happening? What led up to this situation? What are the people thinking about? What will happen later? Murray believed, and many psychologists agree, that as people tell stories about ambiguous pictures, they *project* their needs and motives, as well as their fears, hopes, conflicts, and emotions, onto their characters. For this reason, Murray's test, known as the *Thematic Apperception Test (TAT),* is considered a *projective* method of assessing motives. The test is widely used by clinical psycholo-

Figure 10-9. An ambiguous situation like those depicted in Murray's Thematic Apperception Test.

gists to measure approximately twenty social motives. To evaluate the strength of a given motive, psychologists informally note the storyteller's recurring themes and images or formally score the stories according to specific rules that have been developed for this purpose.

In the 1950s David McClelland, John Atkinson, Russell Clark, and Edgar Lowell, psychologists then at Wesleyan University, adopted the TAT for measuring the achievement motive. First they set up conditions which were designed to arouse the achievement motive, then they presented their subjects with four or five ambiguous TAT pictures which could be interpreted as reflecting an achievement theme. A picture like the one shown in Figure 10-10 appeared on one version of the test and inspired the following stories:

The boy is thinking about a career as a doctor. He sees himself as a great surgeon performing an operation. He has been doing minor first aid work on his injured dog, and discovers he enjoys working with medicine. He thinks he is suited

for this profession and sets it as an ultimate goal in life at this moment. He has not weighed the pros and cons of his own ability and has let his goal blind him of his own inability. An adjustment which will injure him will have to be made [49].

A young fellow is sitting in a plaid shirt and resting his head on one hand. He appears to be thinking of something. His eyes appear a little sad. He may have been involved in something that he is very sorry for. The boy is thinking over what he has done. By the look in his eyes we can tell that he is very sad about it. I believe that the boy will break down any minute if he continues in the manner in which he is now going [50].

Which story contains the most achievement-related imagery (images which reflect competing, striving, winning, accomplishing, and the like)? Although the second story contains few, if any, such images, the first is clearly dominated by them. Subjects' scores on the test are based on the amount of achievement-related imagery which they produce and are believed to reflect the intensity of their need for achievement (this phrase is usually abbreviated n-Ach). Incidentally, McClelland and his associates have established precise scoring criteria for evaluating achievement-related imagery.

The test for n-Ach sounds reasonable, but does it work? Many research findings indicate that it does. When psychologists use the rules developed by McClelland and his group, they can score a given story with high reliability (very consistently). There is also quite a bit of evidence that the test is valid (that it measures what it sets out to measure) (see Chapter 9).

How the Achievement Motive Arises

Like many other social motives, the achievement motive probably arises in response to a combination of cultural and individual learn-

Figure 10-10. Pictures like this one are used to measure the achievement motive. (Rogers, from Monkmeyer.)

ing experiences. An innate need may also influence it. Consider the cultural factor first. Traditionally, Americans have valued high achievement. Slogans such as "work hard," "be first," and "get ahead" spur many people on to excellence in our culture. Moreover, our society frequently rewards achievement by financial gains and high status; so it is hardly surprising that many American children develop a motive to achieve.

If culture were the only determinant of n-Ach, then all Americans would have equally strong achievement motives. But they don't—at least not as measured by the n-Ach test. What causes the differences? Apparently, children—or at least boys (psychologists have studied the achievement motive primarily in boys)—learn the achievement motive in their homes. Research shows that the parents of boys with high n-Ach stress the importance of achievement and reward their sons for achieving—becoming leaders, making friends, attempting difficult tasks by themselves, and persisting to success without help (51). Typically such parents are also emotionally involved in their sons' performances—so much so, in fact, that they may be considered downright pushy and domineering. They also frequently set high standards

of excellence and raise their expectations as their sons grow older. Parents of boys with low n-Ach, in contrast, tend to emphasize virtues such as politeness, cleanliness, and compliance with authority, and they are less likely to encourage and support their son's achievements with any consistency (52).

The achievement motive may also be influenced by physiological factors. Many psychologists believe that the growth motives (see page 280) which lead people to develop and acquire competence and to actualize their basic potential are inborn. The achievement motive, which aims at mastery and excellence, can be seen as a similar motive. It may actually have had survival value for our ancestors. The best hunters probably got the largest and choicest share of the food and the most desirable caves.

Achievement Motives and Behavior: Men Only

Psychologists have accumulated a large body of information on how males with strong achievement motives (as measured by the modified TAT) behave in achievement-related situations. One popular research strategy is to identify large numbers of male subjects who are high or low in n-Ach and then observe their behavior in a controlled laboratory setting to see how they differ. Intelligence is usually taken into account so that investigators can attribute significant differences to the achievement motive alone. Among the many findings are the following: Males with high n-Ach tend to be persistent in achievement situations; for example, they work harder and longer on various problem-solving tasks in the laboratory, and for that reason they tend to be more successful on such tasks than males with low n-Ach (53). Persistence may also be responsible for the finding that male high school and college students high in n-Ach frequently make better grades in school than students low in n-Ach (54). Males with high n-Ach also prefer to attempt problems on which they have a moderate (as opposed to a very high or very low) chance of success. When the possibility of succeeding at a task is small, victory is unlikely, of course. Conversely, when a task is very easy, success appears hollow. So neither extremely high- or low-risk tasks—when they depend primarily on abilities or skills— appeal to the male with high n-Ach (55).

Although these behaviors are generally characteristic of males with high n-Ach, the conduct of any particular male in any particular achievement-related situation is determined by many factors which psychologists John Atkinson, Norman Feather, and their colleagues have been active in specifying. Laboratory findings have led Atkinson and Feather to formulate a model which appears to be useful in predicting how a given individual will *behave* in a particular achievement-related situation. According to this model, the tendency to act to achieve success in a specific setting depends not only on the strength of a particular individual's motive to achieve, but also on the immediate situation—particularly the individual's expectation of reaching an immediate goal, the

value placed on succeeding at that goal, and achievement-related anxiety arising from fear of failing (56).

Achievement Motives and Behavior: Women Only

What about women? Until recently, studies of women's achievement motives were comparatively rare. The research findings that existed were inconsistent. They were also at variance with the data on the achievement motive in men and with theories of achievement motivation in general. Matina Horner, now of Harvard University, was one of the first psychologists to investigate the basis for these sex differences systematically. Looking at the research literature, Horner found that American women consistently showed greater anxiety in test situations than men did. Psychologist Eleanor Maccoby had suggested that "the girl who maintains qualities of independence and active striving (achievement orientation) necessary for intellectual mastery defied the conventions of sex appropriate behavior and must pay a price, a price in anxiety [57]." Horner reasoned that women may feel anxious in achievement-oriented situations for two reasons: They fear the negative consequences of failure, just as men do; in addition, they also fear success, since it is considered unfeminine in our society.

Horner tested her hypothesis on a sample of college men and women at the University of Michigan. In one study each student read a cue and constructed a story around it (a modification of the TAT technique). Women received the cue, "After first-term finals Anne finds herself at the top of her medical school class . . . ." Men received the same cue about John. Horner scored these stories for the *motive to avoid success* (defined as a learned social motive aroused by competitive situations when people fear success will bring negative consequences). Then, she classified the imagery into three categories, as follows:

CATEGORY 1—Success brings strong fear of social rejection. One response in this category read: "Anne doesn't want to be number one in her class. . . . She feels she shouldn't rank so high because of social reasons. She drops down to ninth in the class and then marries the boy who graduates number 1."

CATEGORY 2—Success produces guilt, sadness, and doubt about being normal. For example: "Anne feels guilty. . . . She will finally have a nervous breakdown and quit medical school and marry a successful young doctor."

CATEGORY 3—Success is denied by changing or distorting the cues to absolve the person of responsibility for success. For example: "Anne is a code name for a nonexistent person created by a group of med students. They take turns writing exams for Anne."

In general, the results confirmed Horner's hunch about the motive to avoid success. Approximately 65 percent of the women told stories about Anne that fell in these three categories, whereas fewer than 10 percent of the men told stories about John that fell in these categories (58).

To learn more about the achievement motive and achievement-related behavior of women, psychologists are currently researching such questions as the following: How can the achievement motives of women be more accurately measured? How prevalent is the motive to avoid success? Do women continue to display more achievement-related fears than men? As standards for acceptable feminine conduct change, we should expect to find dramatic changes in women's achievement-related motives and behavior.

Summary: The Achievement Motive

1. The achievement motive, commonly considered a growth or social motive, is measured by having subjects construct stories about TAT pictures which are later scored for achievement-related imagery.
2. The achievement motive appears to be the product of cultural and individual learning factors. An innate need for competence may also underlie this motive.
3. Men with high n-Ach generally persist in achievement situations both in the laboratory and in real life. They also tend to prefer taking moderate risks as opposed to very high or very low ones to achieve success.
4. To predict how specific individuals will perform in particular achievement situations it is necessary to consider their achievement motives, expectations of success in that situation, values placed on task success, and achievement-related fears of failure.
5. Women tend to perform differently than men on TAT measures of the achievement motive and in achievement situations. One explanation is that they are frequently more anxious than men in such settings because both failure and success have negative consequences.

STUDY GUIDE 10

Key Terms. need, motive, drive, instinct, homeostasis, primary drives (basic drives), motives for sensory stimulation and manipulation and exploration, social motives, growth motives, hierarchy of needs, enzymes, glucose, hypothalamus, lateral nucleus ("feeding center"), ventromedial nucleus ("satiety center"), cerebral cortex, external food-related cues, specific hunger, obese, "obesities," hormones, excitement, plateau, orgasm, resolution, fetish, need to achieve (n-Ach), Thematic Apperception Test (TAT), projective test, reliability, validity, motive to avoid success.

Important Research. stomach contractions and hunger pangs (Cannon), cerebral cortex and hunger in rats (Teitelbaum), central processes and hunger in college students (Stellar), early eating practices and obesity (Hirsch), external food-related cues and obesity (Schachter), underexercising and obesity (Mayer), castration and sexual activity (Bremer), physiological responses to sexual excitement (Masters and Johnson), measuring social motives (Murray), measuring the achievement motive (McClelland, Atkinson, Clark, and Lowell), situational determinants of achievement motivation (Atkinson and Feather), sex differences in achievement motivation (Horner).

Basic Theories. McDougall's ideas about instincts, the motivation model, Cannon's concept of homeostasis, Maslow's hierarchy of needs.

Self-Quiz

1. To be classified as an instinct, a behavior pattern must be [**a**] elicited by a particular stimulus; [**b**] largely unlearned; [**c**] typical of all members of a species; [**d**] all of the above.

2. Psychologists call motives which activate behavior aimed at fulfilling basic biological needs [**a**] biologically based motives; [**b**] primary drives; [**c**] homeostatic motives; [**d**] stimulation motives.

3. Monkeys (and children) will learn to work puzzles for no other reward than just working the puzzles. This is considered evidence of a [**a**] cognitive motive; [**b**] curiosity motive; [**c**] superior intellect; [**d**] growth motive.

4. According to Maslow's theory, people are governed by which of the following needs hierarchies? [**a**] physiological, esteem, love, security, self-actualization; [**b**] self-actualization, love, safety, esteem, physiological; [**c**] physiological, safety, love, esteem, self-actualization; [**d**] physiological, safety, esteem, love, self-actualization.

5. Which of the following is *not* a problem in studying human motives? [**a**] People are often unaware of their own motives; [**b**] a single need may be satisfied by a variety of behaviors; [**c**] a single behavior may be provoked by a variety of needs; [**d**] people's needs vary.

6. It is currently believed that stomach contractions occur because [**a**] animals are genetically programmed so that stomachs contract when they are empty; [**b**] brains learn to anticipate regular meals and send neural signals to prepare the stomach muscles to digest the anticipated meal; these muscles then contract; [**c**] as soon as the hypothalamus detects that blood sugar is low, it sends signals directly to the stomach and the stomach contracts to signal people to eat; [**d**] stomach acids cause the stomach to contract when there is no food for them to digest.

7. When the lateral nucleus of the hypothalamus (the "feeding center") is removed from a rat's brain, [**a**] another part of the hypothalamus takes over its functions; [**b**] rats overeat until they become three to four times their normal size; [**c**] rats refuse to eat and may starve to death if they are not force-fed; [**d**] rats rely on hunger signals from the cerebral cortex, the ventromedial nucleus, the stomach, and the throat.

8. To control their eating, which cue are normal-weight people more likely than obese people to use? [**a**] the sight of attractive food; [**b**] the presence of other people eating; [**c**] the times of day associated with meals; [**d**] stomach contractions.

9. Which is *not* a reason that sex is considered a basic physiological drive? [**a**] It is rooted in the nervous and endocrine systems; [**b**] it is directed toward physiological goals—orgasm and reproduction; [**c**] performance of the sex act decreases hormones that would otherwise interfere with health; [**d**] it is necessary for species survival.

10. Masters and Johnson found that the four stages of sexual response occur in which order? [**a**] excitement, plateau, orgasm, resolution; [**b**] excitement, plateau, resolution, orgasm; [**c**] excitement, resolution, plateau, orgasm; [**d**] plateau, excitement, resolution, orgasm.

11. Cross-cultural studies indicate that in societies which are relatively tolerant of children's sexual behavior, adults [**a**] are likely to have a high incidence of adjustment problems; [**b**] rarely complain

of sexual problems; [**c**] engage widely in sexual perversions; [**c**] have little enthusiasm for or interest in sex.

12. Which of the following is currently believed to be *least* likely to influence human sexual preferences? [**a**] cultural expectations; [**b**] genetic predispositions and hormone levels; [**c**] respondent conditioning; [**d**] reinforcement and punishment.

13. The achievement motive is usually measured by [**a**] assessing how much people actually achieve; [**b**] evaluating people's responses to questions about lifestyle and life goals; [**c**] observing people's behavior in an achievement setting, usually in a laboratory; [**d**] scoring people's stories about ambiguous pictures.

14. Men with high n-Ach are likely to do all of the following *except* [**a**] prefer to attempt problems on which they are assured of success; [**b**] earn better grades in school than low n-Ach students; [**c**] be persistent in achievement situations; [**d**] have some anxiety about the possibility of failing.

15. In studying sex differences in achievement motives among college students, Matina Horner found that [**a**] men and women had basically similar needs for achievement; [**b**] women viewed the success of a woman character positively, whereas men viewed it negatively; [**c**] women had stronger achievement motives than men, possibly because it was more difficult for women to get into the college where Horner tested her subjects; [**d**] the majority of women—but less than 10 percent of the men—demonstrated a need to avoid success.

Questions to Consider

1. Consider the motivation model described and illustrated on pages 277–278. How well does it work for physiological motives such as hunger? for curiosity? for social motives? for growth motives? Can you think of any ways to conceptualize motivation that would work well for all types of motives?

2. Describe Maslow's hierarchy of needs. Can you think of any ways to test it?

3. How would you apply Maslow's hierarchy-of-needs concept if you were trying to enhance learning in a third-grade classroom?

4. For a day or two observe the circumstances which immediately precede your own eating. Do you eat primarily in response to internal cues, external cues, or a combination of the two?

5. Based on your reading in this textbook, what practices should parents follow to make certain that their children are not obese either in childhood or later on?

6. Describe how learning has influenced your sexual attitudes and behavior.

7. Make a list of parental behaviors that do and do not encourage the development of the achievement motive, according to the text. Arrange the items on your list in a random order and insert a few unrelated items as distractors. Then ask your parents to rate all items on a one- to five-point scale describing how much they emphasized each practice as you were growing up. Are your parents more similar to the parents of males with high or low n-Ach? Is your own motive for achievement correspondingly high or low? Explain your findings.

Project 10: Studying the Achievement Motives of College Students

Matina Horner's early research suggested that American men seek success, but American women fear it. Horner reached this conclusion in part by analyzing college students' responses to an imaginary success story in which the main character was male for male students and female for female students. The differences Horner found may have been more powerfully influenced by the sex of the character in the story than by the subject's personal motives. For this project you will be repeating part of Horner's study with some modifications to see if you come up with the same results.

Method. Find four cooperative college students, two men and two women. Do not tell them the purpose of the project until after you have collected your observations. You will be testing each subject individually.

Write or type the two versions of the following "stories" on separate sheets of paper. You will need two copies of each of the four "stories." "After first-term finals, Anne (John) finds herself (himself) at the top of her (his) medical school class." "John's (Anne's) law professor has just given him (her) some good news. John's (Anne's) paper on constitutional law has won him (her) a scholarship in a national contest."

You will be presenting two stories to each subject. Half your male and female subjects should read about Ann, the medical student, and John, the law student. The other half should read about John, the medical student, and Anne, the law student. We are using two different stories to minimize suspicion about the real purpose of the study, and we are changing the sex of the protagonist in each story to minimize the effects due to the particular story.

Test each subject in a quiet place free from distractions. Give the subject one paper at a time and ask him/her to "write a story that begins with the sentence(s) on the paper." If the subject asks how long to make the story, indicate that a paragraph would be a good length.

After the subject has written both stories, mark his/her sex on the paper.

Results. Collect all eight stories and read and analyze them for evidence of the achievement motive and the motive to avoid success. Although special training is required to score these stories accurately, you can score them roughly by using the following guidelines. Count one point for each separate idea reflecting one of the motives. To score the achievement motive (AM), look for comments about competing, winning, striving, accomplishing, and succeeding. To score the motive to avoid success (MAS), look for comments implying that success brings social rejection, guilt, sadness, doubt about being normal, or personal problems and denial of success. To practice your scoring, examine the following story and score sentences numbered 1, 2, and 3.

PRACTICE STORY

Anne is delighted with her success because she hopes to be a famous surgeon (no. 1 _____). She is also happy because her parents will be proud of her (no. 2 _____). She is a little worried, though, that her boyfriend may be unhappy because he didn't do as well (no. 3 _____).

You should have scored sentence 1—1 AM, sentence 2—1 AM, and sentence 3—1 MAS.

After scoring your subjects' stories, summarize your results by tallying the total number of points in the categories below.

Category of Story	Number of Stories	Total Points	
		Motive to Achieve	Motive to Avoid Success
1. Male subjects, "John"	2		
2. Male subjects, "Anne"	2		
3. Female subjects, "John"	2		
4. Female subjects, "Anne"	2		

1. To see if you found the same results as Matina Horner, compare categories 1 and 4. Recall that Horner found people in category 1 low on the motive to avoid

success and people in category 4 high on the motive to avoid success.

2. Combine the results of categories 1 and 2 and categories 3 and 4 to see if you found overall differences due to sex of subject (ignoring sex of character).

3. Add the results of categories 1 and 3 and categories 2 and 4 to see if the sex of the character in the story influenced the amount and type of achievement imagery produced.

Discussion. Consider the following questions.

1. Did you find that men and women differed in either motive? How can you explain your findings?

2. Does the sex of the main character influence whether stories contain a predominance of achievement motive or motive to avoid success imagery? How can this result be explained?

3. If you had done a similar study, using stories about achievement in a traditionally feminine role, such as winning a beauty contest or receiving a good mother award instead of achievement in a traditionally masculine role, what results might you have obtained?

4. How could you validate your test of the achievement motive and the motive to avoid success?

Suggested Readings

1. Cofer, C. *Motivation and emotion.* Glenview, Ill.: Scott, Foresman and Company, 1972 (paperback). A brief discussion of how psychologists conceptualize and study motivation and emotion.

2. Schachter, S. "Some extraordinary facts about obese humans and rats." *American Psychologist*, 1971, 26, 129–144. Schachter describes his fascinating research on obese humans and shows some dramatic parallels between their behavior and the behavior of rats with ventromedial hypothalamic lesions.

3. Stuart, R., & B. Davis. *Slim chance in a fat world. The behavioral control of obesity.* Champaign, Ill.: Research Press, 1972 (paperback). Discusses psychological research on obesity and weight loss and describes a program for controlling obesity based on psychological principles.

4. Beach, F. "It's all in your mind." *Psychology Today*, July 1969, 3, 33–35, 60. Discussion of how the brain functions in sexual behavior.

5. Brecher, R., & E. Brecher. *An analysis of human sexual response.* Boston: Little, Brown and Company,

1966 (paperback). Very readable account of Masters and Johnson's early research.

6. Tresmer, D. "Fear of success: popular, but unproven." *Psychology Today*, March 1974, 7, 82–85. A critical look at Horner's original study, at the motive to avoid success, and at recent developments in this research.

Answer Key

SELF-QUIZ
1. d 2. b 3. b 4. c 5. d 6. b 7. c 8. d 9. c 10. a 11. b
12. b 13. d 14. a 15. d

11

EMOTION

The case of Julia P.

When Julia P. was eighteen months old, she had encephalitis, a rare brain infection which was accompanied by a high fever. Although she appeared to recover completely at the time, Julia began having "spells" around the age of ten which seemed to be attributable to the earlier illness. During these "spells" Julia would, suddenly and for no apparent reason, become increasingly terrified. If the "spell" occurred in school, she sometimes attacked a schoolmate. At other times she ran miles until the fear subsided.

A serious incident occurred when Julia was sixteen. While attending a movie with her parents, Julia felt sick and went to the ladies' lounge. When she looked in the mirror, her body seemed to be shriveling up. As she stared in horror at the image, a strange young girl accidentally brushed against her arm. Instantly, Julia grabbed for a small pocket knife which she usually carried with her and stabbed the girl repeatedly.

The stranger's life was saved; Julia was committed to a mental hospital. Despite many valiant attemps to treat her, the problem seemed only to be growing worse. The "spells" occurred more frequently and finally culminated in the stabbing of a nurse with a scissors.

Eventually, Julia's parents decided to take her to a Boston hospital to consult with Vernon Mark and Frank Ervin, two physicians of the Harvard Medical School, who had worked with cases like Julia's before. Measurements of the electrical activity in Julia's brain led Mark and Ervin to suspect that scar tissue deep within the brain was causing Julia's emotional outbursts. To be certain, they implanted radio-controlled electrodes in various parts of Julia's amygdala (the brain region suspected of triggering the attacks) (see Figure 11-3). Using this procedure (which is not painful), Mark and Ervin were able to record from and stimulate Julia's brain as she moved freely about the hospital ward.

As she was sitting in her bedroom one day, the record of brain activity showed that an abnormal epilepticlike seizure was occurring within the amygdala. Moments later, Julia ran to the bedroom wall, her teeth bared, her fists clenched—as if to attack. The seizure activity subsided and Julia returned to normal soon afterwards.

Now that Mark and Ervin had confirmed that the amygdala was involved, they had to locate the specific region that was causing the problem. To do that, they directly stimulated various brain sites to see if they could reproduce these "rage episodes." One day as Julia was sitting in her room playing her guitar, singing enthusiastically, and talking to a young doctor, Mark and Ervin turned the current on at contact 3 in the right amygdala. A few seconds later, Julia stopped singing and a blank stare crept over her face. When asked how she felt, Julia did not respond. Instead, she grabbed the guitar, swung it at the doctor's head, missed narrowly, and smashed it against the wall.

After making certain that the stimulation of the site reliably reproduced the rage outbursts, Mark and Ervin passed a strong current through the electrodes and destroyed the scar tissue. The following year, Julia experienced only two mild rage episodes and no further ones were known to occur after that [1].[1]

Figure 11-1. "Julia ran to the bedroom wall . . . as if to attack." (John Briggs.)

Think of a recent experience which made you feel angry, fearful, or happy, then try to pinpoint the characteristics of an emotion. An *emotion* is another hypothetical construct whose characteristics we infer from behavior. Julia's fear and rage, although induced by scar tissue or by an electrode implanted within the brain, are similar to ordinary emotions

in many respects. Normally, emotions appear *spontaneously*; that is, people rarely try to feel angry, frightened, or overjoyed; the feelings simply occur. Ordinarily, of course, a particular situation or event seems to trigger them. Like Julia's fear and rage, normal emotions also have an *uncontrollable* quality; they are not easily turned on or off. In addition, emotions seem to "command" behavior. It is important to note that although behavior may seem temporarily out of control, our emotions do not compel us to behave in particular ways. Rather, they temporarily increase our arousal, our reactivity, or our irritability. As we will see, learning and the particular social context both influence the behavior that follows.

Our emotions have a number of components. They have a subjective *experiencing* or *feeling* aspect. Rage and fear are both unpleasant feelings, whereas joy is a pleasant one. Emotions also stimulate *physiological arousal*. When we are frightened, for example, our hearts beat faster, we sweat, we flush, our muscles tighten, and so on. Finally, emotions frequently guide subsequent *behavior*. Our verbalizations, gestures, postures, and facial features communicate what we feel. Unpleasant emotions, such as anger and fear, often provoke avoidance or attack, whereas depression typically stimulates withdrawal,

[1]This report of Julia's case is based on statements which Mark and Ervin make in their book *Violence and the brain* (1). The consequences of this type of psychosurgery are very controversial. For a provocative treatment of this topic, see Stephan L. Chorover. "The pacification of the brain." *Psychology Today*, May 1974, 7, 59–69.

and pleasant emotions, such as joy and love, usually trigger approach behavior. Behavior evoked by emotions frequently appears disturbed, irrational, or disorganized; like Julia, people often respond to their emotions by saying or doing things that would ordinarily strike them as inappropriate. We are ready now to define an *emotion* as a seemingly spontaneous and uncontrollable internal state characterized by subjective feelings and physiological arousal which guide expressive gestures and subsequent behavior. To explore the nature of an emotion, we turn to three general questions that psychologists and other scientists continue to investigate: How are physiology and emotions related to one another? How do cognitions influence emotions? What determines people's behavioral responses to their emotions?

Physiology and Emotions

About fifty years ago the American physiologist Walter Cannon demonstrated that emotions were tied up with physiological reactions. Cannon found that when animals were confronted with situations which evoked pain, rage, or fear, they reacted immediately with a particular pattern of physiological responses. In Cannon's words:

Respiration deepens; the heart beats more rapidly; the arterial pressure rises; the blood is shifted away from the stomach and intestines to the heart and central nervous system and the muscles; the processes in the alimentary canal cease; sugar is freed from the reserves in the liver; the spleen contracts and discharges its content of concentrated corpuscles, and adrenalin . . . is secreted from the adrenal medulla . . . [2].

These physiological activities have a purpose. The sugar energizes the muscles. The rapidly beating heart distributes blood quickly to the body parts involved in physical action. And so on. In brief, these physiological reactions prepare animals to meet threats

by running or attacking—increasing the probability that they will survive. These physical changes are generated by both the central and autonomic nervous systems and the endocrine glands.

The autonomic nervous system. During an intense emotion—for example, fear—people are often very aware of a pounding heart, a rapid pulse, tense muscles, a dry throat, perspiration, a need to urinate, trembling, or gastrointestinal pains. These reactions, which can cause people to feel that their emotions are controlling them, are called *autonomic reactions* because they are initiated by the *autonomic nervous system* (ANS) (see Figure 11-2), one branch of the peripheral nervous system.

The ANS consists of nerves that lead from the spinal cord and brain to the smooth muscles of the internal organs, the glands, the heart, and the blood vessels. The ANS is composed of two parts: the *parasympathetic system* and the *sympathetic system*. These systems frequently work in opposition to one another; that is, if one acts to accelerate the action of an organ, the other usually acts to slow the organ down. The parasympathetic system tends to be most active during periods of comparative calm. At these times it controls the performance of routine duties such as decreasing the heart rate and blood pressure and routing additional blood to the digestive system—duties which build up and conserve the body's store of energy. The sympathetic system becomes active during periods of intense emotion. During these "emergencies" it mobilizes the body's resources for action, producing the physiological responses which Cannon described.

The adrenal glands. The sympathetic nervous system stimulates the adrenal glands, glands perched on top of the kidneys, which release the hormones *adrenalin* and *noradrenalin* (see Figure 4-14 on page 112). Adrenalin

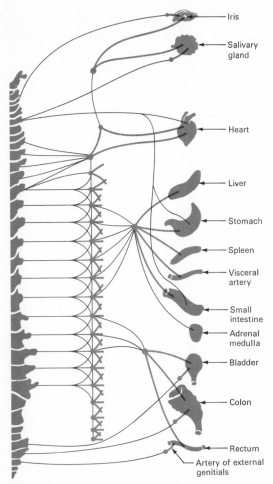

Iris

Salivary
gland

Heart

Liver

Stomach

Spleen

Visceral
artery

Small
intestine

Adrenal
medulla

Bladder

Colon

Rectum

Artery of external
genitials

Figure 11-2. A schematic diagram of the autonomic
nervous system.

the responses that are made during an emotional experience. Let us briefly review the CNS, which is discussed more fully in Chapter 4.

The cerebral cortex. The cerebral cortex, or cortex (see Figure 11-3), identifies, evaluates, and makes decisions about sensory data and subsequent behavior. Learning occurs within the cortex; and thoughts, expectations, and perceptions arise there. These cognitive processes play an important role in maintaining or dissolving emotions and in the behavior which accompanies them. Human emotions are far from simple on-off affairs, as Julia's case might mistakenly lead people to suspect.

The reticular formation. The reticular formation, a network of nerve cells in the brain stem (see Figure 11-3), alerts the cerebral cortex to important sensory information. As potential emotion-arousing events filter through the reticular formation along with other sensory data, they are singled out as important. The reticular formation then arouses the cortex so that it gives them its full attention; so intense arousal characterizes emotional experiences.

The limbic system. The limbic system, a group of interrelated structures deep within the brain's core (see Figure 11-3), also appears to be generally concerned with regulating emotions and motives. The precise function of each structure is not, as yet, clear. It is clear, however, that sensory information passes through the limbic system on its way to the cortex and that the cortex also sends messages down to the limbic system. One limbic structure, the *hypothalamus*, is responsible for activating the sympathetic nervous system during an emergency. Other limbic structures play roles in rage, pleasure, and pain. Recall that stimulation of the *amygdala*, a limbic structure, triggered Julia's rage.

and noradrenalin stimulate many of the same centers that the sympathetic nervous system has already activated, speeding the heart, deepening breathing, and so on. These hormones are continually secreted as long as the body remains highly alert and active—until the emergency passes or the animal is exhausted.

The central nervous system. Many structures within the *central nervous system (CNS)* work at arousing, regulating, and integrating

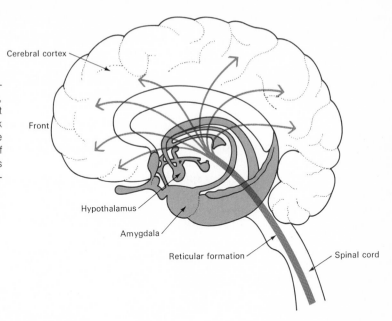

Figure 11-3. A schematic drawing of the central nervous system, showing the limbic system (light blue), the reticular formation (dark blue), and the cerebral cortex. The reticular formation, a network of nerve cells in the brain stem, alerts the cerebral cortex to important sensory information.

Do physiological responses to various emotions differ? Although physiological responses to pain, rage, and fear are similar, psychologists are currently searching for consistent physiological differences between them. Numerous investigators, including Cannon, find no differences. On the other hand, H. G. Wolf and his coworkers at New York Hospital have reported some observations on a man named Tom which suggest that differences may exist. When Tom was nine years old, he drank a cup of scalding clam chowder and damaged his esophagus so severely that it was necessary to bring part of his stomach lining out through an opening in his abdomen so that he might feed himself directly. The surgery left Tom's stomach lining partially exposed. In observing Tom as an adult, scientists noted that when he felt depressed or frightened, his stomach lining became pale and peristaltic movements and hydrochloric acid secretions decreased. When Tom felt angry, his stomach lining reddened and rhythmic contractions and hydrochloric acid secretions increased (3). Re-

search by a psychology team at Harvard University also indicates that fear and anger may elicit different physiological responses. In one study psychologist Albert Ax wired normal adult volunteers for recordings of blook pressure, heart rate, skin conductance (the skin's ability to conduct electricity which is essentially a function of sweating), muscle tension, face and hand temperature, respiration rate, and so on. Then each subject was frightened and angered alternately. The experimenter frightened his subjects by pretending that a dangerous high-voltage short circuit had occurred in the apparatus they were wired to. He angered his subjects by having a rude technician deliver a few choice insults. Fear produced changes such as increased respiration and skin conductance, responses which can also be induced by an injection of adrenalin. Anger produced changes such as increased muscle tension, decreased heart rate, and elevated blood pressure, responses which are typically induced by injections of both adrenalin and noradrenalin (4).

Do people's physiological responses to their emotions differ? People exhibit marked individual differences in their physiological reactions to emotion. These different patterns are apparent at very early ages. First, the intensity of the physiological reaction varies. Soon after birth some infants are autonomically very reactive, whereas others hardly react at all when stressed (see Chapter 3). Second, the predominant autonomic response varies—some people respond primarily by secreting stomach acid; others primarily by accelerating their heart rate; others primarily by elevating their body temperature; and so on (5). Human twin studies and studies of selectively bred rats and dogs show that such different autonomic patterns may be strongly influenced by heredity (6).

Cognitions and Emotions

Suppose that your heart is pounding, your hands are perspiring, and your face is flushed. What emotion are you feeling? If someone had just insulted you, you'd probably label your emotion anger; if you were taking a difficult exam at the time, you'd likely label your feeling fear or anxiety. Had you just been introduced to an exciting and attractive person you might label the feeling "love" or "sexual arousal." In short, many psychologists believe that essentially similar sympathetic nervous system patterns can be labeled in many ways depending on a person's interpretation of the situation. Because this theory emphasizes cognitions, we call it the *cognitive theory of emotion.*

A classic experiment by psychologists Stanley Schachter and Jerome E. Singer supports this theory. Male college student volunteers at the University of Minnesota came individually to a laboratory. They were told that they were participating in a study designed to measure how a vitamin supplement, "supproxin," affected vision. The subjects were divided into four groups. Subjects in the *informed group* received an injection of adrenalin and were told to expect the precise side effects of adrenalin: shaking hands, pounding hearts, and flushed faces. Subjects in the *ignorant group* received an injection of adrenalin but were told nothing about any possible side effects. Subjects in the *misinformed group* also received an adrenalin injection, but they were misled as to its side effects: They were told to expect numbness, itching, and a slight headache. Finally, subjects in a *placebo group* received an injection of a neutral solution (one which produced no side effects) and were told nothing about the injection's possible side effects. Thus, those in the informed group are physiologically aroused, and they can easily explain it. Those in the ignorant and misinformed groups are physiologically aroused, and they cannot easily explain it, whereas those in the placebo group are not aroused at all. Schachter and Singer believed that only the aroused subjects without an adequate explanation for their arousal would seek an emotional label for their state.

After the injection and explanation, an ally of the experimenters was introduced to each subject as a fellow participant in the study. With all the subjects in the misinformed group and half the subjects in each of the other conditions the stooge created a euphoric mood by shooting baskets with crumpled wads of paper, sailing paper airplanes, and hula-hooping. For the remaining subjects the stooge created an angry mood by grumbling and complaining about the experiment and showing increased annoyance with an admittedly exasperating questionnaire which subjects had been asked to fill in. (The questionnaire included such items as "With how many men other than your father has your mother had extramarital relationships?" and "Write the name of a family member who does not bathe or wash regularly.") At the end of the session Schachter and Singer measured the

Group	Injection	Expectations	Resulting state	Model	Effects
Informed	Adrenalin	Told precise side-effects of adrenalin	Not bewildered Aroused	Euphoric	No effect
				Angry	No effect
Ignorant	Adrenalin	Told nothing about side-effects	Bewildered Aroused	Euphoric	Euphoric
				Angry	Angry
Misinformed	Adrenalin	Misled about side-effects	Bewildered Aroused	Euphoric	Euphoric
Placebo	Neutral solution	Told nothing about side-effects	Not bewildered Not aroused	Euphoric	No effect
				Angry	No effect

Figure 11-4. The Schachter-Singer experiment.

emotional state of their subjects by directly observing and rating their behavior and by asking them to complete a self-report questionnaire describing their mood.

The psychologists found that subjects in the misinformed and ignorant groups, those who had no reasonable explanation for their arousal, were more susceptible to the stooge's mood than the others: They behaved more happily and reported more happy feelings with the euphoric stooge and they behaved more angrily and reported more angry feelings with the angry stooge than both the informed and placebo subjects (7) (see Figure 11-4). The Schachter-Singer study clearly supports the theory that cognitions which arise in a particular context influence how people perceive and label a physiologically aroused state.

Clinical observations indicate that cognitions also play a role in determining the intensity and length of people's emotions. A woman who thinks that "her lost lover is the only man suitable for her" and that "she will never be able to find another man because of her own inadequacies" cannot help but feel depressed. She is likely to remain depressed indefinitely if she continually reminds herself of her dismal situation. However, if the woman thinks "there are more men where he came from" and "I'm an attractive person," she is likely to experience a milder depression and recover a lot sooner. Cognitions also affect the intensity and length of anger. Consider the following situation. Your books, coat, and gloves are lying on the couch. Your mother comes home from work, sees the disorder, and yells, "This is not a pig sty. Get your damned books off the couch and hang up your coat." She continues muttering about what a slob you are. At this point you probably pursue one of several lines of thought: (1) You may recount your mother's many failings, say, her thoughtlessness, pettiness, and frequent nagging. These thoughts will probably make you feel increasingly more angry; and as long as you continue to think along these lines, you will probably remain angry. (2) Or you may think to yourself, "Mom had a hard day; she's frustrated and irritable; and it really hurts her to see the house so disorderly when she works so hard to keep it in order." (3) Or you might put the whole scene out of your mind (see Chapter 13.) These last two cognitive strategies will probably cause your anger to vanish rather quickly.

Behavior and Emotions

People and other animals respond to their emotions with various expressive signs— facial expressions and gestures— and with other forms of behavior. What factors influence these responses?

Before reading on, please try to figure out what emotions the faces in Figure 11-5 express. Most people find this exercise rather easy. Apparently, we tend to use certain facial expressions to communicate certain basic emotions ourselves, and, not surprisingly, we recognize these expressions when others use them. Many psychologists and biologists believe that animals are genetically programmed to communicate their basic emotions by particular responses. Consider people. All over the world people, including the aborigines in New Guinea who have never mixed with "civilized" societies, express happiness by smiling or laughing, sorrow by a down-turned mouth, anger by a red face, and so on (8). These facial expressions occur spontaneously in young infants. The congenitally blind and deaf (people who are isolated beginning at birth from the sights and sounds of other's emotions) also express their emotions with these same signs (9). Apparently, genetic factors bias people to respond to their basic emotions with certain facial expressions; however, the final form which the expression takes (how widely people smile and how loudly they laugh, for example) is probably the result of learning.

The form of many facial expressions and gestures are probably influenced little, if at all, by heredity. Much learning occurs as people observe and imitate others. In China children learn to clap their hands when they are worried and scratch their ears and cheeks when they are happy (10), presumably by watching and imitating those around them.

Similarly, members of particular ethnic groups in our own culture learn to use distinctive gestures and facial expressions to communicate their emotions (11).

People's overt behavioral responses to their emotions vary widely. People respond to anger in many ways. One person sulks; a second whines and complains; a third threatens; a fourth yells; and a fifth destroys; a sixth becomes depressed, perhaps even self-destructive; and a seventh looks for a constructive solution to the problem. This behavior is learned, of course. Children frequently learn emotional behavior indirectly—by observing and imitating the behavior of others. They also learn such behavior directly through reinforcement and punishment. Parents, teachers, and others train children to make appropriate behavioral responses to their emotions and to suppress inappropriate ones. Young children, for instance, may be punished until they learn to curb their outbursts of anger. Older children frequently learn by social approval and disapproval when, where, and how to behave when they feel disgusted, angry, or overjoyed, for example. Traditionally, males and females in our culture learn to respond differently to their emotions. Later in this chapter we will look closely at how children learn aggressive behavior.

Summary: The Nature of an Emotion

1. Emotions are accompanied by physiological changes which are triggered by the ANS, CNS, and endocrine systems.
2. Different emotions may be associated with slightly different physiological response patterns.
3. People show large individual differences in the intensity of their physiological reactions and in the predominant physiologi-

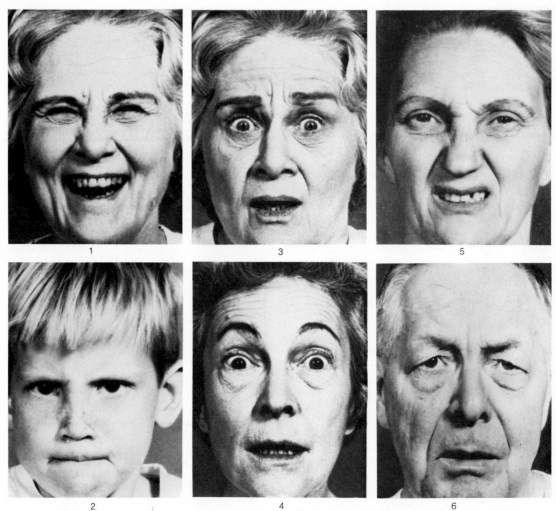

Figure 11-5. What emotion does each of these faces express? See p. 335. (Reproduced from "Universals and Cultural Differences in Facial Expression of Emotion," Paul Ekman in J. K. Cole (Ed.), *Nebraska symposium on motivation*, 1971, University of Nebraska Press, 1972.)

cal system which responds during an emotion.

4. Cognitions appear to influence how people label an aroused bodily state. They also affect the intensity and duration of an emotion.

5. Genetic factors bias people to respond to their emotions with particular facial expressions, although learning undoubtedly influences the final form of the behavior. The majority of overt emotion-related behaviors are probably learned by observation and imitation and by reinforcement and punishment.

We turn now to anxiety.

ANXIETY

That evening as we walked under the skyscrapers it seemed to me I could feel the giant buildings start to sway. Although I knew my fear was preposterous the imagined collapse of these huge giants was utterly terrifying. I was convinced that the towers would split and crash down on me and [I] could already picture the people and traffic crushed under them. The strength sapped out of my legs and they became so weak I felt I could not take a step. It became hard to breathe, and [in order] not to choke I had to gasp for air with my mouth wide open. I felt my vision darkening and a splitting pressure filled my chest. I was afraid the buildings would really crash and at the same time I was afraid my son would notice my panic [12].

This is a picture of *anxiety*, which we define as an emotion characterized by unpleasant subjective feelings of anticipated danger, tension, and distress and attended by sympathetic nervous system arousal. We will be using the words fear and anxiety interchangeably, as many psychologists do. We begin this section by looking at how psychologists measure anxiety and view its causes. Then we examine how cognitions influence the intensity of anxiety. Next we explore the effects of anxiety on learning and, finally, the relationship between tension and the chronic anxiety state, ulcers, heart attacks, and voodoo deaths.

How Psychologists
Measure Anxiety

The items seen in Table 11-1 appear on a widely used anxiety scale. This self-report test is one of the common ways that psychologists measure generalized anxiety. The items shown in Table 11-2 appear on a test which is used to evaluate more specific anxiety reactions. The advantages of self-report tests like these are obvious: They are easy to administer and interpret. The questions simply guide people's responses into a standard format so

TABLE 11-1. ITEMS FROM THE TAYLOR MANIFEST ANXIETY SCALE

I work under a great deal of strain.	True False
I am usually calm and not easily upset.	True False
I sweat very easily even on cool days.	True False
I always have enough energy when faced with difficulty	True False
My sleep is restless and disturbed.	True False

Source: J. A. Taylor. A personality scale of manifest anxiety. *Journal of Abnormal and Social Psychology*, 1953, 48, 285–290.

that they can be quantified and compared with the responses of others. The limitations of self-report measures such as these are discussed in Chapter 2 (see page 39).

Occasionally, psychologists assess anxiety by making direct observations of behavior. For example, they might observe and rate a particular subject on the frequency and intensity of the following signs of tension: trembling, perspiring, nail biting, pacing,

TABLE 11-2. QUESTIONS FROM THE REVISED WILLOUGHBY QUESTIONNAIRE FOR SELF-ADMINISTRATION

0 means "No," "never," "not at all," etc.
1 means "Somewhat," "sometimes," "a little," etc.
2 means "About as often as not," "an average amount," etc.
3 means "Usually," "a good deal," "rather often," etc.
4 means "Practically always," "entirely," etc.

1. Do you get anxious if you have to speak or perform in any way in front of a group of strangers? (0 1 2 3 4)
2. Do you worry if you make a fool of yourself, or feel you have been made to look foolish? (0 1 2 3 4)
3. Are you afraid of falling when you are on a high place from which there is no real danger of falling—for example, looking down from a balcony on the tenth floor? (0 1 2 3 4)
7. Do you feel uncomfortable when you meet new people? (0 1 2 3 4)
13. Does it bother you to have people watch you work even when you do it well? (0 1 2 3 4)

Source: J. Wolpe. *The practice of behavior therapy.* 2d ed. New York: Pergamon Press, 1973. pp. 281–282.

swaying, feet shuffling, blushing, flushing, swallowing, throat clearing, and voice quavering (13). Measuring anxiety by behavioral ratings depends on the assumption that behavior accurately mirrors emotion. Sometimes, it may. But you can probably think of people you know who hide their emotions quite skillfully.

Finally, psychologists often use measurements of physiological responses to assess anxiety. They may monitor bodily reactions such as changes in heart rate, respiration rate, or muscle tension, using electronic equipment. Frequently, several physiological responses are measured by a *polygraph,* an instrument that simultaneously records a number of physiological reactions. The so-called "lie detector" is a well-known instrument of this type (see Figure 11-6). As the subject answers questions, the lie detector records blood pressure, respiration rate, galvanic skin response (skin conductance) and possibly other bodily responses. Employers, national security operations, and law enforcement agencies all use polygraphs to make decisions about people's integrity. Consider how the test works in determining whether a criminal suspect may be lying. Carefully chosen questions ask the subject for routine information, such as "State your name, address, and age," whereas other questions ask for information assumed to be anxiety-provoking but not associated with the crime, such as "Can you document your deductions on your federal income tax returns?" The critical questions are directly associated with the crime, such as "Were you near Fifth Avenue and Thirty-third Street on the night of February 25th, 1975?" After the questioning, the polygraph operator evaluates the magnitude of the physiological changes aroused by each question. The evaluation takes into account the anxiety-arousing potential of each question and the subject's typical level of anxiety. These evaluation procedures are clearly sub-

jective and depend greatly on the operator's skill and experience.

The lie detector test is based on the assumptions that lying arouses anxiety and that anxiety inevitably produces autonomic changes. Neither supposition is completely justifiable. Callous people may not be bothered by critical questions or by lying to others. On the other hand, sensitive people may naturally respond with anxiety to critical questions. After all, going to jail or being fired may depend on the answers. Finally, people can control their autonomic responses, as we saw in Chapter 7.

Physiological measures of anxiety are hard to interpret for several additional reasons: (1) Individuals vary in their physiological reactions to stress, as we noted before. These individual differences must be taken into account in interpreting the physiological

Figure 11-6. As the subject answers questions, this lie detector measures heart rate, blood pressure, respiration rate, and skin conductance. (Wide World Photos.)

data. (2) The physiological patterns for the various emotions overlap. The physiological signs for anger and extreme arousal, for example, are similar to those for anxiety. So although investigators think that they are measuring anxiety, they may, in fact, be observing anger or arousal.

The Causes of Anxiety

What conditions elicit anxiety? Sigmund Freud believed that anxiety arose primarily in two situations: (1) in response to real worldly dangers and (2) in anticipation of punishment for either immoral behavior or the expression of forbidden biological drives, such as sex and aggression. Neobehavioristic psychologists see anxiety as learned—primarily by respondent conditioning and to a lesser degree by observing and imitating the fears of others. We explored the behavioristic view of the origin of fear in Chapter 7. We said that infants appear to be born with innate fears, such as the fear of pain, loud noises, and falling. Additional fears, such as the fear of strangers, develop as the child matures. If a neutral stimulus is repeatedly paired with an anxiety-provoking stimulus, it eventually comes to elicit anxiety all by itself. Such fears may subsequently spread to other objects and events by stimulus generalization (see pages 190 to 193).

Many cognitive and humanistic psychologists view the origin of anxiety quite differently. Some assume that anxiety arises when a person's beliefs, attitudes, perceptions, or concepts conflict with one another, whereas others emphasize *existential anxiety*, anxiety arising from a conflict over how to lead a fulfilling, meaningful life. A middle-aged lawyer might feel existential anxiety in trying to choose between continuing in a conventional role and risking his security and respectability for a more fulfilling life as a farmer.

In short, different psychologists emphasize different sources of anxiety. All these sources—objective dangers, the anticipation of punishment for the violation of moral laws or the expression of taboo drives, the pairing of a neutral stimulus with an anxiety-provoking one, and cognitive conflicts—probably have the potential to arouse the emotional state we call anxiety.

Anxiety and Cognitions

Cognitions have an important influence on anxiety level. When particular stressors are perceived as unfamiliar, for example, they usually lead to greater anxiety than when they are perceived as familiar. Many studies support this notion. In one study college men volunteered for an investigation of the effect of pain (electric shock) on heart rate. The subjects were divided into three groups. Two groups received sample shocks: one mild and the other strong. The third group received no information whatsoever about the nature of the shock. As the men waited for the shock to be delivered, their heart rates were monitored. Those who knew what to expect—be it mild or strong shock—showed only a small increase in heart rate. The heart rates of the uncertain subjects increased dramatically (14).

The predictability of a particular stressor also affects the intensity of anxiety which it arouses. Rats, for example, who are shocked immediately after a tone are less likely to develop ulcers, a severe response to anxiety, than those who are shocked randomly without warning (when the total number of shocks is held constant) (15). More on ulcers later.

Perception of control over a particular stressor also affects anxiety level. Experienced parachutists, for example, show less physiological arousal and report feeling less anxious immediately before a jump than novices (16). Presumably because experienced parachutists have coped successfully in the past, they see themselves in control in the present and consequently feel less threatened. Several psychologists have shown that the *perception of control*, and not necessarily actual control, is the important factor. James Geer and his colleagues at the State University of New York at Stony Brook gave student subjects ten painful six-second electric shocks. After each shock, the subjects pressed a switch immediately. They believed that they were providing an index of their reaction time. At the same time the investigators measured the subjects' sweat gland activity to gauge their anxiety. After the first series of shocks, half the subjects were told that they could control the duration of the next ten shocks: By reacting very quickly, they believed that they could cut the duration of the next shock in half. The other subjects were simply informed that the next ten shocks would be shorter ones. In fact, the subjects all received the same 3-second shocks. It is important to note that half the subjects perceived themselves in control, whereas the other half perceived themselves as helpless victims. As expected, the subjects who perceived themselves in control showed significantly less sweat gland activity than the others (17).

Anxiety and Learning

Anxious students have long claimed that anxiety can disrupt their learning and keep them from preparing properly for exams. During exams such students often report knowing the right answers, but blocking or choking up and being unable to reproduce them. Psychologists have looked closely at how anxious students perform on various learning tasks in the laboratory. The anxiety-learning relationship turns out to be very complicated. People who describe themselves as highly anxious generally perform better on *simple* learning tasks than people who report low anxiety. On *complex* learning tasks the situation is reversed: People who report high anxiety typically do worse than those who report low anxiety (18,19). Additional studies demonstrate that people with high anxiety are especially likely to do poorly on difficult or ambiguous test items, which they are likely to misread or misinterpret (20).

In view of these findings, we'd expect highly anxious students to perform rather poorly in college. Do they? In one study investigators examined the grades and scholastic aptitude test scores of male college students who reported high and low levels of anxiety. They found that anxiety did not appear to affect the academic performance of students with either very low or very high aptitudes: men who scored low on the Scholastic Aptitude Test tended to make relatively poor grades, regardless of reported anxiety level, whereas men who scored high on the test tended to make relatively good grades, regardless of reported anxiety level. Anxiety did affect the great majority of students—those who scored in the middle range on the aptitude test. High-anxiety, middle-aptitude students made poorer grades than low-anxiety, middle-aptitude students (21).

Psychologists have developed programs to help anxious students cope with their anxiety. One program which was initiated by psychologist Charles Spielberger and his associates at Vanderbilt University aimed at helping highly anxious freshmen who were making poor grades. The students were counseled in groups that focused on practical topics such as studying and preparing for exams, figuring out what the instructor wanted, handling individual academic difficulties, managing dorm life, and selecting a vocation. This program proved quite effective in raising the anxious student's grade-point averages (.5 of a grade point!) (22). In Chapter 15 we discuss systematic desensitization, a behavior-therapy procedure that has also been quite successful in helping anxious students cope directly with their anxiety.

Anxiety and the Body

A physician named Hans Selye (b.1907) has spent much of his life studying how acute and chronic stress affect physiology. Early in his career, Selye discovered that environmental stresses (such as intense cold), psychological stresses (such as conflict), and physical stresses (such as injury, bacterial agents, or surgery) all affected the body in the same way. In response to any stress the victim (animal or human) reacts with a *general adaptation syndrome* (GAS). The GAS follows the same pattern each time.

STAGE 1: ALARM REACTION—During stage 1 the sympathetic nervous system and the adrenal glands mobilize the body's defensive forces to handle the emergency; that is, to resist the particular stressor. Selye's stage 1 is the same emergency reaction to danger that Cannon described. If the tension is prolonged, the body enters a second stage.

STAGE 2: RESISTANCE—As the animal continues to resist the specific stressor, the body remains highly aroused but a price is being paid for this emergency-level preparedness. Systems that are ordinarily responsible for growth, repair, and resistance to infection have been shut down; consequently, the body is in a weakened state and very susceptible to other stresses. If the stress continues, the body enters a third stage.

STAGE 3: EXHAUSTION—The body cannot maintain its highly aroused state indefinitely. It gradually begins to show the signs of exhaustion. After the sympa-

thetic nervous system has depleted its energy supply, the parasympathetic system takes over. At this time the activities of the body slow down, and they may even stop altogether. If the stress continues, the worn-out animal will no longer be able to handle it, psychologically or physiologically. At this point continued stress may lead to severe psychological problems, such as deep depression or psychotic behavior, or to serious physical problems, even death.

Selye believes that each exposure to stress brings irreversible consequences: "It uses up reserves of adaptability that cannot be replaced," and it damages body tissue irreparably. Consequently, the animal becomes more susceptible to *psychosomatic disorders* (those that result from the body's autonomic and hormonal responses to stress—such as certain kinds of ulcers and high blood pressure). The cycle of stress, rest, stress, rest, according to Selye, eventually adds up to aging and to the various wear-and tear diseases, such as heart attacks, that most of us eventually die of (23). We focus now on four reactions to which prolonged stress contributes.

Chronic anxiety. The tensions of wartime combat during World War II and the Vietnam war led to a severe stress reaction variously called "combat fatigue," "flying fatigue," and "war weariness." Apparently, prolonged exposure to any stressful situation can produce a chronic anxiety state. People then react to everyday strains and minor stresses (such as loud noises or bright lights) as if they are confronting a major emergency. Their breathing becomes disturbed, their muscles tighten, their hearts beat rapidly, and their bodies recover slowly. The nervous system mechanisms that ordinarily bring the body back to its normal state seem to have broken down (24). Currently, experts believe that some 10 million Americans suffer from chronic anxiety (25).

During World War II researchers found that if they removed soldiers from combat when signs of the stress reaction—lack of appetite, insomnia, increased heart rate, and high irritability—first appeared and allowed them to rest, the soldiers recouped their strength and functioned normally. When soldiers with this stress reaction remained in battle, exposed to continuous tension, they reached a point of no return. They developed chronic anxiety conditions, and rest could no longer relieve the syndrome (26). We will have more to say about chronic anxiety reactions in Chapter 14.

Peptic ulcers. Peptic ulcers will probably afflict 1 in every 10 Americans now living at some time during their lives. A peptic ulcer is a lesion usually in the stomach or duodenum lining produced by the excessive secretion of hydrochloric acid. Ordinarily, hydrochloric acid and enzymes act on food to break it down into components that the body can use. In the case of the peptic ulcer victim, excessive amounts of hydrochloric acid erode the mucus layer that protects the inner wall of the stomach; the acid digests the stomach wall itself.

Stress plays a major role in causing the excessive secretions of hydrochloric acid. Direct evidence comes from observations on Tom, the man with the partially exposed stomach, whom we discussed before. When Tom became angry or tense, his acid production increased and his stomach engorged with blood and began rhythmic contractions. In other words, ordinary digestive functions took place just as if Tom had a stomach full of food. During two weeks of prolonged stress, Tom secreted excessive quantities of gastric juices and his stomach developed bleeding sores (27).

Numerous experimental studies link the ulcers of animals to conditions of severe stress. Similarly, many observations show that when people undergo intense, prolonged tension—during migrations, floods, earthquakes, wars, and rapid social changes—a relatively high percentage develop peptic ulcers or other gastrointestinal disorders (28). Gastrointestinal complaints appear to be common in populations which are facing severe stresses. In our own society, air traffic controllers who contend every day with the extreme stresses involved in making life and death decisions for hundreds of people have an unusually high rate of ulcers (29).

Why is it that stresses do not produce ulcers in *all* people or in *all* laboratory animal subjects? Many scientists believe that ulcer victims are probably predisposed to react to tension with gastric secretions. This predisposition may depend on pepsinogen level. *Pepsinogen,* a substance secreted by the gastric glands in the stomach and later converted into pepsin, functions as a major ingredient in the gastric juices. The level of pepsinogen furnishes a measure of the amount of gastric activity. Research shows that pepsinogen levels appear to be influenced by heredity. Neonates differ markedly in pepsinogen levels and young infants with high pepsinogen levels frequently come from families whose members also have excessively high pepsinogen levels (30).

A high pepsinogen level is also associated with the formation of ulcers. In a careful study psychologist H. Weiner and his colleagues measured the level of pepsinogen in 2,073 newly inducted military draftees. The investigators then selected sixty-three men with the highest and fifty-seven men with the lowest pepsinogen levels for further observation. None of the men had ulcers at the time. When each draftee was reexamined during his eighth and sixteenth week of basic training, nine men were developing ulcers. All nine came from the high-pepsinogen group

(31). A similar association between high-pepsinogen level and ulcer formation has been found in children and civilian adults who were classified earlier as high- or low-pepsinogen secretors (32). In sum, a genetic propensity to secrete gastric juices under stress *and* prolonged tension may combine to produce ulcers.

Heart attacks. Coronary disease kills approximately 700,000 Americans every year (33). The causes of heart disease are multiple and not well understood. Currently, many experts believe that the stresses and strains of life are a contributing factor.

Meyer Friedman and Ray Rosenman, cardiologists at Mount Zion Hospital in San Francisco, have found impressive evidence that heart attacks are related to a particular personality pattern which they designate "type A." Type A people can be male or female. Occupationally, they range from janitors to bank presidents. What they have in common is that they struggle continually to accomplish too many things in too little time or against too many obstacles, and consequently they subject themselves to a great deal of stress. Type A's appear aggressive, ambitious for achievement and power, competitive, and compulsive; they are habitually racing against time; and they almost never "waste time" by relaxing.

What is the evidence for believing that the type A personality pattern relates to coronary heart disease? A massive longitudinal study by Friedman and Rosenman is showing that people with type A personalities will predictably develop heart disease. In 1960, Friedman and Rosenman interviewed 3,500 middle-aged corporate men with no known history of coronary problems; they classified approximately half as type A. Each year all the men returned to the hospital for medical exams. After eight and a half years, 257 of these executives developed heart disease; 70 per-

cent of them had initially been classified type A (34). We might speculate that the personality characteristics of type A people maximize their daily stress and lead to biochemical changes that precipitate coronary heart disease. Of course, there may also be a third factor that predisposes people both to heart attacks and to type A personality characteristics.

Voodoo deaths. In many primitive societies witch doctors are capable of killing as well as curing. They cast their spells by pointing a bone or wand and muttering a curse at the same time. Here is one social scientist's account of the effects of this ritual.

A man who discovers that he is being boned . . . is, indeed, a pitiable sight. He stands aghast, with his eyes staring at the treacherous pointer, and with his hands lifted as though to ward off the lethal medium, which he imagines is pouring into his body. His cheeks blanch and his eyes become glassy, and the expression of his face becomes horribly distorted. . . . He attempts to shriek but usually the sound chokes in his throat, and all that one might see is froth at his mouth. His body begins to tremble and the muscles twitch involuntarily. He sways backwards and falls to the ground, and for a short time appears to be in a swoon; but soon after he begins to writhe as if in mortal agony, and covering his face with his hands, begins to moan. After a while, he becomes more composed and crawls to his wurley [shelter]. From this time onwards, he sickens and frets, refusing to eat, and keeping aloof from the daily affairs of the tribe. Unless help is forthcoming in the shape of a counter-charm . . . his death is only a matter of a comparatively short time [35].

Physiologist Walter Cannon studied many reports of voodoo deaths and then visited Africa to investigate the matter at firsthand. There he was able to confirm the authenticity of more than thirty such deaths (36). How can a voodoo spell cause death? The voodoo spell generates a strong expectation that death is imminent. That expectation arouses intense fear which Cannon believed overstimulated the sympathetic nervous system and led to a heart attack. Recent evidence indicates that Cannon was wrong. The intense anxiety generated by the expectation of dying apparently leads to a state of exhaustion. At this time the parasympathetic nervous system takes over. If the person's belief is strong enough, the tension continues until the parasympathetic system is overstimulated, and it slows the internal organs and eventually stops the heart.[2] Incidentally, a large psychological literature also indicates that expectations can lead to other physical effects, such as recovering from pain or illness.

Summary: Anxiety

1. Psychologists measure anxiety by administering self-report tests, making behavior ratings, and using electronic instruments to monitor physiological indicators of anxiety.
2. Anxiety probably arises under a variety of circumstances—as an innate reaction to danger, when people expect punishment or disapproval for their behavior or thoughts, and when mental conflicts prove severe. Anxiety can also be learned by modeling the fears of others and by the principles of respondent conditioning.
3. Cognitions influence the intensity of anxiety. When people perceive a particular anxiety-arousing stimulus as predictable, familiar, or controllable, they feel less anxious about it, than when they perceive it as unpredictable, unfamiliar, or uncontrollable.
4. Anxiety affects learning in complex ways.

[2]For a fascinating article about deaths that appear to be caused by psychological states (such as giving up on life), see Martin Seligman. "Submissive death: Giving up on life." *Psychology Today*, May 1974, 7, 80–85.

In general, it seems to facilitate the performance of simple tasks and to disrupt the performance of complex tasks.

5. Animals respond to all kinds of stresses with the general adaptation syndrome. Prolonged exposure to stress appears to contribute to chronic anxiety, psychosomatic disorders such as ulcers, and heart attacks, and even death.

ANGER AND AGGRESSIVE BEHAVIOR

On arrival at a small apartment, the officers were informed by an older woman that her married daughter had become enraged, had begun throwing dishes, threatened suicide by jumping out a window, and threatened the complainant and her own 12-year-old child with violence [37].

Figure 11-7. This Brazilian teenager, "possessed by the spirit of the Candomble saint," collapsed during a voodoo ceremony. (United Press International photo.)

This statement, which comes from a police report, links anger and aggression. We define *anger* as an emotion characterized by a high level of sympathetic nervous system activity and by strong subjective feelings of displeasure that are triggered by a real or imagined wrong. We define *aggression* as behavior aimed at hurting. Anger is frequently accompanied by an impulse to retaliate by aggression, but anger and aggression are not always linked. As we mentioned before, anger can lead to sullen, withdrawn, depressed, or constructive behavior, while aggressive behavior can be triggered by states other than anger. In *Little Murders*, a play by Jules Feiffer, for example, people amuse themselves by shooting at one another. Gang members fight savagely to attain status. At My Lai, soldiers murdered to obey orders—at least in part. Keeping this in mind, we nevertheless concentrate on aggressive behavior because, being observable, it has been far more extensively researched than the construct anger. We turn first to the various determinants of aggression.

Are People Instinctively Aggressive?

Sigmund Freud believed that people are born with an instinct to kill and destroy. In his words: "Men are not gentle, friendly creatures wishing for love, who simply defend themselves if they are attacked, but . . . a powerful measure of desire for aggression has to be reckoned as part of their instinctual endowment [38]." Freud also believed that if people were not permitted to express this drive, it accumulated and eventually overflowed, resulting in unexpected violence.

Konrad Lorenz, the prominent Austrian ethologist (see Chapter 3), takes a similar position. Lorenz believes that people are born with aggressive instincts just like other animals. In his view, aggressive instincts are

usually adaptive: They help animals survive, defend their territory, and protect their young. On the other hand, dangerous animals also inherit inhibitions against seriously injuring members of their own species as a built-in safeguard which keeps the species from wiping itself out. Lorenz believes that in the beginning primitive people were ineffectual fighters with a small capacity for destruction, so there was no need for them to develop elaborate inhibitions. Later they invented weapons. Ever since, they have been the most potentially destructive beasts of all, and, unfortunately, they do not appear to have any innate inhibitions about aggressing against each other (39).

Do people have aggressive instincts? So far there is no physiological evidence that a *need to fight arises spontaneously* from within any animal. It appears instead that conditions in the environment must stimulate aggression. One student of animal behavior expressed this idea: "A person who is fortunate enough to exist in an environment which is without stimulation to fight will not suffer physiological or nervous damage because he never fights [40]."

Biology and Aggressive Behavior

Although people may not have an instinct to aggress, biology provides them with the capacity for aggressive behavior. Genes, hormones, and brain mechanisms are all involved. Let's consider heredity first. People can breed bulls, dogs, roosters, rabbits, mice, and fish who fight ferociously with little provocation. Although aggressive behavior is not itself inherited, the many factors that influence it are inherited. Genes influence growth patterns that contribute to size and strength. Larger and stronger animals, of course, become more successful fighters. Similarly, genes affect thresholds of activation which influence reaction time. An animal that reacts quickly also makes a better fighter. Some psychologists believe that animals also inherit thresholds of irritability. The lower the threshold, the more easily the irritability is triggered and the more frequently the individual may feel like aggressing. Genes also influence hormone levels within the human body.

Those internal chemical secretions called hormones are a second biological factor that affects aggressiveness. The androgens, the male sex hormones, determine the patterns of growth which make male animals larger and more powerful, with few exceptions, than female animals. In addition, they influence the propensity to fight. When scientists inject rats, roosters, and other animals with testosterone, the chief androgen, they fight more frequently and more intensely (41,42). When the testosterone level is reduced, animals become gentler. The castrated calf, for example, grows into a benign steer and not a ferocious bull.

The relationship between human aggression and human sex hormones is not as clearcut, but there appear to be some definite connections. During the premenstrual period, at a time when estrogen and progesterone production is low, women typically experience feelings of tension, irritability, and hostility (43). Women also commit a disproportionate number of crimes at this time (44). When men consent to therapeutic castrations, as sex offenders in Denmark sometimes do, the reduction in testosterone level seems to result in "general pacification [45]." These examples suggest that the sex hormones influence human aggression.

The brain mechanisms are a third biological factor that influence aggression. At the beginning of the chapter, we saw that Julia experienced rage and wanted to strike out when her amygdala was stimulated. In a better known and more tragic case a tumor in the amygdala led to a similar effect. Early one morning, a young man named Charles Whitman wrote:

I don't really understand myself these days. I am supposed to be an average, reasonable, and intelligent young man. However, lately, (I can't recall when it started) I have been a victim of many unusual and irrational thoughts. These thoughts constantly recur, and it requires a tremendous mental effort to concentrate. . . . I talked with a doctor once for about two hours and tried to convey to him my fears that I felt overcome . . . by overwhelming violent impulses. . . . After my death, I wish that an autopsy would be performed on me to see if there is any visible physical disorder [46].

Soon after writing these words, Whitman killed his mother, his wife, and fourteen other people before being killed himself. A post mortem revealed a highly malignant tumor in the amygdala.

Scientists now believe that there are many neural systems in the brains of people and other animals that, when stimulated, produce specific kinds of aggressive behavior—defensive behavior, attack behavior, killing, and so on. Under ordinary circumstances these aggressive systems appear to be inactive. Apparently, they can be activated directly by physical, electrical, or chemical stimulation, or by hormones, or indirectly by learned environmental cues.

Learning and Aggressive Behavior

Learning plays a role in the aggressive behavior of many animals. In a classic study Zing Yang Kuo, a psychologist now at Yale University, demonstrated that experience had important effects on the rat-killing behavior of cats. Kuo reared individual kittens under a number of conditions: Some grew up with rat-killing mothers; others with rats as companions; others by themselves. Although 85 percent of the kittens reared with rat-killing mothers became avid rat killers and 45 percent of the kittens reared in isolation later killed rats, only 17 percent of the kittens reared with rats later killed them. Generally, the kittens reared with rats developed strong attachments to their rat companions. Later Kuo took the kittens who'd been reared by themselves and schooled them in rat killing by permitting them to witness an adult cat kill rats. Under these conditions, 82 percent of them converted to rat killing, but only 7 percent of the kittens reared with rats could be induced to kill a rat by example—even under conditions of extreme hunger (47,48).

People also learn aggression. Although their bodily state may make them more or less likely to aggress, learning determines how, against whom, and in what situations people actually do aggress. Much aggressive behavior is learned because it is positively reinforcing. Consider a child who spots a particularly desirable toy bear that a smaller child is playing with. If the large child hits the smaller one, he will probably acquire the bear. Consider the case of a young man growing up in poverty.

He has learned that he had better grab while the grabbing is good, because if he doesn't, one of his brothers and sisters, or his parents, or his peers, will grab instead. . . . Reason has never won a street fight nor enabled him to keep his father from beating his mother when he got drunk. . . . Without immediate action and intense drive, the child may not survive in the tooth-and-claw existence that for him is almost routine. . . . Striking, yelling, and pushing cause others to stand back so that [he] . . . can go ahead [49].

Children also learn aggression by observation and imitation. Parents who punish their children aggressively are particularly effective aggressive models. In fact, there is hardly a better way to teach children aggression for the following reasons: First, the child probably sees aggression working successfully. Second, the aggression occurs in a highly charged emotional climate amidst fear, shame, anger, and exasperation and will probably be memorable. (Research shows that people tend to remember what they learn during a state of moderate arousal.) Third, the behavior is displayed by a powerful model, the loved parent, with whom the child identifies. Fourth, the aggression brings both pain and frustration. As we will see later, both these conditions often lead to more aggression. For all these reasons, we'd expect aggressive parents to have aggressive children. Many studies show that they do (50). In one study, for example, psychologists found that aggressive delinquent boys were likelier than non-delinquent boys to have punitive and rejecting parents (51). It also appears that people who learn aggression from aggressive parents pass the lesson on to their children. When investigators studied sixty sets of parents who had severely battered their young children, they found that the abusing parents had been abused (subjected to constant criticism, unreasonable demands for performance, and in most cases harsh physical punishment) by their own parents— without exception (52).

Many psychologists believe that children also learn aggression from watching television. We examine this issue more closely.

The effects of violent television models. In 1972 a survey indicated that 95 percent of all American homes had television sets and that American children spent more hours watching television than they spent in any other single activity, except sleeping (53). Children who watch American television are exposed to violent models continually. A recent survey found that 80 percent of the programs contained violence (54).

Many psychologists believe that violent television models are dangerous. They reason like this: A person who is watching violence on television is in a heightened emotional state because of the violence and consequently very susceptible to the model's influence. While in this susceptible state, the person is typically exposed to an attractive sympathetic hero whose violence pays off. At the same time unpleasant consequences rarely follow the television hero's aggression. So people who are inclined to be aggressive should behave even more aggressively after observing a violent TV model. This position stems from observation learning studies (see Chapter 7) and is known as the *social learning* view.

Other psychologists believe that watching violence on television may actually benefit both the observer and society. Long ago, Aristotle, the Greek philosopher, speculated that witnessing a drama can cleanse people of strong emotions such as grief, fear, and pity. The *catharsis hypothesis*, derived from Aristotle's theory, assumes that frustration increases the need for aggression. Since frustration is impossible to escape, almost everyone has a need to aggress. Presumably, this need can be satisfied by aggressing oneself, by watching others aggress, or by engaging in fantasy aggression. According to the catharsis hypothesis, then, witnessing violent television models should reduce a person's need to aggress.

We've speculated about two possible effects of observing violence on television. What are the actual effects? Many laboratory studies have been designed to answer this question. The studies follow a similar pattern: The subjects report to the psychology laboratory where they are usually exposed to a frustrating experience. In one study, for example, the subjects took an intelligence test while the experimenter insulted them and berated their performance (55). Sooner or later the experimental subjects view filmed material that features a violent hero, whereas the

control subjects view neutral filmed material. Then each subject is placed in a situation where aggression is encouraged and measured. In the study we just mentioned the subjects were given an opportunity to administer electric shock to the experimenter who had insulted them. The number of shocks and the duration of each shock furnished the measure of aggression.

The vast majority of laboratory studies show that the observation of aggressive filmed models leads to increased aggression when the opportunity is presented. These findings hold true both for children and adults (56), but we cannot yet conclude that watching violent television models causes aggression because there are too many serious problems with these studies. First, the deceptions are contrived, and they may seem unreal to the subjects. Second, behavior in the experimental setting may not be characteristic of real-life behavior. Third, several minutes of television or film is hardly equivalent to a steady diet. Fourth, aggression is invited by the experimenter and apparently acceptable behavior. For all these reasons psychologists cannot hope to understand fully the effects of violent television models if they remain in their laboratories.

So psychologists have turned to field studies—primarily to correlating measures of aggressive behavior with amount of time spent viewing violent television programs. Study after study finds significant positive correlations; that is, children and adolescents who watch many violent programs tend to be more aggressive than those who watch comparatively few violent programs. But what causes what? Does being more aggressive lead children to watch a large amount of violent television? Or does watching all that violence on television make children aggressive? Or does some third factor account for both the aggressive behavior and the steady diet of television violence? An experimental field study is the only way to distinguish between these alternatives.

In the early 1970s Aletha Stein, Lynette Friedrich, and Fred Vondracek, psychologists at Pennsylvania State University, conducted a major field experiment on the effects of violent television models. They worked with ninety-seven preschool children ranging in age from three to five. The children came for nine weeks to a summer nursery school program. As part of the program each child was assigned to one of three television viewing groups. Three times each week for four weeks one group of children watched twenty to thirty minutes of aggressive material (such as "Batman"), while a second group watched twenty to thirty minutes of prosocial material (such as "Mister Roger's Neighborhood"), and a third group watched twenty to thirty minutes of neutral material (diverse children's films with no aggression and little prosocial behavior). Before, during, and after their television viewing the children were observed in the classroom and during free play, and they were rated on aggression, persistence, self-control, and other characteristics. In analyzing their data, Stein, Friedrich, and Vondracek took differences in socioeconomic class, intelligence, and initial level of aggression into account. They found that when children who were above the median initially on aggressive behavior were exposed to a steady diet of television violence, they behaved more aggressively in interpersonal situations. The other groups of children did not appear to be affected (57).

Recent studies indicate that violence on television may have a second unfortunate effect. It may make people insensitive to violence. Several studies show that children who watch a great deal of television stop reacting autonomically to new violence (58). Whether or not this insensitivity carries over into real life is not known for certain, but there remains the frightening possibility that people will become indifferent to brutality.

The Culture and Aggressive Behavior

Some cultures actively discourage aggression. Consider the Hutterites, a religious group of German origin, that has been living in culturally isolated settlements in Montana for about a hundred years. Working primarily as farmers, the Hutterites own their lands in common, live in modest dwellings all furnished alike, and eat their meals in a common dining hall. They also shun luxuries such as television, movies, radio, and jewelry. To preserve their communal way of life, Hutterite children are taught to suppress all outward signs of anger. One result is that murder, arson, severe physical assaults, and sex crimes are extremely rare.

In contrast to the Hutterites, the majority of Americans learn to positively value aggression. Traditionally, Americans glorified the gun-slinging hero of the Wild West and the rifle-bearing pioneer. Today the middle and upper classes value social aggression. People who pursue their goals no matter what, who dominate others and who speak up loudly are more widely respected than less assertive but more sensitive and humane people. Similarly, poor youths sometimes measure human worth by physical strength. One study finds that low-income delinquents perceive themselves as tough, powerful, fierce, and fearless, and that their primary ambition is to become more so (59). The ability to fight hard or to appear to be able to is valued for both status and survival, beginning at an early age.

According to U.S. government statistics, there are about 18,000 murders, 50,000 rapes, and 400,000 violent assaults in our country every year. In addition, some 5,000 children die and another 30,000 are seriously injured as a result of beatings, burnings, or stabbings by their parents (60). One reason for all the violence may be our society's tolerant attitude to aggression.

Provoking Aggression

Biology gives people the capacity to act aggressively. Experience teaches them particular aggressive patterns of behavior; and societies create climates that encourage or discourage the display of that behavior. Still people do not blindly aggress—they must be provoked. Unfortunately, modern life is like a battlefield heavily mined with provocative stimuli. Here are some of them.

Frustration. When an obstacle prevents people from reaching a goal (our temporary definition of frustration), they tend to become angry. If aggression is their usual response to anger, they are likely to aggress. (It is important to note that aggression is not the only possible response to frustration. We will have more to say about this matter in Chapter 13.) Adult frustrations take many forms. Minor conflicts and boredom are daily frustrations for most people. Boredom can be an especially treacherous frustration. When stimulation and excitement are scarce, research shows that dogs, monkeys, rats, and people all try to create their own (61). Some psychologists believe that delinquency may result, at least in part, as a response to the boredom created by too much free time and too little meaningful activity. Gang fights, looting, vandalism, and random cruelty alleviate monotony quickly.

Consider another powerful source of adult frustration, the violation of expectations. Although the American dream has many variations, it frequently goes something like this: When I grow up I'll have a house, two new cars, a nice yard, a satisfying job, money to spend, and self-respect. Many Americans find themselves grown and without. They

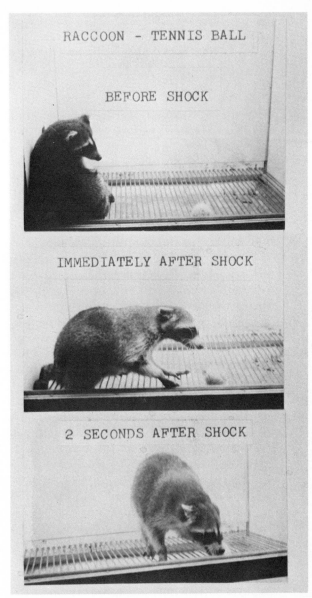

Figure 11-8. The raccoon is responding to electric shock by reflexlike aggression against the only available target: a tennis ball. (Nathan Azrin.)

may have two cramped rooms in a decaying apartment building, an old jalopy, no yard, no money, and a nightmarish job that produces little satisfaction and little self-respect.

Many observers believe that the sharp contrast between expectations and reality leads to much of the anger and aggression seen in contemporary society.

Pain. Rats, raccoons, foxes, cats, ferrets, rattlesnakes, snapping turtles, and squirrel monkeys respond to electric shock in the laboratory with almost reflexlike aggression (see Figure 11-8). When shocked these animals attack almost anything—another male or female animal, a stuffed doll, a tennis ball, a tube. Other pain elicitors such as intense heat and physical blows also elicit aggression. Pain-elicited aggression appears to have survival value in that it is likely to remove noxious stimulation. Although people do not respond to pain with reflexive aggression, there is evidence that they behave more aggressively after receiving physical punishment (electric shock) than after considerate treatment (62). Apparently pain makes people angry and increases their readiness to aggress.

Threats, taunts, or insults. Threats, taunts, or insults appear to be an especially effective provocation to aggression. Hans Toch, a psychologist at the State University of New York in Albany, studied the assault patterns of particularly aggressive (assault-prone) policemen, parolees, and prison inmates. Toch found that many explosive incidents followed a stable scenario: One individual instigated the hostility by taunting or insulting the other. The battle escalated. Eventually, there was a physical confrontation (63). Here is an example of how youths sometimes insult one another in a "game" called "the dozens" designed to provoke aggression:

One of the tormentors will make a mildly insulting statement, perhaps about the mother of the subject, "I saw your mother out with a man last night." Then he may follow this up with "She was drunk as a bat." The subject, in turn, will then make an insulting statement about the tormentor or some member of the tormentor's family. This exchange of insults continues, encouraged by the approval and shouts of the observers, and the insults become progressively nastier and more pornographic, until they eventually include every member of the participants' families and every act of animals and man. . . . Finally, one of the participants, usually the subject, who has actually been combating the group pressure of the observers, reaches his threshold and takes a swing at the tormentor, pulls out a knife or picks up an object to use as a club. This is the sign for the tormentor, and sometimes some of the observers, to go into action, and usually the subject ends up with the most physical injuries [64].

Status. In numerous situations, aggression leads directly to increased status. In the Vietnam war, for example, the American soldier's performance was partially evaluated by his body count (the number of people he killed). The more one killed, the more one was commended and honored. Among gang members and delinquents, brutality frequently leads to increased prestige. In the passage that follows, a chronic assaulter named Sam describes the increase in his stature and self-esteem that resulted from beating a fellow prisoner over a trivial card game incident:

And the dude got up and we were both on him, man. And we beat him to a pulp. Fixed him up bad, man. . . . So we just, once we got going we just wasted the dude. And that was that. Sent him on down to the hospital. And after that I felt like a king, man. I felt like, you know, "I'm the man. You're not going to mess with me." . . . I felt like "The Man," you know. I felt like everybody was looking up to me [65].

The violence of others. New modes of aggression seem to spread like a contagious disease. We have seen epidemics of arson, hijacking, kidnapping, and bombing. An aggressive act appears, attains popularity, and usually dies out as the powers of law and order find effective ways to control it. In any case, these epidemics demonstrate that aggression spreads, possibly because people are more likely to behave aggressively when they see or hear others so engaged.

Laboratory studies show that aggression triggers more of the same. In one study, navy men were made to believe that they were overhearing a discussion between two men, whom we will call Jake and John. Jake took a position that was unacceptable to the subject on several issues. Then the conversation took one of several courses: In one condition John abused Jake. In another condition, John simply disagreed with Jake politely. In a third condition, John's voice was unaudible. At the end of the conversation the subject was asked to describe Jake. Two-thirds of the men who overheard John abusing Jake followed suit—calling him an "ass," saying that he was "nuts," recommending that he be "locked up," "tortured," or "beaten." When John's voice was polite or inaudible, the subjects did not describe Jake aggressively (66). Apparently people are more likely to join in an attack when others are already involved.

Summary: Anger and Aggressive Behavior

1. Genes, hormones, and brain structures all shape an animal's capacity for aggression. Psychologists and physiologists are just beginning to understand how these various mechanisms contribute to aggressive behavior.
2. Although people have the biological capacity for aggression, how, against whom, and under what conditions they aggress depends primarily on learning. People learn aggression because of its positive consequences and through observation.
3. In the United States particular forms of

social and physical aggression are culturally sanctioned. This is probably part of the reason we see so much violence in our country.
4. Frustration, pain, and insults frequently provoke aggression. Aggression is also stimulated by watching others aggress and by incentives like increased status and self-esteem.

JOY: PLEASURE CENTERS AND PEAK EXPERIENCES

At psychology conventions one usually finds a variety of presentations on subjects such as aggression, stress, anxiety, depression, and rage, but comparatively few on subjects such as joy or love. For some reason psychologists have spent far more time studying the negative emotional states than the positive ones. In any case, we now focus briefly on joy. We look first at how the physiological psychologists have localized certain kinds of joy in the pleasure areas of the brain. Then we explore the humanistic psychologists' description of a more intense, more complicated kind of joy—the "peak experience."

The Pleasure Centers

We have seen that when particular areas of the limbic system are electrically stimulated, people feel intensely angry and sometimes they experience a strong desire to attack or destroy. Do the positive emotions also have specific seats in the brain? In 1954 James Olds and Peter Milner, physiological psychologists then at McGill University in Montreal, were exploring another question when they accidentally happened on the answer to this one. Olds and Milner were interested in learning more about the *avoidance areas*, areas deep within the center of the brain which, when stimulated, caused rats to react as if they were experiencing sharp pain and to subsequently avoid anything associated with the stimulation. One day, Olds and Milner implanted an electrode in the wrong area of one rat's brain—without realizing it. As the rat neared the corner of its cage, they turned on the current. They expected the animal to step backward, as other rats did under apparently identical conditions. Instead, the rat moved forward. They stimulated again; and again the rat moved forward. In fact, the rat seemed to be thoroughly enjoying itself. Could the rat be abnormal? What was going on?

When Olds and Milner checked the position of the electrodes, they discovered that they had been implanted in the limbic system and not in the reticular formation, as they had believed. Evidently, the stimulation of that particular limbic site was pleasurable (67). Just how pleasurable became clear in later studies. When a lever was connected to an electric stimulator so that rats could send current to particular limbic sites in their own brains by bar pressing, the animals activated the lever as many as five thousand times in a single hour. Moreover, they preferred particular types of brain stimulation to drinking when they were thirsty, to eating when they were starving, and to mating when they hadn't mated for a while. They also endured intense pain to have an opportunity to stimulate their own brains. In some cases, rats were such gluttons for stimulation that they bar pressed until they literally collapsed of exhaustion some fifteen to twenty-five hours later (68).

Today, psychologists know that many mammals, including people, have pleasure centers—in fact, dozens of them. Furthermore, most animals appear to be genetically programmed so that they can experience at least two distinct kinds of pleasure. The first kind is a pale sort. When we are hungry, thirsty, or sexually frustrated, for example, the alleviation of the need brings a feeling of relief that most of us find at least somewhat pleasurable. The second kind of pleasure is more enjoyable. Food, drink, and sexual activity, for example, not only relieve annoying deprived states, they can also provide intensely enjoyable experiences. Our sensory receptors are apparently connected to specific pleasure sites in the brain. Many psychologists believe that neurons in the pleasure centers may also be activated by positive reinforcement.

Why don't most of us stimulate our pleasure sites all day long by indulging nonstop in eating, drinking, sex, and other sensual pursuits? Evidently, our bodies were designed to minimize this possibility. Typically, the sensory pathways to the pleasure centers are activated only at particular times; in most cases, a biological need must be present to some degree. Under these circumstances, filling the need leads to both relief and joy. In fact, the joy can be viewed as a kind of incentive from the body to persuade us to take care of its needs.

How do people react to direct brain stimulation of the pleasure sites? Since the early 1950s Robert Heath, a physician at Tulane University, has been using brain stimulation therapeutically—to help alleviate pain and gain control of problem behavior. In 1963 Heath and his associates attempted to relieve sudden attacks of deep sleep, muscle weakness, and impulsive activity, the symptoms of two male epileptics, by implanting a number of electrodes in their brains. Six months after the men recovered from surgery, the studies began. The patients could stimulate various sites by depressing a button on a control unit worn on their belts. Stimulation at one site produced the reaction "feels great"; it also elicited "sexual feelings" and eliminated "bad" thoughts. Stimulation at another site, which one patient liked "okay," elicited the response "cool taste." Stimulation at a third site elicited "drunk feelings." The button that produced this state was labeled the "happy button." In general, Heath's studies and those of other researchers indicate that people are a lot less intrigued by pleasure center stimulation than rats appear to be. Heath's patients stimulated the "pleasure centers" for many reasons other than pleasure—such as to pursue a particular memory or to alleviate a particular symptom. And the pleasurable stimulation was not considered as intensely pleasurable as the pleasurable activities themselves would have been (69).

The Peak Experience

Abraham Maslow coined the term "peak experience" for the "best moments of the human being, for the happiest moments of life, for experiences of ecstacy, rapture, bliss, of the greatest joy [70]." These experiences are rare; and they can occur only after basic biological, social, and psychological needs have been fulfilled. Maslow believed that most people were caught up in the constant quest for the basic pleasures we described in the previous section and for the avoidance of pain and that they were not open to "peak experiences."

What are "peak experiences" like? They are intensely pleasant emotional states which can be reached through love, being an involved parent, undergoing a mystic or religious experience, creating beauty, achieving insight, or engaging in other acts of self-fulfillment. During a "peak experience" per-

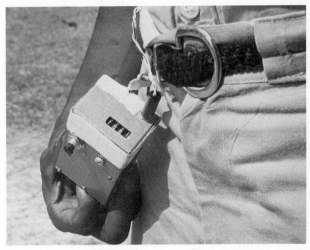

Figure 11-9. Heath's patients could stimulate various brain sites including "pleasure centers" by pressing buttons on a control unit worn on their belts. (Photo courtesy of Dr. Robert Heath.)

ceptions of the world change. People feel so intensely aware of their perceptions that they sometimes experience a sense of union with them. The "peak experience" is valued in and of itself; it is also regarded as a gift or a surprise rather than as something that was consciously produced. Maslow believed that "peak experiences" could change people's lives by making them feel that life was worth living, that "beauty and goodness and excitement and honesty and truth and meaningfulness" existed, even though life was usually "drab, pedestrian, painful, or ungratifying [71]." Note that "peak experiences" resemble certain experiences which people have during meditation (see Chapter 6).

Maslow provided a description of a complex little-known emotional state. Psychologists have a great deal to learn about this and other positive emotions.

STUDY GUIDE 11

Key Terms. emotion, autonomic nervous system (ANS), parasympathetic nervous system, sympathetic nervous system, adrenal glands, adrenalin, noradrenalin, central nervous system, cerebral cortex, reticular formation, limbic system, hypothalamus, amygdala, cognitive theory of emotion, anxiety, polygraph, existential anxiety, perception of control, general adaptation syndrome (GAS), alarm reaction, resistance, exhaustion, psychosomatic disorders, chronic anxiety, peptic ulcers, pepsinogen, type A personality, voodoo death, anger, aggression, social learning, catharsis hypothesis, frustration, peak experience, pleasure centers.

Important Research. physiological responses to emotion (Cannon), different physiological responses to different emotions (Wolf; Harvard research team), cognitions and emotions (Schachter and Singer), cognitions and anxiety (Geer), coping with anxiety (Spielberger), reactions to stress (Selye), anxiety and peptic ulcers (Weiner), personality patterns and heart attacks (Friedman and Rosenman), voodoo deaths (Cannon), learned rat-killing (Kuo), TV violence and aggression (Stein, Friedrich, and Vondracek), assault patterns (Toch), pleasure centers in the brain (Olds and Milner), self-stimulation of pleasure centers (Heath).

Basic Theories. cognitive theory of emotion, the causes of anxiety, aggression as an instinct (Freud and Lorenz), social-learning view of aggression, catharsis hypothesis, Maslow's concept of peak experiences.

Self-Quiz

1. Which phrase is *not* included in the definition of an emotion? [**a**]learned by observation and reinforcement; [**b**] seemingly spontaneous and uncontrollable; [**c**] characterized by subjective feelings and physiological arousal; [**d**] guides expressive gestures and subsequent behavior.

2. The part of the ANS that becomes especially active during intense emotional experiences is the [**a**] parasympathetic nervous system; [**b**] sympathetic nervous system; [**c**] reticular formation; [**d**] limbic system.

3. In their classic study presumably on the effects of supproxin on vision, Schachter and Singer discovered that [**a**] adrenalin causes emotional changes; [**b**] cognitions influence how people perceive and label a physiologically aroused state; [**c**] different physiological states produce different emotions; [**d**] a confederate can influence people's emotions only when they have not taken adrenalin and are not physiologically aroused.

4. Cross-cultural studies support the conclusion that smiling when happy and having a red face when angry [**a**] are learned behaviors; [**b**] are sex-linked characteristics; [**c**] are primarily determined by genetics; [**d**] are common in some societies but not in others.

5. Overt behavioral responses to emotion, such as sulking, whining, yelling, or constructive problem-solving when angry, [**a**] are learned; [**b**] are genetically determined; [**c**] are determined primarily by socioeconomic class; [**d**] occur in a predictable sequence as children grow older.

6. Using a polygraph to measure lying has all of the following problems *except* [**a**] lying does not always arouse anxiety; [**b**] people may learn to control their physiological responses during anxiety; [**c**] blood pressure, respiration rate, and skin conductance cannot be reliably measured; [**d**] the physiological responses during anxiety may be difficult to distinguish from those which occur during other strong emotions, such as anger.

7. Most disagreements among psychologists about anxiety center around [**a**] the physiological effects of anxiety; [**b**] the behavioral signs of anxiety; [**c**] the sources or causes of anxiety; [**d**] the desirability of anxiety.

8. Subjects who are anticipating painful electric shocks are likely to be most anxious if they [**a**] expect very strong shocks; [**b**] expect very frequent shocks; [**c**] know that they must control the delivery of the shocks to themselves; [**d**] do not know what intensity shock to expect.

9. Research shows that anxiety has which general effect on task performance? [**a**] impedes performance; [**b**] improves performance; [**c**] improves performance on easy tasks while impeding performance on difficult tasks; [**d**] improves the performance of students with high scholastic aptitudes but impedes the performance of students with low scholastic aptitudes.

10. According to Selye, environmental stresses cause a general adaptation syndrome that follows which of the following patterns? [**a**] alarm, resistance, exhaustion; [**b**] exhaustion, alarm, resist-

ance; [c] resistance, exhaustion, alarm; [d] alarm, exhaustion, resistance.

11. Studies of World War II soldiers indicated that stress reactions [a] could be reversed if soldiers were allowed to rest when signs of the reaction first appeared; [b] could be reversed at any time, but longer rest was required for soldiers who had been stressed for longer periods of time; [c] eventually disappeared with no special treatment after the war was over; [d] seldom interfered with the soldiers' performance.

12. Friedman and Rosenman have found that people with type A personalities are likely to have heart attacks; a type A personality may be most accurately described as [a] impulsive and egocentric; [b] competitive and compulsive; [c] masculine; [d] stubborn and unimaginative.

13. Which physical factor(s) probably influence human aggression? [a] Hormone levels only; [b] brain mechanisms and hormone levels; [c] genetic inheritance only; [d] hormone levels, genetic inheritance, and brain mechanisms.

14. Stein, Friedrich, and Vondracek found that watching aggressive TV material [a] made boys, but not girls, more aggressive; [b] made aggressive children, but not gentler ones, more aggressive; [c] made younger children, but not older ones, more aggressive; [d] all of the above.

15. When electrodes are implanted in human "pleasure centers" in the brain, electrical stimulation produces [a] moderate pleasure, not the intense pleasure rats apparently experience under similar conditions; [b] no definite emotion, but an increase in sympathetic nervous system activity; [c] no definite emotion, but relief from epileptic symptoms and changes in EEG patterns; [d] strong pleasure, which is apparently addictive.

Exercise

PHYSIOLOGY AND EMOTIONS. To test your knowledge of the role of physiology in emotion, match the following terms with their functions: autonomic nervous system (ANS), parasympathetic nervous system (PNS), sympathetic nervous system (SNS), adrenal glands (AG), adrenalin and noradrenalin (AN), central nervous system (CNS), cerebral cortex (CC), reticular formation (RF), limbic system (LS), hypothalamus (H), amygdala (A).

_____ 1. The part of the CNS that controls cognitive processes in emotion.

_____ 2. The part of the ANS that is responsible for a pounding heart, a dry throat, trembling, perspiring, and tense muscles during a strong emotion.

_____ 3. The part of the limbic system that activates the sympathetic nervous system during an emergency.

_____ 4. Identifies and evaluates responses during an emotional experience.

_____ 5. Stimulated by the sympathetic nervous system; releases hormones that quicken the heartbeat and respiration rate and arouse other centers that have already been activated by the sympathetic nervous system.

_____ 6. Has two subsystems that often work in opposition to each other.

_____ 7. The part of the CNS responsible for learned responses to emotion.

_____ 8. The group of structures in the brain core that helps regulate emotions.

_____ 9. The part of the ANS that is active during calm periods.

_____ 10. The hormones secreted during an intense emotion.

_____ 11. The part of the limbic system directly involved in Julia's rage.

_____ 12. The CNS network that arouses the cortex and has it attend to important events.

_____ 13. The part of the CNS that controls voluntary motor behavior during an emotion.

_____ 14. The part of the ANS that is active during intense emotion.

_____ 15. The nerves that lead from the spinal cord and brain to the smooth muscles, internal organs, glands, heart, and blood vessels.

Questions to Consider

1. In this chapter we discussed several studies which suggested that cognitions influence the intensity of anxiety. How could psychologists study the effects of cognitions on the intensity and/or duration of anger?

2. Cite arguments for and against the use of lie detectors.

3. In his novel The terminal man Michael Crichton describes an "elad" (electrical addict), a person who has had electrodes implanted in the pleasure centers of the brain and has become addicted to electrical stimulation. Based on current research, do you think such brain stimulation would be addicting? What problems would being an elad pose—for the person? for society?

4. How do you think test anxiety might be explained by B. F. Skinner? Sigmund Freud? Abraham Maslow?

5. Design a well-controlled longitudinal study to determine whether watching TV violence causes children to become more aggressive? What problems would you encounter in carrying out such a study?

6. Have you ever had a "peak experience"? If so, what caused it? How did it compare with other positive emotional experiences?

7. Observe your own physiological reactions to anger and fear. Are they similar?

8. Observe how your family members respond behaviorally to anger. How can the similarities and differences in family members' responses be explained?

Project 11: Identifying Emotions from Facial Expressions

People guess the emotions of others partly by interpreting their facial expressions, postures, gestures, etc. Psychologist Robert Rosenthal and his associates have found that certain people make more accurate judgments about the signs of emotion than others. Women tend to be more accurate judges than men; adults tend to be more accurate judges than children. In this project you will be comparing college men and women on their accuracy in quickly sizing up emotions from facial expressions.

Method. Find four cooperative female and four cooperative male college students who are willing to serve as subjects. Inform them that you will be showing them photographs of faces and asking them to judge the emotion that is expressed. Explain the project in full after you have collected all your data. You should test each subject individually in a quiet setting. You will need a table.

Photocopy the six numbered photographs on page 313 and paste each one on a sheet of cardboard. Number each photograph back and front so that they may be quickly identified. Make a data sheet for each subject like the one shown on this page.

Hand the subject the data sheet on which you have indicated the subject's sex. Instruct the subject to circle the number of the caption that best characterizes each photograph. Keep the photographs face down. Beginning with photograph 1, expose each photograph in order (1, 2, 3, 4, 5, 6) for two seconds. Make certain that subjects record one response per photo. (The correct answers appear on page 335.)

Results and discussion. Tally each subject's number of correct responses. Compute a mean number of correct responses for men and women. Also compute a

DATA SHEET (one needed for each subject)

Subject's Sex _____

1. a. Just received an unexpected visitor; surprised.
   b. Just received word that she has been promoted to an important job; joyful.

2. a. His dog is sick; sad.
   b. Can't watch his favorite TV program; angry.

3. a. Just informed daughter has polio; grieved.
   b. Just learned a hurricane is coming; fearful.

4. a. Just learned that her son won a speech contest; surprised.
   b. Just learned that her son ran away from home; unhappy.

5. a. Just saw lots of mold on the pickles she bottled; disgusted.
   b. Just found out that her dog chewed up her favorite rug; angry.

6. a. Son has been disobedient; angry.
   b. Son has flunked math; sad.

mean number of correct responses for photograph 1, photograph 2, etc. Consider the following questions:

1. Were women more accurate in judging emotions from facial expressions than men? vice versa? the same? How can you explain your findings?

2. Were some photographs judged more consistently accurately than others? How can this result be explained?

3. Did any problems occur? How might they have been prevented?

4. Rosenthal found that accuracy of judgments related to certain personality and behavioral characteristics. For example, more accurate subjects reported having fewer but closer friendships than less accurate subjects. How can this finding be explained? What other characteristics might correlate with judging emotions accurately? How could you test your hypotheses?

REFERENCE: Rosenthal, R., et al. "Body language and tone of voice: The language without words." *Psychology Today*, September 1974, 8, 64–68.

Suggested Readings

1. Darwin, C. *The expression of the emotions in man and animals.* Chicago: The University of Chicago Press, 1965 (also available in paperback). In this classic Darwin describes his studies on the ways people, dogs, cats, horses, and monkeys express emotions.

2. Collier, J. L. "Again the truth machines." *The New York Times Magazine*, November 25, 1973, 35, 104,

106–108, 110, 112, 114, 115. A discussion of the lie detector test and the ways it is used today.

3. Edson, L. "The psyche and the surgeon." *The New York Times Magazine*, September 30, 1973. Discusses psychosurgery and the controversies surrounding it.

4. Selye, H. "Stress: It's a GAS." *Psychology Today*, September 1969, 3, 24–26, 56. Selye discusses the research that led to the formulation of the general adaptation syndrome concept.

5. Holmes, T. H., & M. Masuda. "Psychosomatic syndrome." *Psychology Today*, April 1972, 5, 71–72, 106. Discusses how life crises contribute to psychosomatic disorders.

6. Johnson, R. *Aggression in man and animals*. Philadelphia: W. B. Saunders Company, 1972 (paperback). Discusses the fascinating research on the determinants of aggression. Comprehensive.

7. Berkowitz, L. "The case for bottling up rage." *Psychology Today*, July 1973, 7, 24, 26, 28–31. Psychologist argues that venting aggression leads to further aggression.

Answer Keys

SELF-QUIZ
1. a 2. b 3. b 4. c 5. a 6. c 7. c 8. d 9. c 10. a 11. a 12. b 13. d 14. b 15. a

EXERCISE
1. CC 2. SNS 3. H 4. CC 5. AG 6. ANS 7. CC 8. LS 9. PNS 10. AN 11. A 12. RF 13. CC 14. SNS 15. ANS

FACIAL EXPRESSIONS (p. 313)
1. joyful 2. angry 3. fearful 4. surprized
5. disgusted 6. sad

12
PERSONALITY

IN THIS CHAPTER
We focus on personality. We examine
how psychologists have theorized about
personality and how they have studied
morality, one aspect of personality. After
reading this chapter, you should be
able to do the following:

1. Characterize and contrast type, trait,
   psychodynamic, neobehavioristic,
   and self personality theories
2. Describe the personality theories of
   Sheldon, Cattell, Freud, and Mischel
3. Explain Kohlberg's findings about
   the consistency of moral judgments
4. Discuss the evidence concerning the
   consistency of people's moral behavior
5. Explain how family, social environment, formal religion, and moral instruction influence moral behavior
   and judgments

Grope[1]

"Grope was born near Springfield, Illinois, of a middle class family in confortable circumstances. [As a boy he] . . . liked to climb birch trees and swing down again to earth, over and over again. . . . He developed a lot of strength this way, and one day after school he threw down, one by one, every boy in the class. He states that he soon became the best athlete in the school, the best football player, the best drawer, the smartest (with the highest mark on an achievement test), the first person to be elected president of the sixth grade class, and the only person to be elected twice. . . .

"[Grope's] 'fall' began in sixth grade with loss of weight and sluggishness. He had many colds during that summer and when he went back to school in the seventh grade found that he hadn't grown an inch. The following winter he was in bed for two straight months. When he got well, his athletic career was 'shot.' . . .

"[Grope's] friendships were many but casual, never enduring. At college he made no real friends until the end of his sophomore year. Currently, he is extremely fond of one boy, a former member of his card-playing clique.

"From eighth through tenth grade Grope suffered from halitosis, which he believes made him much less popular and thus gave rise to a distressing inferiority complex. He thought he could make himself less offensive by speaking with a minimal expiration of breath, and now, six years later, his voice is habitually so low that his words are not always audible.

"[Grope's] . . . major recurrent fantasy [is] one of landing on a desert island in the Pacific with a band of followers, discovering an inexhaustible spring of fresh water and an abundant food supply, and then founding a new civilization with himself as king and lawgiver. . . . [The chief tenet of Grope's philosophy is] that every person's goal in life is happiness. . . . In his own case, the major sources of prospective happiness . . . are money, power, glory, and fame. . . . [He] writes: 'I am just biding my time and waiting for the day when the "soul" will ignite and this inner fire will send me hurtling (two rungs at a time) up the ladder of success.'

"Grope reports that a few months after his arrival at Harvard he came to the conclusion that he was a 'small frog in a big puddle,' surrounded by many far superior competitors for athletic, social, and academic honors. No hope for glory. Since then he has made the minimum amount of intellectual effort. He studies very little and cuts many of his lectures, especially if they come before noon. As a result, he is on

[1]Grope, the hero of this biographical sketch, participated in experiments, tests, and interviews which were conducted in the 1950s at the Psychological Clinic at Harvard University to study personality.

probation. . . . He has joined no organizations, has accepted no roles or responsibilities, and dates no girls. This abstinence allows him to devote the maximum amount of time to sleep, relaxation, day dreaming, and playing bridge with a small clique of cronies. . . . [1]."

As you read, you may have formulated a mental picture of Grope and his personality. By *personality* we mean the unique pattern of relatively enduring behaviors, feelings, thoughts, motives, interests, and attitudes that characterize a particular individual. Note that personality is a "summary construct": it includes many of the constructs which we have already discussed. Before continuing, try to describe Grope's personality. (You might want to jot down a few notes so that you can refer to your description later.)

Personality psychologists primarily investigate general questions about the nature and origin of personality. Their goal is to describe and explain personality differences between people. Theory has played a particularly prominent role in the study of personality. Some theories grew out of deliberate attempts to describe and measure personality, whereas others arose from efforts to understand and treat troubled people in clinics. Yet others had their origin in laboratory research. We begin by looking at several representative personality theories.

DESCRIPTIVE THEORIES

How did you describe Grope's personality? Many students list traits, such as "insecure," "intelligent," and "moody." *Traits* are characteristics which seem to endure across a wide variety of situations accounting for the regularity of behavior. Another frequent ploy which people use in personality descriptions is "typing." Some students call Grope a "lazy type," or "an ambitious type," or a "neurotic type," or some other type. Categorizing people into *types* assumes that several related personality traits commonly occur together. An "intellectual type," for example, might be high on the traits "snobbish" and "intelligent" and low on the traits "sociable" and "athletic." Both trait and type approaches to personality are similar in that they attempt to analyze the unique wholeness of a personality into enduring core characteristics.

Psychologists have formulated both trait and type theories of personality. We consider trait theories first.

Trait Theories

Trait theorists believe that the existence of a limited number of enduring traits can best explain behavior. Presumably these traits are fairly stable from youth to old age and from situation to situation. Trait theorists also assume that each trait characterizes an individual's personality to a greater or lesser degree. Take the trait "sociability" as an example. Most people fall somewhere in between the extremes very sociable and very unsociable. All traits are perceived as continuous, with people occupying a position in between two extremes. Trait theorists also believe that traits describe different types of personality variables such as temperament ("cheerfulness," "vitality"), adjustment ("psychological health," "self-confidence"), abilities ("intelligence," "creativity"), and values ("idealism," "liberalism"). Finally, whereas certain traits refer to behavior which is relatively easy to observe, others refer to characteristics which appear to be buried beneath the surface. The trait "cheerfulness," for example, can be easily measured by observing how frequently a person laughs or smiles. This relatively superficial characteristic could result from an underlying "warmth" or "distrust" for people. (In the latter case, cheerfulness is a style of interacting which keeps people at a distance.) The traits "warmth" and "distrust" are very difficult to measure. To illustrate how psychologists construct trait theories, we turn briefly to the work of Raymond Cattell.

Cattell's Trait Theory

Raymond Cattell, a psychologist at the University of Illinois, began research aimed at defining and measuring the major components of personality in the 1930s. Cattell and his associates started by compiling a list of some 17,953 English words which were used to describe people. By omitting rare and overlapping words, they managed to reduce the list to 171 words. To compact the list still further, Cattell and his colleagues asked various groups of people to check words on the list which described themselves and their friends. The patterns of adjectives which people used were subsequently analyzed using a mathematical technique known as factor analysis; the list was once again reduced, this time to the sixteen most basic characteristics. Cattell calls the sixteen characteristics shown in Figure 12-1 *source traits*, because they appear to be stable and influenced by genetics and because they determine many superficial behaviors or *surface traits*. Source trait "E," defined at one end by dominance and at the other by submissiveness, for example, seems to be responsible for surface traits such as degree of self-confidence exhibited and amount of boasting. Besides identifying surface and source traits, Cattell and his associates have developed a number of personality tests based on these sixteen source traits which are currently used to characterize the personalities of par-

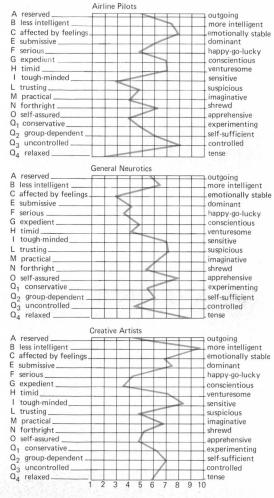

Figure 12-1. Personality profiles of airline pilots, neurotics, and creative artists based on Cattell's source traits. (Reproduced by permission of the Institute for Personality and Ability Testing, Champaign, Illinois.)

ticular individuals and groups of people, such as pilots, neurotics, and artists (see Figure 12-1).

Type Theories

Type theories assume that certain traits commonly cluster together at the core of people's personalities. These same trait "clusters" exist in all countries and in all ages and remain

Figure 12-2. Hippocrates believed that people could be typed according to their temperaments. These medieval woodcuts illustrate two temperament "types." The illustration on the left shows the depressed (melancholic) temperament; the illustration on the right shows the apathetic (phlegmatic) temperament. (National Library of Medicine, Bethesda, Maryland.)

intact from infancy through adulthood and from situation to situation. For example, the Greek physician Hippocrates believed that people's temperaments were typed: depressed, optimistic, apathetic, or irritable. The famous psychoanalyst Carl Jung believed that people could be classified by whether they were predominantly introverted (shy and preoccupied with their own thoughts and feelings) or predominantly extroverted (gregarious). We look closely at the type theory of an American psychologist and physician, William Sheldon.

Sheldon's Type Theory

William Sheldon believed that people with particular *types* of bodies tended to develop particular *types* of personalities. He reasoned that people are genetically endowed with bodily structures that determine the activities at which they may excel and consequently enjoy. If a woman has strong, well-developed muscles, she will probably excel at athletics,

enjoy such activities, and engage in them frequently. Bodies not only influence the activities people enjoy, they also influence the expectations of other people. Fat people, for example, are "supposed to be" jolly, easygoing, and even-tempered. Thin, fragile people are "supposed to be" nervous. And so on. People who look the part tend to be expected to play the role; expectations, as we have repeatedly seen, have important effects on the ways people behave.

Sheldon began looking for the physical components that characterize the male body in the early 1930s. After studying photographs of some four thousand male physiques, Sheldon and his associates came to the conclusion that male bodies could be characterized by three physical components, which they labeled *endomorphy*, *mesomorphy*, and *ectomorphy* (see Figure 12-3).

Because the vast majority of men tend to be mixtures of these characteristics, Sheldon and his associates developed a procedure for rating bodies on each physical component. A body is evaluated first on endomorphy, second on mesomorphy, and third on ectomorphy, and assigned a number ranging from 1 to 7 on each dimension. One represents a minimum, 4 an average, and 7 a maximum amount of that element. The combined scores constitute a *somatotype*. A man with a 6-3-1 somatotype, for example, is high on endomorphy, moderate on mesomorphy, and low on ectomorphy.

After developing a reliable way to identify male (and later female) body types, Sheldon and his associates identified three personality trait patterns which frequently appeared together—*visceratonia, somatotonia,* and *cerebrotonia*:

VISCERATONIA: love of comfort; sociability; gluttony for food, people, and affection; slow reaction time; even temper; tolerance

SOMATOTONIA: assertiveness; aggressiveness; love of action; directness; courage; dominance

CEREBROTONIA: inhibition; seriousness; restraint; secrecy; fear of people; self-consciousness; overly quick reactions; preference for solitude

Sheldon and his associates then attempted to find out if a specific trait pattern was associated with a specific body type. To answer this question they studied two hundred white male college students for five years. The same investigators rated bodies and behavior. At the end of the study they concluded that there were very strong positive correlations (around .80) between physique and personality. That is, a person with a somatotype of 6-1-1 (high endomorphy–low mesomorphy–low ectomorphy) was likely to have a personality described as 6-1-1 (high visceratonia–low somatotonia–low cerebrotonia) (2).

Was Sheldon correct? Do people fit into personality-physique categories? The answer is probably no. Apparently, Sheldon and his associates allowed their personal beliefs to bias their procedures. When other investigators repeat the study, using different sets of trained judges to rate somatotype and personality (to prevent experimenter bias—see Chapter 2), they generally find much smaller correlations between personality and body type. (In most cases they *do* find moderate correlations, supporting Sheldon's belief that our bodies and our personalities are somewhat related.) Sheldon's theory is also criticized for its assumption that somatotypes are stable; they can change and they sometimes do change.

Figure 12-3. William Sheldon's components of physique (*A*) Endomorphy: soft, round, underdeveloped bones and muscles, overdeveloped digestive viscera. (*B*) Mesomorphy: hard, rectangular, strong, resistant to injury, athletic build with highly developed muscles. (*C*) Ectomorphy: tall, thin, fragile, light muscles, large brain, sensitive nervous system.

A. Endomorphy

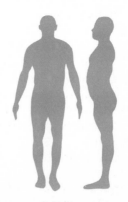
B. Mesomorphy

C. Ectomorphy

Critical Comments

Trait and type theories are both subject to a number of criticisms. Both spend comparatively little time discussing how the various components of personality arise and interact. Type theories in particular may be criticized for distorting personality by abstracting particular characteristics and forcing them into prominence, while neglecting less noticeable, but nonetheless important, propensities. You may have noticed that trait and type theories both emphasize the consistency of personality. Is personality consistent? Consider how your own personality varies as you interact with family members, close friends, strangers, teachers, young children. When we examine the research on moral behavior, we will see quite clearly that people are frequently inconsistent from situation to situation. Lastly, many psychologists believe that the single biggest weakness of trait and type theories may be their overemphasis on inborn determinants of personality and their failure to consider the importance of learning and environment.

PSYCHODYNAMIC THEORIES

The type and trait theories, which we have just examined, emphasize the description of personality and the classification of large numbers of people by objective methods, such as tests and rating systems. *Psychodynamic* personality theories, in contrast, aim at describing how personality develops and at explaining how underlying personality processes interact to determine behavior. They emphasize the importance of forces such as impulses, motives, and emotions; they assume that personality develops as people resolve internal conflicts between these internal forces. Informal techniques, such as in-terviews and clinical observations, are used to gather data on the personality of particular individuals under treatment for psychological problems. Sigmund Freud, Carl Jung, Alfred Adler, Karen Horney, Erich Fromm, Harry Stack Sullivan, and Erik Erikson are among many famous psychodynamic personality theorists. In this section we examine the personality theory of Sigmund Freud, the first psychodynamic theorist.

Freud's Psychodynamic Theory

As Freud treated his neurotic patients, he searched for insights that would enable him to understand the human personality. He also carefully observed his own personality.[2] Gradually, he put together a theory of mental functioning which he continued to check against further observations. Freud believed that personalities could be assessed only by trained experts—like himself—using psychoanalytic procedures in a clinical setting. The experts, known as psychoanalysts, observed their patients as they treated them in almost daily interviews for years. Patients were required to talk about whatever came into their minds and to report their dreams.

---

[2]Freud's own personality is fascinating. He is said to have appeared outwardly shy and inhibited. He also suffered from a number of psychological problems. He was frequently depressed and anxious as a youth. All his life he feared railways and railway travel. His marriage was sometimes stormy. He once wrote to his wife: "Since I am violent and passionate with all sorts of devils pent up that cannot emerge, they ramble about inside or else are released against you [3]." Some psychologists assume that Freud was also hypochondriacal because he often complained about indigestion, constipation, and heart palpitations. Moreover, like numerous other productive people, Freud drove himself compulsively to achieve. At age fifty, he was still working far beyond the capacity of most people—seeing patients from 8 A.M. to 1 P.M. and 3 to 9 P.M. every day and reading, writing, and corresponding from 11 P.M. to 2 A.M. every night. (His published works fill twenty-four volumes!)

The psychoanalyst scrutinized this material and other clues—like the patient's memory lapses, mistakes, and slips of the tongue. Eventually, after analyzing all these sources of information, the psychoanalyst came to understand the "subject's" personality. We will look at these assessment procedures in more detail in Chapter 15.

The main components of personality. Freud believed that people were conscious of only a small number of their own thoughts, feelings, and desires. Others were buried just beneath their awareness where they were fairly easy to retrieve. The vast majority of thoughts, feelings, and desires were completely unconscious and could not become conscious without the aid of a trained specialist. Freud was interested in this buried part. His conception of the *unconscious*, as he called this part of the personality, is extremely complicated; so we will limit our discussion to its bare outlines.

The unconscious, as Freud saw it, contains motives which Freud referred to as "instincts," as well as personality parts or factions, memories of early experiences, and repressed (roughly, pushed out of consciousness) conflicts. Motives—for food, elimination, sex, and aggression—play an important role in Freud's system. They generate the energy for behavior. According to Freud, three personality factions—the id, the ego, and the superego—compete continually for the available energy.

The *id*, the primitive core of the personality, is the domain of the motives and it strives to gratify them. At the earliest stage of infant development, the id monopolizes all the energy, but, like a spoiled child, it is irrational and insensitive to anything but its own desires and incapable of coping with reality, so it cannot satisfy itself.

The *ego* emerges in the developing child, according to Freud, to handle transactions with the environment. One of the ego's main tasks is to locate objects in the real world that are appropriate for the id's needs. The ego deals with both the demands of the id and those of reality. Unlike the childish and irrational id, the ego is controlled, realistic, and logical.

The *superego*, the third personality faction, develops gradually. It is essentially what people call "the conscience," a learned sense of right and wrong and good and bad, which becomes automatic after many years. According to Freud, the superego internalizes the morals, ideals, and standards of parents and society and strives continually for perfection. The superego tries to force the ego to pursue moral goals, instead of simply realistic ones, and to force the id to inhibit its animal impulses.

Freud believed that these personality factions were continually competing against one another for energy. While the id is striving to gratify its motives, the ego is struggling to hold the id and superego in check and to find appropriate objects for the gratification of the id. Simultaneously, the superego is working to restrain the id and to force the ego to carry out its lofty goals. Freud believed that as these factions struggled, dominance continually shifted among them, determining people's behavior. When the id is in charge, people are apt to act like animals; when the ego gains control, like realists; when the superego dominates, like moral reformers. Frustrations, threats, conflicts, and ordinary biological growth keep arousing the personality factions. These events also generate anxiety which the ego learns to handle by using defense mechanisms (see Chapter 13). When the ego is overwhelmed by anxiety, the id sometimes takes over completely. This event causes the individual to display abnormal behavior (see Chapter 14).

How does the personality develop? Freud

Id   Ego   Superego

Figure 12-4. Freud believed that the dominance of the id, ego, or superego determines behavior.

believed that the personality was shaped by early experience as children passed through a series of *psychosexual stages*. During these stages, the id's energy focuses on particular bodily zones—the mouth, the anus, and the genitals. If children are overindulged or deprived at any stage, development is arrested at that stage and the adult personality becomes *fixated on* (centers around) the unresolved difficulty.

Initially infants focus on their mouths—on eating, sucking, and biting. During this *oral stage*, which occurs during the first approximately eighteen months of life, children may be overly gratified or frustrated while nursing. If this happens, adult interests, attitudes, and characteristics may have an "oral" nature. For example, such individuals may be avid smokers, gum chewers, or incessant talkers, or they may exhibit "oral" personality traits (traits which characterize infants in the oral stage) like dependency, passivity, and greediness.

During the second year, toilet training usually begins, and children must learn to control their natural impulses for the first time. This event marks the beginning of the *anal stage*. If toilet training is harsh or if elimination is associated with extreme pleasure, the individual may be fixated in the anal stage and later demonstrate "anal" personality characteristics (traits which characterize chil-

dren during the anal stage): defiance, stubbornness, messiness, and sadism, or submissiveness, excessive orderliness, and cleanliness.

During the *phallic stage* (in the third to fifth year) children discover their genitals. They masturbate, and their fantasies set the stage for a universal crisis—the *Oedipus* and *Electra complexes* (named for the legendary Greek characters who loved the opposite-sexed parent to excess and felt intense rivalry toward the same-sexed parent). If these crises are not adequately resolved, people may reject the socially sanctioned sex role and become homosexuals or lesbians or display antisocial or immoral behavior. In other words, Freud believed that the resolution of these complexes was critical for the development of morality and appropriate sex-role behavior. (We will be considering morality later in the chapter.) Let's examine the boy's plight first. According to Freud, the young boy loves his mother because she gratifies his needs. With the onset of sexual awareness, Freud believed that the young boy directs his erotic fantasies toward his mother—desiring her for himself and perceiving his father as a rival for her love. In fact, according to Freud, the young boy wishes his father would die, and he fantasizes about killing him. Sooner or later the youngster begins to worry. What if his bigger, stronger father should retaliate? In particular, he fears that the father may castrate him to remove the source of his lust. To eliminate this terrifying possibility the boy represses his love for his mother, *identifies* with his father, and strives to become like him. By this maneuver the boy eliminates the threat and simultaneously obtains the *vicarious* gratification of his sexual impulses. (Identified with his father, the boy shares in his father's sexual pleasures.) Freud believed that this identification had far-reaching consequences. It enabled the young boy to take on masculine sex-typed personality characteristics and to incorporate the father's superego.

According to Freud, young girls also face a similar crisis at about the same time in their development. The girl, like the boy, loves her mother since the mother has been gratifying her needs. However, at the beginning of the phallic stage the girl makes a traumatic discovery from which, Freud believed, she never recovers: The girl learns that she has a cavity, instead of a penis, the "more desirable sex organ"; and she blames her mother for this misfortune. To gain control of the valued organ, the girl temporarily transfers her love to her father. Freud never found a satisfactory reason for the girl to repress her love for her father, identify with her mother, assume feminine sex-typed behavior, and adopt her mother's superego. Eventually, he decided that the girl's love for her father and rivalry with her mother simply dissipated slowly with time; so the girl's identification with her mother, unlike that of the boy's with his father, is relatively weak. Freud believed that these developmental circumstances were the cause of numerous character deficiencies in women.[3]

[3]Apparently, Freud had a strong prejudice against women. He characterized them as more envious, self-centered, subject to shame, and dependent than men, as well as less reliable, just, and productive. He believed that these defects could be explained by the woman's

At the conclusion of the phallic stage, at approximately age five, Freud believed that children's personalities were essentially formed. For the next approximately seven years, it seemed to him that the sexual needs became dormant, no important conflicts occurred, and no important personality changes were possible. At the onset of puberty, children's sexual interests reawakened. During adolescence and early adulthood, which roughly coincide with the *genital period*, individuals become oriented toward others, and they begin to participate in the activities of their culture. Up until this time, they have been absorbed in their own bodies and their own immediate needs. Now, as adolescents, they learn to form satisfying relationships with other people. According to Freud, a mature heterosexual relationship is the hallmark of maturity. If energy is tied up—because of excessive gratification or conflicts at lower developmental stages—an adolescent will not be able to meet this challenge. According to Freud, then, the adult personality is primarily shaped during four stages.

Critical Comments

Although Freud's notions about personality were rejected in his day (apparently they shocked and outraged his contemporaries), they are widely accepted by the general public today. Concepts such as "frustrated needs," "unconscious impulses," "Oedipus complex," and "oral personality" are terms which have become so commonplace that they are rarely even associated with Freud's

"genital deficiencies." Because she lacked a penis, the little girl developed personality characteristics such as envy and inferiority feelings. For the same reason, she did not need to identify strongly with her mother, a circumstance which leads to the girl's weak superego. Freud also believed that women longed all their lives for a penis of their own; this longing could only be partially satisfied at best by giving birth to a son.

name. How has Freud's personality theory fared with psychologists? Most psychologists agree with Freud that early experience is important for personality development (see Chapter 3 for the experimental evidence) and that people are often influenced by motives and feelings of which they are unaware. On the other hand, the details of Freud's theories are widely and hotly debated: Is motivation primarily biological in origin? Do children pass through oral, anal, phallic, and genital stages? Are there three parts to the personality? Are unconscious motives the all-important ones? Are the effects of the first five years permanent and irreversible? And so on. Moreover, Freud's theory is generally criticized for having failed to consider social and cultural influences on personality development. Freud assumed, for example, that sexuality was a universal preoccupation, instead of connecting this concern to the social practices of his Victorian society.

What about the psychodynamic theories in general? Like trait and type theories, the psychodynamic ones assume that personality is highly consistent; however, they attribute these consistencies primarily to experiences

Figure 12-5. A person who is "charitable" in a volunteer hospital job may not be charitable when confronted by a panhandler on the street. (From Monkmeyer.)

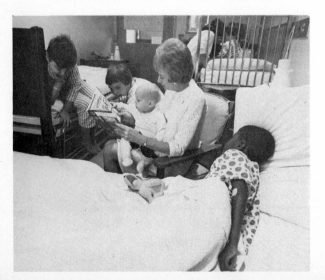

during childhood and secondarily to human heredity which programs people with particular motives. You may also have noticed that psychodynamic explanations of behavior are not parsimonious (see page 33). For example, is messiness most simply explained as the result of a fixation during the anal period? Many psychologists object to this violation of scientific policy. Psychodynamic theories are also criticized for being very difficult (and, in some cases, impossible) to test by scientific methods. How would you operationally define the id, for example? Psychoanalytic theorists maintain that the only meaningful way to test their theories is clinical observation, a method which scientifically oriented psychologists consider lacking in objectivity and precision and incapable of establishing cause-and-effect relationships.

NEOBEHAVIORISTIC THEORIES

Each of the theories we have examined so far supports the popularly held notion that there is something within people—universal types, enduring traits, interacting factions, conflicts, or motives—that cause them to behave in characteristic ways. Neobehavioristic psychologists conceptualize personality quite differently. They focus on what people *do* in particular situations. They avoid drawing inferences about people's motives, traits, feelings, conflicts, or other internal dispositions. They believe that the so-called personality is a fiction: that people infer underlying personality characteristics which simply do not exist. Let's take an example. A young woman contributes several hours each day to various charitable organizations. Many people would view her efforts as triggered by an underlying personality characteristic (say, the trait "generosity" or the motive to help others, "altruism"). Neobehaviorists, in contrast, assume that the woman's behavior is relatively specific to this particular situation (*situation-specific*) and look for environmental conditions which might be responsible for it. The woman's participation in charitable organizations may depend on her parent's approval, her husband's encouragement, an excess of free time, or some combination of factors. Neobehaviorists would not necessarily expect to find this woman "generous" or "altruistic" in other settings since behavior in these other situations would depend on a different set of conditions. She may not give money to beggars because they have been associated with frightening stories; she may not contribute to political campaigns because she believes that all politicians are dishonest. The neobehaviorists believe that behavior in every situation is controlled by many essentially independent causes and conditions, especially current circumstances and past learning. Sometimes they consider the impact of people's cognitions as well. It is important to note that the neobehaviorists particularly stress the basic principles of learning (respondent conditioning, operant conditioning, and observation learning) and perceive learned habits as being the most significant determinants of behavior.

Unlike the psychodynamic theorists, the neobehaviorists emphasize systematic research and deemphasize theorizing which cannot be directly tested. To illustrate the approach, we turn to a case study which was analyzed by Walter Mischel, a neobehavioristic psychologist at Stanford University. B. F. Skinner, Neal Miller, and Albert Bandura, psychologists whom we mentioned in Chapter 7, are also prominent proponents of the neobehavioristic approach to personality.

The case of Pearson Brack

"Pearson Brack was a bombardier in the Tunisian theater of operations during World War II. During Brack's ninth mission his airplane was severely damaged by flak. It suddenly jolted and rolled, and then began to dive. The pilot regained control of the plane just in time to avoid crashing. During the plane's fall, however, Brack was hurled violently against the bombsight and was seriously injured. After his return from this mission he was hospitalized for a month and then, seemingly recovered, was returned to flight duty. On his next two missions, the tenth and eleventh, he fainted and gradually his problem was brought to the attention of a psychodynamically oriented psychiatrist. Direct observation revealed that Brack's tendency to faint seemed specifically linked to being at an altitude of about 10,000 feet.

"After intensive interviews, the psychiatrist concluded that Brack's fainting was connected to deep, underlying anxieties rooted in his childhood experiences. Brack was viewed as a basically immature person with long-standing insecurity who had inadequately identified with his father. The near fatal plane incident was seen as essentially trivial except insofar as it precipitated anxiety in an already insecure and immature individual.

"In contrast, a . . . [neobehavioristic] analysis of the same case emphasized the severe emotional trauma that might have been conditioned to altitude cues during the mishap. That is, if Brack's injury occurred at about 10,000 feet, then any altitude cues present at that time might have become conditioned stimuli capable of eliciting a traumatic reaction (such as fainting). In that case, every time Brack later re-experienced cues connected with the accident (such as being in a plane at a comparable altitude), he would again become emotionally debilitated. . . .

"The . . . [neobehavioristic] view has many implications for the study of persons. Social behavior assessments do not describe the individual in generalized trait terms, sort him into type categories, or infer his conflicts and motives. Instead they sample what the individual does now in relation to the conditions in which he does it. In this sense, behavioral assessment involves an exploration of the unique . . . aspects of the single person by analyzing how he changes in response to changes in stimulus conditions. . . . In the case of bombardier Brack, for example, behavioral assessments would entail studying changes in his emotional response to airplanes as a result of changing and re-arranging altitude cues or other stimuli that seemed to affect his fainting problem most potently [4]."

Critical Comments

The neobehavioristic approach to personality has several important strengths: It emphasizes the necessity of making careful and precise observations of behavior, and it insists that research is the best way to evaluate theories about behavior. On the other hand, the neobehaviorists can be criticised for having carried the "behavior is situation-specific" hypothesis too far. Although many psychologists agree with the neobehaviorists that behavior always depends—at least to some degree—on the situation and on learned habits, many believe that behavior also depends on consistencies within people. As we have seen in previous chapters, research supports the observation that people display behavioral consistencies across diverse situations which appear to be attributable to relatively stable personality variables. People who score high on intelligence tests, for example, often perform well in other academic and social situations (see Chapter 9), and general mood and mode of adaptation to new stimuli are frequently consistent from infancy to adolescence across many situations (see Chapter 3). Many psychologists also see the neobehavioristic approach as narrow because it focuses almost exclusively on environmental conditions and learning and fails to adequately consider (1) important constructs such as motives, emotions, and cognitions and (2) genetic and biologically based influences on behavior.

SELF THEORIES

"Whether beautiful or ugly or just conveniently at hand, the world of experience is produced by the [person] who experiences it [5]." This simple statement expresses the philosophy of the self theorists. These personality theorists focus on the development of the *self*, a unique hypothetical spirit that resides within each person, guiding behavior according to personal concepts and perceptions. Self theorists view people as perceiving, experiencing beings motivated primarily by one need—the need to fulfill their own unique potentialities. Self theorists also stress the importance of the environment. People cannot develop these potentialities unless their environment satisfies their more basic physiological and social needs. When people are hungry, tired, or cold, or when they do not feel safe, accepted, or loved, for example, they are not likely to be interested in pursuing scientific, literary, or artistic goals.

Like the psychodynamic theories, the self theories originated in clinical observations. However, unlike the psychodynamic theories, the self theories gather information about personality by simply asking people to report their feelings and perceptions. Abraham Maslow and Carl Rogers are both prominent representatives of this position. Maslow's self-actualization theory was discussed in Chapter 10 (page 280) and Chapter 1 (page 20). Since we will also examine Carl Roger's view of personality development in Chapter 15, we will not discuss a self theory here.

SUMMARY: THEORIES OF PERSONALITY

Table 12-1 compares the five personality theories which we have examined. In Chapter 15 we will see how psychoanalytic, neobehavioristic, and self theories are applied to the treatment of troubled people. The descriptive approaches to personality are not associated with specific treatment methods.

MORALITY

We turn now from personality theory to personality research on morality. It may strike you as odd that psychologists consider morality to be an aspect of human personality, but, in fact, most people treat morality as a personality characteristic in that they use trait labels such as "sneaky," "honest," "crooked," "saintly," "amoral," and "immoral" to characterize one another. In this section we look at both the consistency and determinants of moral judgments and moral behavior—issues raised by the personality theories which we just examined. We define these terms as follows: *Moral judgments* refer to beliefs about "right" and "wrong," whereas *moral behavior* refers to conduct in situations where people are tempted to behave in ways that they consider "wrong." In general, we use the words "moral" and "immoral" to designate behavior and judgments that conform or fail to conform respectively to the standards of the Judaeo-Christian code. In other words, "moral" is defined by belief in the dignity of life, justice, doing unto others as you would have them do unto you, compassion, and other like concepts.

The Consistency of Moral Judgments

In Europe, a woman was near death from a very bad disease, a special kind of cancer. There was one drug that the doctors thought might save her. It was a form of radium that a druggist in the same town had recently discovered. The drug was expensive to make, but the druggist was charging ten times what the drug cost him to make. He paid $200 for the radium and charged $2,000 for the small dose of the drug. The sick woman's husband, Heinz, went to everyone he knew to borrow the money, but he could only get together about $1,000 which is half of what the drug cost. He told the druggist that his wife was dying, and asked him to sell it cheaper or let

TABLE 12-1. FIVE THEORIES OF PERSONALITY

Theory	Primary Dimensions or Components of Personality	Personality Organization	Major Determinants of Personality	Personality Stability	Major Motives	Method of Assessing Personality
Cattell's Trait Theory	Traits.	Source traits produce surface traits. Interactions between the traits are not well defined.	Genetics, learning, and culture	Source traits: stable. Surface traits: fluid.	None emphasized.	Objective tests.
Sheldon's Type Theory	Personality types related to body structure types.	Not emphasized.	Genetics and social expectations emphasized.	Highly stable.	None emphasized.	Ratings.
Freud's Psychoanalytic Theory	Three interacting systems: id, ego, superego.	Motives supply the energy for behavior. Personality results from the interplay of id, ego, superego, environmental demands, and growth.	Genetics and experience during four psychosexual stages: oral, anal, phallic, genital.	Highly stable.	Sex, aggression, and other "biological" motives.	Psychoanalytic method (analysis of dreams, free associations, memories, memory lapses, mistakes, etc.).

Mischel's Neobehavioristic Approach	Behavior.	Not emphasized.	Behavior is seen as dependent on the situation in which it occurs. Past learning is also considered important and cognitions are also taken into account.	Fluid.	None emphasized.	Descriptive and experimental research methods.
Self Theory	The self.	An optimal environment allows people to grow and fulfill themselves; a less-than-optimal environment arrests the growth process.	Experience.	Fluid.	Self-fulfillment.	Self-report.

him pay later. But the druggist said, "No, I discovered the drug and I'm going to make money from it." So Heinz got desperate and broke into the man's store to steal the drug for his wife. Should [Heinz] . . . have done that? Why?

Suppose that even after taking the drug, Heinz's wife does not recover. Instead, she approaches death very painfully and slowly. Her pain is so great that she is like another person.

She requests her doctor to "mercy kill" her by giving her an overdose of sleeping pills. Should the doctor "mercy kill" a fatally ill woman requesting death because of her pain [6]?

How would you answer these questions? Please jot down your answers before reading further.

Lawrence Kohlberg, a psychologist now at

TABLE 12-2. KOHLBERG'S STAGES OF MORAL DEVELOPMENT

Level	Stage	Motive	Value of a Human Life
1. Premoral	1. Punishment and obedience orientation	Obeys rules to avoid punishment. *Example*: "I don't lie because —if I do—my mother beats me."	The value of a human life is confused with the value of physical objects and is based on the social status or physical attributes of its possessor.
	2. Naive instrumental hedonism	Conforms to obtain rewards, have favors returned, etc. *Example*: "I don't squeal on Joe. That way Joe don't squeal on me."	The value of a human life is seen as instrumental to the satisfaction of the needs of its possessor or of other persons.
2. Conventional Role Conformity	3. Good-boy morality of maintaining good relations, approval of others.	Conforms to avoid disapproval, dislike by others. *Example*: "If my father ever found out that I cheated, he'd never trust me again. So I don't cheat."	The value of a human life is based on the empathy and affection of family members and others toward its possessor.
	4. Authority maintaining morality.	Conforms to avoid censure by legitimate authorities and resultant guilt. *Example*: "The cops might catch you if you shoplift. I'd feel guilty anyway."	Life is conceived as sacred in terms of its place in a categorical moral or religious order of rights and duties.
3. Morality of Self-accepted Moral Principles	5. Morality of contract of individual rights and of democratically accepted law.	Conforms to maintain the respect of the impartial spectator judging in terms of community welfare. *Example*: "If I took fruit, the shopkeeper would be short at the end of the day. He's a person like me. If I don't respect his rights, he won't respect mine. Society can't function unless people respect each other's rights."	Life is valued both in terms of its relation to community welfare and in terms of life being a universal human right.
	6. Morality of individual principles of conscience.	Conforms to avoid self-condemnation. *Example*: "If I killed someone, I couldn't live with myself."	Belief in the sacredness of human life as representing a universal human value of respect for the individual.

the Harvard Graduate School of Education, sees people as "moral philosophers." To put it less eloquently, we all have ideas about what is "right" and "wrong" and why. Much of the time we are not aware of these philosophies, but they emerge rather clearly when we confront a moral dilemma.

Kohlberg began studying in the early 1960s

Sample Responses to Heinz's Dilemma

Pro—If you let your wife die, you will get in trouble. You'll be blamed for not spending the money to save her and there'll be an investigation of you and the druggist for your wife's death.

Con—He may not get much of a jail term if he steals the drug, but his wife will probably die before he gets out so it won't do him much good. If his wife dies, he shouldn't blame himself; it wasn't his fault that she has cancer.

Pro—No one will think you're bad if you steal the drug, but your family will think you're an inhuman husband if you don't. If you let your wife die, you'll never be able to look anybody in the face again.

Con—You're desperate and you may not know you're doing wrong when you steal the drug. But you'll know you did wrong after you're punished and sent to jail. You'll always feel guilty for your dishonesty and law-breaking.

Pro—You'd lose other people's respect, not gain it, if you don't steal. If you let your wife die, it would be out of fear, not out of reasoning it out. So you'd just lose self-respect and probably the respect of others too.

Pro—If you don't steal the drug and let your wife die, you'd always condemn yourself for it afterward. You wouldn't be blamed and you would have lived up to the outside rule of the law but you wouldn't have lived up to your own standards of conscience.

---

the ways people reason about moral issues. In an initial research project, he studied seventy-five American boys between the ages of ten and sixteen. (Later he also observed boys in Canada, Britain, Mexico, and Taiwan.) Kohlberg presented each subject with four to ten moral dilemmas and questions like the ones above. The same material was readministered at periodic intervals over a twelve-year period. Extensive analyses of the data revealed that children all over the world pass sequentially—at varying rates—through six distinct stages of moral thinking. The stages reflect three general moral orientations or levels; each depends on a particular way of valuing human life. As you study Table 12-2 try to categorize your responses to Heinz' dilemma.

Kohlberg finds that people tend to be consistent in the assumptions which underlie their moral judgments; that is, approximately 50 percent of an individual's responses to diverse moral problems can usually be categorized as typical of a particular stage. The remaining responses almost invariably reflect the stage immediately above or below. Generally, young children function at the premoral level, whereas older children and adults function at the conventional level. Approximately one-quarter of the adults Kohlberg has tested reach one of the principled stages—but only 5 to 15 percent ever reach stage 6. To attain the highest moral level, people must apparently confront ethical crises that force them to question the rules of society (7).

Kohlberg, Jean Piaget (the Swiss developmental psychologist), and others believe that moral development is one aspect of cognitive growth. As children struggle to make sense of increasingly complex experiences, they build on past understanding, and their moral thinking becomes more sophisticated. A number of studies show that development proceeds along the following dimensions:

Intentionality. Young children judge behav-

Figure 12-6. A subject of some debate has been the moral level (on Kohlberg's scale) of antiwar demonstrators. (George W. Gardner.)

ior by its physical consequences—without taking intentions into account. For example, a typical eight-year-old judges it morally worse to drop an expensive cup accidentally than to smash a cheap one purposely. A typical fourteen-year-old takes the opposite view.

Relativism. Young children assume that all acts can be classified as absolutely and unconditionally "right" or "wrong." The average eight-year-old may believe that killing is always wrong. Older children judge the same act differently depending on the circumstances. The average fourteen-year-old may view killing as generally wrong, but justifiable under some circumstances—such as in self-defense.

Independence of sanctions. Young children judge the severity of a crime by the severity of the consequences that follow it. Anyone who is spanked is automatically perceived by the young child as having behaved badly. Older children evaluate behavior by the rule that was broken or the harm that was intended.

Use of reciprocity. Young children cannot put themselves in the place of others, and they cannot understand motives that differ from their own. A typical preschooler believes that a bloody nose deserves a bloody nose. The typical adolescent considers the other person's point of view, motives, and so on.

Use of punishment for restitution and reform. The young child believes that bad deeds should be severely punished. Older children endorse the use of mild punishment that results in reform. Punishment, in other words, is justified only when it serves a constructive purpose.

Naturalistic view of misfortunes. Young children perceive accidents and misfortunes as willed by God; older children interpret them as natural (8).

Kohlberg has demonstrated that the assumptions which underlie moral thinking are consistent from judgment to judgment at particular developmental stages, but this does not mean that people are consistently "moral" or "immoral" in their judgments.

The Consistency of Moral Behavior

When confronted with temptation, do people behave in consistently moral or immoral ways? Religious educator Hugh Hartshorne and psychologist Mark May were among the first social scientists to investigate this question experimentally. In 1924 they began studying thousands of children eight to fifteen years of age and of varied social backgrounds. Each child was exposed to diverse temptations, opportunities to cheat, lie, and steal, in several settings such as a classroom, a party, an athletic contest. In one situation, for example, the teacher left the room during a test—making it appear easy to cheat without being detected. Hartshorne and May found moderate consistencies in children's responses to temptation. Children who were intelligent, well mannered, middle-class, enrolled in Sunday School, or infrequent movie goers, cheated less than the others. Generally, however, the children were far from morally consistent. A child might cheat on tests but not during games. A child who stole from a store might not lie to his mother. Almost all the children were dishonest at least some of the time. The characteristics of the situation—the ease, benefits, and safety of dishonest conduct—related more strongly to moral behavior than the child's "moral character" (defined as knowledge of "right" and "wrong," frequent Sunday School attendance, avowed adherence to the Boy Scout oath, etc.) (9). Other investigators find similar results when they study young children (10).

The studies we just cited looked at children who were probably too young to be morally principled—to use Kohlberg's phrase. Recall that people at Kohlberg's stages 1, 2, 3, and 4 conform to moral rules to avoid negative consequences, to attain positive consequences, or to maintain the approval of others. If they are tempted to violate their own ethics and they believe that they can get away with it, there is nothing to hold them back. On the other hand, people at stages 5 and 6 carry their moral principles within; so they should be better able to resist temptation. Doing doctoral research at the University of Chicago in 1967, R. L. Krebs found some support for this hypothesis. After determining the moral-judgment levels of a group of college students and sixth-grade children, Krebs put them in situations that tempted them to cheat. Under these circumstances subjects at the premoral and conventional morality levels were far more likely to cheat than the principled subjects. Krebs also found that moral behavior related to measured intelligence and attention span (11). Apparently, there is no simple answer to our question about moral consistency. Moral behavior depends on the nature of the situation, the maturity of the individual's moral reasoning, and probably on other variables as well. These results suggest that moral behavior may be partly the result of a consistent disposition and partly dependent on the specific situation; so the descriptive, psychoanalytic, and neobehavioristic theories which we examined would all have to stretch a bit to accommodate these results.

Some Factors That Shape Morality

What forces shape moral behavior and moral judgments?

The family. Is there evidence that children learn morality within their families? Freud, you'll recall, believed that the child's moral orientation changed dramatically around the age of five after the resolution of the Oedipus or Electra complex. Is there any evidence that Freud's theory is correct? To date, the research findings on Freud's view are sporadic; the studies that exist do not generally support Freud's hypotheses about how morality develops. For example, Hartshorne and May found no changes in resistance to cheating and stealing as children grew from their nursery to their high school years. Other investigators find that children increase their helping behavior and decrease their stealing and lying around the age of eight (12,13).

Kohlberg also finds changes in moral judgment around this time, but there is no evidence that these changes are linked to the resolution of a universal complex or conflict. Other investigators have checked out Freud's hypothesis that boys are more moral than girls. A review of the research on this subject shows that there are no significant differences between boys and girls on either conformity to internal moral standards or on tendency to feel guilty after a moral transgression (14).

Do people learn moral behavior by simple learning principles within their families, as many neobehaviorists assume? Although a great deal of research indicates that families probably exert an important influence on their children's moral conduct, simple learning principles cannot, by themselves, account for current research findings. The research literature on families and moral behavior has focused on one parental variable, warmth and nurturance versus coldness and rejection. Studies repeatedly find that parental warmth and nurturance are positively correlated with moral behavior in children. In the mid-sixties, for example, the section of Manhattan known as Chinatown was frequently cited as a shining illustration of this phenomenon. Unlike the vast majority of old inner-city neighborhoods, Chinatown had an unusually low crime rate. Parents in Chinatown were characterized by one investigator as affectionate, responsive to their children, and strongly rejecting of antisocial behavior (15); whereas parents of juvenile delinquents were characterized in another study as rejecting, unpredictable, hostile, and frequently antisocial themselves (16).

Social scientists at Yale University have looked at anthropological data on forty-eight nonliterate societies in Africa, North and South America, Asia, and the South Pacific to see if child-rearing practices were associated with the number and types of crimes. Each investigator, independently of the others, analyzed and rated each society for the frequency of personal crimes (those aimed at injuring or killing a person) and thefts. Next they rated each society's child-rearing practices. They were particularly interested in evaluating how nurturant (affectionate, responsive) or strict (severe, anxiety provoking) the parents tended to be. Finally, the two sets of ratings were correlated. The findings included the following: Societies where parents were predominantly nurturant had lower frequencies of theft than those where parents were predominantly strict. Harsh and abrupt training for independence was associated with high rates of personal crime (17).

Parents probably convey warmth to their children by the various disciplinary practices which are used to encourage good behavior and discourage bad behavior. *Love-oriented techniques* refer to disciplinary methods that use praise as a reward for good behavior and reasoning, appeals to pride, withdrawal of love, and displays of disappointment as deterrents or punishments for bad behavior. These techniques communicate the parent's concern about the child's well-being. *Object-oriented techniques* refer to disciplinary methods that use tangible rewards for good behavior and threats, commands, physical force, and withdrawal of privileges as deterrents or punishments for bad behavior. Ordinarily, these techniques are impersonal and do not communicate caring. Numerous studies find that children with strong consciences (those who express feelings of guilt, a sense of responsibility, and a need to confess and atone for wrongdoing) come from homes where warm parents use love-oriented disciplinary techniques predominantly, but children with an external moral orientation (those who are influenced in right and wrong by restrictions and rewards) come from homes where parents use object-oriented techniques predominantly (18).

What do these results mean? Why should parental nurturance and concern be associated with moral behavior? This finding is most

Figure 12-7. Love-oriented vs. object-oriented techniques of discipline.

simply explained by assuming that a combination of learning processes are facilitated by warmth. Research shows that the children of nurturant parents model their parents' values more readily than the children of nonnurturant parents (19). So, if warm, concerned parents are moral themselves, their children are likely to adopt their values. It is also possible that the children of warm parents learn the benefits of considering others firsthand. Similarly, the approval of warm parents may be a more powerful reward for appropriate behavior than the approval of cold parents. At the same time, children may associate their parents' values with their feelings for their parents. Because the moral values of warm parents tend to be associated with pleasant feelings, they may appear more attractive to children than the moral values of cold parents that tend to be associated with unpleasant feelings. You may be able to think of some other reasons for the association of warmth in parents and morality in children.

At least one study shows that empathy training may also be contributing to the effectiveness of the love-oriented techniques. In 1967 Martin Hoffman and Herbert Saltzstein, psychologists then at the Merrill Palmer Institute in Detroit, reported on a study of seventh-graders and their parents. Teachers, parents, and peers rated each child on various dimensions of moral maturity. The children's parents were interviewed concerning their disciplinary practices and later characterized as using mostly *power assertion* (force and threats), *love withdrawal* (direct expressions of anger and disapproval), or *induction* (discussion of the consequences of the child's action for others). For middle-class children a high level of moral maturity was associated with the frequent use of induction and the infrequent use of power assertion. Why should induction lead to moral maturity? Apparently this technique trains children to be empathic (to put themselves in the position of other people) and to consider the welfare of others before acting. For lower-class children there were no consistent relationships between moral development and parental disciplinary styles, possibly because the social environment exerted overriding importance (20).

Social environment. The highest crime rates occur consistently in the delapidated, crowded, and impoverished tenement districts of large cities. There seem to be several related reasons for the association of crime and urban poverty.[4]

[4]We are not saying that all poor inner-city residents are criminals. Nor are we implying that middle- and upper-class people are never criminals. Both statements, of course, are absurd. We are simply asserting that correlational studies find that one kind of immoral behavior—criminal behavior—is high in frequency under the particular living conditions associated with urban poverty.

Figure 12-8. The "Die Hards" of Manchester, New Hampshire. Gang standards are usually antisocial ones that exert strong pressures for law breaking, property destruction, fighting, and sometimes killing. (David Strickler, from Monkmeyer.)

Poverty cannot cause crime but resentment of poverty can, and curiously enough, resentment of poverty is more likely to develop among the relatively deprived of a rich society than among the objectively deprived in a poor society. This is partly because affluent industrial societies are also secular societies; the distribution of goods and services here and now is a more important preoccupation than concerns with eternal salvation. It is also because the mass media . . . stimulate the desire for a luxurious style of life among all segments of the population [21].

Most Americans want social status and financial success. As children, we are taught that if we are ambitious, hard working, thrifty, and virtuous, financial achievement and social status will eventually reward our efforts. Frustration results when children grow up and find that their expectations will not be met. As we saw in Chapter 11, frustration can trigger aggression. Some authorities believe that the explosion of this myth sours poor adolescents on middle-class values. Consequently, they become alienated from mainstream American culture, and they deliberately adopt negative and malicious moral values (22). Powerful peer groups in the inner city, frequently organized as gangs, are the dominant force of social life and may reinforce these values. Each gang is a miniature culture with an elaborate social structure

and a set of standards for behavior (23). Typically, gang standards are antisocial ones which exert strong pressures, particularly on male adolescents, for law breaking, property destruction, stealing, fighting, and sometimes killing (24). At the same time the continual social and economic frustrations that characterize daily life in the inner city prime people for an aggressive life style.

Religion. Countless parents drag their unwilling children to church each week for a moral education. Does frequent exposure to formal religious teachings make people more moral? This is one of the questions that Hartshorne and May were interested in answering. They found that children enrolled in Sunday Schools were generally more honest than others—they stole, cheated, and lied less. But were they honest *because* they attended Sunday School? To investigate this question indirectly, Hartshorne and May looked at the moral behavior of frequent and infrequent Sunday School attenders. As it turned out, frequent Sunday School attenders were no more nor less honest than infrequent ones (25). One way to interpret these findings is to assume that children who had been enrolled in Sunday Schools were more moral to begin with—perhaps because they came from homes where parents were more concerned about moral matters. Sunday School attendance may have been a consequence, not a cause, of their superior morality.

Two sociologists have shown that religious training is associated with one particular kind of moral behavior—*asceticism* (the practice of denying oneself sensual and material pleasures). They asked a large sample of middle-class college students in Florida and California to answer anonymously questions about their moral and religious beliefs and behavior. Students who described themselves as believing in a personal God reported violating fewer ascetic standards than nonbelievers. For example, they gambled less and engaged less frequently in premarital sexual intercourse. But the two groups did not differ on reported numbers or kinds of antisocial moral violations, such as shoplifting, cheating on exams, or striking people when angered (26). Kinsey's well-known study on sexual behavior found similar results: religious people engaged less frequently than nonreligious ones in premarital sex (27). In short, religious training may be likelier to promote asceticism than the practice of society's moral code.

Moral instruction. Lawrence Kohlberg and his colleagues have shown that school children can be trained to make moral judgments one stage above the level at which they are currently functioning. In one study two investigators evaluated the moral reasoning of seventh-grade boys, then they gave half of them practice in role playing moral dilemmas that required reasoning one stage above their current level. Three weeks later, the boys with training were making moral judgments at a more mature level than the others (28). Currently Kohlberg and his associates are developing moral-training programs for inmates in prisons and reformatories. They have had some success with moral-discussion groups. The groups meet informally with a leader and openly discuss moral dilemmas ranging from simple to complex ones. Through the discussion the inmates learn how others reason; they also have a chance to try out alternative ways of thinking. Gradually, some begin to take the feelings of other people into account in making moral decisions. Kohlberg and his associates have seen some persisting changes in moral thinking, but that is not enough, and they are now engineering more ambitious programs for training moral behavior. Here is Kohlberg's description of one such project:

We soon came to realize that we not only had to change the inmates' thinking but also had to effect changes in the institution in order to promote lasting changes in the inmates' behavior. We generally sensed, that the inmates perceived the prison and its staff as operating at about Stage 1—a punishment and obedience level. And they saw the other inmates pretty much at Stage 2—instrumental exchange and manipulation. So the problem was how to change these institutions so that they are at the same or higher level than the inmates and not beneath them. What we did was to set up a "justice community" based upon notions of democracy, self-government and a social contract between the staff and the inmates in which there is an agreement by the two groups as to what the rules and governmental procedures would be. Whenever there's a conflict between individuals—whether among inmates or between inmates and staff—which has importance for the community, a community meeting is called in which the conflict is resolved through group discussion and, if necessary, a vote of the group . . . [29]

If these programs are successful, they will be of enormous benefit to society.

Summary: Morality

1. Children all over the world appear to pass sequentially through distinct stages of moral reasoning. As children develop, their moral judgments become more mature along the following dimensions: in-

tentionality, relativism, independence of sanctions, reciprocity, use of punishment for restitution and reform, and naturalistic view of misfortunes.

2. Although people reason consistently about moral problems, they are not necessarily consistently moral or immoral in their judgments.

3. Moral behavior frequently depends on the characteristics of the specific situation, such as the probability and the consequences of being caught. Moral behavior also depends on some more consistent internal dispositions like the maturity of a person's moral reasoning.

4. When moral parents are nurturant and use love-oriented disciplinary practices,

their children are likely to be mature in their moral behavior and judgments. This finding is most simply explained by assuming that children learn moral behavior by a combination of learning processes which are facilitated by warmth.

5. Several conditions associated with inner-city poverty contribute to antisocial behavior.

6. The main moral effect of formal religious training appears to be the fostering of ascetic behavior.

7. Although specific training programs can increase the maturity of moral thinking, it is not yet clear whether they can increase the frequency of moral behavior.

STUDY GUIDE 12

Key Terms. personality, source traits, surface traits, endomorphy, mesomorphy, ectomorphy, somatotype, visceratonia, somatonia, cerebrotonia, psychoanalyst, unconscious, id, ego, superego, psychosexual stages, oral stage, anal stage, phallic stage, Oedipus complex, Electra complex, identification, genital period, parsimonious, situation-specific behavior, moral judgments, moral behavior, premoral level, conventional level, principled level, intentionality, relativism, sanctions, reciprocity, punishment for restitution and reform, naturalistic view of misfortunes, love-oriented techniques, object-oriented techniques, power assertion, love withdrawal, induction, asceticism.

Important Research. source traits and surface traits (Cattell), somatotypes and personality (Sheldon), clinical studies of personality (Freud), neobehavioristic case study (Mischel), moral judgments (Kohlberg), moral behavior (Hartshorne and May), moral behavior and moral judgments (Krebs), parental practices and crime rates (Yale University research team), parental practices and moral maturity (Hoffman and Saltzstein), moral instruction and moral maturity (Kohlberg).

Basic Theories. trait theories, Cattell's trait theory,

type theories, Sheldon's somatotype theory, psychodynamic theories, Freud's psychodynamic theory, neobehavioristic approach to personality, Mischel's neobehavioristic approach, self theories, Kohlberg's developmental theory of moral judgments.

Self-Quiz

1. Which is *not* part of the definition of personality given in this chapter? [**a**] a unique pattern; [**b**] relatively enduring behaviors, feelings, thoughts, motives, interests, and attitudes; [**c**] developed through learning and resolution of internal conflicts; [**d**] characterizing a particular individual.

2. A personality theory which focuses on describing how personality develops and explaining how underlying personality processes interact to determine behavior is called a _____ theory. [**a**] trait or type; [**b**] self; [**c**] psychodynamic; [**d**] neobehavioristic.

3. A _____ personality theory emphasizes what people do, instead of inner conflicts, desires,

or feelings. [**a**] trait or type; [**b**] self, [**c**] psychodynamic; [**d**] neobehavioristic.

4. In Cattell's theory of personality, an apparently stable characteristic which determines many superficial behaviors is called a(n) _____ trait. [**a**] source; [**b**] determinant; [**c**] surface; [**d**] unconscious.

5. According to Sheldon's theory, [**a**] personality is as stable as height and weight; [**b**] personality is learned and therefore changeable; [**c**] personality depends primarily on distressing experiences in early childhood; [**d**] people with particular types of bodies tend to develop particular types of personalities.

6. In Freud's theory, the id is [**a**] the unconscious; [**b**] the primitive core of the personality that strives to gratify motives; [**c**] the part of the personality that locates objects in the real world to satisfy unconscious motives; [**d**] a learned sense of right and wrong.

7. Freud believed that boys developed masculine personality characteristics [**a**] because of hormones and other genetic influences; [**b**] through operant conditioning; [**c**] by identifying with the father and trying to become like him; [**d**] all of the above.

8. Freud's theory is criticized for all of the following reasons *except* that [**a**] it fails to consider social and cultural influences on personality; [**b**] it places too much emphasis on children's early experiences; [**c**] it cannot be easily tested by scientific methods; [**d**] it is not parsimonious.

9. A neobehaviorist would explain a child's whining and crying behavior as [**a**] due to personality characteristics or traits; [**b**] learned under specific environmental conditions; [**c**] caused by unconscious motives and conflicts; [**d**] an attempt to meet basic needs so that the child can go on to fulfill higher needs.

10. A self theorist would explain a child's whining and crying behavior in terms of which alternative listed under question 9?

11. Kohlberg believes that [**a**] children all over the world pass sequentially through distinct stages of moral thinking; [**b**] children's moral thinking varies, but in no systematic way; [**c**] moral thinking develops at different rates, but virtually all people reach the principled levels by age eighteen; [**d**] children are not capable of making sensible moral judgments until approximately eight to ten years of age.

12. In contrast to younger children, older children tend to [**a**] evaluate the consequences that follow the misbehavior, not the rule broken; [**b**] judge the intentions of the culprit rather than the amount of harm done; [**c**] advocate the "eye for an eye" ethic; [**d**] assume that bad deeds must be punished; whether or not the punishment reforms the wrong doer is irrelevant.

13. Hartshorne and May found that children were *least* likely to cheat if [**a**] they swore that they always adhered to the Boy Scout oath; [**b**] they had strong moral character (knowledge of "right" and "wrong"); [**c**] they were at least one level ahead of their age group on Kohlberg's test; [**d**] the situation made cheating difficult or risky.

14. In a study of moral judgment levels and moral behavior, Krebs found that [**a**] subjects at premoral and conventional levels were far more likely to cheat than subjects at the principled levels; [**b**] subjects at the conventional levels were far less likely to cheat than subjects at the premoral levels; [**c**] cheating on exams depended primarily on how important the test results were to the subject; [**d**] subjects at both the conventional and principled levels were far less likely to cheat than subjects at the premoral levels.

15. Which disciplinary techniques are related to strong conscience development? [**a**] induction and object-oriented; [**b**] power assertion and love-oriented; [**c**] induction and power assertion; [**d**] love-oriented and induction.

Exercises

1. PERSONALITY THEORIES. To test your knowledge of what characterizes the various personality theories, match each description with the appropriate personality theory: trait theories (TRAIT), type theories (TYPE), psychodynamic theories (PT), neobehavioristic theories (NT), self theories (ST).

____ 1. Assume personality develops as people resolve internal conflicts between forces such as impulses and motives.

____ 2. Focus on what people *do* in particular situations.

____ 3. View people as perceiving, experiencing beings.

____ 4. Emphasize the degree to which individuals show particular personality characteristics.

____ 5. Avoid inferences or assumptions about processes underlying behavior.

____ 6. Emphasize clusters of traits.

____ 7. Assume that behavior is situation-specific.

____ **8.** Use informal techniques like interviews and clinical observations; but do not rely on people's self-reports.

____ **9.** Assume that people belong to personality categories such as introvert and extrovert.

____ **10.** Emphasize self-fulfillment as the major human motive.

2. KOHLBERG'S THEORY OF MORAL JUDGMENTS. To test your knowledge and understanding of Kohlberg's stages of moral judgment, match each statement with the stage it represents: punishment and obedience orientation (POO), naive instrumental hedonism (NIH), good-boy morality, approval of others (GBM), authority maintaining morality (AMM), morality of contract of individual rights (MC), morality of individual principles of conscience (MIP).

Why should people pay taxes?

____ **1.** "If you don't pay taxes, your friends and neighbors will consider you cheap; they'll also think that you're trying to get away with something."

____ **2.** "Because otherwise you'll be sent to jail. Who wants to spend his life behind bars?"

____ **3.** "A lot of basic human rights aren't available to poor people unless rich people share their money through taxes. Poor people deserve just as much dignity and respect as anyone else."

____ **4.** "The law says you must pay taxes, so you have to do it."

____ **5.** "The way we've set up our government, taxes are needed to run things. It's something we've all agreed to do to maintain a democratic society."

____ **6.** "Because the government can't keep roads and schools in decent condition without money; tax money helps the government make life pleasant for me."

Is it ever right to hit another person?

____ **7.** "No, hitting someone really is assault, and it's against the law."

____ **8.** "Yes, if that's the only way to get what I want. Sometimes you just can't get something any other way."

____ **9.** "Maybe under very special circumstances. But in general, no—because society couldn't function very well if we all went around hitting each other. We have to agree to respect each other; otherwise life becomes chaotic."

____ **10.** "It's all right to hit somebody bigger than you, because then people don't think you're a bully. It's only if you hit a girl, or somebody smaller, that people don't like you because of it."

____ **11.** "No. Physical force deprives people of basic human rights. Using physical force would really make me feel guilty."

____ **12.** "Yes, my parents never punish me for hitting others, so if someone does something I don't like, I hit them."

Questions to Consider

1. Describe the strengths and weaknesses of each type of personality theory presented in Chapter 12. Which theory do you prefer? Why?

2. Reread the biographical sketch of Grope. Explain how various personality theorists (Sheldon, Cattell, Freud, Mischel, and the self theorists) would analyze Grope's behavior.

3. Design a personality theory of your own, either "from scratch" or by combining elements of existing theories.

4. Consider your social and moral behavior. Are you consistent from situation to situation?

5. Did your own parents use primarily love-oriented or object-oriented disciplinary techniques? Do the relationships described on pages 356–357 seem to be supported in your own family? among families you know?

6. Police, prison guards, lawyers, judges, and others are continually involved in making decisions about people's morality. Should such people be screened for moral judgment level? Should they be trained? Explain.

Project 12: Religiosity and Moral Judgments in Adults

Religion and morality are commonly linked in the public mind; that is, people who consider themselves especially religious are generally expected to behave especially morally. There is, in fact, some empirical support for this relationship. Recall that Hartshorne and May found that children enrolled in Sunday Schools cheated, lied, and stole less than others. Similarly, a study of middle-class college students found that those who reported believing in a personal God reported violating fewer ascetic moral standards than nonbelievers. What about religiosity and moral judgments? Do adults who consider themselves religious make judgments about moral dilemmas at higher moral levels than adults who do not consider themselves religious? This is the question which project 12 attempts to answer.

Method. Administer a copy of the three Rating Scales

to potential subjects (fellow college students). Find six cooperative students to serve as subjects: three who score between 7 and 9 on all three scales and three who score between 1 and 3 on all three scales. We will consider these people "religious" and "nonreligious," respectively. Tell your potential subjects that you are interested in their responses to a story about a moral dilemma and obtain their permission for this project. Do not tell them the full purpose of the project until you have collected all your data.

You should test your subjects individually in a quiet setting that is free from distractions and contains a table and chairs. Have each subject sit behind the table. Give him/her two blank sheets of paper and a pencil and ask him/her to record "r" (for religious) or "non-r" (for nonreligious) and month and day of birth on each sheet of paper so that you can tell which stories were written by the same subject. Now read the story of Heinz (pages 349; 352). Pause after the first question and ask the subject to write a response. Have the subject write an answer to the second question on the second sheet of paper.

Results and discussion. After you have collected responses from all your subjects, determine the moral stage of each answer. See Table 12-2. Then consider the following questions:

1. Are subjects generally consistent in the level of their moral judgments?
2. Were there any problems in our operational definition of religiosity? Would you have done it differently?
3. Are there consistent differences in level of moral judgment between your religious and nonreligious subjects? How can your results be explained?
4. What other factors besides religiosity influenced your data? How could these other factors have been controlled?
5. If you were systematically investigating this subject with a big budget, how else might you improve on this study?

RATING SCALES (one set needed for each subject)

I consider myself

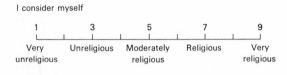

My belief in God is

Religion is

Suggested Readings

1. Hall, C. S., & G. Lindzey. *Theories of personality* (2d Ed.) New York: John Wiley & Sons, Inc., 1970. A thorough discussion of the major personality theories.
2. Wiggins, J. S., K. E. Renner, G. L. Clore, & R. J. Rose. *The psychology of personality.* Reading, Mass.: Addison-Wesley Publishing Company, Inc., 1971. Views personality from many points of view. Focuses on personality research on dependency, aggression, sexuality, and competence.
3. Cattell, R. B. "Personality pinned down." *Psychology Today*, July 1973, 7, 40–42, 44–46. Cattell describes the development of his personality test and the subsequent research that he and his colleagues have done.
4. Cortes, J. B., & F. M. Gatti. "Physique and propensity." *Psychology Today*, October 1970, 4, 42–44, 82–84. Studies on the relationship between personality and somatotype.
5. Puner, Helen Walker. *Freud: His life and mind.* New York: Dell Publishing Co., Inc., 1947 (paperback). An interesting biography that emphasizes the connections between Freud's personality and his theories.
6. Kohlberg, L. "The child as moral philosopher." *Psychology Today*, September 1968, 7, 25–30. Kohlberg describes his theory and research on moral development.

Answer Keys

SELF-QUIZ
1. c 2. c 3. d 4. a 5. d 6. b 7. c 8. b 9. b 10. d 11. a
12. b 13. d 14. a 15. d

EXERCISE 1
1. PT 2. NT 3. ST 4. TRAIT 5. NT 6. TYPE 7. NT 8. PT
9. TYPE 10. ST

EXERCISE 2
1. GBM 2. POO 3. MIP 4. AMM 5. MC 6. NIH 7. AMM
8. NIH 9. MC 10. GBM 11. MIP 12. POO

13

ADJUSTMENT

IN THIS CHAPTER
We examine several attempts to define the concept "good adjustment." Then we look at frustration and conflict, two common stresses that confront people almost daily and affect the quality of their adjustment. Finally, we focus on the coping strategies which people use to help them adjust to their circumstances. After reading this chapter, you should be able to do the following:

1. Outline Erikson's developmental theory of psychological health
2. Describe the characteristics of boys with high and low self-esteem and the personality characteristics of well-adjusted and poorly adjusted middle-aged adults
3. Describe and give examples of four types of conflicts
4. Describe and give examples of four active and six cognitive coping strategies
5. Describe three determinants of coping strategies
6. Describe the consequences of using various coping strategies for anxiety reduction and adjustment.

Caroline Mirthes, a teacher in Public School 15 on the Lower East Side of New York City, had her students write essays about themselves and their lives during the 1967–1968 school year. The following excerpts come from the compositions of a perceptive thirteen-year-old girl named Carmen.

Carmen: Adjustment in a slum

"First of all I want to introduce myself my name is Carmen. Some people call me Smiley. . . .

"On February 9, 1955 my mother was 17 years old and I was born. They named me Carmen. . . . My father was really sick in his brain he tried to smash my head with a rock but my mother didn't let him then my father started telling everybody that I wasn't his daughter. And he used to go and leave my mother and go out with other womens to dances and he use to let me and my mother suffer.

"Once my mother couldn't take it she told him and my father got mad at her so he hit her bad. And she left my house and left me with my grandmother for two years. I was two years old and my grandmother used to treat me like if I was 12 already. I had to take care of myself when I didn't even learn to talk. She was real cruel to me and my father didn't care about me. My cousins and aunts and uncles use to hit me even my neighbors use to hit me. And nobody use to care for me. . . .

"I have a lot of problems in my family but I don't tell anybody what they are. I always try to look happy and sometimes when I can't stand it and I am just about to cry and scream I laugh and laugh. Sometimes I am laughing but I could be angry or sad inside but I still hold myself. But sometimes I feel like getting into a fight so that they will kill me or I will kill somebody. Then maybe I would get out of this world or get out of the problems. . . . Sometimes I think that the only way of getting out of all my problems is killing myself or running away from home and never coming back. But I want to go to school and college. I want to get a good job so that I could help my mother and father live in peace."

Ms. Mirthes writes: "During spring vacation Carmen got into a very bad fight. She saw a group of older girls shoving and hitting her younger brother, and in an attempt to protect him she attacked one of the girls. Six girls jumped her and forced her to the ground. Later her neck stiffened so that she could hardly bend it and her whole face turned black and blue. When she went into her house bleeding and crying, her mother yelled at her, 'What's the matter with you? How could you let those girls beat you up. You're a chicken.'"

When Carmen returned to school, she presented Ms. Mirthes with the following essay:

"On May 4th 1968 a girl decided to write about her opinions of ways to fight. I don't mean fist fight but I mean fight with your mind. What I mean by that is when you have a problem you don't fix it by fist fighting. Instead you fight the problem not the person who gives you the problem. Now let me give you a problem as an example of fighting with your mind. If you don't fight with your mind you will have to fight with your hands.

"Here is the problem. You have a mother who was raised on a slum like I'm on now a mother who is a 3rd grade drop out. She doesn't have understanding for nobody not even her own sons and daughters. Yes she fights but with her hands not with her brain because she was brought up on a slum and she couldn't take it she was weak. The people who were in the slums with her destroyed her brains so she wouldn't use them. But in a way, it was her own fault. She could have fought with her brain.

"Now here goes. The father was brought up in a family who was very strict and they gave him a good education. But, they forgot to give him a heart. He didn't have a heart to care for a family. So you can tell that this is a problem too. . . . How do you fight it? With your fist? You know that with your fist you will lose your figure, face and many other things. And even if you make believe you know how to do it the fist fighters are not always alone. They can gang up on you.

"These examples of problems I gave you are problems to fight but not with your fist. You must fight with your brain and you have got to know how to do it. You can use your brain differently. Like some kids for example they run away from home. Some get married at the age of 13 and you can imagine what kind of life they have. And some other people just separate themselves from life. But that is not the way to fight your fight with your real brain.

"The first thing you should do is try to understand the way other kinds of people live. Then get a good education and then you can have some peace. And if you do that you recognize that you have won the most important fight in the world [1]."

In these writings Carmen focuses on her efforts at adjustment. *Adjustment* refers to the various behaviors and cognitions which people use to adapt to and come to terms with their environment. Carmen has been forced to adjust to treacherous circumstances. Most people have easier conditions to adjust to, but even the most fortunate human being must sometimes face adversity. Kind and loving parents, financial security, and material possessions cannot shield people from illness, accidents, frustrations, pressures, rejection, conflicts, quarrels, disappointments, deaths of loved ones, and so on. Most of us are continually adjusting to various stresses and strains. We begin this chapter by considering the question: What do psychologists mean by the term a "good adjustment"?

Figure 13-1. "I always try to look happy . . ."—Carmen. (Charles Gatewood.)

WHAT IS A "GOOD ADJUSTMENT"?

What characteristics make a person well-adjusted? This question immediately leads to another question: Adjusted for what? To answer these questions one must first commit oneself to a particular goal of life, such as happiness, achievement, self-fulfillment, or service. Second, one must assess which habits and traits equip a person to attain that goal. For example, if happiness is the goal, we

might label qualities such as high self-esteem, vitality, the ability to form lasting, affectionate relationships, and the capacity to cope effectively with adversity "well adjusted." If the goal is achievement, we'd probably emphasize persistence, energy, originality, and productivity. Because answers to the question of what characteristics make a person "well adjusted" depend on a person's subjective life goals, they vary quite a bit. In Chapters 1 and 10, we discussed Abraham Maslow's answer to this question. In this section we focus on three additional attempts to understand the nature of psychological adjustment.

Erik Erikson's Stage Theory

Erik Erikson (b. 1902), an American psychoanalyst and professor of human development at Harvard University, began his career as an artist and teacher. Later he studied psychoanalysis in Vienna under Anna Freud, Sigmund Freud's daughter and a prominent psychoanalyst in her own right. For many years Erikson has been treating and studying children and adults in a number of cultures. His adjustment theory, which we turn to now, evolved from his clinical observations.

According to Erikson, people's personalities form as they progress through eight stages during the course of their lives. At each new stage there is a conflict to face and resolve, and there is a positive and a negative way of resolving it. The positive solution results in healthy interactions with oneself, with others, or with the environment. The

negative solution leads to maladjustment—mistrust, shame, guilt, inferiority, role confusion, isolation, self-absorption, and despair. As Erikson sees it, a person's mental health is continually evolving. The resolution of any conflict depends, in part, on how successfully earlier conflicts were settled, but conflicts are not settled once and for all. Healthy experiences at a later time can sometimes counteract earlier unhealthy ones. Regrettably, unfortunate experiences late in life can undo the effects of a fortunate childhood. Let us now turn to Erikson's eight stages.

During the first year (paralleling Freud's oral stage), infants face a conflict between *basic trust versus mistrust.* At this time their relationship with their mother is all-important. If their mothers feed them, keep them warm and cosy, cuddle, play with, and talk to them, they develop a feeling that the environment is safe and pleasant; they emerge with a sense of their own adequacy and worth. In other words, they learn basic trust. When mothers fail to meet their infants' needs, infants develop fears and suspicions, and they learn to mistrust the world.

During the second and third years (paralleling Freud's anal stage), children face a second crisis, *autonomy versus shame and doubt.* At this time children's capacities are developing rapidly. They like to run, push, pull, hold, and let go. If their parents encourage them "to stand on their own two feet" and allow them to exercise their capabilities, they develop a sense of control—of their muscles, their drives, their environment, and themselves. Erikson calls this sense of control *autonomy.* If parents demand too much too soon or if they prevent their children from using their newly found abilities, children experience shame and doubt.

Children of three to five years of age are active. They run, fight, and climb. They take pride in attacking and conquering their environment. They also take pride in their mental

Figure 13-2. Erik Erickson (b. 1902). (United Press International Photo.)

powers—in their abilities to use language and in their fantasies and make-believe games. At this time children face a new conflict: *initiative versus guilt* (paralleling Freud's phallic stage). If parents try to understand their children, answer their questions, and accept their active play, children learn to approach what they desire; that is, their sense of initiative is reinforced. On the other hand, when parents are impatient and punitive, when they consider their children's questions foolish, their play silly, and their activities wrong, their children feel guilty and uncertain, and they develop a reluctance to act on their own desires.

The six- to eleven-year-old child enters a new world—the school—with its own goals, limits, failures, and achievements. At school children learn something about being workers and providers, as they confront a fourth major challenge, *industry versus inferiority*. When children feel inadequate in comparison with their peers in achievements, skills, and abilities, they develop a sense of inferiority. Successful children, in contrast, emerge with a feeling of competence and pleasure in their own work—a sense of industry.

During adolescence (paralleling Freud's genital stage), the identity crisis occurs— *identity versus role confusion*. Erikson writes:

The growing and developing youths, faced with this physiological revolution within them, and with tangible adult tasks ahead of them are now primarily concerned with what they feel they are, and with the question of how to connect the roles and skills cultivated earlier with the occupational prototypes of the day [2].

The adolescent must integrate various self-images—as youth, friend, student, leader, follower, worker, woman or man—into one image and choose a career and a lifestyle. When youths have achieved a sense of basic trust, autonomy, initiative, and industry, the task of achieving an identity is easier. If the identity crisis is resolved successfully, people emerge with a sense of who they are and what they stand for. The major danger at this time is role confusion, the inability to find a coherent identity.

Erikson believes that the search for identity explains many typically adolescent behavior patterns. He has written:

To keep themselves together [adolescents] temporarily overidentify, to the point of apparent complete loss of identity, with the heroes of cliques and crowds. On the other hand, they become remarkably clannish, intolerant, and cruel in their exclusion of others who are "different," in skin color or cultural background, in tastes and gifts, and often in entirely petty aspects of dress and gesture arbitrarily selected as the signs of an in-grouper or out-grouper. It is important to understand (which does not mean condone or participate in) such intolerance as the necessary defense against a sense of identity diffusion which is unavoidable at a time of life when the body changes its proportions radically, when genital maturity floods body and imagination with all manners of drives, when intimacy with the other sex approaches and is, on occasion, forced on the youngster, and when life lies before one with a variety of conflicting possibilities and choices. Adolescents help one another temporarily through such discomfort by forming cliques and by stereotyping themselves, their ideals, and their enemies [3].

During young adulthood a new challenge arises—*intimacy versus isolation*. Young adults are ready for the formation of lasting social bonds characterized by caring, sharing, and trust. In Erikson's view intimacy ideally requires the development of a sexual relationship with a loved member of the opposite sex "with whom one is able and willing to regulate the cycles of work, procreation, [and] recreation [4]." People who lack a sense of personal identity have a harder time establishing close relationships. Sometimes they seek isolation. Sometimes they form limited ties that lack spontaneity and genuineness.

The conflicts continue. The middle-aged

adult must choose between *generativity versus self-absorption.* The term generativity, coined by Erikson, refers to a commitment to the future and to the new generation. Erikson believes that an active concern about young people and their welfare and about making the world a better place for future generations enhances the self. Self-absorption, on the other hand, leads to stagnation.

Finally, as life nears its end, the elderly adult faces a last crisis, *integrity versus despair.* Integrity arises when people accept their lives as worthy. They look back and feel satisfied. Despair occurs when people see their lives as wasted. They find little meaning and satisfaction in their past. At the same time life is running out, there is little time left, and they fear death (see Table 13-1).

Note that although Erikson's early stages roughly parallel Freud's, Erikson emphasizes the social and interpersonal aspects of each conflict, whereas Freud emphasized their physical and personal aspects. Erikson's em-phasis also is on positive adjustment, whereas Freud's was on maladjustment.

Although they may not agree with all the details of Erikson's stage theory, many psychologists find aspects of the theory attractive, particularly its views of "good adjustment" as continually evolving from early infancy to late adulthood as people grope with old and new conflicts and its optimistic assumption that people are resilient, that unsatisfactory solutions can be reversed, and that early failures can be compensated for. Although Erikson's stage theory is based on clinical observations, it is far too vast to be neatly tested. We turn now to two modest attempts to define "good adjustment" empirically.

Defining "Good Adjustment" Empirically

Sometimes psychologists define "good adjustment" by identifying the characteristic behav-

TABLE 13-1. ERIK ERIKSON'S PSYCHOSOCIAL CONFLICTS

Psychosocial Stage	Approximate Age	Successful Resolution of Conflict Leads to
Basic trust vs. mistrust	First year	Confidence in the environment and in oneself, optimism
Autonomy vs. shame, doubt	2–3 years	Independence, pride in accomplishment, self-control
Initiative vs. guilt	3–5 years	A sense of direction and purpose; a drive to achieve and to explore
Industry vs. inferiority	6 years to puberty	Pleasure in work and a feeling of competence
Identity vs. role confusion	Adolescence	A knowledge of oneself and one's role in life
Intimacy vs. isolation	Early adulthood	An ability to form close personal relationships which combine love and sex
Generativity vs. stagnation	Middle age	Productivity, creativity, and an involvement with the new generation and the future
Integrity vs. despair	Later adulthood	Acceptance of one's life and of mortality, a feeling that one's life has been meaningful

iors of people who appear to be well adjusted. We look at two studies of this type.

Stanley Coopersmith, a psychologist now at the University of California at Davis, began investigating *self-esteem* (an individual's judgment of self worth) in 1959. Many psychologists believe that self-esteem is critical for happiness, competence, creativity, and close interpersonal relationships; consequently, it is part of many definitions of "good adjustment." Initially, Coopersmith and his associates studied middle-class boys ten to twelve years of age from intact families. They assigned each boy to a high, medium, or low self-esteem category, basing their judgments on two bits of information: (1) the teachers' ratings of the boy's self-esteem-related behavior, such as self-assurance, timidity, and reactions to failure and criticism, and (2) each boy's regard for himself as indicated by his performance on a self-esteem inventory (see Table 13-2). Then Coopersmith and his colleagues put the boys through

TABLE 13-2. ITEMS FROM COOPERSMITH'S SELF-ESTEEM INVENTORY

	Like Me	Unlike Me
2. I'm pretty sure of myself.		
3. I often wish I were someone else.		
4. I'm easy to like.		
7. I find it very hard to talk in front of the class.		
14. I'm proud of my school work.		
23. I can usually take care of myself.		
24. I'm pretty happy.		
25. I would rather play with children younger than me.		
49. My teacher makes me feel I'm not good enough.		
53. Most people are better liked than I am.		
58. I can't be depended on.		

TABLE 13-3. CHARACTERISTICS OF BOYS WITH HIGH AND LOW SELF-ESTEEM

Boys with High Self-esteem	Boys with Low Self-esteem
Socially and academically successful	Socially and academically unsuccessful
Eager to express opinions; assertive, vigorous social interactions	Reluctant to express opinions; listen rather than participate
Do not avoid disagreements (socially independent)	Avoid disagreements (fearful of angering others)
Not particularly sensitive to criticism	Sensitive to criticism
Trust perceptions	Distrust perceptions
Optimistic	Discouraged and depressed
Confident	Not confident
Low anxiety	High anxiety
Few personal problems	Preoccupied with personal problems

laboratory and clinical tests and interviews to measure their perceptions, abilities, attitudes, personality characteristics, goal-setting styles, and responses to stress. They also questioned the boys' parents about their son's behavior and their own child-rearing practices (5).

The investigators found striking differences between boys with high and low self-esteem. These differences are summarized in Table 13-3 (6).

What about adults?

During the early 1950s Robert Peck, a University of Texas psychologist, and his colleagues studied the adjustment of middle-aged people. One of their goals was to identify the personality characteristics that distinguish people who make a successful adaptation to life from those who do not. Adaptation and personality characteristics were determined by administering psychological tests and conducting interviews with a

TABLE 13-4. PERSONALITY CHARACTERISTICS OF WELL-ADJUSTED AND POORLY ADJUSTED ADULTS

Well-adjusted	Poorly Adjusted
Pleasant anticipatory set (experience-welcoming)	Distrustful, unpleasant, fearful anticipatory set
Active, initiating	Passive, resigned to external forces
Firm, clear self-concept	Vague, poorly defined self-concept
Sense of competence	Sense of impotence
Emotional stability	Explosive, inappropriate emotionality
Friendly toward others	Hostile towards others
Seeks sharing but not dependent relationships with others	Lonely and isolated, lack of techniques for establishing interpersonal relationships
Reasonable self-indulgence	Excessive demands on others for satisfaction
Blames self for problems	Blames others for problems
Enjoys life	Little enjoyment of life

Source: R. Peck, "Measuring the mental health of normal adults." *Genetic Psychology Monographs*, 1959, 60, 251–252.

representative sample of the Kansas City population. Ten items were found which differentiated people rated high from people rated low in adjustment (see Table 13-4).

"Good Adjustment": An Integration

We have looked at one theoretical and two empirical answers to the question: What is a "good adjustment"? Although the answers vary, they agree on five important issues: Well-adjusted people

1. Have positive feelings about themselves, perceiving themselves as successful or competent
2. Show a sense of autonomy and independence

3. Are active, industrious, and energetic in following their interests
4. Relate well to other people
5. Feel satisfied with their lives, enjoy life, and are not bogged down by problems

Henceforth, when we use the term "good adjustment," we will be referring to these five characteristics.

FRUSTRATION AND CONFLICT

Although few people face as many adversities as Carmen, whose words opened this chapter, no life is without its stresses and strains. In this section we focus on frustration and conflict, two stresses which make life inevitably difficult for us all.

Frustration

Psychologists use the word *frustration* in two ways: (1) to refer to the emotional state that results when an obstacle prevents the satisfaction of a desire, need, goal, expectation, or action and (2) to refer to the obstacle itself. What constitutes a frustration varies from person to person; that is, a particular set of circumstances may be a frustration for one person and not for another because people's desires, needs, goals, expectations, and actions differ.

The obstacles that frustrate people can be physical, personal, or social ones. Sometimes tangible physical barriers keep people from satisfying their needs. In the following passage a school system is viewed as a physical obstacle which frustrates children.

Sitting in a classroom or a home pretending to "study" a badly written text full of false information, adding up twenty sums when they're all the same and one would do, being bottled up for seven hours a day in a place where you decide nothing, having your success or failure depend, a hundred times a day, on the plan, invention and whim of someone else, being put in a position where most of your real desires are not only ignored but actively penalized, undertaking nothing for its own sake but only for that illusory carrot of the future—maybe you can do it, and maybe you can't, but either way, it's probably done you some harm [7].

Sometimes personal capabilities and resources, or the lack thereof, limit satisfactions. Shortness can keep a youngster from reaching a cherished goal, playing on the basketball team. A limited capacity for work due to chronic illness can prevent an otherwise capable student from obtaining an engineering degree. Finally, other people may produce social obstacles which lead to frustration. Continual insults and ridicule from an older sibling may keep a young person from meeting a need for self-esteem.

Conflict

Psychologists define *conflicts* as situations where two or more incompatible needs, goals, or courses of action compete, causing the organism to feel pulled in different directions with an attending sense of discomfort. Since choosing one option in a conflict invariably prevents choosing the other option, at least temporarily, conflicts are sometimes considered frustrations.

Conflicts can occur when a need is incompatible with internal values. For example, a person reared by puritanical parents may feel torn between sexual desires and the strict sexual code that he or she believes in. Conflicts can also occur when motives for incompatible external goals are simultaneously aroused. A student might be conflicted about studying hard to make good marks on an exam and going to a party to socialize with friends. Psychologists usually classify conflicts according to the course(s) of action required to solve them.

Figure 13-3. Approach-approach conflict.

Approach-approach conflicts. When a person is equally attracted to two goals, objects, or courses of action and carrying out one means abandoning the other, the conflict is called an *approach-approach conflict*. Will you buy a car or travel through Europe? Will you attend a party or go to a movie? Will you order a sundae or a malted? Will you buy the brown sweater or the beige sweater? In each situation you may feel simultaneously attracted to two options at once. The donkey of folk literature who was standing midway between two large fragrant haypiles was unable to decide which pile to go to, so it starved to death. Although conflicts are usually difficult to resolve, research shows that people find it easier to resolve approach-approach conflicts than any other kind. Laboratory studies find that approach-approach conflicts are settled in the following way: A person tentatively approaches one goal. As it is approached, its attractiveness increases, and the tendency to approach nearer also increases; at the same time, the other goal becomes more distant, its attractiveness decreases, and the tendency to approach it weakens. Consider shopping for a new sweater. Assume that you see a brown sweater that is very appealing and that soon afterward an attractive beige sweater catches your eye. You may walk back and forth between them, looking at one, then at the other, picturing how each will look with various outfits. As soon as you tentatively choose—say, the brown one—you are likely to emphasize its advantages—say, warm, goes

Figure 13-4. Avoidance-avoidance conflict.

with many outfits, less expensive. Consequently, the appeal of the brown sweater escalates and that of the beige sweater loses ground; so the conflict ends. Approach-approach conflicts may be relatively easy to resolve because one receives something pleasant either way and because the alternatives can frequently be achieved in turn. After all, you may be able to buy the second sweater next month.

Avoidance-avoidance conflicts. When a person is simultaneously repelled by two goals, objects, or courses of action, and one must be selected, psychologists label the conflict an *avoidance-avoidance conflict.* Here are some examples. A student who does not like to study must face studying or flunking. A convicted shoplifter may have to choose between fifteen days in jail or a $200 fine. A finicky child may have to finish her spinach or go to her room. Research shows that as people approach an unattractive choice, it becomes more repellent, and the tendency to avoid it increases in strength. Typically, as people tentatively approach one of the undesirable options in an avoidance-avoidance conflict, it becomes increasingly repellent, causing them to change directions. When the second option is approached, it too becomes increasingly

unpleasant, pushing people toward the other option. Avoidance-avoidance conflicts tend to be more difficult to resolve than approach-approach conflicts because they lead to vacillation and indecision. The student in our example may read one page of his history text and stop abruptly. Flunking may not be so bad after all, he says to himself. But if he flunks, he'll disappoint his parents and ruin his chances of getting into law school. So the student picks up the text once more. Because both alternatives are unpleasant, people frequently try to avoid or escape avoidance-avoidance conflicts. The boy may decide to drop the history course, or he may turn pages, read sentences here and there, and escape into his fantasies. He may even eventually decide on one of his choices—and stick to it.

Approach-avoidance conflicts. When a person is simultaneously attracted to and repelled by the same goal, object, or course of action, psychologists label the conflict an *approach-avoidance conflict.* In reality, most human choices have a bittersweet quality. Thousands of years ago an old Indian prince expressed this idea by saying: One cannot gather roses without being pricked by thorns. An otherwise appealing career may require a lot of education. A sporty car is probably more costly than a conventional model. A luscious dessert is fattening. Intimacy with

Figure 13-5. Approach-avoidance conflict.

another person makes an individual vulnerable.

Sometimes people confront conflicts between two goals, each of which has both good and bad points. This type of conflict is labeled a *double approach-avoidance conflict*. Let's take an example. A young woman is torn between desires to (1) work and (2) attend college. Looking more closely at the situation, we learn that the woman is primarily attracted to work because she needs money, but that she is repelled by the types of jobs for which she is eligible. At the same time she finds college appealing because it will qualify her for a meaningful career, but college is costly. It entails many financial sacrifices, and she dreads many of the courses that are required for her curriculum. Note that both goals have at least one positive and one negative association.

Approach-avoidance and double approach-avoidance conflicts are typically difficult to resolve. Consider the approach-avoidance conflict first. The inviting nature of the goal, say a tempting dessert, leads to approach behavior, but as one reaches for the dessert, the negative characteristics of the goal, all those calories, become more vivid; the person tends to back off. Generally, approach-avoidance conflicts generate a great deal of discomfort and vacillation. In the case of the double approach-avoidance conflict, vacillation from one alternative to the other is likely. Deciding to go to work, the woman in our example may comb the newspaper for employment notices, clip the appropriate ones, and arrange interviews. As the interviews approach, the woman's misgivings are likely to become prominent and powerful, moving her toward the other goal, college. Consequently, she may look through local college catalogues, plan schedules, talk to guidance counselors, and so on. But as registration approaches, the unpleasant aspects of going to college once again become

Figure 13-6. Double approach-avoidance conflict.

prominent, pushing the young woman back to her work goal. Vacillation of this nature can continue indefinitely.

How do people resolve conflicts? On the basis of laboratory research, psychologists have identified several factors which influence people's decisions in all of the conflict situations which we have discussed. *Distance in space* from the goal(s) is one such factor. The tendency to approach or avoid particular goals increases with nearness to those goals. An example is the dilemma of the student who must choose between studying or flunking. Assume that the boy resolves to study every day. One sunny afternoon several friends drop by and invite him to go biking with them. The boy is now torn between studying and socializing. Since his friends are physically present, the student will be strongly pulled toward the outing. If the boy was in the middle of reading when his friends arrived, the pull of studying should also be strong, unless it has aroused strong negative feelings.

Distance in time from the goal(s) is a second factor which influences people's decisions as they confront conflicts. When the goals are distant in time, approach and avoidance tendencies are relatively weak. If the scene between the student and his friends occurs two weeks before an exam, studying may not exert much pull. If the scene occurs the night before an exam, the boy is likelier to be drawn toward the studying option. If the bike outing is scheduled several days in advance, it should also be less compelling and easier to resist.

The *strength of the motives* aroused by the goals also influence decision making during conflicts. As one would expect, goals which are aroused by strong motives exert more pull than those which are aroused by weak motives. In our example, two motives are in conflict: the motive for achievement and the motive for affiliation. The relative strength of these motives will partially determine the outcome of the conflict.

Finally, people's *expectations* about their options in a conflict also influence the outcome of a given conflict. In other words, people usually consider whether the various options really lead to the goals that they are associated with. The student who must choose between studying and socializing may consider how successfully each situation will turn out. The boy may not think very highly of these particular friends and decide biking with them would not really satisfy him, or he might decide that studying for the exam will not help him pass the course.

A word of caution. Conflicts do not always fit neatly into one category. Sometimes a person is faced with more than two choices and more often than not each choice is partly positive and partly negative. Picture yourself sleeping late one Sunday morning when your mother awakens you to ask you to clean the basement, help with lunch, or watch your young nephew. On the surface it looks like a *multiple avoidance conflict*, but is it really? Each alternative may be slightly positive in that it removes you from the conflict itself, and certain alternatives may have advantages— helping with lunch, for example, may mean

sampling your mother's cooking. Now consider yourself vacationing in Florida. Picture trying to choose between four quite pleasant activities—boating in a glass-bottomed boat, scuba diving, swimming, or sightseeing. On the surface we have a *multiple approach conflict*, but, in reality, each choice may have annoying features. Swimming may be unpleasant since you overdid the sun yesterday; scuba diving may be expensive. Moreover, choosing any one goal limits you, reducing the enjoyment you'd normally receive from that activity. In the final analysis most human conflicts are probably best described as *multiple approach-avoidance conflicts*, conflicts between two or more goals where each choice is partly positive and partly negative.

COPING WITH FRUSTRATION, CONFLICT, AND OTHER STRESSES

Frustration, conflict, and other stresses create anxiety, anger, and other unpleasant emotional states. People vary widely in the degree of their emotional reactions, as we saw in Chapter 11. Although some people are only mildly affected by a particular stress or threat, others become panic stricken. People learn to make numerous responses to avoid, escape, or reduce their distress and handle the particular stressor. We call these responses *coping behaviors*; they form an important aspect of a person's adjustment. As we will see in Chapter 14, coping behaviors sometimes complicate and aggravate the initial problem instead of alleviating it.

Richard Lazarus, a psychologist at the University of California at Berkeley, has been studying coping behavior for many years. He believes that it follows an orderly pattern. According to Lazarus, people continually *appraise* (evaluate) their moment-to-moment interactions with the environment. Some events appear benign or positive; others challenging or threatening. When an event is perceived as challenging or threatening, people assess it further—asking themselves such questions as "What kind of action is called for?" and "What resources are currently available to tackle it?" The situation is continually reappraised as new information appears. Whether and to what extent people feel threatened depends on their estimate of their own capacity to manage the threat, which, in turn, depends on their past experiences and their personal characteristics. Once the situation is evaluated, people decide what to do. The decisions may be deliberate or automatic and perhaps unconscious. In general, people cope by action, by cognitive mechanisms, or by a combination of the two (8). We look first at how people cope, second at how coping strategies arise, and finally at the consequences of various coping strategies.

Active Coping Behavior

Actions aimed at coping with threats range from orderly, planned behavior geared to solving a problem constructively to relatively disorganized behavior aimed primarily at self-protection. We turn to several commonly encountered coping behaviors.

Deliberate problem solving. Some people view conflicts, frustrations, and other threats as if they are simply problems to be solved. They evaluate the situation and select appropriate ways of handling it. Usually they make direct preparations to strengthen their resources and reduce the potential harm. Carmen advocated this approach. Another example comes from David Mechanic, a sociology professor at the University of Wisconsin, who studied graduate students as they coped with the threat of comprehensive doctoral examinations—in this case 9 two-hour exams covering the vast literature of nine fields of their discipline. Passing meant that the student would almost assuredly complete the remaining requirements for the doctorate; failing in many cases meant elimination from the program. Students coped similarly. Mechanic wrote:

As examinations drew near, the students' behavior changed considerably. Intensity of study increased, students cut down on recreational activities, and they modified their studying plans as they began to see that their earlier plans were unrealistic. Less effort was devoted to course work and more effort to preparation for examinations [9].

Aggression. Sometimes frustrations, conflicts, and other threats lead to anger and attack even when such actions can in no way remove the source of the problem . In Chapter 11 we discussed the finding that frustration frequently triggers anger and aggression. When the source of frustration is vague, hard to pinpoint, powerful, or dangerous, people sometimes *displace* their aggression and aggress against available targets. *Scapegoating*—blaming innocent victims for one's troubles and making them the object of aggression—is a common example of this practice. Sometimes scapegoating occurs on a personal level. For example, a husband has an especially upsetting day at work, comes home, and yells at his wife and children at the first trivial provocation. Scapegoating also occurs on a national level. During the 1930s, Hitler made Jews the scapegoat for Germany's economic stagnation and political tension. Since the Civil War black Americans have been blamed for numerous social problems and have often been a target for white violence.

Regression. Sometimes people confront threats by returning to immature modes of behavior that characterized them at younger

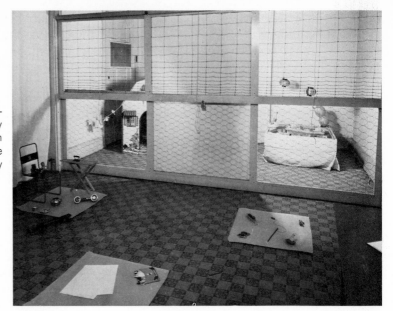

Figure 13-7. In a classic experiment, frustration was induced by having children play in the room in the foreground, separated from the more desirable toys. (The University of Iowa Archives, Iowa City.)

ages. Children who haven't sucked their thumbs or wet their beds in years sometimes react to crises, such as the birth of a new baby, with these immature responses. Regression, according to some psychologists, allows people to escape by returning to past conditions of love and security. Regression could also be explained as an immature way of tackling a problem or a deliberate attempt to attract attention. In a classic study, psychologists Roger Barker, Tamara Dembo, and Kurt Lewin studied the effects of frustration on children's play. The subjects were young children who came, one at a time, to a playroom where they found toys, such as a broken telephone receiver, a sailboat and other water toys (without water), a chair (without a table), and an ironing board and iron (but nothing to iron). Paper and crayons were also available. The children played happily and imaginatively, as psychologists behind a one-way mirror rated their play on its constructiveness. On a second day the same children came to the same playroom. This time a partition in the room had been removed so that the children could play with an unusually attractive set of toys including a large doll house, a toy lake, and a table set for a luncheon. After a brief period of play, the frustration period began. The child was asked to play at one end of the playroom with the original set of toys; a wire partition was put into place separating the child from the desirable toys (see Figure 13-7). Under these circumstances, the children played more roughly, more destructively, and more childishly than previously. For example, they scribbled with the crayons instead of drawing. In fact, their level of play was now characteristic of children about a year and a half younger than their ages. This study indicates that regression may be a common response to frustration (10).

Escape. When people feel overwhelmed by frustration, conflict, or other threats, they sometimes try to escape from the situation. If a particular teacher's sarcasm and derision are very frustrating to a particular student, for example, he may bodily escape by dropping the course or showing up only for tests. Escape responses are very common reactions to avoidance-avoidance conflicts. When complete escape is impossible, people sometimes behave in ways that result in partial escape. *Stereotyped behavior*, behavior that is occasioned by a particular problem event, varies little, and is rarely altered by its consequences, is an example of a partial escape strategy. People sometimes engage in particular rituals to cope with a threat. Consider a young mother who believes that mothers should love their children no matter what. However, some days she feels exasperated; she hates her children and wishes she were free of them. This feeling upsets her so much that she refuses to confront it. Every time she anticipates the feeling, she prevents it from recurring by counting days to Christmas, cracks in the ceiling, books, cans of food in the pantry, or whatever is in sight. By using stereotyped behavior she avoids the conflict.

Even animals cope by stereotyped behavior. In 1949 Norman Maier, a psychologist at the University of Michigan, published a study of stereotyped behavior in rats as a response to conflict. Maier trained rats to jump against one of two cards—one card was associated with a reward (the positive card) and one with a punishment (the negative card). When the rat jumped against the positive card, the card gave way, giving the animal access to food; when it jumped against the negative card, it bumped its nose and fell into a net. As we'd expect, the rats learned to jump consistently against the positive card, no matter what position it occupied. At this point Maier frustrated his subjects. The positive card became half-positive; the negative card half-negative. In other words, each card led to a reward half the time and to punishment half the time; so if the animal continued to choose the original positive card, it was punished half the time.

Under these circumstances, rats tended to form stereotyped habits: They consistently jumped either to the right or to the left; they stopped paying attention to which card was exposed on that side (11). This habit, which was very resistant to change, clearly interfered with the rats' problem-solving abilities, as stereotypic behavior frequently does. We will consider an extreme example of stereotyped behavior—obsessive-compulsive behavior—in Chapter 14.

Dependencies on substances such as alcohol, heroin, barbituates, and amphetamines are another means of partial escape commonly found in our society. Many addicts see their addiction as a way of adjusting. One young suburban heroin addict expressed this belief as follows: "[Heroin] is like a finance plan which allows you to consolidate all of your problems into one—Junk! and then the injection in your arm makes them all go away [12]."

Drug dependency is especially high in inner cities where people long to escape the bleakness of poverty. A twenty-six-year-old Harlem addict put it like this:

I was just born black, poor, and uneducated. And you only need three strikes all over the world to be out, and I have nothing to live for but this shot of dope. . . . That's the only thrill in life for me, you know. I've never had anything, no opportunity, you know to get any money, no nothing. All I can look forward to is what I can get out of this bag, and that's nothing really [13].

Coping Cognitively

Our minds are powerful. As we sit safe and comfortable in the midst of plenty, we can conjure up catastrophic scenes and make ourselves miserable. Similarly, our thoughts can make the grimmest of circumstances endurable. This second power is the subject we turn to now. People use a number of cognitive strategies to cope with conflicts, frustrations, and other unpleasant realities. These attempts are frequently known as *defense mechanisms.* The notion of a defense mechanism came from Sigmund Freud. Freud and his followers believed that people used mental devices unconsciously to falsify and distort threatening situations to prevent or reduce anxiety.

How aware are people of using defense mechanisms? Some psychologists believe that people are completely unconscious of using such devices. Others believe that they are dimly aware. Yet others look on those defensive maneuvers as deliberate, premeditated strategies. The question of awareness is extremely hard to study. Although psychologists usually rely on questionnaires or interviews, measuring awareness in this way has several problems: One is wording the questions without suggesting to subjects what they are supposed to be aware of and, indeed, that they are *supposed* to be aware of anything at all. Then there are the old problems that always crop up with self-report measures: How well do people know themselves? And do they openly reveal what they know?

Psychologists and psychiatrists have described a large number of cognitive mechanisms which people use to cope with stresses. Currently it is not clear whether these mechanisms are used to reduce and/or eliminate anxiety or simply to handle unpleasant experiences. We now turn to some commonly used cognitive mechanisms.

Repression. We define *repression* as the exclusion of anxiety-arousing motives, ideas, conflicts, thoughts, or memories from awareness. Repression is not suppression. When people *suppress* information, they deliberately try to put it "out of mind." Most people are familiar with this kind of coping strategy. You may have tried not to think about a bitter argument with a friend, a frightening opera-

tion, or an approaching test. Suppression, or *cognitive avoidance,* has been well established by laboratory studies. The concept of repression is based on the belief that people do not knowingly hold anything back. In other words, when repression is working, the threatening material does not enter a person's awareness at all. For example, a soldier who saw a friend's body torn apart by shrapnel might become amnesiac (semipermanently forgetful), wander back to his squadron, not knowing where he's been or what has happened, remembering nothing of the battle. Under hypnosis, he might later recall the experience.

Psychologists debate whether threatening material is simply suppressed and eventually forgotten or actually repressed. So far, although many have tried, no experimental study has demonstrated that repression exists—to the satisfaction of all concerned. In one attempt Thomas D'Zurilla, a psychologist now at the State University of New York at Stony Brook, used college students as subjects. He showed them twenty words, then tested their recall to make sure that there were no significant memory differences between them. After that, each subject viewed ten slides. The slides contained one inkblot and two words from the list of twenty. The subjects had to indicate which word best described the inkblot. The experimental subjects were told that the test was designed to detect latent homosexual tendencies. (Presumably homosexuals used one of these two words and heterosexuals used the other to describe each blot.) Control subjects were simply told that they were taking part in the development of a new test. At this point all subjects took a second recall test on the twenty words. Again there were no significant differences between them. Then the experimental subjects were threatened. They were told that they'd chosen nine of ten homosexual responses. The control subjects

	1	2	3	4	5	6	7
Experimental events	All subjects learned a list of twenty words and took a recall test.	Each subject took a "test." They viewed ten slides of inkblots and chose one of two words to describe each one.	Second recall test	Subjects received the results of the "test."	Third recall test	Subjects were enlightened.	Fourth recall test
Experimental subjects	No significant differences	Believed that the "test" showed homosexual tendencies.	No significant differences	"You gave nine out of ten homosexual responses."	Memory worsened. (repression?)	"We deceived you..."	No significant differences
Control subjects		Believed that they were simply helping the experimenter develop a test.		"You did very well."	Memory improved.		

Figure 13-8. The D'Zurilla experiment.

were told that they'd done well. After five minutes subjects took a third recall test. This time there were significant differences between the two groups. The control subjects improved, as we'd expect because of the practice they had had, whereas the experimental subjects did worse than previously. Superficially, this appeared to be the result of repression. Finally, the investigator enlightened the subjects about the deception. On a fourth and final recall test, control and experimental subjects did equally well. This is what repression theory would predict—the experimental group no longer had any need to repress the words. Of course, the critical question is: Did repression actually occur during the third recall test? At best the answer is uncertain. During the five-minute period before the third recall test, the experimental subjects revealed that they had been upset. They'd puzzled over the inkblots, their performance on the test, their past experiences, and their "homosexual tendencies." On the other hand, the control subjects re-

ported that they were not preoccupied with any particular subject at this time. So factors other than repression could have interfered with the experimental subjects' memory (14) (see Figure 13-8).

Denial of reality. When people *deny reality*, they attempt to protect themselves from an aversive experience by ignoring or refusing to acknowledge the existence of the experience. An ambitious student might deny that his favorite teacher believes him a mediocre student. An unwanted child might deny that her parents are indifferent to her. People with fatal illnesses often use denial. In the following example a woman who received fatal burns used this device to make her last few weeks more peaceful.

[W]ithin a few days she developed the attitude that she was not seriously ill at all, but practically well. She then recalled having been afraid of dying immediately after her injury, particularly when she first went to the operating room, but said that when she had survived this ordeal she knew that she would be all right; she felt there was no doubt that she was now practically well, that she would require little further care and would soon be back to a normal family life. . . . She felt that she would be sufficiently improved in a few days so that she would be able to go home and take care of her children. The fact that this patient made such statements calmly and deliberately while she lay helplessly on a Stryker frame—a charred remnant of a woman—had a powerful impact on all observers [15].

A large research literature demonstrates that denial is a common cognitive-coping mechanism.

Fantasy. In *fantasy* people achieve needs or goals in their imagination while escaping unpleasant, anxiety-arousing, or frustrating realities. Both children and adults fantasize. In the following example a twelve-year-old girl fantasizes about "cleaning up" her block.

My block is the most terrible block I've ever seen. There are at least 25 to 30 narcartic people in my block. The cops come around there and tries to act bad but I bet inside of them they are as scared as can be. They even had it in the papers that this block is the worst block, not in Manhattan but in New York City. . . .
   If I could change my block I would stand on Madison Ave. and throw nothing but Teargas in it. I would have all the people I liked to get out of the block and then I would become very tall and have big hands and with my big hands I would take all of the narcartic people and pick them up with my hand and throw them in the nearest river and oceans. I would go to some of those old smart alic cops and throw them in the Ocians and Ribers too. I would let the people I like move into the projects so they could tell their friends that they live in a decent block. If I could do this you would never see 117 street again [16].

Research shows that children's propensities to fantasize may be well formed by the age of five (17). Moreover, frequent fantasizing appears to be associated with some highly constructive habits. One study finds, for example, that when the predisposition to fantasize is great, children tend to be more creative, more flexible, better at concentrating, and less aggressive than when it is small (18).

Rationalization. *Rationalization* involves the use of two related cognitive strategies: One, people think up socially acceptable reasons for past, present, or contemplated behavior to hide the real motives from themselves. Two, they pretend that a bad situation is really good (the sweet lemon strategy) or that a good situation is really bad (the sour grapes strategy). Both kinds of rationalization are common. A young woman who is habitually late might say to herself: "I'd be on time, but I always get involved in something and I can't bear to leave anything unfinished," instead of facing up to the fact that she is behaving selfishly and inconsiderately. A student might tell himself, "I'd have passed that test if the teacher had asked half-intelligent questions," instead of admitting ignorance. Using the sweet lemon, sour grapes strategy, a poor person might adopt the position that people are better off being poor and that "rich people don't know what love and peace and happiness really are [19]."

Reaction formation. When people conceal a real motive or emotion from themselves and express the opposite ones by attitudes and behavior, they are using *reaction formation*—presumably to avoid anxiety associated with the real motive or emotion. Hate is sometimes concealed by a display of love, a sex drive by prudery, and hostility by kindness. The excerpt below illustrates reaction formation. It comes from a letter written by a "kindly" antivivisectionist to a research psychiatrist.

I read [a magazine article] . . . on your work on alcoholism. . . . I am surprised that anyone who is as well educated as you must be to hold the position that you do would stoop to such a depth as to torture helpless little cats in the pursuit of a cure for alcoholics. . . . A drunkard does not want to be cured—a drunkard is just a weak-minded idiot who belongs in the gutter and should be left there. Instead of torturing helpless little cats why not torture the drunks or better still exert your would-be noble effort toward getting a bill passed to *exterminate* the drunks. . . .

My greatest wish is that you have brought home to you a torture that will be a thousand fold greater than what you have, and are doing to the little animals. . . . No punishment is too great for you and I hope I live to read about your mangled body and long suffering before you finally die—and I'll laugh long and loud [20].

Projection. Sometimes people are quick to notice and exaggerate personal characteristics in others that they do not like and do not acknowledge in themselves. Hostile people who do not own up to their own hostility may be quick to note and exaggerate the hostility of others. People threatened by their own sexuality sometimes see others as oversexed. When people use *projection*, they assign their own undesirable characteristics, mistakes, problems, impulses, desires, or thoughts to others—presumably to reduce their own anxiety at having to recognize these characteristics as their own. In 1962 Dana Bramel, a psychologist then at the University of Minnesota, studied projection in the laboratory. A male college student subject interacted socially with another for several minutes. Then each was hooked up to a device that appeared to measure sexual arousal (a fake), as they looked at pictures. The machinery was rigged to suggest to experimental subjects that they were sexually aroused while looking at homosexual pictures. Control subjects did not see an unusual arousal response to such stimuli. After the picture-viewing session, each subject rated his partner's degree of homosexuality. In general, the experimental subjects

attributed a higher degree of homosexuality to their partners than the control subjects attributed to theirs. Presumably, the experimental subjects were threatened by the implications of having homosexual tendencies and they dealt with the threat—at least in part—by attributing the threatening characteristic to their partners (21).

The Determinants of Coping Strategies

What determines how a person responds to frustrations, conflicts, and other threats? Why does one person use problem-solving strategies, another aggression, a third escape? Why does an individual repress or suppress, fantasize, or deny? Psychologists are only beginning to understand the answers to these questions. Currently, it seems that learning, experience in a particular culture, and expectations about a particular situation all play a role in determining how a person copes. Laboratory experiments show that the incidence of a particular type of defensive behavior can be increased or decreased by reinforcement and punishment (22,23). Each adult has a long learning history. If people are generally ignored and/or punished when they talk about threatening events, they probably learn to suppress or repress unpleasant experiences. On the other hand, when people are encouraged to talk about stressful situations, to confront, and to master them, they probably adopt this approach. At least one study shows that children can be actively trained to cope constructively with failure. In 1937 Mary Keister and Ruth Updegraff, psychologists then at the Iowa Child Welfare Research Station, took children who reacted to the frustration of failure by crying, giving up, depending on others, or behaving aggressively and trained them to cope constructively using a series of increasingly difficult tasks. At the end of their training, the children were able to confront relatively difficult tasks in an adaptive way (24).

Coping styles also depend on one's culture—its standards and its customs. Joan Ablon, a medical anthropologist at the University of California Medical School, studied how Samoans handled a disastrous church fire that killed seventeen and injured seventy people. Five years after the disaster she interviewed the survivors, their relatives, doctors, and others who had been in close contact with victims. Their reports indicated that the Samoans had almost, without exception, responded stoically to death, pain, and lasting disfigurement. For example, no one required medication for shock or grief. The patients tended to be silent, and when one of them died, their relatives left quietly after saying a brief prayer. The Samoans, Ablon explains, are a closely knit, deeply religious, family-oriented people that know and support one another. Because of social, family, and religious supports, they may not have experienced the severe emotional problems usually associated with disasters of this kind (25).

Laboratory research shows that the coping mechanisms which people use vary from situation to situation and depend—to some degree—on how people evaluate the situation. Beliefs about one's degree of control seem to be critical. When adversity is inescapable, it may be adaptive to cognitively avoid it. When it can be mastered by the appropriate problem-solving strategy, then being vigilant (attentive) may be a more reasonable approach. Studies suggest that many people take this information into account (26).

The Consequences of Coping Strategies

Although the consequences of the various active coping behaviors cannot be systematically studied in a laboratory, they can be observed and evaluated informally, particu-larly in mental health settings. In the beginning of the chapter we described well-adjusted people as active, competent, and generally happy with their lives. Deliberate problem-solving behavior is most likely to lead to this result. Aggression, regression, and escape behavior usually complicate and aggravate the initial problem and prolong the tension.

The consequences of the cognitive coping mechanisms are much more difficult to evaluate. First we might ask: Can these mechanisms really reduce anxiety and discomfort as Freud believed? We consider this question with regard to denial, the mechanism which has been most thoroughly studied.

Psychologist Richard Lazarus and his associates investigated the question of the anxiety-reducing effects of denial in the laboratory in several ingenious studies. In one study, two films were shown to male college students. One film was neutral, while the other showed subincision rites, the initiation of adolescent boys into manhood in a primitive Australian culture. In this film boys are held down by three or four men to prevent their escape while their penises are stretched and cut on the under side from tip to scrotum with a sharpened flintstone. As subjects watched the films, their heart rates and skin resistance were simultaneously measured as indices of their emotional responses. After the films each subject reported his subjective reactions (see Table 13-5). All subjects showed marked physiological responses, even when they denied being anxious. So Lazarus and his associates concluded that the attempts at denial had been largely unsuccessful (27,28). Note how this study also highlights the fallibility of self-report measures.

In another study Lazarus and his colleagues demonstrated that denial could be successful in the laboratory. They showed the same subincision film under four conditions:

(1) no sound track; (2) a sound track that emphasized the painful, threatening aspects of the operation; (3) a sound track that presented what was happening in an intellectual and detached way; and (4) a sound track that denied that the operation was painful and stressed its social benefits. When the soundtrack played up the painful aspects of the procedure, heart rate and skin resistance were greatest. When the film ran without a sound track, they were moderate. They were lowest when the sound track intellectualized or denied the painful effects of the rites (29).

Denial can also be successful in reducing anxiety in real life. Physicians at the Walter Reed Army Medical Center observed parents whose children were dying of leukemia. Some parents persistently denied that their children were dying and behaved as if they would recover; others did not show this defensive reaction. The researchers found that the mean urinary 17-hydroxycorticosteroid excretion rate (an indicator of stress) was lower in denying parents than in the others. Apparently, denial helped keep anxiety under control (30). This research indicates that denial does help reduce anxiety in situations of stress, but psychologists still lack information about how anxiety-reducing the other cognitive mechanisms are.

Let's consider a related question: Are the cognitive-coping mechanisms adaptive? That is, do they aid or hamper people in their long-term struggle to achieve a good adjustment? Answering this question usually requires a value judgment: Is knowing the truth and suffering better than deceiving oneself and being more comfortable? To decide which is preferable, one must examine the specific context and the positive or negative consequences that accompany the use of a particular cognitive maneuver. Suppression, denial, and fantasy, for example, may keep people from being overwhelmed when they cannot avoid a threat. On the other

TABLE 13-5. DIFFERENT REACTIONS OF ELEVEN EXPERIMENTAL SUBJECTS EXPOSED TO THE SAME STRESSFUL FILM

Subject	Interview Statement of Reaction
1.	"I accepted it as life but I didn't think that this sort of practice still existed on earth today."
2.	"God, I'm shocked! and nauseated. It made me sick."
3.	"I was completely disgusted to the point of almost being ill."
4.	"Shocked—disgusted—I felt like vomiting and wanted to leave."
5.	"Wished I had never seen it for now I feel extremely tense and nervous."
6.	"Interested in customs; disliked poor sanitary conditions of surgery; confused as to basis of custom and its function; curiosity about function of fires; amusement at the dancing; appreciation of stoic control of subjects."
7.	"There were many puzzling parts and I found myself wishing there was sound accompanying it."
8.	"At first I was curious, then I became very interested in what was going on."
9.	"I was bored with the film and felt that watching it was a complete waste of time."
10.	"I thought that it was a rather interesting movie. As a premedical student I was especially curious about the techniques."
11.	"The film was unusual, but it didn't bother me a bit."

Source: R. S. Lazarus, *Patterns of adjustment and human effectiveness.* New York: McGraw Hill, 1969, 73.

hand, when a situation can be mastered or controlled, cognitive mechanisms alone may lead to inaction which is usually unproductive.

Summary: Coping with Frustration, Conflict, and Other Stresses

1. Stresses take a number of forms. Physical, personal, and social barriers can frustrate people. Conflicts can draw people in two or more opposing directions at once.
2. People appear to be continually "on the lookout" for threats. When an event is

appraised as threatening, people decide how to cope with it—sometimes deliberately, sometimes automatically and perhaps unconsciously.

3. People sometimes cope with threats by direct action: deliberate problem solving, aggression, regression, and escape. People also use cognitive-coping mechanisms such as repression, or suppression, denial of reality, fantasy, rationalization, reaction formation, and projection.

4. The choice of particular coping mechanisms appears to be determined, at least in part, by learning, experience in a particular culture, and an appraisal of the particular situation.

5. Deliberate problem-solving strategies usually lead toward the solution of a problem and consequently toward a good adjustment.

6. Denial appears to be able to reduce anxiety. The anxiety-reducing ability of the other cognitive coping mechanisms has not been clearly demonstrated.

7. Cognitive mechanisms can be considered adaptive or maladaptive depending on the context in which they are used and the consequences of their use.

GOOD ADJUSTMENT AND THE GOOD LIFE: AN EPILOGUE

All people face and cope with adversities; some achieve a good adjustment. What can a well-adjusted person expect of life? In studying the adjustment of normal adults, psychologist Robert Peck observed many lives. His observations give some overall perspective to our discussion.

There are times, in studying case after case, when one sadly muses that perhaps Thoreau was literally right. Perhaps most men—and

women—do lead lives of quiet desperation. Certainly, the chaos of bewilderment, the tempers of unreasoning passion, the whine of years-long unhappiness, the tremendous sorrow of engulfing tragedy—these are not strange to the typical American. He, or she, has lived with them and is living with their echoes.

The joy of utter mastery of life? This is a rare experience, encountered by few people. More typical is a quite slightly puzzled sense of some things lacking, some spots of grey where colors ought to be; and all beyond one's comprehension to identify, or one's skill to remedy.

For more than half of us, life is a matter of settling for a good deal less than we want. We know it; we've known it for years; and we are decidedly not happy at the many moments when we think about our losses, our disappointments, and our never-will-be's. For such of us, life is never brilliantly happy. Unalloyed joy is an unknown or forgotten sensation. Too many hurts, big and little, have chipped the bright colors away.

Yet for this "almost average" American, life is not really a matter for despair. On the contrary, he and she pride themselves on "making out," and "getting along"; and what is more, they do get along, and make their way. If they don't have nearly the love, or stature, or pleasure, or security their hearts hunger for, they don't sink into self-pity. If bright happiness is out of reach, a more shaded kind is still attainable. Above all, there is self-respect, dimly but proudly felt, of the person who makes his own way in life.

Are there completely happy people? No. We find no one whose life is and has been, without some hard-hitting frustration or some profound sorrow. When a beloved parent dies, or a just-grown child—what door of escape is there? There is no way out of the grief except to live through it. . . .

Sometimes it seems as if we ask too much of life and of ourselves. We want "perfect" happiness, "perfect" peace of mind, "perfect" mental health. As far as all experience indicates, along with the present data, the best one can reasonably ask for is good health, mental and physical, with which to meet each day [31].

STUDY GUIDE 13

Key Terms. adjustment, good adjustment, self-esteem, frustration, approach-approach conflict, avoidance-avoidance conflict, approach-avoidance conflict, double approach-avoidance conflict, multiple approach-avoidance conflict, coping behaviors, appraise, active coping behavior, deliberate problem solving, aggression, displace, scapegoating, regression, escape, stereotyped behavior, cognitive-coping mechanisms, defense mechanisms, repression, suppression (cognitive avoidance), denial of reality, fantasy, rationalization, reaction formation, projection.

Important Research. self-esteem and personality characteristics in boys (Coopersmith), adjustment and personality characteristics in adults (Peck), students' coping with exams (Mechanic), frustration and regression (Barker, Dembo, and Lewin), frustration and stereotyped behavior in rats (Maier), repression (D'Zurilla), projection (Bramel), training children to cope with frustration (Keister and Updegraff), culture and coping behavior (Ablon), anxiety-reducing effects of denial (Lazarus).

Basic Theories. Erikson's stage theory of adjustment, Lazarus' model of coping behavior.

Self-Quiz

1. Erikson's theory about healthy adjustment [**a**] grew primarily out of naturalistic observations; [**b**] assumes that people must pass through essentially the same stages that Freud believed in; [**c**] states that the stages of the early childhood years are more important for adjustment than those later in life; [**d**] defines adjustment as continually evolving as people face and resolve conflicts at eight stages of life.

2. The main task of adolescence, according to Erikson, is [**a**] developing skills, abilities, and achievements; [**b**] forming an identity; [**c**] learning to make intimate friendships; [**d**] resisting a tendency toward self-absorption.

3. Coopersmith found that boys low in self-esteem [**a**] were continually disagreeing with others; [**b**] distrusted their own perceptions; [**c**] boasted and were generally vulgar; [**d**] were insensitive to criticism.

4. Peck found that adults rated high in adjustment were characterized by all of the following statements *except* [**a**] resigned to external forces; [**b**]

reasonable self-indulgence; [**c**] blames self for problems; [**d**] friendly toward others.

5. Psychologists use the term *frustration* to refer to an emotional state that results when [**a**] a person is confronted by a stressful situation; [**b**] self-esteem is threatened; [**c**] an obstacle prevents the satisfaction of a need or goal; [**d**] an upsetting experience cannot be handled by previously learned coping strategies.

6. A girl cannot decide whether to visit her grandfather who is sometimes pleasant and loving but frequently irritable and rejecting. The girl seems to be experiencing a(n) _____ conflict. [**a**] approach-approach; [**b**] multiple approach-avoidance; [**c**] approach-avoidance; [**d**] double approach-avoidance.

7. Which factor has not been shown to influence the resolution of a conflict? [**a**] the person has positive expectations about all the options; [**b**] the person is physically near the conflicting goals(s); [**c**] the time to make a final decision is near; [**d**] the conflict has existed for years.

8. Most real-life human conflicts are best described as _____ conflicts. [**a**] approach-approach; [**b**] avoidance-avoidance; [**c**] approach-avoidance; [**d**] multiple approach-avoidance.

9. Dependencies on alcohol and other drugs are an example of which coping strategy? [**a**] Stereotyped behavior; [**b**] regression; [**c**] rationalization; [**d**] escape.

10. People who respond to frustration by behaving as they did at an earlier age are displaying [**a**] suppression; [**b**] aggression; [**c**] regression; [**d**] reaction formation.

11. A woman who conceals her dislike for her mother from herself by showering the mother with gifts and attention is engaging in [**a**] reaction formation; [**b**] displacement; [**c**] escape techniques; [**d**] projection.

12. A prudish man who does not acknowledge his own prudery and frequently calls other people prudish is exhibiting [**a**] rationalization; [**b**] projection; [**c**] reaction formation; [**d**] alienation.

13. Which is *not* considered an active coping behavior? [**a**] deliberate problem solving; [**b**] regression; [**c**] rationalization; [**d**] escape.

14. An early research project on children who reacted immaturely to the frustration of failure demonstrated that [**a**] the immature reactions had been

learned by observing and imitating parental coping patterns; [**b**] children could learn constructive coping behavior through training that emphasized confronting increasingly difficult tasks; [**c**] children could learn constructive coping behavior, but it only persisted if parents actively encouraged problem solving responses; [**d**] children could learn constructive coping behavior through observation learning and positive reinforcement principles.

15. In studies using a film which depicted subincision rites in a primitive Australian culture, Lazarus and his associates found that [**a**] men who denied being anxious showed milder physiological reactions than those who admitted being anxious during the film; [**b**] men who admitted being anxious showed milder physiological reactions than those who denied being anxious during the film; [**c**] physiological reactions were mildest when the film was presented without a sound track; [**d**] physiological reactions during the film were mildest when a sound track intellectualized or denied the painful aspects of the film.

Exercise

COPING STRATEGIES. To practice identifying the various coping strategies, label the examples that follow: deliberate problem solving, aggression, regression, escape, repression, denial of reality, fantasy, rationalization, reaction formation, projection.

_____ **1.** After an exasperating day at work, a man comes home and kicks the dog.

_____ **2.** The man's wife is saccharine (syrupy sweet) to the dog, even though she would like to strangle it for digging up her garden.

_____ **3.** The man grumbles, "The dog is really spoiled. All I'm doing is disciplining him. He needs to be disciplined every once in a while."

_____ **4.** Nancy witnesses a terrifying fire in which her home is destroyed. The next day she can't remember anything about the fire.

_____ **5.** Whenever a ten-year-old becomes frustrated, he cries and stamps his foot.

_____ **6.** A pediatrician informs a mother that her child is retarded. The mother says, "Nonsense, she's perfectly all right."

_____ **7.** Jim, who is very dishonest himself, is continually accusing others of lying or trying to trick him.

_____ **8.** Kay excuses her brother's behavior saying that "everyone has little personality quirks."

_____ **9.** Bob's neighbor's stereo keeps him from concentrating on his homework, so he calls the neighbor and politely asks him to turn down the volume.

_____ **10.** When the neighbor increases the volume, Bob has visions of going next door with an ax and demolishing the stereo.

_____ **11.** Bob takes a sleeping pill and falls asleep instead.

_____ **12.** Andrea, who is afraid of her sexual desires, forms a parents' group to ban pornography from the community.

_____ **13.** Andrea daydreams about "appropriate punishments" for people who sell these books.

_____ **14.** When asked if such books really do any harm, Andrea replies that an enormous number of people have potentially uncontrollable sex drives and that these books bring out the worst in them.

_____ **15.** Unable to convince Andrea that she is wrong, Stuart becomes angry, tells her off, and stamps on her foot.

Questions to Consider

1. Think of several people whom you know personally and whom you consider well-adjusted. What kinds of characteristics do they display? How would you define good adjustment? What particular values are inherent in your definition?

2. Recall several conflicts which you have recently experienced. How would they be categorized? How were they resolved? Did distance from the goals in time or space, strength of the motives involved, or expectations about your options influence the resolution? Explain.

3. Try keeping a diary of your own defensive behavior for three or four days. Record incidents which provoke defensive behavior as soon as they happen. What active and cognitive coping strategies do you use to handle stressful situations?

4. List the various coping strategies which you currently use. Do the members of your family use similar strategies? Speculate on how you acquired these mechanisms.

Project 13: Measuring
Self-esteem

Psychologists have devised many ways to measure people's self-esteem. Carl Rogers assumes that self-esteem depends on how closely people's images of themselves correspond to their images of their ideal selves (how they would like to be if they could be any way at all). Generally, Rogers finds that there is a fairly close correspondence between the images of actual and ideal selves in well-adjusted people, although there is little correspondence in maladjusted people. In this project you will be measuring your own self-esteem using a test that is frequently used by Rogers and his followers.

Method. First rank your self-esteem on the following scale.

Now copy the statements in Figure 1 onto index cards. Arrange the cards from one to twenty to indicate how well they currently characterize you. The statement that is most like you should be ordered first, the statement that is second most like you second . . . the statement that is least like you twentieth. Order the remaining statements. Then number the statements from 1 to 20 (lightly in pencil). Record the number beside the letter of the statement under the column labeled "actual self" in Figure 2. (Example: Suppose you ranked item G (I am reliable) eighth among the statements that describe you. You would simply put an 8 beside the G under the column labeled "actual self" in Figure 2.) Two or three days later erase the numbers and shuffle the statements. This time you will arrange them from one to twenty to describe your ideal self (how you would most like to be). Order the statement that best describes your ideal self first; the statement that least describes your ideal self twentieth. Order the remaining statements. Number each statement from 1 to 20. Record the number beside the letter of the statement under the column labeled "ideal self" in Figure 2.

Results. To compare your actual and ideal selves you will be calculating a correlation coefficient to see how strongly your ideal and actual self orderings are associated. The formula for the correlation coefficient which you will compute follows:

$$\text{Correlation coefficient} = 1.00 - \frac{6 \; \Sigma d^2}{N^3 - N}$$

This formula may look difficult, but the calculations are rather simple.

1. You will be working initially with the numbers under ideal self and under actual self in Figure 2. For each row, subtract the smaller number from the larger number and enter the difference in column d. (Example: If statement A is ordered 11 for your actual self and 15 for your ideal self, the difference is 15 − 11 = 4.)

2. Now square each number in the d column by multiplying the number by itself. Record the answer in the column labeled d². (In the example just mentioned d = 4, therefore d² = 4 × 4 = 16.)

3. Add up the twenty numbers in the d² column. This gives you Σd^2.

4. Multiply Σd^2 by 6. Call this quantity A.

5. Divide quantity A by 7,980 (7,980 is obtained by working out the expression $N^3 - N$ where N = 20, the number of statements.) Carry out your division to three decimal places and round off to the second place. Call this result quantity B.

6. Subtract quantity B from 1.00 to arrive at the correlation coefficient.

7. Your correlation coefficient should be a decimal between +1.00 and −1.00. (If your ideal and actual selves corresponded exactly, you would find a perfect positive correlation coefficient, +1.00; if they were exact mirror images of one another, you'd obtain a perfect negative correlation coefficient, −1.00.) If your answer is more than +1.00 or less than −1.00, you've made a mistake, so go back to step 1 and begin again.

Discussion. Consider the following questions:

1. Is the correlation between your ideal and actual selves high or low? To make that judgment you need some norms. J. M. Butler and G. V. Haigh found that the average correlation between actual and ideal selves for a sample of people who had never participated in psychotherapy was .58; for a sample of people who were currently being treated for psychological problems, it was .00. (Since the Butler-Haigh study and this project are quite different in many important ways, the results are only very roughly comparable.)

2. Did your self-report rating of self-esteem roughly agree with your correlation coefficient? Try to explain the reasons for any discrepancies.

3. Does the test used in this project have any advantages over a self-report rating scale? Explain.

4. What factors besides self-esteem may have influenced your findings?

A note of caution: You have taken an abbreviated informal version of a psychological test that is usually evaluated in conjunction with other sources of information. Many factors could have influenced your performance on this test. You should not consider your score a necessarily accurate description of your self-esteem.

FIGURE 1

[**A**] I am impulsive.

[**B**] I have warm emotional relationships with others.

[**C**] I am intelligent.

[**D**] I put on a false front.

[**E**] I have a horror of failing in things I want to do.

[**F**] I usually like people.

[**G**] I am reliable.

[**H**] I am a hard worker.

[**I**] I am ambitious.

[**J**] I express my emotions freely.

[**K**] I am an optimist.

[**L**] I feel apathetic.

[**M**] I often feel tense around others.

[**N**] I want other people to think highly of me.

[**O**] I have an attractive personality.

[**P**] I often do what other people want, even if it is not what I want to do.

[**Q**] I respect myself.

[**R**] I am often hostile.

[**S**] I am self-centered.

[**T**] I have a good sense of humor.

FIGURE 2

	Actual Self	Ideal Self	d	d^2
A				
B				
C				
D				
E				
F				
G				
H				
I				
J				
K				
L				
M				
N				
O				
P				
Q				
R				
S				
T				

$$\sum d^2 =$$

REFERENCE: Butler, J. M., & G. V. Haigh. Changes in the relation between self-concepts and ideal concepts consequent upon client-centered counseling. In C. R. Rogers & R. F. Dymond (eds.) *Psychotherapy and personality change: Coordinated studies in the client-centered approach.* Chicago: The University of Chicago Press, 1954. Pp. 55–76.

Suggested Readings

1. Coleman, J., C. L. Hammen, & L. Fox. *Contemporary psychology and effective behavior.* Glenview, Ill.: Scott, Foresman & Company, 1974. Comprehensive but very readable textbook which addresses itself to questions about finding a meaningful and fulfilling lifestyle.

2. Elkind, D. "One man in his time plays many psychosocial parts—Erik Erikson's eight ages of man." *The New York Times Magazine*, April 5, 1970, 25–27, 84–92, 110–119. An introduction to Erikson's theory of personality development and to his historical studies of Martin Luther and Gandhi.

3. Coopersmith, S. "Studies in self-esteem." *Scientific American*, February 1968, 218, 96–100ff. Coopersmith describes his research on the antecedents of self-esteem.

4. Aronson, E. "The rationalizing animal." *Psychology Today*, May 1973, 6, 46–52. The author discusses rationalization as a method of reducing the discomfort which comes from conflicting beliefs.

5. Pulaski, M. A. S. "The rich rewards of makebelieve." *Psychology Today*, January 1974, 7, 68–74. A survey of research on children who fantasize—what they are like and how they learn to be imaginative.

6. Ray, Oakley S. *Drugs, society, and human behavior.* St. Louis: The C. V. Mosby Company, 1974 (paperback). A psychologist looks at research on drugs, drug abuse, and drug abusers.

Answer Keys

SELF-QUIZ
1. d 2. b 3. b 4. a 5. c 6. c 7. d 8. d 9. d
10. c 11. a 12. b 13. c 14. b 15. d

EXERCISE
1. aggression   2. reaction formation
3. rationalization   4. repression   5. regression
6. denial of reality   7. projection   8. rationalization
9. deliberate problem solving   10. fantasy
11. escape   12. reaction formation   13. fantasy
14. projection   15. aggression

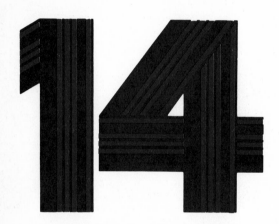

ABNORMAL BEHAVIOR

IN THIS CHAPTER
We look at how psychologists define, explain, and classify abnormal behavior. Then we examine specific abnormal patterns: the relatively mild neurotic disorders, the more severe psychotic disorders, and psychopathic behavior. The treatment of these disorders will be discussed in the next chapter. After reading this chapter, you should be able to do the following:

1. Describe four criteria which psychologists use to assess abnormal behavior
2. Describe the current system of classifying abnormal behavior and discuss its problems
3. Contrast the medical and psychological models of abnormal behavior
4. Differentiate between neurotic and psychotic behavior
5. Describe four neurotic patterns and discuss their possible causes
6. Describe the symptoms of schizophrenia and discuss the possible causes of these disorders
7. Describe psychopathic behavior and discuss its possible causes

Normality is a square circle or
a four-sided triangle

"At New York State University's Upstate Medical Center, a routine
diagnostic interview is in progress. The patient, a dowdy woman in her
late fifties, had been referred for psychiatric evaluation after complaining persistently of a mysterious 'pulling in her head.' In a flat voice she
unfolds a life story so filled with disaster, loss, and sudden death that it
seems more the stuff of theatre than medicine. From time to time, as she
answers the questions of the young resident in psychiatry, she cries
briefly; and yet for the most part she speaks in a curiously emotionless
tone, as though telling someone else's story. The senior psychiatrist on
the case, Dr. Thomas Szasz, sits quietly to one side, jotting on a yellow
note pad. There are some 12 students in the consultation room, all
juniors in the medical school: Their expressions range from slight
embarrassment to stern scientific interest.

" 'Well, what is your diagnosis?' Szasz asks, turning to them after the
patient has been escorted from the room. . . . Uncertain, the students
look at him without answering.

" 'Come now,' he prods ironically. 'You are the doctors and she is the
patient, so that means there must be an illness. Otherwise, we wouldn't
all be here, would we?'

" 'I think,' ventures a young man with a sprouting blond beard, 'that
she's in a chronic depression.'

" 'Oh, a depression,' says the older man, nodding. 'And you?' he asks,
turning to the next student . . . , 'What do you think?'

" 'I think that potentially it's a case of involutional melancholia. But for
right now, I guess I'd concur in a diagnosis of chronic, severe depression.'

"Szasz looks at him with interest. 'And how then would you go about
treating this condition?'

"There is a pause. 'Er . . . isn't there a drug called Elavil that's good
for depression?'

"The psychiatrist blinks several times, parodying extreme amazement:
'So you would treat this sickness she's got with *drugs*?' There are several
uncomfortable, uncomprehending laughs from around the room. 'But
what exactly are you treating? Is feeling miserable—and needing
someone to talk things over with—a form of mental illness?' Szasz gets to
his feet, walks over to a blackboard and picks up a piece of chalk.

" 'I don't understand—We're just trying to arrive at a diagnosis,'
protests the student, his voice confused.

" 'Of what?' demands Szasz. 'Has she got an illness called depression,
or has she got a lot of problems and troubles which make her unhappy?'
He turns and writes in large block letters. 'DEPRESSION' and under-

neath that: 'UNHAPPY HUMAN BEING.' 'Tell me,' he says, facing the class, 'does the psychiatric term say more than the simple descriptive phrase? Does it do anything other than turn "a person" with problems into a 'patient' with a sickness?' [1]"

Is depression an illness or a problem in living? What about abnormal behavior in general? This excerpt highlights the fact that psychiatrists, psychologists, and the other mental health professionals who diagnose and treat disturbed people do not always agree on the answers to these questions. Thomas Szasz, a psychiatrist at the State University of New York Medical School in Syracuse, believes that psychological prob-

lems are simply problems in living. Many traditional psychologists and psychiatrists view psychological problems as very much like illnesses. We return to the problem of how to conceptualize and explain abnormal behavior later in this chapter. First we look at the types of behavior psychologists consider abnormal.

What Does Abnormal Behavior Look Like?

Psychologists frequently employ the following criteria to assess abnormality:

Figure 14-1. "Depression" or "unhappy human being?" (Mimi Forsyth, from Monkmeyer.)

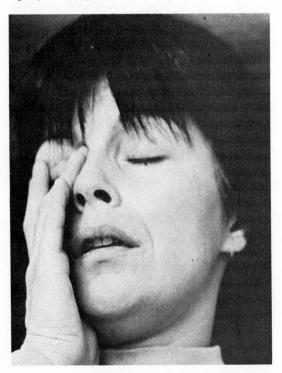

1. Defective Cognitive Functioning—When cognitive capabilities such as the ability to reason, perceive, attend, judge, remember, or communicate are badly impaired, psychologists frequently label the functioning "abnormal."
2. Defective Social Functioning—In each society behavior is regulated by social customs. When behavior deviates grossly from those standards, psychologists are likely to label it "abnormal."
3. Defective Self-control—Although no one has complete control over his or her own behavior, some people exercise extremely little or no control. Extreme lack of control over behavior is considered "abnormal."
4. Distress—All human beings experience strong emotions. Normal people manage to cope with them most of the time. Some people cannot handle anxiety, fear, rage, hate, guilt, depression, or self-pity and experience these feelings in extreme duration and/or quantity. An inability

to cope with emotions is considered "abnormal" (2).

It is important to note that judging abnormality is rarely easy or clear-cut. The guidelines are vague at best and employing them always demands subjective judgments. It is also important to note that there is no clear line separating what is called normal from what is called abnormal. The distinction between normal and abnormal is one of *degree*. People labeled abnormal show *more* cognitive impairment, behave *less* socially appropriately, or demonstrate *less* control over their emotions or themselves than so-called normal people do. Most people experience anxiety and depression, for example, but few experience these emotions with a frequency or intensity that disrupts their lives. Similarly, although most of us have fantasies and delusions, few of us lose our hold on reality. Judgments of normality and abnormality are further complicated by the fact that a given individual may be assessed as abnormal by one or more criteria and normal by the others. For example, a woman might be unable to cope with her extreme anxiety; yet at the same time her cognitive functioning may be quite normal.

Classifying Abnormal Behavior

Currently, psychologists, psychiatrists, and other mental health personnel working in traditional mental health settings employ ten major classifications to categorize abnormal behavior. Each classification is further subdivided into specific behavioral disorders. Table 14-1 presents a brief description of each classification and lists some of the major behavioral disorders which are included under it.

How does the traditional classification system relate to the criteria for abnormal behavior described on page 394? The behavioral disorders in each classification are generally characterized by specific criteria: For example, behavioral disorders included in the classification mental retardation are characterized by defective cognitive and social functioning. Behavioral disorders in the category organic brain syndrome are usually characterized by cognitive impairment and frequently by emotional distress.

Although a classification system can provide a timesaving shorthand for summarizing many facts, the current psychiatric scheme has a number of shortcomings which limit its usefulness. First, its reliability is not high; that is, mental health professionals frequently disagree over how to categorize a given person. To be more precise: Reliability is good when the general classifications are being used and when severe forms of abnormal behavior are encountered. Reliability is poor, however, for the specific behavioral disorders, particularly for the mild disorders (3).

Second, the psychiatric classification system labels frequently cause serious problems for patients. After being labeled, patients begin thinking of themselves as ill; friends and relatives stop treating them as normal human beings. The labels also influence how mental health professionals view people. Once a man is labeled schizophrenic, for example, he is likely to be perceived as hopelessly disturbed and he is actually likely to receive less professional attention than before the label was attached. Moreover, once the labels are attached, they tend to stick.

David Rosenhan, a psychologist at Stanford University, has vividly demonstrated many of the shortcomings of labeling patients according to the current classification system in a very daring and important study. The excerpts on pages 397–398 are taken from Rosenhan's report on this study.

TABLE 14-1. CLASSIFICATION OF BEHAVIORAL DISORDERS ACCORDING TO THE AMERICAN PSYCHIATRIC ASSOCIATION (1968)

Classification	Description of Major Symptoms	Behavioral Disorders
Mental retardation	Cognitive impairment (subnormal intellectual functioning originating at birth or during early childhood) and impairment of social adjustment	Various, ranging from borderline to profound
Organic brain syndrome	Cognitive impairment (impaired orientation, memory, judgment, comprehension, and learning ability) and instability and shallowness of emotion	Nonpsychotic organic brain syndrome Organic brain syndrome accompanied by psychotic symptoms, including alcoholic psychosis, general paresis, senile dementia
Psychosis	Gross impairment of cognitive functioning (including severe perceptual distortions) which result in an inability to fulfill ordinary social demands; dramatic mood swings	Schizophrenia Affective psychoses (marked by extreme depression or elation) Paranoid states
Neurosis	Anxiety, either expressed or controlled; no gross social or cognitive dysfunctioning	Various, including anxiety neurosis, phobic neurosis, obsessive-compulsive neurosis, depressive neurosis, hysteria, neurasthenia, hypochondria
Psychosomatic disorders	Various physical symptoms caused primarily by emotional factors; symptoms usually involve a single organ system controlled by the autonomic nervous system	Various, including skin, musculoskeletal, cardiovascular, gastrointestinal, and genitourinary disorders
Personality disorders	Strongly ingrained behavior patterns generally recognizable by the time of adolescence	Various, including psychopathic personality, sexual deviations, alcoholism, drug addiction or dependence
Special symptoms	Usually a single specific symptom	Various, including speech disorders, specific learning problems, tics, sleep disorders, feeding disorders, enuresis
Transient situational disturbances	Acute but temporary reactions to overwhelming environmental stress; symptoms vary in severity	Various, classified according to developmental stage (for example, adjustment reaction of infancy, childhood, adult life, or old age)
Behavior disorders of childhood and adolescence	More transient than psychoses, neuroses, or personality disorders, but more stable and treatment resistant than transient situational disturbances	Various, including overanxious reaction, runaway reaction, group delinquent reaction
Conditions without manifest psychiatric disorder and nonspecific conditions	Problems of sufficient severity to warrant treatment	Various, including marital maladjustment, occupational maladjustment, dyssocial behavior

On being sane in insane places

"If sanity and insanity exist, how shall we know them? . . . The belief has been strong that patients present symptoms, that those symptoms can be categorized, and, implicitly, that the sane are distinguishable from the insane. More recently, however, this belief has been questioned. . . . The view has grown that psychological categorization of mental illness is useless at best and downright harmful, misleading, and pejorative at worst. Psychiatric diagnoses, in this view, are in the minds of the observers and are not valid summaries of characteristics displayed by the observed.

"Gains can be made in deciding which of these [two opposing views] is more nearly accurate by getting normal people [that is, people who do not have, and have never suffered, symptoms of serious psychiatric disorders] admitted to psychiatric hospitals [where they behaved normally] and then determining whether they were discovered to be sane and, if so, how. . . . This article describes such an experiment.

"Eight sane people gained secret admission to 12 different hospitals. . . . Among them were three psychologists, a pediatrician, a psychiatrist, a painter and a housewife. . . . [Hospital admission was accomplished in the following manner:] After calling the hospital for an appointment, the pseudopatient [a sane person] arrived at the admissions office complaining that he had been hearing voices. Asked what the voices said, he replied that they were often unclear, but as far as he could tell they said 'empty,' 'hollow,' and 'thud.' . . . Beyond alleging the symptoms and falsifying name, vocation, and employment, no further alterations of person, history or circumstances were made. . . . Immediately upon admission to the psychiatric ward, the pseudopatient ceased simulating any symptoms of abnormality. In some cases, there was a brief period of mild nervousness and anxiety, since none of the pseudopatients really believed that they would be admitted so easily. . . . Apart from that short-lived nervousness, the pseudopatient behaved on the ward as he 'normally' behaved. . . . When asked by staff how he was feeling, he indicated that he was fine, that he no longer experienced symptoms. . . . Beyond such activities as were available to him on the admissions ward, he spent his time writing down his observations about the ward, its patients, and the staff. Initially these notes were written 'secretly,' but as it soon became clear that no one much cared, they were subsequently written on standard tablets of paper in such public places as the dayroom. . . . [Nursing] reports uniformly indicate that the patients were 'friendly,' 'cooperative,' and 'exhibited no abnormal indications.'

"Despite their public 'show' of sanity, the pseudopatients were never detected [by the psychiatrists, psychologists, or other mental health professionals with whom they came into contact]. Admitted, except in one case with a diagnosis of schizophrenia, each was discharged with a diagnosis of schizophrenia 'in remission'. . . . Length of hospitalization ranged from 7 to 52 days, with an average of 19 days. Having once been labeled schizophrenic, there [was apparently] nothing the pseudopatient [could] do to overcome the tag. . . . All of his other behaviors and characteristics [were] colored by that label. Indeed, [the schizophrenic] label is so powerful that many of the pseudopatients' normal behaviors were overlooked entirely or profoundly misinterpreted. . . . [For example] Nursing records for three patients indicate that the writing was seen as an aspect of their pathological behavior. . . .

"[The author concludes] . . . The needs for diagnosis and remediation of behavioral and emotional problems are enormous. But rather than acknowledge that we are just embarking on understanding, we continue to label patients 'schizophrenic,' 'manic-depressive,' and 'insane,' as if in those words we had captured the essence of understanding. The facts of the matter are that we have known for a long time that diagnoses are often not useful or reliable, but we have nevertheless continued to use them. . . . [Rather than labeling patients sane or insane,] it seems more useful to limit our discussions to behaviors, the stimuli that provoke them, and their correlates . . . [4]."

Mental health professionals continue to disagree about the utility of the current psychiatric classification system, and the issue has not been resolved. We will be discussing behavioral problems within the traditional framework, keeping in mind, however, the negative aspects of the classification system.

The Incidence of Abnormal Behavior

How common is abnormal behavior? How many Americans are so psychologically troubled that their daily functioning is disrupted? When social scientists interviewed and administered questionnaires to a random sample of 1,660 New Yorkers, they found that approximately 23 percent of their sample reported psychological problems which were severe enough to disturb their daily lives. An additional 58 percent reported mild to moderate psychological disturbances (5). Several

independent investigators have obtained similar results in surveying other communities (6,7). On the basis of these observations there are psychologists who estimate that some 40 million Americans, about one-fifth of the country's population, are psychologically troubled to a marked degree and many more are mildly disturbed.

Explaining Abnormal Behavior

How can abnormal behavior be explained? Greeks and Romans in ancient times believed that evil spirits entered certain people, "possessed" them, and drove them mad. Our ancestors in the Middle Ages also held this belief. In fact, as enlightened a man as the German theologian Martin Luther (1483–1546) wrote: "In cases of melancholy . . . I conclude it is merely the work of the devil.

. . . Those whom . . . [the devil] possesses corporally as mad people, he has permission from God to vex and agitate, but he has no power over their souls [8]."

Emil Kraepelin (1856–1926), a German psychiatrist who studied psychology under Wilhelm Wundt in Leipzig, helped establish the view that natural forces cause abnormal behavior. Kraepelin noted that certain mental symptoms tended to occur together; he concluded that each set of symptoms was a separate and distinct illness, such as measles or smallpox. He also assumed that each "mental disease" had an organic (physiological) basis which would eventually be discovered.

Is mental illness really an illness? Although most mental health professionals would agree that it is not literally an illness, many believe that it resembles an illness. This viewpoint, referred to as the *medical model*, includes these general assumptions:

1. Each disorder is conceptualized as if it were a disease with distinct causes.
2. Treatment aims at identifying the causes of the disease and at selecting the appropriate procedures to restore patients to their normal state.
3. A recognized expert is expected to take charge, to locate the causes of the disease, and to implement the cure. The patient, a passive recipient of treatment, is expected only to cooperate.

Thomas Szasz, whom we mentioned at the beginning of the chapter, is a leading critic of the medical model. Szasz and many psychologists believe that the medical model hinders both the understanding and treatment of abnormal behavior. Szasz writes:

It is customary to define psychiatry as a medical speciality concerned with the study, diagnosis, and treatment of mental illnesses. This is a worthless and misleading definition. Mental illness is a myth. Psychiatrists [psychologists, and

Figure 14-2. During the Middle Ages, evil spirits were believed to possess certain people, a belief illustrated in this fifteenth-century engraving by Martin Schongauer entitled "Saint Anthony Tormented by Demons." (The Metropolitan Museum of Art, Rogers Fund, 1920.)

other mental health professionals] are not concerned with mental illnesses and their treatments. In actual practice they deal with personal, social, and ethical problems in living [9].

The medical model can be criticized for several reasons:

1. It implies that simple, definitive events, such as specific conflicts or crises, are the "germs" which cause complex psychological problems.
2. It implies that techniques specific to treating each syndrome exist.

3. It implies that patients are stricken with illnesses over which they have little control; consequently, treatment must come from an external source.

Many psychologists endorse a *psychological model* of abnormal behavior which assumes the following:

1. Abnormal behavior is similar in kind (though not in degree) to normal behavior. Unlike a disease, it is caused by precisely the same factors which shape normal behavior—cumulative interactions of social, psychological, and biological variables.
2. Treatment is rarely syndrome specific. Rather, essentially the same treatment techniques which aim at helping patients acquire control over their problems and their lives are used for widely diverse symptoms. We will be looking at the major psychological treatment strategies (or psychotherapies as they are called) in the next chapter.
3. Active patient involvement in treatment is important. Suggesting that people are passive recipients of treatment probably compounds their difficulties by preventing them from learning to cope actively with their problems.

As we discuss various abnormal behaviors, we will be presenting both classical psychoanalytic and behavioristic explanations. The former illustrates the medical model approach; the latter illustrates the psychological model approach.

We turn now to three types of abnormal behavior, beginning with the neuroses.

NEUROSES

Psychologists use the term *neuroses* or *neurotic reactions* to refer to mild behavioral disorders which center around anxiety. Typically, neurotic people develop habits which enable them to avoid situations which arouse their anxiety. For example, a woman who finds her critical supervisor threatening may experience such severe nausea and heart palpitations in the supervisor's presence that she is "forced" to look for a new job. A young man may confine himself to his apartment to avoid insects, which frighten him intensely. Even though their lives are severely constricted and limited by their avoidance strategies, neurotic people tend to persevere rigidly in the same maladaptive behavior. Characteristically, they find their symptoms as bewildering as everyone else does, but they feel unable to change them. Their anxieties, symptoms, and inadequacies absorb their attention increasingly—leaving little time or energy for meaningful human relationships or constructive pursuits. Consequently, they usually feel wasted and unhappy. In terms of our criteria of abnormality, neurotic people suffer from severe distress and lack control over their lives. We now explore four of the most frequently seen patterns of neurotic behavior.

Anxiety Neurosis

Anxiety neurotics are almost continually anxious, tense, or worried. Typically, they overreact to every minor stress and strain that comes along; their anxiety cannot be attributed to any specific cause (or causes) so it is said to be *free floating*. Anxiety neurotics frequently complain about muscle tension, digestive problems, and headaches, the physical accompaniments of anxiety. In addition, anxiety attacks often come on suddenly and unexpectedly. An attack begins with an inexplicable and uncontrollable feeling of terror or impending disaster. During the attack breathing becomes difficult; tremors, nausea, excessive perspiration, heart irregularities, and other physical symptoms of anxiety become prominent. The attacks upset the anxiety neurotic; worrying interferes with sleep; lack of sleep and chronic tension lead to irritability, difficulty concentrating, and increased tension. Characteristically, anxiety neurotics try to escape from their tense and anxiety-ridden lives by drinking, taking tranquilizers and other drugs, physically avoiding particular places or situations where the anxiety attacks have occurred, and confining them-selves to a few activities or settings where they feel safe. These escape attempts often severely disrupt the anxiety neurotic's life.

How prevalent are anxiety neuroses today? One investigator estimates that some 10 million Americans currently experience this problem (10). The woman in the following case history was diagnosed as an anxiety neurotic.

Sue

Sue, a recently married, twenty-year-old college student, had been experiencing anxiety attacks for approximately a year when the therapist first saw her. Without warning her heart would begin to pound, her breathing would become difficult, her hands would sweat profusely, her stomach muscles would tighten, and she would feel flushed and feverish. Although she had frequently experienced these sensations, she could not stop herself from feeling that she was about to die. At the same time she knew—somewhere in the back of her mind—that if she only closed her eyes and rested, she'd feel normal again within an hour.

Sue's first anxiety attack had occurred as she was leaving a crowded football stadium. The only previous event that appeared connected with these feelings was a panicky reaction the night before to a TV story about a nightclub fire which trapped and killed thirty people. Her second anxiety attack occurred during an argument with her husband about whether to wear slacks or a dress to a family party. Sue didn't remember the details surrounding the third attack or the fourth or all the others which she had experienced since. The attacks were coming almost every day now—whenever any one disagreed with her, when she encountered strangers, when she drove in congested traffic, when she shopped in crowded stores. They happened at parties and in classes, restaurants, theaters, houses, and even her own apartment. Lately, Sue had been trying to avoid the places where the attacks occurred most often. Consequently, she was spending a great deal of time in her apartment, venturing out into the world primarily to seek help. The many physicians whom she consulted found nothing medically wrong with her and eventually she was referred to a psychiatric clinic.

What causes the anxiety neurosis? Opinions vary. Psychoanalytic theorists believe that its source is an internal conflict between the id and the ego (see Chapter 12). According to Freud's theory, the ego tries to prevent the id from expressing its desires, usually for sex or aggression, because the ego fears that such needs will be punished. This id–ego conflict generates unconscious anxiety. Because the person can neither escape the id impulses nor gratify them, the conflict continues and so does the anxiety. As we saw in Chapter 11, intense stresses do generate extreme anxiety. So an intense conflict of the type Freud postulated could very easily play a causative role in the anxiety neurotic's problem.

In contrast, behavioristic psychologists believe that the anxiety neurotic has simply learned various anxieties in the same way that people learn simple fears through respondent conditioning. During respondent conditioning (see Chapter 7) a neutral stimulus, such as a dog, can be associated with a fear-arousing experience, such as seeing a friend knocked over and bitten by a dog. Because of the association, the previously neutral object, the dog, becomes anxiety arousing. Through stimulus generalization, the anxiety may then spread to all dogs. Behavioristic psychologists believe that the anxieties of the anxiety neurotic result from conditioning and generalization.

Although stress and learning undoubtedly contribute to the anxiety neurotic's problem, genetics may also be involved in some cases. Through twin studies many researchers have found that the tendency to overreact to stress with severe anxiety can have a genetic basis (11). Heredity appears to influence both the speed and intensity with which people respond and the speed with which they stop responding to stress (12,13).

Although psychologists do not agree on the origin of the anxiety neurotic's excessive anxiety, most of them do agree that the maladaptive behavioral responses and the avoidance strategies are learned, probably through reinforcement principles. (One obvious reinforcement is anxiety reduction.)

Figure 14-3. Nightmare-fantasy of an acrophobic, a person with an overwhelming fear of high places. (Jim Jowers, Nancy Palmer Photo Agency.)

Phobic Neurosis

A *phobia* is an excessive or unwarranted fear of a specific object or situation. The person experiencing the phobia is usually aware that the fear is both excessive and unwarranted. Phobias are associated with a wide variety of stimuli, including open places, high places, closed places, crowds, being alone, pain, storms, blood, germs, darkness, disease, snakes, animals, and fire. Although many people have phobias, few are severe enough to qualify as neurotic according to our criteria. On the basis of a recent survey in New England, psychologists estimate that approximately 15 million Americans have phobias but that only a small percentage, some 44,000, have disabling phobias (14). Mild phobias and fears of real potential dangers—such as poisonous snakes or dark al-leys—rarely disrupt living. Phobic neurotics center their lives around avoiding particular feared situations and consequently their pho-bias are extremely disabling, as the following case illustrates.

Martha

Since childhood Martha had been afraid to stay alone. Her fear was traceable to the overzealous efforts of her mother to impress her with the potential dangers of being a lone woman. Martha's mother had fre-quently brought gory newspaper accounts of local robberies, murders, and rapes to her daughter's attention.

Martha never outgrew her fear; it became particularly troublesome when Martha's husband was forced to work the night shift. Although Martha attempted to stay by herself at first, she found her days haunted by fear of the impending evening alone. The nights in the empty house terrified her. When the therapist began treating Martha at the clinic, she was spending each day in a frenzy arranging for relatives, neighbors, neighborhood children, or friends to stay with her for the evening. The neurotic phobia was directing her life.

How do phobias develop? Again, there is no consensus. Psychoanalytic psychologists believe that phobias are displaced anxiety reactions; that is, anxiety has been shifted from an anxiety-arousing experience which initially provoked it to a harmless object. For example, a secretary who fears her boss's sexual advances might develop an elevator phobia which keeps her from working in his office. Behavioristic psychologists believe that both phobias and avoidance behavior are directly learned. Sometimes people observe the fearful behavior of others and model it. Sometimes they acquire phobic behavior by a combination of respondent and operant con-ditioning. After a neutral event becomes anx-iety arousing through respondent condition-ing, an avoidance response is learned because it reduces the anxiety.

But why do only some people develop disrupting neurotic fears? Psychoanalytic theorists believe that the phobic neurotic's specific fear is profoundly upsetting because it reflects basic, deep-rooted, personal con-flicts centering more often than not on sex and aggression. Another possibility is that excessive autonomic reactivity characterizes the phobic neurotic from birth, just as it may characterize the anxiety neurotic. So the pho-bic neurotic's fears may be excessive because of the nature of his or her nervous system and not because of the depth of the internal conflict.

Although the origin of the phobic neurot-ic's excessive anxiety is debatable, the avoid-ance reaction is clearly acquired and probably reflects the neurotic's learning history—parti-cularly the fact that the neurotic individual has never learned constructive ways of coping with fear.

Obsessive-Compulsive Neurosis

The obsessive-compulsive neurotic is tyrannized by *obsessions* (recurring, unwanted thoughts) or *compulsions* (recurring, unwanted, ritualistic acts) or both. For example, a person may worry continually about dirt and germs and wash his or her hands every few minutes, using a particular soap, a specific number of latherings, and so on. The obsessive-compulsive neurotic usually regards the obsessions and compulsions as morbid or irrational but finds them impossible to resist; that is, if they cannot be carried out, intense anxiety results. Most psychologists believe that obsessions and compulsions help the neurotic control anxiety by temporarily blocking out anxiety-arousing thoughts or impulses. Estimates of the incidence of this disorder are disparate—ranging from 40,000 to 2 million Americans—depending on the investigators' criteria for what constitutes a disabling problem (15,16). The following case illustrates the intensity of the obsessive-compulsive neurotic's behavior.

Case 13

"A boy of sixteen, troubled by open conflicts with his fanatically religious father and currently much concerned by his 'secret sin of masturbation,' had developed a number of compulsive rituals which had become annoying to his family. Among these was a peculiar insistence on repeating grace not once, but three times before every meal. The father, enraged by what appeared to be a travesty of the usual family custom, had begun to force the boy to eat without his preliminary prayers. The patient had attempted to comply, but found himself unable to do so because of trembling, palpitation, 'all-gone feeling in the stomach,' sweating, and, more particularly, a 'lump in the throat' that made swallowing impossible. These symptoms abated only slowly if he was ordered from the table, but disappeared promptly if he were permitted to go through his ritual and then discard his first bite of food. Investigation indicated that the three prayers were intoned to expiate guilt not only for his masturbation, but also for 'bad thoughts about mother and father'; so also, he felt compelled to renounce his first mouthful of food before he 'deserved to be given more.' He was sorry that his family 'had to suffer so for my sake—but they will go to heaven and they say I won't—so we'll be even.' When permitted his rituals, he felt little anxiety; when they were proscribed, the symptoms described above inevitably recurred [17]."

Not all obsessions and compulsions are considered neurotic. Normal people have compulsions of various kinds, such as washing the dishes after dinner or checking the doors at night. Normal people also experience recurring thoughts. You may have thought persistently about a mark in a course, an argument, or an eagerly anticipated party. Obsessive-compulsive behavior is considered neurotic only when it serves no constructive purpose, distresses the individual excessively, and interferes generally with the person's life.

The development of the obsessive-compulsive neurosis is not well understood. Psychoanalytic theorists believe that obsessions and compulsions result from a conflict between the id and a defense mechanism and reflect the partially successful operation of the defense mechanism. For example, an individual may resist an id impulse to soil by employing the defense mechanism *reaction formation* (concealing a real motive by expressing the opposite one)—in this case by becoming excessively neat and clean. Similarly, in *undoing* (atoning for immoral desires and thus counteracting them), a person may engage in some magical, ritualistic thoughts to cancel a forbidden id impulse to masturbate.

In contrast to the psychoanalytic theorists, many behavioristic psychologists believe that obsessions and compulsions are learned through reinforcement principles. A person accidentally discovers that performing a particular act or thinking a particular thought blots out a distressing, anxiety-arousing concern. The distraction is consequently substituted consciously and deliberately every time the anxiety-arousing concern occurs. Eventually the obsession or compulsion becomes automatic.

Finally, physiological factors may contribute to the obsessive-compulsive neurosis. In Chapter 3 we mentioned a twin study which indicated that the obsessive-compulsive neurosis is influenced by heredity. Research also shows that people with obsessive-compulsive symptoms frequently exhibit neurological problems (18). Such studies suggest that the nature of the nervous system may make some people likely to ruminate excessively about their experiences. If these people also react to stresses with excessive anxiety, they may be particularly likely to develop this neurotic problem.

Depressive Neurosis

No human being is happy all the time. Over the course of a single day people's moods frequently vary quite markedly. Physical illnesses produce fatigue and frequently mild depressions. Women typically feel unhappy and dissatisfied during their menstrual periods. Depressive reactions are also common responses to disappointments and losses. Neurotic depressions, in contrast, are characterized by excessively prolonged and intense depressive reactions to anxiety or grief, or some combination of the two. Millions of Americans exhibit the symptoms of this neurotic disorder every year, and many psychologists believe that neurotic depressions are more widespread than any other neurotic problem (19). Typically, depressive neurotics feel dejected and hopeless. Time passes slowly for them, and none of their former interests—including food, sex, hobbies, recreation, and loved ones—give them any pleasure. They behave as if they have lost control over the direction of their lives. They neglect their duties and responsibilities. They are the epitome of passivity and lethargy. Their conversation frequently suggests that they feel critical of themselves, guilt-ridden, and irritable. They may also experience chronic fatigue because insomnia is frequently a problem. The following case illustrates some of these behavior patterns.

Mr. J.

"Mr. J. was a fifty-one year old industrial engineer who, since the death of his wife five years earlier, had been suffering from continuing episodes of depression marked by extreme social withdrawal and occasional thoughts of suicide. His wife had died in an automobile accident during a shopping trip which he himself was to have made but was unable to because professional responsibilities changed his plans. His self-blame for her death, which was present immediately after the funeral and regarded by his friends and relatives as transitory, deepened as the months, and then years, passed by. He began to drink, sometimes heavily, and when thoroughly intoxicated would plead to his deceased wife for forgiveness. He lost all capacity for joy—his friends could not recall when they had last seen him smile. His gait was typically slow and labored, his voice usually tearful, his posture stooped. Once a gourmet, he had lost all interest in food and good wine, and on those increasingly rare occasions when friends invited him for dinner, this previously witty, urbane man could barely manage to engage in small talk. As might be expected, his work record deteriorated markedly, along with his psychological condition. Appointments were missed and projects haphazardly started and then left unfinished. When referred by his physician for psychotherapy, he had just been released from a hospital following a near-fatal and intentional overdose of sleeping pills [20]."

What causes the neurotic depressive reaction? That is, why is it that some individuals succumb to severe depression following life stresses and other individuals do not? Freud believed that overly dependent people were prone to depressions. Whenever they experienced an actual loss, such as the death of a loved one, or a symbolic loss, as in rejection by a parent, they displayed the neurotic depressive syndrome. The explanation of behavioristic psychologists is not so very different. Many of them believe that depression occurs when customary reinforcements (such as the presence of a supportive spouse, a satisfying job, or financial success) are suddenly withdrawn. People respond to the event by slowing down their activities. If they are not reinforced for their few constructive efforts, they may slow down even further. Sometimes the pattern of inactivity is reinforced by sympathy or special privileges, which makes the depressive behavior persist. Like their psychoanalytic colleagues, many behavioristic psychologists believe that only particular individuals are prone to neurotic depressions. Martin Seligman, a psychologist at the University of Pennsylvania, has suggested that neurotic depressives share a particular history. They have learned that they are incapable of successful mastery and control over their own lives. In other words, they have learned to regard themselves as helpless. When they confront a great stress, they naturally feel that they are inadequate to cope with it and depression soon replaces anxiety.[1] People who have learned to persist and master difficult problems are much less

[1]Seligman's theories are based on laboratory research on dogs who display behavior similar to that of the neurotic depressive: appetite loss, limited zest for life, and refusal to cope. This canine depressive behavior pattern—which Seligman calls "learned helplessness"—was produced in the following way: One group of dogs was forced to endure shocks without being able to terminate them. Later, when these animals were put in a situation where appropriate behavior would enable them to escape shock, they made very few attempts to do so, submitting

likely to succumb to neurotic depression, according to Seligman.

Seligman's hypothesis makes a great deal of sense and accounts well for suicide statistics. From 50,000 to 70,000 suicides occur annually in the United States (23). As many as 80 percent of these are considered the outcome of a severe depression (24). Suicide is especially prevalent among poor, young males belonging to minority ethnic groups who are likely to have learned that they have little or no control over the good things of American life. Consider an American Indian boy living on a reservation. He is taught that he is helpless at an early age. All his life he is advised: "Listen to him, he's a white man, he's smart." The Indians' squalid living conditions reinforce his perceptions that he is poor and that he will always be poor. On the reservation the boy sees signs of frustration—alcoholism and violence—everywhere. As he reaches adulthood he confronts the bleak choices of his adult life. He can take temporary seasonal work on the reservation, a low-paying job, relief, dependency, poverty, and humiliation, or he can go out into the world of the white man where he has no skills, no experience, and little confidence in himself. The choice is misery or misery, helplessness or helplessness. Accordingly, there is a great deal of depression, and the youthful Indian suicide rate is ten times the national average (25,26).

Finally, physiological processes can also affect moods and lead to depression. Recall the

Figure 14-4. The hopelessness of life on a reservation contributes to a suicide rate ten times the national average among young Indians. (Jesse Alexander, Nancy Palmer Photo Agency.)

research mentioned in Chapter 3 which found evidence that depressive neurosis was influenced by heredity. Genes may determine whether people are predominantly optimistic or pessimistic, which may, in turn, influence their susceptibility to a neurotic depression. In addition, a great many studies indicate that important brain chemicals (particularly the transmitter substance, norepinephrine) play a role in psychotic depressions. Norepinephrine and related substances are frequently depleted during stresses like those which sometimes bring on neurotic depressions. So many investigators currently believe that these physiological deficiencies may contribute to the severe depression of the neurotic.

---

passively instead. A second group of dogs who were never forced to passively endure shock readily learned to escape shock when given the opportunity. Seligman assumed that an initial experience with helplessness had affected the helpless dogs' subsequent capacities to cope constructively (21). Psychologist Jay Weiss of Rockefeller University and his colleagues have discovered that during inescapable shock a transmitter substance called norepinephrine is depleted and that this physiological deficiency seems to be responsible for the behavioral deficits which are subsequently observed in animals (22).

Summary: Neuroses

1. Neurotic people have difficulty handling their anxiety; typically, they react by avoidance responses. More often than not they lack insight into the causes of their symptoms, and they continue to persist in the same maladaptive behaviors. As they become increasingly preoccupied with their anxieties, inadequacies, and symptoms, their work and interpersonal relationships begin to suffer. Consequently, they usually feel unhappy and out of control.

2. Several neurotic patterns—anxiety neurosis, phobic neurosis, obsessive-compulsive neurosis, and depressive neurosis—are frequently seen in clinics. (Incidentally, neurotic individuals often show more than one pattern of symptoms.)

3. Neurotic reactions may be conceptualized as having at least two aspects: a distress or anxiety factor and a behavioral response factor. In some cases the distress factor may have a physiological basis. For example, the excessive autonomic reactivity which characterizes anxiety and phobic neurotics may be rooted in heredity. The distress factor could also be due to prolonged or repeated exposure to stress. Learning plays the major role in determining how neurotics handle their distress.

PSYCHOSES

The official psychiatric classification system states:

Patients are described as psychotic when their mental functioning is sufficiently impaired to interfere grossly with their capacity to meet the ordinary demands of life. The impairment may result from a serious distortion in their capacity to recognize reality. Hallucinations and delusions, for example, may distort their perceptions. Alterations of mood may be so profound that the patient's capacity to respond appropriately is grossly impaired. Deficits in perception, language, and memory may be so severe that the patient's capacity for mental grasp of his situation is effectively lost [27].

Psychotic people are generally far more seriously impaired than neurotic ones. Whereas neurotics are able to function quite normally in many ways, psychotics are frequently totally absorbed in their disturbance, out of contact with reality, and unable to take care of themselves. Moreover, whereas neurotics know that they have problems, psychotics are likely to have little or no perspective about their symptoms.

Although this matter continues to be controversial, many psychologists believe that the psychotic and neurotic disorders differ in kind as well as in degree; that is, when a neurosis worsens, it does not become a mild psychosis. However, the two disorders can sometimes be seen in the same individual. Psychotic people, for example, sometimes show neurotic symptoms such as severe phobias or compulsive rituals.

It is important to note that normal people frequently exhibit psychotic symptoms, though they are usually limited in severity, duration, and number, and they are usually under better control.

Certain psychotic disorders, known as *organic psychoses,* can be traced to specific physical causes such as tumors, head injuries, cerebral arteriosclerosis, hormone deficiencies, alcoholism, and infectious diseases such as syphilis. When psychotic symptoms do not have an obvious physical basis, they are labeled *functional psychoses.* Although the functional psychoses are assumed to have a psychological cause, in actuality their origin is not well understood. The functional psychoses include schizophrenia, severe depressive disorders, manic states (states of agitated excitement), and paranoid conditions. In this section we consider schizophrenia, by far the most prevalent of the functional psychoses.

What Is Schizophrenia?

Most people have the schizophrenic in mind when they use the word "crazy." *Schizophrenia* is the name for a puzzling group of psychotic disorders which are known to occur in all areas of the civilized and primitive world. Of the mental hospital population in the United States 50 percent is schizophrenic. One out of every one hundred people will probably develop schizophrenia at some time during his or her life. Eugen Bleuler, a Swiss psychiatrist, introduced the term schizophrenia (literally: Greek for splitting of the mind) in 1911 to characterize the fragmented, often contradictory quality of the schizophrenic's thoughts and emotions. Although the symptoms of schizophrenia are immensely varied, any individual so labeled is likely to show several of the following patterns (28):

1. Faulty Perceptual Filtering—Schizophrenics frequently have trouble dealing with incoming sensory information. One schizophrenic expressed it like this:

   I can't concentrate. . . . I am picking up different conversations. It's like being a transmitter. The sounds are coming through to me, but I feel my mind cannot cope with everything. It's difficult to concentrate on any one sound [29].

2. Disorganized Thinking—Schizophrenics often have trouble concentrating, associating their thoughts logically, and solving problems. In the words of a schizophrenic:

   My thoughts get all jumbled up. I start thinking or talking about something, but I never get there. Instead I wander off in the wrong direction and get caught up with all sorts of different things that may be connected with the things I want to say . . . [30].

3. Emotional Distortions—The emotional reactions of schizophrenics are often inappropriate to the situation. One schizophrenic commented:

   You see I might be talking about something quite serious to you and other things come into my head at the same time that are funny and this makes me laugh [31].

4. Delusions and Hallucinations—*Delusions* (persistent irrational beliefs) and *hallucinations* (sensory experiences without a basis in reality) are further evidence of the schizophrenic's disorganized thinking, feeling, and perceiving. Here is a schizophrenic's description of these phenomena:

   Shortly after I was taken to the hospital for the first time in a rigid catatonic condition I was plunged into the horror of a world catastrophe. I was being caught up in a cataclysm and totally dislocated. I myself had been responsible for setting the destructive forces into motion, although I had acted with no intent to harm. . . .
   During the first three weeks of hospitalization I saw visions at various times. The first type . . . were entirely projections of inner states of consciousness and appeared before my eyes like a motion picture. . . . The second type could . . . be called visual hallucinations and distortions, sometimes suggested by the play of light and shadow, etc., acting upon an overwrought imagination [32].

5. Withdrawal from Reality—Schizophrenics frequently feel numbed and apathetic about the real world and preoccupied with inner fantasies, reveries, and private experiences. Here is a schizophrenic's description:

   We cannot cope with life as we find it, nor can we escape it or adjust ourselves to it. So we are given the power to create some sort of world we can deal with. The worlds created are as varied as there are minds to create them. Each one is strictly private and cannot be shared by another. It is much more real than reality. For nothing that happens to a

sane mortal in the commonplace world of ordinary living, can approach the startling intensity of things going on in delusion. There
is a sharpness—a shrillness—a piercing intensity which thrusts itself through the consciousness and is so much more convincing
than the blunt edge of reason . . . [33].

6. In addition, the behavior of schizophrenics is sometimes bizarre, as we will see, and
their speech jumbled and incomprehensible, as the following monologue illustrates:

Why nylons, autos, men city people more
cancer—because more polluted meat and
drinks not one single connection with cigs—
never jitters from narcotics or disorganization
of nervous system—"I-am-ity" Megaloma-
nia—why Napoleon had to conquer world—
Hitler and Mussolini and Me Too so now that
I have conquered all mystery diseases (asthma
and rheumatism too/experiment any demen-
tia case) I am going to conquer the Russians/
It is just a mathematical problem/New York,
Cleveland, St. Louis, Detroit, California, Mi-
ami/they have control of now pulling in Cin-
cinnati so I won't die of cancer, or the apparent heart attack/but a couple of bullets—so
KEEP my name out—Please as I know of one
check upon me—mathematics they are watching me see signals in paper. Mathematics if I
disappear they have me—please copy and
send to Hoover—telegraphers mailmen
caught in net [34].

Although schizophrenia may initially appear in childhood or in old age, it usually
becomes apparent first at around age thirty.
Its incidence is approximately the same in
men and women. When schizophrenia develops gradually over many years, as it sometimes does, it is labeled *process schizophrenia.*
People who develop process schizophrenia
d to have been sickly, withdrawn, and
justed as long as anyone can remem-
heir symptoms are usually quite severe,
v are not likely to recover. In contrast,
hizophrenia appears to be triggered
by stress. This disorder is compara-

tively mild, and elements of intense emotional upheaval and confusion tend to be pronounced. The recovery rate from reactive
schizophrenia is higher.

As we mentioned before, schizophrenia is
characterized by variability. Symptoms differ
from schizophrenic to schizophrenic, and a
single individual schizophrenic might behave
in blatantly psychotic ways one day and in
relatively normal ones the next. Some schizophrenics show particular clusters of symptoms called *subtypes.* We consider four of the
ten recognized subtypes. (It is important to
keep in mind that some schizophrenics fit
into more than one subtype and that the
subtype of a particular schizophrenic individual may change over time.)

Paranoid schizophrenia. About half of all
schizophrenics are labeled "paranoid." Characteristically, they feel that they are being
persecuted. The specific delusion may take
many forms: "They want to tie me under a
bridge and then steal my furniture." "An
opium smoker doped me by sticking a needle
in my heel." "The manager of the baseball
team tried to give me syphilis by putting
germs on my sandwich [35]." In addition,
paranoid schizophrenics frequently experience *delusions of grandeur* (beliefs that they are
illustrious, the richest person in the world,
the monarch of England, or Jesus Christ).
Paranoid schizophrenics increasingly center
their lives around their vivid hallucinations
and delusions. Typically, they feel that all
events—even natural or impersonal ones—
are communications meant for them. For
example, if someone coughs or if it happens
to rain, the event may be interpreted as a
message that the Communists are taking over
New York City. Despite their idiosyncrasies,
many paranoid schizophrenics are somewhat
responsive to reality and manage to live in a
marginal way in the outside world. The following case was diagnosed paranoid schizophrenic:

Mel

Mel, a forty-five-year-old bachelor, lived alone in a rented room. He spent his welfare check as soon as it arrived—mostly on books and drawing supplies. He had no umbrella and no winter coat. He often went days without eating anything but chocolate bars. Mel's pleasures were simple: he enjoyed lighting matches; he liked to sketch; he was fond of browsing in bookstores; most of all he loved sitting in coffee houses talking to college students.

Mel described himself as a free-lance inventor, mathematician, scientist, and philosopher. He claimed to have known Einstein and Schweitzer. He insisted that Henry Kissinger sometimes called him for advice. The list of foreign and American presidents who'd consulted him was impressively long; he'd also spoken before the United Nations; and from time to time he'd advised Standard Oil, General Electric, and many other similar corporations. Mel's accomplishments were not confined to advice. He had also invented the color television and the electric can opener; most importantly, he was on the brink of discovering the cure for cancer.

Despite appearances to the contrary, Mel asserted that his inventions had made him rich, a millionaire many times over. But success had brought some heavy burdens with it. As Mel saw it, the heaviest one was envy. Out of envy several state senators were having him tailed and were trying to put him away in a mental hospital.

Simple schizophrenia. Simple schizophrenics become increasingly apathetic about life, usually beginning in adolescence. Their symptoms are not dramatic: They are neither violent nor bizarre. They do not appear to have delusions nor to hallucinate. They are characterized instead by withdrawal and disinterest in the world. They simply want people to leave them alone and let them do as they wish (which usually appears to be nothing). Simple schizophrenics can sometimes fend for themselves in society, but like the paranoid, they are apt to go through life in a marginal role—as a bum or drifter, for example. The following case was diagnosed simple schizophrenic:

Lotte

"Lotte is a forty-year-old woman who was examined and admitted to the hospital at the request of her mother. Shortly before this, her father had died and had left her mother and Lotte with no financial support. Lotte had 'sat around the house' for the previous twelve years, having lost her temporary employment in the office of a government agency because of inefficiency. She had no friends, interests, or hobbies. According to her own account, she did not read or watch television but did occasionally perform a few simple household tasks when pressured by her mother. Her one job had been secured during the manpower shortage of World War II and had consisted of simple filing and sorting of documents. She found this work 'too fast' and was ultimately discharged for incompetence. From her high school days on, Lotte seemed to have no relationship of even a casual kind with men. She did not finish high school; her parents took her out of it 'because it made her nervous.'

"On admission, she was quiet and almost completely passive about the prospect of her hospitalization. She was neat and clean and obedient to the instructions of her mother regarding such matters as where to sit, when to remove her hat, and coat, etc. This pattern of behavior was repeated on the admission ward during the subsequent weeks [36]."

Catatonic schizophrenia. The onset of catatonic schizophrenia is usually sudden; the disorder tends to occur repeatedly as a series of short attacks over the course of many years. Catatonics are most notably character-

Figure 14.5. Sirhan Sirhan, convicted assassin of Robert Kennedy, was diagnosed as a paranoid schizophrenic by psychologists and psychiatrists during his trial. (United Press International Photo.)

ized by peculiar motor behavior. Sometimes they react with excitement, frenzy, hyperactivity, bursts of talkativeness, and violence. Most often they are stuporous—uncommunicative and passive. Occasionally, their limbs are rigid or mannikinlike; that is, they remain in any position that one places them in for minutes and even hours, a characteristic known as *waxy flexibility*. The catatonic schizophrenic's stupor probably masks intense delusional and hallucinogenic experiences, as one patient's observations suggest:

In the stupor many strange events enter the soul. The soul is bewitched. . . . Everything was polar. . . . In order that the sun should shine, the soul had to have psychic trouble, the trouble corresponding in strength in proportion to the strength of the sun. . . .

If you ask a simple question, I hear it, but it's as if from outside the room. People help but the people become transformed into words, and from words people are transformed into a kinemagraphic picture . . . [T]hought stops but for a few fixed points that act as a lighthouse . . . [37].

Hebephrenic schizophrenia. Hebephrenic schizophrenics are severely deteriorated. They are disoriented; their delusions and hallucinations are disjointed and peculiarly unreal, as in the following case:

A hebephrenic divorcée

"The patient was a divorcée, 32 years of age, who had come to the hospital with bizarre delusions, hallucinations, and severe personality disintegration and with a record of alcoholism, promiscuity, and possible incestuous relations with a brother. The following conversation shows typical hebephrenic responses to questioning.

"Dr.: How do you feel today?
"Pt.: Fine.
"Dr.: When did you come here?
"Pt.: 1416, you remember, doctor (silly giggle).
"Dr.: Do you know why you are here?
"Pt.: Well, in 1951 I changed into two men. President Truman was judge at my trial. I was convicted and hung (silly giggle). My brother and I were given back our normal bodies 5 years ago. I am a policewoman. I keep a dictaphone concealed on my person.
"Dr.: Can you tell me the name of this place?
"Pt.: I have not been a drinker for 16 years. I am taking a mental rest after a 'carter' assignment or 'quill.' You know, a 'penwrap.' I had contracts with Warner Brothers Studios and Eugene broke phonograph records but Mike protested. I have been with the police department for 35 years. I am made of flesh and blood—see, doctor (pulling up her dress).
"Dr.: Are you married?
"Pt.: No. I am not attracted to men (silly giggle). I have a companionship arrangement with my brother. I am a 'looner' . . . a bachelor [38]."

Frequently hebephrenic schizophrenics are silly in mannerisms. They do a lot of inappropriate giggling, posturing, gesturing, and grimacing. They may spend hours talking to themselves or to imaginary companions. Their language is usually difficult to understand, as you can see from another hebephrenic's conversation:

No, I never was crazy, a little nervous. Look at my teeth, I came here to have my teeth fixed. We're going to have a strawberry party now. Yesterday I heard voices. They said, "I ran to the drugstore and I am going home tomorrow." I heard J. B. Scott's voice and it came from up here in the air. We've got 39 banks on Market Street. We've got lots of property. Say, take me home and I'll give you three laundry bags . . . [39].

THE CAUSES OF SCHIZOPHRENIA

What causes schizophrenia? Investigators have proposed an enormous number of possible social-psychological and physiological explanations. Psychoanalytic theorists view schizophrenia as a regression to the oral stage of early infancy caused by pathological family relationships and early psychological traumas. Behavioristic psychologists emphasize the schizophrenic's entire learning history. Currently, the majority of psychologists and other mental health experts agree that schizophrenia is probably caused by a combination of *both* genetic and environmental mechanisms.

Figure 14-6. The hebephrenic schizophrenic's behavior is marked by inappropriate giggling and conversations with imaginary companions. (Benyas, from Black Star.)

The Role of Heredity

Evidence suggesting that heredity plays a role in the development of schizophrenic disorders is impressive. Numerous studies show that the relatives of schizophrenics are significantly more likely to be afflicted with this condition than members of the general population. In general, the closer the blood relationship, the greater the chance that two people will be *concordant* (alike) with respect to schizophrenia. Table 14-2 shows that identical twins (individuals with identical sets of genes) are concordant for schizophrenia roughly three to six times more frequently than fraternal twins (siblings with nonidentical sets of genes). These twin studies by themselves do not rule out an environmental explanation of schizophrenia. Because they are the same sex and of similar appearance identical twins may be more likely than fraternal twins to have been exposed to many of the same circumstances, people, routines, learning conditions, pressures, and stresses.

How can social scientists separate the effects of heredity from those of environment?

TABLE 14-2. CONCORDANCE RATES IN THE MAJOR TWIN STUDIES OF SCHIZOPHRENIA*

Study	Source	Identical Twins		Fraternal Twins	
		Number of Pairs	Percent Concordant	Number of Pairs	Percent Concordant
Luxenburger (1928, 1934)	Germany	17–27	33–76.5	48	2.1
Rosanoff et al. (1934)	U.S.A. & Canada	41	61.0	101	10.0
Essen-Möller (1941)	Sweden	7–11	14–71.	24	8.3–17
Kallmann (1946)	New York	174	69–86.2	517	10–14.5
Slater (1953)	England	37	65–74.7	115	11.3–14.4
Inouye (1961)	Japan	55	36–60	17	6–12
Tienari (1963, 1968)	Finland	16	0–6	21	4.8
Gottesman and Shields (1966)	England	24	41.7	33	9.1
Kringlen (1967)	Norway	55	25–38	172	8–10
Fischer (1968)	Denmark	16	19–56	34	6–15
Hoffer et al. (1968)	U.S. Veterans	80	15.5	145	4.4

*In some cases an investigator computed two quite different concordance rates; in these cases two distinct methods of sampling or diagnosis were employed. Note also that whereas the concordance rates vary markedly, in every case—except one—identical twins were considered more concordant than fraternal twins.

In one ingenious study, investigators collected data on individuals who had been permanently separated from their biological mothers in the first month of life and reared primarily in foster and adoptive homes. Approximately half of these individuals had been born to schizophrenic mothers, the other half to parents without a record of psychiatric disturbances. A team of clinicians assessed the mental health of each subject in adulthood through psychiatric interviews and review of available records (school, police, Veterans Administration, and so on). They found a significant excess of schizophrenia and other pathological disorders among those individuals whose biological mothers were schizophrenic. The data are best explained by assuming that these disorders had been transmitted by heredity (40). Many studies have come to the same conclusion.

How could heredity produce schizophrenia? What biological mechanisms may be involved? Although no one knows the answer to this question, there are currently two major types of theories: monogenic-biochemical and diasthesis-stress.

Monogenic-biochemical theories of schizophrenia. The idea that twisted molecules produce twisted minds is behind the monogenic-biochemical theories of schizophrenia. These theories propose that a gene produces a biochemical irregularity and that this irregularity leads, in turn, to schizophrenia. The neurohormone serotonin is among the specific biochemical agents that have been investigated. Attention was first drawn to serotonin when scientists found that LSD 25 and mescaline, drugs structurally similar to serotonin, produced hallucinations, delusions, and other psychoticlike effects (41). Furthermore, when investigators lowered the serotonin level in cats for long periods of time, the cats appeared to hallucinate, alternating between strange and normal behavior in a fashion that resembled schizophrenic

behavior (42). So schizophrenia may be, at least in part, the result of biochemical imbalances resulting from genetic irregularities.

Diasthesis-stress theories of schizophrenia. Diasthesis-stress theories hypothesize that schizophrenics inherit a predisposition to exhibit schizophrenia which develops in full only under adverse circumstances. The diasthesis-stress theory of psychologist Paul Meehl is widely accepted. Meehl believes that existing clinical and genetic studies of schizophrenia support the theory that schizophrenics inherit a neural defect, which he calls *schizotaxia*. Presumably the presence of schizotaxia leads to the formation of a *schizoid personality*, a personality characterized by social distrust, ambivalence, and an inability either to think clearly or to experience pleasure. Meehl also believes that when schizoid individuals inherit a vigorous constitution (physical strength, high resistance to stress, and low autonomic reactivity) and when they have the good fortune to grow up in a favorable interpersonal climate, they manage to escape schizophrenia. Schizoid people with weak constitutions or unfavorable environments or both, according to Meehl, develop full-blown clinical schizophrenia (43).

The Role of Social-psychological Variables

If schizophrenia were completely determined by genetic forces, identical twins would be concordant with respect to schizophrenia 100 percent of the time. The fact that they are not completely concordant suggests that nongenetic factors are operating. Physical traumas such as severe illnesses or brain injuries at an earlier age could be involved, as could social-psychological variables, such as family relationships, cultural pressures, and psychological stresses.

A vast number of studies have focused on

the relationship between schizophrenia and social-psychological factors, particularly the schizophrenic's family. Surveys portray the schizophrenic's mother variously as maladjusted, overprotecting, domineering, weak, rejecting, or smothering. Moreover, observers characterize the marriage of the schizophrenic's parents as chronically tense, lacking in satisfactions, emotionally empty, destructive, or *skewed* (in this last case a relatively healthy parent accepts and supports the pathology of a disturbed one). Psychologists and psychiatrists also find faulty patterns of communication within the schizophrenic's family. In some cases schizophrenics have been bombarded by messages which pull them in two different directions at once, a dilemma known as the *double bind.* Consider an example. A mother claims that she loves her daughter and wants what is best for her, while at the same time she rejects the girl's affection and conversation. This communication pattern probably confuses the child and keeps her from trusting her own experiences. Although many schizophrenics have not experienced warm, healthy family relationships, social scientists cannot conclude that families have significantly contributed to schizophrenia until certain questions are answered; namely:

1. Does the pathology found in the schizophrenic's family tend to be greater than that which is ordinarily encountered in the families of the general population?
2. Does the family pathology precede the development of schizophrenia, or is it simply the result of attending to a sickly or difficult child?
3. Why does the schizophrenic develop schizophrenia, whereas siblings usually do not?
4. Would removing the schizophrenic from the aversive family circumstances significantly decrease the individual's likelihood of developing the disorder? (44)

These questions are very hard to investigate in a real setting. One cannot, for example, remove children from their families for a psychology experiment, even for one of great importance; so the significance of the family in causing schizophrenia cannot yet be specified.

Summary: Psychoses

1. Psychoses are severe disorders characterized by gross social and psychological impairment, emotional instability, and lack of control.
2. Schizophrenia is the most widespread functional psychotic disorder. Typical symptoms include faulty perceptual filtering, disorganized thinking, distorted emotions, delusions, hallucinations, withdrawal from reality, bizarre behavior, and incoherent speech.
3. The onset of schizophrenia may be rapid or gradual. Schizophrenic individuals sometimes show clear-cut symptoms of the paranoid, simple, catatonic, or hebephrenic types.
4. Both hereditary and environmental factors appear to play a role in the development of schizophrenia. The exact mechanisms are still a matter of conjecture.

PSYCHOPATHIC BEHAVIOR

Two 18-year-old youths went to visit a girl at her home. Finding no one there, they broke into the house, damaged a number of paintings and other furnishings, and stole a quantity of liquor and a television set. They disposed of the latter to a mutual friend for a small sum of money. Upon their apprehension by the police, they at first denied the entire venture and then later insisted that it was all a "practical joke." They did not consider their behavior particularly inappropriate, nor did they think any sort of restitution for damage was called for [45].

Individuals with antisocial personalities, or psychopaths as they are frequently called, behave like these two eighteen-year-old youths. They tend to lack the sense of right and wrong which most people acquire at an early age; consequently, they do not follow the moral laws of their culture. The lack of moral convictions leads to a characteristic interpersonal style: Psychopaths usually relate to others as con-artists, extorting and manipulating to obtain what they want without considering the needs or rights of others. Just like very young children, psychopathic people also tend to live in the present, acting for the immediate gratification of their momentary impulses instead of postponing their pleasure when it is appropriate to do so. A psychopathic man who wants a TV set, for example, would be likelier to take one or "con" a friend out of his than to work to earn the money to buy his own. Curiously, unlike professional criminals, psychopaths rarely take pains to conceal their activities; in fact, they often appear to be quite oblivious to the consequences of their actions. As a result, they are frequently caught when they behave illegally. Contrary to what we would expect, punishment does not seem to teach the psychopath restraint. In contrast to the neurotic, the psychopath displays too little anxiety. Clinical observations indicate that people who exhibit psychopathic behavior are frequently intelligent, charming, impressive individuals who put up a good front and show good control over their mental facilities. In terms of our criteria of abnormality, psychopaths exhibit defective social functioning—deviating grossly from accepted social standards.

Psychopathic behavior belongs to a third large category of abnormal behavior, the *personality disorders*, which the psychiatric classification system describes as lifelong maladaptive behavior patterns frequently recognizable by the time of adolescence. Sex-

Figure 14-7. Psychopaths like Hitler's minister Hermann Goering are frequently intelligent, charming persons who violate accepted social and moral standards without anxiety or regret. (Wide World Photos.)

ual deviations, alcohol addiction, and drug dependencies are also included in this general category. A small percentage of psychopaths end up in mental hospitals and clinics—usually because of court referrals. A larger percentage of them turn up in prisons and other penal institutions. The vast majority, it is believed, manage to function in society despite frequent scrapes with the law and other authorities.

The Causes of Psychopathic Behavior

The causes of the psychopath's behavior are not well understood. Some investigators believe that physiological deficits may be at the heart of the problem. Laboratory studies find consistent evidence that psychopaths are relatively insensitive to physical pain (46). Perhaps this is the reason that they rarely acquire the conditioned fears, such as fears of social disapproval or humiliation, which restrain their wrongdoing and develop their sense of right and wrong. There is also some evidence that psychopaths operate at a low level of arousal and do not show variability in their autonomic reactions. These findings suggest that psychopaths may be relatively immune to sensory stimulation and that their impulsive, excitement-seeking behavior may be an attempt to obtain such stimulation (47).

Although the psychopath's behavioral characteristics could be influenced by physiology, they could also have a social-psychological basis. Psychoanalytic theorists have suggested that psychopathic behavior is caused by infantile traumas which generate conflicts that prevent the child from identifying with the like-sexed parent and incorporating his or her moral standards. Behavioristic psychologists believe that psychopathic behavior can result from learning. Some people who display psychopathic behavior come from homes where they are left on their own without discipline or training in moral conduct. Others come from impoverished neighborhoods where they grow up in a climate of alienation. When people believe that they cannot attain "the good life" nor hope to make an impact on their society, they may live for present pleasures and derive their excitement from hostile and destructive acts against the establishment.

The vast majority of psychopaths appear to be the product of middle-class homes. What could middle-class parents be doing to teach their children psychopathic behavior? The parents themselves may be deceitful, manipulative, impulsive, emotionally distant, and self-indulgent; their children may learn these characteristics through observation and modeling. Or the parents might directly reinforce their children for manipulative behavior and deceit by praising or showing approval for these tactics. Another possibility is that the psychopath's parents are arbitrary and harsh in their disciplinary practices and that their children do not trust them. Instead of adopting their standards of right and wrong, they learn instead how to avoid their parents' wrath by lying, cheating, and manipulating. Although all these explanations sound plausible, there is no clear-cut support for any one of them. More research is necessary to establish the causes of this complex pattern of behavior.

STUDY GUIDE 14

Key Terms. abnormal behavior, neuroses, neurotic reaction, anxiety neurosis, free-floating anxiety, phobic neurosis, phobia, obsessive-compulsive neurosis, obsession, compulsion, reaction formation, undoing, depressive neurosis, psychoses, organic psychoses, functional psychoses, manic states, schizophrenia, delusions, hallucinations, process schizophrenia, reactive schizophrenia, paranoid schizophrenia, delusions of grandeur, simple schizophrenia, catatonic schizophrenia, waxy inflexibility, hebephrenic schizophrenia, concordant, serotonin, schizotaxia, schizoid personality, double bind, antisocial personality (psychopath), personality disorders.

Important Research. sane people in insane places (Rosenhan), incidence of psychological problems in New York City, learned helplessness and depression (Seligman), studies of schizophrenia in twins (various).

Basic Theories. Medical model of abnormal behavior, psychological model of abnormal behavior, monogenic-biochemical theories of schizophrenia, diathesis-stress theories of schizophrenia.

Self-Quiz

1. Which criterion for assessing behavior as "abnormal" is not mentioned in this text? [**a**] extreme lack of control over behavior; [**b**] inability to cope with emotions; [**c**] badly impaired cognitive capacities; [**d**] behavior which violates ethical standards.

2. Rosenhan found that sane people who admitted themselves to mental hospitals [**a**] were generally discovered to be sane by the hospital staff during the initial interview; [**b**] were generally discovered to be sane by the hospital staff after two or three days in the hospital; [**c**] were not discovered to be sane by the hospital staff but were eventually released—after a week or two, on the average; [**d**] were not discovered to be sane by the hospital staff but were eventually released—after nearly three weeks on the average.

3. Which of the following statements characterizes the psychological model of abnormal behavior? [**a**] Treatment aims at identifying the causes of the disorder and selecting the most appropriate treatment; [**b**] each disorder is viewed as having distinct causes; [**c**] abnormal behavior is seen as similar in kind (but not in degree) to normal behavior; [**d**] an expert directs the treatment; the patient is primarily expected to cooperate.

4. Psychologists use the term *neuroses* to refer to mild behavioral disorders [**a**] characterized primarily by anxiety; [**b**] characterized primarily by unhappiness; [**c**] characterized primarily by maladaptive social behavior; [**d**] characterized primarily by impaired cognitive abilities.

5. Psychoanalytic theorists believe that the anxiety neurosis is caused by [**a**] an intense conflict between the id and the ego; [**b**] anxiety-arousing experiences in early childhood that are brought to mind by similar experiences later on; [**c**] sexual traumas; [**d**] an actual or symbolic loss experienced by an already overly dependent person.

6. Feelings of hopelessness, guilt, fatigue, and loss of interest in favorite activities are characteristic of [**a**] schizophrenia; [**b**] the psychopathic personality; [**c**] the depressive neurosis; [**d**] the anxiety neurosis.

7. Psychologists generally view schizophrenia as [**a**] an extreme form of the anxiety neurosis; [**b**] a functional psychosis characterized by faulty perceptual filtering, disorganized thinking, distorted emotions, withdrawal from reality, and strange behavior; [**c**] an organic psychosis in which two or more distinct personalities alternate; [**d**] an organic psychosis characterized by severe cognitive, language, emotional, sensory, and behavioral problems.

8. A relatively mild form of schizophrenia brought on suddenly by stress is called _____ schizophrenia. [**a**] reactive; [**b**] process; [**c**] hebephrenic; [**d**] simple.

9. Sudden attacks of panic, nausea, shaking, and breathing difficulties are likeliest to be seen in a person with a diagnosis of [**a**] anxiety neurosis; [**b**] phobic neurosis; [**c**] depressive neurosis; [**d**] obsessive-compulsive neurosis.

10. An excessive life-disrupting fear of the darkness would most likely occur in a person with a diagnosis of [**a**] free-floating anxiety; [**b**] phobic neurosis; [**c**] anxiety neurosis; [**d**] schizophrenia.

11. Seligman produced the symptoms of neurotic depression in dogs by [**a**] rearing them away from their mothers; [**b**] maintaining them on a barely adequate diet; [**c**] giving them electric shocks over which they had no control; [**d**] punishing them for normal puppy sexual behavior.

12. Which is *not* necessarily characteristic of psychotic disorders? [**a**] serious distortions in the capacity to recognize reality; [**b**] badly impaired mental functioning; [**c**] profound changes in mood; [**d**] incapacitating anxiety.

13. According to the diathesis-stress theory of schizophrenia, [**a**] several genes produce a biochemical irregularity which causes schizophrenia; [**b**] a genetic predisposition to schizophrenia is inherited, but the disorder does not develop fully unless the person is subjected to severe stresses and strains; [**c**] several genes produce a biochemical irregularity which interferes with an individual's ability to cope with stress; if stresses occur, the individual will develop schizophrenia; [**d**] an oversupply of serotonin, a chemical similar in structure to LSD or mescaline, is responsible for most schizophrenic disorders.

14. Which of the following is *not* classified as a personality disorder? [**a**] sexual deviations; [**b**] marital problems; [**c**] psychopathic behavior; [**d**] drug dependencies.

15. A study of a random sample of 1660 New Yorkers found that roughly _____ percent suffered from marked psychological impairment, and about twice as many were troubled to some degree. [**a**] 1; [**b**] 5; [**c**] 10; [**d**] 20; [**e**] 30; [**f**] 35.

Questions to Consider

1. Many psychologists view psychological abnormality as extreme deviation from imaginary norms on cognitive and social functioning, self-control, etc. What problems does this type of definition pose? Does this type of definition distinguish, for example, between abnormality and eccentricity? Can it handle the case of an "abnormal culture" like Hitler's Germany? Try to think of a definition of abnormal behavior that has fewer problems.

2. What problems does the current diagnostic system present? Can you think of an alternative scheme? Consider Rosenhan's suggestion. What are its advantages and disadvantages?

3. Ask several people how they conceptualize abnormal behavior (that is, is abnormal behavior different from normal behavior? What causes it? How is it best treated?) Does the general public tend to use a medical or psychological model? Which model seems to you to best describe abnormal behavior?

4. Why is it difficult to study the causes of abnormal behavior?

5. Design a longitudinal study to determine which environmental variables contribute to schizophrenia. What kinds of control group(s) would you use? How could environmental variables be separated from hereditary variables?

6. Based on your reading in this chapter, what sorts of childhood experiences would probably produce a psychopath?

Project 14: Do the Problems of Psychologically Healthy and Psychologically Troubled People Vary in Number, in Kind, or in Severity?

In this project, you will be trying to answer the question: How do the problems of psychologically healthy and psychologically troubled people vary? Specifically, do they vary in number? in kind? in severity? or in some combination of these dimensions? The medical model of abnormal behavior assumes that psychological problems are like distinct illnesses with distinct causes; the psychological model assumes that abnormal behavior is similar in kind (though not in degree) to normal behavior and that they are both caused by interactions of biological, social, and psychological factors. Which model best fits the facts?

Method. Make at least ten copies of the checklist on page 421. Then find a minimum of ten cooperative subjects who are willing to complete them. Try to find five subjects whom you consider troubled and five whom you consider well adjusted. Explain that you are taking a survey on adjustment problems for a psychology project and that people's names will not be identified with their questionnaires.

Your subjects should not write their names on these questionnaires and you should take precautions to conceal their identity. One way to do this is to have all subjects return their questionnaires in similar sealed white envelopes. You should not open any of the envelopes until all have been received so that no one person can be identified.

Results. First look at the ratings on psychological adjustment. Put the questionnaires of people who rated themselves four or less in one pile and the questionnaires of people who rated themselves six or more in a second pile. We will refer to the people who rated themselves four or less as the troubled subjects or the troubled group. We will refer to the people who rated themselves six or more as the well-adjusted subjects or the well-adjusted group.

Now make up two identical data sheets like the one shown on page 422. One for the well-adjusted group and one for the troubled group. Use as many columns on your data sheet as there are subjects in the group. Copy subject 1's rating of each problem onto the data sheet in the appropriate column. Record the remaining subjects' ratings in the appropriate columns. Now count the number of problems that subject 1 rated one or more. Record this number at the bottom of the column in the space marked "Total Number of Problems Reported." Do the same thing for each subject. To compute a mean total number of problems reported for each group, add the total number of problems reported by each subject in that group and divide by the total number of subjects in that group. Put this number in the space labeled "Mean Total Number of Problems Reported."

To fill in the last three columns on the data sheet, work with one row at a time (one problem). First count the number of people who indicated that problem 1 was a problem for them. Put that number in the column under "Number of Subjects Reporting Problem." Divide this number by the number of subjects in the group and multiply the result by 100 percent. This gives you the "Percentage of Group Reporting Problem." Finally, add up the severity ratings for the problem and divide by the number of subjects reporting the problem. Put the result under the column headed "Mean Severity Rating." Repeat this procedure for each of the forty-two problems for each group.

Discussion. Consider the following questions.

1. Do your troubled subjects report a larger number of problems on the average than your well-adjusted subjects? Compare the "Mean Total Number of Problems Reported" by the two groups.

2. Do your troubled subjects report different kinds of problems than your well-adjusted subjects? To answer this question, compare the columns labeled "Percentage of Group Reporting Problem" for the well-adjusted and the troubled groups.

3. Do the troubled and well-adjusted subjects differ on their severity ratings of each problem? To answer this question, compare the columns labeled "Mean Severity Rating" for both groups.

4. Is one model of abnormal behavior supported by your data? Explain.

5. Consider the methods used for this study and comment on sources of error. (Be certain to consider the questionnaire itself, the use of a self-report measure of adjustment, the number of subjects used, their sexes, ages, socioeconomic status, your method of selecting subjects.)

6. If your budget for this research had been unlimited, how might the study have been improved?

A PROBLEM CHECKLIST AND RATING FORM

Please circle the number on the following scale that you believe
most closely describes your own psychological adjustment

1	2	3	4	5	6	7	8	9
Poor		Fair		Average		Good		Excellent

I almost always feel overwhelmed by my own psychological problems.

I frequently feel overwhelmed by my own psychological problems.

I sometimes feel overwhelmed by my own psychological problems.

I infrequently feel overwhelmed by my own psychological problems.

I almost never feel overwhelmed by my own psychological problems.

Below is a list of possible problems. Please check the ones which are currently difficult for you. Then rate each one in terms of how troublesome it has been in the past six months.

1	2	3	4	5
Mildly Troublesome		Moderately Troublesome		Extremely Troublesome

____ **1.** Establishing independence.
____ **2.** Religious doubts.
____ **3.** Forming a close relationship with a member of the opposite sex.
____ **4.** Feeling I really belong.
____ **5.** Repetitive thoughts.
____ **6.** Choosing a vocation.
____ **7.** Anxiety and tension.
____ **8.** Feelings of failure and inadequacy.
____ **9.** Feelings of not being in control of myself.
____ **10.** Concern over physical attractiveness.
____ **11.** Powerful fears.
____ **12.** Academic problems.
____ **13.** Parental demands.
____ **14.** Problems with authority figures.
____ **15.** Thoughts of suicide.
____ **16.** Shyness.
____ **17.** Drugs.

____ **18.** Alcohol.
____ **19.** Finding a direction for my life.
____ **20.** Sexual hang-ups.
____ **21.** Depression.
____ **22.** Needing to perform an action repetitively.
____ **23.** Boredom.
____ **24.** Feelings of powerlessness.
____ **25.** Frequent anger.
____ **26.** Tension headaches.
____ **27.** Criminal behavior.
____ **28.** Apathy.
____ **29.** Feeling tired much of the time.
____ **30.** Feeling worthless.
____ **31.** Unfulfilled needs for love.
____ **32.** Marital problems.
____ **33.** Loneliness.
____ **34.** Being critical of others.
____ **35.** Feeling insecure.
____ **36.** Living in my own world.
____ **37.** Feeling rejected.
____ **38.** Being easily discouraged.
____ **39.** Suspiciousness.
____ **40.** Dishonesty.
____ **41.** Feeling withdrawn.
____ **42.** Hearing voices or seeing images that no one else can hear or see.

Group _____

Problem Number	Severity Ratings Subject Number										Number of Ss Reporting Problem	% of Group Reporting Problem	Mean Severity Rating
	1	2	3	4	5	6	7	8	9	10			
1													
2													
3													
4													
5													
6													
7													
8													
9													
10													
11													
12													
13													
14													
15													
16													
17													
18													
19													
20													
21													
22													
23													
24													
25													
26													
27													
28													
29													
30													
31													
32													
33													
34													
35													
36													
37													
38													
39													
40													
41													
42													

Total Number of Problems Reported ___ ___ ___ ___ ___ ___ ___ ___ ___ ___

Mean Total Number of Problems Reported _____

Suggested Readings

1. Coleman, J. C. *Abnormal psychology and modern life* (4th ed.) Glenview, Ill.: Scott, Foresman and Company, 1972. A large, comprehensive, and unusually interesting textbook on abnormal psychology.

2. Davison, G. C., & John M. Neale. *Abnormal psychology: An experimental clinical approach.* New York: John Wiley & Sons, Inc., 1974. Excellent research-oriented abnormal psychology text of more manageable proportions.

3. Szasz, T. S. "The myth of mental illness." *American Psychologist*, 1960, 15, 113–118. Criticizes the medical model of abnormal behavior.

4. Rosenhan, D. L. "On being sane in insane places." *Science*, vol. 179, no. 4070, January 19, 1973, 1–9.

5. Kaplan, B. (Ed.) *The inner world of mental illness.* New York: Harper & Row, Publishers, Incorporated, 1964 (paperback). A series of first-person accounts on being mentally ill.

6. Seligman, M. E. P. *Helplessness.* San Francisco: W. H. Freeman and Company, 1975. (paperback) An experimental and clinical psychologist discusses research on helplessness and its relation to depression, anxiety, and death.

7. Mednick, S. A. "Birth defects and schizophrenia." *Psychology Today*, April 1971, 4, 49–50, 80–81. Report on original research which suggests that birth complications contribute to schizophrenia.

Answer Key

SELF-QUIZ
1. d   2. d   3. c   4. a   5. a   6. c   7. b   8. a   9. a
10. b   11. c   12. d   13. b   14. b   15. d

15
THE TREATMENT OF ABNORMAL BEHAVIOR

IN THIS CHAPTER
We examine three widely used psychotherapies as they are applied to mild
and neurotic behavioral problems. We
also describe how mental health experts treat the psychotic disorders, particularly chronic schizophrenia. Lastly
we explore a new trend in treatment,
community mental health care. After
reading this chapter, you should be
able to do the following:

1. Explain the nature of psychotherapy
2. Describe and contrast the concepts,
   goals, and procedures of psychoanalytic, behavior, and client-centered
   psychotherapies
3. Describe two promising treatment
   programs for the chronic schizophrenic and discuss the principles
   which they share
4. Describe the goals of primary and
   secondary prevention for community
   mental health

Throughout recorded history all known societies have attempted to treat their psychologically disturbed members. By current standards past treatment was both crude and inhumane. Archeological evidence suggests that about a half-million years ago, Stone Age cavemen cut holes in people's skulls "to let the evil spirits out." Early civilizations in China, Egypt, and Greece prayed, incanted, made noises, flogged, starved, and purged troubled people to force out the demons. During the Middle Ages the clergy used torture. In fact, treating troubled people kindly did not come into vogue until the end of the eighteenth century. Current treatment techniques are undoubtedly a great improvement over past ones, though they are still far from perfect.

Various specialists have treated disturbed people through the ages. In the past, the experts included witch doctors, prophets, priests, medicine men, and physicians. Today the experts include physicians (psychiatrists), psychologists, psychiatric social workers, and psychiatric nurses (see Table 15-1). Prophets, priests, and witch doctors did not agree on the best way to help people cope with their problems, and twentieth-century specialists don't agree either—as we will see.

Psychotherapy Defined

Psychotherapy refers to the various psychological (as opposed to biological) treatment procedures that have been designed to help troubled people solve personal problems. *Counseling*, on the other hand, is usually described as the offering of supportive treatment to essentially normal people with educational, occupational, marital, or other adjustment problems. Some experts feel that the definition of psychotherapy is too broad and that the term psychotherapy (or therapy, as it is usually abbreviated) should be reserved for describing the intensive psychological treatment methods that are used for neurotic or psychotic people. In actuality, the

TABLE 15-1. MENTAL HEALTH EXPERTS

Title and Degree	Function*	Education
Psychologist Ph.D. (usually)	Research, treatment, diagnosis, prevention	Postgraduate study in university psychology department plus internship in psychiatric facility
Psychiatrist M.D.	Treatment, medication, diagnosis, prevention	Medical school plus residency in psychiatric facility
Psychoanalyst M.D. (usually)	Treatment, diagnosis	Apprenticeship training in psychoanalysis (usually after medical school and residency in psychiatric facility).
Psychiatric social worker M.S.W. (Master of Social Work)	Treatment (community orientation), prevention	Postgraduate study in school of social work
Psychiatric nurse R.N.	Treatment (care of hospitalized)	Training in nursing and psychiatry
Mental health technician B.A. or A.A.	Treatment, prevention	Undergraduate education in psychology and mental health
Mental health paraprofessional (none)	Treatment, prevention	Orientation program in service facility

*The functions of these mental health experts are continually changing, and they frequently overlap.

distinctions between normal and abnormal people are often hazy (see Chapter 14), and the methods that counselors and psychotherapists use are frequently quite similar. So we will use the term psychotherapy in the broadest sense, as we defined it above.

The Nature of Psychotherapy

What does psychotherapy involve? Although psychotherapies vary considerably, almost all of them demand the participation of at least two individuals. In most cases a sufferer (sometimes several sufferers) seeks help from a trained, socially approved healer, a mental health expert. Generally, the sufferer thinks well of the healer and has high expectations that the suffering will be alleviated. The healer and sufferer meet regularly and jointly participate in procedures which aim at producing positive changes in the sufferer's behavior, emotions, attitudes, and thoughts. These ingredients, which are also characteristic of primitive healing and religious conversion rites, are basic to psychotherapy (1).

As we saw in Chapter 14, there are significant gaps in psychologists' understanding of the causes of abnormal behavior. This knowledge gap creates a dilemma which may have occurred to you. How can the so-called healers treat problems which they do not fully understand? Although research continues, psychotherapists must act. Generally, they attempt to construct—with varying amounts of help from the patient—experiences that will teach the patient to cope more productively with his or her life.

There are currently many different approaches to psychotherapy. Fifteen years ago thirty-six distinct systems of psychotherapy were identified and described (2). Additional psychotherapy systems could be added today, although it is important to realize that many of these systems might best be described as variations of others. In addition to the formal differences between therapy systems, each individual healer brings additional differences: a distinctive personality, past experience, philosophy of life, and so on; so the psychotherapy that each expert provides is unique.

Contemporary psychotherapy has a mixed reputation. Those psychologists who loathe imprecision look upon psychotherapy as being so sloppy, vaguely defined, and complicated that its effects are impossible to investigate scientifically. Some people view psycho-

therapy as glamorous; in certain social circles being in therapy brings status. Other people view psychotherapy as terrifying; the person in therapy is automatically stigmatized (branded) as "weak-willed," "childish," or "crazy." Psychotherapy seems most profitably viewed as a potentially valuable resource for people who have psychological problems which they cannot resolve without help.

We turn now to three of the most widely encountered basic therapy approaches: psychoanalytic, behavior, and client-centered. Although each of these three psychotherapies aims at restoring a troubled person to healthy functioning, they vary as to (1) concept of troubled behavior, (2) specific goals, and (3) primary procedures. These treatment approaches may be applied to adults and children of varying degrees of disturbance. We focus on how these therapies are applied to the problems of mildly troubled or neurotic adults.

PSYCHOANALYTIC PSYCHOTHERAPY

We begin with the views of Sigmund Freud. Recall that we discussed Freud's theories on the development of personality in Chapter 12 and on the causes of particular abnormal behavior patterns in Chapter 14. Freud believed that repressed internal conflicts between the basic animal drives of the id and the lofty ideals of the superego were the major cause of the neurotic's problems. These conflicts, according to Freud, generated anxiety; the neurotic's ego devoted its energy to building and maintaining defense mechanisms to deal with the anxiety and did not have time to cope constructively with reality.

Freud came to believe that the only way to permanently eliminate the neurotic's *symptoms* (observable abnormal behavior patterns such as ritualistic acts or avoidance habits) was to uncover the source of the unconscious conflicts and bring them to the patient's awareness. Simple intellectual insight was not enough; patients had to relive the intense emotional experiences which had been associated with their conflicts, so that their intellectual insights were firmly rooted in emotional understanding. Once the unconscious conflicts were out in the open, Freud believed that the therapist's job was essentially finished. Presumably, the patient would now resolve the problems realistically and maturely. Freud spent most of his life refining the therapy techniques he used to probe the patient's unconscious and bring unresolved conflicts into the open.

The Procedures of Psychoanalytic Psychotherapy

During psychoanalytic therapy sessions patients typically recline on a couch or sit on a comfortable chair while therapists generally sit off to the side or behind them. The couch seems to be a direct holdover from hypnosis, a technique which Freud had used earlier to probe the neurotic's unconscious mind. Some people think that these elaborate procedures were also motivated by Freud's personal discomfort with face-to-face contact. Whatever their origin, the seating conventions have some distinct advantages. Patients lying on a couch face the ceiling and are not distracted by books, furniture, or the therapist's facial expressions. According to Freud, the absence of face-to-face relationships also helps therapists maintain emotional and intellectual distance, enabling them to better guide their patients to an objective self-understanding.

What do the patients in psychoanalytic therapy do? Their major responsibility is to *free-associate*; that is, to allow their minds to wander freely and to give a completely frank running account of their thoughts and feelings. The patient is asked to say everything and hold nothing back regardless of how nonsensical, trivial, irrelevant, or shameful it appears. Free association forces patients to put their defenses aside and leads to the disclosure of important conflict-related incidents, as the following example illustrates:

That ironing board—my mother was ironing. I jumped off the cupboard, wonderful jump, but I sort of used her behind as support—she was leaning over. She told father I had been disrespectful and he gave me a licking. I was awfully hurt. I hadn't even thought about her old be-

Figure 15-1. During psychoanalytic psychotherapy, the therapist frequently sits behind a patient who is reclining on a couch. (John Briggs.)

hind—it was just a wonderful jump. Father would never let me explain. . . . He was awfully strict. I wish he hadn't died when I was so young—we might have worked things out [3].

Patients in psychoanalytic therapy are also expected to recount their dreams. Dreams are considered to be an important source of information about the patient's unconscious. Presumably, the subject matter of the dream, the *manifest content*, disguises the real meaning, the *latent content*. As we noted in Chapter 6, Freud believed that dreams reflected people's repressed conflicts, motives, wishes, and so on. A person who feels burdened by an aging mother, for example, may repeatedly dream about a car accident in which an old lady is run over and killed. Such a dream could be interpreted as signifying a desire to be free. Psychoanalytic therapists study patient's dreams and free associations to the dreams to further their understanding of the patients' unconscious.

Patients unknowingly engage in several other important behaviors. Characteristically, they develop strong feelings (such as love, hatred, reverence, fear, or contempt) for their therapists. Freud believed that these feelings arose as patients identified their therapists with significant people in their past lives, often people central to their repressed conflicts, usually their parents. This phenomenon is known as *transference*. In the following excerpt from a psychoanalytic therapy session, a male patient describes a transference vividly:

I know this isn't real, but I have a feeling you are my father. I want to reach out and grab my father. He is sitting there, gentle and strong. I want to scream and cry. I want you to come to me. Father, come to me! Please come to me! I want you to kiss me and hold me close. . . . I remember father. He never let me do anything. I always thought I hated him and was afraid to do anything, not even shovel the snow. He acted like he always had to be the boss. Kind of hard

on me. . . . Even now, when I am near him, I am afraid he will hit me. He goes into such a rage. I wonder what would happen if I hit him back. I felt the same way about you. . . . It's funny I never wanted you to touch me. It scares me. It scared me suddenly to realize I want you to treat me like a woman. On the other hand, I want you to touch me. I was afraid for father to touch me. Maybe I felt the same way toward him as toward you. This whole thing must be some way connected with my fear of homosexuality [4].

Freud believed that it was important to help the patient understand the transference, particularly how it related to the patient's past unresolved conflicts and current behavior.

Patients engage unknowingly in a second important practice. As they free-associate, they may pause for long periods of time, change the topic suddenly, forget particular events, or mistakenly use one word instead of another (such as "sex" instead of "six"). Sometimes patients repeatedly arrive late or decide that therapy is doing them no good and want to quit. In all these cases Freud believed that the patient had reached difficult repressed material, felt threatened by the pain of facing it, and was unconsciously resisting the therapy process. Acts which disturb the therapy process are labeled *resistance*. Resistance alerts the psychoanalytic therapist to important material.

By studying the patient's behavior closely, the psychoanalytic therapist locates clues to the patient's conflicts. The therapist then reveals these clues to the patient by comments or *interpretations*. The manner in which interpretations are made is considered critical. Instead of simply blurting out an interpretation spontaneously, the therapist waits until the patient appears receptive. Interpretations are made in such a way that patients feel that they are discovering the unconscious meaning of their own behavior.

Psychoanalytic therapy is a time-consuming and lengthy process. Classical psychoanalysis requires three to five 50-minute sessions every week for several years. Psychoanalytic therapists believe that treatment is inevitably long and difficult because patients resist tracing the troublesome patterns back to their beginning and uncovering the repressed conflicts. The following case history illustrates many aspects of the psychoanalytic approach to treatment:

The businessman: A psychoanalytic case history

"A businessman of forty-two years had suffered for a long time from an uncontrollable jerking of his arms. . . . Neurological examination failed to disclose any sign of brain injury. . . . The patient had a long history of irritability and a domineering attitude which injured his human relationships. At one point his wife divorced him on account of these intolerable traits, but later they were remarried. The immediate occasion for seeking medical help was the fact that his wife was again considering separation. In addition, for a number of weeks he had suffered a complete loss of sexual potency.

"The patient's troubles were discerned to have their origins in his relation to his father. The father had been a self-made man with huge self-confidence and a violent temper. He was a tyrant both at home and in his business. He never tired of making the son feel inferior, and though at times there was sharp conflict between them, the son always gave in. Among other things the father had intimidated the patient in the matter of sexual expression. To meet all this pressure and somehow preserve self-respect, the patient had built up his own assertive and domineering attitude. He was ruled by a vast compensatory need to appear important and strong. When the father died, the patient took over the family glassware works and with great energy expanded it well beyond what his father had been able to accomplish. He felt impelled to surpass his father, yet along with all his competition and rebellion there was a great deal of admiring devotion.

"From the very start the patient reproduced in the therapeutic situation his combined attitudes toward his father. He wanted rules to be made for him, and scrupulously obeyed one or two that had to be suggested. But his conversation was otherwise designed to impress the analyst with his importance, and whenever the analyst explained anything he quickly began to explain something about which he himself was expert: business or sports. He literally tried to force the doctor to become tyrannical so that he could rebel and compete with him. This attitude was so clear that the analyst undertook to create a corrective emotional experience by behaving in just the opposite fashion. He let the patient take the lead, avoided statements that could be thought arbitrary, admitted the limitations of psychiatry, expressed admiration for the patient's good qualities, took an interest in his business and social activities. Under this treatment the patient became distinctly confused. He plainly thrived in the permissive, encouraging atmosphere, but he was unable to check his competitive feelings and still tried to fight battles with the analyst. This offered the perfect opportunity for crucial interpretations. The patient could not help seeing that his aggression was completely out of relation to the analyst's behavior. His chief overdriven striving was exposed and he became able to enter a more genuine relationship with the doctor.

"The change in his attitude toward the therapist was soon reflected at home. He became less domineering and was able to assume a more appropriately benevolent and helpful role toward his son. But his need to make a tyrant out of the analyst finally yielded only after a particularly vivid dream and its aftermath. The patient dreamed that he had manufactured some glassware and that the analyst angrily broke it all to pieces. The dream reminded him of an occasion when his father smashed a set of glassware because he did not like the design. During the hour which began with the reporting of this dream, the analyst asked the patient to tell more about his work. The patient eagerly embarked on a condescending lecture. The corrective emotional experience occasioned by thus assuming authority over the therapist was so great that the patient thereafter recovered his sexual potency. His old role of the now-rebelling, now-submitting son could be outgrown as he found it possible to have a relation of friendly give and take with an authoritative person. As he achieved this new learning on the social plane he outgrew his sexual intimidation.

"The remaining hours of treatment were devoted to fuller discussion of the transference relationship. In childhood the patient had often been obliged to accept help from his father, but the father had always made him feel inferior on such occasions. This led him to react with a compensatory striving to prove that he was really the better man. Accepting help from the analyst had thus reanimated from the start the very core of the neurotic problem. The analyst's radical assumption of exactly the opposite role, giving help along with interest, permissiveness, and a complete lack of the father's dogmatic self-confidence, led to an unusually rapid corrective emotional experience. At the end of treatment the patient's arms no longer jerked, which may be taken as presumptive evidence that the jerking originated from the tension of suppressed rage. His emotional and sexual relations with his wife were better than ever before, talk of separation had ended, and his irritable and domineering tendencies had greatly diminished. The patient was at least much improved, if not fully cured [5]."

Critical Comments

Psychoanalytic therapy has been accepted with almost religious fervor by many therapists and patients. It aims at radically changing the patient's personality, and it exhibits high optimism; once patients attain insight, they are expected to achieve control and change their troublesome life styles. Many patients report that psychoanalytic therapy helps them reach greater self-understanding, relief from anxiety, and improved interpersonal relationships.

There are several problems with the psychoanalytic approach. First, psychoanalytic concepts are hard to define and generally difficult to investigate scientifically. The basic constructs are obscure. Take the conflict between the id and the superego at the heart of the neurosis. How could one objectively study the id? the superego? the conflict? The basic psychoanalytic treatment techniques are also difficult to study. Interpretation is central to the therapy enterprise; so good interpretations should lead to progress and bad ones to no progress. But what is a good interpretation? There is no way to measure objectively the goodness of an interpretation. How could you prove, for example, that a woman in a dream really symbolizes a patient's mother? Although Freud believed that controlled empirical observations had little value,[1] many psychologists are currently trying to investigate psychoanalytic concepts using scientific methods.

A second problem with orthodox psychoanalytic therapy is that because it is an intensive therapy based on attaining intellectual insight, it is primarily suited to a special type of patient—one who is intelligent, adept at

self-expression, in good contact with reality, emotionally strong, oriented toward introspection and self-disclosure, motivated to "get better," and well off financially. Patients of this sort have a high probability of getting better under any kind of therapy (7). Psychoanalytically oriented therapists have been responsive to this problem and many have modified the procedures of orthodox psychoanalytic therapy to make it suitable for more people. These modified psychoanalytic therapies are generally briefer and less intensive; they tend to focus on current interpersonal experiences and to give less emphasis to repressed motives, desires, and conflicts and early childhood experiences.

BEHAVIOR THERAPY

Behavior therapy emerged as a major treatment method in the late 1950s when clinical psychologists began applying the findings of experimental psychology to the treatment of abnormal behavior. In contrast to psychoanalytic therapy which originated in clinical practice, behavior therapy is a product of the psychology laboratory, particularly of research in respondent and operant conditioning; so its roots go back to Pavlov in Russia and Thorndike in America (see Chapter 7).

In contrast to psychoanalytic therapists, behavior therapists regard the patient's symptoms as the problem. Behavior therapists would consider sexual impotence, "intolerable" interpersonal habits, and uncontrollable jerking to be the businessman's problem and not some hypothetical internal conflict. According to the behavior therapist, the symptoms are caused by a combination of psychological, social, biological, and environmental factors, just like the patient's normal behavior. (Behavior therapists view normal personality as the neobehaviorists do. See page 346.) Rather than seeking to uncover a re-

[1]Freud wrote: "The teachings of psychoanalysis are based upon an incalculable number of observations and experiences and no one who has not repeated these observations upon himself or upon others is in a position to arrive at an independent judgment of it [6]."

pressed conflict, behavior therapists usually attempt to identify the present and past circumstances that have contributed to and are currently maintaining the problem so that these conditions can be modified. Consider the businessman again. Many behavior therapists would hypothesize that the businessman learned domineering and irritable behavior by observing and imitating his father and that these behaviors were probably subsequently reinforced. They might see the businessman's impotence as resulting from anxiety over the possible separation from his wife. As we noted in Chapter 10, anxiety interferes with sexual arousal and performance.

The Procedures of Behavior Therapy

Whereas psychoanalytic therapists emphasize discussion and insight, behavior therapists emphasize action. Typically, behavior therapy focuses on new learning: The patient must unlearn maladaptive responses and learn or relearn adaptive ones. Behavior therapists use treatment techniques that have been derived from psychological research (often learning principles) to help people solve the specific problems which both patient

Figure 15-2. A hierarchy for systematic desensitization. (After Wolpe and Lazarus, 1966.)

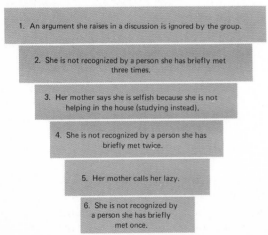

1. An argument she raises in a discussion is ignored by the group.

2. She is not recognized by a person she has briefly met three times.

3. Her mother says she is selfish because she is not helping in the house (studying instead).

4. She is not recognized by a person she has briefly met twice.

5. Her mother calls her lazy.

6. She is not recognized by a person she has briefly met once.

and therapist agree are important. The following procedures are commonly used to treat mildly troubled adults.

Respondent Conditioning. In 1950 Joseph Wolpe, a South African psychiatrist, began using learning principles, primarily those of respondent conditioning, to reduce incapacitating anxiety in children and adults. Wolpe's strategy, known as *systematic desensitization*, or simply *desensitization*, is quite similar to the technique which Mary Cover Jones used to reduce Peter's rabbit anxiety (reported in Chapter 7). In systematic desensitization, the therapist and patient explore and then list those events which provoke the patient's anxiety. These stimuli are arranged from weakest to strongest for each of the patient's fears. The list of ordered anxiety-arousing stimuli is known as a *hierarchy*. One patient's anxiety hierarchy is presented in Figure 15-2. In addition, the therapist trains the patient in deep muscle relaxation; patients then practice relaxing for several weeks until they can achieve very deep relaxation at will.

This is the way desensitization works: The patient relaxes, and while relaxed, is asked to vividly imagine the weakest anxiety stimulus in his or her hierarchy. If any tension at all is felt while imagining the item, the patient must immediately stop imagining it and focus again on relaxing. Eventually, the patient can visualize this weak anxiety stimulus without discomfort. Then the patient and therapist move on to the next weakest anxiety stimulus on the list, and the process is repeated. As a result of this procedure, the patient should eventually be able to picture the most distressing anxiety stimulus in the hierarchy without feeling uncomfortable. Once people can visualize formerly distressing stimuli without feeling distressed, they often feel confident in confronting the actual stimuli. The following behavior therapy case was treated primarily by systematic desensitization:

The case of Mr. N. R.

"Mr. N. R. was a twenty-one-year-old medical student who sought treatment because of an intense anxiety about examinations. It became apparent during the two initial interviews that N. R.'s problem was not restricted to fear of examinations—he also suffered from quite intense social fears of a wide range and type. He was intense, shy, and had great difficulty managing his affairs when they involved other people. His social activities were very restricted.

"In the case of N. R. it was then decided to treat the examination phobia and also his fear of people and specific social situations. Three hierarchies were constructed for this patient, the first consisting of a number of examination situations including preparation for the examination, written and oral examinations, important and not-so-important tests, and so forth. The second hierarchy consisted of a number of people who provoked fear reactions in this patient, and he was asked to imagine himself in various situations coming into touch with these people. The third hierarchy consisted of a series of social situations which ordinarily produced fear and avoidance behavior. The three hierarchies were then desensitized in turn, and considerable progress was made. It should be pointed out, however, that because of the social nature of many of this patient's fears, he was also instructed to use an additional technique. . . . [assertiveness training, a procedure which is discussed on page 434] At the termination of treatment N. R. was able to cope with examination stresses in a normal manner, and had ceased avoiding people who had formerly frightened him, and was able to mix freely in normal social situations [8]."

Positive reinforcement. When the presentation of an event increases the likelihood of a particular behavior, psychologists call the event a *positive reinforcement*. Behavior therapists use the principles of positive reinforcement to increase desirable behavior in a variety of situations including the home when working with the management of problem children, outpatient mental health clinics and mental hospitals, and penal institutions. The following case study shows how positive reinforcement principles were used to treat a case of depression:

The case of Mr. Y.

"Mr. Y. is a 28-year-old married university student and father of two young children. His stated problem was his severe feeling of depression and hopelessness. . . . The intake interview revealed that outside of class attendance, he engaged in very few social interactions. Both he and his wife described him as a "family man" who spent most of his time at home with his family or alone. The need for home observations was readily accepted by Mr. and Mrs. Y., and three separate home observations were conducted. The major findings were as follows: Mrs. Y. directed very few of her actions toward Mr. Y., the object of most of her actions being the children. A significant proportion of her actions and reactions toward him were critical and negative in quality. She generally treated him politely and coldly, occasionally belittling him, not seeming to take what he said very seriously, and rarely praising him or having something pleasant to say to him. . . . In marked contrast, he directed most of his actions toward her. The overwhelming majority of his actions and reactions toward her were positive in quality. . . . This was true even when she was critical of him. . . . Thus . . . there were two main conclusions: (a) he was very inefficient in his interactions; that is, he noncontingently reinforced both positive and negative actions that his wife directed toward him, and (b) it was very clear that his rate of positive reinforcement, both inside and outside the home, was quite low.

"Attempts to involve Mrs. Y. in a joint treatment program were relatively unsuccessful. . . . She was intent on rejoining her former boyfriend. . . . Mr. Y. was provided with feedback about his own behavior, based on the home observations, and he was strongly encouraged to engage in behaviors which would be reinforcing to him outside of the home. The nature of reinforcement was also explained to him and he was encouraged to become more 'efficient' in his relationship with his wife by not reinforcing her critical behavior of him and by reinforcing her when she was emitting more positive actions and reactions toward him. He was asked to develop a list of those activities which he found enjoyable. Within a few sessions, he reported having completed some of these activities and began to note the connection between his engaging in these activities and feeling less depressed. During this period, he became much more critical of his wife, and the subsequent home observation clearly showed that he had been able to achieve some change in his behavior in the desired direction. At the end of the three-month treatment period, Mrs. Y. . . . decided to rejoin her former boyfriend. Mr. Y. accepted this with considerable equanimity. . . . During this period Mr. Y's level of depression as measured by the Depression Adjective Check List . . . remained at a fairly low level. He maintained and increased his activities, both social and academic, and made constructive and realistic plans for the care of his children [9]."

Observation and imitation. People learn many behaviors by observation and imitation or modeling. Problems sometimes occur because people observe and imitate maladaptive behavior or because they have simply never observed adaptive behavior. Behavior therapists use observation learning principles to teach mute patients to speak, to train people to cope appropriately with fears, and to teach children and adults new social skills. In *asser-*

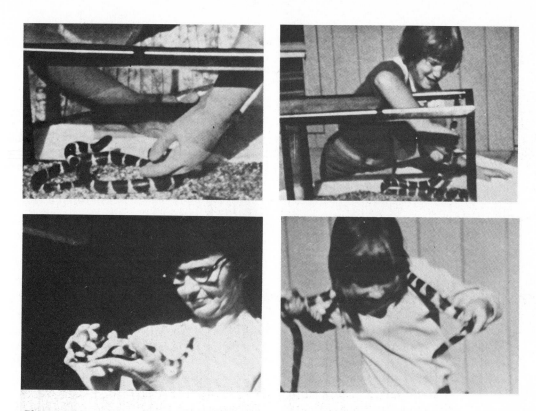

Figure 15-3. When people with snake phobias are exposed to live and filmed models handling snakes increasingly more intimately, their fears are markedly reduced. (Albert Bandura.)

tiveness training adults who experience severe anxiety and inhibitions about expressing their emotions are trained to express themselves more genuinely. Initially, the patient shows the therapist by *role playing* (play acting) the way he or she usually behaves in particularly difficult situations. The therapist generally plays the role of the person whom the patient is confronting. At a later time patient and therapist exchange roles and the therapist behaves in an emotionally expressive (assertive) way to show the patient how it's done. The following dialogue between a behavior therapist and patient demonstrates this procedure:

THERAPIST: . . . This seems to be a good opportunity to do some role playing or what I call "behavior rehearsal." Let me play the role of your father and let's see how well you can handle his onslaughts in a rehearsal situation. . . . Just try to pretend that you really are talking to your father and try to be as realistic as possible. (role playing) Sam, when are you going to grow up, listen to your mother, have a haircut, wear some decent clothes, and be a man?

SAM: (role playing) I am a man.

THERAPIST: (role playing) Men don't go in for fast cars, flashy clothes, and cheap women.

SAM: (role playing) That's your opinion.

THERAPIST: (role playing) Are you questioning my judgment?

SAM: (role playing) No, I'm not questioning

your judgment but I'm also entitled to an opinion.

THERAPIST: Hold it! You are in fact questioning his judgment. Why deny it?

SAM: Yes, yes, I know what you mean. But if I said, "Listen, you old goat, your judgment's way behind the times" nothing except maybe hysteria and a real ugly scene is likely to follow.

THERAPIST: Now that's the aggression or the anger to which I was referring earlier. There's a vast difference between an *assertive* and an *aggressive* response. I think that your anger is legitimate. In fantasy, you can picture yourself going even further than merely hurling verbal insults. You can fantasize punching him and really letting rip. In fantasy, you can even imagine yourself committing murder, but in your real confrontations you don't have to be either submissive or aggressive. Here we should aim for a balanced and rational response. . . . So what I want you to learn is how to express your feelings. . . . Let's reverse roles. Let me be you and you act as your father. Why don't we take it from the part where your father comes on all critically?

SAM: You want me to act as my dad? Okay. (hesitates) Here goes. (role playing) Mother and I deserve better treatment, more respect, and a bit of consideration. Are we any worse than Aunt Hilda and Uncle Mike? And you know how nicely your cousin Herb treats them.

THERAPIST: (role playing) Dad, I wish you wouldn't make comparisons; it makes me feel like a kid. Besides, since Herb is someone I do not particularly admire. . . .

SAM: (role playing) Well you are a kid. You think that being divorced adds up to being a man. And you're always criticizing other people. Believe me, you can learn a lot from Herb.

THERAPIST: (role playing) Dad, I don't wish to get into an argument. I get the message that I am a disappointment to you, that you wish Herb was your son, and that you look upon me as a child who should make no independent decisions but . . .

SAM: (role playing) Don't get smart with me, young man!

THERAPIST: (role playing) Look, Dad. By the time a person reaches my age he has gone beyond the stage where he is open to parental guidance. You and Mother have done the best for me, and if I am a failure and a disgrace in your eyes try to look upon it as my bad luck instead of worrying about the way it reflects on you.

SAM: Actually, I'd like to go further than that and point out to him that ever since I can remember he's never had anything positive to say about me. Whenever he opens his mouth to speak to me he invariably puts me down or finds fault with me.

THERAPIST: Excellent. You should certainly make that point . . . [10].

Aversive learning procedures. Behavior therapists occasionally use *aversive learning procedures* (procedures which employ painful or unpleasant stimuli or deprivation) for problems which fail to respond to other modes of treatment. When aversive techniques are successful, they eliminate unwanted behavior, but they cannot teach constructive responses. Consequently they are almost always combined with techniques which train new adaptive behavior. Aversive therapy is ethically used only when patients agree to its use. In many cases people are willing to put up with unpleasant treatment procedures in hopes that they will relieve a frustrating and stubborn problem. We discussed punishment in Chapter 7. We turn now to *aversive counterconditioning*, a technique based on respondent conditioning principles.

Aversive counterconditioning is used to eliminate socially maladaptive patterns such as excessive drinking, overeating, drug taking, or arousal to inappropriate sexual objects. In aversive counterconditioning, the inappropriate stimulus (such as excessive drinking) is paired with an unconditioned stimulus which automatically produces an unpleasant response (such as a nausea-inducing drug). After repeated pairings, the inappropriate pattern itself begins to produce the same aversive response—if the conditioning is successful. For example, an alcoholic may elect to take the drug Antabuse (disulferim) on a regular basis. When people have Antabuse in their systems, drinking alcohol triggers a violent reaction: Breathing becomes difficult; the heart pounds; and nausea and vomiting usually follow soon afterward. In some cases alcohol itself becomes anxiety-arousing. In other cases, anticipation of these aversive effects deters the alcoholic from drinking. Unfortunately, the alcoholic's problem is not solved so easily. If the alcoholic stops taking Antabuse, drinking will soon regain its reinforcing characteristics. Generally, the effects of aversive learning procedures tend to be limited to the therapy session and short-lived unless patients want to change their behavior and actively attempt to learn and use new behavior patterns.

Critical Comments

Behavior therapy has several important strengths. First, behavior therapists are strongly committed to the scientific method and, consequently, many of them routinely assess their procedures through controlled studies. Second, studies show that behavior therapy is frequently effective with a large variety of problems—at least in the short run (11,12). Although these findings are encouraging, enthusiasm must be cautious since studies are too frequently done on psychologically healthy college students with relatively

trivial problems. Third, behavior therapy tends to be brief in duration; so a large number of people can be treated comparatively inexpensively.

Psychoanalytic therapists originally predicted that although behavior therapists might be able to alleviate particular symptoms, new symptoms would inevitably emerge (*symptom substitution*), since the behavior therapists had not dealt with the "root cause of the symptom, the unconscious conflict." Behavior therapists, as we have noted, do try to modify the determinants of the symptom; they simply see those determinants differently than do the psychoanalytic therapists. Moreover, studies by behavioristic psychologists find little evidence of symptom substitution (13,14).

Although behavior therapy techniques appear to be effective, the reasons for their success are difficult to pinpoint. Simple learning principles cannot easily account for the extremely complex learning of mildly troubled people in clinical settings. Although behavior therapists use learning terms such as "stimulus," "response," "reinforcer," and "respondent conditioning," these terms are used loosely. For example, the imagining of a scene in systematic desensitization—the "stimulus"—is an enormously complex experience, very unlike a light, a tone, or any other typical laboratory stimulus (15). An increasing number of behavior therapists believe that behavior therapy techniques alter people's emotions, motives, expectations, and thoughts and that these internal processes then mediate new behavior.

CLIENT-CENTERED PSYCHOTHERAPY

Psychoanalytic psychotherapy focuses on the deep internal aspects of motivation and personality. Behavior therapy concentrates on human behavior. A third major type of psychotherapy, *client-centered psychotherapy*, focuses on subjective human experience, or on how people see themselves and the events of their lives.

Client-centered psychotherapy was developed by the American psychologist, Carl Rogers (b. 1902), whose ideas were strongly influenced by more than thirty years of clinical experience. Client-centered psychotherapy is "client-centered" in the sense that the client (Rogers' term for patient) determines the content and direction of therapy—in so far as possible.

The Client-centered Therapist's Concept of Troubled Behavior

According to Rogers, clients are people who have neglected their own experiencing and have turned from their "real" selves. The maladaptive patterns begin in childhood when the person learns, probably from parents, that certain impulses, such as sexuality and hostility, are unacceptable. To win parental affection the person denies important aspects of self.

Figure 15-4. Carl Rogers (b. 1902). (The Bettmann Archive.)

Rogers, like Abraham Maslow, believes that human beings have needs to actualize their own potential (see Chapter 10). Because maladjusted adults have long been denying significant aspects of their own identity, they have stopped growing: They are defensive and closed to new experiences; they do not reach for intimate relationships; they do not explore new activities; they do not create; and they do not think well of themselves. According to client-centered theory, neurotic symptoms are the by-products of arrested growth.

The Goals and Procedures of Client-centered Psychotherapy

Client-centered therapy aims at increasing the client's ability to grow in a direction which the client alone determines and at enhancing the client's self-concept. Whereas both behavior and psychoanalytic therapists emphasize the importance of intellectually understanding the troubled person's problem, client-centered therapists avoid diagnosis and evaluation of all kinds. They neither determine what is wrong nor formulate a treatment strategy, and they may not even be interested in the specific events of the client's past or present life. They believe that what really matters is the here-and-now encounter between client and therapist. They assume that if that encounter is characterized by three important conditions, therapeutic change will automatically occur.

First, client-centered therapists must be "genuine"; that is, they must be open to their own experiences and to the experiences of others; they must be able to convey this openness. They must never be guarded or defensive in their interactions with the client. "Genuineness" is supposed to generate an atmosphere that is devoid of deceit or need for pretense—so that clients can be themselves. The following interaction between client and therapist shows what client-centered therapists mean by "genuineness."

> c: I guess you realize that, too, don't you. Or do you? (laughs)
>
> t: Do I realize that? You bet I do! Sure, yeah—I always wanted somebody to take care of me, you know, but I also wanted them to let me do what I wanted to do! Well, if you have somebody taking care of you, then you've got to do what they want you to do [16].

Although therapists in the other therapy orientations are frequently "genuine," the other therapies do not see "genuineness" as a necessary therapeutic condition which leads by itself to behavior change.

Second, client-centered therapists must be emotionally accepting of their clients, accepting all, the good and the bad, without attaching conditions to the acceptance and without evaluating or judging the client's feelings or conduct. In the past the client has met with criticism, censure, and disapproval. In client-centered therapy clients should feel totally secure in the therapist's regard so that they can explore themselves openly. The following therapy excerpt illustrates how the client-centered therapist conveys warmth.

> c: I hated myself so that I didn't, I, I felt that I didn't deserve to have anyone care for me. I hated myself so that I, I, I not only felt that no one did, but I didn't see any reason why they should.
>
> t: I guess that makes some sense to me now. I was wondering why it was that you were shutting other people off. You weren't letting anyone else care. . . .
>
> c: The doctor often goes there on the ward and asks how everyone is and when she'd get about to me, I'd move to a spot that she's already covered . . .
>
> t: You really avoided people.
>
> c: So that, so that she wouldn't, uh, talk with me (t: Uh, hm.) and when—the few times that I refused to see you, it was for the same reason. I didn't think I was worth bothering with, so why waste your time—let's just . . .

> t: Let me ask you, ask you something about that. Do you think it would have been, uh, better if I had insisted that, uh, uh, you come and talk with me?
>
> c: No I don't believe so, doctor. (They speak simultaneously.)
>
> t: I wondered about that; I wasn't sure. (softly) . . . [17].

Psychoanalytic and behavior therapists also accept their patients without morally condemning their behavior, but they tend to be more emotionally aloof than the client-centered therapist. Moreover, both psychoanalytic and behavior therapists judge the appropriateness of their patients' behavior, praising the "adaptive" and labeling the "maladaptive."

Third, client-centered therapists must thoroughly understand their clients' emotional experiences from *moment to moment*, and they must be able to reflect this understanding. Client-centered therapists are sometimes characterized as mirrors of feeling: They verbally reflect the clients' emotional experiences, helping them get in touch with their own feelings. The following excerpt from a client-centered therapy session illustrates this aspect:

> t: I s'pose, one of the things you were saying there was, I may seem pretty hard on the outside to other people but I do have feelings.
>
> c: Yeah, I've got feelings. But most of 'em I don't let 'em off.
>
> t: Mhm. Kinda hide them.
>
> c: (Faintly) Yeah. (Long pause) I guess the only reason that I try to hide 'em, is, seein' that I'm small, I guess I got to be a tough guy or somethin'.
>
> t: Mhm.
>
> c: That's the way I . . . think . . . people might think about me.
>
> t: Mm. Little afraid to show my feelings. They might think I was weak, 'n take advantage of me or something. They might hurt me if they—knew I could be hurt.
>
> c: I think they'd try, anyway [18].

Although behavior and psychoanalytic therapists may be sensitive to their patients' feelings, they do not emphasize moment-to-moment sensitivity as a therapeutic condition that leads by itself to behavior or personality change.

In the following excerpt, psychologist David Murray, a client-centered therapist, describes the procedures that he uses to convey genuineness, warmth, and understanding.

1. I use a lot of simple acceptance. This includes responses such as "Yes," "I see," or "I understand," or the well-known "Um-hum," which can express many things including the message to the patient that "I am here and I am with you."
2. I rephrase or restate what the patient says. He may say, "I could hardly talk; I was shaky, sweaty," and I might reply, "Um-hum, yes, you were so terribly upset that you could hardly function." This, hopefully, shows him that I am understanding him, and if I missed the point, he has a chance to correct me because I have let him know what I thought his meaning was.
3. I encourage the patient to talk: "Go on" or "Would you like to tell me more about how you felt in this situation?" This, I think, shows acceptance; but even more importantly perhaps, by encouraging the patient to talk, it increases the chance for me as a therapist to understand and communicate my understanding to him.
4. I use questions mostly to check on my understanding of what the patient is expressing or, where I am unsure of what he means, to check on just what he does mean. For example, I might say, "When you say that you didn't know what to do, are you indicating that you felt mixed up and confused?" I rarely ask questions to elicit new information. I would be very unlikely to ask things such as "How often have you felt that way?" or "Did you feel that way as a child?" or "Could you tell me what your mother is like?"
5. Affect is labeled, identified, and accepted. I might say, "Yes, I can see that you felt terribly angry," or "Yes, in that situation you are telling me you never felt so happy."
6. Silence is reflected in the same way the patient's verbalizations are, although, of course, it is more difficult to be accurate. I might say to the patient, if he is slow getting started, "It's sort of hard for you to get started today," or I might say, "I guess you just don't feel much like talking right now," or "It seems as though right now you are enjoying sitting and not feeling you have to talk," or perhaps "This silence seems to be making you feel pretty uneasy right now."
7. In general I will not stay quiet too long, though my comments may be very brief. I feel that when the therapist is quiet for long intervals it is much easier for the patient to get a distorted idea of what the therapist is thinking and feeling, to project meaning into the silence. If he is talking about aspects of himself, that he thinks are bad, he is likely to think something like, "I guess this guy just doesn't know what to say to such a terrible person; he must be wishing he had never taken me on as a patient." So I am making comments all along so that he won't think that [19].

How does the relationship between the client and the client-centered therapist lead to therapeutic change? Rogers believes that clients and therapists begin at opposite poles. Clients do not behave in a "genuine" way: They are not able to enter the inner world of other human beings; they cannot accept themselves; they cannot accept others. As clients find themselves listened to, accepted, and understood, they become increasingly able to listen to themselves and to realize what they are experiencing. They listen to feelings and thoughts which were previously excluded because they were terrible or bizarre. They look at hidden and formerly repulsive aspects of themselves for the first time. As clients find that the therapist can accept these aspects of themselves and continue to regard them highly, they become more open to themselves and more able to express all aspects of themselves openly. As clients' insight into themselves increases, new directions and new courses of action become clear. There is a general loosening: rigidity, immaturity, self-centeredness, and defensiveness disappear. Clients begin to like themselves and to feel a readiness to relate to others, to share, and to grow (20).

Critical Comments

Client-centered psychotherapy has been widely accepted by mental health experts who treat moderately troubled people in outpatient settings. Studies by a number of investigators suggest that client-centered therapy is often effective in changing people's self-concepts, negative feelings, and attitudes—especially when it is used with relatively bright and healthy people who have mild problems.

As a theoretical system, client-centered therapy has some problems. For example, Rogers assumes that all troubled people suffer from the same malady, arrested growth. Recall the diverse behavior disorders which we discussed in Chapter 14. Many psychologists find it difficult to believe that all disorders result from precisely the same problem. Many psychologists also question Rogers' assumption that a therapeutic relationship helps clients grow in a direction that *they alone* determine. Studies suggest that all psychotherapists, despite the best of intentions, influence their patients (21).

ECLECTICISM

It may have occurred to you that the psychoanalytic, behavior, and client-centered psychotherapies each have certain strengths which might be fruitfully combined. There is evidence that many therapists do combine the various approaches. A recent survey found, for example, that the majority of responding clinical psychologists regarded themselves as *eclectic*; that is, they reported using whatever techniques and methods appeared most appropriate for a particular patient at a particular time (22). Arnold Lazarus, a clinical psychologist at Rutgers University, has pointed out that no matter how attractive a particular theory is, it is what the therapist *does or does not do* which affects the patient. Lazarus argues, and many psychologists agree, that flexible therapists who fit responsible and effective technology to the needs and problems of the individual sufferer make the most effective therapeutic agents (23).

GROUP VERSUS INDIVIDUAL PSYCHOTHERAPY

Most psychotherapies—including the psychoanalytic, behavior, and client-centered approaches which we have examined—can be used with a single troubled person or with a group of troubled people. Group psychotherapy is generally recommended when an individual suffers from social problems such as difficulty in forming and maintaining interpersonal relationships. Presumably, problems of a social nature can be most satisfactorily resolved in a social setting with the help and support of other people. Group therapy also has the advantage of serving more people with a lower cost per individual.

SUMMARY: THREE PSYCHOTHERAPIES

1. Many psychotherapies are used to treat mildly troubled and neurotic people. Psychoanalytic, behavior, and client-centered therapies are currently among the most widely used.

2. Psychoanalytic psychotherapists assume that neurotic problems are caused by repressed conflicts between primitive biological drives and harsh internal dictates of conscience. The cure consists of a lengthy, intensive exploration of the person's mental life, past and present. Psychoanalytic therapists analyze their patients' free associations and dreams; they also look for and interpret resistance and transference. Through the psychoanalysts' interpretations, patients gain insight into their unconscious conflicts. The insight is assumed to lead automatically to a more constructive adjustment.

3. Behavior therapists assume that neurotic problems are caused by psychological, social, biological, and environmental factors. Behavior therapy is usually brief and involves modifying those factors which appear to be maintaining the problem. Typically, techniques from the experimental psychology laboratory are employed to help people unlearn maladaptive behavior and learn or relearn adaptive behavior.

4. Client-centered psychotherapists assume that neurotic problems occur when people are forced to deny aspects of their own identity and cease to grow. Therapy aims at restoring the self-concept and renewing the growth process. It consists of an intimate here-and-now relationship with a genuine, warmly accepting, and understanding therapist.

TREATMENT APPROACHES TO PSYCHOSES

Unlike the neurotic disorders, the psychotic disorders are usually treated in a hospital. Psychotherapy, as we've discussed it, occupies a small amount of the institutionalized patient's time—perhaps an hour or so a week;

so what patients do for the other 111 waking hours each week is of critical importance for their recovery. What patients do during these hours is determined by the mental hospital. Some mental hospitals offer relatively few structured activities, and mental patients are left largely on their own to occupy themselves. Under these circumstances, they may wander around the building, stare at a TV set, read old newspapers, lie on the grass, play table tennis, and generally kill time. Other mental institutions offer the patient a busy routine. Patients work at simple jobs and attend special activity programs (such as arts and crafts, music, and poetry writing). Many institutions also offer occupational rehabilitation (job training). In addition, medication is almost always an important part of the psychotic's treatment. In this section we will be looking at some aspects of the schizophrenic's treatment—at the medical approach, at traditional hospitalization, at two new promising psychological approaches (milieu therapy and the token economy), and at several alternatives to hospitalization.

The Medical Approach

Physicians have been trying to alleviate the symptoms of schizophrenia for a long time. They have used numerous tactics, including prescribing special diets and massive doses of vitamins, giving drugs which induce violent convulsions, sending the schizophrenic to sleep fifteen hours a day for weeks at a time, administering chemical sedatives, and severing brain connections. Although some of these methods continue to be employed, only the use of chemical agents is *standard* medical practice today.

Major tranquilizers—the *phenolthiazines*, in particular—are highly effective in calming agitated psychotic patients. Two days after the administration of thorazine, for example, schizophrenic patients are noticeably calmer;

within two weeks hallucinations and delusions are usually controlled, sometimes eliminated altogether. Unfortunately, tranquilized schizophrenics are likely to appear drowsier, more lethargic, slower, and less energetic than previously. Many, but not all, mental health experts believe that these side effects are minor, more than balanced by the dramatic reduction in anxiety and disturbed thinking which make the tranquilized schizophrenic more amenable to psychological forms of treatment and to living within the community.[2]

In Chapter 14 we indicated that it was highly likely that schizophrenia had genetic determinants (in addition to environmental ones). Attempts to directly correct the schizophrenic's presumed biological deficiencies are relatively rare, largely because the nature of these deficiencies is not well understood. One such attempt has been made by the *orthomolecular psychiatrists* who administer massive doses of vitamins (particularly niacin) aimed at correcting the schizophrenic's physical condition. Although orthomolecular psychiatrists report many successes, their claims are widely disputed by the medical profession.

The Dilemma of the Chronic Schizophrenic

Approximately one-third of all schizophrenics are currently classified "acute" (24). These people are exhibiting schizophrenic symptoms for the first time. They are newly admitted to the hospital; they have intact ties to family, friends, job, and community. The acutely schizophrenic person can often be treated by medication at home and by psychotherapy and activitity programs in the community.

The chronic, or recurring case, is a second kind of schizophrenic patient. Chronic schizophrenic patients have been sickly and maladjusted since childhood; their ties to family and community are usually badly disrupted or nonexistent, and their chances of recovering sufficiently to function outside the institution are usually poor. Roughly two-thirds of all schizophrenics are currently classified as chronic.

The majority of diagnosed chronic schizophrenics spend much of their lives in state mental institutions. These institutions tend to be large, overcrowded, understaffed, and bleak. In this setting chronic schizophrenics are medicated, and some attempts are made to keep them occupied—frequently they have a menial job, access to a TV set and to various activities of the ashtray, pot-holder, birdhouse-making variety. Mental health experts who have posed as patients and submitted themselves to institutionalization talk of terrible boredom, a boredom which many patients seem to experience as well (25,26). Psychologists also describe institutionalization under these circumstances as "degrading" (27), "depersonalizing" (28), "dehumanizing" (29), and "illness maintaining" (30).

Rehabilitating the Chronic Schizophrenic

Currently, two psychological treatment procedures show promise for rehabilitating the chronic schizophrenic patient. One is social milieu therapy; the other is the token economy. In marked contrast to traditional institutionalization, both share the following characteristics: They emphasize a "resident" as opposed to a "patient" status. They treat the resident like a responsible human being who is expected to follow rules and to participate

[2]This subject is highly controversial. The article "Big brother and psychotechnology" (in the Suggested Readings) argues that drug therapy, behavior modification, psychosurgery, and psychiatry, in general, are used repressively in our society to stamp out social deviance.

Figure 15-5. Some mental hospitals offer relatively few structured activities, and mental patients are left largely on their own to occupy themselves. (Wide World Photos.)

actively in self-care, work, recreation, and social activities. They focus on concrete, realistic behavioral goals—such as managing one's own money, socializing, holding a job, and solving problems for oneself. They provide opportunities for the resident to learn and to practice important vocational, housekeeping, educational, and self-care skills. They make increasing demands for more independence and more responsibility as the resident improves. They also encourage social interactions by supporting large numbers of activities and frequent group meetings. In sum, they structure a good deal of the residents' waking hours with therapeutic activities. In addition, they try to prepare the resident to live in the outside community with support from relatives, friends, and other residents (31).

Social milieu therapy may be described as a set of procedures which are used in a hospital setting to turn a ward into a therapeutic community. Many hospitals offer this kind of program. Physically, the therapeutic community is an ordinary hospital ward that has been "fixed up" with home furniture, doors on rooms and toilet stalls, pictures on walls, and cooking facilities. Both the staff and residents are encouraged to dress in street clothes, and the residents are free to come and go within the community. The "setting" and the "costumes" are designed to force people to see themselves as people involved in an on-going life, not merely sick patients who are there to be taken care of.

Every day the residents participate in jobs, individual and group therapy sessions, and "town meetings." In the town meetings the residents help the staff make decisions about rules, rule infractions, activities, complaints, and recreation. The staff treats the residents with respect and expects them to behave in responsible and healthy ways; these expectations are contagious. Residents soon begin to expect healthy behavior of themselves and one another. Generally, studies show that people in social milieu therapy do begin behaving in healthier ways.

A *token economy*, a behavior therapy procedure, is an elaborate reinforcement system that aims at rehabilitating people by systematically motivating and rewarding healthy and adaptive behavior. In a token economy, a conditioned reinforcer—such as a poker chip, a point, a button, or a slip of paper—is given immediately following healthy behavior. The requirements for positive reinforcement are usually spelled out very clearly so

TABLE 15-2. SELECTED ON-WARD JOBS

Jobs		Tokens Paid
Tooth Brushing:	Brushes teeth or gargles at the time designated for tooth brushing (once daily)	1
Bed Making:	Makes own bed and cleans area around and under bed	1
Exercises:	Assists recreational assistant with exercises; writes names of patients participating in exercises	3
Commissary:	Assists sales clerk assistant; writes names of patients at commissary; records number of tokens patient spent; totals all tokens spent	5
Supplies:	Places ward supplies in supply cabinets and drawers	1
Trash:	Carries empty soft-drink bottles to storage area; empties wastepaper baskets; carries mops outside to dry	1

Source: T. Ayllon & N. Azrin. *The token economy*. New York: Appleton Century Crofts, 1968. Pp. 246, 250.

Figure 15-6. In one "token" economy, the coupons (top) are used to reward patients for participating in therapeutic activities. (Oxnard Community Mental Health Center, California, courtesy of Dr. Robert P. Liberman.)

that the residents know "the rules of the game" (see Table 15-2). Later on the residents can exchange their tokens for privileges and material goods. The token economy was developed in the mid-1960s by two psychologists, Teodoro Allyon and Nathan Azrin, at Anna State Hospital in Illinois. Today token economies exist in scattered mental hospitals, penal institutions, facilities for the retarded, and in ordinary classrooms throughout the United States. We turn to a description of Spruce House, a token economy program primarily for chronic schizophrenics.

Spruce House

In the mid-1960s a psychologist named John Henderson and his associates founded a treatment facility for psychotic men in an old house in the center of downtown Philadelphia and named it Spruce House. Spruce House is dedicated to strengthening the social and vocational coping behavior of its residents to fit them for living in the community.

Life at Spruce House revolves around a token economy. Each time a resident shows healthy, adaptive behavior, it is noted and praised by the staff and other residents; it is also followed immediately by tickets called "chits." Chits are reinforcing because they can be later cashed in for "grickles." A grickle is a positive mark on the resident's program card which has buying power. At Spruce House grickles buy food, tobacco, phone calls, passes, excursions into the community, and money. So residents are very eager to accumulate them; at the same time, of course, adaptive, healthy behavior becomes more and more habitual. At Spruce House maladaptive behaviors like delusions, slovenliness, and childish behavior are ignored in hopes that they will extinguish.[3]

The residents at Spruce House each hold jobs which are assigned on the basis of past work experience, current level of functioning, future job expectations, and the house's current needs. The residents are reinforced by grickles for job-holding skills such as being on time and attaining minimum standards of quality. They can increase their grickle earnings by improving the quantity and quality of their work. The interval between responses and reinforcement is gradually lengthened until payoffs for work approximate a weekly salary—anticipating the resident's eventual return to a real job.

The residents at Spruce House also earn grickles by attending classes where they learn literacy skills, money management, and the use of public transportation. Grickles are also awarded for constructive personal behavior. For example, a hypochondriacal resident might earn grickles for periods during which he doesn't complain about aches and pains, whereas a withdrawn resident might earn grickles for initiating spontaneous conversations with other residents.

Every night there are a wide variety of social programs which Spruce House residents are expected to plan and participate in: films and film discussions, housemeetings, dances, parties, role playing, crafts, physical education, folk singing, group games, current events discussions, and sporting events. And, of course, the residents earn grickles for their constructive social efforts.

Frequent evaluations of Spruce House show that it is more effective than conventional facilities at returning patients to the community in functional roles (32).

[3]Henderson and his associates assume that the schizophrenics' maladaptive behaviors are inadvertently positively reinforced by all the attention they receive. If that is true, removing the reinforcement—the attention—will cause the undesirable behavior to extinguish.

Alternatives to Institutionalization

Because institutions are so frequently associated with stigma and deterioration, mental health experts have looked for other alternatives. One possibility is treating chronic patients in their own homes—if they have one. In Amsterdam, Holland, many people with chronic psychotic disorders are treated at home. Professional personnel are available on a twenty-four-hour-a-day basis to make home visits, to evaluate, and to treat psychological emergencies. This program has been in effect for more than thirty years (33). A similar program, the Psychiatric Home Treatment Service, has been operating in Boston since 1957 and has served more than two thousand psychotic people (34).

Another alternative to institutionalization is the *halfway house*. The halfway house, usually located in an urban community, serves as a treatment facility and home for people who either have been hospitalized or fear that they may have to be hospitalized for psychological reasons. Halfway houses are generally run by a small nonprofessional staff who consult regularly with mental health experts. In the average halfway house about ten residents live together in a familylike atmosphere. Residents contribute a small fee for room and board. Although there are often no written rules, halfway house residents are usually expected to be responsible: to keep themselves clean, to keep their rooms clean, and to do certain chores. In addition, residents are frequently encouraged to find jobs, and many of them consult psychotherapists in the community. Residence in a halfway house is considered temporary. People are expected to be able to function independently in the community after a stay of four to eight months.

Recent studies have demonstrated that chronic schizophrenics can actually live together and administer their own halfway house. A halfway house project, initially started by a psychologist, George Fairweather, and his associates, was gradually turned over to the patients. In addition to administering the house, the patients formed their own business, a handyman service, that produced an income of $50,000 over a three-year period. A follow-up study found that the residents of this halfway house were far better able to hold jobs and manage their own affairs when they returned to the community than patients who had been treated in a hospital by conventional psychotherapy techniques (35).

Summary: Treatment Approaches to Psychosis

1. Chemical therapy with major tranquilizers is highly effective in calming agitated psychotic patients and eliminating hallucinations and delusions, but these drugs have disturbing side effects.
2. Two psychological approaches to the treatment of chronic schizophrenic patients—social milieu therapy and token economies—currently appear promising.
3. Home-treatment programs and halfway houses within the community are two possible alternatives to institutionalization for chronic schizophrenic patients.

COMMUNITY MENTAL HEALTH CARE

We focus now on a new concern in mental health treatment, community mental health care. Since 1963 more than four hundred comprehensive community mental health care centers have been established in urban communities throughout the United States. These centers were created by the federal government to make a wide range of mental health services available to the community and to establish primary and secondary prevention programs.

Primary prevention programs in mental health strive to create a psychologically healthy community by helping essentially normal people utilize their full potential and develop satisfying and effective ways of adjusting to life. Developing the intellectual, emotional, and social competencies of children is one particularly important goal. A second goal is preparing normal people to face potentially distressing life changes—in adolescence, parenthood, middle age, and old age.

In our youth-oriented society, old age can be especially difficult to face. Most old people have to cope with failing health. Poverty can be especially severe in old age. In addition, the elderly are often alone because family members and friends are dead and children have moved away. All too frequently, elderly people find themselves with no role to play in our society—no niche and no future. Under these circumstances the world can become strange, confusing, and frightening.

What can the community do for the elderly? All the problems of old age cannot be alleviated, but the community can—at the very least—do something to reduce the loneliness, the confusion, and the fear. These excerpts from a newspaper article describe a recent community mental health venture for senior citizens.

The needs of the elderly: Primary prevention in Washington, D.C.

"'We wanted to find out from the elderly just what they needed,' explains the senior center project director, Frances Eyster. 'There are lots of places across the country where old people can come to play cards, but we wanted to be of real service . . . [To help keep people out of institutions] we spend $90,000 a year on [visiting] housekeepers. There are so many older people who would literally be found in the gutter and have to go to a nursing home or D. C. Village without help at home.'

"Housekeepers aren't the only answer. For others, Mrs. Eyster and her staff have found foster families for the elderly person to live with. The sponsor, as the family is called, is paid $150 and the elderly person is given $35 a month for spending money. 'We have 35 people in this category,' said Mrs. Eyster. 'If we hadn't found a place for them, they would really be in difficulties, a problem to themselves and the city. These are people who have nowhere else to go. . . . Old people should stay in their own communities. We think the values they bring us are good ones. We should do everything we can to keep them with us. And we have to understand that their families can't always supply the care they need. . . .'

"One of the center's most successful programs costs the least money. Thirty 'friendly visitors,' who were found through churches, each take three people as their responsibility. All are older people who are able to visit as friends, and as volunteers they receive only transportation.

"The center's population is made up of people who haven't had a great many advantages in life. Most of them have never had a real vacation. For these people a six-day trip to Ivakota Association's farm, 250 acres in Fairfax, ranks in life's great experiences. It's not just children who enjoy summer camp.

"The farm has three fishponds, woods, and a dormitory, divided into sections with tie-dyed sheets. Twenty people at a time (180 each summer) go to walk, fish, sing, paint watercolors . . . play bingo and have barbecues. . . .

"Transportation is a serious problem for old people. 'There are about 75 people who wouldn't get to the center at all if we didn't fetch them. . . . We take them to clinics, especially those with wheelchairs and canes. We take them to the farm so they can garden there—one older woman starts plants in little pasteboard boxes, then transplants them at the farm. We pick up people at a housing development once a month and take them to different shopping centers. We've carried them Christmas shopping and to the White House.'

" 'The most important trip, though, is when we take them to have their checks cashed and then on to buy food stamps. They're so afraid to cash their checks and we're able to provide police escort for them.'

"The senior center has employment counselors for those able to work and law students to help with legal aid . . . [36]."

Secondary prevention programs in mental health are designed to identify psychological problems in their early stages and provide immediate treatment before they become serious. Community mental health centers, frequently located in storefront buildings in the heart of the community, offer a wide range of mental health services including hospitalization for the seriously disturbed, psychotherapy for troubled children and adults, emergency and crisis intervention, hotlines, and programs for drug addicts and alcoholics. To detect psychological problems early, *community psychologists* (clinical psychologists with special training in community mental health) frequently work with other community agents such as teachers, clergy, family doctors, and police officers, people who are often in a better position to spot potential problems. One of the best ways to increase the mental health of the community is to make certain that these key community figures deal with troubled people in ways which help alleviate and not aggravate potential problems. We focus on the efforts of psychologists to train therapeutic police officers as one example of secondary prevention in community mental health.

Police as therapeutic agents

Police officers have conflicting roles. On the one hand, they serve the community by retrieving lost children, aiding stranded motorists and helping in emergencies, disasters, and crises. On the other hand, they

Figure 15-7. Community mental health centers offer a wide range of services such as this alcoholism clinic in Michigan. (Andrew Sacks, Editorial Photocolor Archives.)

protect the community by pursuing criminals and upholding the law. Although almost 90 percent of the police officer's time is spent in interactions with other people, the police officer's initial training is centered on practical aspects of law and order (37). "And the police mystique places its highest value on masculinity, usually defined by toughness, imperviousness to feelings, and tight-lipped readiness to neutralize conflict by a quick draw in the middle of Main Street [38]."[4]

Police officers are increasingly recognized as potentially important agents for mental health, since they are frequently in a position to reward good behavior, prevent crime, and influence criminals and potential criminals. In the late 1960s Morton Bard, a psychologist at the City College of New York, began training police officers to better utilize this potential. Specifically, Bard placed eighteen police volunteers in a program to improve their handling of family disputes. Skilled family intervention is important since a high percentage of violent crimes are triggered by arguments among family members and a sizeable proportion of police fatalities and injuries occur during family scuffles. For one month the police attended behavioral science courses and practiced handling mock family disputes staged by professional actors. At the end of the month, the members of the Family Crisis Intervention Unit (FCIU) went out into the community to provide twenty-four-hour coverage by radio car to the Thirtieth Police Precinct in Manhattan—a densely populated area on the upper west side. Two members of the FCIU answered all domestic disturbance calls and attempted to mediate

[4]As the number of women police increases, the police officers' image may gradually change. Female police officers view themselves as more "persuasive, decisive, observant, emotionally stable, intelligent, understanding, and compassionate" than male police officers. So far the women's record on general patrol skills is as good as that of their male counterparts (39)!

the conflicts. When indicated, they referred families to service agencies in the community. In addition, they followed up on each family visited. Each week the police officers consulted with psychologists about their cases.

The officer's comments reveal an increased concern with being therapeutic: "I pick up things much quicker now than before," says FCIU Patrolman John Timothy, "because I'm looking for them. You're actually trying to help people now, whereas before you were simply trying to calm the situation." Says Patrolman Joseph D. Mahoney, summing up some of the new insights that were gained: "You don't prejudge anybody. You never take sides. And you remember that you're in somebody's home, no matter what's going on [40]."

It appears that skilled police intervention paid off. Although the precinct's homicide rate increased 350 percent, there were no homicides in the 962 families visited by the FCIU during the experimental period. Assaults and arrests dropped, and there was only one minor complaint in two years (41).

Through programs like these, community psychologists are trying to prevent serious psychological problems and keep people mentally healthy.

STUDY GUIDE 15

Key Terms. psychotherapy, counseling, psychoanalytic therapy, repressed conflicts, free association, dream analysis, manifest content, latent content, transference, resistance, interpretations, behavior therapy, respondent conditioning, systematic desensitization (desensitization), hierarchy, positive reinforcement, observation learning, assertiveness training, role playing, aversive learning procedures, aversive counterconditioning, symptom substitution, client-centered psychotherapy, actualize, arrested growth, "genuine", accepting, moment-to-moment understanding, eclectic, group therapy, tranquilizers, phenolthiazines, orthomolecular psychiatrists, acute schizophrenic, chronic schizophrenic, social milieu therapy, token economy, halfway house, primary and secondary prevention programs in mental health.

Important Research. Spruce House (Henderson), police as mental health agents (Bard).

Basic Theories. the cause and cure of abnormal behavior (psychoanalytic, behavioristic, and client-centered approaches), eclecticism in psychotherapy.

Self-Quiz

1. The primary goal of psychoanalytic therapy is to [a] help the patient achieve insight into his/her unconscious conflicts; [b] help the patient achieve a greater sense of the meaning of his/her own life; [c] help the patient change specific problem behaviors; [d] help the patient accept him/her self.

2. Identifying the psychoanalytic therapist with a person who was significant in the past, usually a parent, is called [a] free association; [b] symbolic interpretation; [c] resistance; [d] transference.

3. Failing to recall bits of information, forgetting therapy appointments, and arriving late to psychoanalytic therapy are considered evidence that the patient [a] is about ready to terminate (end therapy); [b] has reached difficult repressed material; [c] has strongly identified the therapist with an important person from the past; [d] lacks motivation and is unlikely to complete therapy.

4. A major problem with psychoanalytic therapy is that [**a**] it is rigid and cannot be modified to serve a variety of people and problems; [**b**] it does not allow patients to focus on their current problems; [**c**] it is difficult to study; [**d**] it frequently leads to symptom substitution.

5. A behavior therapist would be most likely to treat the businessman described in the psychoanalytic case history by [**a**] conditioning "away" his maladaptive behavior; [**b**] analyzing the conditions maintaining the maladaptive behavior and helping the businessman unlearn the maladaptive behavior and learn adaptive behavior; [**c**] discussion and insight; [**d**] creating a warm relationship that would help the businessman learn more adaptive interpersonal behavior.

6. Systematic desensitization is based on [**a**] operant-conditioning procedures; [**b**] observation-learning procedures; [**c**] respondent-conditioning procedures; [**d**] aversive counterconditioning procedures.

7. Assertiveness training aims primarily at helping people learn to [**a**] be more aggressive; [**b**] express themselves more genuinely; [**c**] survive in an aggressive dog-eat-dog world; [**d**] argue more effectively.

8. When psychologists pair pictures of attractive men with painful electric shocks to help a homosexual man (who wants to be heterosexual) reduce his sexual arousal to men, they are using _____ procedures. [**a**] sensitization; [**b**] punishment; [**c**] negative reinforcement; [**d**] aversive counterconditioning.

9. A major problem with behavior therapy is [**a**] explaining exactly why the techniques are successful; [**b**] treatment is exceedingly expensive; [**c**] symptom substitution; [**d**] behavior therapists usually treat mild, relatively trivial problems such as snake phobias.

10. A client-centered therapist views neurotic symptoms as [**a**] by-products of arrested psychological growth; [**b**] maladaptive habits; [**c**] signs of a conflict between forbidden impulses; [**d**] signs of an unhappy childhood.

11. In a therapeutic encounter client-centered therapists attempt to convey all of the following except [**a**] emotional acceptance of *all* the client's feelings and behaviors; [**b**] moment-to-moment understanding of the client's emotional experiences; [**c**] wisdom and knowledge; [**d**] genuineness.

12. A major problem with client-centered therapy is that [**a**] it is accepted by comparatively few mental health experts; [**b**] it assumes that all troubled people suffer from the same malady; [**c**] although it helps troubled people feel more positively about themselves, its effects are usually short-lived; [**d**] it neglects the events of early childhood.

13. If you entered a ward in a mental hospital with a homey atmosphere where patients were holding jobs and participating in therapy and in town meetings, you would be most probably observing [**a**] a social economy; [**b**] social milieu therapy; [**c**] a primary prevention effort; [**d**] a run-of-the-mill mental hospital environment.

14. The essential idea behind a token economy is establishing a reinforcement system that [**a**] rewards adaptive behavior and punishes maladaptive behavior; [**b**] is both novel and appealing to the patients so that they will want to cooperate; [**c**] is concrete and specific so that the patients know precisely what is expected of them; [**d**] rehabilitates people by systematically motivating and reinforcing healthy behavior.

15. Which of the following is *not* an example of a primary prevention program? [**a**] "Rap" sessions for essentially normal teenagers; [**b**] a senior citizens' action group; [**c**] Alcoholics Anonymous; [**d**] a program designed for new residents of a public housing development, providing social opportunities and leads on jobs and job-training prospects.

Exercise

TYPES OF PSYCHOTHERAPY. Match the therapy approach with the statements which characterize it. Use the following abbreviations: psychoanalytic (P), behavior (B), client-centered (C).

_____ **1.** Believes that therapists should avoid diagnoses and evaluations.

_____ **2.** Uses learning principles deliberately to bring about specific changes in behavior.

_____ **3.** Believes that what really matters is a here-and-now encounter between therapist and troubled person.

_____ **4.** Developed by Sigmund Freud.

_____ **5.** Assumes that patients usually develop strong feelings for their therapists which reflect feelings for significant people in their past lives.

_____ **6.** Believes that psychotherapy results should be evaluated by objective studies.

_____ **7.** Developed by Carl Rogers.

_____ **8.** Tries to identify and change the conditions that are contributing to the problem.

_____ **9.** Views the desire to quit therapy as unconscious resistance to dealing with repressed conflicts.

____ **10.** Tries to increase the patient's growth in a direction chosen by the patient.

____ **11.** Strives to locate the sources of unconscious conflicts and make the patient aware of them.

____ **12.** Believes that the therapist's genuineness is potentially therapeutic.

____ **13.** Emerged as a major treatment method in the late 1950s.

____ **14.** Asks the patient to free-associate.

____ **15.** Sees the therapist's interpretations of the patient's behavior as an important therapy procedure.

____ **16.** Believes that all the patient's behavior and emotions should be unconditionally accepted.

____ **17.** Focuses on unlearning maladaptive responses and learning adaptive ones.

____ **18.** Views maladaptive behavior as a symptom of an underlying, unconscious conflict.

____ **19.** Assumes that maladaptive behavior is the patient's problem.

____ **20.** Sees the patient's problem as arrested growth.

____ **21.** May be said to have originated in the laboratory.

____ **22.** Analyzes the manifest and latent content of the patient's dreams.

____ **23.** Focuses on the patient's early childhood.

____ **24.** Believes that neurotic behavior will disappear if the patient enters into a genuine, warm, and understanding relationship.

____ **25.** Emphasizes *action* in the present.

Questions to Consider

1. Do you have a preference for one of the three types of psychotherapies which were discussed? If you were making up your own psychotherapy, which elements of each approach would you include?

2. Consider the following case from the point of view of (1) a psychoanalytic, (2) a behavioristic, and (3) a client-centered therapist. In each case tell how you might (a) speculate about the causes of the problem, (b) define goals, and (c) apply treatment methods. "An attractive thirty-year-old woman is quite distressed. Her numerous love affairs have all followed the same pattern. She attracts a man and offers herself to him freely. In most cases she does not know the man very well at the time, and they later turn out to have very little in common. The man soon begins to treat the patient with contempt; eventually he leaves her. At this point the woman usually considers suicide."

3. If you wanted to compare the relative effectiveness of psychoanalytic, behavior, and client-centered thera-

pies, which problems would you encounter? What extraneous variables would have to be controlled?

4. Design a token economy to modify the maladaptive behavior of a group of juvenile delinquents so that they can return to their communities and live a productive life.

5. What kinds of primary prevention programs in mental health are needed in your school? in your community? Choose one that seems to have particularly high priority and outline a program that could fill the need.

Project 15: The Public's Image of Psychological Treatment Methods: A Survey

How much do people know about treatment for psychological problems and how positively do they view such treatment? The purpose of this project is to formulate answers to these questions by surveying the members of your community. Since seeking psychological help is less stigmatizing today than it was thirty or forty years ago, and since information is increasingly available in textbooks like this one, we should expect to find young people more positive in their attitudes and perhaps more generally knowledgeable on this subject than older people.

Method. Find six adult subjects for this project: three in their late teens or early twenties and three in their middle forties or fifties. Explain to each subject that you are taking an opinion poll on psychological treatment for your psychology class and that the subject will not in any way be identified with his/her responses. Do not tell the subject more about the project until your data are collected. It would be best to use subjects who are not sophisticated about psychology and have not been in psychotherapy.

Prepare some answer sheets beforehand. At the top of a ruled sheet of paper write Age Range _____; then number the lines from 1 to 19. You may administer the survey on page 454 to all your subjects at the same time or individually. Have your subjects sit behind a table in a quiet spot that is free from distractions. They should not write their names on their answer sheets, but they should indicate their age bracket (fifteen to twenty-five or forty-five to sixty). Tell your subjects that you will be reading some statements about treating psychological problems and that you want to know their immediate, honest reaction to each statement. They are simply to write A if they agree and D if they disagree with the statement. If they cannot decide, encourage them to indicate whether they lean toward agreeing (A) or disagreeing (D). If they have no opinion whatsoever, instruct them to write NO.

Survey: Psychological Treatment Methods

1. If there were a serious psychological problem in my family, I would prefer to consult a minister (priest, rabbi) or my family doctor as opposed to a psychologist, psychiatrist, counselor, or other mental health professional.
2. Psychotherapy is almost always extremely expensive, so poor people cannot afford it.
3. Mental hospitals do patients a great deal of good.
4. A small percentage of psychiatrists are psychoanalysts.
5. A psychotherapist mainly gives advice.
6. Psychologists do not treat people with psychological problems; they primarily test and diagnose.
7. Almost all modern psychotherapies assume that simply talking about problems eventually leads to their solutions.
8. Tranquilizing drugs can cure most cases of mental illness if used appropriately at the proper time.
9. Mental health professionals (psychologists, psychiatrists, psychiatric social workers, etc.) do not understand psychological problems very well and are rarely helpful.
10. For their own sake people with severe psychological problems should not be isolated from their families and their communities.
11. A person who is basically well adjusted never needs psychotherapy or counseling.
12. Most hospitalized mental patients are eventually cured.
13. Seeking and accepting psychological help is not necessarily a sign of weakness.
14. Psychotherapy usually focuses on the patient's childhood.
15. At a mental hygiene clinic patients usually see the same counselor each time.
16. There are many different kinds of psychotherapy.
17. Counseling is used only for adjustment problems, whereas psychotherapy is only used for deeper emotional problems.
18. It would be more valuable to talk to a counselor about a psychological problem than to a close friend.
19. Most mental hospital patients tend to be about as dangerous to others as an average person.

Results. The statements on the survey can be separated into two categories. Statements 1, 3, 9, 11, 13, and 18 sample people's attitudes toward psychological treatment, and statements 2, 4, 5, 6, 7, 8, 10, 12, 14, 15, 16, 17, and 19 sample how much factual information the person has acquired.

Positive attitude key. A positive attitude is reflected by the following answers: 1. D 3. A 9. D 11. D 13. A 18. A.

Correct information key. Correct information is demonstrated by the following answers: 2. D 4. A 5. D 6. D 7. D 8. D 10. A 12. D 14. D 15. A 16. A 17. D 19. A.

For each subject tally one score for attitude by counting one point every time the subject gives a response in the positive attitude key. Tally a second score for each subject for factual information by counting one point every time the subject gives a response in the correct information key. Note that subjects may score from zero to six on attitude and from zero to thirteen on information.

Discussion. Consider the following questions.

1. Do younger and older people differ in their attitudes toward psychological treatment methods? How can your findings be explained?
2. Do younger and older people differ in their knowledge of psychological treatment methods? How can your findings be explained?
3. What other factors might be expected to relate to people's attitudes toward and knowledge about psychological treatment?
4. What sources of bias may have influenced your results. (Consider your selection of subjects and your own biases.)
5. Is there a need for more information about mental health care in your community? How might people be reached most effectively?

Suggested Readings

1. Strupp, H. H. *Psychotherapy and the modification of abnormal behavior.* New York: McGraw-Hill Book Company, 1971 (paperback). Clear introduction to the major psychotherapy approaches.
2. Maddi, S. R. "The victimization of Dora." *Psychology Today.* September 1974, 8, 91–92, 94, 99, 100. A humanistic psychologist describes and reinterprets one of Freud's most famous clinical case studies.
3. Chorover, S. "Big brother and psychotechnology." *Psychology Today*, October 1973, 7, 43–54. A psychologist argues that drug therapy, behavior modification, and psychiatry itself are often used to suppress social deviance.

4. Pizer, S. A., & J. R. Travers. *Psychology and social change.* New York: McGraw Hill Book Company, 1975 (paperback). Discussion of psychotherapy, encounter groups, prisons, and mental hospitals; and some suggestions for change.

5. Frank, J. D. *Persuasion and healing.* Baltimore: The Johns Hopkins Press, 1961. A comparison of modern psychotherapies, healing rites, religious rituals, and brain-washing techniques.

6. Mikulas, W. L., *Behavior modification: An overview.* New York: Harper & Row, Publishers, Incorporated, 1972 (paperback). A survey of behavior modification techniques.

7. Axline, V. *Dibs: In search of self.* New York: Ballantine Books, Inc., 1964 (paperback). A case history in which the author describes how client-centered therapy techniques are used to treat a troubled child.

8. Kesey, K. *One flew over the cuckoo's nest.* New York: New American Library, Inc., 1962. A novel about life in a mental institution that points up the manner in which many patients are reinforced for unhealthy behavior and punished or ignored for healthy behavior.

Answer Keys

SELF-QUIZ
1. a 2. d 3. b 4. c 5. b 6. c 7. b 8. d 9. a
10. a 11. c 12. b 13. b 14. d 15. c

EXERCISE
1. C 2. B 3. C 4. P 5. P 6. B 7. C 8. B 9. P
10. C 11. P 12. C 13. B 14. P 15. P 16. C
17. B 18. P 19. B 20. C 21. B 22. P 23. P
24. C 25. B

16

SOCIAL PSYCHOLOGY

IN THIS CHAPTER
We focus on social psychology, the study of animals (especially people) as they interact with and influence one another both directly and indirectly. We describe how attitudes (particularly prejudices) are formed and modified. Then we turn to conformity and obedience. Finally, we focus on interpersonal attraction, the study of who likes whom and why. After reading this chapter, you should be able to do the following:

1. Describe the domain of social psychology
2. Discuss the nature of an attitude
3. Describe six factors that influence the formation of racial prejudices and cite supporting evidence
4. Describe three factors that lead to attitude change and cite supporting evidence
5. Discuss cognitive dissonance and give two personal examples
6. Describe situations that elicit conformity and discuss the consistency of conforming behavior
7. Discuss the implications and ethics of Milgram's obedience study
8. Describe five factors that influence interpersonal attraction

A fairy tale about a supernatural traveller who walked about the earth granting the wishes of evil people goes like this:

So too in Wocrahin a swaggering bully came down the street one market day, cuffing aside children with the back of his hand and house-wives with the flat of his sword. "Oh that my way were not cluttered with such riffraff!" he ex-claimed, his shoulder butting into the traveller's chest. "As you wish, so be it," said the traveller, and when the bully turned the corner, the street he walked was empty under a leaden sky—and the buildings either side, and the taverns and the shops. Nor did he again in all eternity have to push aside the riffraff he had cursed; he was alone [1].

Can you imagine a life without people? Can you picture yourself totally alone in the world? The idea is terrifying to most of us. Aristotle wrote, "To live alone one must be either a beast or a god [2]." Accounts of solo flying or sailing experiences and solitary confinements in prisons and monasteries show that social isolation can be a devastating experience. There is little question that peo-ple are social animals, animals that group together, depending on and needing one another physically and psychologically.

Psychologists know comparatively little about social needs (see Chapter 10). In the late 1950s Stanley Schachter, a Columbia University social psychologist, began some important studies on these needs. Picture

Figure 16-1. Can you imagine yourself totally alone in the world? (Mimi Forsyth, from Monkmeyer.)

yourself as a subject[1] in one of his classic studies described below.

[1]In actuality Schachter's subjects were all female, but this detail has no theoretical significance.

Anxiety and affiliation: An experimental study

"[When you arrive at Schachter's laboratory, you find yourself in a group of strangers facing a] gentleman of serious mien, horn-rimmed glasses, dressed in a white laboratory coat, stethoscope dribbling out of his pocket, behind him an array of formidable electrical junk. [This august figure addresses the group:]

Allow me to introduce myself, I am Dr. Gregor Zilstein of the Medical School's Departments of Neurology and Psychiatry. I have asked you all to come today in order to serve as subjects in an experiment concerned with the effects of electrical shock.

"Zilstein pause[s] ominously, then continue[s] with a seven-or-eight-minute recital of the importance of research in this area, citing electro-shock therapy, the increasing number of accidents due to electricity, and so on. He conclude[s] in this vein:"

What we will ask each of you to do is very simple. We would like to give each of you a series of electric shocks. Now, I feel I must be completely honest with you and tell you exactly what you are in for. These shocks will hurt, they will be painful. As you can guess, if, in research of this sort, we're to learn anything at all that will really help humanity, it is necessary that our shocks be intense. What we will do is put an electrode on your hand, hook you into apparatus such as this . . ., give you a series of electric shocks, and take various measures such as your pulse rate, blood pressure, and so on. Again, I do want to be honest with you and tell you that these shocks will be quite painful, but, of course, they will do no permanent damage.

Zilstein next asks you to describe your feelings about participating in the study. Then he continues:

Before we begin with the shocking proper there will be a ten-minute delay while we get this room in order. We have several pieces of equipment to bring in and get set up. With this many people in the room, this would be very difficult to do, so we will have to ask you to be kind enough to leave the room.

Here is what we will ask you to do for this ten minute period of waiting. We have on this floor a number of additional rooms, so that each of you, if you would like, can wait alone in your own room. These rooms are comfortable and spacious; they all have arm chairs, and there are books and magazines in each room. It did occur to us, however, that some of you might want to wait for these ten minutes together with some of the other girls here. If you would prefer this, of course, just let us know. We'll take one of the empty classrooms on this floor and you can wait together with some of the other girls there.

Zilstein passes out a second form so that you can make your preferences known. How would you respond to Zilstein's request?

Please indicate below whether you prefer waiting your turn to be shocked alone or in the company of others.
———— I prefer being alone.
———— I prefer being with others.
———— I really don't care.

Some of the subjects in Schachter's experiment had the experience we just described, whereas others were exposed to Zilstein in the same costume and setting minus the frightening electrical apparatus and the fear-arousing instructions. Zilstein assured these low-anxiety condition subjects that the series of shocks would be "in no way painful," that it would resemble "more a tickle or a tingle than anything unpleasant."

At this point the experiment was essentially over. Zilstein took off his coat and explained the rationale of the study and the reasons for the deceptions.

Schachter found that people in the high-anxiety condition generally preferred to wait together, whereas those in the low-anxiety condition did not show a consistent preference. A number of studies have replicated these findings. Apparently, the more anxious people are, the more eager they are to be near others (3).

Schachter's studies suggest that anxiety-arousing situations influence people's need for others. Do other circumstances elicit social needs? And, more basically, what is it precisely that adults need from one another? Currently, psychologists cannot answer these important questions. Later in this chapter we will be discussing a related subject, the factors that influence people's liking for and affiliation with one another.

We define *social psychology* as the study of animals (especially people) as they interact with and influence one another both directly and indirectly. Social psychologists study a wide range of specific subjects including aggression, conformity, obedience, sex-role differences, helping behavior, crowding, moral behavior, attitude formation and change, prejudice, attraction, leadership, group dynamics, persuasion, and propaganda. We turn first to attitude formation and change.

To Begin: What Is an Attitude?

"Integration is good for society."
"Every human being should learn to read and write."
"Abortions are wrong because they violate the rights of the unborn child."
"Women are best suited for mothering and housework."

These statements express attitudes which you may or may not share. We define an *attitude* as a learned concept which guides (1) thoughts, (2) feelings, and (3) behavior toward a particular object (a person, a group of people, a policy, an event, or an inanimate object). Like many other phenomena we have discussed so far, attitudes are hypothetical constructs which are inferred—usually from verbal statements and overt behavior. Attitudes have several characteristics: They are *evaluative*; that is, they reflect a value judgment. They are *relatively permanent and enduring.* Attitude change is typically slow. Psychologist Herbert Kelman of Harvard University suggests some logical reasons: "[A]ttitudes, once established, help to shape the experiences the person has with the attitude object. They affect the kind of information to which the person will be exposed, the way in which he will organize that information, and often (as in interpersonal attitudes) the way in which the attitude object itself will behave [4]." Although attitude change is generally slow, people do continually form new attitudes and modify old attitudes—as they are exposed to new information and new experiences.

As we noted in our definition, attitudes guide thoughts, feelings, and behavior. People subscribe to particular thoughts or beliefs about the object of the attitude. These

TABLE 16-1. UNIVERSITY STUDENTS' CHARACTERIZATION OF ETHNIC GROUPS, 1933 and 1967

Trait	Percent Checking Trait 1933	1967	Trait	Percent Checking Trait 1933	1967
Americans			Irish		
Industrious	48	23	Pugnacious	45	13
Intelligent	47	20	Witty	38	7
Materialistic	33	67	Honest	32	17
Progressive	27	17	Nationalistic	21	41
Germans			Jews		
Scientific	78	47	Shrewd	79	30
Stolid	44	9	Mercenary	49	15
Methodical	31	21	Grasping	34	17
Efficient	16	46	Intelligent	29	37
Italians			Blacks		
Artistic	53	30	Superstitious	84	13
Impulsive	44	28	Lazy	75	26
Musical	32	9	Ignorant	38	11
Imaginative	30	7	Religious	24	8
Revengeful	17	0			

Source: M. Karlins, T. L. Coffman, & G. Walters. On the fading of social stereotypes: Studies in three generations of college students. *Journal of Personality and Social Psychology*, 1969, 13, 1, 1–16. .

thoughts are generally based on experience, observations, or information. Frequently, people make two or three observations and then generalize. After discovering that three adolescents are able to find summer jobs because of their educational backgrounds, you may conclude that education is generally useful. Or you may know two married women who are perfectly contented to stay at home and care for their houses and children, and jump to the conclusion that all married women are happy when they remain at home. As psychologist Gordon Allport has put it: "Given a thimbleful of facts, . . . [people] rush to make generalizations as large as a tub [5]." When the generalization is overly simple and rigid and concerns people or social groups, it is usually referred to as a *stereotype*. Table 16-1 shows how some common stereotypes are changing. Although the word "stereotype" has negative connotations (associations), it is important to note that generalizations are not always harmful. Frequently, they help people order and simplify

complicated information so that they can act quickly. One or two unpleasant encounters (direct or indirect) with snakes, for example, may lead people to stereotype snakes as dangerous and behave adaptively around them. Generalizations are primarily harmful when people forget that they are based on small samples and therefore invariably unjust when applied indiscriminately to individuals within the population.

Attitudes also influence emotions and behavior. Joel *believes* that married women belong in the home. Typically, he feels *angry* and *yells* whenever his wife mentions looking for a job or whenever the subject of working women comes up.

It is important to note that although the thoughts, feelings, and behavior which are guided by a particular attitude are usually harmonious, they can also be inconsistent. Consider a consistent attitude first. Maria believes that all people benefit from a formal education. She teaches in a small school in a poverty-stricken Appalachian village in

Maryland which would otherwise be without a teacher; whenever the subject of the importance of an education is mentioned, Maria feels happy. Now consider an inconsistent attitude where beliefs, behaviors, and feelings are not harmonious—at least on the surface. These are the words of a dying black grandfather to his young grandson:

Son, after I'm gone I want you to keep up the good fight. I never told you, but our life is a war and I have been a traitor all my born days, a spy in the enemy's country ever since I gave up my gun back in the Reconstruction. Live with your head in the lion's mouth. I want you to over-

come 'em with yeses, undermine 'em with grins, agree 'em to death and destruction, let 'em swoller you til they vomit or burst wide open [6].

We turn now to the question—how are attitudes formed?—focusing on the attitude racial prejudice.

ATTITUDE FORMATION

People are not born with particular attitudes; attitudes are acquired. To see how they are acquired, we examine white-black racial prejudice in America—in detail.

Figure 16-2. Prejudices result in the physical separation of races at a bar and in the exclusion of women from the bastions of finance, religion, and politics. (Top: Jim Jowers, Nancy Palmer Photo Agency; bottom: David Hurn, Magnum.)

Defining the Terms of Racial Prejudice

We define *racial prejudice* as an attitude which reflects a positive or negative prejudgment about a person (or a group of people) based on racial group membership, irrespective of each individual's distinctive strengths or weaknesses. Note that a prejudice may be favorable or unfavorable. *Racial discrimination* refers to behavior consistent with this attitude. When behavior is biased for or against a person or group of people because of their racial group membership and not because of their individual merits or deficiencies, this bias is labeled racial discrimination. A recent poll showed that both blacks and whites in our society demonstrate strong racial prejudices (see Tables 16-2 and 16-3). How are these prejudices formed? We consider two influences: Learning within a family and culture and environmental conditions.

The Lessons of Family and Culture

People learn attitudes from many sources. The first and perhaps most important source is parents.

Parental teaching. Studies show that the racial prejudices of white and black elementary

TABLE 16-2. BLACK PERCEPTION OF WHITES

	Percentage of Blacks Agreeing with Statement
Whites feel blacks are inferior.	81
Whites give blacks a break only when forced.	79
White men secretly want black women.	76
Whites are really sorry that slavery was abolished.	70
Whites have a mean and selfish streak.	68

Source: The Harris Survey, October 4, 1971.

TABLE 16-3. WHITE PERCEPTION OF BLACKS

	Percentage of Whites Agreeing with Statement	
	1971	1963
Blacks are inferior to white people.	22	31
Blacks have less ambition.	52	66
Blacks smell different.	48	60
Blacks have lower morals than whites.	40	55
Blacks breed crime.	27	35

Source: The Harris Survey, October 4, 1971.

school children resemble those of their parents quite closely (7,8). Parents probably teach attitudes in several ways. Sometimes they model prejudiced attitudes. Children may hear their parents talk about "honkies" or "dirty blacks." A white may refuse to hire black employees; a black parent may snub the friendly overtures of a white parent. Parents also positively reinforce behavior which is consistent with their own attitudes. When Susie behaves like her bigoted father, she receives hearty approval; otherwise she is likely to receive disapproval.

Children also learn their parents' values. Social psychologist Milton Rokeach at the University of Western Ontario believes that white middle-class children learn to reject blacks because their parents teach them that blacks scorn middle-class values, such as cleanliness, monogamy, hard work, diligence, and thrift (9). In 1965, David Stein, Jane Allyn Piliavin, and M. Brewster Smith, psychologists at the University of California at Berkeley, tested this hypothesis quite carefully and found some support for it. At the beginning of the experiment the investigators asked high school students to complete value scales indicating to what degree they agreed with statements such as "Teenagers should live up to strict moral standards" or "People should be treated as equals." Two months later, the psychologists returned to the school and asked the same students to read the value-scale responses of four fictitious teen-agers. Two of them—one white, one black—appeared to express values nearly identical to the subjects', but the other two—one white, one black—espoused different views. The subjects were asked to indicate how friendly they'd feel toward each teen (for example, whether they'd invite him/her home to dinner, have him/her date a sister or brother, live in the same apartment house with him/her). In general, subjects felt closest to teens with similar values, regardless of their race. However, race was found to affect the desire for intimate contact, as in dating and marriage. In these situations whites discriminated against blacks with similar beliefs (10). Studies in other parts of the country have replicated these findings. Interestingly, when people know nothing about a person except race, many automatically assume that members of a different race are dissimilar in attitudes and beliefs and members of one's own race are similar (11). So parents may teach their children (1) to dislike people with dissimilar values and (2) to assume that dissimilar racial groups have dissimilar values, a combination of beliefs which can produce racial prejudices.

Simple learning principles can explain how the beliefs and behaviors associated with an attitude arise, but how can the emotional component of an attitude be explained?

Respondent conditioning. Respondent conditioning can explain the acquisition of the emotional component of an attitude. In *higher-order respondent conditioning*, a conditioned stimulus which is currently evoking a conditioned response serves as an unconditioned stimulus for a second neutral stimulus (see Figure 16-3). For example, every time a child gets mud on her clothing, her parents might say, "You're dirty," and soon thereafter punish her. The punishment evokes pain, feelings of doubt, and humiliation. Consequently, the word "dirty" begins to evoke

these same negative, uncomfortable feelings. The emotional responses which many words elicit have probably been acquired in this way. As the child grows older, other stimuli like the names of various groups of people may be repeatedly associated with the conditioned stimulus "dirty" until the stimuli themselves automatically elicit uneasy feelings. As you can see in Figure 16-3, the process can continue further. Once the names of particular groups come to evoke negative feelings, stimuli that are paired with those names may also come to elicit negative feelings through a second higher-order conditioning process.

In some cases emotional components of attitudes are probably learned by simple respondent conditioning and generalization. Suppose two boys—one black, one white—have a vicious fight. Each may subsequently experience fear and anger every time they see one another; these feelings may generalize so that they occur whenever someone of the other race is seen.

The authoritarian personality. Many psychologists believe that childhood experiences shape particular personality characteristics which prime people for prejudice in adulthood. Psychologist Theodor Adorno and his associates believe that this is the best explanation for the prejudices of adults characterized by *authoritarian personalities*. People with authoritarian personalities are described as rigid in their beliefs, conventional in their values, intolerant of weakness in others or themselves, strong believers in punishment, preoccupied with power and being tough, cynical about human nature, and awed by authority figures. They tend to agree with the following statements. (These items appear on a test which Adorno and his associates devised to measure authoritarianism.)

1. "Homosexuals are nothing but degenerates and ought to be severely punished."

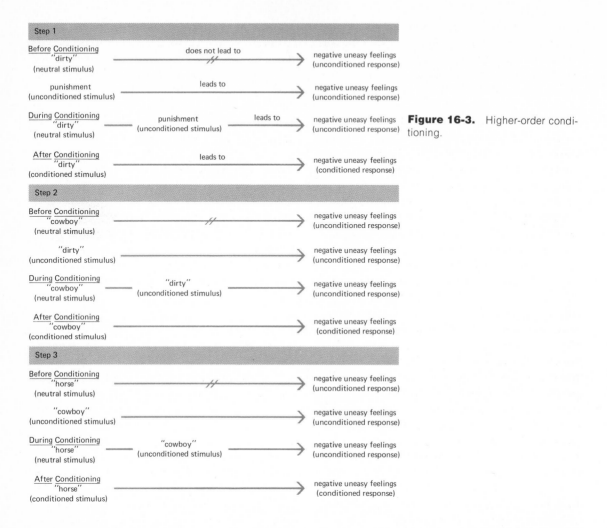

Figure 16-3. Higher-order conditioning.

2. "No weakness or difficulty can hold us back if we have enough will power."
3. "Human nature being what it is there will always be war and conflict."
4. "Obedience and respect for authority are the most important virtues children should learn [12]."

Adorno and his colleagues interviewed a large number of people and found that the ones identified as authoritarian were more likely than the others to have had cold, harsh, unloving, capricious, and severely punish-ing parents. The psychologists speculated that people with authoritarian personalities shared a number of experiences as children. They felt inadequate, and they were frightened of and angry with their parents, but they suppressed these feelings because they feared punishment. According to Adorno and his associates, adults with authoritarian personalities are still insecure and angry, and they handle these feelings with defense mechanisms (see Chapter 13). Specifically, they attribute their own inadequacies to powerless minority groups (projection). They also displace the anger which they feel for their parents onto these groups. Note that the prejudices of authoritarian people could also have been learned in the ways we mentioned earlier.

Peer group influences. People also acquire attitudes from their peers. A well-known field study, the Bennington study, found that people frequently conform to the views of groups that are important to them. In this case political conformity was under investigation. University of Michigan psychologist Theodore Newcomb and his associates studied how Bennington college women changed in their political preferences between 1935 and 1939. In the 1930s Bennington had a politically liberal (Democratic and Socialistic) faculty, whereas most of the students came from politically conservative (Republican) backgrounds. Newcomb found that the longer a student remained at Bennington, the more politically liberal she became. Whereas 62 percent of the freshmen favored the Republican presidential candidate in the 1936 election, only 15 percent of the seniors expressed that preference (13). A twenty-five year follow-up showed that these changed attitudes persisted (14).

Studies on today's college campuses also find that peers influence racial attitudes. When racial prejudice is unfashionable, as it is on many college campuses, investigators find that students display significantly less prejudice with time in the institution—even in the Deep South (15).

How do peer groups influence attitudes? Observation and imitation may be involved. In addition, peer groups may exert strong pressures for *conformity*. After reviewing and conducting a great deal of research, Thomas Pettigrew, a Harvard social psychologist, concluded that conformity is the most reasonable explanation for white-black prejudice among Southerners: "When an individual's parents and peers are racially prejudiced, when his limited world accepts racial discrimination as a given of life, when his deviance means certain ostracism, then his anti-Negro attitudes are . . . socially adjusting [16]."

Environmental Conditions and Attitude Formation

Environmental conditions can shape new attitudes and intensify existing ones. We focus again on racial prejudice in our country. In 1971 a National Opinion Research Center poll showed that poor whites exhibited more prejudice against blacks than did any other group (17). Numerous studies support this finding. Why should poverty be associated with racial prejudice?

Competition. Poor whites and poor blacks compete with one another for jobs, houses, property, social status, and power. Hostility is the almost inevitable outcome of this competition. Psychologists know that competition engenders hostility because when they create competition where it has never existed before, they find hostility where it has never existed before. A classic study provides evidence for this effect. In 1949 and again in 1953 and 1954 a team of social psychologists headed by Muzafer Sherif ran a summer camp for children. The camps were actually experimental field studies. The psychologists personally selected healthy, well-adjusted, white, Protestant, middle-class boys to attend their camp. Their subjects had no idea that they were participating in a psychological study; they saw the psychologists as ordinary camp counselors. The psychologists followed similar procedures in each experiment. They allowed all the campers to mix for several days. Then they divided them into two separate groups, deliberately placing friends in different groups. Initially the psychologists were interested in seeing how each group would develop unity. As the boys cooked, hiked, swam, worked, and played together, they formed friendships with the members of the new group. They selected nicknames for one another and names and symbols for their groups. An informal leader and "lieutenants" soon emerged to lead each group.

During the second phase of the study the psychologists brought the two groups together in baseball, football, tug-of-war, and treasure-hunt tournaments with prizes for the winning team. These competitions, which were characterized by good sportsmanship at first, became increasingly hostile. Name calling accelerated; eventually the members of one group refused to associate with the members of the other group. Soon each side was making threatening posters, planning raids, and hoarding apples as "ammunition for war." Clearly, competition had caused hostility (18). We return to these studies later to see how the friction was eliminated. As you might expect after reading about Sherif's experiment, surveys find that white prejudice against blacks is most pronounced in regions where blacks and whites *compete* for the same jobs (19).

Frustration. Poor people have few of the material niceties that Americans prize, and they lack status and power. If they expect or desire more than they have (and they are likely to), then they will feel frustrated. In Chapter 13 we saw that frustration sometimes leads to aggression and that when the aggression cannot be expressed directly it is sometimes displaced—in some cases, onto a minority group. Many laboratory studies find a link between frustration and displaced aggression or prejudice. In one study young men at a camp were given a long, dull exam that contained very difficult questions. The test ran overtime and forced the men to miss a local theatre event which they'd been looking forward to all week. Both before and after

the exam, the men were asked to check a list of desirable and undesirable traits as being present or absent in either Mexican or Japanese people. After the frustrating exam, the young men checked significantly fewer positive traits and more (but not significantly more) negative traits (20). Presumably, frustration had increased the tendency to aggress, and the aggression which could not be vented against the experimenters had been displaced onto a convenient target.

ATTITUDE CHANGE

Social psychologists have been investigating the conditions that influence attitude change for a long time. Such research has important applications. We focus on research related to one application, reducing racial prejudice.

Conflicting Information

We learn from attitude-change research that when people are confronted by new information which is at odds with their current attitudes, their attitudes sometimes change. Milton Rokeach has used this strategy in numerous attempts to modify the civil rights–related attitudes of college students. In one such study 366 college students at Michigan State University ranked the following values in order of importance: happiness, wisdom, freedom, a world of beauty, salvation, equality, inner harmony, a comfortable life, an exciting life, a sense of accomplishment, a world at peace, family security, mature love, national security, pleasure, social recognition, self-respect, and true friendship. (Before reading on, rank these values in their order of importance to you.) Half the subjects (the control group) were then dismissed. The remaining subjects (the experimental group) were shown a table which depicted how previous Michigan State University students had, on the average, ranked the eighteen values. The experimenter directed the students' attention to the ranking of *freedom* (ranked number 1) and *equality* (ranked number 11). The experimenter expressed the opinion that this ranking indicated that previous Michigan State University students were a lot more interested in their own freedom than in other people's freedom. The subjects were then encouraged to compare their own rankings to these norms. A little later they were asked to rate their sympathy to the aims of civil rights demonstrators. The experimenter produced a second table which showed that people who value the efforts of civil rights groups rank *equality* high in their list of values. The experimenter interpreted these results as follows: "This raises the question as to whether those who are *against* civil rights are really saying that they care a great deal about *their own* freedom but are indifferent to other people's freedom. Those who are *for* civil rights are perhaps really saying they not only want freedom for themselves, but for other people too." Apparently because of self-confrontation and self-questioning, many students changed their attitudes. In some cases their behavior also changed. Several months after the study, the National Association for the Advancement of Colored People contacted all 366 subjects and invited them to join. Of the subjects in the experimental group 28 percent, in contrast to 10 percent of the subjects in the control group, accepted the invitation (21).

Conflicting Social Norms

Psychological research indicates that people tend to conform to the prevailing social norms of the groups to which they belong; so if prejudiced people are exposed to antiracist norms, attitude change should occur. Social psychologists Morton Deutsch and Mary Ellen Collins provide evidence that this is the case. After World War II public biracial housing projects sprang up in a number of cities. Although all of the project dwellers had consented initially to biracial housing, some had been placed in integrated and others in segregated projects. Deutsch and Collins selected two integrated and two segregated projects in the New York City–Newark area for further study.

The norms governing social interactions in the two types of projects differed quite clearly. In the segregated housing projects where whites and blacks lived in the same project in separate buildings, mixing was taboo. One woman reported: "I used to be good friends with a colored woman who worked with me at the factory before I moved here. She lives on the other side of the project, but I never have her over to my side of the project—it just isn't done. Occasionally, I go over and visit her." In integrated housing where blacks and whites lived in adjoining apartments, the social norms sanctioned interracial contact, and the housing authorities clearly favored it.

After people had lived in the projects for some time, Deutsch and Collins interviewed housewives about their interracial attitudes. Of the white housewives in integrated housing 60 percent felt friendly toward their black neighbors. Only 10 percent of those in segregated housing felt that way. The attitudes of the black housewives were very similar (22).

Many social scientists believe that the reduction of white prejudice against blacks and black prejudice against whites depends to a great extent on altering the socialization of young children. One place to begin is in the school. Exposing children to antiracist norms there may make a significant difference. In one study the black racial prejudices of two groups of white middle-class second-grade children were measured and found to be similar. The children were then assigned one of two readers—an ordinary one illustrated with pictures of whites and the same reader

Figure 16-4. Spontaneous, informal contacts between blacks and whites in integrated housing seem to promote favorable attitude change. (George W. Gardner.)

illustrated with pictures of blacks and orientals in addition to whites. After four months with the readers the children's attitudes were remeasured. A significant reduction in reported prejudice had occurred among the children using the multiethnic reader and not among the other children (23); so a comparatively small change in cultural practices had produced a relatively significant attitude change.

Contact with the Object of Prejudice

Suppose you're black and you hate whites and your employer hires a white with whom you must work closely. Will close contact cause you to begin to feel more positively toward whites in general? The question is hard to answer without more information. You'd probably want to know more about the white person: Is he or she different from your negative stereotype of whites? Are you working together cooperatively toward a common goal? Is the person similar to yourself—a "real" human being with whom you

can identify? Is your social and economic status comparable? These are some of the factors that determine whether contact leads to positive attitude change.

Equal status contact. When blacks and whites of equal status come into contact with one another in a noncompetitive situation, their views of one another appear to be likely to change in a positive direction. H. E. O. James, a British psychologist, tested this hypothesis by surveying the attitudes of white thirteen-year-old children toward Africans before and after two weeks' experience with an African teacher. James found that the children developed more favorable attitudes toward Africans in general after this contact (24). In the Deutsch and Collins study blacks and whites were comparable in income and social status—a fact that may have been central to the attitude change that occurred.

Cooperation in the pursuit of a mutual goal. Recall the campers who became hostile toward one another after competing for prizes in a series of tournaments. In the final phase of the Sherif studies, the social psychologists tried to eliminate the hatred. A first effort—bringing the boys together for movies and a delicious meal—ended in failure. The boys merely used this occasion to hurl food and insults and intensify the quarreling. The social scientists then contrived a number of emergencies which were designed to force the boys to cooperate to achieve mutual goals. For example, while on a lake outing the truck that was supposed to pick up lunch in town would not start. The boys got a rope, one that had previously been used in a particularly bitter tug-of-war, and all pulled together to start the vehicle. Joint efforts in emergencies like this one did not immediately eradicate the hostility. Initially, the boys began bickering again as soon as the job was finished, but repeated cooperation over a period of time gradually reduced the friction. Eventually friendships between members of the formerly hostile groups began to develop and the boys actively sought opportunities "to mingle, to entertain and treat each other [25]."

Close personal contact. Contacts between members of hostile groups seem to promote favorable attitude change when the contact enables people to see "common interests and common humanity [26]." Deutsch and Collins suggest that spontaneous, informal contacts between blacks and whites in integrated housing—for example, as people shared elevators and laundry rooms—convinced both groups of their common humanity. One white housewife summed up her feelings like this:

I started to cry when my husband told me we were coming to live here. I cried for three weeks. . . . I didn't want to come and live here where there are so many colored people. I didn't want to bring my children up with colored children, but we had to come; there was no place else to go. . . . Well, all that's changed. I've really come to like it. I see they're just as human as we

are. They have nice apartments; they keep their children clean, and they're very friendly. I've come to like them a great deal. I'm no longer scared of them. [22]

A Combination of Factors

If psychologists deliberately combined all three strategies at once, could they reduce racial prejudice? This is the question that Stuart Cook, a social psychologist at the University of Colorado, tackled. Cook began his research in 1961 when it was very unusual for blacks and whites to eat together or work together in equal status positions in the South. His subjects were intensely prejudiced white Southern female college students in a Southern town. These coeds had accepted a part-time job, two hours a day for forty days, participating in a group task—presumably to train strangers to work together successfully at isolated government bases. The real purpose of the task was to change the subjects' racial attitudes.

Each subject worked with two other students who were, in reality, the experimenters' confederates. One was black and one was white. The confederates set in motion some of the conditions we have already discussed:

1. The black confederate—personable, ambitious, and self-respecting—did not resemble the subject's stereotype of blacks.
2. The social norms encouraged nonprejudice. The white and black confederates were very friendly, and the white confederate obviously disapproved of both segregation and prejudice. Moreover, the supervisor had an obviously competent and responsible black assistant.
3. The black confederate and the white subject were of equal status—both college students, and both teachers and learners in the task.
4. Black and white worked together toward a

common goal. They shared the same successes and failures; and bonus pay rewarded them for cooperating with one another.

5. Finally, lunchtime conversations between the black and white confederates established the humanity of the black by bringing out facts about her family, her plans, her ambitions, her tastes, her fears, and her disappointments.

What happened? The attitudes of approximately 40 percent of the highly prejudiced Southern whites changed very significantly in a positive direction. The attitudes of another approximately 40 percent remained the same, whereas the attitudes of the remaining 20 percent became more prejudiced (27).

Obviously there is still much to understand about changing prejudiced attitudes, but Cook's results are encouraging, especially when we balance eighty hours of antiracist attitude training against a lifetime of racist attitude training. Clearly, social psychologists have pinpointed a number of significant conditions that can change attitudes.

Cognitive Dissonance and Attitude Change

We have described a number of strategies for producing attitude change. All of them involve introducing a conflict or an inconsistency (a discrepancy) between an attitude and either new, challenging information, social norms, or experience. To explain why discrepancies produce attitude change New York University social psychologist Leon Festinger has introduced the concept *cognitive dissonance*. Festinger assumes that when people's cognitions—attitudes, beliefs, perceptions, opinions, thoughts—are dissonant (not in agreement), people become uncomfortable, and they attempt to reduce the tension by reducing the dissonance. Disso-

nance can be reduced in several ways—by seeking new information, by changing attitudes, by altering behavior, by rearranging the environment, and so on. Festinger believes (and studies provide support for the hypothesis) that in the majority of cases people reduce dissonance by cognitive strategies—chiefly by seeking new information or by changing their attitudes and opinions. Let's take an example. Consider a student named George who believes that all construction workers are insensitive and stupid. One day George learns that one of his classmates, a person whom he considers sensitive and intelligent, is a construction worker. Cognitive dissonance theory predicts that the contradiction between George's former attitude and his new perception will generate tension and that he will try to reduce the tension by reducing the dissonance. Two strategies George might consider are (1) avoiding the company of the classmate so that the conflict is avoided or (2) attitude change—in this case deciding that construction workers must be judged as individuals.

Cognitive dissonance is an important concept that seems to be able to account for the ways that people reconcile cognitive conflicts of all kinds. A second example is today's smokers who are confronted by the evidence that smoking causes cancer. That evidence creates a cognitive conflict: the smoker perceives smoking as both pleasurable and dangerous. Typically, smokers reconcile the conflict by choosing one of several strategies: (1) They reduce their smoking behavior, or they quit smoking altogether. (2) They alter the situation, perhaps by smoking only low-nicotine, low-tar, filter-tipped cigarettes which presumably reduce the danger. (3) They change their attitudes. They point to all their friends who continue to smoke and remain healthy and decide that the evidence linking smoking and cancer is inconclusive. Or they argue that they'd rather live a brief, happy cigarette-filled life than a long, miserable life without cigarettes.

Summary: Attitude Formation and Change

1. We defined an attitude as a learned concept that guides thoughts, feelings, and behavior toward a particular object.
2. Attitudes may be acquired by learning from one's family and culture. Environmental conditions may also affect their formation and/or intensity.
3. Positive reinforcement, modeling, direct concept learning, respondent conditioning, peer group pressure, and environmental conditions which foster anger and feelings of inadequacy may all play a role in the formation of racial prejudices in our country. Frustration and competition also contribute to the formation and intensification of racial prejudice.
4. Attitudes such as racial prejudice can be altered by introducing conflicting information, social norms, and/or experiences. The theory of cognitive dissonance is one explanation for why attitudes frequently change in these situations.

We turn now to a second social-psychological subject, conformity.

CONFORMITY

What is conformity? Was Commander Lloyd Bucher of the United States Navy conforming when he signed a statement of guilt to prevent the North Koreans from punishing (possibly torturing) himself and his crew? Is it conforming to wear clothes or eat three meals a day? Is Mary Lou, a high school junior who sacrificed lunch for two weeks to save enough money to buy a class yearbook, conforming? Conversely, is Ned "the rebel," who lets his hair grow down his back to spite his family and the middle-class establishment, nonconforming? The answers to these questions depend, of course, on the definition of conformity. We define *conformity* as a change in behavior, attitudes, or both which results from real or imagined group pressure.

Going back to our examples, we can say that Bucher conformed—at least temporarily. He changed his behavior in response to pressure from the Koreans. You may object, "He had an ulterior motive. He conformed to avoid punishment for himself and his crew." For this reason we label his behavior *compliance*, conformity to gain a reinforcement or avoid a punishment.

Are wearing clothing and eating three meals a day signs of conformity? Not by our definition. These activities are best described

Figure 16-5. Social pressure from peers contributes to conformity in dress and hair style. (Virginia Hamilton.)

as social customs which have been established by conditioning, rather than by group pressure; changes are rarely involved.

Mary Lou's class-yearbook buying behavior is also conforming. Like Commander Bucher, she complies with group pressure. Unlike Bucher, she *privately accepts* her own behavior as appropriate; we label this kind of conformity *internal acceptance*. Finally, there is Ned. He is probably conforming to the standards of his own peer group. Note that we have distinguished two types of conformity: compliance and internal acceptance. In any group situation pressure may lead to one of four possible combinations of these two responses. The cases of Mary Lou and Ned illustrate compliance and acceptance. Commander Bucher's case shows compliance without acceptance. Acceptance without compliance is another possibility. Joel, Mary Lou's boyfriend, would like a class yearbook, but he decides that they're too expensive, and he does not indulge himself. Finally, there is nonacceptance and noncompliance. We call this response *independence*, our definition of true nonconformity. Sarah, for example, decides that class yearbooks are a meaningless extravagance, and she does not buy one.

In this section we will be trying to answer the following questions: Is conformity good or bad? Why do people conform? How do psychologists study conformity? What factors influence conformity? And, finally, are people consistent in conforming or resisting pressures to conform?

Is Conformity Good or Bad?

Do psychologists consider conformity good or bad? For some people, standing out in any way is catastrophic. You may know people who are frightened to wear navy-blue shoes if their friends are wearing black ones. You may also know people who believe that one must never conform—no matter what. They equate conforming with "selling out" or "being ruled by the mob." Whether conformity is good or bad depends, of course, on the specific context in which it occurs and on the consequences which follow it. Conformity has led to cruel and destructive behavior—such as lynchings. On the other hand, nonconformity can also be disastrous. Consider the "nut" who drives fifty miles an hour down the wrong side of the road.

Why People Conform

Why do people conform? Social psychologist Harold Kelley suggests two reasons that make a lot of sense:

1. People rely on two sources for information about the world: their senses and what other people say. Whenever people doubt their sensory impressions or when a situation is unclear or ambiguous, people are more apt to take the opinions of others into account to improve the accuracy of their information. Kelley calls this phenomenon *informational conformity*.
2. People also conform for a more social reason. As a rule, they want to be liked and accepted by others; and they fear embarrassment, rejection, ostracism, or mistreatment. Often, then, people conform to win group support or to avoid group rejection. Kelley labels this phenomenon *normative conformity* (28).

Solomon Asch's Conformity Studies

Rutgers University social psychologist Solomon Asch conducted a series of studies on conformity in the early 1950s. In the past twenty years the large majority of conformity studies have used Asch's basic method or some modification of it; so we examine his method in some detail. Let's assume that you are participating in one of Asch's classic studies. The experimenter tells you that his investigation concerns visual perception. You sit around a table with seven other students, all accomplices of the experimenter. (Of course, you don't know it.) The experimenter props up two large cards on a table in the front of the room. One displays a single vertical line; the other, three vertical lines of varying lengths (see Figure 16-6). Your task is to select the line on the right card which matches the line on the left card. All students are asked to call out their choices. The first pair of cards is easy; so is the second. Everyone is in agreement, and the task begins to appear dull and routine. But not for long. On the third set of cards the first subject gives a wrong response. You stare at the lines again. Is the subject crazy? The next confederate gives the same wrong response. Feeling puzzled, you look again. As the third confederate agrees with the first two, you wonder if something is wrong with your eyes. If you're wearing glasses, you remove them. You tilt your chair backward. If you're brave, you move closer to the cards. You feel alien, strange, and isolated from everyone else. When it comes your turn, what do you say? You may assume that your perceptions are wrong and comply (compliance, acceptance). Or you may go along with the crowd for the heck of it (compliance, nonacceptance). Finally, you may say what you perceive while privately believing you're wrong or right (noncompliance, acceptance or noncompliance, nonacceptance).

Asch measured conformity by counting how many times people gave false judgments. In an early study 33 percent of his subjects never conformed and 8 percent conformed on almost every trial. The average subject conformed 33 percent of the time and remained independent 67 percent of the time (29). Note that Asch's experiment mea-

sures only compliance. Can you spot any other problems?[2]

Factors That Influence Conformity

Studies using Asch's model show that there are quite a few factors that influence conformity. Group unanimity is one. Psychologists find that people are more likely to conform when the majority is unanimous. When there is only one other kindred spirit in the group, the results change dramatically. Apparently, people find it relatively easy to stick with their own beliefs when they have some support (31).

The size of the majority does not matter greatly in the laboratory. To be more precise, a majority of four is just as effective there as one of eight or even sixteen (32). The data are hard to interpret because subjects in laboratory experiments become suspicious when confronted by a large number of people who agree. Naturalistic observations suggest that the tendency to conform in the real world probably increases as the size of the majority grows—largely because the possibility of reprisal becomes more threatening. People also tend to conform when they feel less competent than the other group members (33) and when the tasks are difficult or ambiguous (34). Can you think of something that all these factors—group unanimity, group size, group competence, task difficulty, and task ambiguity—have in com-

[2]Ordinarily people conform in situations where they feel ego involved, but students are not likely to feel ego involved in Asch's artificial laboratory situation. Conformers may simply be saying to themselves, "I may as well go along with this silly study and not sweat it." Moreover, the Asch setting may be losing its power. A recent investigation showed that 75 percent of the subjects felt suspicious of it. Many knew of the study from their reading. Others had heard about it from other students. Yet others suspected that total unanimity had to be some sort of trap (30).

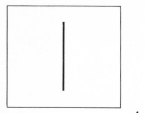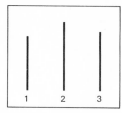

A

B

C

Figure 16-6. (A) Each subject is to select the vertical line on the right-hand card that matches the line on the left-hand card. (B) As the experimenter's confederates give wrong responses, the subject (6) becomes increasingly perplexed. (C) Despite his confusion and concern, the subject does not comply with the unanimous but incorrect verdict. He announces, "I have to call them as I see them." (William Vandivert, *Scientific American.*)

mon? They all play a role in convincing people that the group's judgment may be a more accurate source of information than their own sensory judgments.

When people feel attracted to a particular group, we'd expect them to conform to avoid rejection or embarrassment. In actuality, conformity in this situation seems to depend on the person's status in the group. When people feel exceptionally secure, well liked, and respected, they tend to speak out. The opposite situation has the same effect. After all, there's nothing to lose. In contrast, people with moderate status tend to conform—presumably because they have the most to lose or gain (35). People also tend to conform when they have to speak publicly and everyone will know how they have responded (36). In this situation concern about the consequences of nonconformity may be motivating the conformity.

Who Conforms?

Are people consistent in conforming or in resisting pressures to conform? In a series of studies at the University of California at Berkeley, Richard Crutchfield and his associates found that some people conformed regularly and others conformed relatively rarely in a modified Asch situation. Personality testing allowed Crutchfield and his associates to characterize both groups. Conformers put emphasis on conventional and socially approved values; they showed less ego strength, less tolerance for their own impulses and for ambiguity, less sense of responsibility, less spontaneity, and less self-insight than nonconformists. The nonconformists emerged as the heroes of this research. They were characterized as intelligent, original, capable of coping with stress, self-confident, responsible, and tolerant (37).

Recent studies show that most people are far from consistent in conforming or resisting pressures to conform. In one study a psychologist placed people in four *diverse* group settings. He discovered that only 20 percent of his subjects showed consistent conformity or nonconformity (38). When you stop to think about it, this finding makes sense. We said that people probably conform either because they believe that the group is a better source of information and/or because they want the group's approval. If this is true, then people should conform primarily in situations where the group seems to have better information or when its approval is important to them. Consider a hypothetical student named Sandy who is very good in math. Sandy would not be likely to go along with a wrong math answer no matter how many fellow students supported it. On the other hand, Sandy is unsure of himself in large social settings, so typically he's unwilling to voice an unpopular opinion at parties. Generally, studies find that conformity depends on interactions between the personal characteristics of the individual and the specific characteristics of the situation (39).

OBEDIENCE

Obedience may be considered a special kind of conformity. When people are *obedient*, they conform to the demands of those in authority. Societies, including our own, tend to value obedience. Obedient children are "good children." Obedient citizens and obedient soldiers are highly esteemed. Beginning at an early age Americans are conditioned to obey numerous "legitimate authorities"—parents, grandparents, aunts, uncles, older brothers and sisters, babysitters, elderly people, teachers, doctors, dentists, police, and clergy. We learn to obey rules at home, at school, and in almost every other social situation in which we find ourselves. We also learn to obey laws—traffic laws, criminal laws, tax laws, and so on. Through all this training we probably acquire a general tendency to be obedient. Frequently, the lesson pays off; when everyone follows society's laws, life is safe and orderly. But blind obedience can be dangerous. An American soldier in the Vietnamese war wrote home to his parents:

Dear Mom and Dad:

Today we went on a mission and I am not very proud of myself, my friends or my country. We burned every hut in sight! It was a small rural network of villages and the people were incredibly poor. . . .

The huts here are thatched palm leaves. Each one has a dried mud bunker inside. These bunkers are to protect the family. Kind of like air raid shelters.

My unit commanders, however, chose to think that these bunkers are offensive. So every hut we find that has a bunker, we are *ordered* to burn to the ground. . . . So, everyone is crying, begging and praying that we don't separate them and take their husbands and fathers, sons and grandfathers. The women wail and moan. Then they watch in terror as we burn their homes, personal possessions and food. Yes, we burn all rice and shoot all livestock [40]

In Nazi Germany soldiers systematically slaughtered 6 million to 9 million people in the name of obedience. C. P. Snow, the British author, scientist, and statesman, sums up the situation eloquently: "When you think of the long and gloomy history of man, you will find more hideous crimes have been committed in the name of obedience than in the name of rebellion [41]."

Stanley Milgram's Study of Obedience

When the commands of an authority conflict with moral and humanitarian principles, what does the ordinary person do? This was the first question that social psychologist Stanley Milgram tried to answer when he began conducting extensive investigations of obedience in the early 1960s at Yale University. Milgram's subjects were men twenty to fifty years of age of varied social and educational backgrounds.

If you had been a subject in Milgram's study, you would have appeared for your session along with an older male "subject"

Figure 16-7. The experimenter instructs a subject to administer increasingly severe electric shocks to the "learner" in Milgram's study of obedience. (Stanley Milgram, from the film *Obedience*, distributed by the New York University Film Library.)

who was really the experimenter's accomplice. You're each paid $4.50 as promised, then the experimenter begins the orientation. He tells you that the experiment concerns the effects of punishment on learning. One person will be teaching the other a list of word pairs by using punishment. You and the accomplice draw straws to see who will play the teacher and who will play the learner. The drawing is rigged so that you will play the teacher. The learner follows the experimenter to another room. You follow along and see the learner strapped into a chair. He will be memorizing a list of word pairs.

You return to the laboratory where you are seated before an impressively complex instrument labeled "shock generator." Every time the learner makes a mistake, you will supply the correct response and punish him by administering an electric shock. The experimenter tells you to begin with the switch set at 15 volts. Each time the learner makes an error, you are to increase the shock by one step. There are thirty steps. The highest is labeled "450 Volts Danger: Severe Shock."

In the course of the study the learner gives a great many wrong answers, so you find yourself "punishing him with increasingly intense shock." (Actually, you only think you are punishing him; the shock-generating equipment is phoney.) At 75 volts the learner grunts and moans. (It's a tape recording, but you don't know this.) At 150 volts, the learner demands to be let out of the room. At 180 volts he cries out that he cannot stand the pain. At 300 volts he pounds on the wall and refuses to go on. All along you protest that you want to stop. The experimenter rejoins: "Whether the learner likes it or not, you must go on until he has learned all the word pairs correctly. So please go on." When the learner refuses to answer, the experimenter tells you to treat no answer like a wrong answer; he adds, "You have no other choice, you must go on."

How far would you go? How far do most people go? Forty psychiatrists guessed wrong. They vastly underestimated the number of people who would follow orders in this situation. The fact is that under these circumstances, no subject stopped prior to administering 20 shocks, and approximately 65 percent of the subjects continued to the end (42).

Why was there so much obedience? Could people have complied for the money? Almost certainly not. A sum of $4.50 is not very persuasive; and besides, subjects are paid before the study begins and they are free to walk out without forfeiting their pay. What about fear of reprisal? This alternative is also remote. After all, a respectable Yale University professor is not likely to seek revenge. What about the prestige of Yale University itself? People may have assumed that any experiment which occurred at this highly respected institution of learning was safe and would not jeopardize a person's life. There is some support for this notion. When Milgram conducted the same study in a rundown commercial building at a downtown shopping center in nearby Bridgeport, Connecticut, only 48 percent of the subjects were obedient until the end (as compared to 65 percent under similar conditions at Yale), but that is still a very high rate of obedience. Apparently, many people assume that legitimate authorities have to be obeyed—regardless of their requests (43).

Later studies by Milgram and others at Yale show that obedience also depends on a number of other situational characteristics. The nearer the authority is, the more obedient people are. When the experimenter is not physically present, but delivers his orders over the phone, the subjects obey only 22 percent of the time. The proximity of the victim is also important. When people do not see or hear him, they average a maximum of 275 volts of shock. In contrast, when they sit next to him and must physically restrain him, they give an average maximum of 175 volts. Finally, when subjects see others defy orders, only 10 percent continue to behave obediently (44).

You might wonder about the ethics of Milgram's study. In a review for the *New York Times Literary Magazine*, Steven Marcus, a Columbia University English professor, recently wrote:

There can be no doubt that these experiments were designed—whether consciously or not—to bring out the worst in us. They are brutal and ingenious dramatic inventions, little masterpieces of scientific bad faith. And the cruelty they inflict upon their unwitting subjects is surpassed only by the cruelty they elicit from them. Moreover, the consequences of such an experience for the volunteer subjects are simply incalculable. . . [45].

Was the experiment cruel? In particular, did it have devastating effects on its subjects? Milgram was not insensitive to the ethical dilemma. At the end of each session he explained the study and reconciled the subject and the victim. Moreover, each subject received a detailed report on the objectives and results of the investigation. Milgram also polled his subjects on their feelings toward having participated in the experiment: 84 percent reported that they were glad to have taken part; 15 percent claimed to feel neutral; only 1.3 percent expressed regret (46). Note that interpreting these results requires care; the positive responses could be explained by cognitive dissonance theory— subjects may have been trying to convince themselves that the importance of the study justified their suffering.

Summary: Conformity and Obedience

1. Four different conforming responses can be identified: compliance with acceptance, compliance without acceptance, noncompliance with acceptance, and noncompliance without acceptance.
2. People probably conform to group opinions (1) to improve the accuracy of their

information and (2) to win group support and to avoid group rejection.

3. Conformity is most likely when the rest of the group is unanimous on a particular position.

4. People are also likely to conform when tasks are ambiguous, when they feel that they are less competent than other group members, when they are very attracted to a group and their status with the group is middling, or when they have to respond publicly.

5. In general, few people conform or resist pressure to conform consistently across a wide range of situations. Rather, the characteristics of a specific individual seem to interact with those of a specific situation to determine whether or not the person conforms.

6. When people are confronted by a legitimate authority ordering them to inflict pain and ignore the obvious suffering of a fellow human being, a large percentage of them follow the orders obediently—especially if the authority is nearby, the subject is faraway, and no one is around to support their defiance.

We turn now to our third topic in social psychology, interpersonal attraction.

THE COMPANY OF TWO: WHO IS ATTRACTED TO WHOM? AND WHY?

So far as love or affection is concerned, psychologists have failed in their mission. The little we know about love does not transcend simple observation, and the little we write about it has been written better by poets and novelists [47].

So wrote psychologist Harry Harlow in 1958. Psychologists have learned more about these matters since those words were written. We focus now on the subject of interpersonal attraction, or who is attracted to whom and why?

Think of five people you like. What attracted you to these people in the first place? If you're similar to most of the people psychologists have studied, your reasons will include:

1. They're competent, admirable, likeable, or physically attractive.
2. They like you.
3. They live, work, or attend school near you.
4. Their attitudes, values, beliefs, and interests are similar to your own.
5. Their personalities and interpersonal needs complement your own.

We examine each of these factors more closely.

Desirable Characteristics

To find out what particular characteristics attract people to their friends, Elaine Walster, a social psychologist at the University of Minnesota, and her colleagues gave male and female student subjects personality tests and then matched them randomly for blind dates. Physical attractiveness turned out to be the best predictor, better than intelligence, personality measures, or the complex meshing of needs, of which pairs reported liking one another and making a second date (48); so physical attractiveness appears to be an important influence on attraction between members of the opposite sex in the initial stages of a relationship.

Studies also show that people report liking people who appear to be at least moderately competent. In one such study Elliot Aronson, a social psychologist at the University of Texas, and associates Ben Willerman and Joanne Floyd had male college student subjects listen to a tape recording of a male candidate for a college quiz program. The men listened to one of four different versions of the same interview. In one version the candidate appeared to be a nearly perfect young man. He answered 92 percent of the highly difficult questions and modestly admitted to being an honor student, a yearbook editor, and a member of the track team. The same actor played a mediocre person in a second version of the interview. He answered 30 percent of the questions accurately; he admitted to making average grades, working as a proofreader for the yearbook and failing to make the track team. The third interview was identical to the first except the person clumsily spilled coffee over himself at the end. Similarly, the fourth tape was identical to the second except for the clumsy coffee incident at the end. After listening to the tape, the subjects rated the interviewee's likeability. Best liked was the person on the third tape, the otherwise perfect candidate who spilled the coffee; the perfect candidate was rated second most likeable; and the mediocre candidate who did not spill coffee was rated third. The psychologists concluded that people appear to find competent people who demonstrate some evidence of fallibility most likeable. Presumably the mediocre student had already demonstrated his humanity and his further clumsiness reflected on his incompetence, making him less attractive (49).

Why should people feel attracted to individuals who are physically attractive and at least moderately competent? One possibility is that people learn to admire these characteristics and, consequently, associate people who demonstrate such characteristics with positive feelings. In addition, if the attractive, competent person returns the liking, it may raise the recipient's self-esteem. Nearly perfect people may threaten self-esteem by reminding people of their own inadequacies.

Liking Breeds Liking

Do people like people who like them? In general, the results of many studies suggest that people like being liked and that they like the people who like them, though they have to believe that the other person is sincere and not simply trying to be ingratiating or to win a favor (50). When people feel sad or inadequate, they seem to be especially susceptible to this effect (51). Studies also show that if someone dislikes us and then gradually grows to like us, our attraction may be stronger than if they had liked us the same amount all along. In one study which supported this hypothesis, Elliot Aronson and his associate, Darwyn Linder, had female college student subjects talk to a confederate of the experimenters for several minutes over the course of seven experimental sessions. After each session the subject overheard the confederate make comments about her. In one condition (+ +) the subjects heard only complimentary comments; in a second condition (− −), only nasty and insulting ones. In a third condition (+ −) the remarks were positive at the beginning and gradually became increasingly more negative; in a fourth condition (− +), the remarks began in a negative vein and became increasingly more positive. Later on, the subjects rated their liking for the confederate. Figure 16-8 summarizes the findings. Aronson and Linder suggest that subjects liked the initially negative eventually positive confederate best for a number of reasons: (1) She appeared authentic. (2) She seemed hard to impress and therefore discriminating. Being liked by a discriminating person is, of course, a big boost to self-esteem (52).

Proximity

The best general predictor of who will become friends is physical distance—how far apart people live, work, or attend school. A classic study by social psychologists Leon Festinger, Stanley Schachter, and Kurt Back provides support for the importance of proximity to attraction. The psychologists investigated the friendship formation of couples living in a married student housing project at

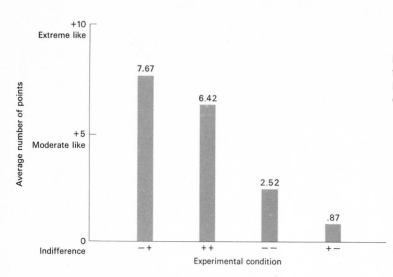

Figure 16-8. Reported liking for the confederate in the Aronson-Linder study. (After Aronson and Linder, 1965.)

the Massachusetts Institute of Technology shortly after World War II. The couples, who had not known one another initially, named their three closest friends within the project. The data showed that even within a single building, people chose friends who lived nearby. Next-door neighbors were more likely to become friends than people two doors apart. In fact, friendships among people four or more units away were relatively rare (53).

Why should proximity enhance liking? Possibly because it allows people to interact and to get together easily for mutually satisfying experiences that reinforce the friendship. Of course, proximity alone is not a sufficient basis for friendship. If a person is objectionable, proximity may make them unbearable. Proximity can also be overdone. When people are constantly underfoot they invade our sense of privacy and become irritating and/or boring.

Similarity

Do birds of a feather flock together, as the old saying goes? If you meet someone at a party and find that you have similar ideas about the current war, farming, religion, and civil rights, will you like one another?

Dozens of studies find that you will—at least initially (54). How do psychologists study such issues? Typically they use social psychologist Donn Byrne's "imaginary stranger" technique. At the beginning of the semester student subjects fill in questionnaires that measure their attitudes about a subject such as politics, religion, or sex. Later in the semester the experiment takes place. The subjects are given questionnaires that have been filled in by an imaginary stranger; they are asked to rate their liking for the stranger. In general, people rate their liking for strangers with similar attitudes higher than that for strangers with dissimilar attitudes.

Why should similar attitudes be important? There are many reasons. They provide a basis for sharing pleasurable activities. They also increase each participant's sense of confidence, making both of them feel more positively about themselves. (If you and I agree, you confirm my belief that I am right; and I confirm your belief that you are right; and we both like that feeling.) People also tend to assume that anyone who agrees with them is a sensible and superior person. In addition, similar attitudes keep people from bickering and quibbling later on. However, just as in the case of proximity too much similarity may

be unattractive; when people are very predictable, the relationship may become quite
dull.

Complementary Personalities

Do opposites attract? The answer to this
question seems to be "Yes, to some degree."
People probably like some measure of *complementarity* (meshing personalities and interpersonal needs) as well as some measure of
similarity.

The research on complementarity and attraction is contradictory, probably because
the matter itself is complicated. Whether people are attracted to people with similar or
complementary characteristics probably depends on the characteristic in question, the
intensity and the type of relationship, and so
forth. Several examples may clarify this
point. In social situations Jane is shy and
Betsy is outgoing; Jane admires Betsy and
Betsy enjoys her opportunity to shine; she
also appreciates Jane's good judgment. But
Jane is neat—she insists on everything in its
place—whereas Betsy is sloppy; she never
makes up her bed and leaves used tissues and
gum wrappers where they happen to fall.
Rooming together could be disastrous for
Jane's and Betsy's friendship. Now consider
the marriage of Irma and Fred. They both
like being in control, but they do not necessarily clash. Each has pursuits outside the
home which satisfy this need. In the home
they divide the control. Irma is dominant on
financial and interpersonal matters; Fred on
matters of household repairs and cooking. So
one sees a subtle complementarity in this
relationship.

A Theory of Friendship

Most of the studies we have examined took
place in the laboratory where two strangers

Figure 16-9. Close interpersonal relationships, such
as the marriage of sex researchers Virginia Johnson and
William Masters, are probably based on both similarity
and need complementarity. (United Press International
Photo.)

encountered one another on a once-in-a-
lifetime basis. They cannot reveal the conditions that lead to lasting relationships. Social
scientists Alan Kerckhoff and Keith Davis
studied couples at Duke University to come to
an understanding of how long-term relationships between men and women evolve.
Kerckhoff and Davis believe that people proceed through successive filters during courtship. Initially, factors such as proximity and
similar social background seem to thrust certain people together, making it more likely
that they will get to know and like one another. Once people have begun to interact, similarity of opinions, beliefs, values, attitudes,
and interests becomes more important. Finally, there is a third filter—need complementarity. When people discover that they are
similar and that they also gratify one another's needs, they begin to contemplate marriage. There is quite a bit of support for this
theory. For example, Kerckhoff and Davis
have found that dating couples whose values
are similar are more likely to progress in their
relationship than couples whose values are
dissimilar. They have also demonstrated that
a test which measures need complementarity
predicts which couples stay together for the
longest time (55)

Summary: The Company of Two: Who Is Attracted to Whom? And Why?

1. Laboratory research shows that people are attracted to people who are moderately competent, physically attractive, nearby, and similar in attitudes, values, beliefs.

2. Long-term male-female relationships may pass through successive filters. First proximity and similar social backgrounds may be important, then similarity in attitudes and values. Finally, need complementarity may determine whether or not the relationship persists.

STUDY GUIDE 16

Key Terms. social psychology, attitude, stereotype, racial prejudice, racial discrimination, higher-order respondent conditioning, authoritarian personality, projection, displaced aggression, peer group, social norms, status, cognitive dissonance, conformity, compliance, internal acceptance, independence, informational conformity, normative conformity, obedience, complementarity.

Important Research. anxiety and affiliation (Schachter), values and prejudice (Stein, Pilliavin, and Smith), authoritarian personalities (Adorno), peer-group influences on attitudes (Newcomb), competition and hostility (Sherif), frustration and prejudice at a camp, information and attitude change (Rokeach), social norms and prejudice (Deutsch and Collins), reduced prejudice after equal-status contact (James), reduced prejudice after cooperation to achieve a mutual goal (Sherif), reduced prejudice after close personal contact (Deutsch and Collins), reduced prejudice after a combination of factors (Cook), conformity to a group (Asch), personality characteristics of conformers (Crutchfield), the consistency of conformity, obedience (Milgram), predictors of interpersonal attraction (Walster), competence and attraction (Aronson, Willerman, and Floyd), liking people who like you (Aronson and Linder), physical distance and attraction (Festinger, Schachter, and Back), similarity and attraction (Byrne), long-term relationships (Kerckhoff and Davis).

Basic Ideas. cognitive dissonance (Festinger), reasons for conformity (Kelley).

Self-Quiz

1. In a classic study of anxiety and affiliation Stanley Schachter found that [**a**] the threat of enduring intense pain appeared to make subjects less talkative than the threat of enduring mild pain; [**b**] the threat of enduring mild pain appeared to make subjects slightly more sociable than the threat of enduring intense pain; [**c**] the threat of enduring intense pain appeared to cause subjects to prefer being near others to being alone; the threat of enduring mild pain did not have this effect; [**d**] affiliation and anxiety are unrelated.

2. Which is *not* characteristic of an attitude? [**a**] reflects a value judgment; [**b**] is directly observable; [**c**] guides thoughts, feelings, and behavior; [**d**] is relatively permanent and enduring.

3. Stein, Piliavin, and Smith found that except in matters of dating and marriage, teenagers felt most friendly toward people [**a**] of the same sex; [**b**] of the same race; [**c**] of the same age; [**d**] with similar values.

4. Authoritarian personalities are characterized by awe of authority, strong prejudices, [**a**] low ego strength, and poor self-control; [**b**] rigid, conventional beliefs, and intolerance of weakness; [**c**] little will power, and low frustration tolerance; [**d**] poor self-images, and insecurity.

5. Sherif and his colleagues created hostility at a boys' camp by dividing the campers into two groups and [**a**] allowing nature to take its course; [**b**] spreading false rumors; [**c**] engaging the boys in wrestling and other aggressive activities; [**d**] arranging baseball tournaments and other competitive activities.

6. In their studies of integrated and segregated housing projects, Deutsch and Collins found *least* favorable attitudes toward members of another race when [**a**] blacks and whites lived in separate buildings; [**b**] blacks and whites had no choice of where to live; [**c**] blacks and whites lived in the same buildings; [d] housing authorities arranged activities to encourage integration.

7. _____ was not mentioned in the text as a factor that encourages favorable racial attitudes. [a] equal-status contact; [b] close personal contact; [c] cooperation to achieve a mutual goal; [d] similar trials and tribulations.

8. According to cognitive-dissonance theory, conflicts between cognitions (beliefs, attitudes, etc.) result in discomfort and usually in [a] an increased use of defense mechanisms; [b] changing one of the cognitions or seeking new information; [c] avoiding both conflicting cognitions; [d] behavior change.

9. Conformity merely to gain a reinforcement or avoid a punishment is called _____; whereas conformity to win group support or avoid group rejection is called _____ conformity. [a] compliance, normative; [b] internal acceptance, compliant; [c] informational conformity, normative; [d] compliance, informational.

10. People are *most* likely to conform to a group's opinion when they [a] have very high status in the group; [b] have very low status in the group; [c] perceive the group's task as difficult and ambiguous; [d] perceive the other members of the group as less competent than themselves.

11. After studying obedience in the laboratory, Milgram concluded that [a] most people assume that legitimate authorities must be obeyed—regardless of their requests; [b] most people are basically sadistic; [c] most people will do anything they are ordered to do as long as a powerful institution seems to be supporting the order; [d] only people with authoritarian personalities tend to obey arbitrary orders.

12. All the following *except* _____ *decreased* obedience in Milgram's studies: [a] having the orders delivered by phone instead of in person; [b] conducting the study in a rundown commercial building instead of in a university laboratory; [c] separating the victim from the subject by putting him in another room; [d] seeing others refuse to obey.

13. Walster found that _____ best predicted the success of a blind date. [a] physical attractiveness; [b] intelligence; [c] similar interests; [d] complementary personalities and needs.

14. Aronson and Lindner found that their subjects rated their liking for a confederate highest when the confederate appeared to _____ them in the beginning and _____ them as their acquaintance continued. [a] like, still like; [b] dislike, still dislike; [c] dislike, like; [d] like, dislike.

15. Kerckhoff and Davis believe that people proceed through which three "filters" (in order) during courtship? [a] Proximity, similarity, mutual regard; [b] proximity and similar social backgrounds, similarity, need complementarity; [c] proximity, mutual regard, similarity; [d] attitudinal similarity, proximity, need complementarity.

Questions to Consider

1. People are considered social animals. Why do adults need one another? Consider the following possibilities: for safety and protection, to divide the labor of daily life, to reduce emotional distresses, to share experiences, to love and be loved, for stimulation, for reproduction, to provide information, to increase self-esteem. Can you think of other reasons? How can this issue be studied?

2. Analyze one of your own attitudes in terms of the components described on page 459. How did you form this attitude? Has it changed?

3. Design a study to investigate the current stereotypes held by people in your community—of women, college students, construction workers, politicians, the elderly, and various ethnic and racial minority groups.

4. Observe how the media (particularly TV and films) represent black people. How does the new media stereotype of blacks differ from the old one?

5. Consider a prejudice of your own. How did you acquire it? Were the factors described on pages 462–466 involved? Do your expectations influence your interactions with the object of your prejudice? Explain.

6. Based on research in this chapter, design procedures to integrate members of a minority group into a second-grade classroom. You might later compare your ideas to those of Elliot Aronson in "Busing and racial tension: The jigsaw route to learning and liking," *Psychology Today*, February 1975, 8, 43–50.

7. Think of some personal examples of cognitive dissonance. How did you reduce the dissonance?

8. Give personal examples of the four types of conformity.

9. Do today's young adults conform more than, less than, or the same amount as their parents to social conventions? How could you design a study to answer this question? How would you define conformity? In what situations would you measure conformity? How?

10. What are the implications of Milgram's research for politics? the military? schools? child-rearing practices?

11. Consider your friends in light of the research on interpersonal attraction. Are the results of the studies described on pages 478–481 consistent with your own experiences? What additional factors might influence the persistence of a long-term, intimate interpersonal relationship?

Project 16: Does Similarity Remain Important in Interpersonal Relationships?

Folklore, psychological research, and the modern computer-dating business all subscribe to the belief that similarity is important for initial interpersonal attraction. Does similarity remain important? That is, are similar people more likely than nonsimilar people to continue to like one another? In this project you will be investigating this question indirectly by measuring similarity and liking between yourself and your friends—to see if they are related.

Method. Find six cooperative subjects, people whom you have known at least a year. (Include people you don't like, some you like very much, and some in between.) Your subjects must be willing to fill in questionnaires describing their interests, attitudes, likes, dislikes, and values; they must not mind your seeing their responses. Tell your subjects that you are studying their attitudes and perceptions for a psychology project. You may want to explain the project in full after your data have been collected.

Before you test your subjects, make seven copies of the Opinion Survey in Figure 2. Fill in one survey by yourself. Then answer the questions on the Liking Scale (see Figure 1) for subject 1. Take a ruled sheet of paper and number the lines from 1 to 9. Read the statements on the Liking Scale and mentally substitute the first subject's name for the blank in each statement and write the number from 1 to 9 that corresponds most closely to your feelings about that subject. Note that an answer of 1 means that you disagree completely with the statement; an answer of 5 means that you agree to some extent; an answer of 9 means that you agree completely. The numbers in between represent intermediate opinions: 7, for example, indicates that you are midway between agreeing to some extent and agreeing completely. Fill in separate scales for each subject in turn.

You are ready now to test your subjects. You may test them individually or in a group. Have each subject sit at a table in a quiet setting that is free from distractions. Pass out copies of the Opinion Survey. Instruct your subjects to write their names on their questionnaires and answer the questions by checking "yes" or "no." If they lean toward "yes," encourage them to check "yes"; if they lean toward "no," encourage them to check "no." If they do not lean one way or the other, they should check "don't know."

Results. You will be computing scores for each subject on liking and similarity. To arrive at a liking score, add the numbers that you circled for each of the nine items on the Liking Scale for subject 1. The total is your liking score for subject 1. Repeat the procedure for each subject. To obtain a similarity score, put subject 1's responses to the Opinion Survey next to your own. Give one point each time they agree on a particular response (yes, no, or don't know). The total number of responses in agreement constitutes the similarity score between you and subject 1. Calculate a similarity score between yourself and each subject.

Discussion. Consider the following questions.

1. Did people with higher liking scores have higher similarity scores? If yes, how can your results be explained? Try to think of several explanations. How could you test these explanations?

2. If you did not find a relationship between similarity and liking, speculate on possible reasons. Consider whether your sample was too small? Were your friends too homogeneous (all relatively similar or all relatively high on the liking scale)? What other factors besides similarity probably influenced the liking scale scores?

3. If you found that low similarity scores were associated with high liking scores, how might you explain your findings? How could you test this hypothesis?

4. Did you see any problems in measuring liking by the Liking Scale? Explain. Can you think of any other ways to measure liking?

5. Are there important aspects of similarity that were not tapped by the questionnaire? Explain. Can you think of other ways to measure similarity?

6. Think of another way to study the question, does similarity remain important in interpersonal relationships?

FIGURE 1: LIKING SCALE

1. I think that _____ is unusually well-adjusted.

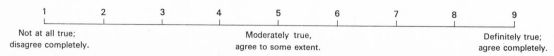

| 1 | 2 | 3 | 4 | 5 | 6 | 7 | 8 | 9 |

Not at all true; disagree completely.   Moderately true, agree to some extent.   Definitely true; agree completely.

2. I would highly recommend _____ for a responsible job.

```
 1        2        3        4        5        6        7        8        9
 └─┴────────┴────────┴────────┴────────┴────────┴────────┴────────┴────────┘
Not at all true;              Moderately true,                Definitely true;
disagree completely.          agree to some extent.           agree completely.
```

3. In my opinion, _____ is an exceptionally mature person.

```
 1        2        3        4        5        6        7        8        9
 └─┴────────┴────────┴────────┴────────┴────────┴────────┴────────┴────────┘
Not at all true;              Moderately true,                Definitely true;
disagree completely.          agree to some extent.           agree completely.
```

4. I have great confidence in _____'s good judgment.

```
 1        2        3        4        5        6        7        8        9
 └─┴────────┴────────┴────────┴────────┴────────┴────────┴────────┴────────┘
Not at all true;              Moderately true,                Definitely true;
disagree completely.          agree to some extent.           agree completely.
```

5. Most people would react favorably to _____ after a brief acquaintance.

```
 1        2        3        4        5        6        7        8        9
 └─┴────────┴────────┴────────┴────────┴────────┴────────┴────────┴────────┘
Not at all true;              Moderately true,                Definitely true;
disagree completely.          agree to some extent.           agree completely.
```

6. I think that _____ is one of those people who quickly wins respect.

```
 1        2        3        4        5        6        7        8        9
 └─┴────────┴────────┴────────┴────────┴────────┴────────┴────────┴────────┘
Not at all true;              Moderately true,                Definitely true;
disagree completely.          agree to some extent.           agree completely.
```

7. _____ is one of the most likable people I know.

```
 1        2        3        4        5        6        7        8        9
 └─┴────────┴────────┴────────┴────────┴────────┴────────┴────────┴────────┘
Not at all true;              Moderately true,                Definitely true;
disagree completely.          agree to some extent.           agree completely.
```

8. _____ is the sort of person whom I myself would like to be.

```
 1        2        3        4        5        6        7        8        9
 └─┴────────┴────────┴────────┴────────┴────────┴────────┴────────┴────────┘
Not at all true;              Moderately true,                Definitely true;
disagree completely.          agree to some extent.           agree completely.
```

9. It seems to me that it is very easy for _____ to gain admiration.

```
 1        2        3        4        5        6        7        8        9
 └─┴────────┴────────┴────────┴────────┴────────┴────────┴────────┴────────┘
Not at all true;              Moderately true,                Definitely true;
disagree completely.          agree to some extent.           agree completely.
```

SOURCE: Z. Rubin, *Liking and loving: An invitation to social psychology.* New York: Holt, Rinehart & Winston, Inc., 1973. (brief version). p. 216.

FIGURE 2: OPINION SURVEY

	Yes	No	Don't Know
1. Do you believe that people should be able to say precisely what they are thinking to intimate friends?			
2. Do you give and receive affection easily?			
3. Do you prefer being alone to being with groups of people?			
4. Do you like to engage in intellectual activities?			
5. Do you believe that stealing can ever be justified?			
6. Do you find yourself happy a great deal of the time?			
7. Do you believe that there are a lot of subjects that should not be discussed socially?			
8. Do you enjoy dirty jokes or stories?			
9. Do you believe that it's important to attend religious services regularly?			
10. Do you prefer socializing with people who talk a lot rather than people who are frequently silent?			
11. Is romance important for your continued happiness?			
12. Do you favor having women run for public offices and hold professional jobs?			
13. Do you prefer to be "on the go" rather than to stay at home?			
14. Do you believe that married couples should try to save a sizeable portion of their income for the future?			
15. Are you more comfortable when people observe social conventions and show proper etiquette than when they don't?			
16. Do you believe that people should remain close to their immediate families even after they marry?			
17. Do you believe that the man should be the dominant partner in a marriage?			
18. Is it important to you to share your hobbies with your close friends?			
19. Do you like children a great deal?			
20. Do you believe that neat (tidy) surroundings are important?			

Suggested Readings

1. Middlebrook, P. N. *Social psychology and modern life.* New York: Alfred A. Knopf, Inc., 1974. A recent social-psychology textbook emphasizing relevant social issues such as aggression, altruism, prejudice, and sensitivity groups.
2. Aronson, E. *The social animal.* San Francisco: W. H. Freeman and Company, 1972 (paperback). A leading social psychologist informally discusses conformity, mass communication, cognitive dissonance, and other topics.
3. Bem, D. *Beliefs, attitudes and human affairs.* Belmont, Calif.: Brooks/Cole Publishing Company, 1970 (paperback). A discussion of the formation of attitudes and beliefs and their effects on behavior.
4. Zimbardo, P. G., & E. Ebbeson. *Influencing attitudes and changing behavior.* Reading, Mass.: Addison-Wesley Press, Inc., 1969 (paperback). Examines the subject of attitude change.
5. Jones, J. M. *Prejudice and racism.* Reading, Mass.: Addison-Wesley Press, Inc., 1972 (paperback). Concise but comprehensive view of these issues. Integrates history, sociology, and psychology.
6. Hall, M. "A conversation with Kenneth B. Clark." *Psychology Today,* June 1968, 2, 19–25. An interview with an eminent black psychologist on some of the problems that confront black people today.
7. The following books (all in paperback) provide insight into the predicament of being a black American: Kozol, J. *Death at an early age.* New York: Bantam Books, Inc., 1968; Little, M. *The autobiography of Malcolm X.* New York: Grove Press, Inc., 1964; Cleaver, E. *Soul on ice.* New York: McGraw-Hill Book Company, 1968.
8. Milgram, S. *Obedience to authority.* New York: Harper & Row, Publishers, Incorporated, 1974. Describes

Milgram's entire research program on obedience, offers a theoretical explanation of the findings, and defends his ethics and the generalizability of the studies.

9. Rubin, Z. *Liking and loving: An invitation to social psychology.* New York: Holt, Rinehart and Winston, Inc., 1973 (paperback). A very readable survey of the research on friendship, mate selection, and inter-group relationships. Rubin looks for the principles behind liking and loving.

Answer Key

SELF-QUIZ

1. c 2. b 3. d 4. b 5. d 6. a 7. d 8. b 9. a
10. c 11. a 12. c 13. a 14. c 15. b

PSYCHOLOGY AND SOCIAL ISSUES

IN THIS CHAPTER
We examine several attempts to apply psychology to the promotion of human welfare in cities, work settings, and prisons. After reading this chapter, you should be able to do the following:

1. Discuss the effects of noise and crowding
2. Discuss the concept of cognitive and sensory overload, describe how people seem to adapt to it, and explain its effects
3. Describe the factors which are associated with job satisfaction and three strategies which are currently being used to increase job satisfaction
4. Describe four functions of prisons and discuss how well each function is served
5. Describe seven aspects of prison life which appear to lead to dehumanization
6. Discuss the characteristics of treatment programs which show promise for rehabilitating criminals and decreasing crime

How can psychology be applied to the promotion of human welfare? In 1969 George Miller, who was then the president of the American Psychological Association, discussed this issue in his presidential address:

The most urgent problems of our world today are the problems we have made for ourselves. They have not been caused by some heedless or malicious inanimate Nature, nor have they been imposed on us as punishment by the will of God. They are human problems whose solutions will require us to change our behavior and our social institutions.

As a science directly concerned with behavioral and social processes, psychology might be expected to provide intellectual leadership in the search for new and better personal and social arrangements. . . .

This is the social challenge that psychologists face. In the years immediately ahead we must not only extend and deepen our understanding of mental and behavioral phenomena, but we must somehow incorporate our hard-won knowledge more effectively into the vast social changes that we all know are coming. [Miller goes on to explain how psychologists should go about contributing to human welfare.]

[T]he secrets of our trade need not be reserved for highly trained specialists. Psychological facts should be passed out freely to all who need and can use them. . . .

Our responsibility is less to assume the role of experts and try to apply psychology ourselves than to give it away to the people who really need it—and that includes everybody. . . .

[I]n the beginning we must try to diagnose and solve the problems people think they have, not the problems we experts think they ought to have, and we must learn to understand those problems in the social and institutional contexts that define them. With this approach we might do something practical for nurses, policemen, prison guards, salesmen—for people in many different walks of life. That, I believe, is what we should mean when we talk about applying psychology to the promotion of human welfare [1].

What roles do psychologists currently play in promoting human welfare? Three major roles are these:

1. Identifying and clarifying existing social and psychological problems
2. Working out potential solutions—programs, procedures, and training methods
3. Evaluating these potential solutions and specifying their costs and benefits through careful research

In this chapter we are concerned with applied psychology. In 1917 when the *Journal of Applied Psychology* was founded, the term *applied psychology* was limited to the application of psychological principles to business and industry. In recent years the term has been broadened and now includes the use of psychology in communities, clinics, counseling centers, mental hospitals, schools, prisons, military institutions, business, industry, consumer affairs, population control, ecology, space travel, and so on. Roughly two-thirds of contemporary psychologists can be considered applied psychologists.

We look first at how psychology can be applied to urban problems.

PSYCHOLOGY AND URBAN PROBLEMS

Just two things of which you must beware;
Don't drink the water and don't breathe the air [2].

These words come from a song describing American cities. Most people would argue that American cities have many more unpleasant aspects. Psychologists would certainly add noise, crowded living conditions, and excessive sensory and cognitive stimulation to the list. In this section we examine the efforts of psychologists to understand the effects of noise, crowded conditions, and overwhelming cognitive and sensory stimulation.

URBANMAN

Anti-power failure headlamp for use in subway tunnels, unlighted streets, etc.

Air-pollution mask

Snowshoes in event of unpredicted heavy snowfall

Scaling rope for lowering self from office buildings during power shutdown

Identification

Emergency drought supply

Briefcase containing emergency cash for sudden tax hikes, fare and toll increases. Also, midtown travel permit, draft card

Change-maker for exact change for buses, pay toilets, tipping waiters, bartenders, etc.

Anti-mugger chain for briefcase

Belt containing skate key and spare skate wheels

Books to read during next newspaper strike and tutoring children during school strike

Pistol, holster, and ammunition for citizen's arrest, if witness to a crime

Aids for getting through demonstrations

Travel aids during transit shutdown

Curb feelers

Figure 17-1. "Urbanman." (Helmer and Eddington, 1973.)

Noise

Cities are noisy places. The honking, screeching, roaring, and rumbling of an almost continual stream of traffic is one major source of noise. Ingenious machines designed to do people's work or at least lighten the burden are another. Even our entertainment is noisy. In fact, rock music is one of the loudest sounds in people's noisy lives. What does noise do to people?

Two psychologists, David Glass of the Uni-

versity of Texas at Austin and Jerome Singer of the State University of New York at Stony Brook, and their associates set out to answer this question. In one investigation they studied forty-eight undergraduate women. Some of them listened to a tape recording of superimposed sounds: a Spanish voice, an Armenian voice, a typewriter, a desk calculator, and a mimeograph machine. Some students heard the cacophony (discordant noise) at high volume; others at low volume. For some the experience occurred at regular (predictable) intervals; for others at random (unpredictable) intervals. After listening to the tape, the subjects were asked to work paper-and-pencil tasks—some of which were insoluble. A third group of subjects, spared the noisy experience altogether, were also asked to work the tasks. What happened? Subjects who had been exposed to any noise at all were less persistent on the insoluble tasks than those who had not been. Moreover, random noise (even when it was soft) decreased people's persistence more than regular noise. In subsequent studies male students and city dwelling residents of both sexes were observed to respond in the same way. Later experiments have shown that when people feel that they can control noise, its aversive effects are reduced. Glass and Singer suggest that unpredictable noise which cannot be controlled leads to a sense of helplessness which decreases people's ability to tolerate frustration and to perform efficiently on complex cognitive tasks (3).

Does noise produce a similar effect in real life? To find out, Glass, Singer, and an associate, Sheldon Cohen, studied elementary school children living in four Manhattan apartment buildings which bordered a heavily traveled highway. They measured noise levels throughout the dwellings and found that the sound was loudest on the first few floors and became increasingly less intense on higher floors. Next the investigators measured the children's reading achievement and their ability to discriminate between linguistic sounds (to distinguish between similar-sounding taped words such as cope and coke). They found that children who had lived in a noisy apartment building a short period of time performed significantly better than those who had lived there four or more years. Moreover, children on upper floors (low-noise environment) scored consistently higher on tests of reading achievement and auditory discrimination than children on lower floors (high-noise environment). These results support the hypothesis that prolonged exposure to intense, unpredictable, and un-controllable noise has measurable adverse effects on cognitive achievement (4). The effects of noise in real life may be due to actual damage to the ear,[1] masking of important auditory information, disrupted learning, frustration, or to some combination of these factors.

Crowding

While observing a crowded baboon colony at the London Zoo, Sally Zuckerman, a London biologist, witnessed a great deal of brutality and violence. The males were so aggressive that no infants survived. Even mature females were sometimes attacked and in some cases literally torn to pieces (6). This is not typical baboon behavior. On the contrary, baboons in Africa are relatively peaceful

beasts who live in orderly and well-organized groups and aggress primarily against preda-tors and intruders (7). Was the brutality the result of crowding? Apparently it was. Ethol-ogists observe similar consequences when other animal species live under crowded con-ditions.

In one important experiment which sup-ports this hypothesis, John Calhoun, a psy-chologist at the National Institute of Mental Health in Bethesda, put domestic white Nor-way rats in a four-chambered cage. From previous studies he knew that they'd split up into groups of ten to twelve, so the cage would hold some forty-eight rats comfort-ably. Calhoun let his rats reproduce until they numbered eighty. He kept them all amply supplied with food, water, and nesting mater-ials, making certain that they lacked nothing except space. What happened? The two most dominant males took charge of the two end pens, gathered harems of eight to ten fe-males, and flourished. This maneuver forced the remaining rats into the middle two pens where severe crowding occurred. Some ani-mals became withdrawn. Many others en-gaged in senseless and unprovoked fighting and in abnormal sexual behavior (homo-sexuality, bisexuality, and hypersexuality). The females neglected their ordinary home-making routines—specifically infant care and nest building. Rats were also affected physi-cally by the crowded conditions. Miscarriages increased significantly, as did premature deaths from stress-related diseases. Appar-ently, the general adaptation syndrome (see Chapter 11) had been triggered by the stress of crowding (8).

How does crowding affect people? There are two ways to study the issue, neither of them completely satisfactory. First, psycholo-gists can compare people who live under crowded conditions to people who live under less crowded conditions on behavioral varia-bles such as adult crime rate, mental hospital

[1]A number of audiological studies show that a high-frequency hearing impairment is more common in older than in younger children. Several investigators believe that this deficit results because older children deliberate-ly surround themselves with a high-intensity sound envi-ronment—rock music. One researcher, David Lipscomb, decided to see how rock music actually affects the ear. He subjected guinea pigs to eighty-eight hours of music at an intensity level approximating that which is frequently measured at rock concerts. One ear of each guinea pig was protected by a plug. Lipscomb found widespread damage in the cochlear cells of the unprotected ear (5).

admissions, and so on. When psychologists do this, they find that density (number of people per unit of space) is positively correlated with crime and other measures of social, physical, and mental breakdown (9,10). But high density is also consistently associated with poverty, lack of education, malnutrition, and other conditions known to be highly related to social, physical, and mental problems; so we don't know if density *per se* is the culprit.

A second approach is the laboratory experiment. Jonathan Freedman, a Columbia University social psychologist, has done many studies of crowding in the laboratory. Typically, he takes volunteer adults and places varying numbers of them (four to nine) in large (180 square feet) and small (25 square feet) rooms so that some groups are very crowded and others are not crowded at all. People sit on fairly comfortable chairs in an air-conditioned room working on various problem-solving tasks generally for four hours at a time. Sometimes they return the next day for a second four-hour stint. Consequently, physical discomfort, restriction of movement, lack of air, offensive odors, and high temperatures—the ordinary accompaniments of crowding in real life—are all minimized. Under these circumstances density does not affect task performance (11). However, when the situation changes slightly and subjects have to interact with one another to solve problems, density affects their interpersonal relationships. Curiously, men and women tend to respond to crowding under these circumstances in distinctly different ways. In general, men become more competitive, negative, suspicious, and aggressive; women become more positive, intimate, friendly, and cooperative (12).

It is important to note that Freedman's laboratory situation is very different from real-life crowding. In the laboratory all subjects have their own approximately equal territory, their own resources, a highly struc-

tured task, and a relatively short time-limited exposure to crowding. Moreover, the interactions in the laboratory occur between strangers. Animal studies suggest that different consequences would result if there were less structure or more congestion, noise, heat, or competition for the available resources (13).

Overload

Cities tend to be both noisy and crowded. We can conceptualize noise as *too much* auditory stimulation, crowding as *too much* interpersonal contact. Large cities also present too much cognitive and sensory data. There is so much information that people cannot process it adequately. Psychologist Stanley Milgram believes that people in cities eventually adapt to continual *sensory and cognitive overload* by various interpersonal strategies:

1. They give little time to each interpersonal encounter.
2. They allow only superficial interpersonal contact. They filter out involvements which demand an emotional investment.
3. They disregard low-priority inputs (incoming information). For example, since they barely have the time or energy for important matters, they can hardly be expected to take time to help a strange woman stranded on the highway with a flat tire or a drunk lying on the sidewalk.
4. They block off their receptivity by looking cold and unfriendly and by such tactics as not listing their phone numbers.
5. They create special institutions, such as charities and welfare, to further reduce the number of inputs that they personally have to handle (14).

Sensory and cognitive overload results in an impersonal world where the great majority of people—even in one small geographical location—do not know one another and each person tends to feel anonymous (unknown).

Studies show that when people feel anonymous, they behave differently than when they feel like individuals. Philip Zimbardo, a Stanford University social psychologist, is responsible for a great deal of the research on this topic. In one of his laboratory studies female students were asked to administer twenty electric shocks to two female victims. Before the shocking trials began, the subjects—in groups of four—listened to a taped interview with each victim. One was "obnoxious, self-centered, conceited, and critical"; the other was "nice, accepting, altruistic, and sweet." The subjects in one condition (the anonymous condition) wore baggy laboratory coats and face-covering hoods and sat in semidarkness. The subjects in the second condition (the individuated condition) saw each others' faces, wore name tags, called each other by name, and, in general, were made to feel like individuals. After the group interactions each subject individually delivered shocks to two victims (confederates of the experimenter trained to convey pain). Girls in the anonymous condition behaved more aggressively (gave longer shocks) than those in the individuated condition, as you can see in Figure 17-3. Moreover, the anonymous subjects did

not seem to be inhibited by either social conventions or perceptions of their victim's virtue. Zimbardo concluded that when people feel anonymous, they orient toward the here-and-now and they tend to act for self-gratification without concern for others (15).

Sensory and cognitive overload may also account for a sense, or absence, of social responsibility. In her book *The Death and Life of Great American Cities*, Jane Jacobs defines the concept of *social* or *public responsibility* like this:

In real life, only from the ordinary adults of the city sidewalks do children learn—if they learn it at all—the first fundamental of successful city life: People must take a modicum of public responsibility for each other even if they have no ties to each other. This is a lesson nobody learns by being told. It is learned from the experience of *having other people without ties of kinship or close friendship or formal responsibility to you* take a modicum of public responsibility for you. When Mr. Lacey, the locksmith, bawls out one of my sons for running into the street, and then later reports the transgression to my husband as he passes the locksmith shop, my son gets more than an overt lesson in safety and obedience. He

Figure 17-2. In Zimbardo's experiment, subjects in the anonymous condition wore hoods and sat in semidarkness. (Philip G. Zimbardo.)

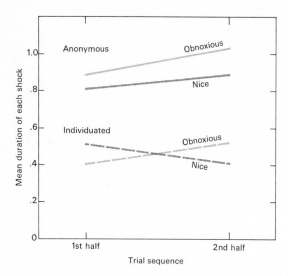

Figure 17-3. The effects of anonymity on aggression as measured by shock duration. (After Zimbardo, 1969.)

also gets, indirectly, the lesson that Mr. Lacey, with whom we have no ties other than street propinquity, feels responsible for him to a degree. . . . [T]he project children who squirt water into house windows and on passers-by, and go unrebuked because they are anonymous children in anonymous grounds [learn a different lesson] [16].

Do people living in cities today feel socially responsible for one another? If we operationally define social responsibility as willingness to intervene in an emergency, we can answer the question by examining studies of bystander intervention in crises (see Chapter 2). In one study conducted in 1969 four investigators—two men and two women—individually rang doorbells, explained that they had misplaced the address of a nearby friend, and asked the resident if they could use the phone. Each investigator made one hundred requests for entry in mid-town Manhattan middle-income housing projects and sixty such requests in nearby towns. As Table 17-1 shows, the social scientists were invited in to make their phone calls more than twice as frequently in towns as in cities. The qualita-

tive observations agreed: In general, town dwellers appeared friendlier and less suspicious than city dwellers. The dangers of city life are at least partially responsible for these findings. Fear probably explains why some 75 percent of Manhattan residents received the investigator's message through a closed door (17).

More recently Milgram and his graduate students used a "less threatening" test of this hypothesis. A nine-year-old child pretended to be lost and asked passersby to help him call home. Significantly more people refused the child's request in cities than in towns (18). Both these studies suggest that people in cities take less responsibility for fellow human beings than people in towns. Why? As we mentioned before, city people adjust to cognitive and sensory overload by social habits which minimize interpersonal contact. In addition, because city people tend to be strangers to one another and because what is strange is frequently fearful, city people may also tend to fear one another to a greater degree than town people do.

If city people feel less responsible for one another than town dwellers do, it is hardly surprising that they also feel less responsible for one another's property. This is one reason we see higher rates of vandalism in cities. To demonstrate this phenomenon Scott Fra-

TABLE 17-1. SUCCESSFUL REQUESTS FOR ENTRY IN BIG CITIES AND SMALL TOWNS

	Percent Entries	
Investigator	**City** (**n** = 100)	**Small Town** (**n** = 60)
Male		
1	16	40
2	12	60
Female		
1	40	87
2	40	100

Source: S. Milgram. The experience of living in cities: A psychological analysis. *Science*, March 13, 1970, 167, 1463.

Figure 17-4. Ten minutes after this car was abandoned in New York City, vandals began to strip it, then to destroy it. In three days, it was a total wreck. (Philip G. Zimbardo.)

ser and Philip Zimbardo abandoned cars near the Bronx campus of New York University in New York City and near Stanford University in Palo Alto, California. The psychologists left the cars without license plates and with their hoods propped up. Observers at nearby buildings filmed all the people who came into contact with the cars. In New York City the action was lively. Ten minutes after the car was abandoned, the first vandals arrived on the scene. A man, a woman, and a young boy—apparently a family—were the first to act. They took the battery; then they used a hacksaw to cut out the radiator. After this incident, a steady stream of people continued stripping the car of all its removable parts. Then random destruction began. As people walked by, they broke windows or lights, dented the hood, the roof, or the door, or slashed the tires. In three days there were twenty-three attacks. (Each family or group counted as one.) After seventy-two hours the New York car had been reduced to "a battered hulk of twisted metal, broken glass, torn tires, [and] ripped out seats." Incidentally, much of the vandalism occurred in broad daylight and was executed by well-dressed, clean-cut adults. The scene in Palo Alto served as a striking contrast. In seven days' time no one molested the car. One passerby lowered the hood to prevent the motor from getting wet when it began raining (19).

Summary: Psychology and Urban Problems

1. Psychologists have only begun to identify the psychological aspects of many city problems. Current information is both incomplete and highly tentative.
2. Cities are noisy. When noise is unpredictable and uncontrollable in the laboratory, it decreases people's ability to tolerate frustration and disrupts their cognitive performance. When children are exposed to intense, unpredictable, uncontrollable noise for long periods of time, they may emerge with lasting cognitive deficits.
3. Cities are crowded. Crowding leads to devastating behavioral consequences in certain animals, including aggression, withdrawal, abnormal sexual behavior, ne-

glect of basic routines, and physiological damage. Crowded conditions are frequently associated with crime and other forms of social, physical, and mental breakdown in people. Studies of crowding in the laboratory find that density *per se* does not affect task performance, but when people have to interact, high density does affect their interpersonal relationships: When crowded, men tend to become more negative, suspicious, competitive, and aggressive; women tend to become more positive, intimate, friendly, and cooperative. Much research still needs to be done to understand the effects of crowding under more realistic circumstances.

4. Cities tend to overload human information processing capabilities. People probably adapt by interpersonal strategies which reduce their contacts with other people. Anonymity and a low level of social responsibility appear to be the result. Both phenomena lead to a disregard for people and property.

We turn now to a second important aspect of contemporary life, a person's work.

PSYCHOLOGY AND WORK

As of April 1973, some 85 million Americans were working full time. On the average a full-time worker spends some 76,000 hours (forty hours a week forty-eight to fifty weeks a year for forty years) at work. Tragically, the majority of people find these hours unpleasant. Many feel that their abilities and skills are wasted. Many are bored—so bored that they stop off in a bar before and after work to tolerate the boredom. Some confront serious occupational dangers and health hazards. Many more labor under conditions of stress

and conflict. We begin by identifying the factors that make work satisfying.

What Factors Make Work Satisfying?

In the early 1970s the Institute for Social Research at the University of Michigan conducted a nationwide study of working conditions and job satisfaction. More than 1,500 people, representatives of those currently employed nationally, were extensively interviewed. In the course of the interview the workers were asked to rate various aspects of work in terms of their importance for job satisfaction (see Table 17-2). The results may be surprising to you if you think workers' satisfactions depend mostly on money. It should be noted that data from people who were either self-employed or working less than thirty-five hours per week were not included in the following analysis.

Of the 5 top-ranked work features, only one had to do with tangible economic benefits. And that one (good pay) was ranked number 5. Interesting work, enough help and equipment to get the job done, enough information to get the job done, and enough authority to do their jobs—all were very important to more workers than was good pay [20].

Friendly and helpful coworkers, opportunities to develop special abilities, job security, seeing the results of work done, and clearly defined responsibilities were rated sixth to tenth in importance. So many people rated interesting, fulfilling work and the resources to do the job well very important. Fewer people considered financial rewards and security important.

Many studies find a positive relationship between job status and job satisfaction. In one survey (see Table 17-3) only 16 percent of unskilled auto workers claimed that they would seek the same job again, where-

TABLE 17-2. IMPORTANCE OF VARIOUS WORKING CONDITIONS (Ordered according to the percentage responding "very important")

1. The work is interesting.
2. I receive enough help and equipment to get the job done.
3. I have enough information to get the job done.
4. I have enough authority to do my job.
5. The pay is good.
6. My coworkers are friendly and helpful.
7. I have an opportunity to develop my special abilities.
8. The job security is good.
9. I can see the results of my work.
10. My responsibilities are clearly defined.
11. My supervisor is competent.
12. I have enough time to get the job done.
13. I am given a chance to do the things I do best.
14. I am given a lot of freedom to decide how I do my work.
15. The hours are good.
16. My fringe benefits are good.
17. Travel to and from work is convenient.
18. I am given a lot of chances to make friends.
19. Physical surroundings are pleasant.
20. I am free from conflicting demands that other people make of me.
21. I can forget about my personal problems.
22. The problems I am asked to solve are hard enough.
23. I am not asked to do excessive amounts of work.

Adapted from *Survey of working conditions: Final report.* Survey Research Center, U. S. Department of Labor, Employment Standards Administration, U. S. Government Printing Office: Washington D.C., 1971, 55, 56.

as 93 percent of urban college professors expressed satisfaction with their vocational choices (21). Studies like this one support our earlier findings. Generally, jobs with high prestige offer variety and opportunities for creativity and independent achievement, factors which probably make them interesting and fulfilling.

Making Work More Satisfying

The research which we have examined so far suggests that if organizations and businesses want to increase their workers' satisfaction, they should stress changes that make work more interesting rather than those that merely increase material rewards and comforts.[2] (Because workers tend to be more productive when they are satisfied, most organizations and businesses are interested in making such changes.)

How can work be made more interesting and fulfilling? Psychologist Robert Kahn, director of the University of Michigan's Survey Research Center, believes that businesses should start by giving their workers greater flexibility in planning the content and scheduling of their jobs. Kahn has proposed an interesting plan which he calls the *work module.* The work module refers to a time-task unit: specifically, to the smallest amount of time which is meaningful economically and psychologically, which, Kahn assumes, is two hours. Accordingly, an eight-hour work day could be broken down into four modules. The employer and employee would work together on scheduling the modules. The system would offer freedom within the constraints dictated both by the job and the employee's skills. A stockman in a supermarket, in conference with his supervisor, might choose to spend two modules a day stamping prices, one module a day at the cash register, and a final module a day learning about inventory control. Moreover, the same man might work five modules on Thursday and leave early on Friday after three modules. Because the program is flexible, it could be easily reevaluated as the needs of the employ-

[2]Current psychological research indicates that pay systems and other extrinsic reinforcements may actually decrease the intrinsic reinforcement value of many tasks (the satisfaction which comes from simply engaging in the activity itself). Many studies show that when children are extrinsically reinforced (usually by tokens or prizes) for work which they formerly did for sheer enjoyment, they subsequently find the work less enjoyable and engage in it less frequently than previously once the rewards are removed (22).

TABLE 17-3. PROPORTIONS IN OCCUPATIONAL GROUPS WHO WOULD CHOOSE
SIMILAR WORK AGAIN

Professional and White-collar Occupations	Percent	Skilled Trades and Blue-collar Occupations	Percent
Urban university professors	93	Skilled printers	52
Mathematicians	91	Paper workers	42
Physicists	89	Skilled auto workers	41
Biologists	89	Skilled steelworkers	41
Chemists	86	Textile workers	31
Firm lawyers	85	Blue-collar workers	24
School superintendents	85	Unskilled steelworkers	21
Lawyers	83	Unskilled auto workers	16
Journalists (Washington correspondents)	82		
Church university professors	77		
Solo lawyers	75		
White-collar workers (nonprofessional)	43		

Occupation and Status. The higher the status of occupation, the more satisfied are persons
who engage in it. Table is based on study of 3,000 workers in sixteen industries, conducted
by the Roper organization; on Wilensky's study of Detroit workers and professionals; and
on a study of Massachusetts school superintendents by Neal Gross, Ward Mason, and W. A.
McEachern.

Source: R. L. Kahn. "The work module—A tonic for lunchpail lassitude." *Psychology Today*,
February 1973, p. 39.

ee or employer change. At the same time
the plan is economically feasible for the
employer (23).

Many big businesses are trying to increase
worker satisfaction by similar strategies. The
following excerpt, which comes from a book
by psychologists Herald Sheppard and Neal
Herrick, describes several current approaches; some start from scratch, others modify
existing practices.

Where have all the robots gone?

"In terms of starting from scratch—in other words, building a new plant
with some of the behavioral science concepts in mind—there are at least
seven plant planning efforts that can be cited: General Foods in Saratoga
and Topeka, Proctor and Gamble and Olin Mathison in Augusta,
Corning Glass and Polaroid in Massachusetts, and General Electric in
Illinois. . . .

"In terms of generalizations, one can note that these new plants
usually eliminate time clocks, have a minimum of rules, engage the
employees in goal setting, and stress communications and team building
[giving workers a role in decision making]. The important point,
however, is that these companies view these plants as *experiments in*

management, with the goal being the creation of a very special organizational climate, one characterized by openness and trust and a strived-for goal congruence between personal and company goals. . . .

[In the second broad category—making changes in existing practices—Sheppard and Herrick list three current approaches which companies are adopting:]

"One is job rotation. Polaroid started the Pathfinder Program in this area some while ago; Edwin Land, President, Chairman and Director of Research at Polaroid, talks about a worthwhile work life as a company goal for every employee. Under Polaroid's job rotation program, some factory people were given the option of moving to the job of laboratory technician. Job rotation was to be a way of life; one was to work half his time on his new exciting job and the other half on his old job, the one that was not so exciting. What was soon learned was that once the employees adapted to the new job, they didn't want to go back to the old job. Job rotation as a way of life didn't work out. Polaroid then moved to a career exposure plan where employees have the opportunity to be exposed to new jobs and when a moment of opportunity arises they can bid for the job. Another large consumer products company tried job rotation in a different way. On a particular packing line it was felt that the inspection job was the high status, interesting, fun job. Inspection which used to be done out in the laboratory was now made part of the packing line and employees rotated through the inspection job so that each employee spent two hours a day as an inspector and the rest of his time on other jobs. Management thought that each employee considered himself an inspector, and job satisfaction went up, productivity went up, and turnover and absenteeism went down. There are lots of interesting things that can be done in the job rotation area.

"The second approach I would like to mention is what I shall call the 'Texas Instruments Approach,' and, again, there is much top management support. Pat Haggerty, Chairman, talks about a worthwhile endeavor. He hopes all the employees in the company will become involved in their jobs. He thinks that if you have an alignment of company and personal goals, the company is in much better shape than if the goals get out of line. Texas Instruments defines a meaningful job as one in which the employee has planning and controlling responsibility in addition to the traditional 'do' part of the job. Vertical job enlargement is stressed at Texas Instruments, and there are a number of jobs, where, for instance, inspection and testing have become part of the job. These are control functions which the employee now has which, formerly, somebody else had. In addition, Texas Instruments has problem-solving–goal-setting sessions where the supervisor and the employees identify the problems of business, form task forces and make recommendations. Being involved in the process can, if it works well, make work a more meaningful experience.

"In contrast, the American Telephone and Telegraph approach

(Work Itself projects) does not employ, at least initially, employee participation; instead, the managers restructure jobs, trying to build in the Herzberg motivators which give employees the opportunity for challenge, recognition, achievement, and responsibility [we call this tactic 'job enrichment']. Managers implement the changes one by one as the employee demonstrates competence to handle the additional responsibilities.

"There are a number of firms that are using AT&T's model of making work more meaningful. One example, at Bankers Trust in New York, took place in the division handling the stock transfer operations. This job involved about 100 employee typists. It used to be their job as typists to type the new stock certificates, after which they went to a production typist to type the transfer sheets. Then there was a person called the 'preparation clerk' who punched the denomination of the stock certificates, dated and stamped the certificates, and a checker who proofread the sheets, checked for production debit and credit totals and then reviewed the certificates. There was a correction typist who corrected the errors.

"After the change, the functions were combined into one, a newly designed typist job. The typist drew the certificate, typed the transfer sheet, prepared the certificate, checked the work, made her own corrections, and, according to an article in the *Boston Globe,* the bank said they saved $300,000 in this one year trial of job enrichment. Among other things, they eliminated much of the quality review force, increased output, improved production quality, and improved job attitudes . . . [24]."

Figure 17-5. In this job-enrichment program at AT&T in Los Angeles, previously fragmented jobs have been expanded as much as possible to make them more interesting. (AT&T Co.)

Summary: Psychology and Work

1. The majority of workers report valuing interesting fulfilling work and sufficient resources to do the job well above other work conditions. As long as they are adequate, wages and security appear to be less important concerns.
2. Many businesses and industries are currently experimenting with programs designed to make work more satisfying. Some promising strategies include job rotation, involving workers in decision making, and job enrichment.

We focus now on a third contemporary social issue—prisons.

PSYCHOLOGY AND PRISONS

In 1973 some eight and one-half million felonies were reported by the Federal Bureau of Investigation. Violent crimes such as murder, rape, and aggravated assault had more than doubled since the early 1960s; so had property crimes (25). The numbers are even more oppressive when you consider that they represent only reported or detected crimes, a much smaller number than those that actually occur.

How do these grim statistics relate to psychology? Crime is a behavior which many psychologists are currently trying to understand. There are several important questions to consider: What factors shape criminal behavior? Who commits crimes? Who gets caught? What roles do police, legal, and judicial systems play in curtailing crime? How does prison affect the criminal's future behavior? In this section we will be concerned with the last question. It is important to note that psychopathic behavior (see Chapter 14) is only one kind of criminal behavior. Many criminals would not be characterized as psychopaths.

Prisons and Their Functions

The American prison system includes city, town, and county jails, reform schools, penal farms, work camps, and state and federal penitentiaries. Over the course of a single year it is estimated that two-and-a-half million Americans spend time in a jail of some kind (26). Some 97 percent of the prison population is male, and minority group members are disproportionately highly represented (27).

Society seems to expect prisons to serve four major functions: (1) to isolate criminals and thereby prevent harm to society, (2) to punish criminals—to make them sorry for what they did and to obtain revenge, (3) to reduce the likelihood of future crime, and (4) to rehabilitate criminals, improving their capacity to function productively in society (28).

Do prisons fulfill these goals? Prisons appear to fulfill the first two goals. Escapes from prison tend to be relatively rare, the reason they make headlines when they occur. Although the pain of imprisonment is impossible to measure, it is undoubtedly severe. Prisoners are deprived of liberty, autonomy, physical security, economic freedom, and heterosexual contact. Psychiatrist Karl Menninger describes the pains of prison life like this: The prisoner lives in a cage on display to every passer-by. The cage contains a toilet bowl, a shelf, a chair, a cot, or a double-decker bed. If the prisoner is lucky, the guards will let him/her out of the cage for meals and for periods of exercise (a euphemism, in many cases, for walking around in a paved enclosure). Some institutions encourage the prisoner to work in a prison industry, a mine, a quarry, or a farm. A small number offer education and job training programs. Run-of-the-mill prisoners live in filthy surroundings and do not receive palatable food. They are also deprived of genuine human relationships, sex, and meaningful work. In a typical prison, the prisoners gamble and take drugs; homosexual rape is commonplace; beatings, torture, and even murder are not unheard of. In short, the prison atmosphere is usually monotonous, brutal, and lonely (29). Although this description is harsh

Figure 17-6. "The prisoner lives in a cage..."
(Charles Gatewood.)

and undoubtedly unjust to some penal institutions, it applies to à great many.[3]

[3]It can be argued that imprisonment is only one penalty that society imposes upon criminals. One recent study of ex-offenders by Hugh Banks, a psychologist at New York University, Stephen Shestakofsky, an attorney at the Citizens Union, and George Carson, director of the Vocational Foundation, Inc., concluded:

History and tradition have worked to create a statutory scheme in this country that imposes a wide range of penalties, over and above direct criminal sanctions, on those convicted of having broken the law. These penalties, known as "civil disabilities," have a critical effect on the lifestyles available to persons released from prison. Directly or indirectly, they deny to the ex-offender the right to pursue various occupations and limit his or her opportunity to earn a living [30].

Do prisons reduce the likelihood of future criminal behavior, and do they equip prisoners to function inside society? Since almost all prisoners (some 99 percent) eventually leave prison (31), both goals are important—for everyone's welfare. First, consider the punishment aspect of prison. Does the punishment of incarceration decrease the likelihood that criminal behavior will be repeated? In Chapter 7 we saw that punishment was most effective in eliminating unwanted behavior when it was consistent, immediate, and brief, and when alternative constructive behavior was positively reinforced. These findings lead many psychologists to believe that prisons probably do not reduce criminal behavior. Additional psychological research leads to the prediction that prison life may actually increase both aggression and crime. Recall that frustration frequently leads to aggression. Also recall that aggressive antisocial behavior increases in frequency when cultures reward aggression and when aggressive models abound (see Chapter 11). All of these conditions typify prison life.

Are psychologists' predictions borne out by psychological research? Does a prison stay increase or reduce the probability of future criminal behavior? To investigate this issue social scientists select a sample of released criminals and follow their "careers" to see what percentage of them return to jail. Since studies of this kind are expensive, time-consuming, and difficult, they are comparatively rare. An accurate overall rearrest rate is not known. Reported rearrest rates vary markedly from study to study ranging from roughly 30 percent to 80 percent. Interpreting these numbers is difficult. The important question is: Would the percentage of rearrests be higher or lower if the prisoner had not been placed in a conventional prison? To answer this question, social scientists must identify two very similar groups of convicted criminals, incarcerate one group and treat the other by an alternative method, then follow their careers to determine how many commit new crimes. Studies of this type are unusual. Recently, one such study was attempted in California. A group of first-time male offenders were randomly assigned to either a prison or a community treatment program; subsequent criminal activity was evaluated after two years. The investigators found that 61 percent of the incarcerated men were later convicted of new crimes, whereas 38 percent of the men in the community treatment program were later convicted of new crimes. Although these results favor community programs, the study has

some methodological problems: The prisoners studied were not representative of prison groups in general since there were no serious offenders and very few minority group members (32). Currently, then, psychologists do not have the systematic experimental data needed to answer the question: Do prisons reduce the probability of future crime?

What about the fourth function of prisons—Do prisons lead to rehabilitation? Social psychologist Philip Zimbardo investigated this issue indirectly by creating a mock prison and observing its effects on normal college students. We turn now to this study.

What does prison life do to people?

With the help of an ex-convict, Philip Zimbardo and several colleagues created a mock prison by converting the basement of the psychology building at Stanford University, into cells with metal bars, cots, and bucket toilets. The prison was designed to run for two weeks. Prisoners and guards were recruited by ads in campus and town newspapers offering $15 a day for participation. Eventually twenty-one intelligent, middle-class, apparently psychologically and physically healthy college students were selected. Eleven of them were randomly assigned to the guard role; ten were randomly assigned to the prisoner role.

The study began dramatically. Each prisoner was unexpectedly picked up by the city police at his home. The arrests were so realistic that some neighbors offered the boys' families their sympathy and support. The police frisked and handcuffed each "suspect," then drove him to headquarters for fingerprinting and booking. Later the police blindfolded the "suspect" and escorted him to Zimbardo's prison.

The mock guards wore khaki uniforms and sunglasses to increase their impersonality. When the "suspects" arrived, they were ordered to strip. They were then skin searched, sprayed with delousing powder, dressed in smocks with their own numbers and ordered to wear stocking caps at all times. A number of arbitrary rules made the prison experience realistic. For example, during meal periods and rest periods the prisoners were forbidden to speak to one another; and silence was again enforced when the lights went out at 10 o'clock. At 2:30 each morning the prisoners were also routinely awakened for head counts.

The prisoners soon began to think up ways to escape or subvert the experiment. On the second day they created a number of disturbances. Some barricaded the door with their beds. Some ripped off their numbers and refused to eat. The guards squashed the rebellion by the strategy—divide and conquer.[4] They provided running water and a special meal for the men in one cell. The rest of them received nothing to eat. One prisoner commented: "If we had gotten together, I think we could have taken over the place. But when I saw the revolt wasn't working, I decided to toe the line. Everyone settled into the same pattern. From then on, we were really controlled by the guards [33]."

The guards behaved with increasing brutality. They abused their charges both verbally and physically. A Stanford University graduate student guard remarked after the experiment: "I was surprised at myself. I was a real crumb. I made them call each other names and clean out the toilets with their bare hands. I practically considered the prisoners cattle, and I kept thinking I have to watch out for them in case they try something [34]."

As he watched his prison become increasingly brutal, Zimbardo became alarmed. He wrote:

At the end of only six days we had to close down our mock prison because what we saw was frightening. It was no longer apparent to most of our subjects (or to us) where reality ended and their roles began. . . . There were dramatic changes in virtually every aspect of their behavior, thinking, and feeling. In less than a week the experience of imprisonment undid (temporarily) a lifetime of learning: human values were suspended, self-concepts were challenged and the ugliest, most base, pathological side of human nature surfaced. . . .

We had to release three prisoners in the first four days because they had such acute situational traumatic reactions as hysterical crying, confusion in thinking and severe depression. . . .

About a third of the guards became tyrannical in their arbitrary use of power, in enjoying their control over other people. . . . Some of the guards merely did their jobs. . . . However, no good guard ever interfered with a command by any of the bad guards; they never intervened on the side of the prisoners, they never told the others to ease off . . . and they never even came to me as prison superintendant or experimenter in charge to complain. . . .

By the end of the week the experiment had become a reality. . . . The consultant for our prison, . . . an ex-convict with 16 years of imprisonment in California's jails, would get so depressed and furious each time he visited our prison because of its pathological similarity to his experiences, that he would have to leave. A Catholic priest, who was a former prison chaplain in Washington, D.C., talked to our prisoners after four days and said they were just like the other first-timers he had seen [35]."

---

[4]Zimbardo believes that guards in real prisons use essentially the same tactic. By tolerating homosexuality and racism, they keep the men or women frightened of one another. Consequently, the prisoners are not likely to unite against the guards.

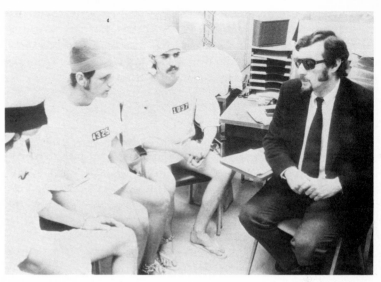

Figure 17-7. "Prisoners" in Zimbardo's Stanford prison experiment meet with the "superintendent." (Philip G. Zimbardo.)

Zimbardo's mock-prison study had many methodological problems. Nonetheless, it suggests that prison is a dehumanizing experience. (*Dehumanization* is defined as "a process which produces a decreased awareness of the human attributes of others and a loss of humanity in interpersonal situations.") Zimbardo has enumerated seven facets of the prison experience which appear to contribute to dehumanization:

1. The physical structure of the prison (steel walls, barbed wire fences, gun towers, and bars) establish the prison as a grim and monotonous place where no decent human being would want to be found.
2. The conditions of prison life reduce the prisoners' sense of their own uniqueness. Conventions force prisoners to wear uniforms and submit to standard hair cuts. All their personal possessions are taken from them. More importantly, they are treated like numbers without unique personalities, needs, past experiences, strengths, and weaknesses.
3. The prisoners are, in many cases, required

to obey petty and arbitrary prison rules which degrade dignity, destroy human trust, and make genuine communication between prisoners and guards or prisoners and prisoners impossible.

4. Prisons produce conditions that cause people to distort, inhibit, and/or suppress emotion for several reasons. First, the expression of emotion is dangerous. Prisoners who express emotion are likely to be labeled potential informers and/or targets for rape. Second, being able to distort, inhibit, or suppress emotion has other tangible rewards. If people feel nothing, no amount of abuse can hurt or disturb them.
5. In an all-male prison world, power and control come through superior physical strength. So prisoners frequently play the role of "tough animal" trying to impress one another as fearless, powerful, unfeeling, totally selfish, and self-gratifying. This role behavior reduces the prisoner's individuality further.
6. The monotony of prison life also dehumanizes. People lose their perspective when time creeps. They find themselves over-

reacting to minor happenings and failing to plan for major ones.

7. Prisoners lose their right to choose. All decisions are made for them and they are stripped of a sense of both self-direction and responsibility for their own behavior (36).

Zimbardo's observations agree with the perceptions of many other authorities. In 1970 Ramsey Clark, former Attorney General of the United States, labeled prisons "factories of crime." The 42nd Annual Assembly, a group of prominent professors, lawmakers, and administrators interested in prison reform, summarized their position in 1972 as follows: "Most correctional institutions are, and can be no more than, mere warehouses that degrade and brutalize their human baggage." The personal reports of many prisoners show that a great many emerge from their stays in prison with new hatred and bitterness, increased cynicism, and more sophisticated and brutal techniques for crime.

Can the Prison System Be Improved?

The conditions of prison life rarely equip prisoners to lead better lives in the outside world. When vocational training exists, it is typically unrealistic, providing low skilled jobs that have little relevance to the outside world. Prison schools are usually inadequate and serve only a small fraction of the inmates. Criminals rarely learn to follow rules and carry out responsibilities in prison. Nor do they receive help with individual problems— a drug habit, aggressive interpersonal behavior, feelings of inferiority, anxieties, or conflicts.

In 1970 it was estimated that approximately 95 percent of all corrections money went into custodial care and security; only 5 percent into health, education, and rehabilitation. If these budgetary priorities were revised, social scientists might be able to rehabilitate prisoners.

How should rehabilitation proceed? Many social scientists believe that community-based work, education, and counseling programs should handle the majority of lawbreakers and that prisons should be the last resort.

Currently, some fifty American cities are experimenting with pretrial intervention programs. The judge, prosecutor, and defense attorney assign low-risk criminals to probation officers. The criminals are expected to either attend school or work. At the same time they receive help with medical, psychological, and family problems. The following reading describes a pretrial intervention project for juveniles.

Pretrial intervention in Baltimore

An experimental Pretrial Intervention Project (PTI) currently in operation in Baltimore promises to be successful in helping to rehabilitate juvenile delinquents here. This is how the system works. Police complaints on all juveniles are referred to the Department of Juvenile Services. An officer of PTI examines and pulls all fifteen- to eighteen-year-old males and excludes those who have been involved in drugs, arson, murder, or armed robbery. Approximately ninety boys are taken into the program every three months. "The typical participant is black, marginally enrolled in school, has had at least one prison offense, has no appreciable skills, and is either unemployed or unemployable."

The immediate purpose of PTI is to keep juvenile offenders from "becoming caught up in the criminal justice system and while doing so, receiving a damaging criminal record and often nonresponsive treatment." In the long run, its purpose, of course, is to prevent crime.

The youthful offenders who have built their reputation and their identity "around stealing, sexual prowess, fancy clothes, or fighting ability" are not easy to reach. They demand a different approach. PTI uses a comprehensive behavior-changing program which includes counseling, education, employment, and positive growth experiences. Carefully trained paraprofessional counselors—frequently ex-offenders from similar backgrounds—seem to work out best. (At the same time the ex-offenders are provided with genuinely meaningful work.) Such counselors can stop the "gaming" early and establish communication. Then counselor and juvenile focus together on issues of authority, aggression, manhood, anger, controls, institutions, self, motivation, family, responsibility, and criminal behavior. The counseling is oriented toward positive action in the present. The counselors use role playing, videotape equipment, and carefully designed exercises to teach their kids to cope actively with difficult situations like job interviews or contacts with the police. The juvenile learns to handle his problems and to gain control over his behavior. Building confidence is considered of prime importance. PTI also offers remedial education and a high school equivalency program. Sometimes the counselors help place their young men in college, in job programs, or in jobs.

When clients remain in the program for ninety days with satisfactory progress, PTI recommends that the charges against them be dropped. So far the results are encouraging. Of the intakes 70 percent complete PTI successfully and have their charges dismissed. The rearrest rate is approximately 13 percent; the conviction rate is lower. In contrast, when kids are simply placed on probation by the court, approximately 80 percent are rearrested. (Note that the two rearrest rates are not strictly comparable because PTI selects their sample of some 400 from 10,000 teenagers arrested each year in Baltimore and only 70 percent of the select group complete the program. Still, these numbers provide a rough indication that PTI's results are impressive) (37).

Summary: Psychology and Prisons

1. Prisons aim at four goals: isolation, punishment, reduction of future crime, and rehabilitation.
2. Although prisons succeed at goals 1 and 2,

psychologists predict and observations provide evidence that prisons do not succeed in reducing the likelihood of future crime or in rehabilitating prisoners.
3. At the present time community-based treatment programs which emphasize job training, lifestyle changes, problem solv-

Figure 17-8. A PTI counselor meets with a young offender in an individual counseling session. (PTI Project.)

ing, and personal counseling appear to be a promising way to reduce crime and rehabilitate criminals.

PSYCHOLOGY AND THE PROMOTION OF HUMAN WELFARE: AN EPILOGUE

In this last chapter we have seen how psychologists try to clarify contemporary problems in cities, work settings, and prisons; we have looked at some solutions to these problems. Actually we've been discussing how psychology can be applied to social problems throughout the text. In Chapter 7 we showed how learning principles were used to manage problem children and reduce fears. In Chapter 12 we looked at programs to train moral thinking and behavior. We examined psychotherapy and community mental health programs in Chapter 15. In Chapter 16 we explored psychologists' efforts to reduce prejudice. At various times in your reading, you may have felt frustrated by the gaps in current psychological knowledge or disappointed at the scarcity of real solutions. For the most part, psychologists have only recently begun the necessary research in these important areas and effective programs are still rare.

You may also have wondered how revolutionary the achievements of psychologists' really are. Helping schizophrenics adjust to life in the community or second graders overcome prejudice hardly seem comparable in their revolutionary consequences to the introduction of the computer, atomic energy, or the wheel. But are they revolutionary? Perhaps people expect too much of psychology. Quoting once again from Miller's presidential address:

[The] behavioral and social sciences cannot be applied to people and institutions in the same way [that] physical and biological sciences are applied to objects and organisms. . . .

[T]he real impact of psychology will be felt, not through the technological products it places in the hands of powerful men, but through its effects on the public at large, through a new and different public conception of what is humanly possible and what is humanly desirable [38].

The revolutionary achievements of psychologists will be comparatively quiet ones consisting largely of placing society in a better position to understand social and psychological problems and to provide more effective and humane solutions.

STUDY GUIDE 17

Key Terms. applied psychology, sensory and cognitive overload, anonymity, social responsibility, bystander intervention, job satisfaction, work module, job rotation, career-exposure plan, vertical job enlargement, job enrichment, dehumanization, pretrial intervention program.

Important Research. noise and cognitive abilities (Glass and Singer; Glass, Singer, and Cohen) crowding and rats (Calhoun), crowding and people (Freedman), requests for entry in cities and towns, helping a "lost" child (Milgram), abandoned cars (Fraser and Zimbardo), determinants of job satisfaction (Institute for Social Research, University of Michigan), work modules (Kahn), increasing job satisfaction (Sheppard and Herrick), lawbreakers treated in prison or community facilities in California, mock prison (Zimbardo), Baltimore Pretrial Intervention Program.

Basic Ideas. adaptation to sensory and cognitive overload (Milgram), psychology and the promotion of human welfare (Miller).

Self-Quiz

1. Applied psychology refers to the use of psychological principles in [**a**] clinics and counseling centers; [**b**] consumer affairs, population control, and ecology; [**c**] business and industry; [**d**] all of the above.
2. Glass, Singer, and Cohen found that children living on noisier floors of apartment buildings _____ than children living on quieter floors. [**a**] scored lower on intelligence tests; [**b**] scored lower on tests of ability to tolerate frustration; [**c**] had more emotional problems; [**d**] scored lower on reading and hearing tests.
3. All the following resulted from Calhoun's overcrowding of rats *except* [**a**] cannibalism; [**b**] abnormal sexual behavior; [**c**] unprovoked fighting; [**d**] neglected infant care and nest building.

4. Freedman's studies show that when people are crowded in a laboratory setting, [**a**] errors on problem-solving tasks increase; [**b**] time to solve problems increases; [**c**] women make fewer errors but men make more on problem-solving tasks; [**d**] problem solving is not affected, but social interactions are: men become more aggressive; women more cooperative.
5. According to Milgram, people in cities adapt to sensory and cognitive overload by [**a**] becoming callous and hardened; [**b**] developing ulcers and other psychosomatic disorders; [**c**] allowing only brief, superficial contacts with other people; [**d**] becoming aggressive.
6. Zimbardo found that college students who were made to feel anonymous behaved _____ than college students who were made to feel like individuals. [**a**] less aggressively; [**b**] more aggressively; [**c**] more aggressively, but only when the victim was perceived as obnoxious; [**d**] less aggressively, but only when the victim was perceived as a decent human being.
7. Comparisons of city dwellers and town dwellers demonstrated all the following *except* [**a**] city dwellers are less likely to help a person who falls down on the street; [**b**] city dwellers are less likely to let a stranger use their telephone; [**c**] city dwellers are less likely to help a lost child; [**d**] city dwellers are more likely to vandalize an abandoned car.
8. In the early 1970s University of Michigan researchers interviewed representatives of those employed nationally in the work force and found that the top ranked work feature was [**a**] interesting work; [**b**] comforts and fringe benefits; [**c**] good pay; [**d**] job security.
9. Kahn's work module plan is primarily intended to [**a**] achieve a greater economic return per unit of time for the employer; [**b**] reduce boredom and

fatigue by scheduling regular breaks; [**c**] give workers more flexibility in planning the content and scheduling of their work; [**d**] expose workers to various work options and opportunities for advancement.

10. The attempts to increase worker satisfaction described by Sheppard and Herrick generally result in [**a**] increased costs to the employer; [**b**] increased costs plus increased productivity yielding no overall loss or gain to the employer; [**c**] increased satisfaction, increased productivity, and decreased turnover and absenteeism—resulting in economic gain by the employer; [**d**] increased satisfaction, but decreased productivity.

11. Which of the following is *not* characteristic of American prisoners? [**a**] Many will return to prison; [**b**] a large percentage will never be released from prison; [**c**] nearly all are male; [**d**] minority group members are disproportionately highly represented.

12. A California study comparing lawbreakers assigned either to a prison or community treatment program produced which results? [**a**] Less than 40 percent of either group committed another crime; [**b**] over 60 percent of the prisoners, but less than 40 percent of the men in the community treatment program, were later convicted of new crimes; [**c**] approximately 60 percent of both groups of offenders committed another crime; [**d**] less than 40 percent of the prisoners, but more than 60 percent of the men in the community treatment program, were later convicted of new crimes.

13. In Zimbardo's mock prison study [**a**] the prisoners and guards both behaved brutally—"suspending a lifetime of learning"; [**b**] consultants with prison experience said that the prison atmosphere resembled a real prison, but was considerably less depressing; [**c**] the guards were brutalized by the experience, but the prisoners did not seem to be affected; [**d**] many of the guards were brutalized, and many of the prisoners showed signs of acute situational trauma.

14. Zimbardo characterizes real prisons as dehumanizing for all the following reasons except [**a**] they rob prisoners of a basic sense of security because they are unsafe; [**b**] they treat the prisoners like numbers and not like people with unique strengths and weaknesses; [**c**] they deprive prisoners of their rights to make decisions and take responsibility for their own behavior; [**d**] they force prisoners to obey petty arbitrary rules.

15. Pretrial intervention projects [**a**] assign low-risk criminals to probation officers; [**b**] expect criminals to work or attend school; [**c**] give personal counseling for medical, psychological, and family problems; [**d**] all of the above.

Questions to Consider

1. How do you think psychologists can best follow George Miller's advice to "give psychology away"? What problems deserve special attention?

2. If you were a city planner, how could you use the research findings presented on pages 489–495 to design a city that minimized the distressing effects of noise, crowding, and sensory cognitive overload.

3. Design a study to compare the three strategies reviewed by Sheppard and Herrick for increasing job satisfaction. How could you avoid the Hawthorne effect?

4. How could the techniques of job rotation, vertical job enlargement, and job enrichment be applied to education to make students more satisfied with school?

5. Design a prison program to rehabilitate criminals and reduce the probability of future crime. Could certain programs that have been successful in rehabilitating chronic schizophrenics be applied to rehabilitating criminals? Explain.

6. If you wanted to study the effects of prisons on real prisoners, what problems would you run into?

7. Consider some of the tactics that psychologists used to gather information in this chapter. In one study a child confederate falsely represented himself as a lost child; in another, adult confederates falsely represented themselves as people who had misplaced a friend's address. Are such procedures ethical? Do they give psychologists a bad public image? On the other hand, could experiments on bystander intervention in emergencies and similar topics be carried out without such deceptions? (For one point of view on this issue, see the suggested reading by Donald Warwick on page 59.)

Project 17: Job Status and Job Satisfaction

A number of studies show that job satisfaction is related to job status: When people's job status is high, they are more likely to be contented with their work. In this project you will be making some measurements to see if these results hold true among people you know. You will also be looking at the particular ingredients of high- and low-status jobs which furnish satisfaction.

Method. Find six cooperative working adults: three with relatively high work status and three with relatively low work status. Do not use people who are self-employed. Tell your subjects that you are doing a psychology project on the job characteristics that make people satisfied with their jobs and enlist their cooperation in filling out a questionnaire. Subjects' responses to the questionnaire will not be identified with their names. Do not tell your subjects the precise nature of the project until after you have collected all your data.

Make six copies of the questionnaire in Figure 1. You may test your subjects individually or in a group. Find a setting that is quiet and free from distractions. Have each subject write his/her occupation at the top of the questionnaire and then rank each job variable on the scale next to it. The subject should circle the number that most closely corresponds to his/her feelings about his/her work.

Results. The answer key on page 514 shows what general characteristic is sampled by each item. Score each subject's questionnaire by separately adding up the circled points on items marked CH (Challenge), RES (Resources), REW (Rewards), and COM (Comfort). Enter each subject's score on each factor in the following table. Now calculate the totals for each factor for the low- and high-status groups and calculate a group mean for each factor by dividing each total by 3, the number of subjects. Next, compute an adjusted group mean by dividing each group mean by the number of items that were included (seven for challenge, four for resources, four for rewards, and six for comfort. Finally, compute a Total Adjusted Mean for Group by adding the four adjusted means for each group.

Job Satisfaction Scores

High-status Job Group	Challenge	Resources	Rewards	Comfort	
Subject 1					
Subject 2					
Subject 3					
Total for Group					
Mean for Group					
Adjusted Mean for Group					Total Adjusted Mean for Group _____
Low-Status Job Group					
Subject 4					
Subject 5					
Subject 6					
Total for Group					
Mean for Group					
Adjusted Mean for Group					Total Adjusted Mean for Group _____

Discussion. Consider the following questions.

1. Did the group means for low-status jobs differ from the group means for high-status jobs on any category of job satisfaction? Were the differences large? Were they expected? How can they be explained?

2. Look at the adjusted means on challenge, resources, rewards, and comfort for each group. Do they vary? How can these findings be interpreted?

3. Compare the total adjusted mean for the high-status job group with the total adjusted mean for the low-status job group. Do they differ? How can this finding be interpreted?

4. What job-related factors besides job status may have influenced your findings?

5. Experimenter bias can be problematic in studies like this one. How might experimenter bias have been controlled in this study?

6. If you had had unlimited financial resources to study the relationship between job status and job satisfaction, what changes would you have made in this study?

7. Assume that you found that challenge, resources, rewards, and/or comforts were definitely positively associated with job status and with job satisfaction, how could psychologists establish cause-and-effect relationships between these variables and job satisfaction?

8. How might unsatisfying jobs be made more satisfying? You might want to discuss this subject with some of your dissatisfied subjects to see if they agree.

FIGURE 1

1. My work is interesting.

2. I have enough authority to do my job.

3. I have enough time to get my work done.

4. My pay is _____.

5. The hours I work are _____.

6. My job responsibilities are clearly defined.

7. My job provides fringe benefits which are

_____.

8. My job security is _____.

9. The problems I am asked to solve at work are challenging enough to hold my interest.

10. I can see the results of my work.

11. My supervisor is competent.

12. I have enough information to get my work done.

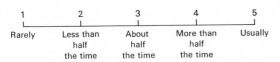

1	2	3	4	5
Rarely	Less than half the time	About half the time	More than half the time	Usually

13. I receive enough help and equipment to get my work done.

1	2	3	4	5
Rarely	Less than half the time	About half the time	More than half the time	Usually

14. I am not asked to do an excessive amount of work.

1	2	3	4	5
Rarely	Less than half the time	About half the time	More than half the time	Usually

15. I have an opportunity to develop my special abilities at work.

1	2	3	4	5
Rarely	Less than half the time	About half the time	More than half the time	Usually

16. My physical surroundings at work are _____.

1	2	3	4	5
Unsatisfactory	Barely satisfactory	Moderately satisfactory	Satisfactory	Very satisfactory

17. I am given a lot of freedom to decide how to do my work.

1	2	3	4	5
Rarely	Less than half the time	About half the time	More than half the time	Usually

18. My supervisor is concerned about employee welfare.

1	2	3	4	5
Rarely	Less than half the time	About half the time	More than half the time	Usually

19. I am given a chance to do the things I do best at work.

1	2	3	4	5
Rarely	Less than half the time	About half the time	More than half the time	Usually

20. Travel time to and from work is _____.

1	2	3	4	5
Unsatisfactory	Barely satisfactory	Moderately satisfactory	Satisfactory	Very satisfactory

21. The chances for promotion are _____.

1	2	3	4	5
Unsatisfactory	Barely satisfactory	Moderately satisfactory	Satisfactory	Very satisfactory

Source: Adapted from *Survey of working conditions: Final report.* Survey Research Center, U. S. Department of Labor, Employment Standards Administration, 1971. U. S. Government Printing Office 2916-0001.

Suggested Readings

1. Ashmore, R. D., & J. B. McConahay. *Psychology and America's urban dilemma.* New York: McGraw-Hill Book Company, 1975 (paperback). Presents research on a number of city problems, including schools, courts, and race relations; some solutions are suggested.

2. Korten, F. F., S. W. Cook, & J. I. Lacey. *Psychology and the problems of society.* Washington, D.C.: American Psychological Association, 1970. A collection of speeches and articles that describe how psychology can be applied to significant social problems. Difficult.

3. Terkel, S. *Working.* New York: Pantheon Books, Inc., 1974. Interviews with more than one hundred working people, focusing on what people do, how they feel about their work, and what they wish they might do instead.

4. Yankelovich, D. "Turbulence in the working world: Angry workers, happy grads." *Psychology Today,* December 1974, 8, 81–87. Discusses five new trends that are changing the American work ethic.

5. Chaneles, S. "Open prisons: Urban convicts can turn ghost towns into rural communities." *Psychology Today*, April 1974, 7, 30, 90–93. An interesting proposal for a new kind of prison by a criminologist and urban sociologist.

6. Zimbardo, P. G., C. Haney, W. C. Banks, & D. Jaffe. "The mind is a formidable jailer: A Pirandellian prison." *The New York Times*, April 8, 1973, 38–53, 56–60. A description of the Stanford University mock prison study and its implications.

Answer Keys

SELF-QUIZ

1. d 2. d 3. a 4. d 5. c 6. b 7. a 8. a 9. c
10. c 11. b 12. b 13. d 14. a 15. d

PROJECT

1. CH 2. CH 3. COM 4. REW 5. COM 6. RES
7. REW 8. REW 9. CH 10. CH 11. RES 12. RES
13. RES 14. COM 15. CH 16. COM 17. CH
18. COM 19. CH 20. COM 21. REW

GLOSSARY

Note: All italicized words are defined in the glossary.

abnormal behavior. *Behavior* is assessed as abnormal when it is characterized by grossly defective cognitive or social functioning or self-control or by uncontrollable distress.

accommodation. The process by which the *lens* system of the eye either thickens or becomes flatter to focus incoming light rays from an object onto the *retina*.

acquisition. In *respondent conditioning*, the learning of a *conditioned response* after a *neutral stimulus* is paired with an *unconditioned stimulus*—usually repeatedly.

acute schizophrenia. Schizophrenia characterized by sudden onset, no prior history of psychosis, and a good chance of recovery. Sometimes called *reactive schizophrenia*.

adaptation. see *adjustment*

adjustment. The various *behaviors* and *cognitions* that people use to adapt to and come to terms with their environment.

adrenal gland. One of a pair of *endocrine glands* located on top of each kidney; one portion of the glands produces *adrenalin* and *noradrenalin*; another produces *sex hormones*, beginning at *puberty*. The adrenal glands produce additional *hormones* that also regulate other bodily functions.

adrenalin. A *hormone* secreted by the *adrenal glands* during stresses to prepare the body to handle an emergency.

aerial perspective. A *monocular depth cue*; as distance increases, colors become grayer and outlines within an image become more blurred.

aggression. *Behavior* aimed at hurting.

alarm reaction. Stage one of the *GAS*; the *sympathetic nervous system* and *adrenal glands* mobilize the body's defensive forces to handle the emergency, to resist the particular stressor.

alpha activity. Electrical activity in the *neural* circuits of the brain in the 8 to 12 *hertz* band associated with pleasantly relaxed feelings.

amygdala. A structure in the *limbic system* that influences *aggression*.

anal stage. According to Freud's *psychodynamic theory*, the second *psychosexual stage* when pleasure is focused on the functions of elimination. If toilet training is harsh or if elimination is associated with extreme pleasure, the individual will show anal characteristics such as messiness or excessive orderliness as an adult.

analytic introspection. A special self-observation procedure employed by *structuralist* psychologists.

androgen-insensitivity syndrome. A disorder caused by a *genetic* defect which prevents the male fetus from utilizing the *androgens*.

androgens. Masculine *sex hormones* that regulate *primary* and *secondary sex characteristics*. During an early *sensitive period* they also alter the *nervous system* and influence subsequent hormonal and behavioral patterns.

anger. An *emotion* characterized by a high level of *sympathetic nervous system* activity and by strong subjective feelings of displeasure that are triggered by a real or imagined wrong.

antisocial personality. See *psychopathic behavior*.

anxiety (fear). An *emotion* characterized by unpleasant subjective feelings of anticipated danger, tension, and distress and attended by *sympathetic nervous system arousal*.

anxiety neurosis. Behavioral disorder characterized by almost continual *anxiety* and tension; anxiety attacks are usually sudden and unexpected.

apparent movement. Visual *perception* of movement, although real physical movement is absent.

applied psychology. The use of psychology in practical settings such as communities, clinics, counseling centers, mental hospitals, schools, prisons, military institutions, business, industry, consumer affairs, population control, ecology, space travel, and so on.

approach-approach conflict. A *conflict* that occurs when a person is simultaneously attracted to two goals, objects, or courses of action and the achievement of one means the abandonment of the other.

approach-avoidance conflict. A *conflict* that occurs when a person is simultaneously attracted to and repelled by the same goal, object, or course of action.

arousal. Degree of alertness.

asceticism. The practice of denying oneself sensual and material pleasures.

assertiveness training. A *behavior modification* technique used to teach adults who experience severe *anxiety* and inhibitions how to express their *emotions* more genuinely; uses *role playing* and *observation learning*.

association area. A region of the *cerebral cortex* that integrates incoming information and coordinates the decision-making process.

attachment. Social bond.

attention. A selective openness to a small portion of impinging *sensory phenomena*.

attitude. A learned concept that guides (1) thoughts, (2) feelings, and (3) *behavior* toward a particular object (a person, a group of people, a policy, an event, or an inanimate object).

autonomic nervous system. A division of the *nervous system*; composed of *nerves* that lead from the brain and spinal cord to the smooth muscles of the internal organs, glands, heart, and blood vessels; composed of *parasympathetic* and *sympathetic nervous systems*.

autonomic reaction. A *physiological* reaction, such as a rapid heartbeat and flushing, that is initiated by the *autonomic nervous system*.

aversive counterconditioning. An *aversive learning procedure* based on *respondent conditioning* principles. Used to eliminate socially maladaptive patterns such as excessive drinking, overeating, gambling, drug taking, or arousal to inappropriate sexual objects. The inappropriate stimulus object is repeatedly paired with an unpleasant *unconditioned stimulus* until the object becomes associated with an unpleasant *conditioned response*.

aversive learning procedure. A learning procedure that employs painful or unpleasant stimulation or deprivation; primarily used by *behavior therapists* for problems which fail to respond to other modes of treatment.

avoidance-avoidance conflict. A *conflict* that occurs when a person is simultaneously repelled by two goals, objects, or courses of action, one of which must be selected.

axon. A branching fiber which protrudes from the *neuron*; its function is to transmit information to other neurons, to muscles, and to glands.

basic drive. See *primary drive*.

behavior. Any human or animal process or activity that can be objectively observed or measured.

behavior genetics. The psychological discipline that attempts to understand how *heredity* influences *behavior*.

behaviorism. A psychological movement founded by John Watson that insists that psychologists study observable *behavior* and use methods of experimentation and observation.

behavior modification. The application of *operant learning* and other experimental laboratory procedures to change human *behavior*.

behavior therapist. A *therapist* who uses *behavior therapy* procedures.

behavior therapy. A *therapy* that assumes that psychological problems are caused by psychological, social, biological, and environmental factors. Behavior therapy is usually brief and involves modifying those factors that appear to be maintaining the problem. Typically, techniques from the experimental psychology laboratory are employed to help people unlearn maladaptive behavior and learn or relearn adaptive behavior.

binocular depth cue. A *depth cue* that depends on the operation of both eyes.

binocular disparity. A *depth cue* that occurs because the eyes are located in different positions, causing each *retina* to register a slightly different visual image.

biofeedback. A technique for teaching a person to control a particular bodily part by providing systematic information or feedback as to what that part is doing.

biological rhythms. Bodily cycles that vary from fractions of a second to a year and even longer (example: the sleep-waking cycle).

bisexuality. Sexual responsiveness to both males and females.

central core. The most primitive part of the brain; regions in the central core control routine, continually operating activities such as digestion and circulation and certain *reflex* movements.

central nervous system (CNS). One of two major subsystems of the *nervous system*; the central information-processing component, consisting of the spinal cord and brain.

central tendency. See *measure of central tendency*.

cerebral cortex. The outer covering of the *cerebrum*; contains *sensory, motor*, and *association areas*.

cerebral hemisphere. One of two nearly symmetrical halves of the *cerebrum* that function as separate brains with their own *sensory* and *motor areas*. The right hemisphere controls the left half of the body, and the left hemisphere controls the right half of the body.

cerebrum. The most recently evolved division of the brain; more highly developed in people than in any other creatures. It *integrates* incoming information with previously acquired information and *mediates* complex *cognitive processes*.

chemical postnatal environment. A chemical influence such as nutrition, water, oxygen, and drugs, to which the animal is exposed after birth.

chemical prenatal environment. The environment which surrounds the developing *fetus*—in people, the *intrauterine* environment.

chromosome. Strands in the *nucleus* of sex and other bodily cells containing *genes*.

chronic schizophrenia. *Schizophrenia* characterized by its recurrent nature, prior history of severe maladjustment, and poor chance of recovery. Sometimes called *process schizophrenia*.

clairvoyance. A form of *extrasensory perception*; seeing something past, present, or future that cannot be seen by the eyes or known by the known *senses*.

classical conditioning. See *respondent conditioning*.

client-centered psychotherapy. A *therapy* approach that assumes that psychological problems occur when people are forced to deny aspects of their own identity and cease to grow. Therapy aims at restoring the *self-concept* and renewing the growth process. It consists of an intimate here-and-now relationship with a genuine, warmly accepting, and *empathic therapist*.

client-centered therapist. A *therapist* who uses *client-centered therapy* procedures.

clinical observation. An observation made as persons are treated in a clinic or office setting to provide insights into private *behavior*.

clinical psychologist. A specialist in normal and abnormal psychology and in the diagnosis and treatment of psychological problems.

closure. Visual *organizing tendency*; incomplete objects are usually seen as complete.

CNS. See *central nervous system*.

cognition. See *cognitive process*.

cognitive-coping mechanism. A mental strategy used to adjust to the environment.

cognitive dissonance. A theory that assumes that when one's *cognitions* conflict, one becomes uncomfortable and attempts to reduce the tension by reducing the dissonance, usually by seeking new information, changing *attitudes*, altering *behavior*, or rearranging the environment. Research shows that in the majority of cases a person seeks new information or changes attitudes or opinions to reconcile the cognitive conflict.

cognitive process. A mental activity such as using language, thinking, reasoning, solving problems, conceptualizing, remembering, imagining, or learning verbal material.

cognitive theory of emotion. A theory that states that essentially similar *sympathetic nervous system* patterns can be labeled in many ways, depending on a person's interpretation of the situation.

community mental health care. Programs designed to bring a wide range of mental health services to people in communities who would not ordinarily utilize them.

compulsion. A ritualistic *behavior* that recurs despite the person's attempts to resist the impulse to perform it.

concordance rate. See *concordant*.

concordant. Alike; a term used in twin studies to indicate that both members of a twin pair exhibit a particular trait or disease. A *concordance rate* indicates the percentage of twin pairs in a study who are concordant.

conditioned. Learned by *respondent* or *operant conditioning* procedures.

conditioned punisher. In *operant conditioning*, a *punisher* that has been learned through *respondent conditioning*—by being paired with a *primary punisher* many times.

conditioned reinforcer. In *operant conditioning*, a

reinforcer which has been learned through *respondent conditioning*—by being paired with a *primary reinforcer* many times.

conditioned response. In *respondent conditioning*, a response evoked by a *conditioned stimulus* that is similar to, but milder than, the *unconditioned response*.

conditioned stimulus. In *respondent conditioning*, the term applied to the *neutral stimulus* after it has been *conditioned* to evoke a new *response*.

conditions. Different groups in an experiment.

conflict. A situation in which two or more incompatible needs, goals, or courses of action compete, causing the organism to feel pulled in different directions with an attending sense of discomfort.

conformity. A change in *behavior*, *attitudes*, or both that results from real or imagined group pressure.

consciousness. See *state of consciousness*.

consolidate. To transform *short-term memories* into *long-term memories*.

constancy. Visual *organizing tendency*; the size, shape, and color of an object are regarded as constant even when the object is viewed from different angles, different distances, or under different conditions of illumination.

constant sensory experience. An experience that occurs either before or after birth that is normally inevitable for all members of a particular species.

contingent. Dependent upon.

continuity. Visual *organizing tendency*; visual elements that form smooth, regular patterns are seen as belonging together.

continuous characteristic. A characteristic that can take on a *continuum* of values. (Also see *discrete characteristic*.)

continuous reinforcement. In *operant conditioning*, *reinforcement* that occurs after every correct response.

continuum. An uninterrupted series.

control. To influence or change a particular behavioral *phenomenon*. Also see *controls*.

control group. One or more groups that are not subjected to changes in the *independent variable* but are otherwise exposed to the same procedures and setting as the *experimental groups* in an *experiment*.

controls. Methods used to keep extraneous factors from interfering with or obscuring the influence of the *independent variable* in an experiment.

convergence. A *depth cue* provided by *kinesthetic* feedback from the eye muscles.

convergent thinking. The ability to follow accepted patterns of thought and arrive at single correct solutions to particular problems; this ability is generally assessed by intelligence, aptitude, and achievement tests. (Compare *divergent thinking*.)

coping behavior. Responses aimed at avoiding, escaping, or reducing distress or handling a particular stressor.

corpus callosum. A massive network of *nerve fibers* which join the two *cerebral hemispheres*, giving each access to the information and memories of the other.

correlation coefficient. A *statistic* used to describe the relationship between two sets of scores; a number between −1 and +1 used to express the strength and direction of the relationship. A positive correlation coefficient indicates that when the score on one *variable* is high, the score on the other variable tends to be high. A negative correlation coefficient indicates that when the score on one variable is high, the score on the other variable tends to be low.

counseling. The offering of supportive treatment to an essentially normal person with educational, occupational, marital, or other *adjustment* problems.

counterconditioning. In *respondent conditioning*, pairing a *conditioned stimulus* with a new *unconditioned stimulus* that evokes a new *unconditioned response* until a new *conditioned response* appears.

creativity. A distinct capacity possessed in varying degrees that enables a person to produce original ideas that are both adaptive (serve a useful function) and fully developed; *divergent thinking* is one aspect of creativity.

critical period. See *sensitive period*.

cross-sectional study. A method of studying several different groups of people, usually by assessing their performance on a test at one point in time. This method is used to establish *norms*.

cue. Noun: A bit of information. Verb: To give information.

culture-fair test. A test that tries to eliminate discrimination against particular ethnic or social groups.

defense mechanism. The Freudian term for a *cognitive* strategy that is used to cope with *conflicts*, *frustrations*, and other unpleasant realities. Freud and his followers believed that persons use these mental devices *unconsciously* to falsify threatening situations in order to prevent or reduce *anxiety*.

dehumanization. A process which produces a decreased awareness of people's individual attributes and a loss of humanity in interpersonal situations.

delusion. A persistent irrational belief that is contrary to evidence and common sense.

denial of reality (denial). A *cognitive-coping mechanism* which occurs when people ignore or refuse to acknowledge the existence of an aversive experience to protect themselves from unpleasantness.

dendrite. A branching fiber attached to the *soma* of the neuron that picks up information from nearby neurons.

deoxyribonucleic acid (DNA). Molecule found in the nuclei of cells which stores *genetic* information.

dependent variable. In an experiment the *variable* whose state is caused by and therefore depends on changes in another variable, called the *independent variable*.

depth cue. A bit of information that signals depth or distance.

depressive neurosis. A behavioral disorder characterized by an excessively prolonged and intense depressive reaction to *anxiety* or grief, or some combination of the two.

descriptive method. A method used to gather facts to put together an accurate picture of a particular *phenomenon*.

determinism. A philosophical doctrine that all events, including human choices, have a cause.

developmental psychology. A branch of *psychology* which investigates the evolution of physical structure, *behavior*, and psychological functioning in people and other animals from any point after conception to any point before death.

directed thinking. Thinking aimed at a particular goal, such as reasoning, problem solving, or concept learning. Usually highly controlled, tied to a specific situation or problem, and evaluated by external standards.

discrete characteristic. A characteristic that an animal either has or does not have. (Also see *continuous characteristic*.)

discrimination. In *respondent* and *operant conditioning* animals learn to respond to one stimulus and to inhibit that response to a second similar stimulus, usually because responses to one stimulus are *reinforced* while responses to the other are *extinguished*.

displaced aggression. Aggression which results from *frustration* and is directed at available targets instead of at the source of the frustration.

divergent thinking. Innovative and original thinking that deviates from customary patterns of thinking and results in more than one correct solution to particular problems; this ability is generally assessed by *creativity* tests. (Compare *convergent thinking*.)

DNA. See *deoxyribonucleic acid*.

double approach-avoidance conflict. A *conflict* between two goals where each choice has good and bad points.

double-blind procedure. A procedure used in an *experiment* to prevent both the experimenter and subject from knowing the subject's group.

drives. Certain *motives*, such as hunger, that appear to arise from fundamental *physiological needs*.

EEG. See *electroencephalograph*.

EEG-REM method. Method used to collect descriptions of dreams in the laboratory: subjects' *EEG* and eye movements are monitored and subjects are awakened for a dream report during or immediately after *REM* periods.

ego. A hypothetical *personality* faction described by Freud that develops to handle transactions with the environment. One of the ego's primary tasks is to fulfill the *id*'s needs. The ego also tries to keep both the demands of the id and the *superego* under control.

elaborated code. A communication style consisting of sentences that are individualized for a specific situation and person, precise, and particular—allowing a more complex range of thought and differentiating between emotional and intellectual content. (Also see *restricted code*.)

Electra complex. In Freudian *psychodynamic theory* the idea that the young girl displays a desire to possess her father sexually during the *phallic stage*.

electrode. A needle or flat metal bit that conducts electricity.

electroencephalogram. A recording of the electrical activity within the *neural* circuits of the brain.

electroencephalograph (EEG). An instrument which measures the electrical activity occurring within the *neural* circuits of the brain.

embryo. An organism in its early prebirth state.

emotion. A seemingly spontaneous and uncontrollable internal state characterized by subjective feelings and *physiological arousal* that guides expressive gestures and subsequent *behavior*.

empathic. Ability to experience the *emotions* and thoughts of another.

empiricism. A philosophical doctrine asserting that *sensory* experiences, particularly *experiments* and *observations*, are the best source of knowledge.

encoding. The initial transformation of the *stimulus-that-is-to-be-remembered* into images or words, so that it can be stored.

endocrine glands. See *endocrine system*.

endocrine system. Internal coordinating system composed of ductless glands that secrete *hormones* into the blood stream, regulating the animal's internal environment.

engram. See *memory trace*.

enzyme. A complex organic substance which controls chemical reactions within the body.

equivalent groups. A method of assigning subjects to groups in an *experiment* so that each group has the same average score on an important characteristic(s); used to *control* extraneous subject *variables*.

estrogens. Feminine *sex hormones* that influence the development of *secondary sex characteristics* and regulate the *estrus cycle*.

estrus cycle. The hormonal cycle in the female related to reproduction.

exhaustion. Stage 3 of the *GAS* in which the body shows signs of exhaustion. After the *sympathetic nervous system* has depleted its energy, the *parasympathetic nervous system* may take over. If the stress continues, severe psychological or physical problems or even death may result.

existential anxiety. Anxiety arising from a *conflict* over how to lead a fulfilling, meaningful life.

experiment. See *experimental method*.

experimental design. A way of investigating how the *independent variable* affects the *dependent variable* in an experiment.

experimental group. One or more groups that are subjected to changes in the *independent variable* in an *experiment*.

experimental method. A method leading to *explanations*. The effect of a deliberately manipulated variable is assessed. The characteristic feature of the experimental method is its attempt to *control* all extraneous factors that can obscure or interfere with the effect of the manipulation.

experimenter bias. A *phenomenon* that occurs when an experimenter unknowingly *cues* the subject and influences *behavior* in the direction of the experimenter's expectations.

extinction. In both *operant* and *respondent conditioning* the gradual decrease in frequency of the *conditioned response* until it occurs no more frequently than it did prior to conditioning; takes place when the *reinforcement* for the response is withdrawn.

extinguish. See *extinction*.

extrasensory perception. *Perception* through means other than the known *senses*.

extrinsic reinforcer. A *positive reinforcer* that is not the natural and inevitable result of simply engaging in a task.

extroverted. Interested in things outside the self; gregarious.

fantasy. A *cognitive-coping mechanism* which occurs when people achieve needs or goals in their imagination while escaping unpleasant, *anxiety*-arousing, or frustrating realities.

fear. See *anxiety*.

fetally androgenized female. A female who has been exposed to excessive *androgen* during an early *sensitive period* shortly before birth.

fetish. A special object that some people consider essential for full sexual satisfaction.

fetus. An organism in its later prebirth state.

figure-ground. A visual *organizing tendency* in which objects (or figures) tend to be seen standing out from a background (or ground).

fire. The production of a *nerve impulse*.

fraternal twins. Twins who come from different fertilized eggs and have different sets of *genes*. (Also see *identical twins*.)

free association. Allowing one's mind to wander freely, giving a completely frank running account of one's thoughts and feelings; a type of *undirected thinking*.

frustration. (1) The emotional state that results when an obstacle prevents the satisfaction of a desire, *need*, goal, expectation, or action; (2) the obstacle itself.

functional fixity. A tendency to see a particular object as fixed in function largely because of past experience and to fail to perceive new and flexible uses for it.

functionalism. A psychological movement of historical interest that concentrated on the mental processes and how they functioned to help people survive in a dangerous world.

functional psychosis. A *psychotic* disorder that does not have an obvious physical basis; currently assumed to be at least partly the result of psychological causes.

GAS. See *general adaptation syndrome*.

gene. The basic unit of *heredity*. By controlling *enzymes* and *protein* production, genes direct the development of internal and external bodily structures, duplicating those that are inherited from the parent.

general adaptation syndrome (GAS). A pattern of *physiological* responses to continued stress; includes three stages: *alarm reaction*, *resistance*, and *exhaustion*.

genetic. Pertaining to the inheritance of physical characteristics through the *genes*.

genetic sex. Determined at conception by sex *chromosomes*; mothers give their *embryos* an X chromosome. If the father contributes a second X chromosome, the embryo develops as a genetic female. If the father contributes a Y chromosome, the embryo develops as a genetic male.

genital period. In Freud's *psychodynamic theory*, the final *psychosexual stage* when sexual interests shift from the self to others.

germ cell. A reproductive cell.

gestalt psychology. A psychological movement founded by Max Wertheimer and his colleagues that argues that psychologists should study whole *phenomena* and focus primarily on people's subjective experiences of the world.

gonad. A sex gland: *ovaries* in the female and *testes* in the male.

grouping. A visual *organizing tendency* in which separate visual elements are unified into patterns.

growth motive. A *motive* that seems to arise from

needs to develop and acquire competence and to actualize one's various potentials.

Hawthorne effect. The influence of attention on performance.

heredity. An animal's physical inheritance.

heritability index. An estimate of the percentage of the variability seen on a psychological test on a particular population that can be accounted for by *genetic* factors.

hermaphrodite. A person with ambiguous sexual anatomy.

hertz. Cycles per second; a measure of frequency.

homeostasis. The body's self-regulating tendency.

hormone. A chemical substance secreted directly into the blood stream by *endocrine glands*.

humanistic psychologists. See *humanistic psychology*.

humanistic psychology. The study of people as wholes, focusing on subjective awareness and tackling significant human problems. Humanistic psychologists aim at enriching human life.

hypersexuality. Excessive or exaggerated sexuality.

hypothalamus. A *limbic system* structure that exerts control over the posterior pituitary gland, and influences sexual physiology and *behavior*, eating, drinking, sleeping, and aggression. Also activates the *sympathetic nervous system* during an emergency.

hypothesis. A tentative explanation to be tested by experimentation.

hypothetical construct. A characteristic, condition, or process such as a thought, *sensation*, *emotion*, *need*, *motive*, *personality* characteristic, or capability that cannot be observed or measured directly and is inferred on the basis of related *behavior*.

id. A hypothetical *personality* faction described by Freud: the domain of the *basic drives* that seek immediate gratification.

identical twins. Twins who develop from the same fertilized egg and have identical sets of *genes*. (Also see *fraternal twins*.)

identification. The perception of self as similar to another; also the process of associating oneself with another person or group of people and accepting their values as one's own.

imitation. See *observation learning*.

immediate reinforcement. In *operant conditioning*, presenting the *reinforcement* immediately after the *behavior* that it is intended to increase.

imprinting. Early following *behavior* seen in many animals that reflects the *learning* of an initial social *attachment*.

independent variable. In an *experiment* the *variable* which is manipulated and causes changes in another variable, called the *dependent variable*.

informational conformity. The conformity that occurs when a person doubts his/her *sensory* impressions or when a situation is unclear or ambiguous; the person is more likely to take the opinions of others into account to improve the accuracy of information.

instinct. A hypothetical inborn *drive* that arouses complex *behavior*; the concept has controversial status.

intelligence. An overall ability to act purposefully, think rationally, and deal effectively with the environment.

intelligence quotient (IQ). A concise way of describing a person's relative performance on an *intelligence test*. The IQ usually indicates how a person compares with others in the same age bracket.

intelligence test. A test which tries to assess particular mental abilities.

intentionality. Pertaining to goals, purposes, or plans; young children judge the morality of *behavior* by its physical consequences—without taking goals, purposes, or plans into account.

interposition. A *monocular depth cue* in which a complete object is perceived as closer than an obstructed object.

interpretation. The presentation of clues to the patient's conflicts by the therapist in *psychoanalytic psychotherapy*.

intrauterine. Within the uterus.

intrinsic reinforcer. A *positive reinforcer* that is the natural and inevitable result of simply engaging in a task.

introverted. Shy and preoccupied with one's own thoughts and feelings.

IQ. See *intelligence quotient*.

kinesthetic sense. A *sense* that informs people about the positioning of the body and its parts as they move; depends on *receptors* in the muscles, tendons, and joints.

language. A systematic relating of symbols (sounds, letters, or signs) to meanings and provision of rules for combining and recombining the symbols to convey various kinds of information.

latent content. Freud's term for the real meaning of a dream that is often hidden in the *manifest content*.

learning. A process that occurs inside the organism and leads to relatively permanent changes in *behavior* that can be attributed to experience.

learning set (learning to learn). A general approach to problem solving that has been acquired through past experience in similar situations.

lens. A part of the eye that helps focus incoming visual images onto the *retina*.

lesion. Change in tissue because of disease, injury, or surgery.

limbic system (old brain). A group of interrelated

structures covering the *central core* and lying below the *cerebrum* that appears to be generally concerned with regulating *emotions* and *motives*.

linear perspective. A *monocular depth cue* produced by an apparent change in the size of objects at different distances from the eye.

localize. To refer particular behavioral functions to particular regions of the *nervous system*.

longitudinal study. A study that measures the same subjects on particular characteristics at several different points in time to pinpoint changes that occur over time.

long-term memory. Semipermanent or permanent memory.

long-term memory system. A memory system that stores semipermanent or permanent memories.

looking chamber. An apparatus used to study the human infant's *perception* of form and pattern.

love-oriented technique. A disciplinary method that uses praise as a reward for good behavior and reasoning, appeals to pride, withdrawal of love, and displays of disappointment as deterrents or *punishments* for bad behavior.

maladjustment. Unsatisfactory adjustment.

manifest content. Freud's term for the events, images, people, and storyline of the dream, as it is remembered.

massed practice. Crowding *learning* into one long practice period without a rest.

matching. A method of assigning subjects to groups in an *experiment* based on equating the subjects in each group on significant characteristics to *control* extraneous subject *variables*.

maturation. The emergence of behavior patterns that depend primarily on the development of body and *nervous system* structures.

mean. A *measure of central tendency*; arithmetic average.

measured intelligence. Performance on an *intelligence test*.

measure of central tendency. A measure of the central value around which a group of scores clusters.

median. A *measure of central tendency*; the middle score in a group of scores; the point that 50 percent of the scores fall above and 50 percent of the scores fall below.

mediating. A link between two processes. Used frequently with reference to *cognitive processes*. Many psychologists believe that environmental *stimuli* do not directly initiate *behavior* but stimulate intervening cognitive processes which activate behavior.

medical model. A model of *abnormal behavior* that assumes that psychological problems resemble physical illness and that (1) each disorder may be traced to distinct causes; (2) treatment must aim at identifying

the causes and selecting appropriate cures; and (3) the patient must primarily cooperate with an expert who applies the appropriate cure.

meditation. A *state of consciousness* brought on by diverse techniques that aim at separating the self from daily life, turning off normal consciousness, and attaining an overall perspective of unity and humanity.

memory trace (engram). A long-lasting physical change in the *nervous system* corresponding to a specific memory; has not yet been observed.

mental age. The concept of mental age is based on the assumption that intellectual ability increases progressively with age and that these increases can be measured. On the basis of relative performance on an intelligence test, individuals are sometimes assigned a mental age score that is assumed to indicate their relative intellectual ability.

method of successive approximations. See *shaping*.

mnemonic strategy. Technique of organizing information by associating it with rhymes, images, and so on, so that it becomes easier to remember.

mode. A *measure of central tendency*; the score that appears most frequently in a group of scores.

modeling. See *observation learning*.

monocular depth cues. *Depth cues* that depend on the operation of only one eye.

motion parallax. A *monocular depth cue* in which close objects seem to move with greater speed than distant objects.

motive. An internal arousing state that results from a *need* and usually activates *behavior* aimed at fulfilling that need.

motive to avoid success. A learned *social motive* aroused by competitive situations in which persons fear that success will bring negative consequences.

motor areas. See *motor regions*.

motor pathways. A collection of *nerve fibers* which convey information from the *CNS* to the muscles or glands.

motor regions. Portions of the *cerebral cortex* that control the skeletal muscles that initiate *behavior*.

multiple approach-avoidance conflict. A *conflict* between two or more goals where each choice is partly positive and partly negative.

n-ach. See *need to achieve*.

naturalistic observation. An observation made in a real-life setting. In psychology, naturalistic observations are frequently used to gather information about realistic behavior.

need. A social-psychological deficiency.

need to achieve (n-ach). A felt social-psychological deficiency that activates a motive to pursue excellence, to accomplish lofty goals, or to be successful on difficult tasks.

negative correlation coefficient. See *correlation coefficient*.

negative reinforcer. In *operant conditioning*, an event whose removal increases the likelihood of a particular behavior.

negative transfer. A result that occurs when past *learning* retards new learning or problem solving.

neobehaviorism. A modern version of *behaviorism* that has become increasingly concerned with complex human processes. Insists on precise, well-delineated questions, scientific methods, and careful, accurate research.

neonate. Newborn human infant.

nerve fibers. *Axons* and *dendrites*.

nerve impulse. An electrochemical change that travels along *nerve fibers*; used for communication throughout the *nervous system*.

nerves. Collections of *nerve fibers* gathered together to carry information to and from the *central nervous system*.

nervous system. An internal coordinating system that organizes the functioning of all living organisms; includes the *central* and *peripheral nervous systems*.

neural. Pertaining to a *nerve* or to the *nervous system*.

neuron. A nerve cell, the basic unit of the *nervous system*.

neurosis (neurotic reaction). A mild behavioral disorder that centers around anxiety. Neurotic people typically have difficulty handling their *anxiety*. They frequently react by avoidance responses. More often than not, they lack insight into the causes of their symptoms; they continue to persist in the same maladaptive behaviors. As they become increasingly preoccupied with their anxieties, inadequacies, and symptoms, their work and interpersonal relationships begin to suffer. Consequently, they usually feel unhappy and out of control.

neurotic reaction. See *neurosis*.

neutral stimulus. In *respondent conditioning*, any event, object, or experience that is paired with an *unconditioned stimulus* and does not initially elicit the *unconditioned response* that is evoked by the unconditioned stimulus.

non-REM sleep. Sleep stages characterized by the absence of rapid eye movements. There are four stages of non-REM sleep.

noradrenalin. A *hormone* secreted by the *adrenal glands* during stresses that prepares the body to handle an emergency.

normative conformity. *Conformity* to win group support or avoid group rejection.

norms. Specific information on the test performance of a large group of people which allows a test examiner to interpret an individual score.

nucleus. A structure within cells in which *chromosomes* are located.

obedience. *Conformity* to the demands of those in authority.

object-oriented technique. A disciplinary method that uses tangible rewards for good *behavior*, and threats, commands, physical force, and withdrawal of privileges as deterrents or *punishments* for bad behavior.

observation learning (imitation, modeling, social learning). The relatively enduring change in *behavior* that results in large part from observing the behavior of another.

obsession. A thought that repeatedly occupies a person's attention despite the fact that the person prefers to be rid of the thought.

obsessive-compulsive neurosis. A behavioral disorder characterized by *obsessions, compulsions,* or both that disrupt the individual's life.

Oedipus complex. In Freudian *psychodynamic theory* the idea that the young boy displays a desire to possess his mother sexually during the *phallic stage*.

old brain. See *limbic system*.

operant. An active response that seems to be under voluntary control.

operant conditioning. The process of altering the frequency of an *operant* by modifying the consequences that follow it.

operant learning. See *operant conditioning*.

operational definition. A precise definition that relates a concept or object to the procedures that are used to observe or measure it.

optic nerve. *Nerve fibers* that connect the *retina* of the eye to the brain.

oral stage. According to Freud's *psychodynamic theory*, the first *psychosexual stage* during which the child's pleasure is focused on the mouth and oral activities such as eating and sucking.

organic psychosis. A *psychotic* disorder that can be traced to specific physical causes such as tumors, head injuries, cerebral arteriosclerosis, hormone deficiencies, alcoholism, and infectious diseases such as syphilis.

organizing tendency. A principle that structures some aspect of the perceptual process; depends on both inborn *physiological* mechanisms and experience.

orgasm. A *physiological* reaction (accompanied by emotional sensations) at the culmination of a sexual act, lasting several seconds and bringing relief to blood-swollen areas and tightened muscles.

ovaries. Female sex glands.

ovum. Mother's *germ cell* or egg.

parasympathetic nervous system. A division of the *autonomic nervous system*; most active during periods of comparative calm in controlling the performance of routine duties that build up and conserve the body's store of energy.

parsimony. A philosophical doctrine stating that the best explanation is the simplest one that fits the observed facts.

partial reinforcement. In *operant conditioning*, *reinforcement* that does not follow each and every correct response.

participant observation. A *naturalistic observation* made while scientists participate in the event or activity being studied.

pavlovian conditioning. See *respondent conditioning*.

peptic ulcer. A lesion (hole), usually in the stomach or duodenum lining, produced by the excessive secretion of hydrochloric acid.

perceived size. A *monocular depth cue* used to judge the distance to a familiar object by noting the size of the retinal image it produces.

perception. The process of extracting information from the environment.

performance. Changes in *behavior* that demonstrate that *learning* has occurred.

peripheral nervous system (PNS). One of two major subsystems of the *nervous system*; composed of the *autonomic nervous system* and the *somatic nervous system*.

personality. The unique pattern of relatively enduring *behaviors*, feelings, thoughts, *motives*, interests, and *attitudes* that characterize a particular individual.

personality disorder. A deeply ingrained maladaptive behavior pattern frequently recognizable by the time of adolescence, including *antisocial personality*, sexual deviations, alcoholic addiction, and drug dependencies.

phallic stage. In Freud's *psychodynamic theory*, the third *psychosexual stage* when pleasure is focused on the genitals and the *Electra* and *Oedipus complexes* arise.

phenomenon. A fact, occurrence, process, event, or condition.

phobia. An excessive or unwarranted fear of a specific object or situation.

phobic neurosis. A behavioral disorder characterized by at least one disabling *phobia*.

phrenology. Outdated brain theory that relates bumps on the skull to the predominance of particular behavioral characteristics.

physiological. Pertaining to the science that deals with the physical functions of living organisms or any of their parts.

physiological psychology. The study of the physical foundations of *sensation*, *perception*, *learning*, memory, *motives*, *emotions*, and other *behaviors*.

placebo. An inert drug or "neutral" treatment used to equalize the effects of expectations between groups in an *experiment*.

polygraph. An instrument used to measure several *physiological* responses, such as heart rate, respiration rate, and muscle tension, at the same time.

population. The entire group under study.

positive correlation coefficient. See *correlation coefficient*.

positive reinforcer. In *operant conditioning*, an event whose presentation increases the likelihood of a particular behavior.

positive transfer. A result that occurs when past *learning* facilitates new learning or problem solving.

precision. Exactness, clarity, and accuracy in definitions and descriptions.

precognition. A form of *extrasensory perception*; knowing a future event that could not be logically inferred.

primary drive (basic drive). A *motive* that activates *behavior* aimed at fulfilling fundamental biological *needs*.

primary prevention. In mental health care, the creation of a psychologically healthy community by helping essentially normal people utilize their full potential and develop satisfying and effective ways of adjusting to life.

primary punisher. In *operant conditioning*, a naturally aversive *punisher* such as a pain-inducing stimulus.

primary reinforcer. In *operant conditioning*, an unlearned *reinforcer* that satisfies a basic *physiological need*.

primary sex characteristics. The sex organs—in females, the *ovaries*, the vagina, and the uterus; in males, the *testes* and the penis.

process schizophrenia (chronic schizophrenia). *Schizophrenia* which develops gradually over many years. Persons with this disorder tend to have been sickly, withdrawn, and maladjusted all their lives. Symptoms are severe and the prognosis is poor.

progesterone. A feminine *sex hormone* whose primary function is to prepare the uterine lining for pregnancy.

projection. A *cognitive-coping mechanism* that occurs when people assign their own undesirable characteristics, mistakes, problems, impulses, desires, or thoughts to others—presumably to reduce their own *anxiety* at having to recognize these characteristics as their own.

projection areas. See *sensory regions*.

projective test. A test in which persons respond to ambiguous stimuli. Many psychologists believe that people project their *needs*, *motives*, fears, hopes, *conflicts*, and *emotions* through their responses.

protein. A complex chemical substance that is necessary for basic life processes.

proximity. A visual *organizing tendency* in which visual elements near one another are seen as belonging together.

psychiatrist. A physician who has specialized in the diagnosis and treatment of behavioral disorders.

psychoanalyst. A person who has been trained in the theory and practice of psychoanalysis. In America most psychoanalysts are *psychiatrists*.

psychoanalytic psychotherapy. A *therapy* approach that assumes that psychological problems are caused by *repressed* conflicts. The cure consists of a lengthy, intensive exploration of the person's mental life, past and present. *Psychoanalytic therapists* analyze their patients, *free associations* and dreams; they also look for and interpret *resistance* and *transference*. Through the psychoanalysts' *interpretations*, patients gain insight into their *unconscious* conflicts. The insight is assumed to lead automatically to a more constructive *adjustment*.

psychoanalytic theory. The general name for Freud's theories about *personality*, abnormality, and treatment.

psychoanalytic therapist. A *therapist* who uses *psychoanalytic* procedures.

psychodynamic theory. A *personality* theory whose aim is to describe how personality develops and explain how underlying personality processes interact to determine behavior. It emphasizes the importance of internal forces such as impulses, *motives*, and *emotions* and assumes that personality develops as persons resolve *conflicts* between these internal forces.

psycholinguistics. The study of how *language* is acquired and used.

psychological model. A model of *abnormal behavior* that assumes that (1) abnormal behavior is similar in kind, though not in degree, to normal behavior; (2) treatment is rarely syndrome specific; (3) active patient involvement in treatment is important.

psychological test. A test which attempts to measure abilities, *personality* characteristics, feelings, *attitudes*, or interests.

psychology. The science of *behavior*.

psychopathic behavior (antisocial personality). A *personality disorder* characterized by *behavior* patterns that bring people into conflict with society. Psychopathic persons neglect the rights of others, behave like con-artists, act for their own immediate gratification, and appear to be oblivious to the consequences of their behavior.

psychosis. A behavioral disorder characterized by severely impaired *cognitive* and *behavioral* functioning. Moods may be profoundly altered. Persons who suffer from psychotic disorders are frequently ab-

sorbed in their disturbance, out of contact with reality, and unable to take care of themselves for long periods of time. They are also likely to have little or no perspective about their symptoms.

psychosexual stages. According to Freud's *psychodynamic* theory, a series of biologically determined developmental stages that shapes *personality*: the *oral stage*, the *anal stage*, the *phallic stage*, and the *genital stage*.

psychosomatic disorder. A disorder that results from the body's *autonomic* and *hormonal* responses to stress, such as *peptic ulcers* and high blood pressure.

psychotherapist. A mental health professional who engages in *psychotherapy*.

psychotherapy. The various psychological (as opposed to biological) treatment procedures that have been designed to help troubled people solve personal problems.

psychotic disorders. See *psychosis*.

punisher. See *punishment*.

punishment. In *operant conditioning*, an event that follows a response and reduces its frequency. Note that punishment is said to occur when, and only when, a specific response is followed by an event which reduces its frequency.

racial prejudice. An *attitude* which reflects a positive or negative prejudgment about a person (or a group of people) based on racial group membership, irrespective of each individual's distinctive strengths or weaknesses.

random assignment. A method of assigning subjects to groups in an experiment based on chance so that each subject has an equal probability of being assigned to any group; used to *control* extraneous subject *variables*.

range. A measure of *variability* computed by subtracting the lowest score from the highest score of a group of scores.

rapid eye movement sleep. See *REM sleep*.

rationalization. A *cognitive-coping mechanism* involving two strategies: (1) Persons think up socially acceptable reasons for past, present, or contemplated *behavior* to hide the real *motives* from themselves, and (2) they pretend that a bad situation is really good or that a good situation is really bad.

reaction formation. A *cognitive-coping mechanism* that occurs when persons conceal a real *motive* or *emotion* from themselves and express the opposite one by *attitudes* and *behavior*—presumably to avoid *anxiety* associated with the real motive or emotion.

reactive schizophrenia (acute schizophrenia). *Schizophrenia* that is triggered suddenly by stress. A relatively mild disorder in which elements of intense emotional upheaval and confusion tend to be pronounced. The recovery rate is higher than that for *process schizophrenia*.

receptor. The detection element of a *sense*; a single cell or group of cells that respond to specific forms of energy.

reciprocity. A mutually giving and receiving relationship. Young children lack a sense of reciprocity; they cannot put themselves in the place of others nor understand *motives* that differ from their own.

reflex. See *reflexive behavior*.

reflexive behavior. A *behavior* automatically elicited by *stimuli* in the environment. A rapid, consistent unlearned response that is not subject to voluntary control under ordinary circumstances.

regression. Coping behavior that occurs when persons confront threats by returning to immature modes of *behavior* that characterized them at younger ages.

reinforcement (reinforcer). An event that increases the probability that a particular response will occur. In *respondent conditioning*, the pairing of the *neutral* and *unconditioned stimulus* reinforces the *conditioned response*. In *operant conditioning*, the response is reinforced by its consequences.

reinforcement schedule. See *schedule of reinforcement*.

relativism. A theory stating that criteria for judgments vary with individuals and environments. Young children tend to assume that all moral acts can be classified as absolutely and unconditionally "right" or "wrong"; they are not relativistic.

reliability. The extent to which repeated measurements of the same *phenomenon* with the same test yield similar results; roughly synonymous with the term "consistency."

REM. Rapid eye movements.

REM sleep. A sleep stage characterized by the occurrence of rapid eye movements; the stage when dreaming occurs.

replicate. To repeat a study to disclose errors or to confirm previous results.

representative sample. A *sample* that mirrors the important characteristics of the *population* under study.

repressed. Excluded from awareness. (Also see *repression*.)

repression. A *cognitive-coping mechanism* that occurs when people exclude *anxiety*-arousing *motives*, ideas, *conflicts*, thoughts, or memories from awareness.

resistance. (1) Acts which disturb the therapy process. Freud believed that such acts occurred when patients reached difficult *repressed* material, felt threatened by the pain of facing it, and unconsciously resisted the therapy process. (2) Stage two of the *GAS*;

the body remains highly aroused and systems responsible for growth, repair, and resistance to infection are shut down.

respondent. An automatic response or *reflex* prewired into an animal.

respondent conditioning (classical conditioning, pavlovian conditioning). A *learning* method used to transfer a *respondent* to a situation where it does not ordinarily occur.

response. Any behavior that is elicited by a *stimulus*.

restitution. Payment for damage or injury. A belief in the necessity for restitution in moral matters characterizes young children.

restricted code. A communication style consisting of sentences that are short, simple, unfinished, implicitly understood, and limited both in concept and in information. (Also see *elaborated code*.)

reticular formation. A massive network of *neurons* located in the *central core* of the brain, one of whose main functions is to warn the *cerebral cortex* of important *sensory* information that requires attention.

retina. The rear inner surface of the eye on which images of objects in the visual field are focused; involved in *transduction* and in information processing.

retrieval. Location of stored information in *long-term memory*.

retrograde amnesia. Memory loss for events and experiences that immediately precede massive disruption of *neural* activity in the brain, but not for more distant memories.

reverberating loop theory. A theory which explains the operation of *sensory* and *short-term memory systems*. Assumes that brain *neurons* are arranged in loops that respond to specific stimuli.

ribonucleic acid (RNA). A molecule that transfers information from DNA to the cells of the body; may also take part in recording *long-term memories*.

RNA. See *ribonucleic acid*.

role playing. "Play acting" a particular role.

sample. The portion of a population that is actually studied in a research investigation. (Also see *representative sample*.)

sampling error. An error that results because the investigator measures a *sample* rather than the entire *population* of interest.

sanction. A law enacting penalties for disobedience or rewards for *obedience*. Young children judge a crime's severity by the severity of its consequences.

schedule of reinforcement. In *operant conditioning*, "rules" that tell when and how *reinforcement* is administered after the occurrence of a particular response. Reinforcement schedules have predictable effects on *behavior*.

schizophrenia. A puzzling group of *psychotic disorders* likely to include many of the following patterns: faulty perceptual filtering, disorganized thinking, emotional distortions, *delusions* and *hallucinations*, withdrawal from reality, bizarre behavior, and jumbled, incomprehensible speech.

secondary prevention. In mental health care, the identification of a psychological problem in its early stages and the provision of immediate treatment before it becomes serious.

secondary sex characteristic. A sex characteristic that develops at puberty, including the growth of breasts and the broadening of hips in young women and the growth of facial and bodily hair and the deepening of the voice in young men.

selective breeding. A procedure for breeding animals used to pinpoint the effects of *genetics* on behavior.

self-actualization. Self-fulfillment.

self concept. An individual's subjective appraisal of his/her own characteristics.

sensation A subjective impression resulting from the stimulation of a *sense*.

senses. Specialized information-gathering systems that enable animals to *perceive* the surrounding environment.

sensitive period (critical period). A period of development when the organism is maximally sensitive to the effects of the environment.

sensory. Pertaining to the *senses*.

sensory and cognitive overload. A state that occurs when a person is exposed to more *sensory* and *cognitive* information than he/she can adequately process; thought to occur frequently in urban environments.

sensory deprivation. Reduced level of *sensory stimulation*; less than the individual's normal range or type of *sensory stimulation*.

sensory isolation. Exposure to a monotonous, relatively unpatterned *sensory* environment for a substantial period of time.

sensory memory. The retention of sensory information for a fraction of a second. (Also see *sensory representation system*.)

sensory pathway. A collection of *nerve fibers* that convey information from *sensory* cells in the skin to the *CNS*.

sensory region (projection area). A portion of the *cerebral cortex* that receives incoming information about the *sensory* world.

sensory representation system. A memory system that makes brief *sensory* representations of all sensory *stimuli*; these sensory representations fade after a fraction of a second.

sensory stimulation. Activation of the senses.

sex hormone. A *hormone* that affects sexual development and sexual *behavior*.

sex-typed behavior. *Behavior* patterns that are characteristic of males or females.

shaping (method of successive approximations). In *operant conditioning*, a *positive reinforcement* strategy for teaching new responses. Reinforcement is *contingent* upon the subject's making closer and closer approximations to the desired *behavior*. The process continues until the desired behavior itself is conditioned.

short-term memory system. A memory system that stores interpretations of *sensory* data for minutes at a time.

similarity. A visual *organizing tendency* in which visual elements with the same color, shape, or texture are seen as belonging together.

single-blind procedure. A procedure used in an *experiment* to prevent the subject's knowing his/her condition.

situation-specific. According to this *neobehavioristic* concept, *behavior* in any given situation is controlled by many essentially independent causes and conditions, especially current circumstances and past *learning*.

Skinner box. A controlled, distraction-free environment introduced by B. F. Skinner for *operant conditioning experiments*.

socialization. Guiding children toward *behaviors*, values, goals, and *motives* that the culture considers appropriate and discouraging those of which the culture does not approve.

social learning. See *observation learning*.

social milieu therapy. A set of procedures that is used in a hospital setting to turn a ward into a therapeutic community.

social motive. A motive that arises from social *needs* to feel loved, accepted, approved, esteemed, and so on.

social psychology. The study of animals (especially people) as they interact with and influence one another, both directly and indirectly.

social punisher. In *operant conditioning*, *punishers* which depend on people's negative reactions such as ridicule, disapproval, or criticism.

social reinforcer. In *operant conditioning*, a *reinforcer* such as approval, prestige, or affection that depends on other people.

soma. The main cell body of the *neuron*.

somatic nervous system. The division of the *nervous system* that contains *sensory* and *motor pathways*.

spaced practice. The distribution of *learning* over short practice periods with rest periods in between.

specific hunger. A hunger that leads animals to seek out actively a substance in which their diets are deficient.

sperm. Father's *germ cell*.

spontaneous recovery. In *operant* and *respondent conditioning*, the reappearance of a response which has been previously *extinguished*; occurs after a rest period.

standard administration. The uniform procedures that are provided by the test designer and to which all test examiners adhere.

standard deviation. A widely used *statistic* that describes *variability*.

Stanford-Binet Intelligence Test. A widely used intelligence test.

state of consciousness. A person's total subjective awareness of world and self.

statistics. Various mathematical techniques which provide ways of organizing, describing, and interpreting numercial data, also refers to the numerical data themselves.

statistical decision. Decision about the significance of statistical results; that is, the decision whether the results are meaningful or likely to be the result of chance.

statistically significant result. A result which the laws of probability predict will occur less than 5 in 100 times simply because of chance.

stereotype. An overly simple and rigid generalization concerning people or social groups.

stereotyped behavior. Behavior that is occasioned by a *conflict*, varies little, has a ritualistic quality, and is rarely altered by its consequences.

stimulus (plural: **stimuli).** An event, object, or situation that evokes a *response*.

stimulus discrimination. In *respondent conditioning*, learning to respond to one *stimulus* and to inhibit that *response* to a second similar *stimulus*.

stimulus generalization. In *respondent conditioning*, the spreading of a *conditioned response* to events that are similar to the *conditioned stimulus* and to aspects of the situation where the conditioned response was initially conditioned.

structuralism. A psychological movement founded by Edward Titchener that states that psychologists should study the mind through introspective studies in the laboratory. (Also see *analytic introspection*.)

superego. A *hypothetical* personality faction described by Freud that incorporates parental and cultural standards of right and wrong.

symmetry (good figure). A visual *organizing tendency* in which visual elements that form regular, simple, symmetrical forms are seen as belonging together.

sympathetic nervous system. A division of the *autonomic nervous system*; most active during periods of intense *emotion* when it mobilizes the body's resources for action.

synapse. The small gap which separates two *neurons*.

systematic desensitization. A strategy that uses *learning* principles, primarily those of *respondent conditioning*, to reduce incapacitating *anxiety* in children and adults. Relaxation is usually paired with the imagining of anxiety-arousing situations, until a person no longer feels anxious when thinking about these situations. Once a person has visualized formerly distressing events without distress, he/she often feels confident in confronting the actual stimuli.

TAT. See *Thematic Apperception Test*.

telegraphic speech. Two-word utterances used by children at approximately $1\frac{1}{2}$ to 2 years of age.

telepathy. A form of *extrasensory perception*; knowing the thoughts of another without using a known means of communication.

testes. Male sex glands.

testosterone. A male *sex hormone*; the major *androgen*.

test-retest reliability. The consistency of a test over time; the *correlation* between two scores, obtained by administering the same test to the same subject several weeks to several months apart. Test-retest reliability is high if the scores are similar, low if the scores vary considerably.

texture gradient. A *monocular depth cue* in which objects in the visual field show gradual changes in texture with distance. They appear coarse nearby and finer as the observer looks farther into the distance.

therapist. See *psychotherapist*.

therapy. See *psychotherapy*.

Thematic Apperception Test (TAT). A *projective test* used to measure twenty *social motives*.

threshold. The minimal *sensory stimulation* level necessary to produce a *response*.

tip-of-the-tongue phenomenon (TOT). State in which a person cannot recall a particular word but feels certain that he/she knows the word.

token economy. A *behavior therapy* procedure that systematically motivates and rewards adaptive *behavior*.

trait. A *personality* characteristic that seems to endure across a wide variety of situations to account for the regularity of *behavior*.

transducer. A device that converts energy from one form to another.

transduction. The process of converting energy from one form to another.

transference. In *psychoanalytic therapy*, the patient's *identification* of the therapist with a person who was significant in the past (usually a parent).

transmitter substance. A chemical secreted by a *neuron* into its *synapses* that causes changes in the membrane of the receiving nerve cell, making it more or less likely to *fire*.

traumatic physical event. An event that destroy's an organism's cells.

twin study method. A method that compares *identical* and *fraternal twins* on a particular characteristic to determine the relative importance of the contributions of *heredity* and environment.

type. A *personality* category to which a person is sometimes assigned. Typing assumes that several related personality *traits* commonly occur together.

unconscious. Unaware; Freud believed that people are unaware of the vast majority of their thoughts, feelings, and desires and cannot become aware of them without the help of a trained specialist.

unconditioned response. In *respondent conditioning*, the *respondent* that is automatically elicited by the *unconditioned stimulus*.

unconditioned stimulus. In *respondent conditioning*, any event, object, or experience that automatically elicits a particular *respondent*.

undirected thinking. Thinking that is aimed at no particular goal, such as *free association*.

unlearned reinforcer. See *primary reinforcer*.

validity. The extent to which a test really assesses what it is supposed to assess.

variability. A concept that describes how widely the scores in a group vary from a central value.

variable. Anything that can change or take on different characteristics.

variable sensory experience. An experience that some members of a species undergo and others do not in the normal course of development.

verbal learning. All *language*-related *learning*; all learning which involves the use of words.

vestibular sense. The *sense* that informs animals about the movement and positioning of the head and body; depends on *receptors* in the boney parts of the skull in both inner ears.

visual cliff. A simulated cliff apparatus used to test depth perception.

WAIS. See *Wechsler Adult Intelligence Scale*.

Wechsler Adult Intelligence Scale (WAIS). A widely used adult *intelligence test*.

zygote. A single cell produced at conception; the uniting of the father's and mother's *germ cells*.

BIBLIOGRAPHY

Chapter 1

1 Bustad, L. K. The experimental subject—A choice not an echo. *Perspectives in Biology and Medicine*, Autumn, 1970, Vol. 14.

2 Bustad, L. K. The experimental subject—A choice not an echo. *Perspectives in Biology and Medicine*, Autumn, 1970, Vol. 14.

3 Titchener, E. *A beginner's psychology.* New York: The Macmillan Company, 1915. P. 9.

4 Miller, G. A. *Psychology: The science of mental life.* New York: Harper & Row, Publishers, Incorporated, 1962. Pp. 20–21.

5 Watson, J. *Psychology from the standpoint of a behaviorist.* Philadelphia: J. B. Lippincott & Company, 1919. Pp. 1–3.

6 Watson, J. *Behaviorism.* New York: W. W. Norton & Company, 1925. P. 82.

7 Freud, S. The origin and development of psycho-analysis. *American Journal of Psychology*, 1910, 21, 182–187.

8 Harlow, H. F. Love in infant monkeys. *Scientific American*, June 1959, 200, 68–70.

9 Bruner, J. S. The act of discovery. *Harvard Educational Review*, 1961, 31, 1, 24–35.

10 Bugenthal, J. F. T. The challenge that is man. In J. F. T. Bugenthal (Ed.), *Challenges of humanistic psychology.* New York: McGraw-Hill Book Company, 1967. P. 7.

11 Maslow, A. Self-actualization and beyond. In J. F. T. Bugenthal (Ed.), *Challenges of humanistic psychology.* New York: McGraw-Hill Book Company, 1967. Pp. 279–280.

12 Maslow, A. H. *Motivation and personality.* (2d ed.) New York: Harper & Row, Publishers, Incorporated, 1970.

13 Vetter, B. M. Manpower in psychology. *American Psychological Association Monitor*, November 1973, 3.

14 Cates, J. Psychology's manpower: Report on the 1968 national register of scientific and technical personnel. *American Psychologist*, 1970, 25, 254–263.

Chapter 2

1 Bachrach, A. *Psychological research: An introduction.* (3d ed.) New York: Random House, Inc., 1972. Pp. 19–20.

2 Crutchfield, R. S., & D. Krech. Some guides to the understanding of the history of psychology. In Leo Postman (Ed.), *Psychology in the making.* New York: Alfred A. Knopf, Inc., 1962. P. 23.

3 Barber, B., & R. Fox. The case of the floppy-eared rabbits: An instance of serendipity gained and serendipity lost. *The American Journal of Sociology*, September 1958, 54, 128–136.

4 Barber, B. Resistance by scientists to scientific discovery. *Scientific Man Power Bulletin*, 1960, 36–47.

5 Rosenhan, D. L. On being sane in insane places. *Science*, 1973, 179, 250–257.

6 Festinger, L., H. W. Riecken, & S. Schachter. *When prophecy fails*. Minneapolis: University of Minnesota Press, 1956.

7 Rosenhan, D. L. On being sane in insane places. *Science*, 1973, 179, 250–257.

8 Festinger, L., H. W. Riecken, & S. Schachter. *When prophecy fails*. Minneapolis: University of Minnesota Press, 1956. P. 140.

9 Corte, H. E., M. M. Wolfe, & B. J. Locke. A comparison of procedures for eliminating self-injurious behavior of retarded adolescents. *Journal of Applied Behavior Analysis*, 1971, 4, 201–213.

10 Freud, S. *The standard edition of the complete psychological works. Vol. 2*. London: Hogarth, 1955. Pp. 175–181.

11 Athanasiou, R., & Shaver, P. Research questionnaire on sex. *Psychology Today*, July 1969, 3, 68–69.

12 Davidoff, L. Unpublished case notes.

13 Latané, B., & J. M. Darley. *The unresponsive bystander: Why doesn't he help?* New York: Appleton Century Crofts, 1970.

14 Roethlisberger, F. J., and Dickson, W. J. *Management and the worker*. Cambridge, Mass.: Harvard University Press, 1939.

15 Rosenthal, R. Clever Hans: A case study of scientific method. In M. S. Gazzaniga & E. P. Lovejoy (Eds.), *Good reading in psychology*. Englewood Cliffs, N.J.: Prentice-Hall, Inc. 1971. Pp. 498–518.

16 Rosenthal, R. *Experimenter effects in behavioral research*. New York: Appleton Century Crofts, 1966.

17 Darley, J. M., & B. Latané. Bystander intervention in emergencies: Diffusion of responsibility. *Journal of Personality and Social Psychology*, 1968, 8, 377–383.

18 Darley, J. M., & C. D. Batson. From Jerusalem to Jericho. A study of situational and dispositional variables in helping behavior. Unpublished study, 1971.

19 Altman, D., M. Levine, M. Nadien, & J. Villera. Trust of the stranger in the city and the small town. Unpublished research, Graduate Center, City University of New York, 1969. cited in S. Milgram The experience of living in cities: A psychological analysis. *Science*, March 13, 1970, 167, 1461–1468.

20 Bryan, J. H., & M. A. Test. Models and helping: Naturalistic studies in aiding behavior. *Journal of Personality and Social Psychology*, 1967, 6, 400–407.

21 Horn, P. The uncaring bystander starts to care. *Psychology Today*, September 1973, 7, 17.

22 Krebs, D. The effect of prior experience on generosity—role taking or modeling. Unpublished manuscript, 1972.

23 Rutherford, E., & P. Mussen. Generosity in nursery school boys. *Child Development*, 1968, 39, 755–765.

24 Ad hoc Committee on Ethical Standards in Psychological Research. *Ethical principles in the conduct of research with human participants*. Washington, D.C.: American Psychological Association, 1973.

25 Baddeley, A. D. Selective attention and performance in dangerous environments. *British Journal of Psychology*, 1972, 63, 4, 537–546.

Chapter 3

1 Hall, G. S. Notes on the study of infants. *Pedagogical Seminary*, 1891, 1, 127–138.

2 James, W. *The principles of psychology*. New York: Henry Holt and Company, Inc., 1890. P. 488.

3 Kessen, W., H. M. Haith, & P. H. Salapatek. Human infancy: A bibliography and guide. In P. Mussen (Ed.), *Carmichael's manual of child psychology*. (3d ed.) New York: John Wiley & Sons, Inc., 1970. Pp. 287–445.

4 Sameroff, A. J. Can conditioned responses be established in the newborn infant? Unpublished paper, 1969.

5 Kagan, J. *Change and continuity in infancy*. New York: John Wiley & Sons, Inc., 1971. P. 3.

6 Hebb, D. O. *Textbook of psychology*. (3d ed.) Philadelphia: W. B. Saunders Company, 1972, Pp. 127–131.

7 Goddard, H. H. *Feeblemindedness: Its causes and consequences*. New York: The Macmillan Company, 1914. Pp. 28–29.

8 Money, J. Two cytogenetic syndromes: Psychological comparison, intelligence, and specific factor quotients. *Journal of Psychiatric Research*, 1964, 2, 223–231.

9 Bock, R. D., & D. Kolakowski. Further evidence of sex-linked major-gene influence on human spatial visualizing ability. *American Journal of Human Genetics*, 1973, 25, 1–14.

10 Bayley, N., L. Rhodes, B. Gooch, and N. Marcus. A comparison of the growth and development of institutionalized and home-reared mongoloids: A follow-up study. In J. Hellmuth (Ed.), *Exceptional infant*. Vol. II. *Studies in abnormality*. New York: Brunner-Mazel, 1971.

11 Tryon, R. C. Genetic differences in maze learning.

Yearbook of the National Society for the Study of Education, 1940, 39, 36–37.

12 Wolff, P. H. Observations on newborn infants. *Psychosomatic Medicine*, 1959, 21, 110–118.

13 Bell, R. Q. Relations between behavior manifestations in the human neonate. *Child Development*, 1960, 31, 463–478.

14 Lipsitt, L. P., & N. Levy. Pain threshold in the human neonate. *Child Development*, 1959, 30, 547–554.

15 Grossman, H. J., & N. H. Greenberg. Psychosomatic differentiation in infancy. *Psychosomatic Medicine*, 1957, 19, 293–306.

16 Thomas, A., S. Chess, & H. Birch. The origin of personality. *Scientific American*, August 1970, 223 (2), 102–109.

17 Thomas, A., S. Chess, & H. Birch. The origin of personality. *Scientific American*, August 1970, 223 (2), 102–109.

18 Vandenburg, S. G. (Ed.), *Methods and goals in human behavior genetics*. New York: Academic Press, Inc., 1965. Pp. 63–74.

19 Cattell, R. B., G. F. Stice, & N. F. Kristy. A first approximation to nature-nurture ratios for eleven primary personality factors in objective tests. *Journal of Abnormal and Social Psychology*, 1957, 54, 143–159.

20 Gottesman, I. I. Differential inheritance of the psychoneuroses. *Eugenics Quarterly*, 1962, 9, 223–227.

21 Gottesman, I. I., & J. Shields. Schizophrenia in twins: Sixteen years, consecutive admissions to a psychiatric clinic. *British Journal of Psychiatry*, 1966, 112, 809–818.

22 Emery, A. E. H. *Heredity, disease, and man: Genetics in medicine*. Berkeley: University of California Press, 1968.

23 Ebbs, J. H., A. Brown, F. F. Tisdall, W. J. Moyle, & M. Bell. The influence of improved prenatal nutrition upon the infant. *Canadian Medical Association Journal*, 1942, 6–8.

24 Davison, A. N., & J. Dobbing. Mylination as a vulnerable period in brain development. *British Medical Bulletin*, 1966, 22, 40–44.

25 Stechler, G. Newborn attention as affected by medication during labor. *Science*, 1964, 144, 315–317.

26 Montagu, M. F. A. Constitutional and prenatal factors in infant and child health. In M. J. E. Senn (Ed.), *Symposium on the healthy personality*. New York: Josiah Macy, Jr., Foundation, 1950. Pp. 148–175.

27 Frazier, T. M., G. H. Davis, H. Goldstein, & I. D. Goldberg. Cigarette smoking and prematurity: A prospective study. *American Journal of Obstetrics and Gynecology*, 1961, 81, 988–996.

28 Thompson, W. R. Influence of prenatal anxiety on emotionality in young rats. *Science*, 1957, 125, 698–699.

29 Sontag, L. W. War and fetal maternal relationships. *Marriage and Family Living*, 1944, 6, 1–5.

30 Laken, M. Personality factors in mothers of excessively crying (colicky) infants. *Monographs Society for Research in Child Development*, 1957, 22 (64).

31 Nissen, H. W., K. L. Chow, & J. Semmes. Effects of a restricted opportunity for tactual, kinesthetic, and manipulative experience on the behavior of a chimpanzee. *American Journal of Psychology*, 1951, 64, 485–507.

32 Provence, S., & R. C. Lipton. *Infants in institutions*. New York: International Press, 1962.

33 Kagan, J. The plasticity of early intellectual development. Paper presented at the meeting of the Association for the Advancement of Science, Washington, D.C., 1972.

34 Kohen-Raz, R. Mental and motor development of the Kibbutz, institutionalized, and home-reared infants in Israel. *Child Development*, 1968, 39, 489–504.

35 Brackbill, Y. *Research and clinical work with children*. Washington, D.C.: American Psychological Association, 1962.

36 Mussen, P. H., J. J. Conger, & J. Kagan. *Child development and personality*. (4th ed.) New York: Harper & Row, Publishers, Incorporated, 1974.

37 Skeels, H. M. Adult status of children with contrasting early life experiences. *Monographs of the Society for Research in Child Development*, 1966, 31 (3).

38 Dennis, W. *Children of the Creche*. New York: Prentice-Hall, Inc., 1974.

39 Rosenzweig, M. R., E. L. Bennett, & R. C. Diamond. Brain changes in response to experience. *Scientific American*, 1972, 227, 22–29.

40 Lorenz, K. *King Solomon's ring*. London: Methuen, 1952.

41 Heinroth, O. In K. Lorenz, *Studies in animal and human behavior*, Vol. 1. Cambridge, Mass.: Harvard University Press, 1970. Pp. 125–126.

42 Harlow, H. F. The nature of love. *American Psychologist*, 1958, 13, 673–685.

43 Harlow, H. F., & M. K. Harlow. Social deprivation in monkeys. *Scientific American*, November 1962, 207 (5), 136–146.

44 Heath, R. G. Electroencephalographic studies in isolation-raised monkeys with behavioral impairment. *Diseases of the Nervous System*, March 1972, 33, 157–163.

45 Suomi, S. J., & H. F. Harlow. Social rehabilitation of isolate-reared monkeys. *Developmental Psychology*, 1972, 6, 487–496.

46 Ambrose, J. A. The development of the smiling

response in early infancy. B. M. Foss (Ed.), *Determinants of infant behavior.* New York: John Wiley & Sons, Inc., 1961. Pp. 179–195.

47 Schaffer, H. R., & P. E. Emerson. Development of social attachments in infancy. *Monographs of the Society for Research in Child Development*, 1964, 29 (3).

48 Ainsworth, M. D., & B. A. Witting. Attachment and exploratory behavior of one year olds in a strange situation. In M. B. Foss (Ed.), *Determinants of infant behavior*, Vol. 4. New York: John Wiley & Sons, Inc., 1971.

49 Goldfarb, W. Effects of early institutional care on adolescent personality: Rorschach data. *American Journal of Orthopsychiatry*, 1944, 14, 441–447.

50 Sewell, W. H., & P. H. Mussen. The effects of feeding, weaning, and scheduling procedures on childhood adjustment and the formation of oral symptoms. *Child Development*, 1952, 23, 185–191.

51 Maslow, A. H., & I. Szilagi Kessler. Security and breast feeding. *Journal of Abnormal and Social Psychology*, 1946, 41, 83–85.

52 Kulka, A. M. Observations and data on mother-infant interactions. *Israel Annals of Psychiatry and Related Disciplines*, 1968, 6, 70–83.

53 Homan, W. E. Parent and child: Mother's milk or other milk. *The New York Times Magazine*, June 6, 1971, 77.

54 Mussen, P. H., J. J. Conger, & J. Kagan. *Child development and personality.* (4th ed.). New York: Harper & Row, Publishers, Incorporated, 1974.

55 MacFarlane, J. W., L. Allen, & M. P. Honzik. *A developmental study of the behavior problems of normal children between twenty-two months and fourteen years.* (*University of California Publications in Child Development*, Vol. II). Berkeley: University of California Press, 1954.

56 Sears, R. R., J. W. M. Whiting, V. Nowlis, & P. S. Sears. Some child-rearing antecedents of aggression and dependency in young children. *Genetic Psychology Monograph*, 1953, 47, 135–234.

57 Bell, S. M., & M. D. S. Ainsworth. Infant crying and maternal responsiveness. *Child Development*, 1972, 43, 1171–1190.

58 Irwin, O. C. Infant speech: Effect of systematic reading of stories. *Journal of Speech and Hearing Research*, 1960, 3, 187–190.

59 Hess, R. D., & V. C. Shipman. Early experience and the socialization of cognitive modes. *Child Development*, 1965, 36 (4), 869–886.

60 White, B. L. Fundamental early environmental influences on the development of competence. Paper presented at 3d Western Symposium on Learning: Cognitive Learning, Western Washington State, 1972. P. 101.

Chapter 4

1 Luria, A. R. *The man with a shattered world.* New York: Basic Books, Inc., Publishers, 1972. Pp. 21, 37, 42–43, 47, 142, 143.

2 Wooldridge, D. E. *The machinery of the brain.* New York: McGraw-Hill Book Company, 1963. P. 22.

3 Wooldridge, D. E. *The machinery of the brain.* New York: McGraw-Hill Book Company, 1963. P. 25.

4 Luria, A. R. *The man with a shattered world.* New York: Basic Books, Inc., Publishers, 1972.

5 Klüver, H., & P. C. Bucy. Psychic blindness and other symptoms following bilateral temporal lobectomy in rhesus monkeys. *American Journal of Physiology*, 1937, 119, 352–353.

6 Penfield, W., & P. Perot. The brain's record of auditory and visual experience—A final summary and discussion. *Brain*, 1963, 86, 595–696.

7 Penfield, W., & P. Perot. The brain's record of auditory and visual experience—A final summary and discussion. *Brain*, 1963, 640–641.

8 Milner, B. Amnesia following operation on the temporal lobes. In C. W. M. Whitty & O. L. Zangwill (Eds.), *Amnesia.* London: Butterworth and Company, 1966.

9 Lashley, K. S. In search of the engram. *Symposium of the Society of Experimental Biology*, 1950, 4, 454–482.

10 Sperry, R. W. Hemisphere disconnection and unity in conscious awareness. *American Psychologist*, 1968, 23, 723–733.

11 Gazzaniga, M. S. *The bisected brain.* New York: Appleton Century Crofts, 1970.

12 Gazzaniga, M. S. *The bisected brain.* New York: Appleton Century Crofts, 1970. P. 107.

13 Ornstein, R. *The psychology of consciousness.* New York: The Viking Press, 1973.

14 Hydén, H. The question of a molecular basis for the memory trace. In K. H. Pribram & D. E. Broadbent (Eds.), *Biology of memory.* New York: Academic Press, Inc., 1970. Pp. 101–119.

15 McConnell, J. V., A. L. Jacobson, & D. P. Kimble. The effects of regeneration upon retention of a conditioned response in the planarian. *Journal of Comparative and Physiological Psychology*, 1959, 52, 1.

16 McConnell, J. V. Cannibalism and memory in flatworms. *New Scientist*, 1964, 21, 465–468.

17 Jensen, G. D., & R. A. Bobbit. Monkeying with the

mother myth. *Psychology Today*, May 1968, 1, 41–43, 68–69.

18 Bell, R. Q. Relations between behavior manifestations in the human neonate. *Child Development*, 1960, 31, 463–477.

19 Money, J. Psychosexual differentiation. In J. Money (Ed.), *Sex research: New developments.* New York: Holt, Rinehart & Winston, Inc., 1965. Pp. 3–23.

20 Levine, S. Sex differences in the brain. *Scientific American*, April 1966, 214, 4, 84–90.

21 Money, J., & A. E. Ehrhardt. *Man and woman boy and girl: The differentiation and dimorphism of gender identity from conception to maturity.* Baltimore: Johns Hopkins University Press, 1972.

22 Money, J., & A. E. Ehrhardt. *Man and woman boy and girl: The differentiation and dimorphism of gender identity from conception to maturity.* Baltimore: Johns Hopkins University Press, 1972.

23 Bardwick, J. M. *Psychology of women: A study of biocultural conflicts.* New York: Harper & Row, Publishers, Incorporated, 1971.

24 Lewis, M. Culture and gender roles: There's no uni-sex in the nursery. *Psychology Today*, 1972, 5, 54–57.

25 Dornbusch, S. M. Afterword. In E. E. Maccoby (Ed.), *The development of sex differences.* Stanford: Stanford University Press, 1966. Pp. 205–219.

26 Stephens, W. N. *The family in cross-cultural perspective.* New York: Holt, Rinehart & Winston, Inc., 1963.

27 Mead, M. *Sex and temperament.* New York: William Morrow and Company, 1935. Pp. 190–191.

Chapter 5

1 Huxley, A. *The doors of perception.* New York: Harper & Row, Publishers, Incorporated, 1954. Pp. 19–20.

2 James, W. *Psychology: Briefer course.* New York: Henry Holt and Company, Inc., 1892. P. 329.

3 Gibson, J. J. *The senses considered as perceptual systems.* Boston: Houghton Mifflin Company, 1966.

4 Rubin, E. Visuell whrgenommere Figuren. Copenhagen: Glydendalske, 1921.

5 Fantz, R. L. The origin of form perception. *Scientific American*, May 1961, 204, 66–84.

6 Gibson, E. J. The development of perception as an adaptive process. *American Scientist*, 1970, 58, 98–107.

7 Gibson, E. J., & R. D. Walk. The visual cliff. *Scientific American*, April 1960, 202, 64–71.

8 Bower, T. G. R. The visual world of infants. *Scientific American*, December 1966, 215, 80–92.

9 Riesen, A. H. Arrested vision. *Scientific American*, July 1950, 183, 17.

10 Chow, K. L., A. H. Riesen, & F. W. Newell. Degeneration of retinal ganglion cells in infant chimpanzees reared in darkness. *Journal of Comparative Neurology*, 1957, 107, 27–42.

11 Hubel, D. H., & T. N. Wiesel. Effects of visual deprivation on morphology and physiology of cells in the cat's lateral geniculate body. *Journal of Neurophysiology*, 1963, 26, 978–993.

12 Blakemore, C., & G. Cooper. Development of the brain depends on the visual environment. *Nature* (London), 1970, 228, 477–478.

13 Held, R., & A. Hein. Movement produced stimulation in the development of visually guided behavior. *Journal of Comparative and Physiological Psychology*, 1963, 56, 872–876.

14 Riesen, A. H. Arrested vision. *Scientific American*, July 1950, 183, 19.

15 Bexton, W. H., W. Heron, & T. H. Scott. Effects of decreased variation in the sensory environment. *Canadian Journal of Psychology*, 1954, 8, 70–76.

16 Heron, W., B. K. Doane, & T. H. Scott. Visual disturbance after prolonged perceptual isolation. *Canadian Journal of Psychology*, 1956, 10, 13–16.

17 Zubeck, J. P. Behavioral and physiological effects of prolonged sensory and perceptual deprivation: A review. In J. Rasmussen (Ed.), *Man in isolation and confinement.* Chicago: Aldine Publishing Company, 1973. Pp. 9–83.

18 Stratton, G. M. Vision without inversion of the retinal image. *Psychological Review*, 1897, 4, 344.

19 Stratton, G. M. Vision without inversion of the retinal image. *Psychological Review*, 1897, 4, 355.

20 Rock, I., & C. S. Harris. Vision and touch. *Scientific American*, May 1967, 216, 96–104.

21 Stratton, G. M. Some preliminary experiments on vision without inversion of the retinal image. *Psychological Review*, 1896, 3, 611–617.

22 Held, R. Plasticity in sensory motor systems. *Scientific American*, November 1965, 213, 84–94.

23 Turnbull, C. Some observations regarding the experiences and behavior of the BaMbuti Pygmies. *American Journal of Psychology*, 1961, 74, 305.

24 Segall, M. H., D. T. Campbell, & M. J. Herskovitz. Cultural differences in the perception of geometric illusions. *Science*, 1963, 139, 769–771.

25 Hastorf, A. H., & H. A. Cantril. They saw a game: A case study. *Journal of Abnormal and Social Psychology*, 1954, 49, 129–134.

36 Lambert, W. W., R. L. Solomon, & P. D. Watson. Reinforcement and extinction as factors in size estimation. *Journal of Experimental Psychology*, 1949, 39, 637–641.

27 Harrison, J. P. Crime busting with ESP. *This Week*, February 26, 1961, 21.

28 Hansel, C. E. M. *ESP: A scientific evaluation.* New York: Charles Scribner's Sons, 1966.

29 Targ, R., & H. Puthoff. Information transmission under conditions of sensory shielding. *Nature*, 1974, 251, 602–607.

30 Hansel, C. E. M. *ESP: A scientific evaluation.* New York: Charles Scribner's Sons, 1966.

Chapter 6

1 Castanada, C. *Journey to Ixtlan.* New York: Simon and Schuster, 1972. Pp. 217, 218, 227.

2 James, W. *The varieties of religious experience.* New York: The New American Library, 1958. P. 298.

3 Luce, G. G. *Body time.* New York: Pantheon Books, Inc., 1971. P. 248.

4 *Time*, January 10, 1972, 48.

5 Mills, J. N. Circadian rhythms during and after three months in solitude. *Journal of Physiology*, 1964, 174, 217–231.

6 Fraisse, P. Temporal isolation, Activity rhythms and time estimation. In J. E. Rasmussen (Ed.), *Man in isolation and confinement.* Chicago: Aldine Publishing Company, 1973. Pp. 85–97.

7 Williams, H. L., G. O. Morris, & A. Lubin. *Illusions, hallucinations, and sleep loss.* In L. J. West (Ed.), *Hallucinations.* New York: Grune and Stratton, 1962.

8 *Luce, G. G. Current research on sleep and dreams*, U. S. Department of Health, Education, and Welfare, U.S. Public Health Service, National Institute of Mental Health, Bethesda, Maryland, 1965.

9 Johnson, L. C., E. S. Slye, W. C. Dement, & G. Gulevich. Psychiatric and EEG observations on a case of prolonged (246 hours) wakefulness. *Archives of General Psychiatry*, 1966, 27, 29–35.

10 Webb, W. B., & H. W. Agnew. *Sleep and dreams.* Dubuque, Iowa: William C. Brown Company, 1973.

11 Webb, W. B., & H. W. Agnew. *Sleep and dreams.* Dubuque, Iowa: William C. Brown Company, 1973.

12 Webb, W. B., & H. W. Agnew. *Sleep and dreams.* Dubuque, Iowa: William C. Brown Company, 1973.

13 Lubin, A. The season of all natures, sleep. *Contemporary Psychology*, 1974, 19, 1, 21.

14 Aserinsky, E., & N. Kleitman. Regularly occurring periods of eye mobility and concomitant phenomena during sleep. *Science*, 1953, 118, 273–274.

15 Vogel, G., D. Foulkes, & H. Trosman. Ego functions and dreaming during sleep onset. *Archives of General Psychiatry*, 1966, 14, 238–248.

16 Evarts, E. Activity of neurons in the visual cortex of the cat during sleep with low voltage fast EEG activity. *Journal of Neurophysiology*, 1962, 25, 812–816.

17 Vaughan, C. J. Behavioral evidence for dreaming in rhesus monkeys. *Physiologist*, 1964, 1, 275.

18 Hall, C. S. What people dream about. *Scientific American*, 1951, 184, 60–63.

19 Hall, C. S., & R. Van de Castle. *The content analysis of dreams.* New York: Appleton Century Crofts, 1966.

20 Van de Castle, R. *The psychology of dreaming.* New York: General Learning Press, 1971.

21 Van de Castle, R. *The psychology of dreaming.* New York: General Learning Press, 1971.

22 Breger, L., I. Hunter, & R. W. Lane. *The effect of stress on dreaming.* New York: International Universities Press, 1971.

23 Dement, W. C., & E. A. Wolpert. The relationship of eye movement, body motility, and external stimuli to dream content. *Journal of Experimental Psychology*, 1958, 55, 543–553.

24 Bokert, E. Effects of thirst and a meaningfully related auditory stimulus on dream reports. Unpublished doctoral thesis, New York University, 1965.

25 Verdone, P. P. Variables related to the temporal reference of manifest dream content. *Perceptual and Motor Skills*, 1965, 20, 1253–1268.

26 Dement, W. C. The effect of dream deprivation. *Science*, 1960, 131, 1705.

27 Dement, W. C. Commentary. In W. B. Webb (Ed.), *Sleep: An active process.* Glenview, Ill.: Scott, Foresman and Company, 1973. Pp. 48–58.

28 Dement, W. C. The biological role of REM sleep. In W. B. Webb (Ed.), *Sleep: An active process.* Glenview, Ill.: Scott, Foresman and Company, 1973. Pp. 33–48.

29 Wyatt, R., D. Kupfer, J. Scott, D. Robinson, & F. Snyder. Longitudinal studies of the effect of monoamine oxidase inhibitors on sleep in man. *Psychopharmacologia*, 1969, 15, 236–244.

30 Kales, A., E. Malmstrom, W. Rickles, J. Hanley, T. LingTan, B. Stadel, & F. Hoedemaker. Sleep patterns of a pentobarbital addict: Before and after withdrawal. *Psychophysiology*, 1968, 5. 208.

31 Dement, W. C. The biological role of REM sleep. In W. B. Webb (Ed.), *Sleep: An active process.* Glenview, Ill.: Scott, Foresman and Company, 1973. Pp. 33–48.

32 Berg, O. M. In R. W. Davidson (Ed.), *Documents on contemporary dervish communities.* London: Hoopoe Limited, 1966. Pp. 10–11.

33 Ornstein, R. E. *The psychology of consciousness,* San Francisco: W. H. Freeman and Company, 1972. P. 140.

34 Rahula, W. *What the Buddha taught.* New York: Grove Press, 1959. P. 71.

35 Maupin, E. W. Individual differences in response to a Zen meditation exercise. *Journal of Consulting Psychology,* 1965, 29, 139–145.

36 Yogi, Maharishi Mahesh *Transcendental meditation: Serenity without drugs.* New York: Signet, 1968.

37 Wallace, R. K., & H. Benson, The physiology of meditation, *Scientific American,* February 1972, 226, 2, 84–90.

38 Lehman, D., G. W. Beeler, & D. H. Fender. EEG responses during the observation of stabilized and normal retinal images. *Electroencephalography and Clinical Neurophysiology,* 1967, 22, 136–142.

39 Cohen, W. Spatial and textural characteristics of the ganzfeld. *American Journal of Psychology,* 1957, 70, 403–410.

40 Weil, A. T., & N. E. Zinberg. Acute effects of marihuana on speech. *Nature,* May 3, 1969, 222, 5153, 434–437.

41 Fort, J. A rap about the gap. *Contemporary Psychology,* April 1974, 19, 4, 321.

42 Jones, R. T., & G. C. Stone. Psychological studies of marijuana and alcohol in man. *Psychopharmacologia* (Berlin), 1970, 18, 108–117.

43 Tart, C. T.. Marijuana intoxication: Common experiences." *Nature,* May 23, 1970, 226, 5247, 701–704.

44 Tart, C. T. *On being stoned: A psychological study of marijuana intoxication.* Palo Alto, Calif.: Science and Behavior Books, 1971.

45 Weil, A. T., N. E. Zinberg, & J. M. Nelsen. Clinical and psychological effects of marijuana in man. *Science,* December 13, 1968, 162, 1234–1242.

46 Melges, F. T., J. R. Tinklenberg, L. E. Hollister, & H. K. Gillespie. Marijuana and temporal disintegration. *Science,* May 29, 1970, 168, 3935, 1118–1120.

47 Weil, A. T., N. E. Zinberg, & J. M. Nelsen. Clinical and psychological effects of marijuana in man. *Science,* December 13, 1968, 162, 1240.

48 Ornstein, R. E. *The psychology of consciousness*, San Francisco: W. H. Freeman and Company, 1972.

Chapter 7

1 Gustavson, C. R., & J. Garcia. Aversive conditioning: Pulling a gag on the wily coyote. *Psychology Today,* August 1974, 8, 68–72.

2 Johnston, M. K., C. Harris, R. Florence, & M. N. Wolf. An application of reinforcement principles to the development of skills of a young child. Unpublished paper cited in D. L. Whaley & R. W. Malott. *Elementary Principles of Behavior.* New York: Appleton Century Crofts, 1971.

3 O'Connor, R. D. Modification of social withdrawal through symbolic modeling. In K. D. O'Leary & S. G. O'Leary (Eds.), *Classroom Management,* New York: Pergamon Press, 1972.

4 Smith, O. H., Jr., & A. D. Geis. Comparative psychology in wildlife conservation. *American Psychologist,* 1956, 11, 183–187.

5 Jersild, A. Emotional development. In Leonard Carmichael, (Ed.), *Manual of Child Psychology* (2d ed.), New York: John Wiley & Sons, Inc., 1954. Pp. 833–917.

6 Jones, M. C. A laboratory study of fear: The case of Peter. *Journal of Genetic Psychology,* 1924, 31, 309.

7 Watson, J. B., & R. Rayner. Conditioned emotional reaction. *Journal of Experimental Psychology,* 1920, 3, 1–4.

8 Jones, M. C. A laboratory study of fear: The case of Peter. *Pedagogical Seminary,* 1924, 31, 310–311.

9 Thorndike, E. L. Animal intelligence: An experimental study of the associative processes in animals. Doctoral dissertation. Columbia University, 1898, 13.

10 Brackbill, Z., & M. S. Kappy. Delay of reinforcement and retention. *Journal of Comparative and Physiological Psychology,* 1962, 55, 14–18.

11 Salzinger, K., R. S. Feldman, J. E. Cowan, & S. Salzinger. Operant conditioning of verbal behavior of two young speech deficient boys. In L. Krasner and L. Ullman (Eds.), *Research in behavior modification.* New York: Holt, Rinehart & Winston, Inc., 1965. Pp. 82–106.

12 Williams, C. D. The elimination of tantrum behavior by extinction procedures. *Journal of Abnormal and Social Psychology,* 1959, 269.

13 Church, R. M. The varied effects of punishment on behavior. *Psychological Review,* 1963, 70, 369–402.

14 Aronfreed, J. The internalization of social control through punishment: Experimental studies of the role of conditioning and the second signal system in the development of conscience. *Proceedings of the 18th International Congress of Psychology,* Moscow, 1966.

15 Solomon, R. L. Punishment. *American Psychologist,* 1964, 19, 239–253.

16 Azrin, N. H., & W. C. Holt. Punishment. In W. K. Honig (Ed.), *Operant behavior: Areas of research and application.* New York: Appleton Century Crofts, 1966.

17 Bernal, M. Training parents in child management. In Robert H. Bradfield (Ed.), *Behavior modification of* *learning disabilities.* San Rafael, Calif.: Academic Therapy Publications, 1971. Pp. 41–67.

18 Miller, N. E. Learning of visceral and glandular responses. *Science*, 1969, 163, 434–445.

19 Mayr, O. The origins of feedback control. *Scientific American*, 1970, 223, 111.

20 Shapiro, D., B. Tursky, E. Gershon, & M. Stern. Effects of feedback and reinforcement on the control of human systolic blood pressure. *Science*, 163, 1969, 588–590.

21 Bandura, A. Analysis of modeling processes. In A. Bandura (Ed.), *Psychological modeling*. Chicago: Aldine Publishing Company, 1971. Pp. 1–62.

22 Washington *Post*, November 1, 1962.

23 Bandura, A., & R. H. Walters. *Social learning and personality development*. New York: Holt, Rinehart & Winston, Inc., 1963.

Chapter 8

1 Milne, A. A. A lost masterpiece. In *If I May*. London: Methuen and Company, 1920. Pp. 122–125.

2 Joyce, J. *Ulysses*. New York: Modern Library, 1961. Pp. 781–782.

3 Piaget, J. *Play, dreams, and imitation in childhood*. New York: W. W. Norton and Company, 1951. P. 124.

4 Piaget, J. *The origins of intelligence in children*. New York: International Universities Press, 1952. P. 335.

5 Glucksburg, S., & R. W. Weisburg. Verbal behavior and problem solving: Some effects of labeling in a functional fixedness problem. *Journal of Experimental Psychology*, 1966, 71, 5, 659–664.

6 Duncker, K. On problem-solving. *Psychological Monographs*, 1945, 58 (5).

7 Köhler, W. *The task of gestalt psychology*. Princeton, N.J.: Princeton University Press, 1969.

8 Scheerer, M. Problem-solving. *Scientific American*. April 1968, 208, 4, 118–128.

9 Harlow, H. F. The formation of learning sets. *Psychological Review*, 1949, 56, 61–65.

10 Luchins, A. Mechanization in problem-solving: The effect of *Einstellung*. *Psychological Monographs*, 1942, 54 (6).

11 Birch, H. G. The role of motivational factors in insightful problem-solving. *Journal of Comparative Psychology*, 1945, 38, 295–317.

12 Miller, G. A. Some preliminaries to psycholinguistics. *American Psychologist*, 1965, 20, 15–20.

13 Listening motion. *Newsweek*, February 18, 1974, 79.

14 Eimas, P., E. R. Siqueland, P. Juscqyk, & J. Vigorito. Speech perception in infants. *Science*, 1971, 171, 303–306.

15 Erwin-Tripp, S. M. Language development. In M.

Hoffman & L. Hoffman (Eds.), *Advances in child development research II*. New York: Russell Sage Foundation, 1966, 55–106.

16 Slobin, D. I. Universals of grammar development in children. In F. D. Arcais & J. M. Lovelt (Eds.), *Advances in psycholinguistics*. Amsterdam, Netherlands: North Holland Publishing Company, 1970. Pp. 174–186.

17 Berko, J. The child's learning of English morphology. *Word*, 1958, 14, 150–177.

18 Gardner, R. A., & B. T. Gardner. Teaching sign language to a chimpanzee. *Science*, August 15, 1969, 165, 664–672.

19 Fouts, R. S. Communication with chimpanzees. In E. Eibl-Eibesfeldt & G. Kurth (Eds.), *Hominisation und Verhalten*. Stuttgart: Gustav Fischer Verlag, 1974, in press.

20 Gardner, R. A., & B. T. Gardner. Teaching sign language to a chimpanzee. *Science*, August 15, 1969, 165, 664–672.

21 Fouts, R. S. Communication with chimpanzees. In E. Eibl-Eibesfeldt & G. Kurth (Eds.), *Hominisation und Verhalten*. Stuttgart: Gustav Fischer Verlag, 1974, in press.

22 Hahn, E. Washoese. *New Yorker*, 1971, 4, (17, 46–97), (24, 46–91).

23 Brown, R. W., & D. McNeill. The "tip-of-the-tongue" phenomenon. *Journal of Verbal Learning and Verbal Behavior*, 1966, 5, 325–337.

24 Lindsay, P. H., & D. A. Norman. *Human information processing: An introduction to psychology*. New York: Academic Press, 1972.

25 Bower, G. H. Organizational factors in memory. *Journal of Cognitive Psychology*, 1970, 1, 18–46.

26 Bower, G. H., & M. C. Clark. Narrative stories as mediators for serial learning. *Psychonomic Science*, 1969, 14, 181–182.

27 Gates, A. J. Recitation as a factor in memorizing. *Archives of Psychology*, 1917, 6, 40.

28 Underwood, B. J. Ten years of massed practice on distributed practice. *Psychological Review*, 1961, 68, 229–247.

29 Krueger, W. C. F. The effect of overlearning on retention. *Journal of Experimental Psychology*, 1929, 12, 71–78.

Chapter 9

1 Boy with IQ of 55 is genius at piano. *New York Times*, August 6, 1971.

2 Wechsler, D. *The measurement and appraisal of adult intelligence* (4th ed.) Baltimore: The Williams & Wilkins Company, 1958, 7.

3 Terman, L. M., & M. A. Merrill. *Stanford-Binet Intelligence scale: Manual for the 3d revision. Form L-M.* Boston: Houghton Mifflin Company, 1960.

4 McNemar, Q. Lost: Our intelligence? Why? *American Psychologist*, 1964, 19, 871–882.

5 Ghisseli, E. E. *The validity of occupational aptitude tests.* New York: John Wiley & Sons, Inc., 1966.

6 Cronbach, L. J. *Essentials of psychological testing.* (3d ed.) New York: Harper & Row, Publishers, Incorporated, 1970.

7 Anastasi, A. A. *Differential psychology.* New York: The Macmillan Company, 1958.

8 McClelland, D. C. Testing for competence rather than intelligence. *American Psychologist*, January 1973, 28, 6.

9 Pinard, A., & E. Sharp. IQ and point of view. *Psychology Today*, June 1972, 66.

10 Lykken, D. T. The "neural efficiency analyzer" scandal. *Contemporary Psychology*, 1973, 18, 10, 462–463.

11 Honzik, M., & J. W. MacFarlane. Personality development and intellectual functioning from 21 months to 40 years. In L. F. Jarvik, C. Eisdorfer, & J. E. Blum (Eds.), *Intellectual functioning in adults.* New York: Springer Publishing Company, 1973.

12 Honzik, M. P. Predicting IQ over the first four decades of the life span. Paper presented at the biennial meeting of the Society for Research in Child Development, Philadelphia, 1973.

13 Baltes, P. B., & K. W. Shaie. Aging and IQ: The myth of the twilight years. *Psychology Today*, March 1974, 7, 10, 35–40.

14 Blum, J. E., J. L. Fosshage, & L. F. Jarvik. Intellectual changes and sex differences in octogenarians: A twenty year longitudinal study of aging. *Developmental Psychology*, 1972, 7, 178–187.

15 Jarvik, L. F., C. Eisdorfer, & J. E. Blum (Eds.). *Intellectual functioning in adults.* New York: Springer Publishing Company, 1973.

16 Sontag, L. W., C. T. Baker, & V. L. Nelson. Mental growth and personality development: A longitudinal study. *Monographs of the Society for Research in Child Development*, 1958, 23 (2).

17 Haan, N. Proposed model of ego functioning: Coping and defense mechanisms in relationship to IQ change. *Psychological Monographs*, 1963, 77 (8).

18 Wechsler, D. *The measurement and appraisal of adult intelligence* (4th ed.) Baltimore: The Williams & Wilkins Company, 1958.

19 Wechsler, D. *The measurement and appraisal of adult intelligence* (4th ed.) Baltimore: The Williams & Wilkins Company, 1958.

20 Tyler, L. E. *The psychology of human differences.* New York: Appleton Century Crofts, 1956.

21 Scarr-Salapatek, S. Race, social class, and I. Q. *Science*, 1971, 174, 1285–1295.

22 Heber, R., & H. Garber. An experiment in the prevention of cultural-familial mental retardation. Unpublished paper, 1970, 19.

23 Rosenthal, R., & L. Jacobson. *Pygmalion in the classroom.* New York: Holt, Rinehart & Winston, Inc., 1968.

24 Rosenthal, R. On the social psychology of the self-fulfilling prophecy: Further evidence for Pygmalion effects and their mediating mechanisms. In *Reading and school achievement: Cognitive and affective influences*, M. Kling (Ed.) Eighth Annual Spring Reading Conference. Rutgers University, 1973.

23 Rosenthal, R., & L. Jacobson. *Pygmalion in the Classroom.* New York: Holt, Rinehart & Winston, Inc., 1968.

26 Leacock, E. Reported in R. Rosenthal, The Pygmalion effect lives. *Psychology Today.* September 1973, 7, 4, 56–63.

27 Shuey, A. M. *The testing of Negro intelligence.* (2d ed.) New York: Social Science Press, 1966.

28 Jensen, A. R. How much can we boost IQ and scholastic achievement? *Harvard Educational Review*, 1969, 39, 1–123.

29 Dobzhansky, T. *Genetic diversity and human equality.* New York: Basic Books, Inc., 1973. P. 221.

30 Scarr-Salapatek, S. Race, social class, and I. Q. *Science*, 1971, 174, 1285–1295.

31 Mozart, W. A. In E. Holmes. *The life of Mozart including his correspondence.* London: Chapman and Hall, Ltd., 1878. Pp. 211–213.

32 Wallach, M. A., & N. Kogan. Creativity and intelligence in children's thinking. *Trans-Action Magazine*, January-February, 1967, 40.

33 Testing creativity: Suppose everyone suddenly doubled in height. *Psychology Today*, December 1973, 7, 7, 128.

34 Vernon, P. E. How to spot the creative. *New Society*, July 1973, 25, 564, 198–200.

35 Barron, F. *Creative person and creative process.* New York: Holt, Rinehart & Winston, Inc., 1969. P. 70.

36 Davis, G. A., & S. E. Houtman. *Thinking creatively: A guide to training imagination.* Unpublished manuscript, 1968, 12.

37 Davis, G. A., & S. E. Houtman. *Thinking creatively: A guide to training imagination.* Unpublished manuscript, 1968, 40

38 Davis, G. A., & S. E. Houtman. *Thinking creatively: A guide to training imagination.* Unpublished manuscript, 1968, 96.

39 Parnes, S. J., & R. B. Noller. *Toward supersanity: Channeled freedom.* Buffalo: D.O.K. Publisher, 1973.

Chapter 10

1 McDougall, W. *An introduction to social psychology* (30th ed., 1950) London: Methuen, 1908.

2 Bernard, L. L. *Instinct: A study in social psychology.* New York: Holt, Rinehart & Winston, Inc., 1924.

3 Holt, E. B. *Animal drive and the learning process.* New York: Holt, Rinehart & Winston, Inc., 1931. P. 4.

4 Boyd, D. A., Jr., & L. W. Nie. Congenital universal indifference to pain. *Archives of Neurology and Psychiatry.* 1949, 61, 402–412.

5 Zuckerman, M. A biological basis for sensation seeking. Paper presented at symposium, "The Sensation Seeking Motive," at the meeting of the American Psychological Association, Montreal, Canada, August, 1973.

6 Butler, R. A. Discrimination learning by rhesus monkeys to visual exploration motivation. *Journal of Comparative and Physiological Psychology*, 1953, 46, 95–98.

7 Sears, R. R., E. E. Maccoby, & H. Levin. *Patterns of child rearing.* Evanston, Ill.: Row, Peterson & Company, 1957.

8 Rohrer, J. H. Interpersonal relations in isolated small groups. In B. E. Flaherty (Ed.), *Psychophysiological aspects of space flight.* New York: Columbia University Press, 1961. Pp. 263–271.

9 Maslow, A. H. *Toward a psychology of being* (2d ed.) Princeton, N.J.: D. Van Nostrand Company, Inc., 1968.

10 Wyden, P. *The overweight society.* New York: William Morrow, 1965.

11 Cannon, W. B. Hunger and thirst. In C. Murchison (Ed.), *Handbook of general experimental psychology.* Worcester, Mass.: Clark University Press, 1934.

12 Morgan, C. T., & J. D. Morgan. Studies in hunger ii: The relation of gastric denervation and dietary sugar to the effect of insulin upon food intake in the rat. *Journal of Genetic Psychology*, 1940, 57, 153–163.

13 Tsang, Y. C. Hunger motivation in gastrectomized rats. *Journal of Comparative Psychology*, 1938, 26, 1–17.

14 Anand, B. K., & J. R. Brobeck. Hypothalamic control of food intake in rat and cat. *Yale Journal of Biological Medicine*, 1951, 24, 123–140.

15 Ferguson, N. B., & R. E. Keesey. Comparison of ventromedial hypothalamic lesion effects upon feeding and lateral hypothalamic self-stimulation in the female rat. *Journal of Comparative and Physiological Psychology*, 1971, 74, 263–271.

16 Teitelbaum, P. The encephalization of hunger. In E. Stellar & J. M. Sprague (Eds.), *Progress in physio-logical psychology.* Vol. 4. New York: Academic Press, Inc., 1971.

17 Stellar, E. Hunger in man: Comparative and physiological studies. *American Psychologist*, 1967, 22, 105–117.

18 Rodgers, W. L. Specificity of specific hungers. *Journal of Comparative and Physiological Psychology*, 1967, 64, 49–58.

19 Richter, C. P. Total self-regulatory functions in animals and human beings. *The Harvey Lectures*, 1942, 38, 63–103.

20 Davis, C. M. Self-selection of diet by newly-weaned infants: An experimental study. *American Journal of Diseases of Children*, October 1928, 36, 4, 651–679.

21 Richter, C. P. The self-selection of diets. In *Essays in Biology*, Berkeley, Calif.: University of California Press, 1943.

22 Creedman, M. Foods and flavors. *Human Behavior*, April 1974, 3, 4, 25–29.

23 Lee, D. Cultural factors in dietary choice. *American Journal of Clinical Nutrition*, 1957, 5, 167.

24 U.S. Public Health Service. *Weight, height, and selected body dimensions of adults: United States, 1960–1962.* Washington, D.C.: U.S. Government Printing Office, 1965.

25 Knittle, J. L., & J. Hirsch. Effect of early nutrition on the development of rat epididymal fat pads: Cellularity and metabolism. *Journal of Clinical Investigation*, 1968, 47, 2091–2098.

26 Hirsch, J., J. L. Knittle, & L. B. Salans. Cell lipid content and cell number on obese and non-obese human adipose tissue. *Journal of Clinical Investigation*, 1966, 45, 1023.

27 Schachter, S., R. Goldman, & A. Gordon. Effects of fear, food deprivation, and obesity on eating. *Journal of Personality and Social Psychology*, 1968, 10, 91–97.

28 Stunkard, A. Obesity and the denial of hunger. *Psychosomatic Medicine*, 1959, 21, 281–289.

29 Schachter, S., R. Goldman, & A. Gordon. Effects of fear, food deprivation, and obesity on eating. *Journal of Personality and Social Psychology*, 1968, 10, 91–97.

30 Schachter, S. Some extraordinary facts about obese humans and rats. *American Psychologist*, 1971, 26, 129–144.

31 Thomas, D. W., & J. Mayer. The search for the secret of fat. *Psychology Today*, September 1973, 7, 4, 74–79.

32 Cagguila, A., & B. Hoebel. Copulation reward site in the posterior hypothalamus. *Science*, 1966, 153, 1284–1285.

33 Beach, F. A. Relative effects of androgen upon the mating behavior of male rats subjected to pre-brain injury or castration. *Journal of Experimental Zoology*, 1944, 97, 249–285.

34 Beach, F. A. Relative effects of androgen upon the mating behavior of male rats subjected to pre-brain injury or castration. *Journal of Experimental Zoology*, 1944, 97, 249–285.

35 Bremer, J. *Asexualization*. New York: The Macmillan Company, 1959.

36 Money, J. Components of eroticism in man I: The hormones in relation to sexual morphology and sexual desire. *Journal of Nervous and Mental Disorders*, 1961, 132, 239–248.

37 Kupperman, H. S. Sex hormones. In A. Ellis & A. Abarbanel (Eds.), *The Encyclopedia of Sexual Behavior*. New York: J. Aronson, 1961. Pp. 494–502.

38 Foss, G. L. The influence of androgens on sexuality in women. *Lancet Magazine*, 1951, 1, 667–669.

39 Gebhardt, P. H. Factors in marital orgasm. *Journal of Social Issues*, April 1966, 22, 2, 88–96.

40 Hariton, E. B. The sexual fantasies of women. *Psychology Today*, March 1973, 6, 10, 39–44.

41 Masters, W. H., & V. E. Johnson. *Human sexual response*. Boston: Little, Brown and Company, 1966.

42 Davenport, W. Sexual patterns and their regulation in a society of the southwest Pacific. In F. Beach (Ed.), *Sex and behavior*. New York: John Wiley & Sons, Inc., 1965.

43 Ford, C. S., & F. A. Beach. *Patterns of sexual behavior*. New York: Harper & Row, Publishers, Incorporated, 1951.

44 Kinsey, A., W. Pomeroy, & C. Martin. *Sexual behavior in the human male*. Philadelphia: W. B. Saunders Company, 1948.

45 Whiting, J. W. M., & I. L. Child. *Child learning and personality*. New Haven, Conn.: Yale University Press, 1953.

46 Kuo, Z. *The dynamics of behavior development: An epigenetic view*. New York: Random House, Inc., 1967.

47 Broderick, C. B. Homosexuality. *World Book Encyclopedia*, 1974.

48 Kolodny, R. C., W. H. Masters, J. Hendryx, & G. Toro. Plasma testosterone and semen analysis in male homosexuals. *New England Journal of Medicine*, 1971, 1170–1174.

49 McClelland, D., J. W. Atkinson, R. A. Clark, & E. L. Lowell. *The achievement motive*. New York: Appleton Century Crofts, 1953. P. 118.

50 McClelland, D., J. W. Atkinson, R. A. Clark, & E. L. Lowell. *The achievement motive*. New York: Appleton Century Crofts, 1953. P. 121.

51 Winterbottom, M. R. The relation of need for achievement to learning experience in independence and mastery. In J. W. Atkinson (Ed.), *Motives in fantasy,*

action and society. Princeton, N. J.: D. Van Nostrand Company, Inc., 1958. Pp. 453–478.

52 Rosen, B. C., & R. D'Andrade. The psychological origins of achievement motivation. *Sociometry*, 1959, 22, 185–218.

53 Atkinson, J. W. *An introduction to motivation*. Princeton, N.J.: D. Van Nostrand Company, Inc., 1964.

54 McClelland, D., J. W. Atkinson, R. A. Clark, & E. L. Lowell. *The achievement motive*. New York: Appleton Century Crofts, 1953.

55 Atkinson, J. W., & G. H. Litwin. Achievement motive and test-anxiety conceived as motive to approach success and motive to avoid failure. *Journal of Abnormal and Social Psychology*, 1960, 60, 52–63.

56 Atkinson, J. W., & N. T. Feather. *A theory of achievement motivation*. New York: John Wiley & Sons, Inc., 1966.

57 Maccoby, E. E. *The development of sex differences*. Stanford, Calif.: Stanford University Press, 1966.

58 Horner, M. Femininity and successful achievement: A basic inconsistency. In J. Bardwick et al. (Eds.), *Feminine personality and conflict*. Belmont, Calif.: Brooks/Cole Publishing Company, 1970. Pp. 44–75.

Chapter 11

1 Mark, V. H., & F. R. Ervin. *Violence and the brain*. New York: Harper & Row, Publishers, Incorporated, 1970. Pp. 97–108.

2 Cannon, W. *The wisdom of the body*, New York: W. W. Norton & Company, Inc., 1932. P. 227.

3 Wolf, S., & H. G. Wolff. Evidence on the genesis of peptic ulcer in man. *Journal of the American Medical Association*, 1942, 120 (9).

4 Ax, A. F. The physiological differentiation between fear and anger in humans. *Psychosomatic Medicine*, 1953 15, (5).

5 Lacey, J. I. Somatic response patterning and stress: Some revisions of activation theory. In M. H. Appley & R. Trumbull (Eds.), *Psychological stress*. New York: Appleton Century Crofts, 1967.

6 Jost, H., & L. W. Sontag. The genetic factor in autonomic nervous system function. *Psychosomatic Medicine*, 1944, 6, 308–310.

7 Schachter, S., & J. Singer. Cognitive, social and physiological determinants of emotional state. *Psychological Review*, 1962, 69, 379–399.

8 Ekman, P. Universal and cultural differences in facial expression of emotion. *Nebraska Symposium on Motivation*, J. K. Cole (Ed.), Lincoln: University of Nebraska Press, 1971.

9 Goodenough, F. Expression of the emotions in a

blind-deaf child. *Journal of Abnormal and Social Psychology*, 1932, 27, 328–333.

10 Klineberg, O. Emotional expression in Chinese literature. *Journal of Abnormal and Social Psychology*, 1938, 33, 517–520.

11 Efron, D. *Gesture, race, and culture*. Atlantic Highlands, N. J.: Humanities Press, 1972.

12 Mischel, W. *Introduction to personality*. New York: Holt, Rinehart & Winston, Inc., 1971. P. 336.

13 Paul, G. L. *Insight vs. desensitization in psychotherapy*. Stanford, Calif.: Stanford University Press, 1966.

14 Elliott, R. Effects of uncertainty about the nature and advent of a noxious stimulus (shock) upon heart rate. *Journal of Personality and Social Psychology*, 1966, 3, 353–356.

15 Weiss, J. M. Psychological factors in stress and disease. *Scientific American*, 1972, 226, 104–113.

16 Fenz, W. D., & S. Epstein. Gradients of physiological arousal in parachutists as a function of an approaching jump. *Psychosomatic Medicine*, 1967, 29, 1, 33–51.

17 Geer, J. H., G. C. Davison, & R. I. Gatchel. Reduction of stress in humans through nonveridical perceived control of aversive stimulation. *Journal of Personality and Social Psychology*, 1970, 16, 731–738.

18 Farber, I. E., & W. K. Spence. Complex learning and conditioning as a function of anxiety. *Journal of Experimental Psychology*, 1953, 45, 120–125.

19 Ganzer, V. J. Effects of audience presence and test-anxiety on learning and retention in a serial learning situation. *Journal of Personality and Social Psychology*, 1968, 8, 194–199.

20 Spielberger, C. D., L. D. Goodstein, & W. G. Dahlstrom. Complex incidental learning as a function of anxiety and task difficulty. *Journal of Experimental Psychology*, 1958, 56, 58–61.

21 Spielberger, C. D. The effects of manifest anxiety on the academic achievement of college students. *Mental Hygiene*, 1962, 9, 195–204.

22 Spielberger, C. D., J. P. Denny, & H. Weitz. The effects of group counseling on the academic performance of anxious college freshmen. *Journal of Counseling Psychology*, 1962, 9, 195–204.

23 Selye, H. *The stress of life*. New York: McGraw-Hill Book Company, 1956.

24 Malmo, R. B. Studies of anxiety: Some clinical origins of the activation concept. In C. D. Spielberger (Ed.), *Anxiety and behavior*. New York: Academic Press, Inc., 1966. Pp. 157–178.

25 Pitts, F. N., Jr. The biochemistry of anxiety. *Scientific American*, 1969, 220, 69–75.

26 Lader, M. H. (Ed.). Studies of anxiety. *British Journal of Psychiatry*. Special Publication Number 3, 1969.

27 Wolf, S., & H. G. Wolff. *Human gastric functions*. New York: Oxford University Press, 1947.

28 Senay, E. C., & F. C. Redlich. Cultural and social factors in neuroses and psychosomatic illnesses. *Social Psychiatry*, 1968, 3 (3), 89–97.

29 Grayson, R. R. Air controllers syndrome: Peptic ulcer in air traffic controllers. *Illinois Medical Journal*, August 1972, 142, 2, 111–115.

30 Mirsky, I. A. Physiologic, psychologic, and social determinants in the etiology of duodenal ulcer. *American Journal of Digestive Diseases*, 1958, 3, 285–314.

31 Weiner, H., M. Thaler, M. F. Reiser, & I. A. Mirsky. Etiology of duodenal ulcer: I. Relation of specific psychological characteristics to rate of gastric secretion. *Psychosomatic Medicine*, 1957, 19, 1–10.

32 Mirsky, I. A. Physiologic, psychologic, and social determinants in the etiology of duodenal ulcer. *American Journal of Digestive Diseases*, 1958, 3, 285–314.

33 A. Golenpaul (Ed.). *1975 Information Please Almanac*. New York: Dan Golenpaul Associates, November 1974. P. 725.

34 Friedman, M., & R. H. Rosenman. Type A Behavior pattern: Its association with coronary heart disease. *Annals of Clinical Research*, 1971, 3, 300–317.

35 Basedow, R. H. *The Australian aborigine*. Adelaide, Australia: F. W. Peerce and Sons, 1925. Pp. 178–179.

36 Cannon, W. B. "Voodoo" death. *American Anthropologist*, 1942, 44 (2), 169–181.

37 Bard, M. The study and modification of intra-familial violence. In J. L. Singer (Ed.), *The control of aggression and violence*. New York: Academic Press, Inc., 1971. P. 160.

38 Freud, S. *Civilization and its discontents*. (trans. by Joan Riviere). London: The Hogarth Press, Ltd., 1957. Pp. 85–86.

39 Lorenz, K. *On aggression*. New York: Harcourt Brace Jovanovich, 1966.

40 Scott, J. P. *Aggression*. Chicago: University of Chicago Press, 1958.

41 Levy, I. V., & I. A. King. The effects of testosterone propionate on fighting behavior in young C57 BL/10 mice. *Anatomical Record*, 1953, 117, 562.

42 Allee, W. C., N. Collias, & C. Z. Lutherman. Modification of the social order among flocks of hens by injection of testosterone propionate. *Physiological Zoology*, 1939, 12, 412–420.

43 Hamburg, D. A. Effects of Progesterone on Behavior. In R. Levine (Ed.), *Endocrines and the central nervous system*. Baltimore: The Williams & Wilkins Company, 1966.

44 Moyer, K. E. The physiology of aggression and the implications for aggression control. In J. L. Singer

(Ed.), *The control of aggression and violence.* New York: Academic Press, Inc., 1971.

45 LeMaire, L. Danish experiences regarding the castration of sexual offenders. *Journal of Criminal Law and Criminology*, 1956, 47, 294–310.

46 Charles Whitman; in R. N. Johnson, *Aggression in man and animals.* Philadelphia: W. B. Saunders Company, 1972. P. 78.

47 Kuo, Z. Y. The genesis of the cat's responses to the rat. *Comparative Psychology*, 1930, 11, 1, 1–35.

48 Kuo, Z. Y. Further study on the behavior of the cat toward the rat. *Comparative Psychology*, 1938, 25, 1, 1–8.

49 McCandless, B. R. *Children: Behavior and development.* (2d ed.) New York: Holt, Rinehart & Winston, Inc., 1967. P. 587.

50 Bandura, A. *Aggression: A social learning approach.* Englewood Cliffs, N.J.: Prentice-Hall, Inc., 1973.

51 McCord, J., & W. McCord. The effects of parental role models on criminality. *Journal of Social Issues*, 1958, 14, 66–74.

52 Steele, B. F., & C. B. Pollock. A psychiatric study of parents who abuse infants and small children. In R. E. Helfer & C. H. Kempe (Eds.), *The battered child.* Chicago: University of Chicago Press, 1968. Pp. 103–133.

53 Stein, A. H., & L. K. Friedrich. Television content and young children's behavior. In J. P. Murray, E. A. Rubinstein, & G. A. Comstock (Eds.), *Television and social behavior.* Volume II: *Television and social learning.* Washington, D.C.: U.S. Government Printing Office, 1972. Pp. 202–317.

54 Baker, R. K., & S. J. Ball (Eds.), *Violence and the media*, Vol. 9. Washington, D.C.: U.S. Government Printing Office, 1969.

55 Berkowitz, L. Some aspects of observed aggression. *Journal of Personality and Social Psychology*, 1965, 2, 359–369.

56 Liebert, R. M., & R. A. Baron. Some immediate effects of televised violence on children's behavior. *Developmental Psychology*, 1972, 6, 3.

57 Stein, A. H., & L. K. Friedrich. Television Content and Young Children's Behavior. In J. P. Murray, E. A. Rubinstein, & G. A. Comstock (Eds.), *Television and social behavior.* Volume II: *Television and social learning.* Washington, D.C.: U.S. Government Printing Office, 1972. Pp. 202–317.

58 Cline, V. B., R. G. Croft, & S. Courrier. Desensitization of children to television violence. *Journal of Personality and Social Psychology*, 1973, 27, 3, 360–365.

59 Fannin, L. F., & M. B. Clinard. Differences in the conception of self as a male among lower and middle class delinquents. *Social Problems*, 1965, 13, 205–214.

60 A. Golenpaul (Ed.), *1975 Information Please Almanac.* New York: Dan Golenpaul Associates, November 1974. P. 730.

61 Kish, G. B. A developmental and motivational analysis of stimulus-seeking. Paper presented at American Psychological Association, Montreal, Canada, 1973.

62 Azrin, N. H., R. R. Hutchinson, & D. F. Hake. Avoidance and escape reactions to aversive shock. *Journal of the Experimental Analysis of Behavior*, 1967, 10, 131–148.

63 Toch, H. *Violent men.* Chicago: Aldine Publishing Company, 1969.

64 Berdie, R. Playing the dozens. *Journal of Abnormal and Social Psychology*, 1947, 42, 120.

65 Toch, H. *Violent men.* Chicago: Aldine Publishing Company, 1969. Pp. 91–92.

66 Cited in J. Frank. *Why men fight.* New York: Random House Vintage Books, 1968.

67 Olds, J., & P. Milner. Positive reinforcement produced by electrical stimulation of septal area and other regions of the rat brain. *Journal of Comparative and Physiological Psychology*, 1954, 47, 419–427.

68 Olds, J. Differential effects of drives and drugs on self-stimulation at different brain sites. In D. E. Sheer (Ed.), *Electrical stimulation of the brain.* Austin: University of Texas Press, 1961.

69 Heath, R. G. Electrical self-stimulation of the brain in man. *American Journal of Psychiatry*, 1963, 120, 571–577.

70 Maslow, A. Fusion of facts and values. *American Journal of Psychoanalysis*, 1963, 23, 117–181.

71 Maslow, A. Cognition of being in the peak experiences. *Journal of Genetic Psychology*, 1959, 94, 43–66.

Chapter 12

1 Murray, H. A. American Icarus. In A. Burton & R. E. Harris (Eds.), *Clinical studies in personality.* Vol. 2. New York: Harper & Row, Publishers, Incorporated, 1955. Pp. 615–641.

2 Sheldon, W. H., with collaboration of S. S. Stevens. *The varieties of temperament: A psychology of constitutional differences.* New York: Harper & Row, Publishers, Incorporated, 1942.

3 Freud, S. In E. Jones, *The life and work of Sigmund Freud. Volume 1: The formative years and the great discoveries.* New York: Basic Books, Inc., 1953. Pp. 195–196.

4 Mischel, W. *Introduction to personality.* New York: Holt, Rinehart & Winston, Inc., 1971. Pp. 75–76.

5 Neisser, U. *Cognitive psychology*. New York: Appleton Century Crofts, 1967. P. 3.

6 Kohlberg, L. Stage and sequence: The cognitive-developmental approach to socialization. In D. A. Goslin (Ed.), *Handbook of socialization theory and research*. Chicago: Rand McNally, 1969.

7 Kohlberg, L. Continuities in childhood and adult moral development. In P. B. Baltes & K. W. Schaie (Eds.), *Life-span developmental psychology: Personality and socialization*. New York: Academic Press, Inc., 1973.

8 Kohlberg, L. Development of moral character and moral ideology. In M. L. Hoffman & L. W. Hoffman (Eds.), *Review of child development research*. New York: Russell Sage Foundation, 1964. Pp. 383–431.

9 Hartshorne, H., & M. A. May. Studies in deceit. In Columbia University, Teachers College, *Studies in the Nature of Character*, Volume 1. New York: The Macmillan Company, 1928.

10 Hartup, W. W., & A. Yonas. Developmental psychology. In *Annual Review of Psychology*, Vol. 22. Palo Alto, Calif.: Annual Review, Inc., 1971. Pp. 337–392.

11 Krebs, R. L. Some Relationships between Moral Judgment, Attention and Resistance to Temptation. Unpublished Ph.D. dissertation, University of Chicago, 1967.

12 Krebs, D. Altruism: An examination of the concept and a review of the literature. *Psychological Bulletin*, 1970, 73, 258–302.

13 MacFarlane, J., L. Allen, & M. Honzik. *A developmental study of behavior problems of normal children between twenty-one months and four years*. Berkeley: University of California Press, 1954.

14 Kohlberg, L. Moral development and identification. In H. Stevenson (Ed.), *Child psychology, 62nd yearbook of the National Society for the Study of Education*. Chicago: University of Chicago Press, 1963. Pp. 277–332.

15 Sollenberger, R. T. Why no juvenile delinquency? Paper presented at the American Psychological Association, New York, 1966.

16 Glueck, S. & E. Glueck. *Toward a typology of juvenile offenders: Implications for therapy and prevention*. New York: Gruen and Stratton, 1970.

17 Bacon, M. K., I. L. Child, & H. Barry. III. A cross-cultural study of some correlates of crime. *Journal of Abnormal and Social Psychology*, 1963, 66, 291–300.

18 Sears, R. R., E. E. Maccoby, & H. Levin. *Patterns of child rearing*. Evanston, Ill.: Row, Peterson & Company, 1957.

19 Bandura, A., & A. C. Huston. Identification as a process of incidental learning. *Journal of Abnormal and Social Psychology*, 1961, 63, 311–318.

20 Hoffman, M. L., & H. D. Saltzstein. Parent discipline and the child's moral development. *Journal of Personality and Social Psychology*, 1967, 45–57.

21 Toby, J. Affluence and adolescent crime. In President's Commission on Law Enforcement and Administration of Justice. *Task Force Report: Juvenile Delinquency and Youth Crime*. Washington, D.C.: U.S. Government Printing Office, 1967. Pp. 143–144.

22 Merton, R. K. *Social theory and social structure*. (rev. ed.) Chicago: The Free Press of Glencoe, Ill., 1957.

23 Geis, G. *Juvenile gangs*. Washington, D.C.: U.S. Government Printing Office, 1965.

24 Tannenbaum, A. J. Alienated youth. *Journal of Social Issues*, 1969, 25 (entire).

25 Hartshorne, H., & M. A. May. Studies in deceit. In Columbia University, Teachers College, *Studies in the Nature of Character*. Volume 1. New York: The Macmillan Company, 1928.

26 Middleton, R., & S. Putney. Religion, normative standards, and behavior. *Sociometry*, 25, 141–152.

27 Kinsey, A. C., W. B. Pomeroy, & C. E. Martin. Sexual behavior in the human male. Philadelphia: W. B. Saunders & Company, 1948.

28 Tracy, J. J., & H. J. Cross. Antecedents of shift in moral judgment. *Journal of Personality and Social Psychology*, 1973, 26, 238–244.

29 Kohlberg, L. An interview with Lawrence Kohlberg. In *Psychology 73–74 Text*. Guilford, Conn.: The Dushkin Publishing Group, Inc., 1973. Pp. 89–90.

Chapter 13

1 Carmen. In C. Mirthes and the children of P. S. 15, *Can't you hear me talking to you?* New York: Bantam Books, Inc., 1971. Pp. 23, 24, 25, 74, 75, 88, 89.

2 Erikson, E. Eight ages of man. In *Childhood and society*. (2d ed.) New York: W. W. Norton & Company, Inc., 1963. P. 261.

3 Erikson, E. Identity and the life cycle. *Psychological Issues*, 1959, 1 (1), 92.

4 Erikson, E. Eight ages of man. In *Childhood and society*. (2d ed.) New York: W. W. Norton & Company, Inc., 1963. P. 266.

5 Coopersmith, S. *The antecedents of self-esteem*. San Francisco: W. H. Freeman and Company, 1967.

6 Coopersmith, S. Studies in self-esteem. *Scientific American*, February 1968, 218, 96–100.

7 Herndon, J. *The way it spozed to be*. New York: Bantam Books, Inc., 1969. P. 197.

8 Lazarus, R. S. The self-regulation of emotion. Paper delivered at symposium, Parameters of Emotion, in Stockholm, Sweden, June 4–6, 1973.

9 Mechanic, D. *Students under stress*. New York: The Free Press, 1962.

10 Barker, R. G., T. Dembo, & K. Lewin. Frustration and regression: An experiment with young children. In R. G. Barker, J. S. Kounin, and H. F. Wright (Eds.), *Child behavior and development*. New York: McGraw-Hill Book Company, 1943. Pp. 441–458.

11 Maier, N. R. F. *Frustration: A study of behavior without a goal*. New York: McGraw-Hill Book Company, 1949.

12 Vaillant, G. E. The natural history of narcotic drug addiction. *Seminars in Psychiatry*, 1970, 2, 486–498.

13 Clark, K. B. *Dark ghetto*. New York: Harper and Row, Publishers, Incorporated, 1965. P. 95.

14 D'Zurilla, T. Recall efficiency and mediating cognitive events in "experimental repression." *Journal of Personality and Social Psychology*, 1965, 1, 253–257.

15 Hamburg, D. A., B. Hamburg, & S. de Goza. Adaptive problems and mechanisms in severely burned patients. *Psychiatry*, 1953, 16, 9.

16 Neomia. In H. Kohl, *Thirty-six children*. New York: New American Library, 1968. Pp. 36, 40.

17 Pulaski, M. A. S. Play as a function of toy structure and fantasy predisposition. *Child development*, 1970, 41, 2, 531–537.

18 Singer, J. L. *The child's world of make-believe: Experimental studies of imaginative play*. New York: Academic Press, Inc., 1973.

19 Elisa. In C. Mirthes and the children of P. S. 15, *Can't you hear me talking to you?* New York: Bantam Books, Inc., 1971. P. 62.

20 Masserman, J. *Principles of dynamic psychiatry*. Philadelphia: W. B. Saunders Company, 1961. P. 38.

21 Bramel, D. A dissonance theory approach to defensive projection. *Journal of Abnormal and Social Psychology*, 1962, 64, 121–129.

22 Dulany, D. E., Jr. Avoidance learning of perceptual defense and vigilance. *Journal of Abnormal and Social Psychology*, 1957, 55, 333–338.

23 Eriksen, C. W., & J. L. Kuethe. Avoidance conditioning of verbal behavior without awareness: A paradigm of repression. *Journal of Abnormal and Social Psychology*, 1956, 53, 203–209.

24 Keister, M. E., & R. Updegraff. A study of children's reactions to failure and an experimental attempt to modify them. *Child development*, 1937, 8, 243–248.

25 Ablon, J. Reactions of Samoan burn patients and families to severe burns. *Social Science and Medicine*, 1973, 7, 167–178.

26 Mischel, W., E. Ebbesen, & A. Raskoff. Cognitive and attentional mechanisms in delay of gratification. Unpublished manuscript, Stanford University, 1971.

27 Lazarus, R. S., & J. C. Spiesman. A research case history dealing with psychological stress. *Journal of Psychological Studies*, 1960, 11, 167–194.

28 Lazarus, R. S., J. C. Speisman, A. M. Mordkoff, & L. A. Davison. A laboratory study of psychological stress produced by a motion picture film. *Psychological Monographs*, 1962, (34) 76, Whole No. 553.

29 Speisman, J. C., R. S. Lazarus, A. Mordkoff, & L. Davison. Experimental reduction of stress based on ego-defense theory. *Journal of Abnormal and Social Psychology*, 1964, 68, 4, 367–380.

30 Wolff, C. T., S. B. Friedman, M. A. Hoffer, & J. W. Mason. Relationship between psychological defenses and mean urinary 17-Hydroxycorticosteroid excretion rates. 1. A Predictive study of parents of fatally-ill children. *Psychosomatic Medicine*, 1964, 26, 576–591.

31 Peck, R. Measuring the mental health of normal adults. *Genetic Psychology Monographs*, 1959, 60, 251–252.

Chapter 14

1 Scarf, M. Normality is a square circle or a four sided triangle. *The New York Times Magazine*, October 3, 1971, 16, 17.

2 Page, J. D. *Psychopathology: The science of understanding deviance*. Chicago: Aldine-Atherton, 1971.

3 Schmidt, H. O., & C. P. Fonda. The reliability of psychiatric diagnosis: A new look. *Journal of Abnormal and Social Psychology*, 1956, 52, 262–267.

4 Rosenhan, D. L. On being sane in insane places. *Science*, January 19, 1973, 179 (4070), 1–9.

5 Srole, L., T. S. Langner, S. T. Michael, M. K. Opler, & T. A. C. Rennie. *Mental health in the metropolis: Midtown Manhattan study*. Vol. 1. New York: McGraw-Hill Book Company, 1962.

6 Philips, D. L. The "true prevalence" of mental illness in a New England state. *Community Mental Health Journal*, 1966, 2, 35–40.

7 Pasamanick, B. A. A survey of mental disease in an urban population. IV: An approach to total prevalence rates. *Archives of General Psychiatry*, 1961, 5, 151–155.

8 Luther, M. *Colloquia mensalia*. Cited in J. C. Coleman, *Abnormal Psychology and Modern Life*. Glenview, Ill.: Scott, Foresman and Company, 1972. P. 33.

9 Szasz, T. *The myth of mental illness*. New York: Delta Books, Dell Publishing Co., Inc., 1961. P. 296.

10 Pitts, F. N., Jr. The biochemistry of anxiety. *Scientific American*, 1969, 220, 69–75.

11 Slater, E. & J. Shields. Genetic aspects of anxiety. In

M. H. Lader (Ed.), *Studies of anxiety*. Ashford, England: Headley Broteis, 1969.

12 Vandenburg, S. G., P. J. Clark, & I. Samuels. Psychophysiological reactions of twins: Heritability factors in galvanic skin resistance, heartbeat, and breathing rates. *Eugenics Quarterly*, 1965, 12, 7–10.

13 Lader, M. H., & L. Wing. Physiological measures, sedative drugs, and morbid anxiety. *Maudsley Monographs No. 14*, London: Oxford University Press, 1966.

14 Agras, S., D. Sylvester, & D. Oliveau. The epidemiology of common fears and phobias. Unpublished manuscript, 1969.

15 Coleman, J. C. *Abnormal psychology and modern life*. (3d ed.) Glenview, Ill.: Scott, Foresman and Company, 1964.

16 Goodwin, D. W., S. B. Guze, & E. Robbins. Follow-up studies in obsessional neurosis. *Archives of General Psychiatry*, 1969, 20, 182–187.

17 Masserman, J. H. *Principles of dynamic psychiatry*. (2d ed.) Philadelphia: W. B. Saunders Company, 1961. P. 48.

18 Grimshaw, L. Obsessional disorder and neurological illness. *Journal of Neurology, Neurosurgery, and Psychiatry*, 1964, 27, 229–231.

19 Public Health Service Statistical Note 68, *National Institute of Mental Health Department of Health Education and Welfare Publication HSM 73-9005*, February 1973, Table A, P. 6.

20 Davison, G. C., & J. M. Neale. *Abnormal psychology: An experimental clinical approach*. New York: John Wiley & Sons, Inc., 1974. P. 174.

21 Seligman, M. E. P. Fall into Helplessness. *Psychology Today*, June 1973, 7, 43–46, 48.

22 Weiss, J. M., H. I. Glazer, & L. A. Pohorecky. Neurotransmitters and helplessness: A chemical bridge to depression? *Psychology Today*, December 1974, 8, 58–62.

23 Coping with Depression. *Newsweek*, January 8, 1973, 51–54.

24 Motto, J. A. Langley Porter receives grant to study depression and suicide. *University of California: University Bulletin*, 1969, 17 (36), 180.

25 Coping with Depression. *Newsweek*, January 8, 1973, 51–54.

26 Curlee, W. V. Suicide and self-destructive behavior on the Cheyenne River reservation. In *Suicide among the American Indians*. Public Health Service Publication No. 1903, Washington, D.C.: U.S. Government Printing Office, June 1969. Pp. 34–36.

27 *Diagnostic and Statistical Manual of Mental Disorders*. (2d ed.) Washington, D.C.: American Psychiatric Association, 1968. P. 23.

28 Coleman, J. C. *Abnormal psychology and modern life*. (4th ed.) Glenview, Ill.: Scott, Foresman and Company, 1972.

29 McGhie, A., & I. Chapman. Disorders of attention and perception in early schizophrenia. *British Journal of Medical Psychology*, 1961, 34, 104–106.

30 McGhie, A., & I. Chapman. Disorders of attention and perception in early schizophrenia. *British Journal of Medical Psychology*, 1961, 108.

31 McGhie, A., & I. Chapman. Disorders of attention and perception in early schizophrenia. *British Journal of Medical Psychology*, 1961, 109–110.

32 Anonymous. Autobiography of a schizophrenic experience. *Journal of Abnormal and Social Psychology*, 1955, 51, 677–689.

33 Jefferson, L. *These are my sisters*. Tulsa: Vickers Publishing Co., 1948. Pp. 51, 52.

34 Kisker, G. W. *The disorganized personality*. (2d ed.) New York: McGraw-Hill Book Company, 1972. P. 318.

35 Kisker, G. W. *The disorganized personality*. (2d ed.) New York: McGraw-Hill Book Company, 1972. P. 314.

36 Maher, B. *Principles of psychopathology: An experimental approach*. New York: McGraw-Hill Book Company, 1966. P. 304.

37 Luce, G. G. *Body time*. New York: Pantheon Books, Inc., 1971. P. 245–246.

38 Coleman, J. C. *Abnormal psychology and modern life*. (4th ed.) Glenview, Ill.: Scott, Foresman and Company, 1972. P. 280, 281.

39 Zax, M., & G. Stricker. *Patterns of psychopathology: Case studies of behavioral dysfunction*. London: The Macmillan Company, 1963. P. 69.

40 Heston, L. The genetics of schizophrenia and schizoid disease. *Science*, January 1970, 167, 249–256.

41 Hoffer, A., H. Osmond, & J. Smythies. Schizophrenia: A new approach II: Result of a year's research. *Journal of Mental Science*, 1954, 100, 29–45.

42 Dement, W. C., V. Zarione, J. Ferguson, H. Cohen, T. Pivile, & J. Barchas. Some parallel findings in schizophrenic patients and serotonin-depleted cats. Paper presented at the Schizophrenia Conference, November 1968.

43 Meehl, P. Schizotaxia, schizotypy, schizophrenia. *American Psychologist*, 1962, 17, 827–838.

44 Page, J. D. Psychopathology: The science of understanding deviance. Chicago: Aldine-Atherton, 1971.

45 Coleman, J. C. *Abnormal Psychology and Modern Life*. (4th ed.) Glenview, Ill.: Scott, Foresman and Company, 1972. P. 366.

46 Eysenck, H. J. *Behavior therapy and the neuroses*. London: Pergamon Press, 1960.

47 Fenz, W. D. Heart rate responses to a stressor: A comparison between primary and secondary psychopaths and normal controls. *Journal of Experimental Research in Personality*, 1971, 5 (1), 7–13.

Chapter 15

1 Frank, J. D. *Persuasion and healing.* Baltimore: The Johns Hopkins Press, 1961.

2 Harper, R. A. *Psychoanalysis and psychotherapy: 36 systems.* Englewood Cliffs, N.J.: Prentice-Hall, Inc., 1959.

3 Munroe, Ruth L. *Schools of psychoanalytic thought.* New York: Dryden Press, 1955.

4 Wolberg, L. *The technique of psychotherapy.* (2d ed.) New York: Grune and Stratton, 1967. Pp. 689–690.

5 White, R. W., & N. F. Watt. *The abnormal personality.* (4th ed.) New York: The Ronald Press Company, 1973. Pp. 262, 263, 264.

6 Nash, E. H., R. Hoehn-Saric, C. C. Battle, A. R. Stone, S. D. Imber, & J. D. Frank. Systematic preparation of patients for short-term psychotherapy. II. Relation to characteristics of patient, therapist, and the psychotherapeutic process. *Journal of Nervous and Mental Disease*, 1965, 140, 374–383.

7 Strupp, H. H. *Psychotherapy and the modification of abnormal behavior: An introduction to theory and research.* New York: McGraw-Hill Book Company, 1971.

8 Rachman, S. *Phobias: Their nature and control.* Springfield, Ill.: Charles C. Thomas, 1968. P. 49.

9 Lewinsohn, P. M., & M. Schaffer. Use of home observation as an integral part of the treatment of depression: Preliminary report and case studies. *Journal of Counseling and Clinical Psychology*, 1971, 37, 92–93.

10 Lazarus, A. A. *Behavior therapy and beyond.* New York: McGraw-Hill Book Company, 1971. Pp. 123, 124, 125, 126.

11 Paul, G. L. *Insight vs. desensitization in psychotherapy.* Stanford, Calif.: Stanford University Press, 1966.

12 Lang, P. J., A. D. Lazovik, & D. J. Reynolds. Desensitization, suggestibility and pseudotherapy. *Journal of Abnormal and Social Psychology*, 1965, 70, 395–402.

13 Paul, G. L. *Insight vs. desensitization in psychotherapy.* Stanford, Calif.: Stanford University Press, 1966.

14 Lang, P. J., A. D. Lazovik, & D. J. Reynolds. Desensitization, suggestibility and pseudotherapy. *Journal of Abnormal and Social Psychology*, 1965, 70, 395–402.

15 Breger, L., & J. L. McGaugh. Critique and reformulation of "learning-theory" approaches to psychotherapy and neurosis. *Psychological Bulletin*, 1965, 63, 338–358.

16 Truax, C. B., & R. R. Carkhuff. *Toward effective counseling and psychotherapy: Training and practice.* Chicago: Aldine Publishing Company, 1967. P. 72.

17 Truax, C. B., & R. R. Carkhuff. *Toward effective counseling and psychotherapy: Training and practice.* Chicago: Aldine Publishing Company, 1967. Pp. 67, 68.

18 Truax, C. B., & R. R. Carkhuff. *Toward effective counseling and psychotherapy: Training and practice.* Chicago: Aldine Publishing Company, 1967. P. 57.

19 Rogers, C. R. Client-centered psychotherapy. In A. M. Freedman and H. I. Kaplan (Eds.), *Comprehensive textbook of psychiatry.* Baltimore: The Williams and Wilkins Company, 1967. Pp. 1225–1228.

20 Murray, D. Client-centered therapy. In L. Hersher (Ed.), *Four psychotherapies.* New York: Appleton Century Crofts, 1970. Pp. 13, 14.

21 Rosenthal, D. Changes in some moral values following psychotherapy. *Journal of Consulting Psychology*, 1955, 19, 431–436.

22 Wildman, R. W., & R. W. Wildman, II. The practice of clinical psychology in the United States. *Journal of Clinical Psychology*, 1967, 23, 292–295.

23 Lazarus, A. A. *Behavior therapy and beyond.* New York: McGraw-Hill Book Company, 1971.

24 Jones, K., & R. Sidebotham. *Mental hospitals at work.* London: Routledge and Kegan Paul, 1962.

25 Goldman, A. R., R. H. Bohr, & T. A. Steinberg. On posing as mental patients: Reminiscences and recommendations. *Professional Psychology*, Vol. 1, 1970, 427–434.

26 Rosenhan, D. L. On being sane in insane places. *Science*, January 19, 1973, 179, 4070, 1–9.

27 Sarbin, T. R. On the futility of the proposition that some people are labeled "mentally ill." *Journal of Consulting Psychology*, 1967, 31, 445–453.

28 Rosenhan, D. L. On being sane in insane places. *Science*, January 19, 1973, 179, 4070, 1–9.

29 Goffman, E. *Asylums.* Garden City, N.Y.: Doubleday & Company, Inc., 1961.

30 Schwartz, M. S. Functions of the team in the state mental hospital. *American Journal of Orthopsychiatry*, 1960, 30, 100–102.

31 Paul, G. L. The chronic mental patient: Current status—Future directions. *Psychological Bulletin*, 1969, 71, 81–94.

32 Henderson, J., K. Kelley, R. Hibbert, & J. A. Samuels. Community based operant learning environment. In R. D. Rubin (Ed.), *Advances in behavior therapy.* New York: Academic Press, Inc. 1969. Pp. 233–271.

33 Egan, M. H., & O. L. Robinson. Home treatment of severely disturbed children and families. In A. J. Bindman & A. D. Spiegel (Eds.), *Perspectives in* *community mental health.* Chicago: Aldine Publishing Company, 1969. Pp. 538–544.

34 Weiner, L., A. Becker, & T. T. Friedman. *Home treatment: Spearhead of community psychiatry.* Pittsburgh, Pa.: University of Pittsburgh Press, 1967.

35 Fairweather, G. W., D. H. Sanders, H. Maynard, & D. L. Cressler. *Community life for the mentally ill: An alternative to institutionalization.* Chicago: Aldine Publishing Company, 1969.

36 Conroy, S. B. Needs of the elderly. *Washington Post,* September 3, 1972, M2.

37 Bard, M. Family intervention police teams as a community mental health resource. Paper presented at the American Psychological Association Annual Convention, San Francisco, Calif., September 3, 1968.

38 The compassionate cop. *Time,* March 23, 1970, 58.

39 Bloch, P., D. Anderson, & P. Gervais. *Policewomen on patrol,* First Report, Vol. 1. Washington, D.C.: A Police Foundation Paper, February 1973.

40 The compassionate cop. *Time,* March 23, 1970, 58.

41 Bard, M. Alternatives to traditional law enforcement. In F. Korten, S. W. Cook, & J. I. Lacey (Eds.), *Psychology and the problems of society.* Washington, D.C.: American Psychological Association, 1970. Pp. 128–132.

Chapter 16

1 Brunner, J. Break the doors of hell. In H. S. Santesson (Ed.), *The mighty swordsmen.* New York: Lancer, 1970. Pp. 86–131.

2 Aristotle. Politics, Book I, Chapter II, line 29.

3 Schachter, S. *The psychology of affiliation.* Stanford, Calif.: Stanford University Press, 1959. Pp. 12–19.

4 Kelman, H. C. Attitudes are alive and well and gainfully employed in the sphere of action. *American Psychologist,* May 1974, 29, 5, 316.

5 Allport, G. *The nature of prejudice.* Garden City, N.Y.: Doubleday and Company, Inc., 1958. P. 9.

6 Ellison, R. *Invisible man.* New York: Random House, Inc., 1952. Pp. 13, 14.

7 Horowitz, E., & R. Horowitz. Development of social attitudes in children. *Sociometry,* 1938, 1, 301–338.

8 Epstein, R., & S. Komorita. Childhood prejudice as a function of parental ethnocentrism, punitiveness, and outgroup characteristics. *Journal of Personality and Social Psychology,* 1966, 3, 259–264.

9 Rokeach, M. *Beliefs, attitudes, and values.* San Francisco: Jossey and Bass, 1968.

10 Stein, D. D., J. A. Hardyck, & M. B. Smith. Race and belief: An open and shut case. *Journal of Personality and Social Psychology,* 1965, 1, 4, 281–289.

11 Stein, D. D., J. A. Hardyck, & M. B. Smith. Race and belief: An open and shut case. *Journal of Personality and Social Psychology,* 1965, 1, 4, 281–289.

12 Adorno, T., E. Frenkel-Brunswik, D. Levinson, & R. Sanford. *The authoritarian personality.* New York: Harper & Row, Publishers, Incorporated, 1950.

13 Newcomb, T. *Personality and social change.* New York: The Dryden Press, Inc., 1943.

14 Newcomb, T., K. Koenig, R. Flacks, & D. Warwick. *Persistence and change: Bennington College and its students after 25 years.* New York: John Wiley & Sons, Inc., 1967.

15 Caffrey, B., S. Anderson, & J. Garrison. Changes in racial attitudes of white southerners after exposure to the atmosphere of a southern university. *Psychological Reports,* 1969, 25, 555–558.

16 Pettigrew, T. Social psychology and desegregation research. *American Psychologist,* 1961, 16, 109.

17 Greeley, A. M., & P. B. Sheatsley. Attitudes toward racial integration. *Scientific American,* December 1971, 225, 6, 13–19.

18 Sherif, M. Experiments in group conflict. *Scientific American,* November 1956, 195, 32, 54–58.

19 Greeley, A. M., & P. B. Sheatsley. Attitudes toward racial integration. *Scientific American,* December 1971, 225, 6, 13–19.

20 Miller, N., & R. Bugelski. Minor studies of aggression: II. The influence of frustrations imposed by the in-group on attitudes expressed toward out-groups. *Journal of Psychology,* 1948, 25, 437–452.

21 Rokeach, M. Long-range experimental modification of values, attitudes, and behavior. *American Psychologist,* 1971, 26, 453–457.

22 Deutsch, M., & M. E. Collins. *Interracial housing: A psychological evaluation of a social experiment.* Minneapolis: University of Minnesota Press, 1951.

23 Lichter, J. H., & D. W. Johnson. Changes in attitudes toward Negroes of white elementary school students after use of multi-ethnic readers. *Journal of Educational Psychology,* 1969, 60, 148–152.

24 James, H. E. O. Personal contact in school and change in intergroup attitudes. *International Social Science Bulletin,* 1955, 7, 66–70.

25 Sherif, M. Experiments in group conflict. *Scientific American,* November 1956, 195, 32, 54–58.

26 Allport, G. *The nature of prejudice.* Garden City, N.Y.: Doubleday & Company, Inc., 1958. P. 267.

27 Cook, S. W. Motives in a conceptual analysis of attitude-related behavior. In W. J. Arnold & D. Levine (Eds.), *Nebraska Symposium on Motivation,* 1969, Lincoln: University of Nebraska Press, 1970. Pp. 179–231.

28 Kelley, H. Two functions of reference groups. In G. Swanson, T. Newcomb, & E. Hartley (Eds.), *Readings in social psychology.* (2d ed.) New York: Holt, Rinehart & Winston, Inc., 1952. Pp. 410–414.

29 Asch, S. *Social psychology*. New York: Prentice-Hall, Inc., 1952.

30 Glinski, R., B. Glinski, & G. Slatin. Nonnaivety contamination in conformity experiments: Sources, effects, and implications for control. *Journal of Personality and Social Psychology*, 1970, 16, 478–485.

31 Asch, S. Effects of group pressure upon the modification and distortion of judgment. In M. H. Guetzkow (Ed.), *Groups, leadership, and men*. Pittsburgh: Carnegie Press, 1951. Pp. 117–190.

32 Asch, S. *Social psychology*. New York: Prentice-Hall, Inc., 1952

33 Ettinger, R., C. Marino, N. Endler, S. Geller, & T. Natziuk. Effects of agreement and correctness of relative competence and conformity. *Journal of Personality and Social Psychology*, 1971, 19, 204–212.

34 Asch, S. *Social psychology*. New York: Prentice-Hall, Inc., 1952.

35 Dittes, J., & H. Kelley. Effects of different conditions of acceptance upon conformity to group norms. *Journal of Abnormal and Social Psychology*, 1956, 53, 100–107.

36 Deutsch, M., & H. Gerard. A study of normative and informational influence upon individual judgment. *Journal of Abnormal and Social Psychology*, 1955, 51, 629–636.

37 Crutchfield, R. S. Conformity and character. *American Psychologist*, 1955, 10, 191–198.

38 Vaughn, G. M. The trans-situational aspect of conforming behavior. *Journal of Personality*, 1964, 32, 335–354.

39 Nord, W. R. Social exchange theory: An integrative approach to social conformity. *Psychological Bulletin*, 1969, 71, 174–208.

40 Hampden-Turner, C. *Radical man: The process of psycho-social development*. Cambridge, Mass.: Schenkman Publishing Company, 1970. Pp. 100–101.

41 Snow, C. P. Either/Or. *Progressive*, February 1961, 24.

42 Milgram, S. Behavioral study of obedience. *Journal of Abnormal and Social Psychology*, 1963, 67, 371–378.

43 Milgram, S. Some conditions of obedience and disobedience to authority. *Human Relations*, 1965, 18, 57–76.

44 Milgram, S. Some conditions of obedience and disobedience to authority. *Human Relations*, 1965, 18, 57–76.

45 Marcus, S. Obedience to authority. *New York Times Book Review*, January 13, 1974, sec. 7, 1–3.

46 Milgram, S. Some conditions of obedience and disobedience to authority. *Human Relations*, 1965, 18, 57–76.

47 Harlow, H. F. The nature of love. *American Psychologist*, 1958, 13, 673.

48 Walster, E., V. Aronson, D. Abrahams, & L. Rottman. Importance of physical attractiveness in dating behavior. *Journal of Personality and Social Psychology*, 1966, 5, 508–516.

49 Aronson, E., B. Willerman, & J. Floyd. The effect of a pratfall on increasing interpersonal attractiveness. *Psychonomic Science*, 1966, 4, 227–228.

50 Berscheid, E., & G. Walster, Liking reciprocity as a function of perceived basis of proffered liking. Cited in E. Berscheid and E. Walster. *Interpersonal attraction*. Reading, Mass.: Addison Wesley Publishing Company, Inc., 1969. Pp. 58–59.

51 Walster, E. The effect of self-esteem on romantic liking. *Journal of Experimental Social Psychology*, 1965, 1, 184–197.

52 Aronson, E., & D. Linder. Gain and loss of esteem as determinants of interpersonal attractiveness. *Journal of Experimental Social Psychology*, 1965, 1, 156–171.

53 Festinger, L., S. Schachter, & K. Back. *Social pressures in informal groups: A study of human factors in housing*. New York: Harper & Row, Publishers, Incorporated, 1950.

54 Byrne, D. *The attraction paradigm*. New York: Academic Press, Inc., 1971.

55 Kerkhoff, A. C., & K. E. Davis. Value consensus and need complementarity in mate selection. *American Sociological Review*, June 1962, 27, 3, 295–303.

Chapter 17

1 Miller, G. A. Psychology as a means of promoting human welfare. *American Psychologist*, 1969, 24, 1063, 1070, 1071, 1073.

2 Lehrer, T. *Tom Lehrer's second song book*. New York: Crown Publishers, Inc., 1968. P. 26.

3 Glass, D. C., & J. E. Singer. *Urban stress*. New York: Academic Press, Inc., 1972.

4 Cohen, S., D. C. Glass, & J. E. Singer. Apartment noise, auditory discrimination, and reading ability in children. Unpublished manuscript, University of Texas at Austin, 1972.

5 Lipscomb, D. M. High intensity sounds in the recreational environment. *Clinical Pediatrics*, 1969, 8, 63–68.

6 Zuckerman, S. *The social life of monkeys and apes*. New York: Harcourt, Brace, 1932.

7 DeVore, I. (Ed.), *Primate behavior*. New York: Holt, Rinehart, & Winston, Inc., 1965.

8 Calhoun, J. B. A "behavioral sink." In E. L. Bliss (Ed.), *Roots of behavior*. New York: Harper & Row, Publishers, Incorporated, 1962.

9 Schmitt, R. C. Density, delinquency, and crime in Honolulu. *Sociology and Social Research*, 1957, 41, 274–276.

10 Schmitt, R. E. Density, health, and social disorganization. *Journal of American Institute of Planners*, 1966, 32, 38–40.

11 Freedman, J. L., S. Klevansky, & P. R. Ehrlich. The effect of crowding on human task performance. *Journal of Applied Social Psychology*, 1971, 1, 1, 7–25.

12 Freedman, J. The effects of crowding on human performance and social behavior. Paper read at American Psychological Association, Miami Beach, September 1970.

13 Loo, C. M. Deriving hypotheses for researching the effects of crowding in experimental settings. Paper presented to the symposium on *Problems of Human Crowding: Theory, Findings, and Needed Research* at the American Psychological Association Convention, Montreal, Canada, August 1973.

14 Milgram, S. The experience of living in cities: A psychological analysis. *Science*, March 13, 1970, 167, 1461–1468.

15 Zimbardo, P. G. The human choice: Individuation, reason, and order versus deindividuation, impulse, and chaos. In W. J. Arnold & D. Levine (Eds.), *Nebraska Symposium on Motivation*. Lincoln: University of Nebraska Press, 1969.

16 Jacobs, J. *The death and life of great American cities.* New York: Random House, Inc., 1961. P. 82.

17 Altman, D., M. Levine, M. Nadien, & J. Villena. Trust of the stranger in the city and the small town. Unpublished research, Graduate Center, City University of New York, 1969, cited in reference 14.

18 Tavris, C. The frozen world of the familiar stranger, A conversation with Stanley Milgram. *Psychology Today*, June 1974, 8, 70–74.

19 Fraser, S., & P. G. Zimbardo. Unpublished research cited in P. G. Zimbardo, The human choice: Individuation, reason, and order versus deindividuation, impulse, and chaos. In W. J. Arnold & D. Levine (Eds.), *Nebraska Symposium on Motivation*. Lincoln: University of Nebraska Press, 1969.

20 Sheppard, H. L., & N. Q. Herrick. *Where have all the robots gone? Worker dissatisfaction in the 70s.* New York: The Free Press, 1972. Pp. 10, 11.

21 Robinson, J. P., & P. E. Converse. Social change reflected in the use of time. In A. Campbell & P. E. Converse (Eds.), *The human meaning of social change*. New York: Russell Sage Foundation, 1971.

22 Levine, F. M., & G. Fasnacht. Token rewards may lead to token learning. *American Psychologist*, November 1974, 29, 816–820.

23 Kahn, R. L. The work module—A tonic for lunchpail lassitude. *Psychology Today*, February 1973, 6, 35–39.

24 Sheppard, H. L., & N. Q. Herrick. *Where have all the robots gone? Worker dissatisfaction in the 70s.* New York: The Free Press, 1972. Pp. 171, 172, 173.

25 *The 1975 world almanac and book of facts.* New York: Doubleday and Company, Inc., 1974. P. 966.

26 Goldfarb, R. L., & L. R. Singer. *After conviction.* New York: Simon & Schuster, 1973.

27 Geller, W. The problem of prisons—A way out? *The Humanist*, May-June 1972, 32, 3, 24–33.

28 Cressey, D. Cited in E. Goffman, *Asylums*. Garden City, N.Y.: Doubleday & Company, Inc., 1961. P. 83.

29 Menninger, K. *The crime of punishment*. New York: The Viking Press, Inc., 1968. P. 31.

30 Banks, H. C., S. R. Shestakofsky, & G. Carson. Civil disabilities of ex-offenders, a team project report sponsored by the John Hay Whitney Foundation, February 1975.

31 Glaser, D. *The effectiveness of a prison and parole system*. Indianapolis: The Bobbs-Merrill Company, Inc., 1964.

32 Wilson, J. Q. If every criminal knew he would be punished if caught . . . *New York Times Magazine*, Sunday, January 28, 1973, 9ff.

33 Faber, N. I almost considered the prisoners as cattle. *Life*, October 15, 1971, 71, 82–83.

34 Faber, N. I almost considered the prisoners as cattle. *Life*, October 15, 1971, 71, 82–83.

35 Zimbardo, P. G. Pathology of Imprisonment. *Society*, April, 1972, 9, 4, 4–6.

36 Zimbardo, P. G. The dehumanization of imprisonment. Unpublished paper, 1973.

37 Harrison, E. M. Baltimore pre-trial intervention project: A project summary, 1974.

38 Miller, G. A. Psychology as a means of promoting human welfare. *American Psychologist*, 1969, 24, 1066.

ACKNOWLEDG-MENTS

In addition to the references cited in the text, we wish to make special acknowledgment as follows:

FIGURES AND TABLES

Chapter 2

P. 38   Athanasiou, R., and Shaver, E. P. Research questionnaire on sex, *Psychology Today,* July 1969, pp. 64–71, questions 81 and 99. Copyright © 1969 Ziff-Davis Publishing Company. All rights reserved.

P. 47   Bibb Latané and John M. Darley, THE UNRESPONSIVE BYSTANDER: Why Doesn't He Help?, © 1970, p. 97. By permission of Prentice-Hall, Inc., Englewood Cliffs, New Jersey.

Chapter 3

P. 68   Erlenmeyer-Kimling, L., and Jarvik, L. F. Genetics and intelligence: A review. *Science*, 1963, **142**:1478. Copyright 1963 by the American Association for the Advancement of Science.

Chapter 4

P. 96   Adapted from *Introduction to Psychology*, 6th Edition, by Hilgard, E. R., Atkinson, R. C., and Atkinson, R. L., copyright © 1975 by Harcourt Brace Jovanovich, Inc., and reproduced with their permission.

P. 117   Adapted from Hennessee, J. A., and Nicholson, J. "NOW Says: TV Commercials Insult Women," *The New York Times Magazine,* May 28, 1972, p. 13. © 1972 by the New York Times Company. Reprinted by permission.

Chapter 5

P. 145   Segall, M. H., Campbell, D. T., and Herskovitz, M. J. Cultural differences in perception of geometric illusions. *Science*, 1963, **139**:770. Copyright 1963 by the American Association for the Advancement of Science.

Chapter 6

P. 171   Copyright 1965 by the American Psychological Association. Reprinted by permission.

P. 176   Tart, C. *On Being Stoned: A Psychological Study of Marijuana Intoxication.* Palo Alto, Calif.: Science and Behavior Books, 1971.

Chapter 7

P. 185   From *Psychology: Its Principles and Meanings*, by Lyle E. Bourne, Jr., and Bruce R. Ekstrand. Copyright © 1973 by The Dryden Press. Adapted and reprinted by permission of The Dryden Press.

P. 189   Adapted from R. Keith Van Wagenen and Everett E. Murdock, "A Transistorized Signal-Package for Toilet Training of Infants," *Journal of Experimental Child Psychology*, 1966, **3**, pp. 312–314. Reproduced by permission.

P. 192   Copyright 1920 by the American Psychological Association. Reprinted by permission.

P. 202   Williams, C. D. The elimination of tantrum behavior by extinction procedures. *Journal of Abnormal and Social Psychology*, 1959, **269**. Copyright 1959 by the American Psychological Association. Reprinted by permission.

Chapter 8

P. 220   Duncker, K. On problem-solving. *Psychological Monographs*, 1945, **58** (5). Copyright 1945 by the American Psychological Association. Reprinted by permission.

P. 220   Glucksberg, S., and Weisburg, R. W. Verbal behavior and problem-solving: Some effects of labeling in a functional fixedness problem. *Journal of Experimental Psychology*, 1966, **71** (5):659–664. Copyright 1966 by the American Psychological Association. Reprinted by permission.

P. 221   *The Task of Gestalt Psychology* by Wolfgang Köhler (copyright © 1969 by Princeton University Press; Princeton Paperback 1972), p. 150. Reprinted by permission of Princeton University Press.

P. 225   Luchins, A. S. Mechanization in problem-solving: The effect of Einstellung. *Psychological Monographs*, 1942, **54** (6). Copyright 1942 by the American Psychological Association. Reprinted by permission.

P. 225   Copyright 1942 by the American Psychological Association. Reprinted by permission.

P. 230   From Berko, J. The child's learning of English morphology. *Word*, Vol. 14, 1958, pp. 150–177. Reprinted by permission of Johnson Reprint Corporation.

P. 236   Bower, G. H. Organizational factors in memory. *Journal of Cognitive Psychology*, 1970, **1**:18–46. Reprinted by permission of Academic Press.

Chapter 9

P. 239   Copyright 1929 by the American Psychological Association. Reprinted by permission.

P. 254   Adapted from Wechsler, D. *Manual for the Wechsler Adult Intelligence Scale,* The Psychological Corporation, 1955. Modified and reproduced by permission. Copyright 1947, © 1955 by The Psychological Corporation, New York, N.Y. All rights reserved.

P. 255   Adapted from Wechsler, D. *Manual for the Wechsler Adult Intelligence Scale,* The Psychological Corporation, 1955. Reproduced by permission. Copyright © 1955 by The Psychological Corporation, New York, N.Y. All rights reserved.

P. 257   R. B. Cattell, "Are IQ Tests Intelligent?" *Psychology Today*, March 1968, pp. 56–62. Reprinted by permission of the Institute for Personality and Ability Testing, University of Illinois, Champaign, Ill.

P. 263   Heber, R., Garber, H., Harrington, S., Hoffman, C., and Falender, C. *Rehabilitation of Families at Risk for Mental Retardation,* December 1972 Progress Report; Madison, Wisconsin: Rehabilitation Research and Training Center in Mental Retardation.

P. 266   From *Newsweek*, "The Chitling Test," July 15, 1968. Copyright Newsweek, Inc., 1968 reprinted by permission.

P. 269   Wallach, M. A., and Kogan, N. Creativity and intelligence. *Trans-Action,* Jan.–Feb. 1967, p. 40. Published by permission of Transaction, Inc., from *Transaction*, Jan/Feb. Copyright © 1967, by Transaction Inc.

P. 270   Parnes, S. J., and Noller, R. B. *Toward Supersanity Channeled Freedom;* Buffalo, N.Y.: D.O.K. Publishers, 1973. Copyright 1973; reprinted by permission.

Chapter 10

P. 277   After N. Tinbergen, *The Study of Instinct;* Oxford: The Clarendon Press, 1951. Reprinted by permission.

Chapter 11

P. 314   Taylor, J. A. A personality scale of manifest anxiety. *Journal of Abnormal and Social Psychology*, 1953, **48**:285–290. Copyright 1953 by the American Psychological Association. Reprinted by permission.

Chapter 12

Pp. 352–353   Table 1 from "Development of Moral Character and Moral Ideology," by Lawrence Kohlberg in *Review of Child Development Research,* edited by Martin L. Hoffman and Lois Wladis Hoffman, Vol. 1, © 1964 by Russell Sage Foundation.

Chapter 13

P. 370   Reprinted from *Childhood and Society,* Revised, Second Edition, by Erik H. Erikson. By permission of W. W. Norton & Company, Inc. Copyright 1950, © 1963 by W. W. Norton & Company, Inc.

Chapter 15

P. 425   From *Psychology: Its Principles and Meanings* by Lyle E. Bourne, Jr., and Bruce R. Ekstrand. Copyright © 1973 by The Dryden Press. Adapted and reprinted by permission of The Dryden Press.

Chapter 17

P. 494   Milgram, S. The experience of living in cities: A psychological analysis. *Science,* 1974, **167**:1461–1468. Copyright 1974 by the American Association for the Advancement of Science.

P. 494   Reprinted from *Nebraska Symposium on Motivation*, 1969, by Philip G. Zimbardo.

P. 498   Reprinted from *Psychology Today* Magazine, February 1973. Copyright © 1973 Ziff-Davis Publishing Company. All rights reserved.

TEXT QUOTATIONS

Chapter 1

Pp. 18–19   Jerome S. Bruner, The Act of Discovery, *Harvard Educational Review*, **31**, Winter 1961, 21–32. Copyright © 1961 by President and Fellows of Harvard College.

Chapter 2

Pp. 29–30   Barber, B., and Fox, R. The case of the

floppy-eared rabbits, *American Journal of Sociology,* **54**, 1958. Copyright 1958 by the University of Chicago Press.

Chapter 4

Pp. 92–93 *The Man with a Shattered World: The History of a Brain Wound,* by A. R. Luria, translated from the Russian by Lynn Solotaroff, © 1972 by Basic Books, Inc., Publishers, New York.

Chapter 6

P. 158 Luce, G. G. *Body Time: Physiological Rhythms and Social Stress.* New York: Pantheon Books, a Division of Random House, Inc., © 1971.

p. 170 Reprinted by permission of Grove Press. © 1959 by Walpola Rahula.

P. 175 Weil, A. T., Zinberg, N. E., and Nelsen, J. M. Clinical and psychological effects of marihuana in man, *Science,* **162**, 1968. Copyright 1968 by the American Association for the Advancement of Science.

Chapter 8

P. 217 Joyce, J. *Ulysses.* New York: Modern Library, Copyright 1961 by Random House, Inc.

P. 218 Reprinted from *The Origins of Intelligence in Children* by Jean Piaget. By permission of International Universities Press, Inc. Copyright 1952 by International Universities Press, Inc.

Chapter 9

Pp. 246–247 "Boy with IQ of 55 Is Genius at Piano," *The New York Times,* August 6, 1971. © 1971 by The New York Times Company. Reprinted by permission.

Chapter 11

P. 328 Berdie, R. Playing the dozens. *Journal of Abnormal and Social Psychology,* 1947, **42**:120–121. Copyright 1942 by the American Psychological Association. Reprinted by permission.

Chapter 12

Pp. 337–338 From "American Icarus" by Henry A. Murray in *Clinical Studies of Personality:* Vol. II edited by Arthur Burton and Robert E. Harris (originally published as Vol. II of *Case Histories in Clinical and Abnormal Psychology* under the editorship of Gardner Murphy). Copyright © 1955 by Harper & Row, Publishers, Inc. By permission of the publishers.

P. 359 Reprinted by permission of the publisher from *Psychology 73/74* (revised and retitled 1975, *The Study of Psychology*) by the Dushkin Publishing Group, Inc. Guilford, Ct.

Chapter 13

Pp. 365–366, 382 Excerpts from *Can't You Hear Me Talking to You?* by Caroline Mirthes and the Children of P.S. 15, copyright © 1971 by Bantam Books, Inc. Reprinted by permission of Bantam Books, Inc.

Pp. 372–373 Copyright © 1965, 1968 by James Herndon. Reprinted by permission of Simon and Schuster.

Chapter 14

Pp. 393–394 *Normality Is a Square Circle or a Four-Sided Triangle* by Maggie Scarf, Copyright © 1971 by Maggie Scarf. Reprinted by permission of Brandt and Brandt.

Pp. 397–398 Rosenhan, D. On being sane in insane places. *Science,* 1973, **179**:250–258. Copyright 1973 by the American Association for the Advancement of Science.

Pp. 405–406 Davison, G. C., and Neale, J. M. *Abnormal Psychology: An Experimental Clinical Approach.* Copyright © 1974 by John Wiley & Sons, Inc. Reprinted by permission of John Wiley & Sons, Inc.

P. 412 Luce, G. G. *Body Time: Physiological Rhythms and Social Stress.* New York: Pantheon Books, a Division of Random House, Inc., © 1971.

P. 412 Zax, M., and Stricker, G. *Patterns of Psychopathology: Case Studies of Behavioral Dysfunction.* © 1963 by Macmillan Co., Inc.

Pp. 413, 416 From *Abnormal Psychology and Modern Life* by James C. Coleman. Copyright © 1972, 1964, by Scott, Foresman & Company. Reprinted by permission of the publisher.

Chapter 15

P. 428 Wolberg, L. *The Technique of Psychotherapy,* Second Ed., New York: Grune & Stratton, 1967. Reprinted by permission of the publisher.

P. 440 Freedman, A. M., and Kaplan, H. I. (Eds.), *Comprehensive Textbook of Psychiatry,* Rogers, C. R. "Client-Centered Psychotherapy." Copyright 1967, The Williams & Wilkins Co. Reproduced by permission.

P. 450 The compassionate cop, March 23, 1970. Reprinted by permission from *Time,* The Weekly Newsmagazine; Copyright Time Inc.

Chapter 16

P. 459 Kelman, Herbert. Attitudes are alive and well and gainfully employed in the sphere of action. *American Psychologist,* 1974, **29**:316. Copyright 1959 by the American Psychological Association. Reprinted by permission.

Chapter 17

P. 489 Taken from *Tom Lehrer's Second Song Book* by Tom Lehrer. Used by permission of Crown Publishers, Inc.

Pp. 496, 498–500 Sheppard, H. L., and Herrick, N. Q. *Where Have All the Robots Gone? Worker Dissatisfaction in the 70's,* Copyright 1974 by the Free Press, a Division of Macmillan Co., Inc.

P. 504 Published by permission of Transaction, Inc. from *Society,* Vol. 9, No. 6. Copyright © 1972 by Transaction, Inc.

INDEX

she said.

"Of course, you did." His eyes opened halfway and he looked at her through the slits. "If you were still an innocent, you would have said so. 'How dare you suggest I am not, sir.' Something like that. 'I am unmarried. Of course, I am untouched. You are an inexcusable rogue to imply otherwise.' Or, perhaps, 'To address such a subject is beyond indelicate and an insult. I must demand you leave this carriage and ride up with the coachman.'"

She felt her face growing hotter with each response she had not given. Perhaps he saw that, because he unwound himself, sat upright and leaned toward her. "As I said, it in no way alters my opinion of you. My conclusion was a logical one, owing to your person and manner, but one never knows, what with the peculiar ideas the world has on such things."

"It is of absolutely no consequence to me how you feel about whatever erroneous conclusions you may have drawn from this extremely odd conversation."

"Not so odd." He looked her right in the eyes. "After all, a woman of some experience presents no conundrum, but an innocent — I wouldn't begin to know what to do then."